AESTHETICS TODAY

AESTHETICS TODAY

REVISED EDITION

Edited by Morris Philipson and Paul J. Gudel

A MERIDIAN BOOK
NEW AMERICAN LIBRARY
TIMES MIRROR
NEW YORK AND SCARBOROUGH, ONTARIO

PERMISSIONS ACKNOWLEDGMENTS

Bouwsma, O. K.: "The Expression Theory of Art." From AES-
THETICS AND LANGUAGE, edited by William Elton (New
York: Philosophical Library, 1954). Reprinted by permission of
the author and publisher.

(The following pages constitute an extension of this copyright page.)

iv

v

Mehlman, Jeffrey: "Poe Pourri: Lacan's Purloined Letter." From Semiotext(e), Vol. 1, #3. Copyright 1975 by Semiotext(e).

Melville, Stephen: "Psychoanalysis Demands a Mind." Copyright © 1980 by Stephen Melville. Reprinted by permission of the author.

Meyer, Leonard B.: "Some Remarks on Value and Greatness in Music." From THE JOURNAL OF AESTHETICS AND ART CRITICISM, Vol. XVII, No. 4 (June 1959). Reprinted by permission of the author and THE JOURNAL OF AESTHETICS AND ART CRITICISM.

Miller, J. Hillis: "Stevens' Rock and Criticism as Cure." Copyright © 1976 by J. Hillis Miller, appeared originally in THE GEORGIA REVIEW, Spring and Summer 1976, and will be reprinted in revised form in the author's THE LINGUISTIC MOMENT, to be published by Princeton University Press. Reprinted by permission of the Princeton University Press.

Said, Edward W.: "The Problem of Textuality: Two Exemplary Positions." From CRITICAL INQUIRY, Vol. 4, No. 4 (Summer 1978). Copyright © 1978 by The University of Chicago Press. Reprinted by permission of The University of Chicago Press.

Schapiro, Meyer: "Style." Reprinted from ANTHROPOLOGY TODAY, edited by A. L. Kroeber, by permission of The University of Chicago Press. Copyright 1953, by The University of Chicago.

Sircello, Guy: "Arguing About 'Art.'" From LANGUAGE AND AESTHETICS, pages 65–86, edited by Benjamin R. Tilghman. Reprinted by permission of Regents Press of Kansas.

Wollheim, Richard: "Minimal Art." From ON ART AND THE MIND: ESSAYS AND LECTURES (Allen Lane, 1973), pp. 101–111. Collection copyright © Richard Wollheim, 1973. Reprinted by permission of Penguin Books Ltd.

For
Edith Alderman Philipson
and
Samuel Philipson, M.D.
of
New Haven, Connecticut,
with love and gratitude

CONTENTS

INTRODUCTION   1

I. ART AND CULTURAL PURPOSES   7

Introduction   7
Robert Cumming: *The Literature of Extreme Situations*   9
Frederic Jameson: *T. W. Adorno; or, Historical Tropes*   45
Edward W. Said: *The Problem of Textuality: Two
  Exemplary Positions*   87

II. STYLE: FORM AND CONTENT   135

Introduction   135
Meyer Schapiro: *Style*   137
E. H. Gombrich: *Meditations on a Hobby Horse: or, the
  Roots of Artistic Form*   172
Nelson Goodman: *Art and Authenticity*   187
Richard Wollheim: *Minimal Art*   203
Michael Fried: *Art and Objecthood*   214

III. EXPRESSION AND COMMUNICATION   241

Introduction   241
O. K. Bouwsma: *The Expression Theory of Art*   243
Leonard B. Meyer: *Some Remarks on Value and Greatness
  in Music*   267
Marcia M. Eaton: *Liars, Ranters, and Dramatic Speakers*   287

IV. ART AND KNOWLEDGE   305

Introduction   305

Nelson Goodman: *Art and Inquiry*   307
Arthur C. Danto: *Artworks and Real Things*   322
Paul de Man: *Criticism and Crisis*   337

V. PSYCHOLOGY AND AESTHETICS   353

Introduction   353
Kenneth Burke: *Freud—and the Analysis of Poetry*   357
Jacques Lacan: *Seminar on "The Purloined Letter"*   382
Jeffrey Mehlman: *Poe Pourri: Lacan's Purloined Letter*   413
Stephen Melville: *Psychoanalysis Demands a Mind*   434

VI. AESTHETICS AS A PHILOSOPHICAL DISCIPLINE   457

Introduction   457
W. E. Kennick: *Does Traditional Aesthetics Rest on a Mistake?*   459
Guy Sircello: *Arguing About "Art"*   477
J. Hillis Miller: *Stevens' Rock and Criticism as Cure*   497
Stanley Cavell: *Music Discomposed*   537

BIBLIOGRAPHY   569

INTRODUCTION

In 1961, when the first edition of *Aesthetics Today* appeared, aesthetics was just emerging from a very bleak period of its history. The impact of the logical positivism of the 1930s and 1940s included an organization of philosophical energies toward the solution of certain "central" problems in metaphysics, epistemology, and the philosophy of science; aesthetics, along with ethics and other "value-oriented" areas, was relegated to a distinctly penumbral realm. It is true that this economy of energy had preceded positivism to an extent, but positivism's effects also included what seemed to be the final extinction of the "systematic" philosopher who would, as a matter of course, write on aesthetics as well as metaphysics as part of his traversal of all forms of human experience. The trend of twentieth-century philosophy toward division of labor and specialization, so that one says that one "does aesthetics" or "does epistemology," combined with a certain accepted hierarchy of the possible specializations, ensured that until recently few philosophers of real quality would devote themselves to problems of aesthetics. In the 1950s, what is known as "ordinary language philosophy" stimulated a certain revival of interest in aesthetics, but most of the work done during that decade was of the ground-clearing variety. Many pages were devoted to unmasking the linguistic confusions upon which traditional aesthetics, from Plato to Collingwood, was thought to have rested. Little effort was devoted to constructive work in the philosophy of art. Only in the past fifteen or so years has aesthetics moved toward some degree of equality with the more firmly entrenched philosophical disciplines, with the result that, perhaps for the first time in this century, those who are considered to be among the best philosophers of our time are giving serious attention to issues in aesthetics.

If aesthetics has moved closer to the "center" of philosophy, it is at least in part because aesthetics has come to seem particularly relevant to philosophy's more recent attempt to recover a sense of its own unity and purpose. That this attempt is being made at all is without doubt due to the twin impact of Wittgenstein and Heidegger. These writers propelled philosophy into its modern crisis of self-questioning and self-doubt, following a period in which it had seemed possible to achieve philosophical "progress," based on a model of shared assumptions and cooperative work with a common method, a model borrowed from the physical sciences and equally deeply entrenched in the otherwise divergent traditions of logical positivism and transcendental phenomenology. Philosophy today is thrown into a state of confusion. It is no longer sure of its proper object or its proper audience; its desires and goals no longer seem evident. It is no longer taken for granted that philosophy represents an activity which is, in the classic sense, "healthy," or even whether it represents an activity which is properly human.

In many ways, this is not a novel situation. It certainly goes back at least as far as Plato and that massive corpus of texts revolving around the central action of the trial and death of the philosopher, an action in which the issues of the nature, value, audience, and authority of philosophy are crystallized. It is not news that the only real problem of philosophy is philosophy. What is new is that in the modern period this problem has appeared in the guise of what might be taken for an aesthetical problem; specifically, the problem has thematized itself as one of philosophical *textuality* and *writing*.

Let us agree for the moment to take Hegel as the point at which the problem of writing explicitly poses itself to philosophy for the first time. The Preface to Hegel's *Phenomenology of Spirit* is the point at which that text would lay out the rules for the reading of itself, so as to guarantee the closure of beginning and end which constitutes the Absolute. The Preface is the place at which the *Phenomenology* would assure its own ultimate unity and self-identity, by giving the rules by which the *Phenomenology* would be wholly self-mastering and autonomous. This Preface must of necessity be subsumable itself under the logic of reading for which it would provide a foundation (hence Hegel's attack on the idea of "prefaces" in general within it), but at the same time it must be somehow exterior to, prior to, one's entry into that logic. Thus the Preface is, in its own terms, unreadable.[1]

It is the failure of this claim to the self-mastery and autonomy of philosophical discourse which determines the structure of the "post-Hegelian": for we who follow Hegel, philosophical discourse is no longer possible, or (what is the same thing) is only possible as the transgression of its own proper limits.

This is the point at which the situation of philosophy is illuminated by that of literature, because we have come to recognize a similar "impossibility" at work in literature. Let us say that the literary work presents an implicit claim to identity with itself, to a self-reading autonomy. The work so conceived can be thought of as double: something to be read and all the rules necessary to its reading, together in the same text. These rules may be variously conceived: we can speak of key or organizing metaphors, of genre markers, of deep structures, of psychoanalytic symbology. In each case, we have traditionally attempted to show that the text-as-ruler coincides with the text-as-ruled. We have assumed that the text must *read itself*, as Hegel's Preface attempted to assert in a rigorous way that the *Phenomenology* in fact *did* read itself, thereby rendering the reader superfluous. In the event that we fail to close the gap "between" the text, we tend to attribute the failure to the "richness" of literature, or the approximative nature of criticism, or both. In so doing, we implicitly recognize the noncoincidence of the text with itself, and then explicitly deny that noncoincidence.

That approach to literature known as New Criticism may be said to have held such a view of the text. For a truly competent reader, the poem read itself completely; it did not "mean"—it *"was."* Criticism merely showed that this was so; it was a secondary, technically unnecessary activity and existed only because we were not all competent readers and needed to be educated. Thus the great emphasis on New Critical methodology as a way of teaching as well as a way of doing criticism. For New Criticism, criticism was nothing more than a contingent detour in the face of the poetic text.

To put our point conversely, if any text were wholly adequate to itself there would be no occasion for criticism, which is to say, for *reading.* Criticism *as* a response to literature locates itself precisely within the gap between text-as-ruler and text-as-ruled. Why, after all, *is* there criticism rather than silent appreciation? Why are there so many supplementary words?[2] The answer lies in our recognition of the inner discontinuity in literature which demands (and also repels) the supplementary language of criticism. Criticism is a necessary and "original" complication of literature, to the point that we cannot imagine some Paradise of literature which would have existed before some criticial Fall. If this is so, criticism is not a logically dispensable adjunct of literature but a completion of it. Following the logic of reading, literature must find its completion in what is "not literature." And what does philosophy find its completion in?

Let us go back to the reasons for our selection of Hegel as the pivotal figure for modern philosophy. Hegel's fundamental importance derives from his location at the moment at which philosophy's relation to its past undergoes a radical change. With Hegel, the characteristic mode of the philosopher's refutation of his predecessor's doctrines is cast off, and the relation he bears to his predecessors locates itself for the first time at the heart of his own philosophy. One could say that, with Hegel, the philosophical past ceases to be a body of doctrines and becomes instead a field of texts. In the nearly two centuries since Hegel, philosophy has been increasingly forced, under a variety of guises, to reflect on its own past and on its nature *as* a discipline constituted by the possession of such a past. (Examples of this form of reflection are Heidegger's "retrieve," Derrida's "deconstruction," and Stanley Cavell's "acknowledgement."[3])

Central to all these enterprises is the sense that philosophy can only save itself as an *historical* discipline and that such salvation is only possible as the most radical criticism of its own history. The paradox is recognizable as that which also inhabits modern art—the traditions against which *alone* modern art is able to define itself can only be conserved by being subjected to the most searching criticism possible.[4] Since modern art and philosophy *are* the disciplines which are now only recognizable by their possession of (or by) these traditions, this criticism is also a self-criticism. It is not surprising in the light of their parallel paralogical structures that some of the most exciting recent work in aesthetics has been concerned with problems relating specifically to modernist art. We have tried to give this strain of contemporary aesthetics as full a representation as possible in this volume.

In its self-reflection on its own textual past, philosophy has adopted more and more the procedures of what we have been taught to call literary criticism. This critical approach to its texts has seemed to rob philosophy of its "critical" function. It is no longer possible to lodge the easy charge that another philosopher's writings are "false"— the prototypical philosopher's criticism.[5] In one of those doublings which haunts the modern writer, one of the difficulties of philosophy adopting the methods of literary or artistic criticism is precisely the fact that what has been hitherto known as "philosophy" has, in its quest for truth, always arrogated to itself the right, and the need, to level the charge of falsehood. It may be relatively easy, if not indeed soothing, to give up the right, but it is difficult if not impossible to escape the need. Philosophy's exploration of its own desires entails an exploration of the ways in which it differs from literature, and from criticism, and how each of these differs from the other, and from themselves. Again, aesthetics has been the field in which these tendencies have been most clearly manifested.[6] It seems only right that what has traditionally been viewed as the most peripheral and marginal of philosophical fields should become the locus of philosophy's self-subversive desire.

In this revised edition of *Aesthetics Today*, we have retained the same system of organization into subtopics which was used in the first edition. We have also chosen the selections for this edition on the same principle as the first edition, namely, not to !imit ourselves strictly to papers by "professional philosophers" (what a decade or so ago would have been called "talk about talk about art") but to include papers by as wide a range of critics of the various arts as possible. These papers will bear as much philosophical discussion, we feel, as those of a more orthodox philosophical style. In this way, what we consider the distinctive flavor of the first edition is preserved.

There is an enormous range of material published on the issues discussed in this volume. Confronted with such quantity, we have had to be guided by considerations of accessibility as well as importance in compiling the bibliography. The sectional introductions include further bibliographical data relating to each of the selections; we have tried to provide some listing which, along with other works by the author of the selection, will allow the reader to at least begin to follow up some of the issues involved. When the name of an author with more than one listing in the bibliography is given with no number in parentheses following his name, that means that all the author's listed works are relevant to the topic in question.

The editors gratefully acknowledge the assistance of Ms. Estelle Stinespring in preparing this anthology for publication.

—*Paul J. Gudel*
Stephen Melville

NOTES

1. Cf. G. Spivak, "Introduction" to Derrida (8), pp. ix–xiii.
2. Cf. J. Hillis Miller, "Stevens' Rock and Criticism as Cure, Part II."
3. Cf. Stanley Cavell, "Foreword: An Audience for Philosophy" and "Knowing and Acknowledging" in Cavell (4).

4. Cf. Michael Fried, "Art and Objecthood" and Fried (6).
5. Cf. Stanley Cavell, "Austin at Criticism" in Cavell (4).
6. It is a striking fact that Jacques Derrida, a very technical philosophical writer, has had his major impact in the English-speaking world in literary circles. In America, Derrida's works are read almost exclusively in departments of literature, particularly departments of comparative literature.

I. ART AND CULTURAL PURPOSES

Introduction

No matter what the differences between the Anglo-American and Continental philosophical traditions in this century, they have at least one feature in common: both received their initial impetus in a situation of reaction against the system-building philosophies of the previous century. Stanley Cavell has remarked that "it is striking that the terms 'analytic' and 'existential' were initially coined to purify philosophy of the identical fool's gold in its tradition—the tendency to issue in speculative systems." [Cavell (1)]

This purification has taken the general form of a deep critique of the notion of "theory," a critique which involves raising the question of the degree to which philosophical "theories" (separated from any "practice") can answer the human needs which philosophy would like to answer. This critique is engaged in by both Wittgenstein and Heidegger. To some, this can seem to constitute a betrayal of philosophy itself, since philosophy has so often, since antiquity, been identified with *theoria*. Modern philosophy can seem to be *sophia* without the *philia*, replacing the idea of the philosopher as "the highest form of life" (as in Plato) with the pathetic image of the fly in the bottle. This phenomenon first manifests itself, not coincidentally, in the wake of the system to end all systems, with the attempts of Kierkegaard and Marx to stand Hegel on his head.

Some of the most penetrating work on the uneasy relation between theory and practice has been in the area of the philosophy of art and criticism, since the topic of art and society is of particularly long standing, predating the specifically modern attempts to locate some framework within which art could be systematically related to other cultural and social phenomena. The three essays in this section all work with a double problematic: the (philosophical) investigation of the larger contexts in which (artistic) texts are embedded is inextricably linked to a (textual) investigation of the contexts in which philosophy is embedded. In all three essays, we are forced to confront

7

and acknowledge the fact *both* that we are engaging in a theoretical discussion of the relation between theory and practice *and*, at the same time, we have no neutral, "purely" theoretical standpoint, no metalanguage in which to describe this relation. Our discussions must be "impurely theoretical": cast, for example, in the mode of reflection on *other* philosophers' texts. These essays are therefore philosophical in an exemplary way—they are three attempts at self-knowledge through the uncovering of the implications of one's own position.

The essays here represent three influential twentieth-century strategies: existentialism, Marxism, and structuralism. For more on existentialism, see Cavell (1), Kaelin, and the section on Sartre in Mehlman (5); on Marxism, see Arvon, Baxandall, and Eagleton. Felman (1) is another fine discussion of the controversy between Foucault and Derrida, from the side of Derrida rather than Foucault. Professor Said's essay should be read in conjunction with J. Hillis Miller's essay in Section VI.

The Literature of Extreme Situations

Robert Cumming

THE POSTWAR MOOD

A philosophy with a label is usually no longer a philosophy. A philosophy proposes some coherent way of handling problems that cuts across their previous arrangement. But the popular acknowledgment of a label marks the impact of a philosophy on what would have been thought had its influence never been exerted. Its cutting edge is blunted as it encounters older recalcitrant and incompatible ways of thinking, which reclaim or rearrange its problems. The question that should then force itself on our attention, I raise specifically with regard to the philosophy labeled "existentialism": Is it merely what it has largely become—a miscellaneous assortment of aches and pains of the human spirit?

Even to reach this question we have first to get past two popular interpretations of existentialism, the theological and the sociological, which pose problems in ways which are not native to existentialism itself. On the one interpretation, existentialism is coping with a profoundly novel spiritual problem, What is one to do with his soul, now that God is dead? But this announcement, before it was Nietzsche's, was a Lutheran hymn, and a moment in the Christian revelation (not to mention more ancient faiths), so that it is hardly surprising if existentialist soul-searching seems the sapping of human faith by an "old despair." On the other interpretation, such novelty as existentialism retains can be traced to a different intimation of mortality, which finds expression in a less ambiguous announcement, *"Nous autres, civilisations, nous savons maintenant que nous sommes mortelles."*[1] Existentialism then becomes a relatively new despair; a date can be added to the label, identifying existentialism as a postwar mood. But to accept this identification is to interpret existentialism as a transient emotional reaction which never achieved the sustained cogency and articulation of a philosophy, and which can be explained away by the

9

social circumstances of its vogue—the crumbling of bourgeois society.

Furthermore, the arrangement of problems that this sociological interpretation brings with it is incompatible with the theological interpretation. The social historian is not inclined to accept the depths of a soul as fundamental; what happens there is merely evidence of what is happening to the structure of society. Soul-searching as such he is likely to regard as evidence of social disintegration; in a more integrated society men know, without searching, what to do with their souls, they put them at the disposal of their fellow men.

But where does this sociological disparagement and dismissal of existentialism lead us? Existentialism first attained its popular vogue after World War I in Germany. If we interpret Heidegger's despairing preoccupation with death and nothingness as the preoccupation of the German bourgeoisie, whose sense of their social reality was undermined by war and inflation, which left them with nothing—if we similarly interpret Sartre's existentialism as a moral backwash (like black-marketeering) from the French experience of invasion and resistance during World War II—we can then expect existentialism to become the mood of America after World War III, when the mortality of our civilization should be amply evident. In other words, the sociological framework of explanation, which sustains the convictions on which we are relying when we dismiss existentialism as a phenomenon of social disintegration, may not itself survive the cumulative disintegration of the structure of our society. Soul-searching might instead come into popular favor as a method of social research.

There is, however, something more obviously awkward about the social historian's dismissal of existentialism as a postwar mood than any anticipation which might disturb our present confidence, it can't happen here. Even if we overlook God's possible role in the soul-searching of the existentialists, we have to recognize that existentialism was not originally a postwar mood. What happened after World War I in Germany, when Heidegger played upon the terms *Stimmung* and *bestimmen* and found that such moods as anxiety and despair define man's *Sein zum Tode*, was in part the revival of a largely neglected thinker, Kierkegaard, whose thoughts had not originally been conceived under postwar circumstances, or indeed with any reference to social circumstances. When after World War II existentialism re-emerges out of the French resistance, Sartre analyzes this public experience by re-employing terminology which had originally been shaped by Kierkegaard's private experience. Kierkegaard's mood of despair over the Fall of Man, when he analyzed the intricacies of the human soul in *Sickness Unto Death*, becomes despair over the Fall of France in Sartre's *La Mort dans l'âme*. Kierkegaard encountered his despair in his anxious struggle to reach some final verdict on himself—*Guilty/Not-Guilty*. And he describes this struggle metaphorically as a "self-torturing" process of putting himself "on trial." This struggle to reach inner clarity withdrew him, moreover, from any contact with matters of public concern, and he describes his withdrawal with the further metaphor of "self-imprisonment." Thus Kierkegaard was self-tortured, self-tried, self-imprisoned. He was never menaced with an actual trial, with actual torture, with actual imprisonment. It took nearly a century for social history to catch up with Kierkegaard's private moods and to supply his metaphors with the literal public references which we find in Sartre's writings to the tortures, trials, and imprisonments actually instituted by the Gestapo in occupied France, and by the French army in Algeria. What were originally Kierkegaard's metaphorical descriptions of his introspective withdrawal have been pulled inside out by the eventual course history has taken. Life has imitated his art.

But Sartre's transformation of existentialism from self-scrutiny into social commentary is not completely unambiguous. For the public drama of a social struggle to the death in Sartre still derives some of its plot from the private theatricals of Kierkegaard's inner struggle. When Sartre, for example, writes of "Torture in the Twentieth Century," his indignation obtains much of its righteousness from the involutions of introspective moral implication which the original existentialist metaphors still retain, even when they have been partially uncoiled to describe the overt activities of an Algerian prison camp.

It is because existentialism has undergone this transformation from a private mood into a postwar mood, from self-scrutiny into social commentary, that it lends itself to both of the two interpretations with which we began. But neither interpretation adequately draws our attention to the process of transformation itself, which is not only characteristic of the long-range evolution of existentialism from Kierkegaard to Sartre, but also takes place (though in a less pronounced fashion) in the writings of each of these thinkers. Kierkegaard's introspective withdrawal originally took the form of a private journal. In an entry for 1837 Kierkegaard finds the prospect of publishing his thoughts "revolting." But in this journal, he explains to himself, "I can let my thoughts appear with the umbilical cord of their first mood."[2] Nevertheless Kierkegaard's private mood later became his postwar mood.

During the Schleswig-Holstein war, the tremors of the social revolutions of 1848 reached quiet Denmark, and in an entry for 1849 Kierkegaard envisages the prospect that his journal "might be published after my death under the title, *The Book of the Judge.*"[3] It will then no longer be a question, as in *Guilty/Not-Guilty*, of an individual who is putting himself on trial. Kierkegaard's private court of appeal—his journal—is to become posthumously the book of a judge issuing verdicts on society, and Kierkegaard in fact adopted this public role in such works as his *Attack on Christendom* and on *The Present Age.*

There was also a prewar Sartre as well as a postwar Sartre. His first novel, *Nausea*, was published before World War II began and ostensibly takes the form of a private journal which (like Kierkegaard's) was never intended for publication. For this journal was kept by someone who was "merely an individual without social significance," and his bouts of nausea, are the moods of revulsion which sweep over him whenever he pretends to significance. But after World War II, Sartre takes to public journalism and wrestles with the socially significant. The private revulsion of a mere individual in *Nausea* becomes a revolutionary protest against bourgeois society; it becomes in *Les Séquestrés d'Altona* the bad "taste" our whole epoch leaves in the mouth of the protagonist when he anticipates its trial and the eventual verdict of history.

EXISTENCE AND COMMUNICATION

My selecting Kierkegaard and Sartre to exhibit the transformation of existentialism from self-scrutiny into social commentary has rendered even more embarrassing our initial effort to consider existentialism as a philosophy—as a coherent way of handling some range of problems. For they are the foremost representatives of the two major factions into which existentialism is split. The inability of the prevailing interpretation of existentialism to mend this split is well illustrated by Lowrie's denial of any philosophical relationship between them. Lowrie is incensed that the same label, "existentialist," should have become popularly affixed to both their philosophies. He is convinced that when one has "heard in the very words of Kierkegaard what he understood by *existence*, one must feel bewildered by the claim that Sartre is his legitimate successor." So he suspects "a monstrous hoax," when he concludes that "between these two men there is hardly enough likeness to make it easy to define the difference."[4]

I am not concerned to retrieve the popular label "existentialist."

The packaging and labeling of an intellectual product, and its consignment to a destination determined by prevailing intellectual commonplaces, rather than by the writer's very words—this monstrous hoax, I have suggested, is played on almost any philosophy which receives common acknowledgment. But the intellectual complacency of this hoax is hardly consistent with the existentialists themselves finding communication so troublesome a problem.

The trouble begins, of course, when thoughts are cherished so long as they remain entangled with the umbilical cord of their first mood, and indeed could not have been conceived had they been originally intended for publication. But the novelty of existentialism does not reside in this moment of self-scrutiny, which is a romantic version of a venerable theological and philosophical tradition with which Kierkegaard identifies himself as a "Christian Socrates." Nor is it displayed by existentialist social commentaries; after all, Sartre's comments on society are largely Marxist. Nor is the bold attempt to lend self-scrutiny the scope of social commentary itself unique to existentialism. The novelty of existentialism is to be sought rather in the way Kierkegaard and Sartre solve the problem of communication that arises in the course of their making this attempt. The respects in which they are both existentialists can be discovered, I shall argue, if we examine the ways in which they are both forced, by their otherwise quite different philosophies, to adopt literary works as a means of communicating these philosophies.[5]

Of course the fact has often been recognized that the actual intellectual influence exercised by existentialists cannot be accounted for by their philosophical writings without reference to their literary writings, but only by the way the prestige of their employment of the one genre enhances the popular appeal of the other. Yet this fact might only betray the flippancy of intellectual fashion. Thus Lowrie himself concedes that "Sartre shows a certain resemblance to Kierkegaard in the fact that he has sought to popularize his views by creating a novelistic literature." But Lowrie deprives this resemblance of any philosophical significance. It does not seem to him to require explanation in terms of their own views of the problem of communication; he offers instead merely extraneous comment on such philosophically inconsequential characteristics of popular mentality as its romantic readiness in the nineteenth century to be tantalized by the minor raptures of Kierkegaard's *Seducer's Diary* and its whetting its jaded appetite in the twentieth with the virulent obscenities of Sartre's novels. But a hostile interpreter of existentialism, who prefers common sense and thinks of himself as a steadier philosopher than Kierkegaard or Sartre, may entertain unflattering suspicions of their stooping to literature in order to conquer the popular mind. He may suspect that their philosophies are merely literary gestures, indistinguishable in intellectual content from their literary works. Thus De Ruggiero allots no role to Sartre's philosophy besides that of waving "a banner for the diffusion of his dramas."[6] I shall try to get behind such references as Lowrie's and De Ruggiero's to existentialism as a popular literary vogue, in order to demonstrate that Kierkegaard's and Sartre's literary efforts are indispensable to, yet distinguishable from, their philosophies. This demonstration will enable me to deal with the other issues I have been raising regarding existentialism, including the claims of common sense.

REFLECTION AND ACTION

The least which a summary exposition of Kierkegaard's very words should make clear are his puzzling terminology and titles. Each of Kierkegaard's literary works, which he himself refers to as his "aesthetic production," he published under a pseudonym, along with an ethical-religious work in his own name. But the relation of these pseudonymous aesthetic works to the ethical and religious philosophy which he acknowledges as his own, is complicated by his distinguishing, in these aesthetic works themselves, three *Stages on Life's Way*. For he draws a particularly sharp distinction between the first stage, which he identifies as itself "aesthetic," and the two succeeding stages, the "ethical" and the "religious." Thus in his first aesthetic work, *Either/Or*, the points of view of the aesthetic and ethical stages are distinguished in terms of the principle of contradiction which this title dramatizes. But the distinction is not evenly balanced. Although *Either/Or* solicits a choice between these two points of view, the defining trait of the aesthetic point of view is its hospitable reconciliation of all different points of view, and its evasion of this particular choice between the aesthetic and ethical points of view; while uncompromising choice is the defining trait of the ethical point of view, and the decisive ethical choice is the refusal to compromise with the aesthetic point of view. But despite the fact that the distinction between these points of view is thus itself an ethical and not an aesthetic distinction, it comes up for clarification in works which Kierkegaard chracterizes as aesthetic.

Such paradoxes have encouraged the presumption that existentialism is too incoherent to be considered a philosophy. But for Kierkegaard the problem of existence itself is its fundamental incoherence

—"the doubleness characteristic of existence." He explains, "Life must be understood backward, but . . . it must be lived forward."[7] This paradox has the additional interest for us of having been the first existentialist formula to catch the attention of an Anglo-Saxon philosopher. It is cited by William James, who found it in Höffding.[8] Needless to say, James's commitment to scientific prediction, as a way of understanding forward, enables him to dispose promptly of the paradox. But in Kierkegaard the formula implies that the reflective movement of self-scrutiny is inherently introspective and retrospective, in that it can be continued undisturbed only so long as one is abstracting from the actual "external conditions" of one's life, which are continually changing.[9]

What for Kierkegaard is distinctively *aesthetic* is this movement with which reflection "throws away" these actual "external conditions," in the sense that they dissolve into merely imaginary ideal possibilities as soon as they have been reflected upon.[10] What is distinctive of any individual who remains at the *aesthetic stage of existence* is the "illusion" that while he is reflecting he also actually "exists." So long as he is "dabbling" in imaginary possibilities, he is employing reflection as a means for "keeping existence away."[11] In contrast, the individual who makes a "choice" and acts upon it is an "existing individual." He is "as bifrontal as existence itself," because he respects its "doubleness" by performing a double movement: the aesthetic movement of reflection and the "contradictory" ethical movement of choice and action, which is his "persistent striving" to "reduplicate" himself—to reach a "historical conclusion" that "reproduces" concretely, in the setting of the actual external conditions of the life he is living forward, an abstract imaginative possibility which his reflection has produced.[12]

Despite the fact that the individual's arrival at the ethical stage of existence thus presupposes his previous imaginative passage through the aesthetic stage, the *Either/Or* of ethical choice that demarcates these two stages is not itself blurred. On the one hand, the regressive movement of reflection is inherently inconclusive: a choice, when reflected upon instead of being acted upon, remains a possible choice, and undergoes, so long as reflection continues, imaginative dissolution into further possibilities. Meantime the forward movement of the individual's life also continues: "The ship is all the while making its usual headway." His life "drifts on" until the possibility of choosing itself finally eludes him, for the drift is his succumbing to social pressure: "If he forgets to take into account the headway, there comes at last a moment when there is no longer any question of an either/or . . . because others have chosen for him, because he has lost his self."[13] On the other hand, the movement of ethical action halts and reverses this regressive movement of reflection. To gain a self, the individual must "choose himself" by turning himself around and "pressing" himself "back" into "the most intimate connection and the most exact coherence" with the actual historical conditions of his life, from which he has been abstracting during the course of his reflection.[14] It is this pressure from within which is his "persistent striving" to reach a "historical conclusion" that will lend coherence to his life. He becomes a self—an "existing individual."

The distinction of these two movements acquires emphatic philosophical implications in Kierkegaard's major philosophical work, *Concluding Unscientific Postscript to the Philosophical Fragments*, where he takes "A Glance at a Contemporary Effort in Danish Literature." The effort referred to by this chapter title is that represented by his own pseudonymous aesthetic works. In this chapter he glances at *Either/Or* in order to disparage Hegel's reflective philosophical system as merely "aesthetic." It leaves no place for the distinctively ethical movement of reaching a historical conclusion, since it is ostensibly a philosophy of *history*—the progressive realization by reflection of its ideal possibilities as historical conditions. The ethical principle of contradiction is superseded by the aesthetic principle of synthesis. Along with all other antitheses, the reflective movement of Hegel's philosophy melts the fundamental antithesis, "either" reflection "or" action, into a conciliatory "both" reflection "and" action. But because this reconciliation itself is merely reflective, the coherence of Hegel's philosophical system is merely abstract. In contrast Kierkegaard's philosophy is fragmentary, because the intrusion of the *Either/Or* shatters any reflective philosophical system and substitutes for its abstract coherence the concrete coherence of the life of an existing individual.

Hegel's reflective philosophy displays, from the point of view of Kierkegaard's philosophy of action, all the liabilities of reflection. From this point of view reflection is a regressive and inconclusive movement which cannot move forward with history; Hegel's reflective philosophy therefore "turns back upon itself" and again "turns back," so that when Hegel ostensibly reaches a historical conclusion, he is in fact being "wise only after the event."[15] Furthermore, in order to maintain this retrospective point of view undisturbed, Hegel must construct his reflective system by abstracting from the forward moving history of his own life. He is "like a man who constructs an enormous castle and lives in a shack close by."[16] His system "fails to express the situation of the knowing subject in existence," who must act in order to bring his reflection to some conclusion; it expresses instead the illusory aesthetic status of an "imaginary subject" who has withdrawn from existence "by way of recollection."[17]

The same aesthetic characteristics of reflection which attach to Hegel's philosophy, from Kierkegaard's ethical point of view, also attach to Kierkegaard's own aesthetic works. The characteristic form they assume is that of "recollections." This is the reason that Kierkegaard has to shoulder the existential problem of bringing his "esthetic production" to a conclusion by writing *The Concluding Unscientific Postscript*, not as still another aesthetic work, despite its backward "glance" at his aesthetic works, but as embodying an ethical choice which marks a "turning-point in his authorship."[18] Only a glance is permissible, since he is halting with this work the regressive movement of his reflection and hence his writing of aesthetic works. Moreover, he does not glance back at these aesthetic writings as his own works but as a "Contemporary Effort in Danish Literature," because he is "only imaginatively their author."[19] In writing these works he has abstracted from his own life and has, therefore, presented them pseudonymously, as if each were written by an "imaginary subject."

It is from *The Concluding Unscientific Postscript* that Lowrie cites in order that we may hear "in the very words of Kierkegaard what he understood by existence" and feel "bewildered by the claim that Sartre is his legitimate successor." When Lowrie examines Sartre's philosophy he finds that Kierkegaard's criticism of Hegel's philosophy as "aesthetic" equally applies to Sartre's systematic *L'Etre et le néant*. But unlike Hegel and like Kierkegaard, Sartre writes literary as well as philosophical works. Lowrie's extension to Sartre of Kierkegaard's ethical criticism of the aesthetic neglects the paradox that Kierkegaard initially undertakes this criticism in literary works which he himself characterizes as aesthetic. If Kierkegaard's own aesthetic works are to be shielded from a similar extension of his ethical criticism in these works of the aesthetic evasion of the problem of existence, a second problem must be distinguished—the problem of communication.

REFLECTION AND COMMUNICATION

Despite his criticism of the aesthetic from the ethical point of view of his philosophy, it is from this ethical point of view that Kierkegaard adopts aesthetic works as a means of communicating this philosophy. The situation which poses the problem of communication

is more complicated than the contradictory relationship, between reflection moving backward and life moving forward, which poses the
problem of existence. Two individuals are now on the move:

> To stop a man on the street and stand still while talking to him
> is not so difficult as to say something to a passer-by in passing,
> without *standing still* and without *delaying* the other, without
> attempting to persuade him *to go the same way*, but giving him
> instead an *impulse to go his own way*.[20]

The first individual's existential situation has already been delineated. His "standing still" is existentially impossible, for if he respects
the forward movement of his life, he is persistently striving toward a
conclusion that coheres with its particular limiting conditions. Since
this ethical action of persistent striving is self-differentiating, the
"existential reality" he acquires by it is "subjective" and "incommunicable."[21] A second individual now enters the range of Kierkegaard's concern. Kierkegaard's not "delaying the other" is the
existential tact he must display in communicating his subjective ethical philosophy to another individual whose life is also moving forward. To attempt to communicate "directly" his own "existential
reality" would be to attempt to persuade the other individual "to go
the same way." For instance, in an ordinary novel, one of the characters may be presented as exemplifying the writer's own particular
ethical choice and as "having already realized the possibility" the
writer himself is striving toward in his own life. But if the writer
attempts to supply social pressure in this way, the reader is relieved
of the performance of his own subjective act of self-differentiating
choice. Someone else has chosen for him, and he has lost his individuality—the prospect of ethical coherence. In order to give the
reader instead "an impulse to go his own way," Kierkegaard in his
aesthetic works "places the possibility between the example [the particular character in the novel that exemplifies this possibility] and the
observer as something they both [the writer and the observing
reader] have in common." This mode of communication is "indirect," inasmuch as it "operates in terms of the ideal, not the differentiated ideal, but the universal ideal."[22] The writer and reader can
therefore reflect together upon this ideal possibility, even though they
must act separately, each differentiating the ideal possibility by his
own subjective choice. An ideal possibility that is merely universal
floats in the pressureless vacuum of the imagination. Its "aloofness"
from the particular conditions of both their lives leaves it up to the

reader to "choose himself" by supplying the pressure of realizing the ideal possibility under the limiting conditions of his own life.

Kierkegaard's literary works are aesthetic in that his characters do in fact exemplify abstractly possible ideal points of view. He has abstracted imaginatively from the particular conclusions which they might reach, in relation to each other, in the course of their lives. No concrete historical limitations restrict the imaginary scope of their possibilities. He explicitly contrasts this procedure in *Either/Or* with the techniques of the ordinary novel:

> One sometimes chances upon novels in which certain characters exemplify opposing views of life. Such novels usually end by one of them persuading the other. Instead of allowing these views to speak for themselves, the reader is enriched by being told the historical conclusion. I regard it as fortunate that these papers contain no such information. . . . When the book is read then A and B are forgotten. Only their views confront one another.[23]

Their views confront each other as an "either/or" which awaits the reader's own act of self-differentiating choice of the particular limiting conditions of his own life, instead of theirs.

In adopting an aesthetic means of communication, Kierkegaard is not disavowing his ethical criticism of Hegel's philosophy as aesthetic. Rather he is, in effect, criticizing Hegel for writing a philosophy of history instead of literary works. Like Kierkegaard's literary works, Hegel's *philosophy* is aesthetic in that it is an abstract process of reflection from which universal ideals emerge. But as a philosophy *of history* it leaves no place for an ethics, since it presents this abstract process of reflection as at the same time the concrete historical realization of these universal ideals under particular conditions. Since Hegel is failing to distinguish, in the first place, between the abstract aesthetic movement of reflection and the concrete ethical movement of action, he also is failing to distinguish, in the second place, the abstract aesthetic process of reflective communication from the concrete ethical process of self-differentiation, by which the individual acquires "subjective reality." Hegel thereby is failing to distinguish, in the third place, between the different individuals who are involved in the process of communication. Thus he not only abstracts in his philosophy (as Kierkegaard abstracts in his literary works) from the differentiating conditions of his own life as an individual, but he also "confuses himself with humanity as a whole,"[24] including his readers, for he assumes the "objective reality" of the social community as the agent at once of reflection and of historical action. In his literary works Kierkegaard remains a pseudonymous "imaginary subject." Just as his philosophy respects the "doubleness," the incoherence, of existence by distinguishing the movement of reflection from the movement of action, so his merely reflective means of communicating this philosophy respects the distinction of the two different individuals who are on the move by "holding" the writer and the reader "devoutly apart from each other." They are not "permitted to fuse or cohere into objectivity,"[25] since they are merely reflecting together. In order to acquire "subjective reality" and achieve the coherence of "an existing individual," each must still act independently of the other and "realize" concretely the imaginative possibility they have reflected upon in common.

LITERATURE AND LIFE

Sartre, like Kierkegaard, faces problems which he is not satisfied to treat either philosophically or by employing ordinary literary techniques:

> The problems which the present age poses . . . can be treated *abstractly by philosophical reflection*, but we whose purpose it is to *live* these problems—i.e., sustain our thinking by those *imaginative* and *concrete* experiences which are novels—have available at the outset only techniques . . . which are radically opposed to our purpose.[26]

Sartre's conception of philosophy as abstract reflection derives from Husserl's procedure of "bracketing" the actual conditions of existence in order to carry out an analysis of the structure of consciousness. But Sartre rejects the "transcendental ego," to which the structure of consciousness is firmly anchored in Husserl's phenomenology, so that the procedure of bracketing becomes in Sartre the dialectical movement of consciousness itself, as analyzed in Hegel's phenomenology.[27] Although Sartre accordingly admits that "the reflective consciousness is Hegelian," he also insists that "this is its greatest illusion."[28] For the prerogatives of the actual conditions of existence, as over against the pretensions of philosophical reflection, are reinforced by Sartre's deriving, from Heidegger's reaction against Husserl, a conception of the historical structure of human existence, and from Marx's reaction against Hegel, a sociological conception of the actual movement of history. As a result of this mixed inheritance, rather than of any noteworthy familiarity with Kierkegaard, Sartre's philosophy betrays the inadequacy of its reflective procedure of bracketing the actual conditions of existence, in much the same way as Kierkegaard's literary works, where reflection "throws away" its "external conditions."

The existential requirement remains to be met of "living the problems" which philosophy merely reflects upon abstractly. This requirement is met in Sartre by the novel, insofar as it is not merely an "imaginative" but a "concrete" experience of "a progressive action." (We shall discover later who it is that is acting and having this experience.) It was Kierkegaard's philosophy, not his literary works, that embodied the experience of an "existing individual" who has not merely reflected but who also acts, as his life moves forward, to bring his reflection to some conclusion. These traits of an existing individual's experience in Kierkegaard's philosophy are, in effect, transferred by Sartre to characterize the experience of the novel. What this curious transference of opposed traits suggests is that while Kierkegaard's philosophy of action is distinctively existential, in contrast with his merely reflective literary works, Sartre's novels of action are distinctively existential, in contrast with his merely reflective philosophy. Kierkegaard's "either/or" opposed to the abstract movement of reflection the movement of action, which reproduces concretely the imaginative product of reflection. When he carried this contradiction over into his criticism of the reflective coherence of Hegel's philosophy, he was criticizing Hegel for failing to acknowledge "the doubleness characteristic of existence." Unlike Hegel, both Kierkegaard and Sartre respect this incoherence of existence by reserving for a different genre their abstract reflective analysis, so that it does not intrude upon their treatment, in the other genre, of the distinctively existential problem of securing by action the coherence reflection cannot lend our lives.

When Lowrie sought to interpret their existentialisms, he found "between these two men hardly enough likeness to make it easy to define the difference," even though he admitted that they alike wrote literary as well as philosophical works. So far I have been making a somewhat schematic attempt to prepare the comparison that he denies is feasible. If my resorting to similarities between Sartre's philosophical works and Kierkegaard's literary works, on the one hand, and between Sartre's literary works and Kierkegaard's philosophical works, on the other hand, seems perverse legerdemain, this may be partly due to our traditional preconceptions as to what philosophy is, what literature is, and what can plausibly happen when the two genres are linked by a writer. Thus we are ready to recognize literary philosophy or philosophical novel. But these genres are merely blends, which can be interpreted on the assumption that reflection and life are perhaps not so very far apart after all. Such interpretations of existentialist writings have flooded the market and encouraged the facile presumption that an existentialism is a philosophy of life, albeit a disturbing philosophy of a distraught life. But one of the more significant influences of existentialism should be its disturbance of our traditional preconceptions of the possible relations between philosophy and literature. Although we are ready to recognize blends, we are not so ready to recognize the maneuver which I am suggesting has taken place during the development of existentialism: philosophy and literature have retained distinct intellectual functions and yet exchanged places, so that the one genre performs within Sartre's intellectual scheme what in significant respects resembles the other's function for Kierkegaard. If my suggestion seems perverse, it is no more perverse than Kierkegaard's and Sartre's own use of literary works to criticize Hegel's philosophy, and I am making this suggestion in the hope of eventually explaining their perversity.

EXTREME SITUATIONS

If my suggestion is correct, we can expect that Sartre's treatment of the problem of existence will be illustrated by the literary techniques he employs in handling the characters in his novels, rather than by his philosophical procedure of abstract reflection. And we can further expect that similarities to Kierkegaard's treatment of this problem can be found by comparing Sartre's characters with the "existing individual" of Kierkegaard's philosophy, rather than with the characters in Kierkegaard's literary works. Let us, however, first give way to common sense, accept for the moment the traditional distinction of genre, and attempt a comparison of their literary techniques.

The traditional literary techniques which Sartre disdains as "radically opposed" to the existential requirement of "living . . . the problems which the present age poses," he attributes to what he calls the "retrospective novel," where the events usually take place in the past, as if they had already happened and were only being recollected by the writer.[29] Sartre concedes that the retrospective novel is able to encompass "average situations," but the more strenuous techniques which he himself employs he justifies as an effort to "create a literature of extreme situations."[30] He finds the appropriateness of this effort in the fact that the present age "has forced us to reach, like itself, the limits."[31] Now it is true that Kierkegaard also draws a contrast between the traditional novelist's handling of his characters and the extreme treatment accorded in his own literary works:

A little psychology, a little observation of so-called real men, they [the readers of psychological novels] still want to have, but when this science or art follows its own devices, when it looks away from the various expressions of psychological states which reality offers . . . then many people grow weary. As a matter of fact in real life emotions, psychological states, are only carried to a certain point. This too delights the psychologist, but he has a different sort of delight in seeing emotion carried to its abstract limits.[32]

The emotions of Kierkegaard's characters, however, reach different limits than Sartre's, and by a different movement. The "abstract limits," to which Kierkegaard here refers, are not the historical limits which in Sartre's view the present age has forced us to reach. The extreme situation in Kierkegaard can in fact only be reached when the writer has abstracted from what might have been the concrete historical conclusions of his characters' lives, had they really existed. Kierkegaard's crucial example of the movement by which the abstract limits of an extreme situation are reached is "The Psychological Experiment" performed by the "self-torturer," whose unremitting imagining himself *Guilty/Not-Guilty* pushes him along an infinite regress of reflection without his ever confronting this "either/or" in the fashion required for action. He never actually arrives at a verdict that would bring his imagined trial to some conclusion. Such a psychological experiment, inasmuch as it "leaves the reader in a lurch by not allowing him any conclusion," satisfies Kierkegaard's requirement for reflective communication by making the reader "still more completely contemporary [i.e., in the psychological sense of participating in the reflections of the self-torturer] than he would be with a real contemporary event."[33] But we shall find that in Sartre real contemporary events dominate the relations of his readers to his characters. In fact, they will be contemporaneous with each other, as a consequence of the common orientation of their lives by the same events.

For the present we need only notice that while Kierkegaard is always prompt with the mock apology that "nothing ever happens" to his characters themselves in his literary works, Sartre defines his "literature of extreme situations" as a "literature of great events."[34]

Instead of abstracting from the historical conclusions of his characters' lives, so that their reflections remain an inconclusive movement toward abstract possibilities, Sartre allows this movement to be brought to a halt within the concrete limits imposed by historical situations. As we noted at the beginning of this essay, the crucial examples of these situations in Sartre are not the imaginary self-imposed trials and tortures of introspection, but the trials and tortures actually instituted by the Gestapo in occupied France. Sartre's claim that a novel is not merely an "imaginative" experience but a "concrete" experience as well thus receives some of its meaning from the experience of his characters themselves. Because his novels "evolve on the eve of great events which transcend predictions, frustrate expectations, upset plans,"[35] his characters are eventually viewed, not merely in terms of the imaginative evolution of the possibilities they predict, expect, and plan for, but also (in Kierkegaard's phrase) as "living forward" toward these events. The approach of these events forces them to act and dominates their action. Their reflections interpreting the course of their action in the novel are therefore "in movement—*dragged* along by the action itself that is interpreted."[36] To find an existential situation that is similar in Kierkegaard, we cannot avoid turning from his merely reflective literary works, which evolve as the unimpeded exercise of his characters' imaginations, to the "existing individual" of his philosophical works, who respects the actual forward movement of his life by his action, which halts the abstract and inconclusive movement of his reflection.

Nonetheless there still remains a difference between Kierkegaard and Sartre which cannot be probed while assuming, without qualification, that the term "existential" retains identical implications if applied, in Sartre's case, to the experience of the individual characters in his novels, and reserved, in Kierkegaard's case, for the experience of the "existing individual" of his philosophy. Although the term in both cases serves to distinguish the double movement of imaginative reflection and concrete action from the single abstract movement of imaginative reflection, the two movements are not identically related for the two writers. Kierkegaard's individual halts the regressive movement of his reflection when he no longer lives "drifting" forward until he has succumbed to social pressure but, instead, persistently "strives" forward toward a "historical conclusion." But we have just noted that the reflections of Sartre's characters are "dragged" forward by the action of the novel, since it takes place on the eve of some overwhelming event. In Kierkegaard the movements of reflection and action are both initiated by the individual himself, are simply his movements in opposite directions. The movement of his reflection starts from, but "throws away," the external historical conditions of his life, in the sense that these conditions become merely imaginary in retrospect as soon as reflected upon. This introspective movement is not only halted but also reversed by the movement of his action, which starts from his choice of an imagined self, which has been produced as a possibility by his reflection, and "presses" this self "back" into "the most exact coherence" with the actual conditions of his life. The pressure of the action thus comes from within the individual, is his "persistent striving" toward a historical conclusion. Although the action could also be said to press Sartre's characters back into the most exact coherence with actual historical conditions, its pressure comes no less persistently from the relentless approach of the external event. The two movements are not simply opposed as the contradictory movements of an individual pivoting himself first in one direction and then in the opposite direction. The movement of action is eventually oriented by the approaching external event, independently of the inwardly and regressively oriented movement of the individual's own reflection, and therefore does not simply halt and reverse this reflective movement but overlaps and drags it forward. Because of this overlap and drag on his reflection, each of Sartre's characters is incapable of the choice of an imagined self that is the prerogative of Kierkegaard's individual. Sartre's characters are, in fact, "unable to decide within themselves if the changes in their destiny come from their own strivings, from their own failings, or from the course of external events."[37]

Furthermore, it is "their destiny" and not, as in Kirkegaard, the historical destination of a single individual that is at stake. The reflections of all Sartre's characters are overlapped and dragged forward by the action, for the different relation between reflection and action in Sartre involves a different relation between individuals who are reflecting and acting. Although the individual "exists" for both Kierkegaard and Sartre only insofar as he acts as well as reflects, *action* is for Kierkegaard a means of self-differentiation, but becomes ultimately for Sartre a common action. Kierkegaard's individual, when he acts, escapes from social pressure and differentiates himself from others, so that the "reality" which he acquires by his action is "subjective" and "incommunicable." When each of Sartre's characters acts, he is not acting merely under the pressure of his own choice and striving forward toward a different historical destination from that of the other characters, in the fashion in which Kierkegaard's individual "chooses himself" and destines himself for his own particular historical conclusion. "The pressure of a gas on the walls of the container," Sartre reminds us, "does not depend on the individual history of the molecules which compose the gas."[38] Since the different actions of Sartre's individual characters are all oriented by the same impending historical event, they eventually compose a common destiny.

At the same time, *reflection* ultimately becomes for Kierkegaard a means of communication, but is for Sartre an effort at self-differentiation. Each of Sartre's characters, when he reflects upon himself, is attempting to abstract from the course of external events, which he shares in common with the other characters, in order to differentiate his own point of view from theirs. Nevertheless he then finds himself in the same existential predicament, in relation to them, that he finds himself in when he reflects upon and interprets the action and attempts to maintain the point of view of his interpretation against its forward drag. He cannot disentangle his point of view on himself from theirs any more successfully than he can disentangle his point of view on the common action from its movement, which drags all their points of view forward together toward the impending event. The "reality" of each of Sartre's characters is thus not the merely "subjective reality" which Kierkegaard's individual acquires by his self-differentiating action.

Sartre does not become, however, the Hegelian Lowrie suspects him of being. He remains an existentialist, insofar as each of his characters remains an individual. Even though the impending event is itself objective, the "reality" of his characters does not therefore also become objective in the sense this term had in Kierkegaard's criticism of the "objective reality" of the community which Hegel assumed as the historical agent of his philosophical reflection. If their "reality" were "objective" in this sense, the distinction between the process of reflection and the process of historical action would have been removed, and Sartre would be writing a philosophy of history, like Hegel, instead of historical novels. The "reality" of Sartre's characters, he himself explains, "is the *snarled* and *contradictory* fabric of the interpretations each of them passes on all the others, including himself, and that all pass on each."[39] Although the actions of Sartre's characters receive a common orientation from the objective historical event, their reflective points of view on their actions do not thereby receive a collective reconciliation, do not (in Kierkegaard's phrase criticizing Hegel) "fuse or cohere into objectivity," but remain "contradictory" and only become "snarled together," as a consequence of the dialectical fashion in which the common course of the action in the novel supervenes and drags his own reflections along with theirs towards the same historical event.[40]

ACTION AND COMMUNICATION

Since both Kierkegaard and Sartre employ their literary works as a means of communication, the differences between their handling of the relations of their characters to each other turn out to be more fundamentally differences between their handling of their own relations as writers to their readers. When Kierkegaard writes his aesthetic literary works, he views himself as reflecting. Because the movement of reflection is introspective, he becomes, as he writes, increasingly self-enclosed and remote from the presence of other individuals, whose actual selves his reflection "throws away" along with the rest of the "external conditions" of his own actual self. They therefore become, when they enter his literary works as characters, merely imaginary possibilities of himself as a writer; and their relations to each other become the correspondingly imaginary relations between the successive phases of his own introspective process of self-enclosure. Thus the major characters in *Either/Or* are imaginatively related to each other as one possibility enclosed within the other, until the writer himself is reached regressively as enclosing within himself each of these possibilities, "like the boxes," Kierkegaard points out, "in a Chinese puzzle box."[41] Although when the existential problem of action is posed, B's aesthetic papers in *Either/Or* exemplify a possibility which is opposed as its contradiction to the possibility exemplified by A's ethical papers and must, therefore, have been written by a different individual, both sets of papers can also be "looked at from a new point of view, by considering all of them as the work of one individual . . . who had reflected upon" both possibilities.[42] This one individual, the writer, not only encloses within himself all the possibilities which his characters exemplify, but in order to do so, he must also have become himself an imaginary possibility—a mere pseudonym who is even more abstractly imaginary, because more inclusive and more remote from the actual conditions of anyone's life, than all these other possibilities.

Sartre, however, challenges the writer who pretends to enjoy an aloof imaginary status. "Where is he himself then—in mid-air?" Sartre asks of the retrospective novelist, who is abstracting from the existential problem of action when he writes a novel where the events take place in the past as if they were his recollections. Such a novel's resulting inconclusiveness for the reader, who in turn must face the problem of action as his life moves forward, is evidence for Sartre that the writer is also failing to face the problem of communication: his novel is "only a hesitant guide who stops halfway and allows the reader to continue his own way alone."[43] But although Sartre's criticisms of the retrospective novel resemble Kierkegaard's criticisms, from the point of view of his existential philosophy of action, of the aesthetic individual's merely imaginary status, Kierkegaard's criticisms did not apply to his own aesthetic literary works as a means of facing the problem of communication. Kierkegaard adopted the retrospective point of view of reflection in these works precisely in order to abstract from the problem of action. By merely reflecting as a writer, Kierkegaard stopped halfway in his own life—i.e., stopped short of the existential problem of action. If this left him in mid-air with the merely imaginary status of a pseudonymous writer, his aloofness allowed the reader to go forward his own way alone and to reach his own conclusion independently. For since the reader exists in movement, he must not be "delayed," in his performance of the concrete action which the particular conditions of his own life require, by having his attention diverted to the "historical conclusion" which some one else is striving to reach under different conditions. What the communication furnishes the writer and the reader in common is merely the abstract possibility they both reflect upon. They do not act in common. "Existential reality is incommunicable"; the community of reflection, established by the communication, is merely transitional and breaks down as soon as the existential problem of action is faced and reflection itself is halted. Therefore when Kierkegaard views himself as an "existing individual," he not only denies that he is the writer of his literary works by substituting their pseudonymous authors, he even insists on the paradox that he is only "a reader" of these works.[44] As the writer he becomes, during the process of communication, the series of imaginary possibilities exemplified by his characters. To become an "existing individual" he must retain, over against the reflective process of communication, what this process has been designed to enable a reader to retain—his existential initiative in action.

I have also already noted that Sartre regards the novel as "progressive action" instead of as abstract reflection, just as he treats its characters as acting instead of merely reflecting. Like Kierkegaard, Sartre models his treatment of his readers on his treatment of the problem of existence and distinguishes in terms of this model his own status as the writer from that of his readers. But since Sartre's problem of existence is woven out of a different relation between reflection and action, a different relationship is also involved between the writer and his reader as well as between his characters. Sartre therefore copes with a different paradox—that "the writer cannot read what he writes," for "he knows the words he is writing before writing them."[45] In this sense, Sartre's writer, like Kierkegaard's writer, merely recollects. Like Kierkegaard's reader, Sartre's readers exist in movement. But they do so, not only in the course of their lives, but also in the course of reading a novel in which they "live" its problems. For they do not know the words they are reading before reading them. They are in suspense—"always ahead of the sentence they are reading." For their reflections, like those of the characters, "can always be frustrated instead of confirmed" by the impending events of the novel.[46] So long as the literary work is merely what it is for Kierkegaard, an imaginary product of the writer's reflection, it is not for Sartre actually a literary work, even though it may have been transferred to paper. The writer's reflection by itself is "only an inconclusive and abstract moment of the production of a literary work; if the writer existed alone, he could write as much as he pleased, the novel would never emerge. . . . The literary work is a curious kind of top which only exists in movement; for it to emerge a concrete action known as reading is necessary."[47] This action of Sartre's readers, like the action of Kierkegaard's reader independently of his reading, is the concrete realization of a possibility previously imagined by the writer. But for Sartre the possibility realized is the novel itself. Their reading is not merely imaginative reflection but "a concrete action" which carries over into overt political acts, performed by his readers, who come together as members of the community established by the novel as a communication.[48] Thus the abstract movement of Sartre's reflection as a writer does not remain an abstract movement but is overlapped by the reflections of his readers and dragged forward by their common action, in the same way that the reflection of each of his characters does not remain an abstract movement (like that of each of Kierkegaard's aesthetic characters) but is overlapped by the reflections of the other characters and "dragged" forward by the action they share in common.

In other words, the problems of existence and communication, which I have argued must be distinguished in interpreting Kierkegaard, cannot ultimately be distinguished in interpreting Sartre. His existence, as the writer of his novels, is in this way as dependent on the action of his readers, as Kierkegaard's existence, as a reader of his literary works, is independent of their reflective pseudonymous writers. Because they both model the relation between the writer and the reader on the existential relationship between reflection and action, the difference between Kierkegaard, who is only "a reader" of his literary works, and Sartre, who "cannot read what he writes," is the difference between Kierkegaard's "existing individual," who can acquire "subjective reality" only by his own action independently of other individuals, and Sartre's individual character, who cannot acquire "reality" by reflecting on himself independently of the other characters. The difference is no arbitrary literary convention. It is implicit in the different term each uses for the individual. Kierkegaard's characteristic description of the "existing individual" as an "exception" implies the individual's acquisition of "subjective reality" by a self-differentiating action, which slips him outside of the scope of any abstractly universal possibility that he could reflect upon in common with others. Sartre's individual characteristically reflects that he has become "superfluous" (de trop). For his sense of his own individual existence is his reflection upon his loss of initiative, which has passed into the hands of others.

ANXIETY AND DESPAIR

The different relationship between reflection and action in Kierkegaard and Sartre is illustrated not only by the different relationship between the individual and others but also by the different way in which the individual's anxiety evolves dialectically into despair. For such existentialist moods are not the miscellaneous assortment we suspected they might be at the beginning of this essay. In Kierkegaard anxiety is merely the self-consciousness that accompanies all reflection. To reflect is not to become conscious of one's actual self, which is limited by "external conditions"; reflection instead produces a possible self, by "throwing away" these "external conditions," in the sense that they become imaginary as soon as they have been reflected upon. Anxiety in Kierkegaard is the recognition that the self has thereby lost its footing in the external world. This feeling of precariousness Kierkegaard compares to the giddiness felt on the edge of an abyss.[49] In Sartre too self-consciousness is the anxious recognition of the precariousness of the self one is conscious of. But the reflection involved in this recognition is reflection upon one's possible performance of an action, to which the actual limitations imposed by external conditions remain relevant. The giddiness felt on the edge of an abyss in Sartre is itself anxiety over the possibility of throwing oneself into the abyss, and the actual presence of a physical abyss and the law of gravity in accordance with which all bodies fall, are indispensable external conditions.[50] But the abyss in Kierkegaard's use of this example of an extreme situation is merely a metaphor for the imagined depths of the reflective self-consciousness—its infinite inwardness. The individual's metaphorical throwing away the external conditions of his actual self, and his metaphorical falling into the abyss between his actual self and a possible self, are one and the same movement of reflection.

In Kierkegaard anxiety ripens into melancholy when this self-enclosing movement of reflection also becomes an effort to imagine some external condition, which—if it could be retrieved—would provide an exit from the process of reflection and a mode of self-disclosure. In Sartre the movement of reflection is instead an effort to withdraw inwardly from the presence and pressure of an external condition which cannot be thrown away. The forms of psychological sickness which correspond in Sartre to Kierkegaard's "melancholy of morbid introversion," are nausea and shame. Something external has invaded the field of consciousness and remains present to self-consciousness—something faintly disgusting which consciousness cannot stomach but can neither digest nor disgorge.[51] If unassimilable by one's own consciousness, it is at the same time one's intimate exposure to the consciousness of others. To become self-conscious for Sartre is to become ashamed of the self that others are conscious of from observing one's physical actions.[52]

We have reached a juncture in the evolution of anxiety where we again realize that the differences between Kierkegaard's and Sartre's analyses of consciousness illustrate not only their different rendering of the relationship between reflection and action but also the implications of this relationship for the individual's relationship to others. Kierkegaard's account of the way the reflecting individual falls into the imaginary abyss between his actual self and some possible self, enables him to explain that the Fall of Man was Adam's dawning self-consciousness and cannot be imputed to the intervention of anyone else—God, Satan, or Eve—stacking the external conditions against Adam.[53] But the revealing moment in Genesis for Sartre is the moment when Adam and Eve "knew that they were naked."[54] Burning shame indicates that "Hell is other people." There are no private hells; the Fall of Man takes place in the presence of his fellow man.

In Kierkegaard melancholy at not finding an exit from reflection and some mode of self-disclosure, finally evolves into despair over the impossibility of finding an exit. This is the predicament of the seducer —not the physical seducer who merely leads others astray—but a "reflective seducer" who has led himself away from himself:

> The lost traveler always has the consolation that the scene is constantly changing before him, and with every change there is born the hope of finding a way out. He who goes astray inwardly has not so great a range. . . . It is in vain that he has many exits from his hole, i.e., imaginary possibilities of exits; at the moment his anxious soul believes that it already sees daylight breaking through it turns out to be a new entrance . . . and he constantly seeks a way out and finds only a way in, through which he goes back to himself.[55]

Such despair, since it is a product of reflection, is not despair over any event external to the self, but is "a sickness in the self."[56] The despairing individual eventually reaches that terminal phase of his inability to find an exit and disclose himself which Kierkegaard describes as "inwardness with a jammed lock."[57] Just as "the troll disappears through a crack which no one can observe," so the despairer "dwells behind an external appearance where it ordinarily would never occur to anyone to look for him." He has "behind reality an enclosure, a world for himself locking all else out."[58]

Kierkegaard's *Sickness Unto Death* identifies this sickness with despair; "the torture of despair is precisely this, not to be able to die."[59] Despair is a "self-consuming gnawing canker; but it is impotent self-consumption."[60] The despairing individual cannot "get rid of himself," because the effort of his reflection to do so is itself the production of still another imaginary self, who has only gotten rid of the previous self. In this ultimate impossiblity of psychological suicide, Kierkegaard finds proof of the "indestructibility" of the self, of its immortality.

If the melancholy of Kierkegaard's anxious individual thus evolves into the despairing recognition of the self's psychological indestructibility, the nausea of Sartre's anxious individual evolves into despairing recognition of the physical "fragility" of his exposed self, of its physical "vulnerability," its physical mortality. The affliction of the despairing consciousness in Kierkegaard is a canker gnawing within; in Sartre it is a "hemorrhage." For instead of disappearing through a crack which no one else can observe, Sartre's individual is "pierced by a crack in the middle of his being, through which he is constantly draining out."[61] Instead of having behind reality a private enclosure where no one can look for him—a world for himself locking all else out—Sartre's individual is exiled; his "world flows forth towards the other," as soon as he is "looked at" by another individual, who organizes an alien and antagonistic world out of his own perceptions, oriented by his own body. Instead of being "self-consumed by his own suicidal consciousness of himself," Sartre's individual has his sense of vitality drained off by others' homicidal consciousness of him. The soul's sickness unto death in Sartre is not merely Kierkegaard's sickness inside the self but the exposed self's inability to escape menacing external events. This is the theme of Sartre's *La Mort dans l'âme*. The protagonist reads FRAGILE, stamped on a discarded packing case, into his reflections upon his own superfluousness, which are dominated by his despair over the Fall of France. In Kierkegaard the ostensibly historical details of the account in Genesis of the Fall of Man, merely "represent externally what occurred inwardly," and are therefore to be taken as metaphorical descriptions of what happens when Adam, or any individual, reflects upon himself. But for Sartre the Fall of Man is instanced by the Fall of France, as a historical and public event which Frenchmen reflected upon in the presence of others—the German invaders. "Death" in Sartre's title has the metaphorical psychological significance of Kierkegaard's title. But it also acquires a literal reference. *La Mort dans l'âme* ends with the action of the Germans shooting a French prisoner attempting to escape, and with "the French and the Germans looking at each other across the body." If the end of the phoney war can then be signalized by the concluding realization, *"Enfin, c'était la guerre,"* it is because their struggle has at this moment finally reached the psychological level of their consciousness of each other.

In analyzing the evolution of anxiety, Kierkegaard drew a contrast between the physical changes in the external scene, which give the lost traveler some hope of recovering his sense of direction, and the psychological changes in the "reflective seducer" himself, who has gone astray inwardly and must despair of recovering his sense of direction, because he can no longer refer to the external conditions that his reflection has "thrown away." This metaphorical description itself embodies the reflective procedure of "throwing away" the external conditions. Indeed all of Kierkegaard's descriptions of episodes in the process of reflection—seduction, the abyss, the Fall, torture, trials, death—are metaphors which reflection itself has produced by discarding their literal external reference. Just as Kierkegaard offers mock apologies for the absence of external events in his reflective literary works, so he also offers mock apologies for the lack of scenery: "It is scenery which gives variety, and . . . a reading public needs events, landscapes, and many people."[62] Sartre, however, not only writes novels which are eventful, populous, and dependent for their existence as novels on a reading public, but he also argues that the scenery in a novel should be designed "to plunge things into the action," for "the density of the reality of things is measured by the multiplicity of practical relations they sustain with the characters."[63]

Sartre's use of language to overwhelm us with the consciousness of reality of things provides us with a further illustration of the way the movement of reflection, which in Kierkegaard is a separate movement from that of action, is overlapped in Sartre by the movement of action. According to Kierkegaard, a word can only be understood when its meaning is detached by the individual's reflection, which "throws away," as its external condition, the physical sensation of what is heard or read. But Sartre assumes that language is "a prolongation of our physical senses," that our use of language is a development of our use of our bodies as instruments of action, and that a word, as "a particular moment in the course of action . . . cannot be understood apart from the action."[64] This difference in their conception of language is apparent from the different metaphors each prefers. In Kierkegaard there is no scenery in that reflection substitutes an imaginary scene; visual imagery predominates his metaphorical descriptions of the reflective consciousness. But Sartre's use of language prolongs other senses besides sight, for in the case of visual perception, reflection has played a preponderant part in abstracting from and interpreting physical sensations. In order to emphasize the way in which the body, as the instrument of human action, grips or even clogs the process of reflection, Sartre disdains visual imagery, which has been the stock in trade of the traditional philosophical analysis of intellectual perception, and employs instead clumsier and murkier metaphors that incorporate those sensations of touch or taste or even visceral sensations—the "nonaesthetic senses," which the philosophical tradition has discounted in epistemology as well as in aesthetics.

This emphasis of Sartre's metaphors, along with the other implications of his treatment of the relation between reflection and action, carries over into his analysis of the way the individual reflects upon his relation to others, where the metaphors still derive from processes of manipulation, seduction, and digestion. Even the seducer's raptures in Kierkegaard are entirely visual as well as entirely metaphorical; even in describing intellectual vision, Sartre resorts to the metaphor of rape.[65] Man in Sartre is no longer the rational animal of the philosophical tradition, but "the only being who can touch other beings."[66] I suspect that the feeling of the body's intrusion within the field of consciousness and the feeling of the resistance of things became for Sartre clues to social relationships, even before the German invasion and the French resistance gave the social historian the opportunity to interpret Sartre's existentialism as a product of World War II. His obscenities are not, as Lowrie assumes, extraneous to his philosophy. The sensory for Sartre is sensual. Sartre's analysis of the way we look at each other, in effect, translates into the indicative mood Valéry's exclamations: *"Que de'enfants si le regard pouvait féconder, que de morts s'il pouvait tuer: Les rues seraient pleines de cadavres et de femmes grosses."*[67]

The considerations now raised by Sartre's use of language were previously raised by his use of literary works, when we found that Sartre's reflective philosophical analysis of the relation between reflection and action was a merely abstract rendering of this relationship, and had to be completed by the concrete rendering provided by his literary works. Now that we have recognized that the use of language itself is for Sartre a development of our use of our bodies as instruments of action, we also recognize that the metaphors of his reflective philosophical analysis undergo a brutal inversion in his realistic novels of action, where they become concrete by acquiring literal physiological implications.[68] Although Sartre extends metaphorically the meaning of nausea, he still insists that his reference to this feeling of something lying heavily on the stomach is "not merely metaphorical." And this theme of the individual's consciousness of his relation to his body is worked out with literal detail in *Nausea*. The metaphor of "hemorrhage" suggests in *L'Etre et le néant* the individual's consciousness that his relationship with others is abortive, and this suggestion is literally carried out by the theme of abortion in *L'Age de raison*.

PHILOSOPHICAL COMMUNICATION

Kierkegaard's and Sartre's different rendering of the relation between reflection and action receives still a further illustration as the difference between the way in which Kierkegaard's philosophy of action is related to his reflective literary works and the way in which Sartre's reflective philosophy is related to his novels of action. In order to render what is for him the blunt opposition of the movement of historical action to the movement of reflection, Kierkegaard adopted the procedure of publishing in his own name a work embodying his concrete ethical and religious philosophy at the same time as he published pseudonymously each of his abstract aesthetic works. Sartre is faithful to his edict that though "the problems which the present age poses can be treated abstractly by philosophical reflection . . . we whose purpose it is to live those problems" must "sustain our thinking by those imaginative and concrete experiences which are novels." Hence his usual procedure is to publish alternatively philosophical and literary works. The abstract movement of his philosophical reflections upon a problem is sustained and indeed dragged forward, when it is followed up in a novel as a literary version of the same problem. Sartre's philosophical reflections thus become concrete when they become the reflections of the readers of his literary works, who then "live" the problems of action which the extreme situations of the present age pose.

We have already recognized that Kierkegaard's and Sartre's resort to philosophy and literature as two distinct genres is a criticism of Hegel for his failure to confront the problem of *existence* which emerges when they distinguish the abstract movement of reflection from the concrete movement of historical action. Their mutual employment of the literary genre, as a means of communicating this criticism of Hegel, is itself a further criticism of Hegel for assuming that a historical community is the agent at once of the movement of reflection and of the movement of action, and of his resulting failure to confront the problem of *communication*. Nonetheless their criticisms differ, because each envisages a different community. Although both their philosophies pose a problem of communication, in Kierkegaard's case this problem is posed by the concrete character of his philosophy, while in Sartre's case, it is posed by the abstract character of his philosophy. In his literary works, Kierkegaard enters with his readers into a community of reflection by abstracting from the historical conditions of their separate lives. But it is because Sartre and his readers are ultimately unable to abstract by reflection from the historical conditions of their lives together that they enter in his novels into a community of action. Since the communities established by the process of communication are different, the publication of each of their literary works, in the sense that it marks the point of entry into these communities, takes on different implications itself, as well as in relation to the timing of the publication of their philosophical works. In Kierkegaard the individual enters the aesthetic stage of existence by initiating a reflective process of self-enclosure. He "throws away" the "external conditions" of his life, which include his actual relations to others. Kierkegaard therefore is not just being tiresomely whimsical when he respects the introspective orientation of his aesthetic works by assigning pseudonyms to their publishers as well as to their writers, by denying that they were actually intended for publication, and by congratulating himself over their poor sales. In Sartre, however, it is impossible for us to maintain an introspective orientation. As soon as we initiate a reflective process of self-enclosure, we are promptly reoriented outwardly and disclosed to others. Instead of our throwing away the conditions external to our reflection, we are ourselves, when we reflect, "thrown onto the highroad in a menacing world under a blinding light."[69] This light is focused on us by others' reflections upon the action which we share in common with them. We are blinded by their reflections, because our exposure to external conditions is "our liberation from the inner life" of our own reflection. In the light of this publicity we recognize that "ultimately everything is external, even ourselves—outside in the world, among others." This recognition is for Sartre the "restoration" of aesthetic experience.[70] Thus the characters in the novels that compose Sartre's tetrology, *Les Chemins de la liberté*, travel the successsive stages of liberation from the inner life of reflection which they led in the first novel, *L'Age de raison*. Since the writer's aesthetic experience is his exposure to the pressure of the community into which he is dragged by historical events, it becomes for him a public way in which he "lives" with his readers the menacing "problems which the present age poses." Thus Sartre's novels are journalistic and appropriately read in the context of Sartre's journal, which proclaims itself *Les Temps modernes*. And it is here, in fact, that portions of *Les Chemins de la liberté* were first published.

Kierkegaard might have found himself thrown into Sartre's highroad when the exposures of the Danish journal *Corsair* focused the light of publicity on his own inner life. These exposures gleaned concrete information about the history of his own life from the pseudonymous aesthetic works he imagined he had written by abstracting from his life. But for Kierkegaard, unlike Sartre, aesthetic experience could not be menaced from outside by the pressure of publicity. He had spoken of it as "my castle, which like an eagle's nest is built high upon the mountain peaks among the clouds; nothing can storm it." His introspective entry here had been the liberation of his inner life from its external conditions: "From it [the castle] I fly down to reality to seize my prey, but I do not remain down there; I bring it home, and this prey is a picture I weave into the tapestries of my palace."[71] Kierkegaard's aesthetic experience had been this weaving of his recollections. Since withdrawn from the individuating external conditions of his own life, these recollections could take the form of aesthetic works which were intended to serve as a means of communication with others. Thus Kierkegaard's reaction to the publicity of the *Corsair* was a counterattack on journalism itself and on *The Present Age* as journalistic—as outwardly oriented, instead of reflective, in its preferred means of communication.

THE INDIVIDUAL AND THE COMMUNITY

I have regained this essay's starting point—the public impact of existentialism. But I have in the meantime supplied Kierkegaard's and Sartre's different interpretations of what is at stake in its occurrence. Since I have held my comparison close to their "very words," I may perhaps now borrow some of these words in order to describe the existential situation of the contemporary intellectual who has felt this impact and made existentialism fashionable. The problem of action confronts him as an individual either as a problem of self-differentiating action or as a problem of common action; he either feels that he must (in Kierkegaard's words) "strive" to become an "exception," by halting the social "drift" of his life before others have chosen for him, or he feels that he must (in Sartre's words) discount his individuality as "superfluous" and respond publicly to the "drag" of social history.

In either case the individual remains alienated from the community, and this situation retains its existential significance despite the discrepancy between the vehemently antisocial theological conclusion of Kierkegaard's dialectic and the vehemently atheistic sociological conclusion of Sartre's dialectic. This discrepancy does not serve to distinguish Kierkegaard and Sartre as existentialists: Lutheranism has traditionally been indifferent to social arrangements; communism has traditionally been atheistic. What is existentially significant is that neither the theological conclusion Kierkegaard is "striving" toward nor the sociological conclusion Sartre is "dragged" toward can actually be reached. Theological interpreters of Kierkegaard often display less patience than God Himself, who (according to Kierkegaard) said of Kierkegaard, "as a fisherman says of a fish, 'Let it run awhile, it is not yet the moment to pull it in.' "[72] Kierkegaard reiterates that he is "not a Christian," and explains that "the problem of the religious stage of existence" is "the problem of *becoming* a Christian." Sartre's remonstrances that he is not a Communist can similarly be taken to mean that his existential problem is rather the problem of *becoming* a Communist. For neither the Christian church, in Kierkegaard's case, nor the Communist party, in Sartre's, is a community that can overcome their alienation as individuals by reconciling the conditions of reflection and action.

In presenting his theological version of the problem of existence, Kierkegaard encounters a version of his problem of communication; his treatment of the problem of becoming a Christian is complicated by the fact that the Christian church is no longer Christian. Thus his attack on *The Present Age* culminates in an *Attack Upon Christendom*: the ostensibly Christian community is actually only the social "drift" of the present age. In presenting his sociological version of the problem of existence, Sartre similarly encounters a version of his problem of communication; the Communist party is no longer Communist, in the sense that its Marxism has atrophied and is no longer an evolving response to the "drag" of social history. Just as Kierkegaard feels himself debarred from obtaining official status in the Christian community as a clergyman and stresses that he acts as an individual "exception" who is "without authority," so Sartre feels himself debarred from official membership in the Communist party and denies himself, or any member of the intellectual bourgeoisie (an Albert Camus, for example), the authority to reflect on behalf of the proletariat. For Sartre's dialectic of reflection and action sharpens the reflective individual's sense of alienation from the historical conditions of mass action. If Kierkegaard is only a passer-by, Sartre is only a fellow traveler.

COMMON SENSE

It is not, however, just the individual who finds himself in extreme situations in Kierkegaard and Sartre. Philosophy itself is *in extremis*. At the beginning of my exposition of Kierkegaard, I challenged the frequent supposition that existentialism, because of its orientation toward action, resembles traditional pragmatism. I noted that William James's reliance on scientific prediction enables him to dispose of the paradoxical relationship in which Kierkegaard is caught between the regressive movement of reflection and the progressive movement of action. Now that we have gone on from this relationship to the relationship between the individual and others, we can at last suggest what happens to the philosophical tradition in existentialism. William James defends "the common-sense notion of minds sharing the same objects," explaining, "Our minds meet in a world of objects which they have in common." He labels his assertion, "Two Minds Can Know One Thing," the doctrine of the "co-consciousness," the "co-terminousness" of different minds.[73] The same physical object is an identical point of arrival where two different minds can meet. In this common world, there is no problem of communication. We can identify objects by pointing.

Kierkegaard would concede that there is a common world of physical objects which can be pointed out and located with spatio-temporal co-ordinates. In this common world the moves of the traveler can be mapped, since "he changes his situation without changing himself." He can accordingly give a direct report of his travels to someone else. He can say, "I left Peking and arrived at Canton on the 14th and stayed there." But Kierkegaard adds a metaphorical description of the world of the reflective consciousness, where "the various stages are not like towns on a route of travel."[74] Here a change of situation, as we have already seen in the case with the "reflective seducer," involves a change in the individual himself. Self-identity cannot be achieved in the way physical objects can be identified. The individual's moves cannot be mapped, and he cannot in any simple designative way supply someone else with his own sense of direction.

With this change of scene, we have left behind James's commonsense world where minds can meet and individuals can communicate directly; we have entered a world where individuals must pass each other by and only communicate indirectly. In Sartre too common sense is undermined and communication becomes difficult, inasmuch as the individual cannot rely on his visual perceptions. But in Sartre, in contrast with Kierkegaard, the individual's relation to things, as well as to other men, is complicated by the intrusion of his body within the field of his consciousness. The characteristic human gesture toward things is not pointing but handling, so that the individual cannot even identify physical objects as readily as he can in Kierkegaard.

The modern philosophical tradition has been a working-partnership between philosophy and science. To the extent that this partnership might be said to begin with Descartes's philosophical reconstruction of the science of physics, its commitments can be detected in his *Discourse*, which opens with his assertion that "sense," which Descartes specifies is "the ability to distinguish the true from the false," is "common" to all men, and ends with an appeal for funds to promote collective scientific research. A scientific prediction is not uniquely valid for the individual observer who originally proposes it. In principle its validity can be tested by anyone. It is unencumbered by the umbilical cord of the first observer's first mood. From the point of view of this modern philosophical tradition, existentialism is nonsense, for it is a revolt against common sense—against the assumption that an individual's experience makes sense and can be verified or falsified, only insofar as it can be shared in common with other men. Since "truth is subjective" for Kierkegaard, the ability to distinguish the true from the false is not a common sense but a sense of irony—the ability to retain for oneself and withhold from others the meaning of what one says and does.[75] Sartre reformulates the traditional problem of truth, which was raised by Descartes as a problem of our knowledge of the external world. The problem becomes, in Sartre's analysis of insincerity (*mauvaise foi*), what we colloquially describe as the problem of being true to oneself.

If the existentialist can transform his self-scrutinizing search for truth into social commentary, this is partly due to the philosophical range of his initial revulsion against common sense. The Kierkegaard who in his journal found the prospect of publishing his reflections "revolting," is brandishing the umbilical cord of his first mood, not only on behalf of his private self-consciousness, but also in revolt against the whole development of modern philosophy, beginning with Descartes, as a development in which the self-consciousness of the philosopher has finally become Hegel's *Absolute Mind*, which exposes its process of reflection publicly in the form of the historical development of Western society. It is therefore only a relatively short step from Kierkegaard's initial revulsion against publication to his later denunciation of *The Present Age* for its illusion of fulfilling, as it "drifts," the historical role assigned it by Hegel's dialectic. Similarly Sartre's initial mood of nausea is not just a revulsion the individual privately feels when he becomes conscious of the difficulty of digesting his physiological and social experiences. This sense of revulsion is also a philosophical surrogate for Descartes's process of reflection, and becomes a revolt against the facility with which Hegel's reflective dialectic digests the whole range of human experience, without remainder. It is therefore only a relatively short step from this initially private revulsion to Sartre's later Marxist theory of social revolution, in terms of which he denounces Hegel's universal dialectic for embodying the bourgeois illusion of an homogeneous society from which no social group remains excluded.

Although existentialism may therefore seem dependent for its scope on the philosophical tradition against which it is revolting, it is yet a revolution which subverts the entire fabric of human experience accepted and articulated by this tradition. The individual's relation to things and even the relation between his different sensations of things, the individual's relation to other men and even the relation between his different moods in relation to other men—these relationships, I have shown, all become twisted because they are caught up in the existentialist readjustments of the relation between reflection and action. But any attempt like mine to state what is involved in these readjustments is itself complicated by their effects on the relation between philosophy and science and between philosophy and literature, which are the genres that we use when we attempt to understand all the other relationships and to communicate what we understand to other men. The traditional alliance between philosophy and science has been subverted in favor of an alliance between philosophy and literature. Indeed we have seen that even our language itself, which insofar as it has been shaped by direct communication is the instrument of common sense, does not survive this revolution unscathed.

NOTES

1. Paul Valéry, *Variété* (Paris: 1924), p. 11.
2. *Journals* (London: 1938), p. 48.
3. Ibid., p. 301.
4. Walter Lowrie, "Existence as Understood by Kierkegaard and/or Sartre," *Sewanee Review*, 1950, p. 389.
5. Though I shall restrict my examination to Kierkegaard and Sartre, the role the interpretation of Hölderlin assumes in the exposition of Heidegger's philosophy, of literary classics generally in Jasper's philosophy, of his own dramatic works in Marcel's philosophy, suggests I have located an expedient common to the major existentialists.
6. Guido de Ruggiero, *Existentialism* (London: 1946), p. 1.
7. *Journals*, p. 127.
8. *Essays in Radical Empiricism* (New York: 1912), pp. 238 ff.
9. We shall see that Kierkegaard describes this movement as "recollection." The etymology of the Danish *Erindring* brings out the fact that this is an introspective as well as retrospective movement.
10. *Either/Or* (London: 1946), II, 161.
11. *Concluding Unscientific Postscript* (Princeton: 1944), p. 226.
12. Ibid., p. 83.
13. *Either/Or*, II, 139.
14. Ibid.
15. *Concluding Unscientific Postscript*, p. 34.
16. *Journals*, p. 156.
17. *Concluding Unscientific Postscript*, p. 242.
18. *The Point of View* (London:1939), p. 97.
19. *Concluding Unscientific Postscript*, p. 552.
20. Ibid., p. 247. Italics throughout the essay are mine.
21. Ibid., p. 320.

22. Ibid., p. 321.
23. *Either/Or*, I, 46. Since *Either/Or*, as an aesthetic work, provides a solution to Kierkegaard's problem of communication, the proponents of the aesthetic and ethical points of view are denominated "A" and "B" in order to suggest their merely imaginary status as abstract possibilities. But "B" as the proponent of the ethical point of view, must "exist" and be identifiable as a particular individual (Judge William), while "A" as the proponent of the aesthetic point of view has neither name, which would imply personal identity, nor occupation, which would imply particular conditions for his life.
24. *Concluding Unscientific Postscript*, p. 113.
25. Ibid., p. 73.
26. *Situations* (Paris: 1948), II, 251.
27. "*Transcendence de l'ego*," *Recherches philosophiques*, VI (1936–1937), pp. 85–123.
28. *L'Etre et le néant* (Paris: 1943), p. 201.
29. *Situations*, II, 179.
30. Ibid., p. 250.
31. Ibid., p. 251.
32. *Stages on Life's Way* (London: 1945), p. 184.
33. *Concluding Unscientific Postscript*, p. 257.
34. *Situations*, II, 251.
35. Ibid., 241.
36. *Situations*, I, 46.
37. *Situations*, II, 253.
38. *Situations*, I, 23.
39. *Situations*, II, 253.
40. These relations between reflection and action, and therefore between individuals who are reflecting and acting, are implicit in the prescriptions from Sartre's critical writings that I have been citing. They are also exhibited by Sartre's actual handling of his characters in his projected tetrology, *Les Chemins de la liberté*. In the first volume, as its title *L'Age de raison* suggests, his characters reflect. In the second volume, as its title *Le Sursis* suggests, they are in suspense. Their reflections are halted, for they find themselves (as his critical writings prescribe) "on the eve of a great event [World War II] which will transcend [their] predictions, frustrate [their] expectations, upset [their] plans." The period of halted reflection is Munich Week, during which the characters are "unable to decide within themselves if the changes in their destiny will come from their own strivings, from their own failings, or from the course of external events." The approach of a common destiny is rendered by Sartre's overlapping the episodes in their lives. The shifts from one character to another occur disconcertingly in the middle of a paragraph or even of a sentence. But these episodes do not, in fact, as Edmund Wilson has carelessly suggested, when he has offered misleading comparison with James Joyce, "melt back and forth into each other." Their streams of consciousness are not tributary to each other but remain "contradictory" and are only "snarled" together by the approaching event. In the third volume, *La Mort dans l'âme*, their reflections are "dragged" forward by the actual events of the war.
41. *Either/Or*, I, 8.
42. Ibid., p. 11. The ethical movement of action excludes, as a movement in

the opposite direction, the aesthetic movement of reflection. But the aesthetic point of view includes the ethical point of view of action among the possible points of view that can be reflected upon. In contrast with Sartre, there is therefore no overlapping of these points of view, but instead a relationship "either" of exclusion "or" of inclusion in the Chinese puzzle-box fashion.

43. *Situations*, II, 10, 239.
44. "In the pseudonymous works there is not a single word which is mine. I have no knowledge of their meaning except as a reader." (*Concluding Unscientific Postscript*, p. 551.)
45. *Situations*, II, 92.
46. Ibid.
47. Ibid., pp. 91, 93.
48. Sartre's later phraseology, in *Les Communistes et la paix*, describing the social function of the Communist Party is therefore virtually identical with the phraseology I am citing here describing the social function of the novel.
49. *Le Concept d'angoisse* (Paris: 1935), p. 108.
50. *L'Etre et le néant*, p. 67.
51. Ibid., p. 404.
52. Ibid., pp. 275 ff.
53. *Le Concept d'angoisse*, pp. 91 ff.
54. *L'Etre et le néant*, p. 349.
55. *Either/Or*, I, 255.
56. *Sickness Unto Death*, pp. 26 ff.
57. Ibid., p. 116.
58. Ibid., p. 117.
59. Ibid., p. 28.
60. Ibid., p. 27.
61. *L'Etre et le néant*, p. 319.
62. *Concluding Unscientific Postscript*, p. 255.
63. *Situation*, II, 264.
64. Ibid., pp. 65, 67.
65. *L'Etre et le néant*, p. 666.
66. *Les Temps modernes*, Jan. 1948, p. 1154.
67. Paul Valéry, *Choses tués* (Paris: 1930), p. 187.
68. Sartre's analysis of social relationships derives from Heidegger's analysis of man's relationship to things in the mode of *zuhandenheit*. The implications of this metaphor, Sartre, on the one hand, spells out with tactile imagery, and, on the other hand, expands into a Marxist *technological* analysis.
69. *Situations*, I, 33.
70. Ibid., p. 34.
71. *Either/Or*, I, 34.
72. *The Point of View*, p. 82.
73. *Essays in Radical Empiricism*, pp. 123 ff.
74. *Concluding Unscientific Postscript*, p. 250.
75. *Der Begriff der Ironie mit ständiger Rücksicht auf Sokrates*, trans., W. Rutemeyer (Munich: 1929).

T. W. Adorno; Or, Historical Tropes *

Frederic Jameson

To whom can one present a writer whose principal subject is the disappearance of the public? What serious justification can be made for an attempt to summarize, simplify, make more widely accessible a work which insists relentlessly on the need for modern art and thought to be difficult, to guard their truth and freshness by the austere demands they make on the powers of concentration of their participants, by their refusal of all habitual response in their attempt to reawaken numb thinking and deadened perception to a raw, wholly unfamiliar real world?

It is as though everything in the life work of T. W. Adorno were designed to arouse and exacerbate the very socio-economic phenomenon that it denounces: the division of labor, the fragmentation of intellectual energies into a host of seemingly unrelated specialized disciplines. So it is that Adorno's critique of modern culture, one of the most thoroughgoing and pessimistic that we possess, cannot be conveniently scanned in a passing hour between appointments. Indeed, for reasons which we will fully appreciate only later on, it is unavailable as a separate thesis of a general nature, for it is at one with Adorno's detailed working through of the technical specifics of his various preoccupations: those of the professional philosopher, the Hegelian critic of phenomenology and existentialism; of the composer and theoretician of music, "musical adviser" to Thomas Mann during the writing of *Doctor Faustus*; of the occasional but lifelong literary critic; and finally, of the practicing sociologist, who ranged from a pioneering investigation of anti-Semitism in the monumental *Authoritarian Personality* to a dissection of the "culture industry" (the term is his) and of so-called popular music.

But although these various and distinct fields of study have their own structures and laws, their own independent traditions, their own

* Originally published as Chapter One of *Marxism and Form* (Princeton, 1971).

45

precise technical terminology, although they are to be thought of as something more and other than the epiphenomena, the false consciousness, that we associate with the word ideology, they nonetheless share an uneasy existence, an uncertain status, as objects afloat in the realm of culture.

Adorno's treatment of these cultural phenomena—musical styles as well as philosophical systems, the hit parade along with the nineteenth-century novel—makes it clear that they are to be understood in the context of what Marxism calls the *superstructure*. Such thinking thus recognizes an obligation to transcend the limits of specialized analysis at the same time that it respects the object's integrity as an independent entity. It presupposes a movement from the intrinsic to the extrinsic in its very structure, from the individual fact or work toward some larger socio-economic reality behind it. To put it another way, the very term superstructure already carries its own opposite within itself as an implied comparison, and through its own construction sets the problem of the relationship to the socio-economic base or *infrastructure* as the precondition for its completeness as a thought.

The sociology of culture is therefore first and foremost, I would like to suggest, a *form*: no matter what the philosophical postulates called upon to justify it, as practice and as a conceptual operation it always involves the jumping of a spark between two poles, the coming into contact of two unequal terms, of two apparently unrelated modes of being. Thus in the realm of literary criticism the sociological approach necessarily juxtaposes the individual work of art with some vaster form of social reality which is seen in one way or another as its source or ontological ground, its Gestalt field, and of which the work itself comes to be thought of as a *reflection* or a *symptom*, a characteristic *manifestation* or a simple *by-product*, a *coming to consciousness* or an imaginary or symbolic *resolution*, to mention only a few of the ways in which this problematic central relationship has been conceived.

Clearly, then, a sociology of literature has its origins in the Romantic era along with the invention of history itself, for it depends on some prior theorization about the unity of the cultural field: whether the latter is thought of in terms of political regimes (the character of monarchic, as opposed to despotic or republican, society), historical periods (the classic, the medieval, the modern-romantic), the organic language of national character (the English, French, or German temperament), or in the more recent language of cultural personality or socio-economic situation (the postindustrial, the industrializing, the underdeveloped). At first, of course, this type of thinking about the arts, this dawning historicity in the realm of taste, was the property of Right and Left alike, for it has its existential origins in the very convulsions of the revolutionary period itself, and royalists like Chateaubriand were as profoundly aware of the relativity of cultures and the historicity of human experience as was Madame de Stael, whose *Literature Considered in Its Relation to Social Institutions* (1800) may stand, after Vico and Montesquieu, as the first full-blown treatise on the subject. Indeed, we shall have to concern ourselves later with the problem of distinguishing a sociological, "value-free" approach to literature, which counts the Romantics among its ancestors, from the specifically Marxist form of literary analysis to be presented here.

Once some such notion of cultural unity has been acquired, however, the two essential elements of the sociological operation—work and background—begin to interact in dialectical and indeed almost chemical fashion, and this fact of sheer interrelationship is prior to any of the conceptual categories, such as causality, reflection, or analogy, subsequently evolved to explain it. Such categories may therefore be seen as the various logical permutations or combinations of the initial model, or as the alternating visual possibilities of the Gestalt into which it is organized: the attempts of the mind, after the fact, to account for its ability to subsume two such disparate terms within the framework of a single thought.

In this context, it becomes possible to place the vexed question of determinism by social being, or by "race, moment, milieu," between parentheses, and such issues as those which seemed to oppose Marxism and the Weberians turn out to be optical illusions. For from this point of view, the Marxist analysis of a phenomenon such as Puritanism—that it is one of the ideologies of early capitalism, or in other words that it reflects and is determined by its social context—and that of Max Weber, for whom Puritanism is precisely one of the *causes* or contributing factors in the development of capitalism in the West, are essentially variations on the same model, and have far more in common with each other as *ideograms*—in which a form of consciousness is superposed against the pattern of a collective and institutional organization—than with what we may call the two-dimensional treatments of the separate elements involved, such as works on the theology of the reformers, or on changes in the structure of sixteenth-century commerce.

Such thinking is therefore marked by the will to link together in a single figure two incommensurable realities, two independent codes or systems of signs, two heterogeneous and asymmetrical terms: spirit and matter, the data of individual experience and the vaster forms of institutional society, the language of existence and that of history. Let the following passage from Adorno's *Philosophy of the New Music* stand, therefore, not so much as an implied philosophical proposition, or as a novel reinterpretation of the historical phenomena in question, but rather as a metaphorical composition, a kind of stylistic or rhetorical trope through which the new historical and dialectical consciousness, shattering the syntactic conventions of older analytical or static thought, comes to its truth in the language of events:

> It is hardly an accident that mathematical techniques in music as well as logical positivism originated in Vienna. The fondness for number games is as peculiar to the Viennese mind as the game of chess in the coffee house. There are social reasons for it. All the while intellectually productive forces in Austria were rising to the technical level characteristic of high capitalism, material forces lagged behind. The resultant unused capacity for figures became the symbolic fulfillment of the Viennese intellectual. If he wanted to take part in the actual process of material production, he had to look for a position in Imperial Germany. If he stayed home, he became a doctor or a lawyer or clung to number games as a mirage of financial power. Such is the way the Viennese intellectual tries to prove something to himself, and—bitte schön!—to everyone else as well.[1]

Psychoanalysis of the Austrian character? Object lesson in the way society resolves in the *imaginary* realm those contradictions which it cannot overcome in the real? Stylistic juxtaposition of music, symbolic logic, and financial sheets? The text under consideration is all of these things, but it is first and foremost a complete thing, I am tempted to say a poetic object. For its most characteristic connectives ("it is no accident that") are less signs of some syllogistic operation to perform than they are equivalents of the "just as . . . so" of the heroic simile.

Nor does the sudden exchange of energy involved really tell us anything new about either of the elements juxtaposed: indeed, we must already know what each of them is, in its own specificity, to appreciate their unexpected connection with each other. What happens is rather that for a fleeting instant we catch a glimpse of a unified world, of a universe in which discontinuous realities are nonetheless somehow implicated with each other and intertwined, no matter how remote they may at first have seemed; in which the reign of chance briefly refocuses into a network of crossrelationships wherever the eye can reach, contingency temporarily transmuted into necessity.

It is not too much to say that through such a historical form there is momentarily effected a kind of reconciliation between the realm of matter and that of spirit. For in its framework the essentially abstract character of the ideological phenomenon suddenly touches earth, takes on something of the density and significance of an act in the real world of things and material production; while there flashes across the material dimension itself a kind of transfiguration, and what had only an instant before seemed inertia and the resistance of matter, the sheer meaninglessness of historical accident—in the determining factors in Austrian development, the chance agents of geography or foreign influence—now finds itself unexpectedly spiritualized by the ideality of the objects with which it has been associated, reorganizing itself, under the pull of those mathematical systems which are its end product, into a constellation of unforeseen uniformities, into a socio-economic style which can be *named*. Thus the mind incarnates itself in order to know reality, and in return finds itself in a place of heightened intelligibility.

It is, however, one of the most basic lessons of dialectical method that the potentialities for development of a given mode of thought lie predetermined and, as it were, fore-ordained within the very structure of the initial terms themselves, and reflect the characteristics of its point of departure. The limits on any large-scale projection of the sociological figure here described are therefore implicit in the nature of the objects synthesized. Like wit, the Adorno trope drew its force from the instantaneity of the perception involved,[2] and it is only too clear that to juxtapose against its historical background a cultural item understood in an isolated, atomistic way—whether it be an individual work, a new technique or theory, even something as vast as a new movement understood as a separate entity, or a period style detached from its historical continuum—is to ensure the construction of a model that cannot but be static.

Thus the full-scale study of superstructures, the construction of the historical trope, not to lyrical but rather to extended and epic proportions, presupposes a transcendence of the atomistic nature of the cultural term: it is essentially the difference between the juxtaposition of an individual novel against its socio-economic background, and the *history* of the novel seen against this same background. In effect, at this point a relationship which was that of form to background, of point to field, gives place to the superposition of two fields, two series, two continua; the language of causality gives way to that of analogy or homology, of parallelism. Now the construction of the microcosm, of the cultural continuum—whether it be the formal history of costume or of religious movements, the fate of stylistic conventions or the rise and fall of epistemology as a philosophical issue —will include the analogy with the socioeconomic macrocosm or infrastructure as an implied comparison in its very structure, permitting us to transfer the terminology of the latter to the former in ways that are often very revealing. Thus it turns out that as a marketable commodity on the spiritual level, the nineteenth-century novel may also be said to have known its version of a stage of "primitive accumulation of capital": the names of Scott and Balzac may be associated with this initial stockpiling of social and anecdotal raw material for processing and ultimate transformation into marketable, that is to say *narratable*, shapes and forms.

At the same time, inasmuch as the cultural is far less complex than the economic, it may serve as a useful introduction to the real on a reduced, simplified scale. Thus Engels spoke of Balzac's "complete history of French society from which, even in economic details (for instance, the rearrangement of real and personal property after the Revolution) I have learned more than from all the professed historians, economists, and statisticians of the period together."[3] Traditionally, indeed, Marxist literary criticism has furnished a convenient introduction both to the subtleties of the dialectical method and to the complexities of Marxist social and economic doctrine. But what Engels learned from the content, a modern Marxist literary criticism ought to be able to demonstrate at work within the form itself: so it is the model that now helps us to read the bewildering and massive substance of the real of which it began by being the projection.

I

The ideal material for a full-scale demonstration of such historical models would no doubt be drawn from spheres as distant from everyday life as possible: non-Euclidean geometry, for example, or the various logical worlds of science fiction, in which our own universe is reduplicated at an experimental level. Illustrations derived from the history of the visual arts or from the development of mathematics are thus more useful for our purposes than the more representational modes of literature or philosophy. For in dialectical treatments of the latter, there tends to take place a kind of slippage from form into content which cannot but blur the methodological points to be made.

Thus our characterization of Balzac's primitive accumulation of raw material above was intended to function on a formal level, to underscore a parallel between two formal processes. Yet the analogy is complicated by the fact that Balzac's raw material, his *content*, happens to be precisely that primitive accumulation of capital with which we compared the form: for the origins of the first businesses and the first fortunes are among the archetypal stories he has to tell. As a model, therefore, literature is not so useful as the more abstract arts, and the parallels with developments in the novel will in what follows be underlined as *analogies* to the central model to be presented, rather than as historical projections in their own right.

Yet even the specialized is sometimes taken for granted, even highly sophisticated techniques can come to seem natural in the general indistinction of everyday life. So it turns out that to assess the full originality of Adorno's historical vision, we must try to bring a new unfamiliarity to some of the social phenomena we are accustomed to take for granted: to stare, for instance, with the eyes of a foreigner at the row upon row of people in formal clothing, seated without stirring within their armchairs, each seemingly without contact with his neighbors, yet at the same time strangely divorced from any immediate visual spectacle, the eyes occasionally closed as in powerful concentration, occasionally scanning with idle distraction the distant cornices of the hall itself. For such a spectator it is not at once clear that there is any meaningful relationship between this peculiar behavior and the bewildering tissue of instrumental noises that seems to provide a kind of background for it, like Arab musicians playing behind their curtain. What is taken for granted by us is not apparent to such an outsider, namely that the event around which the concert hall is itself established consists precisely of attention to that stream of sound patterns entering in at the ear, to the organized and meaningful succession of a nonverbal sign-system, as to a kind of purely instrumental speech.

For Western polyphonic music is "unnatural" precisely to the degree to which it has no institutional equivalent in any other culture. Though it has its origins in ritual, though its earliest forms are not essentially distinct from the dance and chant, the pure monody of other cultures, Western music in its most characteristic forms has severed its ties with those primitive musical activities in which the musical substance, still involved in concrete life and social reality, may be said to have remained representational, to have preserved something like a content. There is no longer a mere difference in degree, but rather an absolute one in kind, between the older, functional music and this, which has developed an autonomy of its own, has acquired the status of an event in its own right, and requires its participants to suspend their other activities in the exercise of some alert but nonverbal mental capacity which had never been used before, with the conviction that something real is taking place during fifteen or twenty minutes of practical immobility. It is as if a new sense has been invented (for the active, interpretive concentration which marks such listening is as distinct from ordinary hearing as is mathematical language from ordinary speech), as if a new organ had been developed, a new type of perception formed. What is particularly noteworthy is the poverty of the materials from which such new perception has been fashioned; for the ear is the most archaic of the senses, and instrumental sounds are far more abstract and inexpressive than words or visual symbols. Yet in one of those paradoxical reversals that characterize the dialectical process, it is precisely this primitive, *regressive* starting point that determines the development of the most complex of the arts.

Finally, we must observe that inasmuch as Western music is not natural but historical, inasmuch as its development depends so intensely upon the history and development of our own culture, it is mortal as well, and has it in it to die as a genuine activity, to vanish when it has served its purpose and when that social need which it once answered has ceased to exist. The fact that the production of so-called classical records has become a big business in the present day should not make us lose sight of the privileged relationship between the golden age of Western music and a Central Europe in which a significant proportion of the collectivity performed music and knew it from the inside, in a qualitatively different fashion from the passive consumers of our own time. In much the same way such a genre as the epistolary novel loses its very reason for being and its social as well as linguistic basis in a period when letter writing is no longer an important everyday activity and an institutionalized form of communication. So also certain types of lyric poetry vanish from cultures in which conversation and verbal expression are colorless and without life, lacking in any capacity for those twin forms of expansion which are eloquence or figuration.

So it is that Western music at the very outset marks itself off from the culture as a whole, reconstitutes itself as a self-contained and autonomous sphere at distance from the everyday social life of the period and developing, as it were, parallel to it. Not only does music thereby acquire an internal history of its own, but it also begins to duplicate on a smaller scale all the structures and levels of the social and economic macrocosm itself, and displays its own internal dialectic, its own producers and consumers, its own infrastructure.

In it, for instance, as in the larger world of business and industry, we find a tiny history of inventions and machines, what might be called the engineering dimension of musical history: that of the instruments themselves, which stand in the same ambiguous relationship of cause and effect to the development of the works and forms as do their technological equivalents (the steam engine) in the world of history at large (the industrial revolution). They arrive on the scene with a kind of symbolic fitness: "it is not for nothing that the newly soulful tone of the violin counts among the great innovations of the age of Descartes."[4] Throughout its long ascendancy, indeed, the violin preserves this close identification with the emergence of individual subjectivity on the stage of philosophical thought. It remains a privileged medium for the expression of the emotions and demands of the lyrical subject, and the violin concerto, much like the *Bildungsroman*, stands as the vehicle for individual lyric heroics, while in other forms the massed orchestral strings conventionally represent the welling up of subjective feeling and of protest against the necessities of the objective universe. By the same token, when composers begin to suppress the singing violin tone and to orchestrate without strings or to transform the stringed instrument into a plucked, almost percussive device (as in the "ugly" pizzicati, the strummings and "weird" falsetto effects of Schoenberg), what happens to the violin is to be taken as a sign of the determination to express what crushes the individual, to pass from the sentimentalization of individual distress to a new, postindividualistic framework.

In a similar way, the rise of the saxophone, in that commercial music which replaces the older folk art of the masses, has symbolic value: for with it vibration, the oscillation back and forth in place, supersedes the soaring of the violin as an embodiment of subjective excitement in the modern age, and a metallic sound, all pipes and valves, yet "sexually ambivalent" to the degree to which it "mediates between brass and woodwinds" ("being materially related to the former, while it remains woodwind in its mode of performance"),[5] replaces the living warmth of the older instrument, which expressed life, where the newer one merely simulates it.

And if musical forms evolve in response to their public (church and salon music being little by little supplanted by middle-class spectator forms), so also they are influenced by the changing social functions of their performers as well. Wagner, himself a great conductor, for the first time undertakes to compose music in which the role of the virtuoso conductor is foreseen and built into the structure of the score. As in parliamentary demagoguery, the listening masses submit to the conductor with a kind of hypnotized fascination. The quality of their listening deteriorates; they lose that autonomy of judgment and intensity of concentration which the earlier generations of the triumphant middle class brought to their practice of the art. Thus they are increasingly unable to follow anything as thoroughly organized as a Beethoven sonata, and instead of the theme and variations with its development and resolution in time, Wagner offers them something cruder and easier to grasp: the repetition of easily recognizable themes not unlike advertising slogans, "fatefully" underlined for the listener's benefit by the dictatorial gesture of the conductor.

At the same time, the development of the leitmotif must be understood in terms of the autonomous dialectic of the musical tradition itself, as one of the stages in that slow working out of musical laws and of the possibilities inherent in the musical raw material. From this point of view, the Wagnerian theme, with its rigidity and its nondeveloping character, must be seen as a regression from the themes of Beethoven, which were functionally inseparable from their context. If there is for music something like a "heresy of paraphrase" —in the brutal wrenching of melody or theme from a texture in which alone it has its reason for being—then it must be added that such a practice finds its initial stimulus not so much in the caprice or formal ignorance of the individual listener as in the deeper equivalence—or cleavage—between form and content in the very structure of the work itself.

For Beethoven the sonata represented a complex solution to the problem of musical identity and musical change. The characteristics of the form—the dispatching of the theme to the most distant and unexpected keys (in order that it may return, this time with a kind of finality, to its point of origin), the thoroughgoing metamorphoses it is made to undergo in variation after variation (in order to demonstrate the more surely its identity with itself)—are at one with the very establishment of the tonal system itself, for they amount to a concrete reenactment before the listener of tonality as a self-evident law, reconfirmed through the form.

For Wagner, however, the problem is that of setting up a relationship between leitmotifs which cannot be varied in the old sense, for it is now the leitmotif rather than the basic key of the composition which is the element of permanence. To make a virtue of necessity: the expression fixes the very essence of the dialectical process at the same time that it defines Wagner's freedom with respect to the historical situation. In order to devise a constructional principle capable of dealing with the archaic and cumbersome phenomenon of static repetition, Wagner finds himself obliged to invent something which bears in itself the seeds of the most advanced and progressive of future musical techniques. To be sure, the manner in which the sheer vertical sonority of the Wagnerian orchestra edges up or down the half-tones separating the various leitmotifs from each other must ultimately complete the destruction of the sonata form and of the tonality on which it is based. Yet at the same time this new *chromaticism* points, even beyond atonality, toward the future resystematization of the twelve-tone row, and may thus serve as an object lesson in the way in which the historically new is generated out of the contradictions of a particular situation and moment, and as an illustration of the function, in dialectical analyses, of such terms as *progressive* and *regressive*, by means of which elements of a given complex are distinguished only in order to reidentify them the more surely in their inseparability and to make possible a differential perception of the place of a given moment in the historical continuum.

The Wagnerian invention of chromaticism, therefore, as an example of development within an autonomous system, offers a small-scale model of the changes we might expect to find in the macrocosm of socio-economic history itself. So it is, for instance, that the economic backwardness of nineteenth-century Germany was responsible for the failure of the attempts to develop parliamentary government which issued from the Revolution of 1848, and led to that notorious and fateful separation between German nationalism and the more progressive Western-style democratic aspirations of the middle classes. Thus socio-economic backwardness resulted in political authoritarianism; yet inasmuch as the latter was able to stimulate industrial development far more effectively than parliamentary regimes elsewhere, the initial lag ultimately results in a dialectical leap which leaves Germany abreast of its greatest rival in production by the end of the nineteenth century, and in possession of the newest industrial plant in Europe.

And what obtains in the infrastructure yields an analogy for developments in the other arts as well. I choose more or less at random from the history of the novel the example of Proust, where an initial predilection for the essay as a mode of discourse combines with an initial predisposition to the long static scene as an existential experience of the present to produce an unexpected organizational innovation: for Proust expands his formal scene to the point where the essay-style digressions and disquisitions may be intercalated in succession with as little disruption as might be produced by the change of subject or of conversation partner in the course of a long afternoon reception. Meanwhile the scenes themselves, as immense as they are, are now reconnected by *topic*, in much the same static fashion in which the essay preselected its subject matter: by means of the hours of the day or the stops on a train, or ultimately indeed, by the very geographical identity of the Swann and Guermantes ways themselves. Yet the result of this rather static organization, initially determined by a storytelling *deficiency* in the Proustian imagination, is a more complex rendering of the passage of time than had hitherto been possible in conventional linear narration.

For Adorno, therefore, the names of the artists stand as so many moments in the history of the form, as so many lived unities between situation and invention, between contradiction and that determinate resolution from which new contradictions spring. A whole vision of the movement of modern history is built implicitly into the lens through which we watch the progression of music from Beethoven to Schoenberg and Stravinsky. In particular, these two final figures illustrate what is for Adorno an exemplary, archetypal opposition, standing as the twin symbolic possibilities of twentieth-century creation—as the very prototypes, indeed, above and beyond art itself, of the alternatives remaining to thought and action in a henceforth totalitarian universe. It is therefore to his influential and seminal study of these two figures, under the title of *Philosophy of the New Music*, that we now turn.

II

It has often been pointed out that the increasing tempo of artistic change since Romanticism and the conquest of power by the middle classes involves a modification of the functional value of the new within the artistic process.[6] Novelty is now felt to be not a relatively secondary and *natural* by-product, but rather an end to be pursued in its own right. Now knowledge of the innovations of the past furnishes a new kind of stimulus for the construction of the individual works themselves, so that technical revolutions such as that of Schoenberg must henceforth be read on two levels: not only as one more moment in that gradual and autonomous evolution of material which has characterized the whole history of music, but also, and above all, as an object lesson in a peculiarly modern phenomenon: the attempt to think your way, through sheer formal invention, into the very future of history itself.

The evolution of musical sound may therefore initially be understood against the background of the aging of musical effects in general, which have as it were their own inner life, know their moment of maturation, and suffer debility and ultimately a kind of natural death. The common triad, for instance, struck the ear of its earliest listeners with an intensity which it will never again possess; and for us such sounds, which were originally heard in the context of a polyphonic system and as the triumph of tonal harmony over it, are henceforth nothing but insipid consonance in a world in which the cause of harmony has long since been won and its initial audacities long since become commonplace.

In much the same way we can speak of something like a progress in the history of writing: one which, however, is less a matter of individual stylistic innovation than of the habits of the reading public, to be gauged against the sheer quantity of words with which a given historical environment is saturated. It is clear, for instance, that a few bare names and plain nouns, a minimum of description, had a suggestive value for the readers of earlier centuries that they now no longer possess in that overexposure to language which is characteristic of our own time. Thus style resembles the Red Queen, developing ever more complicated mechanisms in order to sustain the power to say the same thing; and in the commercial universe of late capitalism the serious writer is obliged to reawaken the reader's numbed sense of the concrete through the administration of linguistic shocks, by restructuring the overfamiliar or by appealing to those deeper layers of the physiological which alone retain a kind of fitful *unnamed* intensity.

In the musical realm, of course, the problem of the intensity of effects at a given historical moment may be described in positive or negative terms, inasmuch as the continuing value of a given system of consonance is at one with the effects of the dissonances that obtain within it as well. Yet these effects, as Adorno shows us, largely transcend the musical scheme of things, to the degree to which dissonance as such has symbolic social value, comparable to "the role which the concept of the unconscious plays throughout the history of middle-class *ratio*." The transgression of the consonant therefore functions "from the very outset as the disguised representation of everything that has had to be sacrificed to the taboo of order. It substitutes for the censored instinctual drive, and includes, as tension, a libidinal moment as well, in its lament over enforced renunciation."[7] Thus the Wagnerian diminished seventh at its inception expressed unresolved pain and sexual longing, the yearning for ultimate release as well as the refusal to be reabsorbed into bland order; yet having grown familiar and tolerable over the years, it now stands as a mere period sign of feeling or emotiveness, as a manner rather than a concrete experience of negation.

Such absorption and accommodation of repressed material has of course always been one of the social functions of art; yet at the time of Wagner it undergoes a modification not unrelated to the shift in the role of innovation described above. For where in the past dissonance had existed only in order to confirm and ratify more strongly the positive tonal order on which it depended, now its character as "self-glorifying subjectivity" and as protest "against the social instance and its normative laws" tends to become an end in itself. "All energy is now invested in dissonance; by comparison the individual resolutions become ever thinner, mere optional decor or restorative asseveration. Tension becomes the fundamental organizing principle to the degree that the negation of the negation, the utter canceling out of the debt of each dissonance, is as in some gigantic credit system indefinitely postponed."[8] This phenomenon is to be seen against the background of that vaster repression of the negative in present-day society of which Adorno's colleague Herbert Marcuse is the leading theoretician. It manifests itself in the literary realm by the increasingly antisocial character of the greatest works, and by the accompanying attempt on the part of society to reabsorb and neutralize the impulses they release. Thus in *Beyond Culture* Lionel Trilling has underscored the contradiction between the institutionalization of such modern "classics" by the American university and the profoundly subversive spirit of the works themselves, which originate in a refusal and a negation of just such institutionalization in the first place.

That the work of Schoenberg is deeply marked by this situation may be judged by the disproportionate place of both positive and negative in it: absolute freedom, violent liberation from harmonic constraint in what may be called his expressionistic or atonal period; and renewed order, the self-imposed rigidities of the twelve-tone system, which involves compulsions far beyond anything dreamed of in that tonal order which Schoenberg first abolished and then replaced. Yet both moments can in the long run be understood only in the context of the concrete historical situation: in the light of that regression of hearing in the modern world in general, where, bathed in the very element of debased sound and canned music from one corner to the other of the civilized universe, we tend to adjust our perceptions to the level of their object, with the resultant deterioration in that ability to listen with which the composer must work.

So it is that we now hear not the notes themselves, but only their atmosphere, which becomes itself symbolic for us: the soothing or piquant character of the music, its blueness or sweetness, is felt as a signal for the release of the appropriate conventionalized reactions. The musical composition becomes mere psychological stimulus or conditioning, as in those airports or supermarkets where the customer is aurally tranquilized. The musical accompaniment has moreover become intimately linked in our minds with the advertising of products, and continues, in both "popular" and "classical" music alike, to function as such long after the advertisement is over: at this point the sounds *advertise* composer or performer and stand as *signs* for the pleasure about to be derived from the product, so that the work of art sinks to the level of consumers' goods in general. Compare in this regard the subliminal role of music in the movies, as a means of guiding our "consumption" of the plot, with the relationship of score to narrative in opera as an art form. And when, after this, we recall the high technical quality of present-day commercial composition in general, we begin to understand the destructive effect of such background music on the inherited concert repertoire, vast portions of which are eroded and emptied of their intrinsic vitality without our so much as realizing that it had ever been otherwise.

In this situation, therefore, the new in the older sense is not enough: art no longer has to do with a change in taste resulting from the succession of the generations alone, but with one intensified and raised to the second power by a new commercial exploitation of artistic techniques in every facet of our culture. The new music must come to terms not only with our hearing, as did the old, but with our nonhearing as well. Hence concrete music, which seeks to transform the unconscious contents of our daily perceptual life, the unheard aural stress of the industrial city, into a conscious object of perception. Hence the willed "ugliness" of modern music in general, as if, in this state of pathological hebetude and insensibility, only the painful remained as a spur to perception.

The parallel with language is only too clear, and it is enough to evoke the fad for rapid reading and the habitual conscious or unconscious skimming of newspaper and advertising slogans, for us to understand the deeper social reasons for the stubborn insistence of modern poetry on the materiality and density of language, on words felt not as transparency but rather as things in themselves. So also in the realm of philosophy the bristling jargon of seemingly private languages is to be evaluated against the advertising copybook recommendations of "clarity" as the essence of "good writing": whereas the latter seeks to hurry the reader past his own received ideas, difficulty is inscribed in the former as the sign of the effort which must be made to think real thoughts.

It is not only our hearing that is affected, but also the works themselves. In strict correlation with our own fitful attention, our lowered capacity for concentration, our absentmindedness and general distraction, the work of art suffers distortion, is broken down and fetishized. The whole comes to be replaced by the part, and instead of perceiving music as an organized structure, we are content to hear it while doing something else just as long as we can salute the principal melodies and themes in passing. What was once a complete and continuous discourse has become an indistinguishable blur intermittently illuminated by vulgar theme songs, motifs that have crystallized into objects and tokens, like clichés in speech. Our emotion comes to be magically invested in these entities: they are the source of a purely subjective pathos which has nothing to do with the original, integral work itself, but which is rather a result of its disintegration and of the absence of any whole response. No wonder, therefore, that modern music is so unmelodious, so resolutely unlyrical, so suspicious of the illusions of individual subjectivity and of the song in which it is supposed to affirm itself.

It is this breakdown of extended form in general to which the expressionistic music of Schoenberg is a memorial: a reaction against the idea of the completed work of art, a refusal of the very possibility of the self-sufficient masterpiece existing in and for itself. With the disappearance of the organizational value of the form as a whole the surface of the work is shattered and no longer presents an unbroken and homogeneous appearance (*Schein*), no longer stands complete and suspended, as it were, over against the world, but rather falls into it, becoming one object among others. Thus the musical work loses its most fundamental precondition: that autonomous time in which the themes live as in an element of their own, in which they were able to develop according to their own internal laws in that thorough interaction with each other, that leisurely drawing out of all the formal consequences known to aesthetics as *Spiel*. The shattering of the tonal framework frees the individual notes themselves from whatever had previously given them meaning; for the note, essentially a neutral and nonsignifying element like the phoneme in speech, derived its functional value as an intention—whether as consonance or dissonance, continuation in a given key or modulation toward some new one—from the overall system itself. So in tonality the mind held a kind of musical past and future together, whereas in the new atonal universe the note exists only insofar as it is part and parcel of a musical statement in the present. The new form must remain almost physically in touch with all of its components at any given moment: atonality is a kind of musical nominalism.

Now, therefore, the part has become the whole, and the themes become the music itself, which is over when they are over; so that the works shrink alarmingly and the revolutionary piano pieces that make up Opus 23 last only a few seconds apiece, each contained in a scant page of sheet music. (And in this context, the next step would seem to be single notes, and then silence: thus Webern may be seen as the logical completion of this tendency in early Schoenberg.) Hence the term expressionism, for where the motifs involved no longer find a formal justification within the larger relational system of the work itself they are obliged to be somehow *self-justifying*: pure expression, as autonomous and intelligible as a cry, an instant bounded by the limits of the mind's capacity to hold a single thought together. Such a situation places new stress on both listener and composer alike: for each of these works reinvents all of music within itself, like a speech each sentence of which would involve the simultaneous recreation of a new grammar to govern it.

And what holds for the form is visible on the level of *content* as well. One of the most striking features of Schoenberg's early music is undoubtedly that *fin de siècle* neurosis style which he shares with the other Austrian artists of his period, and through which his world seems so profoundly akin to that of Freud. The thinly disguised sexual longing of *Verklaerte Nacht* or *Gurre-Lieder*, the monodrama of female hysteria (*Erwartung*), lead little by little to a new flood of unconscious material.

This is no longer the mimesis of passions, but rather the undisguised registration through the musical medium of bodily impulses from the unconscious, of shocks and traumas which assault the taboos of the form inasmuch as the latter attempt to impose their censorship on such impulses, to rationalize them and to transpose them into images. Thus Schoenberg's formal innovations were intimately related to the changes in the things expressed, and helped the new reality of the latter to break through to consciousness. The first atonal works are transcripts, in the sense of the dream transcripts of psychoanalysis. . . . The scars of such a revolution in expression are, however, those blots and specks which as emissaries of the id resist the conscious will of the artist in both painting and music alike, which mar the surface and can as little be cleansed away by later conscious correction as the bloodstains in fairy tales. Real suffering has left them behind in the work of art as a sign that it no longer recognizes the latter's autonomy.[9]

Thus the work of art, during the expressionistic period, would seem to be reduced to the status of testimony and symptom, of charts, graphs, X-ray plates. Yet what if the Freudian raw material (now thought of not so much as the elements of theory or scientific hypothesis, but rather as a peculiar type of content in its own right: dreams, slips of the tongue, fixations, traumas, the Oedipal situation, the death wish) were itself but a sign or symptom of some vaster historical transformation? In this context, the Freudian topology of the mental functions may be seen as the return of a new type of allegorical vision and as the disintegration of the autonomous subject, of the cognito or self-governing consciousness in Western middle-class society. Now such characteristically Freudian phenomena are no longer seen as permanent mental functions awaiting throughout human history their discovery and revelation by Freud, but rather as new *events* of which Freud was at once contemporary and theorist. They mark, indeed, the gradual alienation of social relations and the transformation of the latter into autonomous and self-regulating mechanisms in terms of which the individual or independent personality is little by little reduced to a mere component part and, as it were, a locus of strains and taboos, a receiving apparatus for injunctions from all levels of the system itself. The former subject no longer thinks, he "is thought," and his conscious experience, which used to correspond to the concept of *reason* in middle-class philosophy, becomes little more than a matter of registering signals from zones outside itself, either those that come from within and "below," as in the drives and bodily and psychic automatisms, or from the outer circles of interlocking social institutions of all kinds. At the same time, the surviving remnant of the ego now falls victim to the illusion of its own continuing centrality: that which no longer is "in itself" continues to exist "for itself," and the subject wrongly continues to assume that there exists some correspondence between its inner monadic experience and that purely external network of circum-stances (economic, historical, social) which determines and manipu-lates it through mechanisms beyond the horizon of individual experience.

(It is at this point, of course, that the novel, as a meaningful identification between the individual and social dimensions, begins to come apart at the seams as a form. Now that individual experience has ceased to coincide with social reality, the novel is menaced by twin contingencies. If it holds to the purely existential, to the truth of subjectivity, it risks turning into ungeneralizable psychological ob-servation, with all the validity of mere case history. If, on the other hand, it attempts to master the objective structure of the social realm, it tends to be governed more and more by categories of abstract knowledge rather than concrete experience, and consequently to sink to the level of thesis and illustration, hypothesis and example.)

Yet atonality, however much it may testify to the loss of rational control in modern society, at the same time carries within itself the elements of a new kind of control, the requirements of a new order as yet still only latent in the historical moment. For whatever the will toward total freedom, the atonal composer still works in a world of stale tonality and must take his precautions with regard to the past. He must, for example, avoid the kind of consonance or tonal chord which would be likely to reawaken older listening habits, and to reorganize the music into noise or wrong notes. Yet this very danger is enough to awaken in atonality the first principle of a new law or order. For the taboo against accidentally tonal chords carries with it the corollary that the composer should avoid any exaggerated repeti-tion of a single note, for fear such an insistence would ultimately tend to function as a new kind of tonal center for the ear. It is necessary only to pose the problem of avoiding such repetition in a more formal way for the entire twelve-tone system to show itself upon the horizon. For ultimately the only logical solution is that of not repeating a given note until all of the other eleven notes of the scale have first been touched on, and with this the twelve-tone "row" is born and replaces tonality. Henceforth, each work shall be composed not in a key but "in" a particular and unique row, or arrangement of all twelve notes of the scale, devised for it alone, so that in a sense the twelve-tone work is "nothing more" than an immense theme and variations with the individual row as theme, a repetition over and over again of the same series of twelve notes, but this time in either the horizontal or the vertical dimension.

For the new system has the merit of abolishing one of the most ancient and fundamental contradictions in music, that between harmony and counterpoint, between the vertical and the horizontal, between the traditions of a massive orchestral sonority, on the one hand, and those which appeal back to a rather archaic polyphony, with its fugues and canons, on the other. Hitherto, it is as though there had existed mutually exclusive vertical and horizontal types of perception, which had alternated in a kind of Gestaltlike interference with each other, obliging the listener to choose between two hearings of a given superposition of sounds, either as a momentary intersection of voices in movement or as the massive intertwining of harmonic levels in a chord structure. Now, in the seething texture of Schoenberg's mature works, this opposition is abolished, and the row, which may at first have resembled an intricate, lengthy, highly articulated theme or melody, also serves, like some elaborate and complex molecule, as the building block for the vertical dimension of the score.

Thus the twelve-tone system serves as a kind of unified field theory for music, in which the data of harmony and that of counterpoint can now be translated back and forth into each other. And with this, other inherited dilemmas are solved as well: henceforth no element is too small to require its place in the overall scheme of things, no detail too insignificant to be made to furnish its credentials and to embody a meaning. Such relatively traditional matters as instrumentation are, for example, now codified, so that in the notion of *Klangfarbenmelodie* a given succession of instrumental timbres (such as the sequence violin, trumpet, piano) takes on the functional value of a sequence of notes in a melody. Thus there is carried to completion in the musical realm that basic tendency of all modern art in general toward a kind of absolute *overdetermination* of all of its elements, toward an abolition of chance, a kind of total absorption of the last remnants of sheer contingency in the raw material, which are henceforth painfully assimilated into the structure of the work itself.

(In the form of the novel this evolution follows a rigorous and exemplary internal logic: the earliest realistic novels justify their contingent elements—descriptions, historical background, choice of a particular subject such as the life of a soap manufacturer or a doctor —on the purely empirical grounds that such phenomena already exist in the world around us, and that they therefore need no justification. With Zola, however, this empirical, purely descriptive motivation is joined by a second one, which rises oddly behind it like the symptom-formation of a repressed impulse: this is the tendency to turn such facts, which seem to have no intrinsic self-justifying meaning in themselves, into symbols or grossly materialized pictures of meanings. Thus it is as if the mind, unable to bear the sheer contingency of this empirical reality, instinctively reckoned into such phenomena that unconscious, mythical, symbolic dimension which it denied them on the conscious level. Finally, with Joyce's *Ulysses*, which seemed at the time so naturalistic and conclusive a slice of life, this impulse has become a conscious intention, and the literary materials lead a double life on two separate levels, that of empirical existence and that of a total relational scheme not unlike the twelve-tone system itself, where each empirical fact is integrated into the whole, each chapter dominated by some basic symbolic complex, the motifs of the work related to each other by complicated charts and cross-references, and so forth.)

Thus, in a situation where subjective and objective have begun to split apart, Schoenberg's originality was to have driven the subjective and expressionistic to its outer limit, to the point at which the nerve-pictures and traumata of the latter slowly veer, under the pressure of their own internal logic, into the new objectivity, the more total order, of the twelve-tone system. The specificity of this solution may be better gauged against the diametrically opposed one of Stravinsky, who may be thought of as having worked out from the other, *objective* pole of the modern dilemma.

For already the privileged form in which Stravinsky works, the ballet, may be seen as a kind of applied music, which even more drastically than the "program music" that is contemporary with it reinvents a kind of distance between content and form within a medium that is otherwise nonrepresentational. Thus it is able to avoid the problems of self-justification and self-determination faced by pure music and resolved by Schoenberg in the way described above: for its musical practice is, as it were, already justified by the visual tableau itself, and after the fact by the physical movements of the dancers, which ratify it and of which it comes to seem the *accompaniment*.

And what happens to the form of these works is reproduced on the level of the content itself, particularly in the Russian ballets. Both *Petrouchka* and the *Rite of Spring* dramatize the sacrifice of individual subjectivity to an inhuman collectivity, and their deliberate primitivism (with its appeal to folk culture in *Petrouchka* or *L'Histoire du soldat*, and with its elemental, archaic, well-nigh prehistoric rhythms in the *Rite of Spring*) solicit the regression of their sophisticated listener/spectator toward a kind of sacrifice of the intellect in the sheer emotionalism of mass response. This ultrasophisticated primitivism or musical demagoguery (Adorno will go so far as to compare it as a phenomenon to Fascism) is inscribed in the technique of the works themselves, which, as opposed to the total organizational principles of Schoenberg, favors a kind of massive and discontinuous verticality. Its ritualistic beats and repetitions are broken by lapses and silences which create a syncopation with the returning shock waves of the listener's bodily reactions. Unlike Schoenberg, Stravinsky organizes the elements involved according to categories extrinsic to the musical structure, such as the isolated colors or qualities of the instruments themselves, or the psychological effects of their oppositions (loud and soft, piercing or massive).

To be sure, Stravinsky, and particularly the Stravinsky of the early ballets, is as influential and primal a musical phenomenon as Schoenberg himself; but it is instructive to compare the respective historical situations from which the innovations of each composer derived, and in particular "those 'Russian' characteristics of Stravinsky which have been so often and abusively stressed":

> It has often been observed that Moussorgsky's songs are distinguished from German lieder by the absence in them of a poetic *subject* or organizational point of view, each poem being treated as the composer of operas does his arias, not as an immediately subjective expression, but rather as a kind of objectification and distantiation of whatever emotion is involved. The artist fails to coincide with the lyrical subject. The category of the subject was nowhere near so solidly established in pre-middle-class Russia as in the Western countries. Whence the alienness of a Dostoyevsky, for instance, which stems from the lack of identity of the ego with itself: none of the brothers Karamazov is a 'character' in the sense of Western literature. Now this preindividuality stands the late-capitalist Stravinsky in good stead, in his legitimation of the collapse of the individual subject.[10]

His modernness is therefore the result of a kind of optical illusion, of a historical paradox in which pre- and post-individualism seem to meet, and are distinguished only by the deeper motivations at work beneath the surface. Thus where Schoenberg's expressionism was designed as a shock absorber for the unconscious material and ultimately as a means of mastering it and assimilating it to the form, Stravinsky's aim is to reproduce such effects directly as psychic events by assault on the nerve ends of his audience.

The value and direction of Stravinsky's artistic practice may be judged ultimately by the long series of neoclassical pastiches which succeed the Russian period. For here the bias toward musical objectivity may be openly observed at work in the way in which the composer renounces his own voice, abdicating that personal style which has become problematical in modern times and speaking through the fossilized subjectivity of dead composers, in a kind of witty stylistic masquerade reviving ghostly forms from a past when musical composition was still relatively free of internal contradictions. Thus Stravinsky's "way" ends in sterile imitation, in the writing of music about music (Palestrina with wrong notes, as someone has said); and indeed, in some ultimate squaring of the circle, we find him composing in the twelve-tone idiom itself, and taking his metaphysical adversary Schoenberg as his final avatar. (In literature, the theoretical justification for the use of such pastiche and parody has been made by Thomas Mann, for whom the act of speaking with irony through a dead style permits speech in a situation where it would otherwise be impossible. Joyce, once again, embodies an exemplary progress from a derivative personal style—showing period affinities with Walter Pater—through the multiple pastiches of *Ulysses*, toward something which transcends both style and pastiche altogether and which, like the twelve-tone system in the musical realm, may stand as a distant representation of some future linguistic organization of a postindividualistic character.)

It should not, however, be thought that Adorno finds Schoenberg's ultimate solution any less inherently contradictory in the long run than that of Stravinsky. How could it be otherwise, when the very inner tension and authenticity of Schoenberg's music result from the way that it at one and the same time both reflects and refuses the historical moment of which it is the memorial? This is perhaps the point at which to say something about Adorno's conception of the relationship of the work of art to its immediate historical situation, where indeed he appears to bet on all sides at once, simultaneously adopting mutually exclusive alternatives or variations on the basic model. The work of art "reflects" society and is historical to the degree that it *refuses* the social, and represents the last refuge of individual subjectivity from the historical forces that threaten to crush it: such is the position of that lecture on "Lyric and Society" which is one of Adorno's most brilliant essays. Thus the socioeconomic is inscribed in the work, but as concave to convex, as negative to positive. *Ohne Angst leben*: such is for Adorno the deepest and most fundamental promise of music itself, which it holds even at the heart of its most regressive manifestations.

On the other hand, the repeated characterization of Schoenberg's system as a "total" one deliberately underscores the relationship between that work and the totalitarian world in which it comes into being. For it is no less true that this drive toward a total organization of the work which we find operative in the twelve-tone system is symptomatic of an objective tendency in the socio-economic structure of the modern world itself. Indeed, it is hardly surprising that this music, which finds its reason for being in a reaction against the debasement of hearing in general, should as in a mirror image develop all the strengths and weaknesses of its adversary, in a kind of point by point correlation. And inasmuch as that phenomenon is itself profoundly social, and is at one with the commercialization of the modern world, modern music finds itself at once deeply implicated in a social struggle without so much as straying from the internal logic of pure musical technique, and reproduces the structure of the alienated society in miniature in the intrinsic language of the musical realm.

Thus the total organizational principle of Schoenberg's system reflects a new systematization of the world itself, of which the so-called totalitarian political regimes are themselves only a symptom. For in the later stages of monopoly or postindustrial capitalism not only the multiplicity of small business units, but also distribution, and ultimately the last free-floating elements of the older commercial and cultural universe, are now assimilated into a single all-absorbing mechanism. Now, when the entire business system with its projections in government and in the military and judicial branches depends for its very existence on the automatic sale of products which no longer correspond to any kind of biological or indeed social need and which are moreover for the most part identical with each other, marketing psychology obliges it to complete its conquest of the world by reaching down into the last private zones of individual life, in order to awaken the artificial needs around which the system revolves. Thus the total organization of the economy ends up by alienating the very language and thoughts of its human population, and by dispelling the last remnant of the older autonomous subject or ego: advertising, market research, psychological testing, and a host of other sophisticated techniques of mystification now complete a thorough *planification* of the public, and encourage the illusion of a life-style while disguising the disappearance of subjectivity and private life in the old sense. Meanwhile, what remains of the subjective, with its illusions of autonomy and its impoverished satisfactions, its ever diminishing images of happiness, is no longer able to distinguish between external suggestion and internal desire, is incapable of drawing a line between the private and the institutionalized, and finds itself therefore wholly delivered over to objective manipulation.[11]

This new totalitarian organization of things, people, and colonies into a single market-system is now duplicated by the planification of the work of art itself, whether in Joyce or in Schoenberg: the absolute conscious control which modern artists seek to establish over the last remnants of free-floating contingency reflects this increasing autonomy of institutions, this increasing "conquest" of both nature and society that they feel at work in the historical moment around them. It is no wonder, then, that Adorno's description of the relationship between art and society is ambiguous. The ambiguity had already been underlined in Thomas Mann's *Doctor Faustus*, whose theoretical sections Adorno inspired, and where the life of the twelve-tone composer Leverkühn stands in sharp allegorical parallel to the disintegration of Weimar Germany and its passage into Fascism. By which Thomas Mann meant to emphasize not the "evil" of modernism, after the fashion of a Wyndham Lewis, but rather the nature of tragedy in modern times: the possession of man by historical determinism, the intolerable power of history itself over life and over artistic creation, which is not free not to reflect what it reacts against.

In such a way, the contradictions of the age reenter the microcosm of the work of art and condemn it to ultimate failure also. Thus the system of Schoenberg, the product of an inhumanly systematized society, becomes itself a kind of straitjacket, a constraint rather than a liberating convention. The row does not replace tonality after all, but only sets itself to imitating it, and instead of evolving new forms, the new music returns to the composition of sonatas in twelve tones. But the old forms represented a triumph over the resistance of things, the result of a kind of stubborn logic in their raw material: these new ones are as distant from nature as the postindustrial universe itself, their matter as preformed and as lacking in any genuine internal logic as plastic. Nor is the identification of vertical with horizontal really achieved, but only willed: its symbol would appear to be that massive chord of all twelve tones which ends Berg's *Lulu* in a kind of blank indistinction or deathly synthesis of all the elements.

Finally, the listener's ability to hear cannot be fully regenerated, and the concrete experience of the simultaneity of the whole and its parts is no longer possible in modern times. The most successful audition of a work by Schoenberg yields, not a plenitude, but rather a kind of shadow work, an optical illusion in which the whole somehow floats above the concrete parts, not really at one with any of them in any given moment; in which the parts themselves flee hearing and extend beyond the present, are dissociated from the physical notes through which they are expressed and rise beyond them as a kind of blur or image superimposed: the distorted result of an attempt to imagine wholeness in a period that has no experience of it, under circumstances that doom the attempt to failure from the very start.

III

We are thus led little by little to reflect on the connection between such a dialectical vision of historical change, in which the various moments are articulated according to the various possible relationships between subject and object, and some hypothesis of a historical moment of plenitude or completion against which the other historical stages are judged and weighed. Such a moment is of course first and foremost nothing but a *logical* possibility: the concept of what Adorno calls *Versoehnung* or reconciliation between the subject and objectivity, between existence and the world, the individual consciousness and the external network of things and institutions into which it first emerges. The naïve projection of such a logical possibility into the realm of historical chronology can only result in metaphysical nostalgia (the golden age before the fall, the blissful state of primitive man) or in Utopianism. Yet in some more subtle fashion all so-called "theories of history" tend to organize themselves around the covert hypothesis of just such a moment of plenitude: think of Jeffersonian America or of the "unity of sensibility" of the Metaphysical poets; of the humaneness of medieval economic doctrine or of the organic continuity of an *ancien régime* unsullied by regicide or by the hubris of political self-determination; not to speak of the innumerable ideological exploitations of ancient Greece.

In the cultural realm, however, where the essential working opposition between subject and object is transposed into terms of form and content, such hypotheses have perhaps greater validity, and are in any case more verifiable. For if we are in no position to judge the concreteness of life at any given moment of the past, at least we can evaluate the adequacy of form to content in its cultural monuments, and are able to measure the reconciliation of intention and medium and the degree to which all visible matter is form, and all meaning or expression concrete embodiment.

So it is that for Adorno the work of Beethoven stands as a kind of fixed point against which earlier or later moments of musical history will be judged. It is, of course, not a question of degrees of genius, but rather of the inner logic of historical development itself, and of a kind of accumulation of formal possibilities of which Beethoven is the beneficiary and which suddenly makes possible an unexpected carrying through to their conclusion of all the unfinished trends, a filling out of all the hitherto empty spaces, and an actualization of the potentialities latent in the musical raw material itself.

In musical terms, that unique reconciliation which is Beethoven's historical opportunity takes the form of a precarious equilibrium between melody and development, between a new and richer thematic expression of subjective feeling and its objective working through in the form itself, which no longer has anything of that relatively mechanical and a priori, applied execution of eighteenth-century music. For the sheer volume of the production of the great eighteenth-century composers resulted in part from the presence to hand for them of relatively simple schemes and formulae of execution. Nor had orchestration yet become so complicated and individualistic an affair: the court orchestras of feudal principalities do not yet have the variety of instruments, let alone the sheer technical virtuosity, of the later middle-class stage orchestra. For all these reasons the themes of the eighteenth-century composers cannot be said to have achieved a genuine fullness of subjective being: a melody of Mozart is not yet self-sufficient and remains functionally conceived, bearing traces of the form of which it is an indivisible component.

Nor, on the other hand, does the Beethoven melody ever reach that extreme autonomy and overripeness of those devised by the hyper-subjective composers of the later nineteenth century—let Tchaikovsky stand as their archetype—for whom the contrapuntal work is reduced to a bare minimum, the working through of themes to perfunctory and monitory repetition, and in whose work the center of gravity of musical invention moves to sheer instrumental expressiveness and orchestral coloration.

Standing between these two extremes, the Beethoven melody represents a short-lived synthesis of the functional and the expressive: lengthy and articulate, it presents the appearance of autonomy while being at the same time shrewdly disposed and preformed with a view to the various developments, polyphonic or variational, which it is about to undergo. Reciprocally, the various subvoices of the development are still relatively independent and intrinsically meaningful, which cannot be said for those of late Romanticism; and they have something individual and personal about them which distinguishes them from their rather schematic and mechanical equivalents in earlier music. Thus subjectivity and the personal inform the score down to its smallest elements, but do so by working through the objective, suffusing and vivifying it, rather than by blotting it out and smothering it with the overwhelming harmonic and coloristic bias of later music. And what is true of the part holds, as we have already seen above, for the form as a whole, for the sonata as a short-lived possibility of meaningful organization on a large scale, in which the mind is momentarily able to glimpse a concrete totality, completely present at every instant of its unfolding.

Even though there is no exact literary equivalent for Beethoven and what he represents in the history of Western music, literary judgments ultimately depend on the presuppositions about form and content described above. Thus the privileged position of a Tolstoy in the history of the novel proves on closer examination to have an analogous basis. The relatively late development of middle-class literature in Russia leaves the nineteenth-century Russian novelist in a position of great freedom: everything remains to be done in the area of Russian themes, there is not the oppressive fact of earlier generations of novelists and of shelves of novels that weighs on the successors of Balzac or Dickens. Yet these Russian novelists, by their very tardiness, are contemporary with all that is most sophisticated in novelistic technique—with Maupassant and the naturalists—so that the Russian realistic novel in general and Tolstoy in particular can be born fully grown. Technique elsewhere laboriously acquired can here seem flowing and natural, resulting in that peculiar and characteristic reconciliation between the subjective intention and the novel's objective social material which we associate with the name of Tolstoy and in which both social and individual experience issue from the novelist's hand as though equally his own creations.

The dialectical structure of our negative judgments is even more apparent: think of the grimace and caricature to which we object in Balzac—is it anything more than a too hasty attempt to assimilate the objective social material—characters, furniture, institutions—to the personal enthusiasms of the author himself, imperiously deforming and distorting it for his own purposes? Think, on the other hand, of the rather metallic brittleness of Flaubert, which results from too rigid and surgical a suppression of the subjective dimensions of the work, until the hero becomes as vacuous as a recording eye, in *L'Education sentimentale*, and the work is finally, in *Salammbô*, degraded into cinematographic phantasmagoria. Think of the "mannered" quality of Henry James: those great pauses between meaningful half-sentences, the close-ups of small areas of objectivity in an attempt to infuse them with subjective intention, in the way a random word surrounded by a "pregnant" silence becomes ominous with meaning. Think of the precariousness of the synthesis of Joyce, in which matter once again seems momentarily reconciled with spirit, all the objects and detritus of the city luminous and as though informed by subjectivity—except that the seams show; there is something willful and arbitrary about the relationship of the individual chapters to each other, and the new reconciliation is paid for as dearly as that of Schoenberg in music. The novel is always an attempt to reconcile the consciousness of writer and reader with the objective world at large; so it is that the judgments we make on the great novelists fall not on them, but on the moment of history which they reflect and on which their structures pass sentence.

There can therefore be no doubt that the privileged synthesis of Beethoven's works corresponds to some peculiar freedom in the social structure of his time. Historical freedom, indeed, expanding and contracting as it does with the objective conditions themselves, never seems greater than in such transitional periods, where the life-style has not yet taken on the rigidity of a period manner, and when there is sudden release from the old without any corresponding obligation to that which will come to take its place. The dominant figure of Napoleon himself is symbolic of the basic ambiguity of this moment which follows the collapse of the feudal order in Europe and precedes the definitive setting up of the new ethical, political, and economic institutions of the middle classes which triumphed over it. He combines something of the fading values of feudality and sacred kingship with the frankly secular and propagandistic appeal of the charismatic political leaders of later middle-class society, yet at the same time can be assimilated neither to the bewigged absolute monarchs of the sixteenth and seventeenth centuries nor to the demagogues of the twentieth. Even the neoclassicism of the Napoleonic period is significant and points in two directions: for it seems to have been the last of the great Continental styles which—Gothic or Renaissance, baroque or rococo—swept across Europe in successive waves, leaving the sediment of monuments behind them; while on the other hand, it is the first form of modernism as well, in that it is secretly pastiche, art about art, and registers the contradictions of the middle-class world through its own inner contradictions in a way that will be characteristic of every artistic movement to follow.

Thus Beethoven's reconciliation between the subjective and the objective faithfully registers the enlarged horizons of the revolutionary transition period itself, when the positive and universalistic thinking of the middle class during its struggle for power has not yet given way to the *esprit de sérieux* of money, business, and *Realpolitik*; when the abstract idea of human freedom, whose optimism and heroics are eternalized in *Fidelio*, has not yet been transformed into an ideological defense of class privilege. And what is true for music holds for thought as well: philosophy, freed from the long constraint of theology, has not yet undergone the positivistic reduction to scientific empiricism, has not yet abdicated its rights to such newly invented academic disciplines as sociology or psychology, let alone begun to question its own validity in the manner of twentieth-century logical positivism. At this point in history thought is still out for the largest things, and it is to such a moment of possibility, such a moment of suspension between two worlds, that the philosophy of Hegel is the most ambitious and profoundly characteristic monument.

The problem of the role Hegelianism is called upon to play in a Marxist framework is clearly at one with the relationship between the values of the older middle-class revolution and the revolutionary consciousness and needs of the present day. Yet it is at once evident that the very principle at work in the dialectical analyses which we have described above—that of the adequation of subject and object, and of the possibility of reconciliation of I and Not-I, of spirit and matter, or self and world—is itself the very premise of Hegel's system and may be claimed to be virtually Hegel's intellectual invention.

For Hegel made concrete the merely abstract and empty affirmations of his predecessors that the objective external world is identical with that of spirit, and set out to demonstrate the multiplicity of ways in which such an identity is realized. From the objective point of view, the *Phenomenology of Spirit* is just such a demonstration of identity, showing how the most seemingly external or material phenomena (such as the objects of our sense perception and of our scientific research) are all informed with spirit, all profoundly involved with and penetrated by ideality. But from the subjective point of view, the *Phenomenology* is the story of an ascent and a development, a description of the successive stages through which consciousness enriches and solidifies itself, and from its most individualistic and subjectively limited moments gradually arrives at the condition of Absolute Spirit, in which it learns that it ultimately includes within itself all the abundance and multiplicity of the external and objective universe. Hegel is able to overcome the separation between subject and object by finding his starting point in a moment when that separation has not yet taken place: in the moment of experience itself, where the subject, still at one with its object, has not yet attained self-consciousness, has not yet learned to distinguish itself as a separate and abstractly independent entity, has not yet been able to draw back and look across a void toward the separate, equally abstract entity of things in themselves.

The dialectical method is precisely this preference for the concrete totality over the separate, abstract parts. Yet it is more complicated than any objective apprehension of a merely external kind of totality, such as takes place in the various scientific disciplines. For in these the thinking mind itself remains cool and untouched, skilled but un-self-conscious, and is able to forget about itself and its own thought processes while it sinks itself wholly in the content and problems offered it. But dialectical thinking is a thought to the second power, a thought about thinking itself, in which the mind must deal with its own thought process just as much as with the material it works on, in which both the particular content involved and the style of thinking suited to it must be held together in the mind at the same time. The dialectical thinking through of a mathematical problem, for example, would involve, besides the awareness of the problem on its own terms, an implicit comparison between the way the mind felt performing the mathematical transaction and its feel during the experience of other, entirely different scientific and nonscientific operations. Dialectical thought is therefore profoundly comparative in its very structure, even in its consideration of individual, isolated types of objects; and the chapter sequence of the *Phenomenology* is merely the objective working out of the set of comparisons already inherent in it. Yet comparison involves difference, and the movement from one chapter to another, from one form of consciousness to another, is that of a series of leaps, of a constant passage from one kind of raw material to another seemingly unrelated to it.

Indeed, the most striking aspect of the *Phenomenology* for the modern reader is that it presents, to use the terminology of the novel, no unity of point of view. The transitions between the chapters are not necessarily equivalent to moments of growth and change in the life of an individual. The content of the various chapters is quite heterogeneous, some of it coming from collective or historical experience, some from individual or ethical, some relating to action, some to pure knowledge. Corresponding to these two structural irregularities, the attacks on the Hegelian system have tended to fall into two distinct groups. On the one hand, the existential objection to Hegel has always been that there is a vital difference between the knowing of a transition between two moments and the living of it: the salvation of the slave may lie in a stoicism which will result in a whole new inner life for humanity, but generations of individual slaves must die before the qualitatively new moment is achieved. Nor, on the other hand, is the *Phenomenology* ultimately any more satisfying when examined from the objective point of view, where it seems to fall apart into a series of random observations and analyses, historical notes, psychological, philosophical, scientific, artistic data which would have to be analyzed separately by the various disciplines in question before their validity could be assumed.

Yet these criticisms are based on our own historical vantage-point. They presuppose the increasing intellectual specialization of the sciences in defining their various fields and methods, as well as a greater psychological awareness of the structure and value of individual life. They represent, therefore, not so much an intrinsic, logical critique of Hegel, as an almost physical discrepancy between his moment in time and our own, and it is this paradox which is at the center of Adorno's reading of Hegel. From our inability to realize the Hegelian vision of totality it does not follow that this vision is not fuller and richer, more concrete, than anything we can presently imagine. The impossibility of the Hegelian system for us is not a proof of its intellectual limitations, its cumbersome methods and theological superstructure; on the contrary, it is a judgment on us and on the moment of history in which we live, and in which such a vision of the totality of things is no longer possible.

Just as the Beethoven sonata stood as the precarious synthesis of whole and part, so the philosophy of Hegel is one long tension between the organization of the overall dialectic, with Absolute Spirit as the end result of the process, and the individual moments, the steps of the dialectic, the concrete analyses of the various kinds of experience along the way. The two components depend on each other and cannot be considered separately: a satisfactory reading of Hegel's thought at any point resembles in structure the listening demanded by the Beethoven sonata, where the part, the note or phrase, must be apprehended both in itself and in its position with respect to the whole, as variation, modulation, reprise, and so forth. It is therefore impossible to select individual insights from the system, to separate the valid from the no longer relevant. The terminology and the intellectual equipment of the various chapters presuppose a generalizing attitude toward experience, one which demands expansion if it is to be understood at all. The key ideas of self-consciousness and recognition, of the general and the concrete, of the concept and the notion, cannot be analyzed by themselves, for they all depend on and are part of the larger ideal of Absolute Spirit, of a consciousness for which the supreme value is a development of its own powers by the assimilation of the world outside until at length it reaches the point where it recognizes in itself seeds of everything in the objective universe, where it is able somehow to recognize the latter as being of the same substance with itself.

Yet the overall organization is no longer comprehensible for us. The organizational framework, the notion of an Absolute Spirit, the possibility for the isolated subjectivity to achieve an entire self-contained world, an equivalence with the real world itself, has become inadmissible and even unthinkable in modern society, where the highly restricted worth of the individual subjectivity is only too clear, where people are at once irrevocably interrelated to each other and condemned to view the whole through the distorting windows of their own positions in it. Thus, even though one can reread Hegel, we are never able to reach the vantage point of that last chapter which would finally permit us to catch a glimpse of the work as a whole. The synthesis remains imperfect, a mere imperative to unity, a dead letter: and this imperfect focus holds true even down to the reading and rendering of the individual sentences. The very indifference to publication, the unrevised and approximate versions in which the system has come down to us and which offer the paradox of "a thought of such boundless assertions renouncing the attempt to perpetuate itself in definitive and determinate form" suggest Hegel's own awareness of this dilemma. "In the sense in which we nowadays speak of antimatter," Adorno says, "the Hegelian texts are antitexts."[12] Such a structure accounts for the unique difficulty presented by a philosopher who can only be read in fragments and only understood in the light of the whole.

What happened was that the transitional indeterminacy of the period in which Hegel lived granted him a fortunate mirage, the optical illusion of Absolute Spirit; and this idealistic, abstract, and indeed imaginary concept was able to serve as the organizational framework for a profoundly realistic set of analyses of the world itself. For the work done depends not so much on the cast of mind of the philosopher as on the possibilities for development inherent in the organizational principle available to him. When Marx, for example, sets back on its feet this "dialectic standing on its head," as he called the idealism of Hegel, a reversal takes place in which his own material is at once more humanistic and less humane, in which he finds himself limited to the highly technical subject matter of economics. He grounds Hegel in reality but at the same time engages himself in a specialization from which it is difficult to reemerge into the wider possibilities opened up by his predecessor.

That system into which Hegel organized his thoughts and which he thought to be a property of things themselves was therefore latent in them only, and had not yet been realized in the actual historical world. A completely embodied philosophical system, a concrete intellectual reconciliation between the I and the Not-I, the subject and the world, would be possible only in a society in which the individual was already reconciled in fact with the organization of things and people around him: the concrete reconciliation would have had to precede the abstract formulation of it. So it is no wonder Hegel's system fails, just as it is no wonder that the vast artistic syntheses which are its equivalent in the twentieth century all cracked under the strain of their elaborate universalized pretense. But they already take place at a lower level of language, no longer on the level of understanding but rather on that of more elemental and immediate physical and emotional perceptions: and the real wonder is not so much that the Hegelian system fails as that it could be conceived and executed even to that degree of concreteness which it still possesses.

IV

Perhaps the only way to keep faith with the Hegelian spirit of systematization in a fragmented universe is to be resolutely unsystematic. In this sense Adorno's thought is profoundly Hegelian, thinking its motifs through in a genuinely Hegelian spirit, facing thereby its principal formal problem: How to write chapters of a phenomenology when there is no longer any possibility of a whole? How to analyze the part as a part when the whole is not only no longer visible but even inconceivable? How to continue to use the terms subject and object as opposites which presuppose, in order to be meaningful, some possible synthesis, when there is no synthesis even imaginable, let alone present anywhere in concrete experience? What language to use to describe an alienated language, to what systems of reference to appeal when all systems of reference have been assimilated into the dominant system itself? How to see phenomena in the light of history, when the very movement and direction that gave history its meaning seem to have been swallowed up in sand?

Adorno himself, now in the guise of a theoretician of the essay as a form, has attributed its lack of development in Germany to the reluc-

tance of German writers to surrender themselves to the almost frivolous and inconsequential freedom it presupposes, to make the painful
apprenticeship of an intellectual life amidst the fragmentary and the
ephemeral, to resist the ontological consolations of the *Hauptwerk*
and the monumental and to stand in the very river of history itself,
suffering their provisory constructions to undergo those ceaseless
metamorphoses which make up the life of an idea in time.

For the fundamental formal problem of the dialectical writer is
precisely that of continuity. He who has so intense a feeling for the
massive continuity of history itself is somehow paralyzed by that very
awareness. as in some overloading of perception too physical to be
any longer commensurable with language. Where all the dimensions
of history cohere in synchronic fashion, the simple linear stories of
earlier historians are no longer possible: now it is diachrony and
continuity which become problematical, mere working hypotheses.
Adorno's larger form will therefore be a construct rather than a
narrative. In the work on Schoenberg, of which we have given a brief
account above, the formal continuity is not that of Schoenberg's
chronological development (although a loose feeling of chronology is
maintained), but rather that of a series of abstract moments, of the
internal generation out of each other of the fundamental elements or
parts of Schoenberg's work seen as a total system. The individual
work of art is therefore understood as a balance between inner organs,
as an intersection of what we can call determinate categories of a
stylistic nature, separate yet profoundly interdependent on each other,
such that a modification of one (such as the intensity of instrumental
coloration) immediately involves a shift in the proportions of the
others (temporal dimensions of the work, contrapuntal development,
and so forth). Change takes place in an artist's development as a
result of such a modification in the relationships that obtain between
the fundamental categories of the work itself; the dialectical *critic*,
however, will plot this change on his graph as a series of moments
which generate each other out of their own internal contradictions.[13]

When we turn now to the shorter pieces, and particularly to that
series of *Notes on Literature* which is perhaps Adorno's masterpiece,
we find that as mental operations they consist precisely in the perceptual registering and isolation, indeed in a virtual invention and naming for the first time, of those categories or component parts of which
the larger dialectical form had been an interlocking construction. Let
the subjects of some of them—the relation of titles to works, sensitivity to punctuation, the uses of interlarded foreign words and phrases,

the physical impression books make—illustrate the working method itself: they imply dialectical self-consciousness, a sudden distancing which permits the most familiar elements of the reading experience to be seen again strangely, as though for the first time, making visible the unexpected articulation of the work into determinate categories or parts. The premise remains that of the most thoroughgoing network of internal relationships, so that it is precisely the apprehension of the apparently discrete and external—the predilection in a novelist, for instance, for epigraphs to his chapters—which as a heuristic principle leads to those deeper formal categories against which the surface is organized. These essays are therefore the concrete working out of that formal category of Adorno's own production which we have described earlier under the sign of the *footnote*: an observation which may itself be thought of as a tribute to his method insofar as it amounts to a pastiche of it.

Such essays are thus the fragments of or footnotes to a totality which never comes into being; and what unites them, I am tempted to say, is less their thematic content than it is on the one hand their style, as a perpetual present in time of the process of dialectical thinking itself, and on the other their basic intellectual coordinates. For what as fragments they share in spite of the dispersal of their raw material is the common historical situation itself, that moment of history which marks and deforms in one way or another all the cultural phenomena which it produces and includes, and which serves as the framework within which we understand them. To this concrete situation itself the language makes fateful and monitory allusion: *the* administered world, *the* institutionalized society, *the* culture industry, *the* damaged subject—an image of our historical present which is Adorno's principal sociological contribution and which yet, as we have pointed out above, is never expressed directly in the form of a *thesis*. Rather, it intervenes as a series of references to a state of things with which our familiarity is already presupposed, a reality with which we are presumed to be only too well acquainted. The mode is that characteristic German sarcasm which may be said to have been Nietzsche's contribution to the language and in which a constant play of cynical, colloquial expressions holds the disgraced real world at arm's length, while abstractions and buried conceptual rhymes compare it with the impossible ideal.

At the same time, there seems to me to be a profoundly stylistic motivation behind such indirection. We have said that for Adorno— as indeed for Hegel, as for all dialectical thinkers to the degree that they are genuinely dialectical—thinking dialectically means nothing more or less than the writing of dialectical sentences. It is a kind of stylistic obedience analogous to that which governs the work of art itself, where it is the shape of the sentences themselves, above and beyond all conscious reflection, that determines the choice of the raw material. So here also the quality of the idea is judged by the type of sentence through which it comes to expression. For insofar as dialectical thinking is thought about thought, thought to the second power, concrete thought about an object, which at the same time remains aware of its own intellectual operations in the very act of thinking, such self-consciousness must be inscribed in the very sentence itself. And insofar as dialectical thinking characteristically involves a conjunction of opposites or at least conceptually disparate phenomena, it may truly be said of the dialectical sentence what the Surrealists said about the image, namely, that its strength increases proportionately as the realities linked are distant and distinct from each other.

Thus, if the work of Adorno nowhere yields that bald statement about the administered world which would seem to be its presupposition, if he nowhere takes the trouble to express in outright sociological terms that theory of the structure of the "institutionalized society" which serves as a hidden explanation and essential cross-reference for all the phenomena under analysis, this is to be explained not only by the fact that such material belongs to a study of the infrastructure rather than of ideological materials, and that it is already implicit in classical Marxist economics, but above all by the feeling that such outright statements, such outright presentations of sheer *content*, are stylistically wrong, this stylistic failure being itself a mark and a reflection of some essential failure in the thought process itself. For in a purely sociological presentation the thinking subject eclipses himself and seems to let the social phenomenon come into view objectively, as a fact, as a thing in itself. Yet for all that the observer does not cease to have a position with respect to the thing observed, and his thoughts do not cease to be conscious operations even when he ceases to be aware of them as such. Thus the overt presentation of content in its own right, whether in sociological or in philosophical writing, stands condemned as a fall back into that positivistic and empirical illusion which dialectical thinking was designed to overcome.

Yet if what Sartre would have called the "untotalizable totality" of Adorno's system, its absent center, cannot be conceptually described as a positivistic "theory of society" in its own terms, if the placelessness of so-called objective thought is ruled out by the very commitment of the system to self-consciousness, there is nonetheless another way in which such an absent totality may be evoked. It is to this ultimate squaring of the circle that Adorno came in his two last and most systematic, most technically philosophical works, *Negative Dialectics* and *Aesthetic Theory*. Indeed, as the title of the former suggests, these works are designed to offer a theory of the untheorizable, to show why dialectical thinking is at one and the same time both indispensable and impossible, to keep the idea of system itself alive while intransigently dispelling the pretensions of any of the contingent and already realized systems to validity and even to existence.

The essential argument of *Negative Dialektik*, and Adorno's ultimate philosophical position, seems to me to be an articulation on the theoretical level of that methodology which we have seen at work in a concrete, practical way in the earlier aesthetic essays and critical writings. For there we found that in the long run the content of a work of art stands judged by its form, and that it is the realized form of the work which offers the surest key to the vital possibilities of that determinate social moment from which it springs. Now the same methodological discovery proves valid in the realm of philosophical thought itself; and the practice of negative dialectics involves a constant movement away from the official content of an idea—as, for example, the "real" nature of freedom or of society as things in themselves—and toward the various determinate and contradictory forms which such ideas have taken, whose conceptual limits and inadequacies stand as immediate figures or symptoms of the limits of the concrete social situation itself.

So it is, at the very outset, with the idea of the dialectic itself, which had in Hegel "as its foundation and its result the primacy of the subject, or, in the well-known language of the introductory remarks to the *Logic*, the identity of identity and nonidentity."[14] But the very mark of the modern experience of the world itself is that precisely such identity is impossible, and that the primacy of the subject is an illusion, that subject and outside world can never find such ultimate identity or atonement under present historical circumstances. Yet if that ultimate synthesis toward which dialectical thought moves turns out to be unattainable it must not be thought that either of the terms of that synthesis, either of the conceptual opposites which are its subject and object, are any more satisfactory in their own right. The object considered in itself, the world taken as directly accessible content, results in the illusions of simple empirical positivism, or in an academic thinking which mistakes its own conceptual categories for solid parts and pieces of the real world itself. In the same way, the exclusive refuge in the subject results in what is for Adorno the subjective idealism of Heideggerian existentialism, a kind of ahistorical historicity, a mystique of anxiety, death, and individual destiny without any genuine content. Thus a negative dialectic has no choice but to affirm the notion and value of an ultimate synthesis, while negating its possibility and reality in every concrete case that comes before it.

Such thought therefore aims at maintaining contact with the concrete, painfully continuing a process of thinking about the world itself, at the same time that it rectifies its own inevitable falsifications at every moment, thus appearing to unravel everything it had been able to achieve. Yet not altogether: for the genuine content acquired remains, albeit in what Hegel would have called a canceled and transcended fashion; and negative dialectics does not result in an empty formalism, but rather in a thoroughgoing critique of forms, in a painstaking and well-nigh permanent destruction of every possible hypostasis of the various moments of thinking itself. For it is inevitable that every theory about the world, in its very moment of formation, tends to become an object for the mind and to be itself invested with all the prestige and permanency of a real thing in its own right, thus effacing the very dialectical process from which it emerged: and it is this optical illusion of the substantiality of thought itself which negative dialectics is designed to dispel.

So it is, for instance, that in a classic essay on society Adorno shows not only how every possible idea we form about society is necessarily partial and imperfect, inadequate and contradictory, but also that those very *formal* contradictions are themselves the most precious indications as to how we stand with respect to the concrete reality of social life itself at the present moment of time. For society is clearly not some empirical object which we can meet and study directly in our own experience: in this sense the neopositivistic criticism, which considers the idea of society an inadmissible abstract construct or a mere methodological hypothesis with no other kind of real existence, is justified. At the same time society—precisely in the form of such an impossible, suprapersonal abstraction—is present in the form of an ultimate constraint upon every moment of our waking lives: absent, invisible, even untenable, it is at the same time the most concrete of all the realities we have to face, and "while the notion of society may not be deduced from any individual facts, nor on the other hand be apprehended as an individual fact itself, there is nonetheless no social fact which is not determined by society as a whole."[15] Thus the contradictions of pure thought turn out to reflect the contradictions of their object as well, and that in the very moment when those initial conceptual contradictions seemed to forbid us any access to the real object to which they were supposed to correspond. Similarly, in the posthumous *Aesthetische Theorie*, the traditional foundations of aesthetic philosophy are at once discredited and given fresh justification by a constant shuttling back and forth between the historical facts of the world of artistic practice and the abstract conceptual categories through which that practice is perceived, at the same time that they reflect it.

We may therefore say that "the negative dialectic" represents an attempt to save philosophy itself, and the very idea of philosophizing, from a fetishization in time, from the optical illusion of stasis and permanency. Such antisystematic systematization, with all the deep inner contradictions it involves, reminds me of nothing quite so much as those equally contradictory monuments of modern art and literature which in their attempt to say everything end up saying only that one thing; which in their convulsive effort to present themselves, in almost medieval fashion, as the very book of the world itself, end up being but one book among others in a universe so disparate that no single thought can encompass it. Thus Barthes' observation about Proust, "whose whole work constitutes a simultaneous approach to and postponement of Literature itself," might also be applied to Adorno's philosophical position: "The writer thereby falls again into the power of time, for it is impossible to negate within the temporal continuum without at the same time elaborating a positive art which must be destroyed in its turn. Thus the greatest modern works linger as long as possible, in a kind of miraculous suspension, on the very threshold of Literature itself, in that waiting-room situation in which the density of life is given and protracted without yet being destroyed by the creation of an order of signs."[16]

It is therefore not to the discredit of *Negative Dialektik* to say that it is in the long run a massive failure; or, in different terms, that it stands as a kind of hyperconscious abstraction of that genuine totality of thought which Adorno's works taken as a whole embody. No doubt the emphasis on method and on the theory rather than the practice of negative dialectics risks giving an exaggerated and distorted importance to the moment of failure which is present in all modern thinking: and it is this overemphasis, more than anything else, which seems to me to account for that lack of political commitment with which radical students reproached Adorno at the end of his life. Yet his concrete studies remain incomparable models of the dialectical process, essays at once both systematic and occasional, in which pretext and consciousness meet to form the most luminous, if transitory, of figures or tropes of historical intelligibility: "like its object, knowledge remains shackled to the determinate contradiction."[17]

NOTES

1. T. W. Adorno, *Philosophie der neuen Musik* (Frankfurt, 1958), pp. 62–63.
2. This should not, however, be taken as evidence for the presence of two alternating and imperfectly assimilated modes of dialectical thought in Adorno's own work. There, on the contrary, an almost physical cause may be said to account for the structural peculiarity of the text in question, which is neither more nor less than a complete *footnote*: and the abundance, as well as the stylistic and philosophical quality, of the footnotes to *Philosophie der neuen Musik* is itself "no accident" and has symptomatic value. The footnote in this context may indeed be thought of as a small but autonomous *form*, with its own inner laws and conventions and its own determinate relationship to the larger form which governs it—something on the order of the moral of a fable or the various types of digressions which flourished within the nineteenth-century novel. In the present instance, the footnote as a lyrical form allows Adorno a momentary release from the inexorable logic of the material under study in the main text, permitting him to shift to other dimensions, to the infrastructure as well as to the wider horizons of historical speculation. The very limits of the footnote (it must be short, it must be complete) allow the release of intellectual energies, in that they serve as a check on a speculative tendency that might otherwise run wild, on what we will later describe as the proliferation of "theories of history." The footnote as such, therefore, designates a moment in which systematic philosophizing and the empirical study of concrete phenomena are both false in themselves; in which living thought, squeezed out from between them, pursues its fitful existence in the small print at the bottom of the page.
3. Marx and Engels, *Über Kunst und Literatur* (Berlin, 1953), p. 122.
4. T. W. Adorno, *Versuch über Wagner* (Frankfurt, 1952), p. 8.
5. T. W. Adorno, *Moments musicaux* (Frankfurt, 1964), p. 123.
6. See, for example, Renato Poggioli's *Theory of the Avant-Garde* (Cambridge, Mass., 1968).
7. *Philosophie der neuen Musik*, p. 147.
8. *Versuch über Wagner*, p. 67.
9. *Philosophie der neuen Musik*, pp. 42–43.
10. *Philosophie der neuen Musik*, pp. 134–135.
11. For the most comprehensive description of this process, see Paul Baran and Paul Sweezy, *Monopoly Capital* (New York, 1966), esp. Chaps. V, X, and XI.
12. T. W. Adorno, *Drei Studien zu Hegel* (Frankfurt, 1957), p. 136.
13. For more on this problem, which concerns the relative validity of Hegelian

and Marxist dialectics, see the final chapter of my *Marxism and Form.*
14. T. W. Adorno, *Negative Dialektik* (Frankfurt, 1966), p. 17.
15. T. W. Adorno, "Society," *Salmagundi,* Nos. 10–11 (Fall 1969–Winter 1970), p. 145.
16. Roland Barthes, *Le Degré zéro de l'écriture* (Paris, 1953), pp. 58–59.
17. *Philosophie der neuen Musik,* p. 33.

The Problem of Textuality:
Two Exemplary Positions

Edward W. Said

The pages that follow work through two powerful, contemporary "ways" of considering, describing, analyzing, and dealing theoretically with the problem of textuality, a manifestly central problem for anyone concerned with criticism and theory. These "ways"—with only the slightest allusion to Proust's "ways" intended—are Foucault's and Derrida's. My analysis of these two theories is part of an attempt to characterize an exemplary critical consciousness as situated between, and ultimately refusing both, the hegemony of the dominant culture and what I call the sovereignty of systematic method. Moreover, I will argue that for both these critics, critical work is a cognitive activity, a way of discovery, not by any means a purely contemplative activity; indeed, I will go so far as to say that in our present circumstances criticism is an adversary, or oppositional, activity. Finally—and I am depressingly aware that these prefatory comments are far too schematic—I will discuss Derrida's *mise en abîme* and Foucault's *mise en discours* as typifying the contrast between a criticism claiming that *il n'y a pas d'hors texte* and one discussing textuality as having to do with a plurality of texts, and with history, power, knowledge, and society. Far from mediating or reconciling these vividly contrasting theses about textuality, whose protagonists serve me as but two instances of a very wide theoretical divergence polarizing contemporary criticism, my position uses both in what is its own best interest since both strike me as indispensable to any cogent critical position.

I

Derrida and Foucault are opposed to each other on a number of grounds, and perhaps the one specially singled out in Foucault's at-

tack on Derrida—that Derrida is concerned only with "reading" a
text and that a text is nothing more than the "traces" found there by
the reader—would be the appropriate one to begin with here.[1] According to Foucault, if the text is important for Derrida because its
real situation is literally an abysmally textual element, *l'écriture en
abîme* with which (Derrida says in "La double séance") criticism so
far has been unable really to deal,[2] then for Foucault the text is
important because it inhabits an element of power (*pouvoir*) with a
decisive claim on actuality, even though that power is invisible or
implied. Derrida's criticism therefore moves us *into* the text, Foucault's *in* and *out* of it.

Yet neither Foucault nor Derrida would deny that what unites
them—more, even, than the avowedly revisionist and revolutionary
character of their criticism as theory, performance, pedagogy—is
their attempt to *make visible* what is customarily invisible in a text,
namely, the various mysteries, the rules, and the "play" of its textuality. Except for one word, Foucault would not, I think, disagree with
the rather abrupt definition of textuality advanced by Derrida at the
opening of *La Pharmacie de Platon*, that "a text is a text only if at first
glance and to the first comer it hides the law of its composition and
the rule of its internal play. Besides a text always remains imperceptible. Its law and its rule do not merely shelter themselves inside
something so inaccessible as a secret, because they quite simply do
not ever give themselves up (*elles ne se livrent jamais*), at least at
present, to anything that we might rigorously call a perception."[3] The
rather troublesome word is "jamais," although it is so subtly qualified
by Derrida as partly to lose its interdictory force: so I shall ignore the
qualifiers and retain the obvious assertiveness of the statement. To
say that the text's textual intention and integrity are invisible is to say
that the text hides something, that the text implies, perhaps also
states, embodies, represents, but *does not immediately disclose* something. At bottom, this is a gnostic doctrine of the text to which, in
quite different ways, Foucault and Derrida both assent.

Foucault's whole enterprise has taken it for a fact, however, that if
the text hides something, or if something about the text is *invisible*,
these things can be *revealed* and *stated*, albeit in some other form,
mainly because the text is part of a network of power whose textual
form is a purposeful obscuring of power beneath (or in) textuality
and knowledge (*savoir*). Therefore the countervailing power of criticism is to bring the text back to a certain visibility. More: that if
some texts, particularly those in the later phases of a discursive development, *assume* their textuality because their sources in power

have either been incorporated into the text's authority as text or obliterated, it is the archaeologist's task to serve as a countermemory for the text, to put the network around and, finally, *before* the text, where it can be seen. Derrida works more in the spirit of a kind of negative theology.[4] The more he grasps textuality for itself, the greater the detail of what is *not* there for him; as will become evident shortly, I consider his key terms, *"dissémination," "supplément," "pharmakos," "trace," "marque,"* and the like, to be not only terms describing "la dissimulation de la texture" but also quasi-theological terms ruling and operating the textual domain his work has opened.

In both cases, nevertheless, the critic challenges the culture and its apparently sovereign powers of intellectual activity, which we may call "system" or "method," when in dealing with texts these powers aspire to the condition of science. The challenge is delivered in characteristically large gestures of differentiation: Derrida refers everywhere to Western metaphysics and thought, Foucault in his earlier work to various periods, epochs, *epistémès*, that is, those totalities which build the dominant culture into its controlling, incorporating, and discriminating institutions. Each "way," Foucault's and Derrida's, attempts not only to *define* these challenged entities but also in some persistent fashion to *dedefine* them, to attack the stability, authority, presence, power of their rule, to dissolve them if at all possible. For both writers, their work is meant to replace the tyranny and the fiction of direct *reference*—of what Derrida calls *presence*, or the transcendental signified—with the rigor and practice of textuality mastered on its own highly eccentric ground in Derrida's case, and in Foucault's, *in* its highly protracted, enduring, systematized, and sustained persistence. Dedefinition and antireferentiality are Derrida's and Foucault's common response to the *positivist* ethos which they both abhor. On the other hand both have constantly appealed to empiricism and to the nuanced perspectivism they seem to have derived from Nietzsche.

There is some irony in the fact that both Derrida and Foucault are solicited nowadays for literary criticism, since neither of them is in fact a literary critic. One is a philosopher, the other a philosophic historian. Their material, however, is generically hybrid: quasi-philosophical, quasi-literary, quasi-scientific, quasi-historical. Similarly, their positions in the academic or university world are anomalous in ways that need no very elaborate description here. I suppose that what I am drawing attention to is a fundamental uncertainty in their works as to what they are doing, theorizing over the problem of textuality or—and this is egregiously obvious in Derrida's case, especially since *Glas*, but also noticeable in Foucault's—practicing an alternative textuality of their own. Later I propose to discuss the doctrinal and didactic aspects of their works; now I want simply to state that, at least since *De la grammatologie* (or at least more explicitly *since* than before it), Derrida has attempted what he has called a form of *écriture double*, one half of which "provoque un renversement," a complete overturning of the cultural domination he everywhere identifies with metaphysics and its hierarchies, the other half of which "causes a form of writing to explode right in the middle of speech itself, thereby disorganizing all accepted convention of order and invading the whole field."[5] This unbalanced and unbalancing (*decalée et decalante*) writing is intended by Derrida to mark the admittedly uneven and undecidable fold (*pli*) in his work between the description of a text, which he deconstructs, and the enactment of a new one, with which his reader must now reckon. Similarly in Foucault's case, there is a "double writing" (which is not the name he gives it) intended first to describe (by *re*presenting) the texts he studies, as discourse, archive, statements, and the rest, then later to present a new text, his own, doing and saying what those other "invisible" texts have repressed, doing and saying what no one else will say and do.

This simultaneous, intertextual before and after in their writing is designed by both Derrida and Foucault to dramatize the differences between what they do and what they describe, between the logocentric and discursive worlds, on the one hand, and the Derridean and Foucauldian critique, on the other. In both their cases there is a postulated and repeatedly proved culture against which their definitions are directed. Their characterizations of the culture are ample of course, but so far as I am concerned one aspect of these characterizations is extremely problematic.

First Foucault. As he outlines it in *L'Archéologie du savoir* and *L'Ordre du discours*, the archaeological method is supposed to reveal how discourse—impersonal, systematic, highly regulated by enunciative formations—overrides society and governs the production of culture. Foucault's thesis is that *individual* statements, or the chances that individual authors *can* make individual statements, are *not* really likely. Over and above every opportunity for saying something there stands a regularizing collectivity which in his more recent work Foucault has called a discourse, itself governed by the archive. Thus his studies of delinquency, the penal system, and sexual repression are studies of a certain *anonymity* during and because of which, Foucault says in *Surveiller et punir*, "le corps humain entre dans une machinerie de pouvoir qui le fouille, le désarticule et le recompose." The responsibility for this *machinerie* is a *discipline*, a turn taken by discourse when it enters the ranks of administrative justice; but here too Foucault dissolves individual responsibility in the interests not so much of collective responsibility as of institutional will:

> The human body was entering a machinery of power that explores it, breaks it down, and rearranges it. . . . These methods, which made possible the meticulous control, of the operations of the body, which assured the constant subjection of its forces and imposed upon them a relation of docility-utility, might be called "disciplines."[6]

In a variety of ways, therefore, Foucault is concerned with *assujettissement,* the subjugation of individuals in society to some suprapersonal discipline or authority. He is obviously anxious to avoid vulgar determinism in explaining the workings of the social order, yet the whole category of intention is pretty much ignored by Foucault. He is conscious of this difficulty, I think, and his account of something called a will to knowledge (and power)—*la volonté de savoir*—attempts in some way to redress the asymmetry in his work between the blindly anonymous and the intentioned. Yet the problem of the relationship between individual subject and collective force (which reflects also the problem of the dialectic between voluntary intention and determined movement) is still an explicit difficulty, and it is acknowledged by Foucault as follows:

> Can one speak of science and its history (and therefore of its conditions of existence, its changes, the errors it has perpetrated, the sudden advances that have sent it off on a new course) without reference to the scientist himself—and I am speaking not merely of the concrete individual represented by a proper name, but of his work and the particular form of his thought? Can a valid history of science be attempted that would retrace from beginning to end the whole spontaneous movement of an anonymous body of knowledge? Is it legitimate, is it even useful, to replace the traditional "X thought that . . ." by a "it was known that . . ."? But this is not exactly what I set out to do. I do not wish to deny the validity of intellectual biographies, or the possibility of a history of theories, concepts, or themes. It is simply that I wonder whether such descriptions are themselves enough, whether they do justice to the immense density

of scientific discourse, whether there do not exist, outside their customary boundaries, systems of regularities that have a decisive role in the history of the sciences. I should like to know whether the subjects responsible for scientific discourse are not determined in their situation, their function, their perceptive capacity, and their practical possibilities by conditions that dominate and even overwhelm them.[7]

This is shrewd, perhaps even disarming, self-criticism, but the questions have yet to be answered. Certainly Foucault's work since the *Archéologie du savoir,* and since the two long interviews given in 1968 to *Esprit* and *Cahiers pour l'analyse,*[8] has progressed in the directions suggested by his remark about individuals, "I wonder whether such descriptions are themselves enough." That is, he has provided a prodigiously detailed set of possible descriptions whose main aim is, once again, to overwhelm the individual subject or will and to replace it instead with minutely responsive rules of discursive formation, rules that no one individual can either alter or circumvent. These rules *exist,* and they are to be complied with mainly because discourse is not mere formalization of knowledge; its aim is the control and manipulation of knowledge, the *body* politic, and ultimately (although Foucault is evasive about this) the State.

Foucault's dissatisfaction with the subject as sufficient cause of a text and his recourse to the invisible anonymity of discursive and archival power are curiously matched by Derrida's own brand of involuntarism. This is a very complex and, to me, deeply troubling aspect of Derrida's work. On the one hand, there are Derrida's frequent references to Western metaphysics, to a philosophy of presence and all that it entails and explains about a fairly wide variety of texts, from Plato, through Descartes, Hegel, Kant, Rousseau, Heidegger, and Lévi-Strauss; on the other hand, there is Derrida's attention to the minutiae, the inadvertent elisions, confusions, circumspections on certain key points, to be found in a number of important texts. What his readings of a text are meant to uncover is silent complicity between the superstructural pressures of metaphysics and an ambiguous innocence about a detail at the level of base, for example, Husserl's merely verbal distinction between expressive and indicative signs or the vacillation (discussed in *"Ousia* et *Grammé"*) between Aristotle's *nun* and *ama.*[9] Yet the mediating agency between the level of detail and the superstructural level is neither referred to nor taken into account. In some cases, including the two I have mentioned, Derrida's implication is that the writer deliberately eluded the problems sprung on him by his own verbal behavior, in which event we are to suppose perhaps that he is being pressured involuntarily by the superstructure and the teleological biases of "metaphysics." In other instances, however, the writer's own complex textual practice is divided against itself; the undecidability of a term—for example, *"pharmakos," "supplément,"* or *"hymen"*—is built into the text and its workings. Yet as to whether or not the writer was aware of this undecidability is a question posed explicitly only once by Derrida, and then dropped. Here is his rather allusive treatment of the problem in *Of Grammatology*:

> In Rousseau's text, after having indicated—by anticipation and as a prelude—the function of the sign "supplement," I now prepare myself to give special privilege, in a manner that some might consider exorbitant, to certain texts like the *Essay on the Origin of Languages* and other fragments on the theory of language and writing. By what right? And why these short texts, published for the most part after the author's death, difficult to classify, of uncertain date and inspiration?
>
> To all these questions and within the logic of their system, there is no satisfying response. In a certain measure and in spite of the theoretical precautions that I formulate, my choice is in fact *exorbitant*.[10]

What Derrida is really asking himself is whether what he does and whether the texts he has chosen for this analysis of Rousseau have anything to do with Rousseau, what Rousseau did or intended to do, or not. Did Rousseau value and emphasize the *Essay on the Origin of Languages*, or not? Moreover, in posing the questions and then saying that there is no satisfying response, isn't Derrida himself still relying on the very notion of intention which he tried to make exorbitant to his method? For despite his insistent criticism of such terminalistic or barrier ideas as *source* and *origin*, Derrida's own writing, in a passage like this one, is full of them. His word "privilege" for what he does, like his escape at the end of the passage into "exorbitance," does not diminish his reliance upon the notion of "Rousseau" as an author having a specifiable life span, an evident canon of texts, datable and classifiable works and periods, and so forth. There is also an eighteenth century, an age of Rousseau, and a much larger closure called Western thought—all of which seem to exert some influence on what texts mean, on their *vouloir-dire*. What "Rousseau" designates in all this is something clearly more than

Derrida can ignore, even when he puts quotation marks around the name. To what extent is the phrase "my choice" to be understood as indicating mere intellectual willfulness and to what extent a methodological act of philosophical liberation from "the totality of the age of logocentrism?" Is the word "supplement" emphasized *before* Derrida's exorbitance, and is his passage therefore prepared for in part by Rousseau himself out of the logocentric world; or is the choice made *exorbitantly*, and hence *from exteriority*, in which case we must ask how (since method is the issue) one can systematically place oneself outside "the logocentric world" when every other writer somehow cannot. And what is the content of the will enabling such a translation of verbally ensnared philosopher into a new, efficient reader?

The severity of these questions is validated by Derrida himself, who in his critique of Foucault had barraged the *Historie de la folie* with objections to its cavalier indifference about its own discursive complicities. In accusing Foucault of not having dealt sufficiently with the philosophic and methodological problems of discussing the silence of unreason in a (more or less) rational language, Derrida opens up the question of Foucault's rigor. For even if Foucault claims to be himself using a language maintained in a "relativity without recourse," Derrida is entitled to ask

On what in the final analysis he has caused this language to depend, as if without seeming in fact to depend on anything this language pronounces its own nonrecoursability? Who has written and who must listen to this language, in what specific language and as a result of what historical situation of the *logos* must one understand how this language was written and how it was intended to be received? . . .[11]

The issue here is Foucault's claim to be liberating folly from its forcible enclosure inside Western culture. To which claim Derrida's answer is:

I would therefore to tempted to say that Foucault's book is itself a powerful gesture of protection and enclosure. It is a twentieth-century Cartesian gesture. It is a sort of recovery of negativity. For apparently it is reason itself which it has enclosed, but just as Descartes did, Foucault has chosen as his target, not the possibility of meaning in general but a sort of yesterday's reason.[12]

For what Derrida claims to have found Foucault doing is reading Descartes naively, mistaking Descartes and domesticating notions of doubt, making it appear that Descartes had severed folly from reason; whereas, according to Derrida, a close reading of Descartes' text shows the contrary, that Descartes' hyberbolic theory of doubt included the idea of "Malin Génie," whose function it was not to banish but to include folly as part of the originating and originary flaw undermining the order of rationality itself. It is this troubling economy between reason, madness, silence, on the one hand, and language, on the other, that Derrida accuses Foucault of overlooking as he seems to announce the exteriority of the archaeological method to the structures of imprisonment and enclosure he describes.

I have simplified a very complicated argument, and I shall not now rehearse Foucault's response to Derrida's criticism; that response properly belongs to a later account of Foucault's work. For the moment my interest is in Derrida's positing of the metaphysical, logocentric world and in how the writers he examines as instances of that world become a part of it. This is a question that I take very seriously. For it is never really clear how the logocentric fallacy—which takes many different forms: binary, axiological oppositions with one apparently equal term controlling the other, paternally organized hierarchies, ethnocentric valorization, phallic insemination—how the logocentric prejudice insinuates itself to begin with, nor how it becomes (as it frequently is referred to) the larger thing that is *Western metaphysics.* Neither is it apparent how metaphysical biases, including the neglect of the sign and the nostalgia for presence, can be ascribed, on the one hand, to the inadvertencies of a writer (in some cases), his elisions, his sliding from one term to another (*dérapage*) and, on the other hand, to the clearly (but only implicitly) *intentioned* designs of Western metaphysics upon its adherents. For on the one hand there is Derrida's vigilance in exposing the small mistakes, the significant lapses made by writers going from one thing to the next heedlessly and, on the other, there is Derrida appealing to the influence of a philosophy of presence, which acts—it seems—as an agent of something still larger and more prevalent called Western metaphysics.

If we are not to say that the point of a philosophy of presence is to accomplish certain things not only in the text but beyond the text—in the institutions of society, for example—then are we forced to say that the accomplishments of Western metaphysics are (*a*) the infection of philosophic prose by certain errors of false logic and (*b*), by a kind of irony, the deconstruction of Western texts by Derrida? As reader of these texts, then, Derrida's own will realizes itself, a process which is theoretically infinite because the number of texts to be deconstructed is as large as Western culture, and hence practically infinite. Is it entirely inaccurate to say that Derrida's elimination of voluntarism and of intention, in the interests of what he calls infinite substitution, conceals, or perhaps smuggles in, an act of Derrida's will in which the deconstructive strategy, based on a theory of undecidability and desemanticization, provides (and has already provided) a new semantic horizon, and hence a new interpretive opportunity associated with a *Derridean* philosophy? To the extent that Derrida's disciples have availed themselves of this strategy and its "concepts" (about which I shall have something to say later) a kind of new orthodoxy has come into existence, no less held in by certain doctrines and ideas than is "Western metaphysics." For this of course Derrida is not responsible.

But I am not convinced that such orthodoxies exist in any very simple, almost passive way. That is, it seems much more likely (and difficult to describe) that any philosophy or critical theory exists and is maintained in order not merely *to be there, passively around everyone and everything*, but in order to be taught and diffused, to be absorbed decisively into the institutions of society or to be instrumental in maintaining or changing or perhaps upsetting these institutions and that society. To these latter ends Derrida and Foucault have been variously responsive—and this is, I believe, what recommends them to our attention. Each in his own way has attempted to devise what is (in aim at least) a form of critical openness and repeatedly renewed theoretical resourcefulness, designed first to provide knowledge of a very specific sort, second, to provide an opportunity for further critical work itself and, third, to avoid if possible both the self-confirming operations of culture and the wholly predictable monotony of a disengaged critical system. I should like now to consider these things in Derrida's work.

Ever since his earliest considerations of the various programs put forward by critical and philosophical methods, Derrida has stalked a certain self-serving quality in these methods. The military and hunting metaphor is apt, I think, since Derrida has recently spoken in such terms of what he does: I refer not only to the interviews published in *Positions* but also to his essay "Où commence et comment finit un corps enseignant" published in the collection *Politiques de la philosophie*.[13] What has attracted his aggressive intentions is the almost visual aspect of these methods by which the text, or the problem to be discussed by the method, seems to be *entirely* doubled, or duplicated—and hence deceptively resolved—in the text of the critic or philosopher. But this can only take place (and there are several conditions to be met) if the original text or problem is represented by the critic schematically in order that, second, the critical text can accommodate the problem completely so that, third, the critical text appears to stand alongside the original text, appearing also to absorb, explain, account for everything in it.

Derrida's entire procedure is to show, either in the pretended rapport between critical and original texts or in the representation of a problem by a text, that far from criticism being able to account for everything by a doubling or duplicating representation, there is always something that escapes. Because writing itself is a form of escape from every scheme designed either to shut it down, hold it in, frame it, or parallel it perfectly, any attempt to show writing as capable in some way or the other of being *secondary* is also an attempt to prove that writing is *not original*. The military operation involved in deconstruction therefore is in one respect an attack on a party of colonialists who have tried to make the land and its inhabitants over into a realization of their plans, an attack in turn partly to release prisoners and partly to free land held forcibly. What Derrida shows over and over is that writing (*écriture*)—and here we must note that whether he admits it openly or not, Derrida does introduce oppositions, themes, definitions, and hierarchies between different sorts of writing, for there are, after all is said and done, various sorts of writing, some better than others—what Derrida shows is that *ècriture* is not so much only a process of production and effacement, tracing and retracing, but essentially a process of excess, overflowing, of bursting through, just as his own work itself attempts to burst through various conceptual barriers, enclosures, repressions.

In the *Grammatology*, Derrida speaks of "a self-effacing and respectful redoubling [of the text] by commentary,"[14] the idea being that when reading a given text traditionally a critic will respect its supposed stability and securely reproduce that stability in a critical commentary that—figuratively speaking—stands alongside the original text. Similarly, a formalist reading of a poetic text will posit the form as being principally there to receive—hence, formally, to double —the text's meaning. The visual equivalent of such a procedure is described quite brilliantly by Derrida as geometrical, one text ("square," "circular," or having an irregular contour) reproduced in another text whose shape corresponds exactly to that of the first. Between them the pair of texts presumably allows the critic to have "the tranquil assurance that jumps over the text toward its presumed content, toward its pure signified."[15] The teleology of the whole business is what Derrida legitimately questions, as when he describes Jean Rousset's "teleological structuralism": "Rousset seems not to have posited the notion that every form is beautiful, but only the notion that every form is congruent with meaning, a notion that we can feel congruent with too because it makes common rational cause with the whole idea of what meaning is. Therefore, once again, why believe that the geometer's ideas are the correct ones in this case?"[16]

Such neatness as Rousset's can do nothing with the irreducible primordial shock delivered by all writing, an initial violence common to all *écriture*. So whether a critic doubles a text or says about a text that its form coincides perfectly with its content, the neatness is a repressing one, and it has been Derrida's remarkable project everywhere to open language to its own richness, thereby to free it from the impositions of helpful schemata.

But Derrida has been no less perspicacious in lifting off the covers of a great many assertions which, more recently in his work, he has called *thèmes*, or *catégorèmes*—words that claim to refer to something definite and unshakable outside themselves for which they are supposed to be exact duplicates. These words involve a great deal of purely linguistic maneuvering hidden behind their calm Apollonian façade. Not for nothing was Derrida's first extended work a study of Husserl's *Logische Untersuchungen* of 1900–1901 (a date with almost vulgar significance for phenomenology as a science of "pure principle" or primordiality), a set of investigations whose stated effort was to understand meaning and its implements more radically than ever before. Into every one of Husserl's important and not so important definitions Derrida insinuates his technique of trouble; he shows generally that Husserl's denigration of the sign, his subordination of the sign to a meaning it existed economically to express, was an unsuccessful attempt to "eliminate signs by making them derivative";[17] and still more important Husserl's attitude to signs (and to language) pretended that signs were mere modifications of "a simple presence," as if in using language, presence could ever be present except as *re*presence (or representation), reproduction, repetition— to all of which signs were not only inevitable but, paradoxically, the only presence, a represence proclaiming the absence of what the sign presented. Derrida's role is that of an investigative reporter "attentive to the instability [and the messy quality] of all these [philosophers'] moves, for they pass quickly and surreptitiously into one another." Far from being a set of neat radical distinctions between one thing and another, Husserl's whole science of origins thus turns out instead to be "a purely teleological structure" designed mainly to eliminate signs, and other trivia, and restore "presence." And what is presence, but "an absolute will-to-hear-oneself-speak"?[18] The self-confirmation not only of philosophy but also of a kind of lumpish, pure, and undifferentiated presence to oneself (ontological egoism) simply ignores language which while being used to bring about "presence" is being denied simultaneously. For despite Husserl's desperate scramble to keep it secondary and a serviceable double for presence, language manufactures the very meanings that philosophy desires to produce, plus of course more meanings that philosophy desires to suppress as embarrassing, marginal, accessory. Thus for every big word like "god" or "reality," there are small words like "and" or "between" or even "is," and Derrida's philosophic position is that the big words don't mean anything outside themselves: they are significations attached for their entire sense to all the small words (the *chevilles syntaxiques*, as he calls them) which in turn signify more than they can adequately be understood to be *expressing*.

What, in my opinion, Derrida refers to portentously as Western metaphysics is a *magical* attitude licensed ironically by language and so far as I know is not *necessarily* a Western attitude. (But perhaps that is a small point.) Derrida's argument stresses the (again visual) thesis that the valorization of voice, or presence, of ontology is a way of not *looking* at writing, of pretending that expression is immediate and does not rely upon the signifying visual chain, which is *écriture*, writing. The grammatological attitude—and with it the strategy of deconstruction—therefore is a visual, theatrical one, and its consequences for intellectual production (Derrida's in particular) are quite specific and quite special.

II

I should like to begin this section with what may seem a somewhat irrelevant quotation from *Great Expectations*. Pip and Herbert go off to watch a performance of *Hamlet* in which Mr. Wopsle, Pip's fellow townsman, has the leading role; the performance comes before Pip finds out who his benefactor is, so the near farce (which, incidentally, anticipates Beckett quite brilliantly) of what he and Herbert see on the stage is meant to be a mocking allusion to Pip's own pretensions at being a gentleman.

On our arrival in Denmark, we found the king and queen of that country elevated in two arm-chairs on a kitchen-table, holding a Court. The whole of the Danish nobility were in attendance; consisting of a noble boy in the wash-leather boots of a gigantic ancestor, a venerable Peer with a dirty face, who seemed to have risen from the people late in life, and the Danish chivalry with a comb in its hair and a pair of white silk legs, and presenting on the whole a feminine appearance. My gifted townsman stood gloomily apart, with folded arms and I could have wished that his curls and forehead had been more probable.

Several curious little circumstances transpired as the action proceeded. The late king of the country not only appeared to have been troubled with a cough at the time of his decease but to have taken it with him to the tomb, and to have brought it back. The royal phantom also carried a ghostly manuscript round its truncheon, to which it had the appearance of occasionally referring, and that, too, with an air of anxiety and a tendency to lose the place of reference which were suggestive of a state of mortality. It was this, I conceive, which led to the Shade's being advised by the gallery to "turn over!"—a recommendation which it took extremely ill. . . . The Queen of Denmark, a very buxom lady, though no doubt historically brazen, was considered by the public to have too much brass about her; her chin being attached to her diadem by a broad band of that metal (as if she had a gorgeous toothache), her waist being encircled by another, and each of her arms by another, so that she was openly mentioned as "the kettledrum." . . . Lastly, Ophelia was a prey to such slow musical madness, that when, in course of time, she had taken off her white muslin scarf, folded it up, and buried it, a sulky man who had long been cooling his impatient nose against an iron bar in the front row of the gallery, growled, "Now the baby's put to bed, let's have supper!" Which, to say the least of it, was out of keeping.

Upon my unfortunate townsman all these incidents accumulated with playful effect. Whenever that undecided Prince had to ask a question or state a doubt, the public helped him out with it. As for example; on the question whether 'twas nobler in the mind to suffer, some roared yes, and some no, and some inclining to both opinions said "toss up for it;" and quite a Debating Society arose. When he asked what should such fellows as he do crawling between earth and heaven, he was encouraged with loud cries of "Hear, hear!" . . . On his taking the recorders . . . he was called upon unanimously for Rule Britannia. When he recommended the player not to saw the air thus, the sulky man

said, "And don't *you* do it, neither; you're a deal worse than
him!"[19]

The comedy of this is immediately obvious: Dickens takes a well-
known play, never mentions it by name, and proceeds to describe the
somewhat demeaning incongruities that occur when it is being staged
by an incompetent and ridiculous company. The technique of Dickens' description, however, bears a little more analysis. In the first
place, several levels of action are formed in the scene which, because
Dickens describes a staged performance at a theatre, we expect to be
kept distinct from each other. There are Pip and Herbert; there is an
audience; there are several vociferous members of the audience who
stand out; there are bad actors; there is a stage setting which is
supposed to be Denmark; and finally, very far away it seems, there is
supposed to be a play written by Shakespeare commanding the entire
proceedings (although the actor playing the part of the ghost carries
the text with him).

Now in the second place, these levels are hardly distinct from each
other during the performance. That is why the whole business is so
funny. Since nothing and no one—actors, spectators, setting, Pip and
Herbert—does what is expected of him, we come to realize without
much difficulty that no one and nothing fits the part assigned to him.
The fit between actor and role, the fit between audience and performer, between speaker and words, between supposed setting and
actual scene: all these are out of joint with each other and behave
differently than they would if, for example, actor and part were perfectly matched. In short, nothing during this hilariously inept performance perfectly represents what we expect to be represented. For
in our heads we have a picture telling us that Hamlet ought to look
noble, that the audience ought to be quiet, that the ghost ought to be
ghostlike, and so on. The effect of these foiled expectations is a
travesty of a great play which, despite the abuses, nevertheless manages to weave its way more or less into everything Dickens describes
and inform the entire proceedings. Indeed it would be quite accurate
to say that Shakespeare's play, its text, is there offstage, and what
happens onstage is a result of the text's imperfect or insufficient
power to command this particular performance. For what goes wrong
is in some measure due not only to the company's and the audience's
incompetence but also to the text's insufficient authority to make a
representation or performance of itself work "properly."

One more thing. Not only are the levels scrambled, not only is
there no correspondence between original text and its realization, there

is also the fact that *Hamlet* the play is everywhere in Dickens' account of this disastrous evening. I mentioned this a moment ago, but now I must add that what Dickens gives us is in fact a double scene or, to use a musical analogy, a theme and variations in which one text (or theme) and a confused, new version of it take place simultaneously in his prose. Dickens' narrative somehow manages to portray *Hamlet* and *Hamlet* travestied, *together*, not just as montage, but as criticism, a criticism which opens the venerated masterpiece to its own vulnerability, which forces a monument of literature to accept and actually accommodate the fact of its written, and hence unprotected, consequence: each time the play is performed, the performance is a substitute for the original, and so on to infinity, and each time the original becomes a more and more hypothetical "original." So at one and the same time Dickens narrates a dramatic text in the process of its performance as it wants or as it intends to be performed as well as the same text in a new configuration as it is *being* performed and grossly travestied. The old and the new can cohabit this way for us only because Dickens puts the two together and lets them happen together in his text according to a relatively strict method of comic exfoliation. If we say that *Hamlet* as Shakespeare wrote it is at the center, or the origin, of the whole episode, then what Dickens gives us is a comically literal account of the center not only unable to hold, but *being* unable to hold, producing instead a number of new, devastatingly *eccentric* multiples of the play. Thus the power of the text turns out to be the exact reverse of what I said about it earlier; the text commands and indeed permits, invents, all the misinterpretations and misreadings which are functions of itself.

Since the beginning of his career Derrida has been fascinated with the possibilities of this sort of thing. Some of his philosophic ideas about presence, about the privilege given by Western metaphysics to voice over writing, about the disappearance of the idea of center or origin in modern thought are assumed in a most unphilosophic way by Dickens. For him the simple incontrovertible fact that Shakespeare may have been the author of a great play called *Hamlet* but is not around to prevent *Hamlet* from being taken over and literally redone by anyone who has a mind to do so is an assumption resembling Derrida's notion that ideas of voice, presence, and metaphysical "origins" are simply inadequate for the performative actualities of language. The other side of this view is the paradoxical one that Shakespeare's *text* is about its travesties of course, but those have to do with the text's powers, which are tied to its written state and the exigencies of performance and not to Shakespeare's presence as a once alive human being.

The technique of showing how these myths about voice and presence persist in our thinking, and in much writing (whose whole status is undermined and debased by the idea that writing is simply a reflection for something, like thought or a voice, which it is expected to represent), is Derrida's as much as it is Dickens' in the scene I've been discussing and—to mention another example—Mark Twain's in *A Connecticut Yankee in King Arthur's Court.* Derrida himself has made the point that such debunkings as his in a sense revalidate the old myths, just as Dickens' parody of *Hamlet* is an act of homage to Shakespeare. This is what Derrida means when he speaks of his philosophy as a form of *paleonymy.* For Derrida the reason the old ideas have this "hold" (the word he uses in *La Voix et le phénomène* is *prise*) on us and him is that they have preempted our thinking more or less completely, they have caused certain notions (which he calls *impensé*) to become uncritically accepted, and—this is perhaps more important—as a philosopher he has been unable to discover a new way of thinking that totally liberates us from old or persistent ideas. Derrida has been extremely scrupulous about saying that he is not attempting to replace the old ideas with new ones since he apparently does not intend to become the promulgator of a new orthodoxy to replace the old one. Whether this new orthodoxy emerges or not in his work is something I shall come back to a little later; however, it is an important question and one, I think, unfortunately ignored by Derrida and by his disciples.

But what is Derrida's philosophic strategy of deconstruction, as he calls it, and why are its techniques helpfully illuminated by the scene in *Great Expectations*? Let us start with *representation*, one of the key problems in all criticism and philosophy. Most accounts of representation, including Plato's, involve an original and a copy or representation, the first coming first in time and higher in value, the second later in time and lower in value, the first determining the second; in principle, a representative representation is meant to be a sometimes unavoidable, sometimes merely convenient substitute for the original, which for any number of reasons cannot be present to be itself, and act itself. The representative or substitute is thus qualitatively different from the original, in part because an original is itself and not contaminated by its difference. I simplify greatly of course, but Derrida's philosophic position is that difference—as between original and representative—is not a quality merely added to a representation or secondary object in the way that language is often considered to be a substitute for the real thing (since, for example, it is commonly supposed that language *re*presents an idea or a person not immediately present). Rather, Derrida says that difference on one level is added to objects when they are designated as representative, but on another level, the strictly verbal level of designation itself, difference is already differed, and therefore cannot be thought of as a quality or an idea or a concept having originals and copies. Difference is something wholly intrinsic to language, which *is* diacritical, and is the very activity of language itself when it is perceived not phonetically but graphically, and for this purely graphic linguistic activity Derrida invents the word *différance*, an unnameable (or unpronounceable) name.

> What is unnameable here is not some ineffable being that cannot be approached by a name; like God, for example. What is unnameable is the play that brings about the nominal effects, the relatively unitary or atomic structures we call names, or chains of substitutions for names.[20]

To name something is to specify an idea, object, or concept by giving some priority to the very activity of naming and, of course, to the name. Derrida wants us to see—if not to understand—that so long as we believe that language is mainly a representation of something else, we cannot see what language *does*; so long as we are expecting to understand language in terms of some primitive essence to which it is a functional addition, then we cannot see that any use of language means not only representation but, paradoxically, the end or permanent deferring of representation and the beginning of something else, which he calls writing. So long as we do not see that writing, more accurately and materially than speaking, signifies language being used not simply as a substitute for something better than itself but as an activity all its own, we cannot recognize that "something better" is a fundamental illusion (for if it could be there, it would be there). In short we will remain in the grip of "metaphysics."

Written language in fine involves representation, just as the play that Pip sees is a representation; yet to say that language—or rather *writing*, since that is what Derrida is talking about always—and the performance are representations is not to say that they could be something else. They cannot be because, as I said earlier, the play by Shakespeare called *Hamlet* is also an instance of writing, and all writing is not a replacement for anything but an admission that there is only writing when language is to be used, at least so far as the possibility of sustained, repeatable representation is concerned. All of a sudden we see that the very notion of representation acquires a new uncertainty, just as, if one thinks about it, every performance of *Hamlet*—no matter how zany—confirms the play's own verbal and even thematic instability. What we find Derrida doing is what we saw Dickens doing, allowing the very notion of representation to represent itself on a stage (which is a profoundly apt locale, obviously) where at least two versions of a familiar text get in each other's way and "on top of each other" (in Norman O. Brown's phrase), one reversing the other, the new version supplementing the old, and the whole thing happening within Dickens' prose, which is where and only where it can happen. Thus Derrida's endless worrying of representation involves him in a kind of permanent but highly economical tautology. He uses his own prose to represent certain ideas of presence, as well as their representations, at work in a whole series of texts from Plato to Heidegger; then in representing these texts he rereads and rewrites them, enabling us to see them not as representations of something, as references to a transcendental signified outside them, but as texts representing only themselves in, for a text, perfectly representative ways.

This is an extremely bald and inadequate summary of what is by all odds one of the most sophisticated and complex theories of meaning and textuality available today. My main reason for doing the summary as I did is to emphasize a small number of Derrida's ideas (by no means his system, if there is such a thing) in order to speak about them in a little more detail. I believe that these ideas have a special interest for the critic today who may wish to place himself skeptically between culture, as a massive body of self-congratulating ideas, and system or method, anything resembling a sovereign technique that claims to be free of history, subjectivity, or circumstance. In addition Derrida's work has some urgency for my notion that if it is not to be merely a form of self-validation, real criticism (which his is) must intend knowledge and, what is more, it must attempt to deal with, identify, and produce knowledge as having something to do with will and with reason.

Many of Derrida's essays employ not only the spatial metaphors I've been describing but, more specifically, theatrical ones. Writing, *écriture*, is seen in Freud's work, for example, to have a kind of textuality that attempts to emulate a stage setting. Derrida's two remarkable essays on Artaud in *L'Ecriture et la différence* exploit Artaud's interest in an infinitely repeatable representation in order both to explicate Derrida's own idea about writing being an infinite substitution of one trace for another and to define the space of a text as being activated by play, *jeu*; similarly, Derrida shows the irreducible ambiguity in Artaud's notions of the theater, that on the one hand he needed—like Derrida—to see everything in terms of a theater, although "Artaud also wished for the impossibility of theater, and wanted himself to obliterate the stage, as well as not wanting to see what was taking place in a spot which was eternally inhabited or haunted by the father and subject to the repetition of an original murder."[21] The quasi-montage technique I have described earlier is characterized by Derrida as having something uniquely to do with all writing, *where* (the preposition is relevant here) the graphological process traces, retraces, and effaces itself constantly, the old and the new combining in what Derrida calls *la double scène*; and later, employing one of the pun series he exploits insistently in his later work, he calls what he does with it a *double science*, which itself recalls his two-part lecture on Mallarmé's writing, *la double séance*.

All this establishes a sort of perpetual interchange in Derrida's work between the page and the theater stage, yet the locale of the interchange—itself a page and a theater—is Derrida's prose, which in his recent work attempts to work less by chronological sequence, logical order, and linear movement than by abrupt, extremely difficult to follow lateral and complementary movement.[22] The intention of that movement is to make Derrida's page become the apparently self-sufficient site of a critical reading in which traditional texts, authors, problems, and themes are presented in order to be dedefined and dethematicized more or less permanently. Thus textuality is seen to be the written equivalent of a stage for which, paradoxically, there are boundaries only to be jumped over, actors only to be decomposed into numerous parts, spectators who enter and exit with impunity, and an author who cannot decide whether he writes, or rewrites, or reads on one side of the stage page or the other. (The resemblances with Pirandello and Beckett here are worth quickly remarking.)

The polemical burden of Derrida's verbal exhibitions is virtually to rethink what he considers to be the mainstays of philosophical (and even popular) thought: and of these it is, he believes, the idea of an authorizing presence as "substance/essence/existence [*ousia*]"[23] and with it the commanding fiction of such guiding notions as Platonic ideas, teleological processes like Hegelian synthesis, and all literary critical totalizing that have now served their time and must be seen as having been valorized not by some "outside" power but by a misreading of texts. And a misreading of texts is made possible by texts themselves, for which—in the best of them—every meaning-possibility exists in a raw unresolved state. This notion is Derrida's principal philosophic idea, out of which his announced but not practiced science called *grammatology* is made initially possible. Yet Derrida's work also eliminates the possibility of deciding what is *in* a text, of being able to determine whether a critical text can so easily be detached from its parent text as critics have often believed, of being able to contain the meaning of a text in the notion of meaning itself, of being able to read texts without a commanding suspicion that all texts—the greater the text, and perhaps the critic, the more skillfully —attempt to hide their almost androgynous style in a whole structure of misleading directions to the reader, fictional objects, ephemeral appeals to reality, and the like.[24] For since we have only writing to deal with writing, our traditional modes of understanding have to be altered considerably.

An important instance of Derrida's manner of muddling traditional thought beyond the possibility of its usefulness is found in this passage on the genealogy of a text:

> We know that the metaphor that would describe the genealogy of a text correctly is still *forbidden* [that is, if we try to think where a text comes from, we will be left with some outside notion like "author," and this forbids us from trying to grasp the text's specifically textual origins, an altogether different matter]. In its syntax and its lexicon, in its spacing, by its punctuation, its lacunae, its margins, the historical appurtenance of a text is never a straight line. It is neither causality by contagion, nor the simple accumulation of layers. Nor even the pure juxtaposition of borrowed pieces. And if a text always gives itself a certain representation of its own roots, those roots live only by that representation, by never touching the soil, so to speak [this is something with which it is possible to disagree completely because Derrida goes too quickly over the way in which texts are connected to other texts, to circumstances, to reality]. Which undoubtedly destroys their *radical essence,* but not the necessity of their *racinating function.*[25]

The effect of such logic (the *mise en abîme*) is to reduce everything that we think of as having some extratextual leverage in the text to a textual function. What matters in a text is that its textuality transgresses even its own explicit statements about such things as its "roots" in, or affiliations with, reality. For rather than being mystified by the obvious analogy between the production of writing and the production of organic life (as the similarity is permitted to stand in the parallel between *seme* and *semen*, for example), Derrida breaks the similarity down, reverses matters. The culturally permitted idea of the book is that of a totality—whose greatest exemplar is the encyclopedia—and the totality enables, produces a family of ideas conceived by, inseminated with some single Original, which like a self-delighting pedagogue or father makes meaning *cyclical*, derived from and imprisoned by the one source. Every *concept* testifies to auto-insemination, the one confirming and reconfirming every other.[26] Against this set of concepts—the sexual language usually used to discuss meanings and texts is very much at the center of Derrida's most consistently interesting book, *La Dissémination*—Derrida sets and reenacts an opposite movement (as the actors in Wopsle's *Hamlet* are set *in* Shakespeare's *Hamlet*). This movement he calls *dissémination*, which is not a concept at all but what he elsewhere describes as the power of textuality to burst through semantic horizons.

Dissemination does not *mean*. It does not require the notion of a return to a source or origin or father; quite the contrary, it entails a certain figurative castration: showing the text in its writing, dissemination is capable of emasculating the Platonic idea informing our views of meaning and representation as well as the Hegelian triangle resolved in synthesis. Dissemination *maintains* the perpetual disruption of writing, *maintains* the fundamental undecidability of texts whose real power resides not in their polysemousness (which can after all be collected hermeneutically under the heading of several themes, the way Jean-Pierre Richard's account of Mallarmé collects all his work under the much varied rubric of "un monde imaginaire")[27] but texts whose power lies in the possibility of their infinite generality and multiplicity.

> Dissemination inscribes, with a regulated extension of the concept of the text, another kind of law governing the effects of meaning or of reference (anteriority of the thing to the word, reality, objectivity . . .), another kind of relationship between writing (in the metaphysical sense of that word) and what is "exterior" to it. . . . (Dissemination explains itself *too* . . . but altogether differently. . . . Heterogeneity and the absolute exteriority of "seed," seminal *différance* constitutes itself into a program, although a nonformulizable program. For formulizable reasons. The infinity of its code, and its rupture, so to

speak, therefore do not have the same sort of form saturated with presence that in its circular form, the encyclopedia does. . . .)[28]

Every one of Derrida's extraordinarily brilliant readings since and including *De la grammatologie* therefore builds from and around that point in a text around which its own heterodox textuality, distinct from its message or meanings, is organized, the point also *toward* which the text's textuality moves in the shattering dissemination of its unorganizable energy. These points are words that are anticoncepts, bits of the text in which Derrida believes, and where he shows, the text's irreducible textuality to lie. These anticoncepts, antinames, counterideas escape definite or decidable classification. That is why they are only textual and why also they are heterodox. Derrida's method of deconstruction functions then to release them, just as the climactic moment in each of *his* texts is a *performance* by these anticoncepts, these *mere* words. Thus what Derrida points toward is "a scene of writing set inside a scene of writing and so on without end, by virtue of a structural necessity marked in the text."[29] Only words that are *syncatégorèmes*—words having, like the copula, a snytactic function but capable of serving semantic ones too[30]—can reveal textuality in its element. These words are of an infinite, hence disseminative, pliability: they mean one thing *and* another (rather like Freud's antithetical primal words), but Derrida's interest in them is that it is they, and not the big ideas, that *make* a text the uniquely written phenomenon that it is, a form of *supplementarity* to (or something necessarily in excess of) formulable meaning. And this supplementarity is. that property of the text capable of repeating itself (*a*) without exhausting itself and (*b*) without keeping anything (for instance, a secret hoard of meaning) in reserve. Thus Derrida's reading of the *Phaedrus* is an explication of the word *"pharmakos,"* whose use for Plato is to make him able to write in such a way as to produce a text where truth and nontruth coexist as instances not of ideas but of textual repetition.[31]

Of these privilege words of his, these textual runes, Derrida says:

What goes for "hymen" goes, *mutatis mutandis*, for all those signs which, like *pharmakon, supplément*, and *différance* and a few others, have a double, contradictory, and undecidable value, which is always linked to their syntactical form, whether that might be somehow "interior" and articulating and combining two incompatible significations under the same yoke, hyphen (*uph'en*), or whether it might be "exterior," dependent on the code by which the word is made to operate. But the syntactical composition or decomposition of the sign makes the question of interior or exterior quite irrelevant. What we have to do with therefore are more or less larger syntactical operating units, and with differing economies of condensation. Without in fact making these distinctions very clear, we can acknowledge a certain law governing the serial pivoting of these signs in place, a place never mediated, mastered, restored or dialectized by *Erinnerung* or *Aufhebung*. Is it an accident that all these effects of play and pivoting, these "words" that manage to escape the grip of philosophic mastery have, in very different historical contexts, an extremely marked relation to writing? These "words" admit into the space of their play both contradiction and noncontradiction (as well as the contradiction and noncontradiction between contradiction and noncontradiction). Without dialectical relief, without even any respite, they belong somehow both to the consciousness and to the unconscious, of which Freud has told us that it is tolerant of as well as insensitive to contradiction. To the extent then that the text depends on these "words," that it is *folded* around them, the text therefore acts out a *double scene*. It operates in two absolutely different places, even if they are only separated by a veil, passed through and not passed through at one and the same time, slightly ajar. The double science to which these two theaters must give birth would have been called *doxa* and not *epistémè* by Plato, because of the indecision and instability fundamental to it.[32]

What all the words share is not so much a common meaning but a common structure, very much like the word *"hymen"* that Derrida uses to guide his reading of Mallarmé, or like the word *"tympan"* used to open *Marges*.[33] The word's undecidable meaning—*"hymen"* can be decomposed by a stroke of the pen into *"hymne,"* for example —is like a hypersensitive, permeable membrane marking its different significations, different positions, different sides (as of a folded piece of paper) but easily penetrable, easily rupturable by the very seductive activity it gets started, attracts, and finally is compelled to release *through* it. Derrida's key words furthermore are unregenerate signs: he says that they cannot be made more significant than signifiers are. In some quite urgent way then there is something *frivolous* about them, as all words that cannot be accommodated to a philosophy of serious need or utility are futile or unserious.[34]

Basing his enterprise on a suggestion in Condillac, and then also on the ceaseless alteration in Nietzsche's writing between instructive philosophy and seemingly careless song, fable, aphorism, or prophetic utterance, Derrida has inaugurated a style of philosophic criticism and analysis that quite literally and self-consciously wanders (Derrida's word is *errance*, with its cognates in *erreur*, for instance) into corners neglected by supposedly serious criticism and philosophy. The form of his work, which like Lukács' is cast in essays purposely vulnerable to the charge that they are *only* essays, is disseminative; and the intention of his work is to multiply sense, not to hold it down. The habitual amenities of exposition are cast aside, and the skidding from allusion to pun to neologism is sometimes impossible to follow. But in a strict sense, Derrida's deconstructive technique is a form of discovery (I use Mark Schorer's famous phrase advisedly) whose material is not merely the textuality of texts, nor the text's peculiar verbal eccentricities that do not fall into categories, nor even the unresolvable uncertainties in structure between the writing and the asserted meaning of some texts, but the opposition between *diction* and *scription*, between the absent/present word and its limitless repetition in writing. What he wants to bring to performance is "the written proposition or form of logocentrism; the simultaneous affirmation of its being-outside the outside and its sneaky intrusion into the inside, or interior."[35] Invariably, this conundrum will be found lodged not in a stable veridic discourse but, and here Derrida is affirmatively Nietzschean, in a discourse whose hidden instruments and agencies are the figural powers of *literature*. It is this latter point that Derrida emphasizes in his essay "La Mythologie blanche."[36] What each of Derrida's works tries to do is to reveal the *entame*—the tear, or perhaps the incision—in every one of the solid structures put up by philosophy, an *entame* already inscribed in written language itself by its persistent desire to point outside itself, to declare itself incomplete and unfit without presence and voice. Voice thus appears secondary to writing since writing's *facility* is precisely the facility of all fiction to *authorize*, even create, its opposite and then act subordinate to and become invisible for it.

The range of texts chosen by Derrida for analysis and discovery—unlike the much more restricted range of texts chosen by Derrida's disciples and imitators for their analyses—is relatively wide, from Plato to Heidegger, Philippe Sollers, Maurice Blanchot, and Georges

Bataille. Insofar as his readings seek to unsettle prevalent ideas in Western culture, his texts seem to have been chosen because they embody the ideas influentially: thus Rousseau, Plato, and Hegel are revealed to be unavoidable examples of logocentric thought enmeshed in and exemplifying its noncontradictory contradictions. More recent authors—Lévi-Strauss and Foucault, for example—are chosen with what seems to be a fairly straightforward polemical goal in mind. However, even a superficial reading of all Derrida's work will reveal an implicit hierarchy, the more conventional for its *not* being stated than for Derrida's brilliant uncoverings of new significance in his texts. Therefore, for Derrida, Plato, Hegel, and Rousseau either inaugurate epochs, inhabit them, or solidify them; Mallarmé initiates a revolutionary poetic praxis; Heidegger and Bataille wrestle openly with problems they both canonize and restate. The way these figures are characterized historically would support any list compiled by a teacher of "humanities" or masterpieces of Western thought. Yet there is no explanation why what Derrida calls the age of Rousseau should not also be known as the age of Condillac, nor why Rousseau's theory of language should receive precedence over Vico's, or Jones', or even Coleridge's. But Derrida doesn't go into these issues, although I think that they are not problems of historical interpretation *marginal* to what Derrida does; on the contrary, they seem to me to lead to the major questions raised by Derrida's work.

It will be recalled that I introduced my remarks on Derrida and Foucault by saying that although they represented divergent views on criticism, both of them consciously attempt to take revisionist, if not adversary, positions toward a reigning cultural hegemony—and for such a position their criticism provides an account of what cultural hegemony is—and, moreover, they have formulated a reflective critical position while aware of the danger that what they do might itself turn into a critical orthodoxy, an unthinking system of thought impervious to change and insensitive to its own problems. Now Derrida's position and his entire production have been devoted to exploring both the misconceptions and the uncritically repeated notions central to Western culture. On at least one occasion he has also pointed out that a teacher of philosophy working in a state-run institution bears a special responsibility for understanding the system by which ideas get passed on mechanically from teacher to student and back again. This defines the teaching position he happens officially to occupy, to the ironies of whose name he is wryly sensitive: *agrégé-répétiteur.* In addition he also belongs to the *corps enseignant,* and to the meaning of this somewhat compromising position he is also sensitive:

> My body is glorious, and it concentrates all the light on itself. First of all the light coming from the projector above me. Then it radiates out toward and attracts to it all public scrutiny. But it is also glorious inasmuch as it is not simply a body. In the representation of at least one other body it sublimates the teaching corps of which it is at the same time a part and the whole: a member making it possible to see the whole of the teaching corps which in its turn produces itself by effacing the barely visible and wholly transparent philosophical and sociopolitical corpus, the contract between these various bodies never itself being exhibited openly to public view.[37]

The theatrical metaphor is well employed here and elsewhere in Derrida's only explicit analysis of the institutional, historical, and political consequences and realities of being what he is, a philosopher and a teacher with a particular and identifiable project of his own. Yet he has stopped the characterization of this special and privileged position of his rather short, I think. It is enough to say that the deconstructive method must not attempt to differentiate between "long or scarcely moving" and "short and quickly outdated" series of philosophical ideas but rather concern itself in a very general way with how "the multiple powers of the oldest intellectual apparatus [in this case he refers to the whole operative structure of Western thought as exemplified in the philosophical tradition], can always be re-used and exploited in new situations"?[38] My feeling is that so long as it is referred to generally, or even if it is found concretely in individual texts, Western thought is going to remain an abstraction and *as it is*, not because Derrida does not oppose it—he does, and does not, in some of the subtle ways I've tried to describe—but because Western thought is something more differentiated, incorporative and, most important, *institutionally representative* than Derrida seems to allow.

The problem does not end here, however. To the extent that Derrida has been most careful to say that even his affirmative deconstructive technique is not a program to replace the old-style philosophic system, he has also gone to extraordinary lengths to provide his readers (and his students, here and in France) with a set of what I would call counterconcepts. The main thing claimed by the Derrideans for these words, and indeed about his deconstructive method, is that they are not reducible to a limited semantic lexicon. Neither are they supposed to be mirror opposites of the oppositions, dogmas, ideas endemic to Western metaphysics that they challenge. *"Différance,"* for example, is first "defined" in 1968 as having two and perhaps three root meanings, all of them different from *différence.*[39] In 1972, he said of *"différance,"* however, that it resembled "a configuration of concepts that I consider to be systematic and irreducible; thereafter each intervenes, and is more marked, at decisive moments in the work of a text."[40] I think I understand him to be saying that *"différance,"* or some aspect of it, depends for its exact meaning on its use at a given moment in reading a text. Yet we are left wondering how something can be practical, contextual, systematic, recognizable, irreducible and, at the same time, not really a fixed doctrine, nor a concept, nor an idea in the old sense of those words. Can we remain poised indefinitely between an old and a new sense? Or will not this median undecidable word begin to corral more and more meanings for itself, just like the old words? Similarly, if the texts he has read and organized around key words do not necessarily elevate those words into universal key words (in Raymond Williams' sense) they are not simply *neutral* words. *"Supplément"* is a perfect example, since out of the word he finds in Rousseau Derrida has built a small repertory of words, including *"suppleméntarité"* and the *"supplément"* of one thing and the other, all of which have had evident uses in the reading of other texts. More and more, a word like *"supplément"* gathers status and history; to leave it without some attention to its vital *positional* use in his work is, for Derrida, I think, a strange negligence.

My point is that Derrida's work has had and continues perforce to have a cumulative effect *on him*, to say nothing of the obvious effect on his disciples and any of his readers. I rather doubt that, in wisely attempting to avoid the wholly compromising fall into systematic method to which as a powerful philosophic teacher he is more than likely to succumb, he has been successful in avoiding the natural consequence of *accumulating* a good deal that resembles a method, a message, a whole range of special words and concepts. Since it is incorrect (and even an insult) to say that Derrida's accumulation of knowledge in the course of his published work is no more than a mood, or an atmosphere, we shall have to accept it then as constituting a position, which is a word that he himself has used comfortably. As a position it is of course specifiable but Derrida's *programmatic* hesitation toward his historical situation, toward his work's affiliation with certain types of work and not with others, both (again) pro-grammatically deny it its own considerable position and influence. Likewise, the texts to which this position has been applied by Derrida have also been denied their historical density, specificity, weight. Der-rida's Plato, Rousseau, Mallarmé, and Saussure: are all these just texts, or are they a loose order of *knowledge* from the point of view of a liberal believer in Western culture; how have they a *professional significance* for a philosopher, linguist, and literary critic; how are they *events* for an intellectual historian? The refinements are greatly extendable, just as the complex apparatus diffusing Plato, Rousseau, and the others, in the universities, in the technical language of various professions, in the Western and non-Western worlds, in the rhetoric of possessing minorities, in the application of power, in the creation or rupture of traditions, disciplines, and bureaucracies is an ap-paratus with power and a lasting historical, actual imprint on human life. But all this needs some greater degree of specification than Derrida has given it.

I will not go so far as to say that Derrida's own position amounts to a new orthodoxy. But I can say that it has not, from its unique vantage point, illuminated *in sufficient detail* the thing he refers to in his account of *le corps enseignant*, that is, *le contrat entre ces corps* (bodies of knowledge, institutions, power), a contract hidden be-cause *jamais exhibé sur le devant de la scène*. All of Derrida's work has magnificently demonstrated that such a contract exists, that texts demonstrating logocentric biases are indications that the contract exists and keeps existing from period to period in Western history and culture. But it is a legitimate question, I think, to ask what keeps that contract together, what makes it possible for a certain system of metaphysical ideas, as well as a whole structure of concepts, praxes, ideologies derived from it, to maintain itself from Greek antiquity up through the present. What forces keep all these ideas glued together? What forces get them into texts? How does one's thinking become infected, then get taken over, by those ideas? Are all these things matters of fortuitous coincidence, or is there in fact some relevant connection to be made, and *seen*, between the instances of logocen-trism and the agencies perpetuating it in time? In one of his writings Borges says: "I used to marvel that the letters in a closed book did not get mixed up and lost in the course of a night." And so in reading Derrida's work, we marvel at what keeps the ideas of Western meta-physics there in all the texts at night and during the day, for so long a period of time. What makes this system *Western*? Above all, what keeps the contract hidden and, more important, lets its effects appear in a highly controlled, systematized way?

The answers to these questions cannot be found by reading the texts of Western thought *seriatim*, no matter how complex the reading method and no matter how faithfully followed the series of texts. Certainly any reading method like Derrida's—whose main ambition is both to reveal undecidable elements in a text in lieu of some simple reductive message the text is supposed to contain and to shy away from making each reading of a text part of some cumulatively built explicit thesis about the historical persistence of and the agencies for Western metaphysical thought—certainly any method like that will finally be unable to get hold of the local material density and power of ideas as historical actuality. For not only will those ideas be left unmentioned, they cannot even be named—and this, any reader of Derrida will know, is highly consonant with the entire drift of Derrida's antinominalism, his dedefinitional philosophy, his desemanticizing of language. In other words, the search *within* a text for the conditions of textuality will falter and fail at that very point where the text's *historical presentation* to the reader is put into question and made an issue for the critic.

Here one can make the divergence between Derrida and Foucault very dramatic. It is not enough to say, as I implied, that Foucault moves the text out from a consideration of "internal" textuality to its way of inhabiting and remaining in an extratextual reality. It would be more useful to say that Foucault's interest in textuality is to present the text stripped of its esoteric or hermetic elements and to do this by making the text assume its affiliation with institutions, offices, agencies, classes, academies, corporations, groups, guilds, ideologically defined parties and professions. Foucault's descriptions of a text, or discourse, attempt by the detail and subtlety of the description to *resemanticize*, and forcibly to redefine and reidentify, the particular interests that all texts serve. A perfect case in point is his answer to Derrida to which I have referred several times. Foucault is not only able to show very polemically that on one crucial point Derrida has apparently misread Descartes by employing a French translation that adds words not present in Descartes' Latin original; he is also able apparently to "prove" that Derrida's whole argument about Descartes is wrong, even capricious. Why? Because, true to his method and not to the text's semantic sedimentation, Derrida insists on trying to prove that Foucault's thesis about Descartes, in which Descartes separated folly from dreaming, was *really* not that at all but an argument about how dreams were more extravagant even than folly, folly being but a weak instance of dreaming. And that argument, according to Foucault, merely *read* the text: it allowed the reader's (i.e., Derrida's) opinions, uncertainties, ignorance to override an almost invisible but *present* and functioning system of ideas which makes the text *say* specifically that *madness* is forcibly to be distinguished and excluded from the system of normal human activity, which includes dreaming.

The trouble with this evident overriding of the text, as Foucault is at very great pains to show, is that Derrida's reading of Descartes does not read matters in the text that have the *plainly intended force* of active juridical and medical authority, of specific professional interests at work. Moreover, the form of Descartes' text rigorously follows the pattern of two discourses, the meditative exercise and a logical demonstration, in both of which the positional status of the objects discussed—dream and folly—as well as the positional role of the subject (the philosopher who holds and conducts both discourses in his text) constitute and even determine the text. Derrida's textualization has the effect therefore of "reducing discursive practice to textual traces," a reduction which has given rise to a pedagogy associated with Derrida:

> It is an historically sufficiently determined little pedagogy which manifests itself most visibly. A pedagogy that tells the pupil that there is nothing outside of the text, but that within it, in its interstices, in its white spaces and unspokennesses, the reserve of its origin reigns; it is not at all necessary to search elsewhere, for exactly here, to be sure not in the words, but in words as erasures, in their *grill*, "the meaning of being" speaks itself. A pedagogy that conversely gives to the voice of the teacher that unlimited sovereignty which permits them to read the text indefinitely.[41]

This extremely bitter climax of Foucault's reply to Derrida is to some extent a way of registering anger that Derrida's pedagogy, and not so much his method, seems easily teachable, diffusable and, at present, potentially more influential than Foucault's work. The personal animus informing Foucault's judgment also supplies it with a rhetoric of furious, perhaps even unseemly, denunciation. But isn't Foucault's intellectual point that Derrida's reading of a text does not allow for the role of information at all, that in reading a text and placing it *en abîme* in a wholly textual ether, Derrida does not seem willing to treat a text as a series of discursive events ruled not by a sovereign author but by a set of constraints imposed on the author by the kind of text he is writing, by historical conditions, and so forth? For if one believes that Descartes merely *wrote* his text, and that his text contains no problems raised by the fact of its textuality, then one eludes and elides those features of Descartes' text that bind it willingly to a whole body of other texts (medical, juridical, and philosophical texts) and imposes upon Descartes a certain process of produced meaning which *is* his text and for which as author he accepts legal responsibility. Derrida and Foucault therefore collide on how the text is to be described, as a *praxis* whose existence is a fact of highly rarefied and differentiated historical power, associated not with the univocal authority of the author but with a discourse constituting author, text, and subject which gives them a very precise intelligibility and effectiveness. The meaning of this collision is, I think, remarkably significant for contemporary criticism.

The significance of Derrida's position is that in his work he has raised those questions uniquely pertinent to writing and to textuality that tend to be ignored or sublimated in metacommentary on texts. The very elusiveness of texts, and the tendency to see them homogeneously either as functions of, or as parasitic on, some schematic philosophy or system on which they are dependent (as illustrations, exemplifications, expressions): these are the things on which Derrida's considerable dedefinitional energies are directed. In addition he has developed a particularly alert and influential reading method. Yet his work embodies an extremely pronounced self-limitation, an ascesis of a very inhibiting and crippling sort. In it Derrida has chosen the lucidity of the undecidable in a text, so to speak, over the *identifiable power* of a text; as he once said, to opt for the sterile lucidity of the performative *double scène* in texts is perhaps to neglect the implemented, effective power of textual *statement*.[42] Derrida's work thus has not always been in a position to accommodate descriptive information of the kind giving Western metaphysics and Western culture a more than repetitively allusive meaning; neither has it been interested systematically and directly in dissolving the ethnocentrism of which on occasion it has spoken with noble clarity; neither has it demanded from its disciples any binding engagement on matters pertaining to discovery and knowledge, freedom, oppression, or injustice. For if everything in a text is always open equally to suspicion and to affirmation, then the differences between one class interest and another, or between oppressor and oppressed, one discourse and another, one ideology and another are virtual in—but never crucial to making decisions about—the finally reconciling element of textuality.

If for Derrida the *impensé* in criticism which he has frequently attacked signifies a lazy, imprecise understanding of signs, language, and textuality, then for Foucault the *impensé* is what at a specific time and in a specific way cannot be thought because certain other things have been imposed upon thought instead. In those two meanings of *impensé*, the one passive, the other active, we must be able not only to see the opposition between Derrida and Foucault—but thereafter to take our position as critics doing something which it may be possible to describe and defend.

For Foucault, as much as for Derrida, textuality is a more variable and interesting category than the somewhat lifeless one imposed on it by the canonizing rituals of traditional literary criticism. Ever since the beginning of his career Foucault has been interested in texts as an integral, and not merely an accessory, part of the social processes of differentiation, exclusion, incorporation, and rule. He has said of a text, his own included, that it is an "object-event," which "copies itself, fragments itself, repeats itself, simulates itself, doubles itself and finally disappears without its author ever being able to claim that he is its master." More specifically:

> I would like for a book not to give itself the sort of status that would make of it a text which pedagogues and critics would then be able to reduce; rather I would want a text to have the casual bearing, as it were, in order to present itself only as discourse; that it be at the same time battle and arms, strategy and shock, struggle and trophy (or wound), conjecture and vestiges, irregular encounter and repeatable performance.[43]

The conflict in each text between its author and the discourse of which, for various social, epistemological, and political reasons, he is a part is central for Foucault's textual theory. Far from agreeing with Derrida's contention that Western culture has valorized speech over writing, Foucault's project is to show precisely the opposite, at least since the Renaissance, and to show also that writing is no private exercise of a free scriptive will but rather the activation of an immensely complex tissue of forces for which a text is a place among other places (including the body) where the strategies of control in society are conducted. Foucault's entire career from *Histoire de la folie* through *La Volonté de savoir*[44] has been an attempt to describe these strategies with, on the one hand, greater and greater detail and, on the other, a more and more effective general theoretical apparatus of description. It is arguable, I think, that he has been more successful in the former than in the latter, and that such books as *Surveiller et punir* are of a greater intrinsic interest and power than *L'Archéologie du savoir*. But what is not arguable is Foucault's ability somehow to put aside his enormously complex theoretical apparatus (as it emerges in *L'Archéologie du savoir*) and let the material he has dug up create with him its own order and its own theoretical lessons. Certain basic theoretical categories, assumptions, working principles have remained near the center of what he does, however, and I should like now to sketch them briefly.

Some of them are clearly derived from temperament. Foucault is a scholar for whom no corner is too obscure to be looked into, especially when he investigates the machinery of corporeal and mental control throughout Western history. While it is true that he has been mainly interested in two sides of the same coin—the process of exclusion by which cultures designate and isolate their opposites and its obverse, the process by which cultures designate and valorize their own incorporative authority—it is now certain that Foucault's greatest intellectual contribution is to an understanding of how the appetite for or will to exercise dominant control in society and history has also discovered a way to clothe, disguise, rarefy, and wrap itself systematically in the language of truth, discipline, rationality, utilitarian value, and knowledge. And this language, in its naturalness, authority, professionalism, assertiveness, antitheoretical directness, is what Foucault has called *discourse*. The difference between discourse and such coarser, yet not less significant, fields of social combat as the class struggle is that discourse works its productions, discriminations, censorship, interdictions, and invalidations on the intellectual at the level of base, not of superstructure. The power of discourse is that it is at once the object of struggle and the tool by which the struggle is conducted: in penology, for example, the juridical language identifying the delinquent and the intellectual schema embodied in the prison's physical structure are instruments controlling, identifying, incarcerating felons as well as the powers (withheld from felons obviously) to keep freedom for oneself and deny it to others. The goal of discourse is to maintain itself and, more important, to manufacture its material continually; thus, as Foucault has said provocatively, prisons are a factory for creating criminals. Temperamentally, and no doubt because he is an intellectual uniquely gifted to see that intellectuals are part of the system of discursive power, he has written his books in solidarity with society's silent victims to make visible the actuality of discourse and to make audible the repressed voice of its subjects.

The master discourse of society is what Foucault in *L'Ordre du discours* has called *le discours vrai* or *le discours de vérité*.[45] He has not described this even in *L'Archéologie du savoir*, but I assume that he is referring to that most mysterious and general of all elements in discourse that makes its individual utterances appear to be speaking for, about, and in truth. Yet each branch of discourse, each text, each statement has its own canons of truth, and it is these that designate such matters as relevance, propriety, regularity, conviction, and so forth. Foucault is perfectly correct to note that when one writes as a philologist, say, or philologically *what* one writes, its form, its shape, its *statement*, is made rigorously *apt*, fitting, appropriate by a set of enunciative possibilities unique to philology at that time and in that place. These regional but productive constraints upon the writing and subsequently the interpretation of texts make Foucault's reading of texts a very different process than Derrida's, but theoretically they also *situate* or *locate* texts and what they enact far more dramatically than is possible in Derrida's theater or representations.

Foucault's most interesting and problematic *historical* and philosophical thesis is that discourse, as well as the text, *became* invisible, that discourse *began* to dissemble and appear merely to be writing or texts, that discourse hid the systematic rules of its formation and its concrete affiliations with power, not at some point in time, but as an *event* in the history of culture generally, and of knowledge particularly. Here as elsewhere in his work, Foucault makes a rigorous effort to be specific even though we are not sure whether what Foucault tries to describe is an event in the common sense meaning of that word, or an event in a rather more special sense, or both together. My inclination is to think that Foucault is identifying a phase through which culture must have passed at a period in time that is approximately locatable. Because this phase presumably lasted for a long period, the event then can be characterized as a gradual alteration in the essentially spatial relationship between language and representation. Once again we are in the theatrical space, although it has a considerably thicker historical dimension to it than Derrida's. In *Les Mots et les choses (The Order of Things)* Foucault builds his descriptions of the event around a contrast of a fairly simple and instrumental sort. At least until the end of the eighteenth century, he says, it was believed that discourse (that is, language as representative of an order of Being) "ensured the initial, spontaneous, unconsidered deployment of representation within a table" or, we might well add, within a quasi-theatrical space. Now this at least seems to be the case *before* the event Foucault is about to describe, so completely and dramatically has that event altered, and made difficult even to grasp, the kind of relationship that obtained between language and reality before the event.

The change occurred when "words ceased to intersect with representations and to provide a spontaneous grid for the knowledge of things."[46] Discourse then became problematic and seemed to efface itself since it was no longer obligated immediately to represent anything other than itself; this is the moment that Foucault calls "the discovery of language," albeit a dispersed language. What he describes is something we can understand a little better in terms of the scene from *Great Expectations*. Dickens nowhere says that what he is representing is a theater nor, as I said earlier, is *Hamlet* (Shakespeare's play—the text on which the whole performance is based) named. The comedy of the situation is that we somehow know that the characters are trying to act a play they obviously have an imperfect grasp of. But we know this because Dickens' language obliquely directs the entire scene, represents the stage and its actors, clues our responses as readers. And all this is possible because of the novelistic convention in which a special referentiality and a quasi-realistic use of language are permissible and to which readers bring quite specialized expectations and responses. In other words, the theater Dickens describes exists in the *language of the novel*, which has absorbed and taken over reality so much as to be completely responsible for it. Novelistic convention, however, is language released from the burden of representing reality exclusively in a table or grid; rather, the table or, in this case, the theater is *a* use for novelistic convention, which is obligated to perform as novels do, to refer to things novelistically and in no other way. As for philological convention, it views words quite differently. There are therefore many kinds of language, each doing things in its own way, each requiring a different discipline to produce, transmit, or record, each existing according to rules available only after much investigation. These special languages are the modern form of discourse.

At the beginning of the nineteenth century, [words] . . . rediscovered their ancient, enigmatic density; though not in order to restore the curve of the word which had harbored them during the Renaissance, nor in order to mingle with things in a circular system of signs. Once detached from representation, language has existed, right up to our own day, only in a dispersed way . . .[47]

The witnesses of this dispersion of language—who between them map the space possible for language to act in—are Nietzsche and Mallarmé: the first sees language as wholly determined by history, by circumstance, by the individual using language at any given moment, by the terms of the speaker; the latter sees language as pure Word, which "in its solitude, in its fragile vibration, in its nothingness, [is] the word itself—not the meaning of the word, but its enigmatic and precarious being." Therefore "the whole curiosity of our thought now resides in the question: What is language, how can we find a way around it in order to make it appear in itself, in all its plenitude?" And since language is situated between the two poles articulated by Nietzsche and Mallarmé, Foucault situates his work between them, there he says "to discover the vast play of language contained once more within a single space."[48] The imperative is to make language and, if possible, discourse once again appear within that field of invisible dispersion that since the end of the Classical Age language has become.

The passages I have been quoting from *Les Mots et les choses* are, I think, typical of the early—or at least the earlier—Foucault. To make language and discourse reappear is in the earlier book, we note, a task for the intellectual historian; even the disappearance of discourse is not described as anything but an archaeological event, so to speak. All of Foucault's work since *Les Mots et les choses* has been a rephrasing of the question "How, when and why did language and discourse disappear," and he has turned it into a political and methodological question of the greatest urgency. By replying that discourse did not simply disappear but that it became invisible, Foucault begins his answer to the question, adding that if it disappeared it did so for political reasons, the better for it to be used to practice a more subtle, more insidious form of control over its material and its subjects. Thus the very effectiveness of modern discourse is linked to its invisibility and to its rarity. Each discourse, each language—of psychiatry, penology, criticism, history—is to some degree a jargon, but it is also a language of control and a set of institutions within the culture which it constitutes as its special domain.

The major shift that occurred in Foucault's thought in 1968—after *Les Mots* and before *L'Archéologie*—is the one reconceiving the problem of language not in an ontological but in a political or ethical framework, the Nietzschean framework. Thus we can best understand language by making discourse visible not as a historical task but as a political one; the model ought then to be a *strategic* and not finally a linguistic one.

> The further I go in my work, the more it seems to me that the formation of discourse and the genealogy of knowledge ought to be analyzed not in terms of types of consciousness, modalities of perception or as forms of "ideology," but as tactics or strategies of power. These tactics and strategies are deployed by means of implantations, distributions, sections, control of territory, organization of domains, which taken together could constitute a sort of geopolitics, at which point my own preoccupations and methods as a scholar meet up with yours [Foucault is addressing a group of revisionist geographers]. There is one theme that in the years to come I would like to study: the army as a matrix of organization and of knowledge—this entails the necessity of studying the fortress, the campaign, the military movement, the colony, the territory. I think geography must very well be right at the heart of what it is I do.[49]

Between the power of the dominant culture on the one hand and the impersonal system of disciplines and methods (*savoir*) on the other stands the critic. We are back now to my first formulation and, I hope, to a greater awareness of what such a *geopolitical* position as Foucault's might mean. Whereas Derrida's theory of textuality brings criticism to bear upon a signifier freed from any obligation to a transcendental signified, Foucault's theories move criticism from a consideration of the signifier to a description of the signifier's *place*, a place rarely innocent, dimensionless, or without the affirmative authority of discursive discipline. In other words, Foucault is concerned with describing the force by which the signifier *occupies* a place, so in *Surveiller et punir* he can show how penal discourse in its turn was able to assign felons to their places in the structural, administrative, psychological, and moral economy of the prison's panoptical architecture.

Now the value of such a strictly historical view of the signifier in the text is not only that it is historical. Its greatest value is that it awakens criticism to the recognition that a signifier occupying *a* place, signifying *in* place *is*—rather than *represents*—an act of will with ascertainable political and intellectual consequences and an act fulfilling a strategic desire to administer and comprehend a vast and *detailed* field of material. The nonrecognition of this act of will is what one finds the deconstructor not recognizing, thereby denying or overlooking it. Thus by virtue of Foucault's criticism we are able to understand culture as a body of disciplines having the effective force of knowledge linked systematically, but by no means immediately, to power.

Foucault's lesson is that while in one sense he *complements* Derrida's work, in another he takes a step in a new direction. The vision of history he has been propounding takes as its starting point the great shift in knowledge at the end of the eighteenth century from a despotic to a strategic articulation of power and of knowledge. The disciplines that arose in the nineteenth century were specialized ones in which the human subject was first collapsed into swarming detail, then accumulated and assimilated by sciences designed to make the detail functional as well as docile. From these disciplines evolved a diffuse administrative apparatus for maintaining order and opportunities for study. Thus what Foucault proposes is, I think, a criticism as catholic and as detailed in its descriptions as the knowledge it seeks to understand. For Foucault where there is knowledge and discourse, there must criticism also be, to reveal the exact places—and displacements—of the text, thereby to see the text as a process signifying an effective historical will *to be present*, an effective desire to *be* a text and to be a *position taken*.

While severed consciously from cultural hegemony, this sort of criticism is a meaningful activity *within* the culture. It releases one from the barriers imposed formalistically on one by departments, by disciplines, or by moribund traditions of scholarship and opens up the possibility of an aggressive study of the realities of discourse, which at least since the eighteenth century has ruled the production of texts. Yet despite the extraordinary worldliness of this work, Foucault takes a curiously passive and sterile view not so much of the uses of power but of how and why power is gained, used, and held onto. This is the most dangerous consequence of his disagreement with Marxism, and its result is the least convincing aspect of his work. Even if one fully agrees with his view that what he calls "the micro-physics" of power "is exercised rather than possessed; it is not the 'privilege', acquired or preserved, of the dominant class, but the overall effect of its strategic positions,"[50] the notions of class struggle and of class itself cannot therefore be reduced—along with the forcible taking of state power, economic domination, imperialist war, dependency relationships—to the status of superannuated nineteenth-century conceptions of political economy. However much power may be a kind of indirect bureaucratic discipline and control, there are ascertainable changes stemming from who holds power, who dominates whom, and so forth.

In short, power can be made analogous neither to a spider's web without the spider nor to a smoothly functioning flow diagram; a great deal of power remains in such coarse items as relations of production, wealth and privilege, monopolies of coercion, and the central state apparatus. In understandably wishing to avoid the crude notion that power is unmediated domination, Foucault more or less eliminates the central dialectic of opposed forces that still underlies modern society, despite the apparently perfected methods of "technotronic" control and seemingly nonideological efficiency that seem to govern everything. What one misses in Foucault therefore is something resembling Gramsci's analyses of *hegemony*, historical blocks, ensembles of relationships done from the perspective of an engaged political worker for whom the fascinated description of exercised power is never a substitute for trying to change power relationships within society.

To a great extent Foucault's flawed attitude to power derives from his insufficiently developed attention to the problem of historical change. While he is right in believing that history cannot be studied exclusively as a series of violent discontinuities (produced by wars, revolutions, great men), he surely underestimates such motive forces in history as profit, ambition, ideas, the sheer love of power, and he does not seem interested in the fact that history is not a homogeneous French-speaking territory but a complex interaction between uneven economies, societies, ideologies. Much of what he has studied in his work makes greatest sense not as an ethnocentric *model* of how power is exercised in modern society but as part of a much larger picture involving, for example, the relationship between Europe and the rest of the world. He seems unaware of the extent to which the ideas of discourse and discipline are assertively European and how, along with the use of discipline to employ masses of detail (and of human beings), discipline was used also to administer, study, reconstruct—and then subsequently to occupy, rule, and exploit—almost the whole of the non-European world. This dimension is wholly absent from Foucault's work even though his work helps one to understand it; since it strikes me as being a definitive part of modern history, some account of this European hegemony over the world needs to be taken.

The simple fact is that between 1815, when European powers were in occupation of approximately 35 percent of the earth's surface, and

1918, when that occupation had extended to 85 percent, discursive power increased accordingly. One can very well ask—as I have tried to[51]—what makes it possible for Marx, Carlyle, Disraeli, Flaubert, Nerval, Renan, Quinet, Schlegel, Hugo, Rückert, Cuvier, and Bopp all to employ the word "Oriental" in order to designate essentially the same corporate phenomenon, despite the enormous ideological and political differences between them. The principal reason for this was the constitution of a geographical entity—which, were it not for the Europeans who spoke for it and represented it in their discourse, was otherwise merely passive, decadent, obscure—called the Orient, and its study called Orientalism, that realized a very important component of the European will to domination over the non-European world and made it possible to create not only an orderly discipline of study but a set of institutions, a latent vocabulary (or a set of enunciative possibilities), a subject matter, and finally—as it emerges in Hobson's and Cromer's writing at the end of the nineteenth century—subject races. The parallel between Foucault's carceral system and Orientalism is striking. For as a discourse Orientalism, like all discourses, is "composed of signs; but what they [discourses] do is more than use these signs to designate things. It is this 'more' that renders them irreducible to the language and to speech. It is this 'more' that we must reveal and describe."[52]

In the discourse and discipline of Orientalism this "more" to which Foucault refers is the power to make philological distinctions between "our" Indo-European languages and "their" Semitic languages (with a clear evaluation of one over the other expressed in the distinction) and the institutional force to make statements about the Oriental mentality, the inscrutable Oriental, the unreliable and degenerate Oriental, and so forth. Moreover the enormous growth in Oriental professorships all across Europe, the mushrooming of books on the Orient (for the Near East alone, estimated at 60,000 books between 1850 and 1950), the springing up of Oriental societies, Oriental Exploration Funds, geographical societies and, finally, the creation of a vast colonial bureaucracy, government departments, and research facilities—all this is far "more" than the Orient to which the sign "Orient" seems innocently to refer. Above all Orientalism had the epistemological and ontological power virtually of life and death, or presence and absence, over everything and everybody designated "Oriental." In 1833 Lamartine visited the Orient and wrote his experiences in his *Voyage en Orient*, which contains the record of many discussions with natives, of visits to their villages, of meals taken with them. Yet how is one to explain his statement in the "Resumé politique" attached to the *Voyage* that the Orient is at present a territory without real citizens, nations, or frontiers—except by the force of Orientalist discourse assigning Europeans and Orientals to ontologically different categories of existence and nonexistence. For like all discourses Orientalism is correlated with juridical discourse—say, Emer de Vattel's theory about legally inhabited territories and the right of Europeans to expropriate and render useful territory that had no real inhabitants; Orientalism is correlated with biological discourse, not only Cuvier's typology of races but Geoffroy Saint-Hilaire's teratology of the study of deviant, monstrous types; with pedagogical discipline of the sort expressed in Macaulay's 1835 report on Indian education.

Above all it is as a discipline of detail, and indeed as a theory of Oriental detail by which every minute aspect of Oriental life testified to an Oriental essence which it expressed, that Orientalism had the eminence, the power, and the affirmative authority over the Orient that it had. In Orientalism the accumulation of texts, by which enormous caches of Oriental manuscripts were transported westwards to be made the subject of remarkably detailed study, and more and more during the nineteenth century the accumulation of human bodies, by which the Oriental races and their territories were acquired for European suzerainty: these two went hand in hand, as did the discipline of their management. If we believe that Kipling's jingoistic White Man was simply an aberration, then we cannot see the extent to which the White Man was merely one expression of a science—like that of penal discipline—whose goal was to understand, and to confine, nonwhites in their status as nonwhites, in order to make the notion of whiteness—as its apex is embodied in European culture—clearer, purer, stronger. If we cannot see this, then we will be seeing a good deal *less* than every major European intellectual and cultural figure of the nineteenth century saw, from Chateaubriand, Hugo, and the other early romantics, to Arnold, Newman, Mill, to T. E. Lawrence, Forster, Barrès, William Robertson Smith, Valéry, and countless others. What they saw was the necessary, valuable connection between the affirmative powers of European discourse—the European signifier, if you like—and constant exercises of disciplined authority, affirmation, and overcoming, in short, exercises of strength with everything designated as non-European, or nonwhite. I am referring of course to the hegemony of an imperialistic culture, but what is alarming is the extent to which much contemporary criticism that is lost in the "abysmal" element of textuality seems utterly blind to the impressive constitutive authority in textuality of such power as that of a broadly based *cultural* discipline, in Foucault's sense of the word.

I can conclude on a more positive—if somewhat summary—note. I have been implying that criticism is, or ought to be, a cognitive activity, and that it is a form of knowledge. I now find myself saying that if, as Foucault has tried to show, all knowledge is contentious, then criticism, as activity and knowledge, is or ought to be openly contentious, too. My interest is to reinvest critical discourse with something more than contemplative effort or an appreciative technical reading method for texts as undecidable objects. There is obviously no substitute for reading well, and *that* of course criticism, is one of the branches exemplified by Derrida, does try to do and does try to teach. My sense of the contemporary critical consciousness is that having initially detached itself from the dominant culture, having thereafter adopted a situated and responsible adversary position for itself, this consciousness begins its meaningful cognitive activity in attempting to account for, and rationally to discover and know, the force of statements in texts: statements and texts, that is, as doing something more or less effective, with consequences that criticism should make it its business to reveal. For if texts are, as indeed in many but not all cases they are, a form of *impressive* human activity, they must be correlated with (not reduced to) other forms of impressive, perhaps even repressive and displacing, forms of human activity.

Criticism cannot assume that its province is merely the text, nor even the great literary text. It must see itself, as well as other discourse, inhabiting a much contested cultural space in which what has counted in the continuity and transmission of knowledge has been the signifier as an event that has left lasting traces upon the human subject. Once we take that view, then literature as an isolated paddock in the broad cultural field disappears, and with it too the harmless rhetoric of self-delighting humanism. Instead we will be able, I think, to read and write with a sense of the greater stake in historical and political effectiveness that literary, as well as all other, texts have had.

NOTES

1. Michel Foucault's attack on Derrida is to be found in an appendix to the later version of *Folie et déraison: Histoire de la folie à l'âge classique* (Paris, 1972), pp. 583–603; the earlier edition has been translated into

English: *Madness and Civilization: A History of Insanity in the Age of Reason*, trans. Richard Howard (New York, 1965).

2. Jacques Derrida, *La Dissémination* (Paris, 1972), p. 297.

3. "Un texte n'est un texte que s'il cache au premier regard, au premier venu, la loi de sa composition et la règle de son jeu. Un texte reste d'ailleurs toujours imperceptible. La loi et la règle ne s'abritent pas dans l'inaccessible d'un secret, simplement elles ne se livrent jamais, au *présent*, à rien qu'on puisse rigoureusement nommer une perception." Ibid., p. 71. Here, as elsewhere in the text, my translation unless otherwise cited.

4. One should cite, as an instance of negative theology, the powerfully moving early chapters of *De la grammatologie* (Paris, 1967); in English, *Of Grammatology*, trans. Gayatri Chakravorty Spivak (Baltimore, 1976).

5. ". . . laisse détonner une écriture à l'intérieure même de la parole, désorganisant ainsi toute l'ordonnance reçue et envahissant tout le champ." Derrida, *Positions: Entretiens avec Henri Ronse, Julia Kristeva, Jean-Louis Houdebine, Guy Scarpetta* (Paris, 1972), pp. 57–58.

6. "Ces méthodes qui permettent le contrôle minutieux des opérations du corps, qui assurent l'assujettissement constant de ses forces et leur imposent un rapport de docilité-utilité, c'est cela qu'on peut appeler les 'disciplines.'" Foucault, *Surveiller et punir: Naissance de la prison* (Paris, 1975), p. 139; in English, *Discipline and Punish: The Birth of the Prison*, trans. Alan Sheridan (New York, 1978), pp. 137–38.

7. Foucault, *Les Mots et les choses: Une Archéologie des sciences humaines* (Paris, 1966); in English, *Sciences*, trans. anonymous (New York, 1970), pp. xiii–xiv.

8. Foucault, "Réponse à une question," *Esprit* 5 (May 1968): 850–74; "Réponses au cercle d'épistémologie," *Cahiers pour l'analyse* 9 (Summer 1968); 9–40.

9. Derrida, *Marges de la philosophie* (Paris, 1972), pp. 31–78.

10. Derrida, *Of Grammatology*, p. 161.

11. ". . . nous sommes en droit de nous demander à quoi en dernier recours il a appuyé ce langage sans recours et sans appui: qui énonce le non-recours? qui a écrit et qui doit entendre, dans quel langage et à partir de quelle situation historique du logos, qui a écrit et qui doit entendre cette histoire de la folie?" Derrida, *L'Ecriture et la différence* (Paris, 1967), p. 61.

12. ". . . [J]e serais tenté de considérer le livre de Foucault comme un puissant geste de protection et de renfermement. Un geste cartésien pour le XXe siècle. Une récupération de la négativité. En apparence, c'est la raison qu'il renferme à son tour, mais, comme le fit Descartes, c'est le raison d'hier qu'il choisit comme cible, et non la possibilité du sens en général." Ibid., p. 85.

13. Derrida, "Où commence et commet finit un corps enseignant," in *Politiques de la philosophie: Chatelet, Derrida, Foucault, Lyotard, Serres*, ed. Dominique Grison (Paris, 1976).

14. ". . . le redoublement effacé et respectueux du commentaire . . ." Derrida, *De la grammatologie*, p. 227.

15. ". . . la tranquille assurance qui saute par-dessus le texte vers son contenu présumé, du côté du pur signifié." Ibid., p. 228.

16. "Or Rousset ne semble pas poser . . . que toute forme soit belle, mais seulement celle qui s'entend avec le sens, celle qui se laisse entendre de nous parce qu'elle est d'abord d'intelligence avec le sens. Alors pourquoi,

encore une fois, ce privilège du géomètre?" Derrida, *L'Ecriture et la différence*, p. 35.

17. *La Voix et le phénomène: Introduction au problème du signe dans la phénoménologie de Husserl* (Paris, 1967); in English, Derrida, *Speech and Phenomena, and Other Essays on Husserl's Theory of Signs*, trans. David B. Allison (Evanston, Ill., 1973), p. 51.

18. Ibid., pp. 101–2.

19. Dickens, *Great Expectations* (1861; reprint ed., Indianapolis, Ind., 1964), chap. 31, pp. 273–75.

20. Derrida, *Speech and Phenomena*, p. 159.

21. ". . . Artaud a aussi désiré l'impossibilité du théâtre, a voulu effacer lui-même la scène, ne plus voir ce qui se passe dans une localité toujours habitée ou hantée par le père et soumise à la répétition du meurtre." Derrida, *L'Ecriture et la différence*, p. 336.

22. There is a very fine account of *Glas* and of Derrida's verbal brilliance to be found in Geoffrey Hartman's two essays on Derrida, "Monsieur Texte: On Jacques Derrida, His *Glas*," *Georgia Review* 29 (Winter 1975): 759–97, and "Monsieur Texte II: Epiphony in Echoland," *Georgia Review* 30 (Spring 1976): 169–97.

23. Derrida, *Of Grammatology*, p. 12.

24. Derrida's most extended analysis of style and sexuality is to be found in his "La Question du style," in *Nietzsche aujourd'hui?* 2 vols. (Paris, 1973), 1:235–99.

25. Derrida, *Of Grammatology*, p. 101.

26. Derrida, *La Dissémination*, pp. 55–61.

27. See ibid., pp. 277–317.

28. "La dissémination inscrit, avec une extension réglée du concept de texte, une autre loi des effets de sens ou de référence (antériorité de la "chose," réalité, objectivité . . .), un autre rapport entre l'écriture au sens métaphysique et son "dehors". . . . (La dissémination s'explique *aussi* . . . mais tout autrement. . . . Hétérogénéite, extériorité absolue de la sémence, la différance séminale se constitue en programme mais en programme non formalisable. Pour des raisons formalisables. L'infinité de son code, sa rupture, donc, n'a pas la forme saturée de la présence à soi dans le cercle encyclopédique. . . ." Ibid., pp. 49, 60.

29. ". . . une scène d'écriture dans une scène d'écriture et ainsi sans fin, par necessité structurelle marquée dans le texte." Ibid., p. 252.

30. See Derrida, "Le Supplément de copule," *Marges de la philosophie*, pp. 209–46.

31. Derrida, *La Dissémination*, p. 154.

32. "Ce qui vaut pour hymen vaut, *mutatis mutandis*, pour tous les signes qui, comme *pharmakon, supplément, différance*, et quelques autres, ont une valeur double, contradictoire, indécidable qui tient toujours à leur syntaxe, qu'elle soit en quelque sorte 'intérieure,' articulant et combinant sous le même joug, uph'en, deux significations incompatibles, ou qu'elle soit 'extérieure,' dépendant du code dans lequel on fait travailler le mot. Mais la composition ou décomposition syntaxique d'un signe rend caduque cette alternative de l'intérieur et de l'extérieur. On a simplement affair à de plus ou moins grandes unités syntaxiques au travail, et à des différences économiques de condensation. Sans les identifier entre eux, bien au contraire, on peut reconnaître une certaine loi de série à ces lieux de pivotement indéfini: ils mar-

quent les points de ce qui ne se laisse jamais médiatiser, maîtriser, relever, dialectiser par *Erinnerung* et *Aufhebung*. Est-ce par hasard que tous ces effets de jeu, ces 'mots' qui échappent à la maîtrise philosophique, ont, dans les contextes historiques fort différents, un rapport très singulier à l'écriture? Ces 'mots' admettent dans leur jeu la contradiction et la non-contradiction (et la contradiction et la non-contradiction entre la contradiction et la non-contradiction). Sans relève dialectique, sans relâche, ils appartiennent en quelque sorte à la fois à la conscience et à la inconscient dont Freud nous dit qu'il est tolérant ou insensible à la contradiction. En tant qu'il dépend d'eux, qu'il s'y *plie*, le texte joue donc une *double scène.* Il opère en deux lieux absolument différents, même s'ils ne sont séparés que d'un voile, à la fois traversé et non traverse, entr'ouvert. La double science à laquelle ces deux théâtres doivent donner lieu, Platon l'aurait nommée, en raison de cette indécision et de cette instabilité, *doxa* et non *epistémè.*" Ibid., pp. 250–51.

33. Derrida, "Tympan," *Marges de la philosophie,* pp. i–xxv.
34. Derrida, "L'Archéologie du frivole," introductory essay for Condillac's *Essai sur l'origine des connaissances humaines* (Paris, 1973), p. 90.
35. ". . . la proposition ecrite du logocentrisme; l'affirmation simultanee de l'etre-dehors et de son intrusion nefaste dans le dedans." Derrida, *La Dissémination,* p. 183.
36. Derrida, *Marges de la philosophie,* pp. 247–324.
37. "Mon corps est glorieux, il concentre toute la lumière. D'abord celle du projectuer au-dessus de moi. Puis il rayonne et attire à lui tous les regards. Mais il est aussi glorieux en tant qu'il n'est plus simplement un corps. Il se sublime dans la représentation d'un autre corps, au moins, le corps enseignant dont il devrait être à la fois une partie et le tout, un membre donnant à voir l'assemblé du corps; qui à son tour se produit en effaçant comme la représentation à peine visible, toute transparente du corpus philosophique et du corpus socio-politique, le contrat entre ces corps n'étant jamais exhibé sur le devant de la scène." Derrida, "Où commence et comment finit un corps enseignant," pp. 87–88.
38. ". . . des chaines longues ou peu mobiles . . . des chaines courtes et vites perimées . . . les pouvoirs multiples de la plus vieille machine peuvent toujours êtres réinvestis et exploités dans une situation in-édites." Ibid., p. 73.
39. In his essay "La Différance," *Marges de la philosophie,* pp. 1–29.
40. ". . . une configuration de concepts que je tiens pour systématique et ir-réductible et dont chacun intervient, s'accentue plutôt, à un moment décisif du travail." Derrida, *Positions,* p. 17.
41. ". . . je dirai que c'est une petite pédagogie historiquement bien déterminée qui, de mainière très visible, se manifeste. Pédagogie qui enseigne à l'élève qu'il n'y a rien hors du texte, mais qu'en lui, en ses interstices, dans ses blancs et ses non-dits, règne la réserve de l'origine; qu'il n'est donc point nécessaire d'aller chercher ailleurs, mais qu'ici même, non point dans les mots certes, mais dans le mots comme ratures, dans leur grille, se dit *'le sens de l'être.'* Pédagogie qui inversement donne à la voix des maîtres cette souveraineté sans limite qui lui permet indéfiniment de redire le texte." Foucault, *Histoire de la folie,* p. 602; see also Spivak's introduction to her translation of Derrida's *Grammatology,* pp. lxi–lxii.
42. I have referred to this, citing Derrida, in "Roads Taken and Not Taken in Contemporary Criticism," *Contemporary Literature* 17 (Summer 1976): 334.

43. "Je voudrais qu'un livre ne se donne pas lui-même ce statut de texte auquel la pédagogie ou la critique sauront bien le reduire; mais qu'il ait la désinvolture de se présenter comme discours: à la foi bataille et arme, stratégie et choc, lutte et trophée ou blessure, conjonctures et vestiges, rencontre irregulière et scène répétable." Foucault, *Histoire de la folie*, p. 8.
44. Foucault, *La Volonte de savoir* (Paris, 1977).
45. Foucault, *L'Ordre du discours* (Paris, 1971), p. 22 and *passim*. An English translation, *The Discourse on Language*, is included in a translation of *L'Archéologie du savoir* (see No. 52).
46. Foucault, *The Order of Things*, p. 304.
47. Ibid.
48. Ibid., pp. 305–7.
49. "Plus je vais, plus il me semble que la formation des discours et la généalogie du savoir ont à être analysées à partir non des types de conscience, des modalités de perception ou des formes d'idéologies, mais des tactiques et stratégies de pouvoir. Tactiques et strategies qui se déploient à travers des implantations, des distributions, des découpages, des contrôles de territories, des organisations des domaines qui pourraient bien constituer une sorte de géopolitique, par ou mes préoccupations rejoindraient vos méthodes. Il y a un thème que je voudrais étudier dans les années qui viennent: l'armée comme matrice d'organisation et de savoir—la nécessité d'étudier la fortresse, la 'campagne,' le 'mouvement,' la colonie, le territoire. La géographie doit bien être au coeur de ce dont m'occupe." "Questions à Michel Foucault sur la géographie," *Hérodote* (January–March 1976), p. 85.
50. Foucault, *Discipline and Punish*, p. 26.
51. In my *Orientalism* (New York, 1978).
52. Foucault, *L'Archéologie de savoir* (Paris, 1969); in English, *The Archaeology of Knowledge*, trans. A. M. Sheridan Smith (New York, 1972), p. 53.

II. STYLE: FORM AND CONTENT

Introduction

The distinction between form and content or form and matter is one of the oldest in aesthetics, but since the time of Kant (who is often mistakenly thought to have established it even more firmly) there has been a growing tendency to try to surmount this dichotomy. One strategy for so doing was the elaboration, during the nineteenth and early twentieth centuries, of various conceptions of style. The history of such conceptions shows a desire to correlate form and content as closely as possible within the unity of a style. This history probably culminates in Clement Greenberg's thoroughgoing attempt to consider the representational "content" of visual art as merely one element of its formal construction, an attempt which at last recaptures the full sense of the "formalism" of Kant's aesthetics. Ironically, at the moment at which Greenberg wrote, the visual arts were preparing to transcend the form/content distinction in a wholly different way; far from absorbing content into form, art seemed to reverse the priority and present us with the brute givenness of a content on which the artist had imposed no form at all. The results were the "ready made" and the phenomenon known as minimal art. The essays by Schapiro, Wollheim, and Fried trace out this evolution in art and aesthetics.

Also included in this section are two essays, by E. H. Gombrich and Nelson Goodman, which touch on the problem of representation in general, the problem of how a certain formal arrangement *can* present itself as a content. "Art and Authenticity" is an excerpt from Professor Goodman's extremely influential book, *Languages of Art*, and gives the reader at least a glimpse of the approach embodied therein.

On theories of style generally, see particularly Harlow, and also Ackerman, Frank, Friedrich, and Lang (5). On the issues of pictorial representation raised by Gombrich and Goodman, see Bach, Bedford, Falk, Howell, Kjørup, Manns (2), Meager (1), Polanyi, Roskill,

135

Ross, Walton (1, 5), and Wollheim (3); on the issue of fakes and forgeries in particular, see Fell, Radford (2), and Sagoff. General discussions of Nelson Goodman's *Languages of Art* will be found in Carrier (2), Howard, Neill, Savile (1), Sparshott (3), Walton (4), Webster, Weitz (4), and Wartofsky. For more on the problems concerning modern art raised by Wollheim and Fried, see in particular Greenberg and Cavell (4, 6); also Carrier (1), M. Cohen (4), Fisher, Moffett, Poggioli, Rosand, Rosenberg, Rubin, and Steinberg.

Style

Meyer Schapiro

By style is meant the constant form—and sometimes the constant elements, qualities, and expression—in the art of an individual or a group. The term is also applied to the whole activity of an individual or society, as in speaking of a "life-style" or the "style of a civilization."

For the archaeologist, style is exemplified in a motive or pattern, or in some directly grasped quality of the work of art, which helps him to localize and date the work and to establish connections between groups of works or between cultures. Style here is a symptomatic trait, like the nonaesthetic features of an artifact. It is studied more often as a diagnostic means than for its own sake as an important constituent of culture. For dealing with style, the archaeologist has relatively few aesthetic and physiognomic terms.

To the historian of art, style is an essential object of investigation. He studies its inner correspondences, its life-history, and the problems of its formation and change. He, too, uses style as a criterion of the date and place of origin of works, and as a means of tracing relationships between schools of art. But the style is, above all, a system of forms with a quality and a meaningful expression through which the personality of the artist and the broad outlook of a group are visible. It is also a vehicle of expression within the group, communicating and fixing certain values of religious, social, and moral life through the emotional suggestiveness of forms. It is, besides, a common ground against which innovations and the individuality of particular works may be measured. By considering the succession of works in time and space and by matching the variations of style with historical events and with the varying features of other fields of culture, the historian of art attempts, with the help of common-sense psychology and social theory, to account for the changes of style or specific traits. The historical study of individual and group styles also discloses typical stages and processes in the development of forms.

For the synthesizing historian of culture or the philosopher of history, the style is a manifestation of the culture as a whole, the visible sign of its unity. The style reflects or projects the "inner form" of collective thinking and feeling. What is important here is not the style of an individual or of a single art, but forms and qualities shared by all the arts of a culture during a significant span of time. In this sense one speaks of Classical or Medieval or Renaissance Man with respect to common traits discovered in the art styles of these epochs and documented also in religious and philosophical writings.

The critic, like the artist, tends to conceive of style as a value term; style as such is a quality and the critic can say of a painter that he has "style" or of a writer that he is a "stylist." Although "style" in this normative sense, which is applied mainly to individual artists, seems to be outside the scope of historical and ethnological studies of art, it often occurs here, too, and should be considered seriously. It is a measure of accomplishment and therefore is relevant to understanding of both art and culture as a whole. Even a period style, which for most historians is a collective taste evident in both good and poor works, may be regarded by critics as a great positive achievement. So the Greek classic style was, for Winckelmann and Goethe, not simply a convention of form but a culminating conception with valued qualities not possible in other styles and apparent even in Roman copies of lost Greek originals. Some period styles impress us by their deeply pervasive, complete character, their special adequacy to their content; the collective creation of such a style, like the conscious shaping of a norm of language, is a true achievement. Correspondingly, the presence of the same style in a wide range of arts is often considered a sign of the integration of a culture and the intensity of a high creative moment. Arts that lack a particular distinction or nobility of style are often said to be style-less, and the culture is judged to be weak or decadent. A similar view is held by philosophers of culture and history and by some historians of art.

Common to all these approaches are the assumptions that every style is peculiar to a period of a culture and that, in a given culture or epoch of culture, there is only one style or a limited range of styles. Works in the style of one time could not have been produced in another. These postulates are supported by the fact that the connection between a style and a period, inferred from a few examples, is confirmed by objects discovered later. Whenever it is possible to locate a work through nonstylistic evidence, this evidence points to the same time and place as do the formal traits, or to a culturally associated region. The unexpected appearance of the style in another region is explained by migration or trade. The style is therefore used with confidence as an independent clue to the time and place of origin of a work of art. Building upon these assumptions, scholars have constructed a systematic, although not complete, picture of the temporal and spatial distribution of styles throughout large regions of the globe. If works of art are grouped in an order corresponding to their original positions in time and space, their styles will show significant relationships which can be co-ordinated with the relationships of the works of art to still other features of the cultural points in time and space.

II

Styles are not usually defined in a strictly logical way. As with languages, the definition indicates the time and place of a style or its author, or the historical relation to other styles, rather than its peculiar features. The characteristics of styles vary continuously and resist a systematic classification into perfectly distinct groups. It is meaningless to ask exactly when ancient art ends and medieval begins. There are, of course, abrupt breaks and reactions in art, but study shows that here, too, there is often anticipation, blending, and continuity. Precise limits are sometimes fixed by convention for simplicity in dealing with historical problems or in isolating a type. In a stream of development the artificial divisions may even be designated by numbers—Styles I, II, III. But the single name given to the style of a period rarely corresponds to a clear and universally accepted characterization of a type. Yet direct acquaintance with an unanalyzed work of art will often permit us to recognize another object of the same origin, just as we recognize a face to be native or foreign. This fact points to a degree of constancy in art that is the basis of all investigation of style. Through careful description and comparison and through formation of a richer, more refined typology adapted to the continuities in development, it has been possible to reduce the areas of vagueness and to advance our knowledge of styles.

Although there is no established system of analysis and writers will stress one or another aspect according to their viewpoint or problem, in general the description of a style refers to three aspects of art: form elements or motives, form relationships, and qualities (including an all-over quality which we may call the "expression").

This conception of style is not arbitrary but has arisen from the experience of investigation. In correlating works of art with an individual or culture, these three aspects provide the broadest, most stable, and therefore most reliable criteria. They are also the most pertinent to modern theory of art, although not in the same degree for all viewpoints. Technique, subject matter, and material may be characteristic of certain groups of works and will sometimes be included in definitions; but more often these features are not so peculiar to the art of a period as the formal and qualitative ones. It is easy to imagine a decided change in material, technique, or subject matter accompanied by little change in the basic form. Or, where these are constant, we often observe that they are less responsive to new artistic aims. A method of stone-cutting will change less rapidly than the sculptor's or architect's forms. Where a technique does coincide with the extension of a style, it is the formal traces of the technique rather than the operations as such that are important for description of the style. The materials are significant mainly for the textural quality and color, although they may affect the conception of the forms. For the subject matter, we observe that quite different themes—portraits, still lifes, and landscapes—will appear in the same style.

It must be said, too, that form elements or motives, although very striking and essential for the expression, are not sufficient for characterizing a style. The pointed arch is common to Gothic and Islamic architecture, and the round arch to Roman, Byzantine, Romanesque, and Renaissance buildings. In order to distinguish these styles, one must also look for features of another order and, above all, for different ways of combining the elements.

Although some writers conceive of style as a kind of syntax or compositional pattern, which can be analyzed mathematically, in practice one has been unable to do without the vague language of qualities in describing styles. Certain features of light and color in painting are most conveniently specified in qualitative terms and even as tertiary (intersensory) or physiognomic qualities, like cool and warm, gay and sad. The habitual span of light and dark, the intervals between colors in a particular palette—very important for the structure of a work—are distinct relationships between elements, yet are not comprised in a compositional schema of the whole. The complexity of a work of art is such that the description of forms is often incomplete on essential points, limiting itself to a rough account of a few relationships. It is still simpler, as well as more relevant to aesthetic experience, to distinguish lines as hard and soft than to give measurements of their substance. For precision in characterizing a style, these qualities are graded with respect to intensity by comparing different examples directly or by reference to a standard work.

Where quantitative measurements have been made, they tend to confirm the conclusions reached through direct qualitative description. Nevertheless, we have no doubt that, in dealing with qualities, much greater precision can be reached.

Analysis applies aesthetic concepts current in the teaching, practice, and criticism of contemporary art; the development of new viewpoints and problems in the latter directs the attention of students to unnoticed features of older styles. But the study of works of other times also influences modern concepts through discovery of aesthetic variants unknown in our own art. As in criticism, so in historical research, the problem of distinguishing or relating two styles discloses unsuspected, subtle characteristics and suggests new concepts of form. The postulate of continuity in culture—a kind of inertia in the physical sense—leads to a search for common features in successive styles that are ordinarily contrasted as opposite poles of form; the resemblances will sometimes be found not so much in obvious aspects as in fairly hidden ones—the line patterns of Renaissance compositions recall features of the older Gothic style, and in contemporary abstract art one observes form relationships like those of Impressionist painting.

The refinement of style analysis has come about in part through problems in which small differences had to be disengaged and described precisely. Examples are the regional variations within the same culture; the process of historical development from year to year; the growth of individual artists and the discrimination of the works of master and pupil, originals and copies. In these studies the criteria for dating and attribution are often physical or external—matters of small symptomatic detail—but here, too, the general trend of research has been to look for features that can be formulated in both structural and expressive-physiognomic terms. It is assumed by many students that the expression terms are all translatable into form and quality terms, since the expression depends on particular shapes and colors and will be modified by a small change in the latter. The forms are correspondingly regarded as vehicles of a particular affect (apart from the subject matter). But the relationship here is not altogether clear. In general, the study of style tends toward an ever stronger correlation of form and expression. Some descriptions are purely morphological, as of natural objects—indeed, ornament has been characterized, like crystals, in the mathematical language of group theory. But terms like "stylized," "archaistic," "naturalistic," "mannerist," "baroque," are specifically human, referring to artistic processes, and imply some expressive effect. It is only by analogy that mathematical figures have been characterized as "classic" and "romantic."

III

The analysis and characterization of the styles of primitive and early historical cultures have been strongly influenced by the standards of recent Western art. Nevertheless, it may be said that the values of modern art have led to a more sympathetic and objective approach to exotic arts than was possible fifty or a hundred years ago.

In the past, a great deal of primitive work, especially representation, was regarded as artless even by sensitive people; what was valued were mainly the ornamentation and the skills of primitive industry. It was believed that primitive arts were childlike attempts to represent nature—attempts distorted by ignorance and by an irrational content of the monstrous and grotesque. True art was admitted only in the high cultures, where knowledge of natural forms was combined with a rational ideal which brought beauty and decorum to the image of man. Greek art and the art of the Italian High Renaissance were the norms for judging all art, although in time the classic phase of Gothic art was accepted. Ruskin, who admired Byzantine works, could write that in Christian Europe alone "pure and precious ancient art exists, for there is none in America, none in Asia, none in Africa." From such a viewpoint careful discrimination of primitive styles or a penetrating study of their structure and expression was hardly possible.

With the change in Western art during the last seventy years, naturalistic representation has lost its superior status. Basic for contemporary practice and for knowledge of past art is the theoretical view that what counts in all art are the elementary aesthetic components, the qualities and relationships of the fabricated lines, spots, colors, and surfaces. These have two characteristics: they are intrinsically expressive, and they tend to constitute a coherent whole. The same tendencies to coherent and expressive structure are found in the arts of all cultures. There is no privileged content or mode of representation (although the greatest works may, for reasons obscure to us, occur only in certain styles). Perfect art is possible in any subject matter or style. A style is like a language, with an internal order and expressiveness, admitting a varied intensity or delicacy of statement. This approach is a relativism that does not exclude absolute judgments of value; it makes these judgments possible within every framework by abandoning a fixed norm of style. Such ideas are accepted by most students of art today, although not applied with uniform conviction.

As a result of this new approach, all the arts of the world, even the drawings of children and psychotics, have become accessible on a common plane of expressive and form-creating activity. Art is now one of the strongest evidences of the basic unity of mankind.

This radical change in attitude depends partly on the development of modern styles, in which the raw material and distinctive units of operation—the plane of the canvas, the trunk of wood, toolmarks, brushstrokes, connecting forms, schemas, particles and areas of pure color—are as pronounced as the elements of representation. Even before nonrepresentative styles were created, artists had become more deeply conscious of the aesthetic-constructive components of the work apart from denoted meanings.

Much in the new styles recalls primitive art. Modern artists were, in fact, among the first to appreciate the works of natives as true art. The development of Cubism and Abstraction made the form problem exciting and helped to refine the perception of the creative in primitive work. Expressionism, with its high pathos, disposed our eyes to the simpler, more intense modes of expression, and together with Surrealism, which valued, above all, the irrational and instinctive in the imagination, gave a fresh interest to the products of primitive fantasy. But, with all the obvious resemblances, modern paintings and sculptures differ from the primitive in structure and content. What in primitive art belongs to an established world of collective beliefs and symbols arises in modern art as an individual expression, bearing the marks of a free, experimental attitude to forms. Modern artists feel, nevertheless, a spiritual kinship with the primitive, who is now closer to them than in the past because of their ideal of frankness and intensity of expression and their desire for a simpler life, with more effective participation of the artist in collective occasions than modern society allows.

One result of the modern development has been a tendency to slight the content of past art; the most realistic representations are contemplated as pure constructions of lines and colors. The observer is often indifferent to the original meanings of works, although he may enjoy through them a vague sentiment of the poetic and religious. The form and expressiveness of older works are regarded, then, in isolation, and the history of an art is written as an immanent development of forms. Parallel to this trend, other scholars have carried on fruitful research into the meanings, symbols, and iconographic types of Western art, relying on the literature of mythology and religion; through these studies the knowledge of the content of art has been considerably deepened, and analogies to the character of the styles have been discovered in the content. This has strengthened the view that the development of forms is not autonomous but is connected with changing attitudes and interests that appear more or less clearly in the subject matter of the art.

IV

Students observed early that the traits which make up a style have a quality in common. They all seem to be marked by the expression of the whole, or there is a dominant feature to which the elements have been adapted. The parts of a Greek temple have the air of a family of forms. In Baroque art, a taste for movement determines the loosening of boundaries, the instability of masses, and the multiplication of large contrasts. For many writers a style, whether of an individual or a group, is a pervasive, rigorous unity. Investigation of style is often a search for hidden correspondence explained by an organizing principle which determines both the character of the parts and the patterning of the whole.

This approach is supported by the experience of the student in identifying a style from a small random fragment. A bit of carved stone, the profile of a molding, a few drawn lines, or a single letter from a piece of writing often possesses for the observer the quality of the complete work and can be dated precisely; before these fragments, we have the conviction of insight into the original whole. In a similar way, we recognize by its intrusiveness an added or repaired detail in an old work. The feel of the whole is found in the small parts.

I do not know how far experiments in matching parts from works in different styles would confirm this view. We may be dealing, in some of these observations, with a microstructural level in which similarity of parts only points to the homogeneity of a style or a technique, rather than to a complex unity in the aesthetic sense. Although personal, the painter's touch, described by constants of pressure, rhythm, and size of strokes, may have no obvious relation to other unique characteristics of the larger forms. There are styles in which large parts of a work are conceived and executed differently, without destroying the harmony of the whole. In African sculpture an exceedingly naturalistic, smoothly carved head rises from a rough, almost shapeless body. A normative aesthetic might regard this as imperfect work, but it would be hard to justify this view. In Western paintings of the fifteenth century, realistic figures and landscapes are set against a gold background, which in the Middle Ages had a spiritualistic sense. In Islamic art, as in certain African and Oceanic styles, forms of great clarity and simplicity in three dimensions—metal vessels and animals or the domes of buildings—have surfaces spun with rich mazy patterns; in Gothic and Baroque art, on the contrary, a complex surface treatment is associated with a correspondingly complicated silhouette of the whole. In Romanesque art the proportions of figures are not submitted to a single canon, as in Greek art, but two or three distinct systems of proportioning exist even within the same sculpture, varying with the size of the figure.

Such variation within a style is also known in literature, sometimes in great works, like Shakespeare's plays, where verse and prose of different texture occur together. French readers of Shakespeare, with the model of their own classical drama before them, were disturbed by the elements of comedy in Shakespeare's tragedies. We understand this contrast as a necessity of the content and the poet's conception of man—the different modes of expression pertain to contrasted types of humanity—but a purist classical taste condemned this as inartistic. In modern literature both kinds of style, the rigorous and the free, coexist and express different viewpoints. It is possible to see the opposed parts as contributing elements in a whole that owes its character to the interplay and balance of contrasted qualities. But the notion of style has lost in that case the crystalline uniformity and simple correspondence of part to whole with which we began. The integration may be of a looser, more complex kind, operating with unlike parts.

Another interesting exception to the homogeneous in style is the difference between the marginal and the dominant fields in certain arts. In early Byzantine works, rulers are represented in statuesque, rigid forms, while the smaller accompanying figures, by the same artist, retain the liveliness of an older episodic, naturalistic style. In Romanesque art this difference can be so marked that scholars have mistakenly supposed that certain Spanish works were done partly by a Christian and partly by a Moslem artist. In some instances the forms in the margin or in the background are more advanced in style than the central parts, anticipating a later stage of the art. In medieval work the unframed figures on the borders of illuminated manuscripts or on cornices, capitals, and pedestals are often freer and more naturalistic than the main figures. This is surprising, since we would expect to find the most advanced forms in the dominant content. But in medieval art the sculptor or painter is often bolder where he is less bound to an external requirement; he even seeks out and appropriates the regions of freedom. In a similar way an artist's drawings or sketches are more advanced than the finished paintings and suggest another side of his personality. The execution of the landscape backgrounds behind the religious figures in paintings of the fifteenth century is sometimes amazingly modern and in great contrast to the precise forms of the large figures. Such observations teach us the importance of considering in the description and explanation of a style the unhomogeneous, unstable aspect, the obscure tendencies toward new forms.

If in all periods artists strive to create unified works, the strict ideal of consistency is essentially modern. We often observe in civilized as well as primitive art the combination of works of different style into a single whole. Classical gems were frequently incorporated into medieval reliquaries. Few great medieval buildings are homogeneous, since they are the work of many generations of artists. This is widely recognized by historians, although theoreticians of culture have innocently pointed to the conglomerate cathedral of Chartres as a model of stylistic unity, in contrast to the heterogeneous character of stylelessness of the arts of modern society. In the past it was not felt necessary to restore a damaged work or to complete an unfinished one in the style of the original. Hence the strange juxtapositions of styles within some medieval objects. It should be said, however, that some styles, by virtue of their open, irregular forms, can tolerate the unfinished and heterogeneous better than others.

Just as the single work may possess parts that we would judge to belong to different styles, if we found them in separate contexts, so an individual may produce during the same short period works in what are regarded as two styles. An obvious example is the writing of bilingual authors or the work of the same man in different arts or even in different genres of the same art—monumental and easel painting, dramatic and lyric poetry. A large work by an artist who works mainly in the small, or a small work by a master of large forms, can deceive an expert in styles. Not only will the touch change, but also the expression and method of grouping. An artist is not present in the same degree in everything he does, although some traits may be constant. In the twentieth century, some artists have changed their styles so radically during a few years that it would be difficult, if not impossible, to identify these as works of the same hand, should their authorship be forgotten. In the case of Picasso, two styles—Cubism and a kind of classicizing naturalism—were practiced at the same time. One might discover common characters in small features of the two styles—in qualities of the brushstroke, the span of intensity, or in subtle constancies of the spacing and tones—but these are not the elements through which either style would ordinarily be characterized. Even then, as in a statistical account small and large samples of a population give different results, so in works of different scale of parts by one artist the scale may influence the frequency of the tiniest elements or the form of the small units. The modern experience of stylistic variability and of the unhomogeneous within an art style will perhaps lead to a more refined conception of style. It is evident, at any rate, that the conception of style as a visibly unified constant rests upon a particular norm of stability of style and shifts from the large to the small forms, as the whole becomes more complex.

What has been said here of the limits of uniformity of structure in the single work and in the works of an individual also applies to the style of a group. The group style, like a language, often contains elements that belong to different historical strata. While research looks for criteria permitting one to distinguish accurately the works of different groups and to correlate a style with other characteristics of a group, there are cultures with two or more collective styles of art at the same moment. This phenomenon is often associated with arts of different function or with different classes of artists. The arts practiced by women are of another style than those of the men; religious art differs from profane, and civic from domestic; and in higher cultures the stratification of social classes often entails a variety of styles, not only with respect to the rural and urban, but within the same urban community. This diversity is clear enough today in the coexistence of an official-academic, a mass-commercial, and freer avantgarde art. But more striking still is the enormous range of styles within the latter—although a common denominator will undoubtedly be found by future historians.

While some critics judge this heterogeneity to be a sign of an unstable, unintegrated culture, it may be regarded as a necessary and valuable consequence of the individual's freedom of choice and of the world scope of modern culture, which permits a greater interaction of styles than was ever possible before. The present diversity continues and intensifies a diversity already noticed in the preceding stages of our culture, including the Middle Ages and the Renaissance, which are held up as models of close integration. The unity of style that is contrasted with the present diversity is one type of style formation, appropriate to particular aims and conditions; to achieve it today would be impossible without destroying the most cherished values of our culture.

If we pass to the relation of group styles of different visual arts in the same period, we observe that, while the Baroque is remarkably similar in architecture, sculpture, and painting, in other periods, e.g., the Carolingian, the early Romanesque, and the modern, these arts differ in essential respects. In England, the drawing and painting of the tenth and eleventh centuries—a time of great accomplishment, when England was a leader in European art—are characterized by an enthusiastic linear style of energetic, ecstatic movement, while the architecture of the same period is inert, massive, and closed and is organized on other principles. Such variety has been explained as a sign of immaturity; but one can point to similar contrasts between two arts in later times, for example, in Holland in the seventeenth century where Rembrandt and his school were contemporary with classicistic Renaissance buildings.

When we compare the styles of arts of the same period in different media—literature, music, painting—the differences are no less striking. But there are epochs with a far-reaching unity, and these have engaged the attention of students more than the examples of diversity. The concept of the Baroque has been applied to architecture, sculpture, painting, music, poetry, drama, gardening, script, and even philosophy and science. The Baroque style has given its name to the entire culture of the seventeenth century, although it does not exclude contrary tendencies within the same country, as well as a great individuality of national arts. Such styles are the most fascinating to historians and philosophers, who admire in this great spectacle of unity the power of a guiding idea or attitude to impose a common form upon the most varied contexts. The dominant style-giving force is identified by some historians with a world outlook common to the whole society; by others with a particular institution, like the church or the absolute monarchy, which under certain conditions becomes the source of a universal viewpoint and the organizer of all cultural life. This unity is not necessarily organic; it may be likened also, perhaps, to that of a machine with limited freedom of motion; in a complex organism the parts are unlike and the integration is more a matter of functional interdependence than of the repetition of the same pattern in all the organs.

Although so vast a unity of style is an impressive accomplishment and seems to point to a special consciousness of style—the forms of art being felt as a necessary universal language—there are moments of great achievement in a single art with characteristics more or less isolated from those of the other arts. We look in vain in England for a style of painting that corresponds to Elizabethan poetry and drama; just as in Russia in the nineteenth century there was no true parallel in painting to the great movement of literature. In these instances we recognize that the various arts have different roles in the culture and social life of a time and express in their content as well as style different interests and values. The dominant outlook of a time—if it can be isolated—does not affect all the arts in the same degree, nor are all the arts equally capable of expressing the same outlook. Special conditions within an art are often strong enough to determine a deviant expression.

V

The organic conception of style has its counterpart in the search for biological analogies in the growth of forms. One view, patterned on the life-history of the organism, attributes to art a recurrent cycle of childhood, maturity, and old age, which coincides with the rise, maturity, and decline of the culture as a whole. Another view pictures the process as an unfinished evolution from the most primitive to the most advanced forms, in terms of a polarity evident at every step.

In the cyclical process each stage has its characteristic style or series of styles. In an enriched schema, for which the history of Western art is the model, the archaic, classic, baroque, impressionist, and archaistic are types of style that follow in an irreversible course. The classic phase is believed to produce the greatest works; the succeeding ones are a decline. The same series has been observed in the Greek and Roman world and somewhat less clearly in India and the Far East. In other cultures this succession of styles is less evident, although the archaic type is widespread and is sometimes followed by what might be considered a classic phase. It is only by stretching the meaning of the terms that the baroque and impressionist types of style are discovered as tendencies within the simpler developments of primitive arts.

(That the same names, "baroque," "classic," and "impressionist," should be applied both to a unique historical style and to a recurrent type or phase is confusing. We will distinguish the name of the unique style by a capital, e.g., "Baroque." But this will not do away with the awkwardness of speaking of the late phase of the Baroque style of the seventeenth century as "baroque." A similar difficulty exists also with the word "style," which is used for the common forms of a particular period and the common forms of a phase of development found in many periods.)

The cyclical schema of development does not apply smoothly even to the Western world from which it has been abstracted. The classic phase in the Renaissance is preceded by Gothic, Romanesque, and Carolingian styles, which cannot all be fitted into the same category of the archaic. It is possible, however, to break up the Western development into two cycles—the medieval and the modern—and to interpret the late Gothic of northern Europe, which is contemporary with the Italian Renaissance, as a style of the baroque type. But contemporary with the Baroque of the seventeenth century is a classic style which in the late eighteenth century replaces the Baroque.

It has been observed, too, that the late phase of Greco-Roman art, especially in architecture, is no decadent style marking a period of decline, but something new. The archaistic trend is only secondary beside the original achievement of late imperial and early Christian art. In a similar way, the complex art of the twentieth century, whether regarded as the end of an old culture or the beginning of a new, does not correspond to the categories of either a declining or an archaic art.

Because of these and other discrepancies, the long-term cyclical schema, which also measures the duration of a culture, is little used by historians of art. It is only a very rough approximation to the character of several isolated moments in Western art. Yet certain stages and steps of the cycle seem to be frequent enough to warrant further study as typical processes, apart from the theory of a closed cyclical form of development.

Some historians have therefore narrowed the range of the cycles from the long-term development to the history of one or two period styles. In Romanesque art, which belongs to the first stage of the longer Western cycle and shares many features with early Greek and Chinese arts, several phases have been noted within a relatively short period that resemble the archaic, the classic, and the baroque of the cyclical scheme; the same observation has been made about Gothic art. But in Carolingian art the order is different; the more baroque and impressionistic phases are the earlier ones, the classic and archaic come later. This may be due in part to the character of the older works that were copied then; but it shows how difficult it is to systematize the history of art through the cyclical model. In the continuous line of Western art, many new styles have been created without breaks or new beginnings occasioned by the exhaustion or death of a preceding style. In ancient Egypt, on the other hand, the latency of styles is hardly confirmed by the slow course of development; an established style persists here with only slight changes in basic structure for several thousand years, a span of time during which Greek and Western art run twice through the whole cycle of stylistic types.

If the exceptional course of Carolingian art is due to special conditions, perhaps the supposedly autonomous process of development also depends on extra-artistic circumstances. But the theorists of cyclical development have not explored the mechanisms and conditions of growth as the biologists have done. They recognize only a latency that conditions might accelerate or delay but not produce. To account for the individuality of the arts of each cycle, the evident difference between a Greek, a western European, and a Chinese style of the same stage, they generally resort to racial theory, each cycle being carried by a people with unique traits.

In contrast to the cyclical organic pattern of development, a more refined model has been constructed by Heinrich Wölfflin, excluding all value judgment and the vital analogy of birth, maturity, and decay. In a beautiful analysis of the art of the High Renaissance and the seventeenth century, he devised five pairs of polar terms, through which he defined the opposed styles of the two periods. These terms were applied to architecture, sculpture, painting, and the so-called "decorative arts." The linear was contrasted with the picturesque or painterly (*malerisch*), the parallel surface form with the diagonal depth form, the closed (or tectonic) with the open (or a-tectonic), the composite with the fused, the clear with the relatively unclear. The first terms of these pairs characterize the classic Renaissance stage, the second belong to the Baroque. Wölfflin believed that the passage from the first set of qualities to the others was not a peculiarity of the development in this one period, but a necessary process which occurred in most historical epochs. Adama van Scheltema applied these categories to the successive stages of northern European arts from the prehistoric period to the age of the migrations. Wölfflin's model has been used in studies of several other periods as well, and it has served the historians of literature and music and even of economic development. He recognized that the model did not apply uniformly to German and Italian art; and, to explain the deviations, he investigated peculiarities of the two national arts, which he thought were "constants"—the results of native dispositions that modified to some degree the innate normal tendencies of development. The German constant, more dynamic and unstable, favored the second set of qualities, and the Italian, more relaxed and bounded, favored the first.

In this way, Wölfflin supposed he could explain the precociously *malerisch* and baroque character of German art in its classic Renaissance phase and the persistent classicism in the Italian Baroque.

The weaknesses of Wölfflin's system have been apparent to most students of art. Not only is it difficult to fit into his scheme the important style called "Mannerism" which comes between the High Renaissance and the Baroque; but the pre-Classic art of the fifteenth century is for him an immature, unintegrated style because of its inaptness for his terms. Modern art, too, cannot be defined through either set of terms, although some modern styles show features from both sets—there are linear compositions which are open and painterly ones which are closed. It is obvious that the linear and painterly are genuine types of style, of which examples occur, with more or less approximation to Wölfflin's model, in other periods. But the particular unity of each set of terms is not a necessary one (although it is possible to argue that the Classic and Baroque of the Renaissance are "pure" styles in which basic processes of art appear in an ideally complete and legible way). We can imagine and discover in history other combinations of five of these ten terms. Mannerism, which had been ignored as a phenomenon of decadence, is now described as a type of art that appears in other periods. Wölfflin cannot be right, then, in supposing that, given the first type of art—the classic phase —the second will follow. That depends perhaps on special circumstances which have been effective in some epochs, but not in all. Wölfflin, however, regards the development as internally determined; outer conditions can only retard or facilitate the process, they are not among its causes. He denied that his terms have any other than artistic meaning; they describe two typical modes of seeing and are independent of an expressive content; although artists may choose themes more or less in accord with these forms, the latter do not arise as a means of expression. It is remarkable, therefore, that qualities associated with these pure forms should be attributed also to the psychological dispositions of the Italian and German people.

How this process could have been repeated after the seventeenth century in Europe is a mystery, since that required—as in the passage from Neo-Classicism to Romantic painting—a reverse development from the Baroque to the Neo-Classic.

In a later book Wölfflin recanted some of his views, admitting that these pure forms might correspond to a world outlook and that historical circumstances, religion, politics, etc., might influence the development. But he was unable to modify his schemas and interpretations accordingly. In spite of these difficulties, one can only admire

Wölfflin for his attempt to rise above the singularities of style to a general construction that simplifies and organizes the field.

To meet the difficulties of Wölfflin's schema, Paul Frankl has conceived a model of development which combines the dual polar structure with a cyclical pattern. He postulates a recurrent movement between two poles of style—a style of Being and a style of Becoming; but within each of these styles are three stages: a preclassic, a classic, and a postclassic; and in the first and third stages he assumes alternative tendencies which correspond to those historical moments, like Mannerism, that would be anomalous in Wölfflin's scheme. What is most original in Frankl's construction—and we cannot begin to indicate its rich nuancing and complex articulation—is that he attempts to deduce this development and its phases (and the many types of style comprehended within his system) from the analysis of elementary forms and the limited number of possible combinations, which he has investigated with great care. His scheme is not designed to describe the actual historical development—a very irregular affair—but to provide a model or ideal plan of the inherent or normal tendencies of development, based on the nature of forms. Numerous factors, social and psychological, constrain or divert the innate tendencies and determine other courses; but the latter are unintelligible, according to Frankl, without reference to his model and his deduction of the formal possibilities.

Frankl's book—a work of over a thousand pages—appeared unfortunately at a moment (1938) when it could not receive the attention it deserved; and since that time it has been practically ignored in the literature, although it is surely the most serious attempt in recent years to create a systematic foundation for the study of art forms. No other writer has analyzed the types of style so thoroughly.

In spite of their insights and ingenuity in constructing models of development, the theoreticians have had relatively little influence on investigation of special problems, perhaps because they have provided no adequate bridge from the model to the unique historical style and its varied developments. The principles by which are explained the broad similarities in development are of a different order from those by which the singular facts are explained. The normal motion and the motion due to supposedly perturbing factors belong to different worlds; the first is inherent in the morphology of styles, the second has a psychological or social origin. It is as if mechanics had two different sets of laws, one for irregular and the other for regular motions; or one for the first and another for the second approximation, in dealing with the same phenomenon. Hence those who are most concerned with a unified approach to the study of art have split the history of style into two aspects which cannot be derived from each other or from some common principle.

Parallel to the theorists of cyclical development, other scholars have approached the development of styles as a continous, long-term evolutionary process. Here, too, there are poles and stages and some hints of a universal, though not cyclical, process; but the poles are those of the earliest and latest stages and are deduced from a definition of the artist's goal or the nature of art or from a psychological theory.

The first students to investigate the history of primitive art conceived the latter as a development between two poles, the geometrical and the naturalistic. They were supported by observation of the broad growth of art in the historical cultures from geometric or simple, stylized forms to more natural ones; they were sustained also by the idea that the most naturalistic styles of all belonged to the highest type of culture, the most advanced in scientific knowledge, and the most capable of representing the world in accurate images. The process in art agreed with the analogous development in nature from the simple to the complex and was paralleled by the growth of the child's drawings in our own culture from schematic or geometrical forms to naturalistic ones. The origin of certain geometrical forms in primitive industrial techniques also favored this view.

It is challenging and amusing to consider in the light of these arguments the fact that the Paleolithic cave paintings, the oldest known art, are marvels of representation (whatever the elements of schematic form in those works, they are more naturalistic than the succeeding Neolithic and Bronze Age art) and that in the twentieth century naturalistic forms have given way to "abstraction" and so-called "subjective" styles. But, apart from these paradoxical exceptions, one could observe in historical arts—e.g., in the late classic and early Christian periods—how free naturalistic forms are progressively stylized and reduced to ornament. In the late nineteenth century, ornament was often designed by a method of stylization, a geometrizing of natural motives; and those who knew contemporary art were not slow to discern in the geometrical styles of existing primitives the traces of an older more naturalistic model. Study shows that both processes occur in history; there is little reason to regard either one as more typical or more primitive. The geometrical and the naturalistic forms may arise independently in different contexts and coexist within the same culture. The experience of the art of the last fifty years suggests further that the degree of naturalism in art is not a sure indication of the technological or intellectual level of a culture. This does not mean that style is independent of that level but that other concepts than those of the naturalistic and the geometrical must be applied in considering such relationships. The essential opposition is not of the natural and the geometric but of certain modes of composition of natural and geometric motives. From this point of view, modern "abstract" art in its taste for open, asymmetrical, random, tangled, and incomplete forms is much closer to the compositional principles of realistic or Impressionist painting and sculpture than to any primitive art with geometrical elements. Although the character of the themes, whether "abstract" or naturalistic, is important for the concrete aspect of the work of art, historians do not operate so much with categories of the naturalistic and geometrical as with subtler structural concepts, which apply also to architecture, where the problem of representation seems irrelevant. It is with such concepts that Wölfflin and Frankl have constructed their models.

Nevertheless, the representation of natural forms has been a goal in the arts of many cultures. Whether we regard it as a spontaneous common idea or one that has been diffused from a single prehistorical center, the problem of how to represent the human and animal figure has been attacked independently by various cultures. Their solutions present not only similar features in the devices of rendering but also a remarkable parallelism in the successive stages of the solutions. It is fascinating to compare the changing representation of the eyes or of pleated costume in succeeding styles of Greek, Chinese, and medieval European sculpture. The development of such details from a highly schematic to a naturalistic type in the latter two can hardly be referred to a direct influence of Greek models; for the similarities are not only of geographically far separated styles but of distinct series in time. To account for the Chinese and Romanesque forms as copies of the older Greek, we would have to assume that at each stage in the post-Greek styles the artists had recourse to Greek works of the corresponding stage and in the same order. Indeed, some of the cyclical schemas discussed above are, in essence, descriptions of the stages in the development of representation; and it may be asked whether the formal schemas, like Wölfflin's, are not veiled categories of representation, even though they are applied to architecture as well as to sculpture and painting; for the standards of representation in the latter may conceivably determine a general norm of plasticity and structure for all the visual arts.

This aspect of style—the representation of natural forms—has been studied by the classical archaeologist Emmanuel Löwy; his little book on *The Rendering of Nature in Early Greek Art*, published in 1900, is still suggestive for modern research and has a wider application than has been recognized. Löwy has analyzed the general principles of representation in early arts and explained their stages as progressive steps in a steady change from conceptual representation, based on the memory image, to perspective representation, according to direct perception of objects. Since the structure of the memory image is the same in all cultures, the representations based on this psychological process will exhibit common features: (1) The shape and movement of figures and their parts are limited to a few typical forms; (2) the single forms are schematized in regular linear patterns; (3) representation proceeds from the outline, whether the latter is an independent contour or the silhouette of a uniformly colored area; (4) where colors are used, they are without gradation of light and shadow; (5) the parts of a figure are presented to the observer in their broadest aspect; (6) in compositions the figures, with few exceptions, are shown with a minimum of overlapping of their main parts; the real succession of figures in depth is transformed in the image into a juxtaposition on the same plane; (7) the representation of the three-dimensional space in which an action takes place is more or less absent.

Whatever criticisms may be made of Löwy's notion of a memory image as the source of these peculiarities, his account of archaic representation as a universal type, with a characteristic structure, is exceedingly valuable; it has a general application to children's drawings, to the work of modern untrained adults, and to primitives. This analysis does not touch on the individuality of archaic styles, nor does it help us to understand why some cultures develop beyond them and others, like the Egyptian, retain the archaic features for many centuries. Limited by an evolutionary view and a naturalistic value norm, Löwy ignored the perfection and expressiveness of archaic works. Neglecting the specific content of the representations, this approach fails to recognize the role of the content and of emotional factors in the proportioning and accentuation of parts. But these limitations do not lessen the importance of Löwy's book in defining so clearly a widespread type of archaic representation and in tracing the stages of its development into a more naturalistic art.

I may mention here that the reverse process of the conversion of naturalistic to archaic forms, as we see it wherever works of an advanced naturalistic style are copied by primitives, colonials, provincials, and the untrained in the high cultures, can also be formulated through Löwy's principles.

We must mention, finally, as the most constructive and imaginative of the historians who have tried to embrace the whole of artistic development as a single continuous process, Alois Riegl, the author of *Stilfragen* and *Die spätrömische Kunstindustrie*.

Riegl was especially concerned with transitions that mark the beginning of a world-historical epoch (the Old Oriental to the Hellenic, the ancient to the medieval). He gave up not only the normative view that judges the later phases of a cycle as a decline but also the conception of closed cycles. In late Roman art, which was considered decadent in his time, he found a necessary creative link between two great stages of an open development. His account of the process is like Wölfflin's, however, though perhaps independent; he formulates as the poles of the long evolution two types of style, the "haptic" (tactile) and the "optic" (or painterly, impressionistic), which coincide broadly with the poles of Wölfflin's shorter cycles. The process of development from the haptic to the optic is observable in each epoch, but only as part of a longer process, of which the great stages are millennial and correspond to whole cultures. The history of art is, for Riegl, an endless necessary movement from representation based on vision of the object and its parts as proximate, tangible, discrete, and self-sufficient, to the representation of the whole perceptual field as a directly given, but more distant, continuum with merging parts, with an increasing role of the spatial voids, and with a more evident reference to the knowing subject as a constituting factor in perception. This artistic process is also described by Riegl in terms of a faculty psychology; will, feeling, and thought are the successive dominants in shaping our relations to the world; it corresponds in philosophy to the change from a predominantly objective to a subjective outlook.

Riegl does not study this process simply as a development of naturalism from an archaic to an impressionistic stage. Each phase has its special formal and expressive problems, and Riegl has written remarkably penetrating pages on the intimate structure of styles, the principles of composition, and the relations of figure to ground. In his systematic account of ancient art and the art of the early Christian period, he has observed common principles in architecture, sculpture, painting, and ornament, sometimes with surprising acuteness. He has also succeeded in showing unexpected relationships between different aspects of a style. In a work on Dutch group portraiture of the sixteenth and seventeenth centuries, a theme that belongs to art and social history, he has carried through a most delicate analysis of the changing relations between the objective and the subjective elements in portraiture and in the correspondingly variable mode of unifying a represented group which is progressively more attentive to the observer.

His motivation of the process and his explanation of its shifts in time and space are vague and often fantastic. Each great phase corresponds to a racial disposition. The history of Western man from the time of the Old Oriental kingdoms to the present day is divided into three great periods, characterized by the successive predominance of will, feeling, and thought, in Oriental, Classical, and Western Man. Each race plays a prescribed role and retires when its part is done, as if participating in a symphony of world history. The apparent deviations from the expected continuities are saved for the system by a theory of purposive regression which prepares a people for its advanced role. The obvious incidence of social and religious factors in art is judged to be simply a parallel manifestation of a corresponding process in these other fields rather than a possible cause. The basic, immanent development from an objective to a subjective standpoint governs the whole of history, so that all contemporary fields have a deep unity with respect to a common determining process.

This brief summary of Riegl's ideas hardly does justice to the positive features of his work, and especially to his conception of art as an active creative process in which new forms arise from the artist's will to solve specifically artistic problems. Even his racial theories and strange views about the historical situation of an art represent a desire to grasp large relationships, although distorted by an inadequate psychology and social theory; this search for a broad view has become rare in the study of art since his time. And still rarer is its combination with the power of detailed research that Riegl possessed to a high degree.

To summarize the results of modern studies with respect to the cyclical and evolutionary theories:

(1) From the viewpoint of historians who have tried to reconstruct the precise order of development, without presuppositions about cycles, there is a continuity in the Near East and Europe from the Neolithic period to the present—perhaps best described as a tree with many branches—in which the most advanced forms of each

culture are retained, to some extent, in the early forms of succeeding cultures.

(2) On the other hand, there are within that continuity at least two long developments—the ancient Greek and the Western European medieval-modern—which include the broad types of style described in various cyclical theories. But these two cycles are not unconnected; artists in the second cycle often copied surviving works of the first, and it is uncertain whether some of the guiding principles in Western art are not derived from the Greeks.

(3) Within these two cycles and in several other cultures (Asiatic and American) occur many examples of similar short developments, especially from an archaic linear type of representation to a more "pictorial" style.

(4) Wherever there is a progressive naturalistic art, i.e., one which becomes increasingly naturalistic, we find in the process stages corresponding broadly to the line of archaic, classic, baroque, and impressionist in Western art. Although these styles in the West are not adequately described in terms of their method of representation, they embody specific advances in range or method of representation from a first stage of schematized, so-called "conceptual," representation of isolated objects to a later stage of perspective representation in which continuities of space, movement, light and shadow, and atmosphere have become important.

(5) In describing the Western development, which is the model of cyclical theories, historians isolate different aspects of art for the definition of the stylistic types. In several theories the development of representation is the main source of the terms; in others formal traits, which can be found also in architecture, script, and pottery shapes, are isolated; and, in some accounts, qualities of expression and content are the criteria. It is not always clear which formal traits are really independent of representation. It is possible that a way of seeing objects in nature—the perspective vision as distinguished from the archaic conceptual mode—also affects the design of a column or a pot. But the example of Islamic art, in which representation is secondary, suggests that the development of the period styles in architecture and ornament need not depend on a style of representation. As for expression, there exist in the Baroque art of the seventeenth century intimate works of great tragic sensibility, like Rembrandt's, and monumental works of a profuse splendor; either of these traits can be paralleled in other periods in forms of nonbaroque type. But a true counterpart of Rembrandt's light and shadow will not be found

in Greek or Chinese painting, although both are said to have baroque phases.

VI

We shall now consider the explanations of style proposed without reference to cycles and polar developments.

In accounting for the genesis of a style, early investigators gave great weight to the technique, materials, and practical functions of an art. Thus wood carving favors grooved or wedge-cut relief, the column of the tree trunk gives the statue its cylindrical shape, hard stone yields compact and angular forms, weaving begets stepped and symmetrical patterns, the potter's wheel introduces a perfect roundness, coiling is the source of spirals, etc. This was the approach of Semper and his followers in the last century. Boas, among others, identified style, or at least its formal aspect, with motor habits in the handling of tools. In modern art this viewpoint appears in the program of functionalist architecture and design. It is also behind the older explanation of the Gothic style of architecture as a rational system derived from the rib construction of vaults. Modern sculptors who adhere closely to the block, exploiting the texture and grain of the material and showing the marks of the tool, are supporters of this theory of style. It is related to the immense role of the technological in our own society; modern standards of efficient production have become a norm in art.

There is no doubt that these practical conditions account for some peculiarities of style. They are important also in explaining similarities in primitive and folk arts which appear to be independent of diffusion or imitation of styles. But they are of less interest for highly developed arts. Wood may limit the sculptor's forms, but we know a great variety of styles in wood, some of which even conceal the subtance. Riegl observed long ago that the same forms occurred within a culture in works of varied technique, materials, and use; it is this common style that the theory in question has failed to explain. The Gothic style is, broadly speaking, the same in buildings; sculptures of wood, ivory, and stone; panel paintings; stained glass; miniatures; metalwork, enamels, and textiles. It may be that in some instances a style created in one art under the influence of the technique, material, and function of particular objects has been generalized by application to all objects, techniques, and materials. Yet the material is not always prior to the style but may be chosen because of an ideal of expression and artistic quality or for symbolism. The hard substances of Old Egyptian art, the use of gold and other precious luminous substances in arts of power, the taste for steel, concrete, and glass in modern design, are not external to the artist's first goal but parts of the original conception. The compactness of the sculpture cut from a tree trunk is a quality that is already present in the artist's idea before he begins to carve. For simple compact forms appear in clay figures and in drawings and paintings where the matter does not limit the design. The compactness may be regarded as a necessary trait of an archaic or a "haptic" in Löwy's or Riegl's sense.

Turning away from material factors, some historians find in the content of the work of art the source of its style. In the arts of representation, a style is often associated with a distinct body of subject matter, drawn from a single sphere of ideas or experience. Thus in Western art of the fourteenth century, when a new iconography of the life of Christ and of Mary was created in which themes of suffering were favored, we observe new patterns of line and color, which possess a more lyrical, pathetic aspect than did the preceding art. In our own time, a taste for the constructive and rational in industry has led to the use of mechanical motives and a style of forms characterized by coolness, precision, objectivity, and power.

The style in these examples is viewed by many writers as the objective vehicle of the subject matter or of its governing idea. Style, then, is the means of communication, a language not only as a system of devices for conveying a precise message by representing or symbolizing objects and actions but also as a qualitative whole which is capable of suggesting the diffuse connotations as well and intensifying the associated or intrinsic affects. By an effort of imagination based on experience of his medium, the artist discovers the elements and formal relationships which will express the values of the content and look right artistically. Of all the attempts made in this direction, the most successful will be repeated and developed as a norm.

The relationship of content and style is more complex than appears in this theory. There are styles in which the correspondence of the expression and the values of the typical subjects is not at all obvious. If the difference between pagan and Christian art is explained broadly by the difference in religious content, there is nevertheless a long period of time—in fact, many centuries—during which Christian subjects are represented in the style of pagan art. As late as 800, the *Libri Carolini* speak of the difficulty of distinguishing images of Mary and Venus without the labels. This may be due to the fact that a general outlook of late paganism, more fundamental than the religious doctrines, was still shared by Christians or that the new religion, while important, had not yet transformed the basic attitudes and ways of thinking. Or it may be that the function of art within the religious life was too slight, for not all concepts of the religion find their way into art. But even later, when the Christian style had been established, there were developments in art toward a more naturalistic form and toward imitation of elements of ancient pagan style which were incompatible with the chief ideas of the religion.

A style that arises in connection with a particular content often becomes an accepted mode governing all representations of the period. The Gothic style is applied in religious and secular works alike; and, if it is true that no domestic or civil building in that style has the expressiveness of a cathedral interior, yet in painting and sculpture the religious and secular images are hardly different in form. On the other hand, in periods of a style less pervasive than the Gothic, different idioms or dialects of form are used for different fields of content; this was observed in the discussion of the concept of stylistic unity.

It is such observations that have led students to modify the simple equation of style and the expressive values of a subject matter, according to which the style is the vehicle of the main meanings of the work of art. Instead, the meaning of content has been extended, and attention has been fixed on broader attitudes or on general ways of thinking and feeling, which are believed to shape a style. The style is then viewed as a concrete embodiment or projection of emotional dispositions and habits of thought common to the whole culture. The content as a parallel product of the same viewpoint will therefore often exhibit qualities and structures like those of the style.

These world views or ways of thinking and feeling are usually abstracted by the historian from the philosophical systems and metaphysics of a period or from theology and literature and even from science. Themes like the relation of subject and object, spirit and matter, soul and body, man and nature or God, and conceptions of time and space, self and cosmos are typical fields from which are derived the definitions of the world view (or *Denkweise*) of a period or culture. The latter is then documented by illustrations from many fields, but some writers have attempted to derive it from the works of art themselves. One searches in a style for qualities and structures that can be matched with some aspect of thinking or a world view. Sometimes it is based on a priori deduction of possible world views, given the limited number of solutions of metaphysical problems; or a typology of the possible attitudes of the individual to the world and to his own existence is matched with a typology of styles. We have seen how Riegl apportioned the three faculties of will, feeling, and thought among three races and three major styles.

The attempts to derive style from thought are often too vague to yield more than suggestive *aperçus*; the method breeds analogical speculations which do not hold up under detailed critical study. The history of the analogy drawn between the Gothic cathedral and scholastic theology is an example. The common element in these two contemporary creations has been found in their rationalism and in their irrationality, their idealism and their naturalism, their encyclopedic completeness and their striving for infinity, and recently in their dialectical method. Yet one hesitates to reject such analogies in principle, since the cathedral belongs to the same religious sphere as does contemporary theology.

It is when these ways of thinking and feeling or world views have been formulated as the outlook of a religion or dominant institution or class of which the myths and values are illustrated or symbolized in the work of art that the general intellectual content seems a more promising field for explanation of style. But the content of a work of art often belongs to another region of experience than the one in which both the period style and the dominant mode of thinking have been formed; an example is the secular art of a period in which religious ideas and rituals are primary, and, conversely, the religious art of a secularized culture. In such cases we see how important for a style of art is the character of the dominants in culture, especially of institutions. Not the content as such, but the content as part of a dominant set of beliefs, ideas, and interests, supported by institutions and the forms of everyday life, shapes the common style.

Although the attempts to explain styles as an artistic expression of a world view or mode of thought are often a drastic reduction of the concreteness and richness of art, they have been helpful in revealing unsuspected levels of meaning in art. They have established the practice of interpreting the style itself as an inner content of the art, especially in the nonrepresentational arts. They correspond to the conviction of modern artists that the form elements and structure are a deeply meaningful whole related to metaphysical views.

VII

The theory that the world view or mode of thinking and feeling is the source of long-term constants in style is often formulated as a theory of racial or national character. I have already referred to such concepts in the work of Wölfflin and Riegl. They have been common in European writing on art for over a hundred years and have played a significant role in promoting national consciousness and race feeling; works of art are the chief concrete evidences of the affective world of the ancestors. The persistent teaching that German art is by nature tense and irrational, that its greatness depends on fidelity to the racial character, has helped to produce an acceptance of these traits as a destiny of the people.

The weakness of the racial concept of style is evident from analysis of the history and geography of styles, without reference to biology. The so-called "constant" is less constant than the racially (or nationally) minded historians have assumed. German art includes Classicism and the Biedermeier style, as well as the work of Grünewald and the modern Expressionists. During the periods of most pronounced Germanic character, the extension of the native style hardly coincides with the boundaries of the preponderant physical type or with the recent national boundaries. This discrepancy holds for the Italian art which is paired with the German as a polar opposite.

Nevertheless, there are striking recurrences in the art of a region or nation which have not been explained. It is astonishing to observe the resemblances between German migrations art and the styles of the Carolingian, Ottonian, and late Gothic periods, then of German rococo architecture, and finally of modern Expressionism. There are great gaps in time between these styles during which the forms can scarcely be described in the traditional German terms. To save the appearance of constancy, German writers have supposed that the intervening phases were dominated by alien influences or were periods of preparation for the ultimate release, or they conceived the deviant qualities as another aspect of German character: the Germans are both irrational and disciplined.

If we restrict ourselves to more modest historical correlations of styles with the dominant personality types of the cultures or groups that have created the styles, we meet several difficulties; some of these have been anticipated in the discussion of the general problem of unity of style:

(1) The variation of styles in a culture or group is often considerable within the same period.

(2) Until recently, the artists who create the style are generally of another mode of life than those for whom the arts are designed and whose viewpoint, interests, and quality of life are evident in the art. The best examples are the arts of great monarchies, aristocracies, and privileged institutions.

(3) What is constant in all the arts of a period (or of several

periods) may be less essential for characterizing the style than the variable features; the persistent French quality in the series of styles between 1770 and 1870 is a nuance which is hardly as important for the definition of the period style as the traits that constitute the Rococo, Neo-Classic, Romantic, Realistic, and Impressionist styles.

To explain the changing period styles, historians and critics have felt the need of a theory that relates particular forms to tendencies of character and feeling. Such a theory, concerned with the elements of expression and structure, should tell us what affects and dispositions determine choices of forms. Historians have not waited for experimental psychology to support their physiognomic interpretations of style but, like the thoughtful artists, have resorted to intuitive judgments, relying on direct experience of art. Building up an unsystematic, empirical knowledge of forms, expressions, affects, and qualities, they have tried to control these judgments by constant comparison of works and by reference to contemporary sources of information about the content of the art, assuming that the attitudes which govern the latter must also be projected in the style. The interpretation of Classical style is not founded simply on firsthand experience of Greek buildings and sculptures; it rests also on knowledge of Greek language, literature, religion, mythology, philosophy, and history, which provide an independent picture of the Greek world. But this picture is, in turn, refined and enriched by experience of the visual arts, and our insight is sharpened by knowledge of the very different arts of the neighboring peoples and of the results of attempts to copy the Greek models at later times under other conditions. Today, after the work of nearly two centuries of scholars, a sensitive mind, with relatively little information about Greek culture, can respond directly to the "Greek mind" in those ancient buildings and sculptures.

In physiognomic interpretations of group styles, there is a common assumption that is still problematic: that the psychological explanations of unique features in a modern individual's art can be applied to a whole culture in which the same or similar features are characteristics of a group or period style.

If schizophrenics fill a sheet of paper with closely crowded elements in repeat patterns, can we explain similar tendencies in the art of a historic or primitive culture by a schizophrenic tendency or dominant schizoid personality type in that culture? We are inclined to doubt such interpretations for two reasons. First, we are not sure that this pattern is uniquely schizoid in modern individuals; it may represent a component of the psychotic personality which also exists in other temperaments as a tendency associated with particular emotional contents or problems. Secondly, this pattern, originating in a single artist of schizoid type, may crystallize as a common convention, accepted by other artists and the public because it satisfies a need and is most adequate to a special problem of decoration or representation, without entailing, however, a notable change in the broad habits and attitudes of the group. This convention may be adopted by artists of varied personality types, who will apply it in distinct ways, filling it with an individual content and expression.

A good instance of this relationship between the psychotic, the normal individual, and the group is the practice of reading object forms in relatively formless spots—as in hallucination and in psychological tests. Leonardo da Vinci proposed this method to artists as a means of invention. It was practiced in China, and later in Western art; today it has become a standard method for artists of different character. In the painter who first introduced the practice and exploited it most fully, it may correspond to a personal disposition; but for many others it is an established technique. What is personally significant is not the practice itself but the kinds of spots chosen and what is seen in them; attention to the latter discloses a great variety of individual reactions.

If art is regarded as a projective technique—and some artists today think of their work in these terms—will interpretation of the work give the same result as a projective test? The tests are so designed as to reduce the number of elements that depend on education, profession, and environment. But the work of art is very much conditioned by these factors. Hence, in discerning the personal expression in a work of art, one must distinguish between those aspects that are conventional and those that are clearly individual. In dealing with the style of a group, however, we consider only such superindividual aspects, abstracting them from the personal variants. How, then, can one apply to the interpretation of the style concepts from individual psychology?

It may be said, of course, that the established norms of a group style are genuine parts of an artist's outlook and response and can be approached as the elements of a modal personality. In the same way the habits and attitudes of scientists that are required by their profession may be an important part of their characters. But do such traits also constitute the typical ones of the culture or the society as a whole? Is an art style that has crystallized as a result of special problems necessarily an expression of the whole group? Or is it only in the special case where the art is open to the common outlook and everyday interests of the entire group that its content and style can be representative of the group?

A common tendency in the physiognomic approach to group style has been to interpret all the elements of representation as expressions. The blank background or negative features like the absence of a horizon and of consistent perspective in paintings are judged to be symptomatic of an attitude to space and time in actual life. The limited space in Greek art is interpreted as a fundamental trait of Greek personality. Yet this blankness of the background, we have seen, is common to many styles; it is found in prehistoric art, in Old Oriental art, in the Far East, in the Middle Ages, and in most primitive painting and relief. The fact that it occurs in modern children's drawings and in the drawings of untrained adults suggests that it belongs to a universal primitive level of representation. But it should be observed that this is also the method of illustration in the most advanced scientific work in the past and today.

This fact does not mean that representation is wholly without expressive personal features. A particular treatment of the "empty" background may become a powerful expressive factor. Careful study of so systematic a method of representation as geometrical perspective shows that within such a scientific system there are many possible choices; the position of the eye-level, the intensity of convergence, the distance of the viewer from the picture plane—all these are expressive choices within the conditions of the system. Moreover, the existence of the system itself presupposes a degree of interest in the environment which is already a cultural trait with a long history.

The fact that an art represents a restricted world does not allow us to infer, however, a corresponding restriction of interests and perceptions in everyday life. We would have to suppose, if this were true, that in Islam people were unconcerned with the human body, and that the present vogue of "abstract" art means a general indifference to the living.

An interesting evidence of the limitations of the assumed identities of the space or time structure of works of art and the space or time experience of individuals is the way in which painters of the thirteenth century represented the new cathedrals. These vast buildings with high vaults and endless vistas in depth are shown as shallow structures, not much larger than the human beings they enclose. The conventions of representation provided no means of re-creating the experience of architectural space, an experience that was surely a factor in the conception of the cathedral and was reported in contemporary descriptions. (It is possible to relate the architectural and pictorial spaces; but the attempt would take us beyond the problems of this paper.) The space of the cathedrals is intensely expressive, but it is a constructed, ideal space, appealing to the imagination, and not an attempt to transpose the space of everyday life. We will understand it better as a creation adequate to a religious conception than as one in which an everyday sentiment of space has been embodied in architecture. It is an ideological space, too, and, if it conveys the feelings of the most inspired religious personalities, it is not a model of an average, collective attitude to space in general, although the cathedral is used by everyone.

The concept of personality in art is most important for the theory that the great artist is the immediate source of the period style. This little-explored view, implicit in much historical research and criticism, regards the group style as an imitation of the style of an original artist. Study of a line of development often leads to the observation that some individual is responsible for the change in the period form. The personality of the great artist and the problems inherited from the preceding generation are the two factors studied. For the personality as a whole is sometimes substituted a weakness or a traumatic experience which activates the individual's will to create. Such a view is little adapted to the understanding of those cultures or historical epochs that left us no signed works or biographies of artists; but it is the favored view of many students of the art of the last four centuries in Europe. It may be questioned whether it is applicable to cultures in which the individual has less mobility and range of personal action and in which the artist is not a deviant type. The main difficulty, however, arises from the fact that similar stylistic trends often appear independently in different arts at the same time; that great contemporary artists in the same field—Leonardo, Michelangelo, Raphael—show a parallel tendency of style, although each artist has a personal form; and that the new outlook expressed by a single man of genius is anticipated or prepared in preceding works and thought. The great artists of the Gothic period and the Renaissance constitute families with a common heritage and trend. Decisive changes are most often associated with original works of outstanding quality; but the new direction of style and its acceptance are unintelligible without reference to the conditions of the moment and the common ground of the art.

These difficulties and complexities have not led scholars to abandon the psychological approach; long experience with art has established as a plausible principle the notion that an individual style is a personal expression; and continued research has found many confirmations of this, wherever it has been possible to control statements about the personality, built upon the work, by referring to actual information about the artist. Similarly, common traits in the art of a culture or nation can be matched with some features of social life, ideas, customs, general dispositions. But such correlations have been of single elements or aspects of a style with single traits of a people; it is rarely a question of wholes. In our own culture, styles have changed very rapidly, yet the current notions about group traits do not allow sufficiently for corresponding changes in the behavior patterns or provide such a formulation of the group personality that one can deduce from it how that personality will change under new conditions.

It seems that for explanation of the styles of the higher cultures, with their great variability and intense development, the concepts of group personality current today are too rigid. They underestimate the specialized functions of art which determine characteristics that are superpersonal. But we may ask whether some of the difficulties in applying characterological concepts to national or period styles are not also present in the interpretation of primitive arts. Would a psychological treatment of Sioux art, for example, give us the same picture of Sioux personality as that provided by analysis of Sioux family life, ceremony, and hunting?

VIII

We turn last to explanations of style by the forms of social life. The idea of a connection between these forms and styles is already suggested by the framework of the history of art. Its main divisions, accepted by all students, are also the boundaries of social units—cultures, empires, dynasties, cities, classes, churches, etc.—and periods which mark significant stages in social development. The great historical epochs of art, like antiquity, the Middle Ages, and the modern era, are the same as the epochs of economic history; they correspond to great systems, like feudalism and capitalism. Important economic and political shifts within these systems are often accompanied or followed by shifts in the centers of art and their styles. Religion and major world views are broadly coordinated with these eras in social history.

In many problems the importance of economic, political, and ideological conditions for the creation of a group style (or of a world view that influences a style) is generally admitted. The distinctiveness of Greek art among the arts of the ancient world can hardly be separated from the forms of Greek society and the city-state. The importance of the burgher class, with its special position in society and its mode of life, for the medieval and early Renaissance art of Florence and for Dutch art of the seventeenth century, is a commonplace. In explaining Baroque art, the Counter-Reformation and the absolute monarchy are constantly cited as the sources of certain features of style. We have interesting studies on a multitude of problems concerning the relationship of particular styles and contents of art to institutions and historical situations. In these studies ideas, traits, and values arising from the conditions of economic, political, and civil life are matched with the new characteristics of an art. Yet, with all this experience, the general principles applied in explanation and the connection of types of art with types of social structure have not been investigated in a systematic way. By the many scholars who adduce piecemeal political or economic facts in order to account for single traits of style or subject matter, little has been done to construct an adequate comprehensive theory. In using such data, scholars will often deny that these "external" relationships can throw any light on the artistic phenomenon as such. They fear "materialism" as a reduction of the spiritual or ideal to sordid practical affairs.

Marxist writers are among the few who have tried to apply a general theory. It is based on Marx's undeveloped view that the higher forms of cultural life correspond to the economic structure of a society, the latter being defined in terms of the relations of classes in the process of production and the technological level. Between the economic relationships and the styles of art intervenes the process of ideological construction, a complex imaginative transposition of class roles and needs, which affects the special field—religion, mythology, or civil life—that provides the chief themes of art.

The great interest of the Marxist approach lies not only in the attempt to interpret the historically changing relations of art and economic life in the light of a general theory of society but also in the weight given to the differences and conflicts within the social group as motors of development, and to the effects of these on outlook, religion, morality, and philosophical ideas.

Only broadly sketched in Marx's works, the theory has rarely been applied systematically in a true spirit of investigation, such as we see in Marx's economic writings. Marxist writing on art has suffered from schematic and premature formulations and from crude judgments imposed by loyalty to a political line.

A theory of style adequate to the psychological and historical problems has still to be created. It waits for a deeper knowledge of the principles of form construction and expression and for a unified theory of the processes of social life in which the practical means of life as well as emotional behavior are comprised.

Meditations on a Hobby Horse, or
The Roots of Artistic Form

E. H. Gombrich

The subject of this article is a very ordinary hobby horse. It is neither metaphorical nor purely imaginary, at least not more so than the broomstick on which Swift wrote his meditations. It is usually content with its place in the corner of the nursery and it has no aesthetic ambitions. Indeed it abhors frills. It is satisfied with its broomstick body and its crudely carved head which just indicates the upper end and serves as holder for the reins. How should we address it? Should we describe it as an "image of a horse"? The compilers of the *Oxford Pocket Dictionary* would hardly have agreed. They defined *image* as "imitation of object's external form" and the "external form" of a horse is surely not "imitated" here. So much the worse, we might say, for the "external form," that elusive remnant of the Greek philosophical tradition which has dominated our aesthetic language for so long. Luckily there is another word in the *Dictionary* which might prove more accommodating: *representation*. To *represent*, we read, can be used in the sense of "call up by description or portrayal or imagination, figure, place likeness of before mind or senses, serve or be meant as likeness of . . . stand for, be specimen of, fill place of, be substitute for." A portrayal of a horse? Evidently not. A substitute for a horse? Yes. That it is. Perhaps there is more in this formula than meets the eye.

I

Let us first ride our wooden steed into battle against a number of ghosts which still haunt the language of art criticism. One of them we even found entrenched in the *Oxford Dictionary*. The implication of its definition of an image is that the artist "imitates" the "external form" of the object in front of him, and the beholder, in his turn, recognizes the "subject" of the work of art by its "form." This is what

172

might be called the traditional view of representation. Its corollary is that a work of art will either be a faithful copy, in fact a complete replica, of the object represented or that it constitutes a degree of "abstraction." The artist, we read, abstracts the "form" from the object he sees. The sculptor usually abstracts the three-dimensional form and abstracts *from* color, the painter abstracts contours and colors, and *from* the third dimension. In this context one hears it said that the draftsman's line is a "tremendous feat of abstraction" because it does not "occur in nature." A modern sculptor of Brancusi's persuasion may be praised or blamed for "carrying abstraction to its logical extreme." Finally the label of "abstract art" for the creation of pure forms carries with it the same implications. Yet we need only look at our hobby horse to see that the very idea of abstraction as a complicated mental act lands us in curious absurdities. There is an old music hall joke describing a drunkard who politely lifts his hat to every lamppost he passes. Should we say that the liquor has so increased his power of abstraction that he is now able to isolate the formal quality of uprightness from both lamppost and the human figure? Our mind, of course, works by differentiation rather than by generalization, and the child will for long call all four-footers of a certain size "gee-gee" before it learns to distinguish breeds and "forms"![1]

II

Then there is the age-old problem of universals as applied to art. It has received its classical formulation in the Platonizing theories of the Academicians. "A history-painter," says Reynolds, "paints man in general; a portrait-painter a particular man, and therefore a defective model."[2] This, of course, is the theory of abstraction applied to one specific problem. The implications are that the portrait, being an exact copy of a man's "external form" with all "blemishes" and "accidents," refers to the individual person exactly as does the proper name. The painter, however, who wants to "elevate his style" disregards the particular and "generalizes the forms." Such a picture will no longer represent a particular man but rather the class or concept "man." There is a deceptive simplicity in this argument but it makes at least one unwarranted assumption: that every image of this kind necessarily refers to something outside itself—be it individual or class. But no such reference need be implied if we point to an image and say "this is a man." Strictly speaking that statement may be interpreted to mean that the image itself is a member of the class "man." Nor is that interpretation as farfetched as it may sound. In fact our hobby horse would submit to no other interpretation. By the logic of Reynolds's reasoning it would have to represent the most generalized idea of horseness. But if the child calls a stick a horse it obviously means nothing of the kind. It does not think in terms of reference at all. The stick is neither a sign signifying the concept horse nor is it a portrait of an individual horse. By its capacity of serving as a "substitute" the stick becomes a horse in its own right, it may graduate into the class of "gee-gees" and even receive a proper name of its own.

When Pygmalion blocked out a figure from his marble he did not at first represent a "generalized" human form, and then gradually a particular woman. For as he chipped away and made it more lifelike the block was not turned into a portrait—not even in the unlikely case that he used a live model. So when his prayers were heard and the statue came to life she was Galatea and no one else—and that regardless of whether she had been fashioned in an archaic, idealistic, or naturalistic style. The question of reference, in fact, is totally independent of the degree of differentiation. The witch who made a "generalized" wax dummy of an enemy may have meant it to refer to someone in particular. She would then pronounce the right spell to establish this link—much as we may write a caption under a generalized picture to do the same. But even those proverbial replicas of nature, Madam Tussaud's effigies, need the same treatment. Those in the galleries which are labeled are "portraits of the great." The figure on the staircase made to hoax the visitor simply represents "an" attendant, a class. It stands there as a "substitute" for the expected guard—but it is not more "generalized" in Reynolds's sense.

III

The idea that art is "creation" rather than "imitation" is sufficiently familiar. It has been proclaimed in various forms from the time of Leonardo, who insisted that the painter is "Lord of all Things,"[3] to Klee, who wanted to create as Nature does.[4] But the more solemn overtones of metaphysical power disappear when we leave art for toys. The child "makes" a train either of a few blocks or with pencil on paper. Surrounded as we are by posters and newspapers carrying illustrations of commodities or events, we find it difficult to rid ourselves of the prejudice that all images should be "read" as referring to some imaginary or actual reality. Only the historian knows how hard it is to look at Pygmalion's work without comparing it with nature. But recently have we been made aware how thoroughly we misunderstand primitive or Egyptian art whenever we make the assumption that the artist "distorts" his motif or that he even wants us to see in his work the record of any concrete experience.[5] In many cases these images "represent" in the sense of "substitution." The clay horse or servant buried in the tomb of the mighty takes the place of the living. The idol takes the place of the God. The question whether it represents the "external form" of the particular divinity or, for that matter, of a class of demons does not come in at all. The idol serves as the substitute of the God in worship and ritual—it is a man-made God in precisely the sense that the hobby horse is a man-made horse; to question it further means to court deception.[6]

There is another misunderstanding to be guarded against. We often try instinctively to save our idea of "representation" by shifting it to another plane. Where we cannot refer the image to a motif in the outer world we take it to be a portrayal of a motif in the artist's inner world. Much critical (and uncritical) writing on both primitive and modern art betrays this assumption. But to apply the naturalistic idea of portrayal to dreams and visions—let alone to unconscious images—begs a whole number of questions.[7] The hobby horse does not portray our idea of a horse. The fearsome monster or funny face we may doodle on our blotting pad is not projected out of our mind as paint is "ex-pressed" out of a paint tube. Of course any image will be in some way symptomatic of its maker, but to think of it as of a photograph of a pre-existing reality is to misunderstand the whole process of image making.

IV

Can our substitute take us further? Perhaps, if we consider how it could become a substitute. The "first" hobby horse (to use eighteenth-century language) was probably no image at all. Just a stick which qualified as a horse because one could ride on it. . . . The *tertium comparationis*, the common factor, was function rather than form. Or, more precisely, that formal aspect which fulfilled the minimum requirement for the performance of the function—for any "ridable" object could serve as a horse. If that is true we may be enabled to cross a boundary which is usually regarded as closed and sealed. For in this sense "substitutes" reach deep into biological layers that are common to man and animal. The cat runs after the ball as if it were a mouse. The baby sucks its thumb as if it were the breast. In a sense the ball "represents" a mouse to the cat, the thumb a breast to the baby. But here too "representation" does not depend on formal, that is geometrical, qualities beyond the minimum requirements of function. The ball has nothing in common with the mouse except that it is chasable. The thumb nothing with the breast except that it is suckable. As "substitutes" they fulfill certain demands of the organism. They are keys which happen to fit into biological or psychological locks, or counterfeit coins which make the machine work when dropped into the slot. In the language of the nursery the psychological function of "representation" is still recognized. The child will reject a perfectly naturalistic doll in favor of some monstrously "abstract" dummy which is "cuddly." It may even dispose of the element of "form" altogether and take to a blanket or an eiderdown as its favorite "comforter"—a substitute on which to bestow its love. Later in life, as the psychoanalysts tell us, it may bestow this same love on a worthy or unworthy living substitute. A teacher may "take the place" of the mother, a dictator or even an enemy may come to "represent" the father. Once more the common denominator between the symbol and the thing symbolized is not the "external form" but the function; the mother symbol should be lovable, the father-imago fearable, or whatever the case may be.

Now this psychological concept of symbolization seems to lead enormously far away from the more precise meaning which the word "representation" has acquired in the figurative arts. Can there be any gain in throwing all these meanings together? Possibly there is. For anything seems worth trying to get the function of symbolization out of its isolation. The "origin of art" has ceased to be a popular topic. But the origin of the hobby horse may be a permitted subject for speculation. Let us assume that the owner of the stick on which he proudly rode through the land decided in a playful or magic mood— and who could always distinguish between the two?—to fix "real" reins and that finally he was even tempted to "give" it two eyes near the top end. Some grass could have passed for a mane. Thus our archartist "had a horse." He had made one. Now there are two things about this fictitious event which have some bearing on the idea of the figurative arts. One is that, contrary to what is sometimes said, communication need not come into this process at all. He may not have wanted to show his horse to anyone. It just served as a focus for his fantasies as he galloped along—though more likely than not it fulfilled this same function to a tribe to which it "represented" some horse-demon of fertility and power.[8] We may sum up the moral of this "Just So Story" by saying that substitution may precede portrayal, and creation communication. It remains to be seen how such a general theory can be tested. If it can, it may really throw light on some concrete questions. Even the origin of language, that notorious problem of speculative history,[9] might be investigated from this angle. For what if the "pow-wow" theory, which sees the root of language in imitation, and the "pooh-pooh" theory, which sees it in emotive interjection, were to be joined by yet another? We might term it the "niam-niam" theory, postulating the primitive hunter lying awake in hungry winter nights and making the sound of eating, not for communication but as a substitute for eating—being joined, perhaps, by a ritualistic chorus trying to conjure up the phantasm of food.

V

There is one sphere in which the investigation of "representational" functions of forms has made considerable progress of late, that of animal psychology. Pliny, and innumerable writers after him, have regarded it as the greatest triumph of naturalistic art for a painter to have deceived sparrows or horses. The implication of these anecdotes is that a human beholder easily recognizes a bunch of grapes in a painting because for him recognition is an intellectual act. But for the birds to fly at the painting is a sign of a complete "objective" illusion. It is a plausible idea, but a wrong one. The merest outline of a cow seems sufficient for a tsetse trap, for somehow it sets the apparatus of attraction in motion and "deceives" the fly. To the fly, we might say, the crude trap has the "significant" form—biologically significant, that is. It appears that visual stimuli of this kind play an important part in the animal world. By varying the shapes of "dummies" to which animals were seen to respond, the "minimum image" that still sufficed to release a specific reaction has been ascertained.[10] Thus little birds will open their beak when they see the feeding parent approaching the nest but they will also do so when they are shown two darkish roundels of different size "representing" the silhouette of the head and body of the bird in its most "generalized" form. Certain young fishes can even be deceived by two simple dots arranged horizontally, which they take to be the eyes of the mother fish in whose mouth they are accustomed to shelter against danger. The fame of Zeuxis will have to rest on other achievements than his deception of birds.

An "image" in this biological sense, then, is not an imitation of an object's external form but an imitation of certain privileged or rele-

vant aspects. It is here that a wide field of investigation would seem
to open. For man is not exempt from this type of reaction.[11]   The
artist who goes out to represent the visible form is not simply faced
with a neutral medley of forms he seeks to "imitate." Ours is a
structured universe whose main lines of force are still bent and fashioned by our biological and psychological needs, however much they
may be overlaid by cultural influences. We know that there are certain privileged motifs in our world to which we respond almost too
easily. The human face may be outstanding among them. Whether by
instinct or by very early training, we certainly are ever disposed to
single out the expressive features of a face from the chaos of sensations that surrounds it and to respond to its slightest variations with
fear or joy. Our whole perceptive apparatus is somehow hypersensi-
tized in this direction of physiognomic vision[12] and the merest hint
suffices for us to create an expressive physiognomy that "looks" at us
with surprising intensity. In a heightened state of emotion, in the
dark, or in a feverish spell the looseness of this trigger may assume
pathological forms. We may see faces in the pattern of a wallpaper,
and three apples arranged on a plate may stare at us like two eyes
and a clownish nose. What wonder that it is so easy to "make" a face
with two dots and a stroke even though their geometrical constellation may be greatly at variance with the "external form" of a real
head? The well-known graphic joke of the "reversible face" might
well be taken as a model for experiments which could still be made in
this direction. It shows to what extent the group of shapes that can be
read as a physiognomy has priority over all other readings. It turns
the side which is the right way up into a convincing face and disinte-
grates the one that is upside down into a mere jumble of forms which
is accepted as a strange headgear.[13] In good pictures of this kind it
needs a real effort to see both faces at the same time. Our automatic
response is stronger than our intellectual awareness.

Seen in the light of the biological examples discussed above there is
nothing surprising in this observation. We may venture the guess that
this type of automatic recognition is dependent on the two factors of
resemblance and biological relevance and that the two may stand in
some kind of inverse ratio. The greater the biological relevance an
object has to us the more will we be attuned to its recognition—and
the more tolerant will therefore be our standards of formal correspondence. In an erotically charged atmosphere the merest hint of
formal similarity with sexual functions creates the desired response
and the same is true of the dream symbols investigated by Freud. The
hungry man will be similarly attuned to the discovery of food—he

will scan the world for sensations likely to satisfy his urge. The starving may even project food into all sorts of dissimilar objects—as Chaplin does in *Gold Rush* when his huge companion suddenly appears to him as a chicken. Can it have been some such experience which stimulated our "niam-niam" chanting hunters to see their longed-for prey in the patches and irregular shapes on the dark cave walls? Could they perhaps gradually have sought this experience in the deep mysterious recesses of the rocks, much as Leonardo sought out crumbling walls to aid his visual fantasies? Could they finally have been prompted to fill in such "readable" outlines with colored earth —to have at least something "spearable" at hand which might "represent" the eatable in some magic fashion? There is no way of testing such a theory, but if it is true that cave artists often "exploited" the natural formations of the rocks,[14] this, together with the "eidetic" character of their works,[15] would at least not contradict our fantasy. The great naturalism of cave paintings may after all be a very late flower. It may correspond to our late, derivative, and naturalistic hobby horse.

VI

It needed two conditions, then, to turn a stick into our hobby horse: first, that its form made it just possible to ride on it; secondly —and perhaps decisively—that riding mattered. Fortunately it still needs no great effort of the imagination to understand how the horse could become such a focus of desires and aspirations, for our language still carries the metaphors molded by a feudal past when to be chival-rous was to be horsy. The same stick that had to represent a horse in such a setting would have become the substitute of something else in another. It might have become a sword, scepter, or—in the context of ancestor worship—a fetish representing a dead chieftain. Seen from the point of view of "abstraction," such a convergence of meanings onto one shape offers considerable difficulties, but from that of psychological "projection" of meanings it becomes more easily intelligible. After all a whole diagnostic technique has been built up on the assumption that the meanings read into identical forms by different people tell us more about the readers than about the forms. In the sphere of art it has been shown that the same triangular shape which is the favorite pattern of many adjoining American Indian tribes is given different meanings reflecting the main preoccupations of the peoples concerned.[16] To the student of styles this discovery that one basic form can be made to represent a variety

of objects may still become significant. For while the idea of realistic
pictures being deliberately "stylized" seems hard to swallow, the
opposite idea of a limited vocabulary of simple shapes being used for
the building and making of different representations would fit much
better into what we know of primitive art.

VII

Once we get used to the idea of "representation" as a two-way
affair rooted in psychological dispositions we may be able to refine a
tool which has proved quite indispensable to the historian of art and
which is nevertheless rather unsatisfactory: the notion of the "conceptual image." By this we mean the mode of representation which is
more or less common to children's drawings and to various forms of
primitive and primitivist art. The remoteness of this type of imagery
from any visual experience has often been described.[17] The explanation of this fact which is most usually advanced is that the child (and
the primitive) do not draw what they "see" but what they "know."
According to this idea the typical children's drawing of a manikin is
really a graphic enumeration of those human features the child remembered.[18] It represents the content of the childish "concept" of
man. But to speak of "knowledge" or "intellectual realism" (as the
French do)[19] brings us dangerously near to the fallacy of "abstraction." So back to our hobby horse. Is it quite correct to say that it
consists of features which make up the "concept" of a horse or that it
reflects the memory image of horses seen? No—because this formulation omits one factor: the stick. If we keep in mind that representation is originally the creation of substitutes out of given material we
may reach safer ground. The greater the wish to ride, the fewer may
be the features that will do for a horse. But at a certain stage it must
have eyes—for how else could it see? At the most primitive layer,
then, the conceptual image might be identified with what we have
called the minimum image—that minimum, that is, which will make
it fit into a psychological lock. The form of the key depends on the
material out of which it is fashioned, and on the lock. It would be a
dangerous mistake, however, to equate the "conceptual image" as we
find it used in the historical styles with this psychologically grounded
minimum image. On the contrary. One has the impression that the
presence of these schemata is always felt but that they are as much
avoided as exploited.[20] We must reckon with the possibility of a
"style" being a set of convictions born out of complex tensions. The
man-made image must be complete. The servant for the grave must

have two hands and two feet. But he must not become a double under the artist's hands. Image-making is beset with dangers. One false stroke and the rigid mask of the face may assume an evil leer. Strict adherence to conventions alone can guard against such dangers. And thus primitive art seems often to keep on that narrow ledge that lies between the lifeless and the uncanny. If the hobby horse became too lifelike it might gallop away on its own.[21]

VIII

The contrast between primitive art and "naturalistic" or illusionist" art can easily be overdrawn.[22] All art is "image-making" and all image making is rooted in the creation of substitutes. Even the artist of an "illusionist" persuasion must make the man-made, the "conceptual" image of convention his starting point. Strange as it may seem he cannot simply "imitate an object's external form" without having first learned how to construct such a form. If it were otherwise there would be no need for the innumerable books on "how to draw the human figure" or "how to draw ships." Wölfflin once remarked that all pictures owe more to other pictures than they do to nature.[23] It is a point which is familiar to the student of pictorial traditions but which is still insufficiently understood in its psychological implications. Perhaps the reason is that contrary to the hopeful belief of many artists the "innocent eye" which should see the world afresh would not see it at all. It would smart under the painful impact of a chaotic medley of forms and colors.[24] In this sense the conventional vocabularly of basic forms is still indispensable to the artist as a starting point, as a focus of organization.

How, then, should we interpret that great divide which runs through the history of art and sets off the few islands of illusionist styles, of Greece, of China, and of the Renaissance, from the vast ocean of "conceptual" art?

One difference, undoubtedly, lies in a change of function. In a way the change is implicit in the emergence of the idea of the image as a "representation" in our modern sense of the word. As soon as it is generally understood that an image need not exist in its own right, that it refers to something outside itself and is therefore the record of a visual experience rather than the creation of a substitute, the basic rules of primitive art can be transgressed with impunity. No longer is there any need for that completeness of essentials which belongs to the conceptual style, no longer is there the fear of the casual which dominates the archaic conception of art. The picture of a man on a

Greek vase no longer needs a hand or a foot in full view. We know it is meant as a shadow, a mere record of what the artist saw and we are quite ready to join in the game and to supplement in our imagination what the real motif undoubtedly possessed. Once this idea of the picture as a sign referring to something outside itself is accepted in all its implications—and this certainly did not happen overnight—we are indeed forced to let our imagination play around it. We endow it with "space" around the figure, which is only another way of saying that we understand that the reality to which it referred was three-dimensional, that the man could move and that even the aspect momentarily hidden "was there."[25] When medieval art broke away from that narrative conceptual symbolism into which the formulas of classical art had been frozen, Giotto made particular use of the figure seen from behind which stimulates our "tactile" imagination by forcing us to imagine it in the round.

Thus the idea of the picture as a representation of a reality outside itself leads to an interesting paradox. On the one hand it compels us to refer every figure and every object shown to that imaginary reality which is "meant." This mental operation can only be completed if the picture allows us to infer not only the "external form" of every object represented but also its relative size and position. It leads thus to that "rationalization of space" we call scientific perspective by which the picture plane becomes a window pane through which we look into the imaginary world the artist creates there for us. In theory, at least, painting becomes synonymous with geometrical projection.[26]

The paradox of the situation is that once the whole picture is conceived as the representation of a slice of reality, a new context is created in which the conceptual image plays a different part. For the first consequence of the "window" idea is that we cannot conceive of any spot on the panel which is not "significant," which does not represent something. The empty patch thus comes easily to signify light, air, and atmosphere, and the vague form is interpreted as enveloped by air. It is this confidence in the representational context which is given by the very convention of the frame which makes the development of impressionist methods possible. The artists who tried to rid themselves of their conceptual knowledge, who conscientiously became beholders of their own work and never ceased matching their created images against their impressions by stepping back and comparing the two—these artists could only achieve their aim by shifting something of the load of creation on to the beholder. For what else does it mean if we are enjoined to step back in turn and watch the colored patches of an impressionist landscape "spring to life"? It means that the painter relies on our readiness to take hints, to read contexts, and to call up our conceptual image under his guidance. The blob in the painting by Manet which stands for a horse is no more an imitation of its external form than is our hobby horse. But he has so cleverly contrived it that it evokes the image in us—provided, of course, we collaborate.

Here there may be another field for independent investigation. For those "privileged" objects which play their part in the earliest layers of image making recur—as was to be expected—in that of image reading. The more vital the feature that is indicated by the context and yet omitted, the more intense seems to be the process that is started off. On its lowest level this method of "suggestive veiling" is familiar to erotic art. Not, of course, to its Pygmalion phase, but to its illusionist applications. What is here a crude exploitation of an obvious biological stimulus may have its parallel, for instance, in the representation of the human face. Leonardo achieved his greatest triumphs of lifelike expression by blurring precisely the features in which expression resides, thus compelling us to complete the act of creation. Rembrandt could dare to leave the eyes of his most moving portraits in the shade because we are thus stimulated to supplement them.[27] The "evocative" image, like its "conceptual" counterpart, should be studied against a wider psychological background.

IX

My hobby horse is not art. At best it can claim the attention of iconology, that emerging branch of study which is to art criticism what linguistics is to the criticism of literature. But has not modern art experimented with the primitive image, with the "creation" of forms, and the exploitation of deep-rooted psychological forces? It has. But whatever the nostalgic wish of their makers the meaning of these forms can never be the same as that of their primitive models. For that strange precinct we call "art" is like a hall of mirrors or a whispering gallery. Each form conjures up a thousand memories and afterimages. No sooner is an image presented as art than, by this very act, a new frame of reference is created which it cannot escape. It becomes part of an institution as surely as does the toy in the nursery. If—as might be conceivable—a Picasso would turn from pottery to hobby horses and send the products of this whim to an exhibition, we might read them as demonstrations, as satirical symbols, as a declaration of faith in humble things or as self-irony—but one thing would be denied even to the greatest of contemporary artists: he could not make the hobby horse mean to us what it meant to its first creator. This way is barred by the angel with a flaming sword.

NOTES

1. In the sphere of art this process of differentiation rather than abstraction is wittily described by Oliver Wendell Holmes in the essay *"Cacoethes Scribendi,"* from *Over the Teacups* (London: 1890): "It's just my plan . . . for teaching drawing. . . . A man at a certain distance appears as a dark spot—nothing more. Good. Anybody . . . can make a dot. . . . Lesson No. 1. Make a dot; that is, draw your man, a mile off. . . . Now make him come a little nearer. . . . The dot is an oblong figure now. Good. Let your scholar draw an oblong figure. It is as easy as to make a note of admiration. . . . So by degrees the man who serves as a model approaches. A bright pupil will learn to get the outline of a human figure in ten lessons, the model coming five hundred feet nearer every time."

2. *Fourth Discourse* (Everyman Edition), p. 55. I have discussed the historical setting of this idea in *"Icones Symbolicae," Journal of the Warburg and Courtauld Institutes*, XI (1948), p. 187, and some of its more technical aspects in a review of Charles Morris, *Signs, Language, and Behavior* (New York: 1946) in *The Art Bulletin*, March 1949. In Morris's terminology these present meditations are concerned with the status and origin of the "iconic sign."

3. Leonardo da Vinci, *Paragone*, edited by I. A. Richter (London: 1949), p. 51.

4. Paul Klee, *On Modern Art* (London: 1948). For the history of the idea of *deus artifex* cf. E. Kris and O. Kurz, *Die Legende vom Künstler* (Vienna: 1934).

5. H. A. Groenewegen-Frankfort, *Arrest and Movement: An Essay on Space and Time in the Representational Art of the Ancient Near East* (London: 1951).

6. Perhaps it is only in a setting of realistic art that the problem I have discussed in *"Icones Symbolicae,"* loc. cit., becomes urgent. Only then the idea can gain ground that the allegorical image of, say, Justice, must be a portrait of Justice as she dwells in heaven.

7. For the history of this misinterpretation and its consequences, cf. my article on "Art and Imagery in the Romantic Period," *The Burlington Magazine*, June 1949.

8. This, at least, would be the opinion of Lewis Spence, *Myth and Ritual in Dance, Game, and Rhyme* (London: 1947). And also of Ben Jonson's Busy, the Puritan: "Thy Hobbyhorse is an Idoll, a feirce and rancke Idoll: And thou, the *Nabuchadnezzar* . . . of the *Faire*, that set'st it up, for children to fall downe to, and worship." (*Bartholomew Fair*, Act. III, Scene 6).

9. Cf. Géza Révész, *Ursprung und Vorgeschichte der Sprache* (Bern: 1946).

10. Cf. Konrad Lorenz, *"Die angeborenen Formen möglicher Erfahrung,"* *Zeitschrift für Tierpsychologie* V (1943), and the discussion of these experiments in E. Grassi and Th. von Uexküll, *Vom Ursprung und von den Grenzen der Geisteswissenschaften und Naturwissenschaften* (Bern: 1950).

11. K. Lorenz, loc. cit. The citation of this article does not imply support of the author's moral conclusions. On these more general issues see K. R. Popper, *The Open Society and Its Enemies,* esp., I, pp. 59 ff. and p. 268.

12. F. Sander, *"Experimentelle Ergebnisse der Gestaltpsychologie,"* *Berichte über den 10. Kongress für Experimentelle Psychologie* (Jena: 1928), p. 47, has shown that the distance of two dots is much harder to estimate in its variations when these dots are isolated than when they are made to represent eyes in a schematic face and thus attain physiognomic significance.

13. For a large collection of such faces cf. Laurence Whistler, *Oho! The Drawings of Rex Whistler* (London: 1946).

14. G. H. Luquet, *The Art and Religion of Fossil Man* (London: 1930), pp. 141 f.

15. G. A. S. Snijder, *Kretische Kunst* (Berlin: 1936), pp. 68 f.

16. Franz Boas, *Primitive Art* (Oslo: 1927), pp. 118–28.

17. E.g., E. Löwy, *The Rendering of Nature in Early Greek Art* (London: 1907), H. Schaefer, *Von aegyptischer Kunst* (Leipzig: 1930), Mr. Verworn, *Ideoplastische Kunst* (Jena: 1914).

18. Karl Buehler, *The Mental Development of the Child* (London: 1930), pp. 113–17, where the connection with the linguistic faculty is stressed. A criticism of this idea was advanced by R. Arnheim, "Perceptual Abstraction and Art," *Psychological Review,* LVI (1947).

19. G. H. Luquet, *L'Art primitif* (Paris: 1930).

20. The idea of avoidance (of sexual symbols) is stressed by A. Ehrenzweig, "Unconscious Form-creation in Art," *The British Journal of Medical Psychology,* XXI (1948) and XXII (1949).

21. E. Kris and O. Kurz, loc. cit., have collected a number of legends reflecting this age-old fear. Thus a famous Chinese master was said never to have put the light into the eyes of his painted dragons lest they would fly away.

22. It was the intellectual fashion in German art history to work with contrasting pairs of concepts such as haptic-optic (Riegl), paratactic-hypotactic (Coellen), abstraction-empathy (Worringer), idealism-naturalism (Dvorak), physioplastic-ideoplastic (Verworn), multiplicity-unity (Wölfflin), all of which could probably be expressed in terms of "conceptual" and "less conceptual" art. While the heuristic value of this method of antithesis is not in doubt it often tends to introduce a false dichotomy. In my book *The Story of Art* (London: 1950) I have attempted to stress the continuity of tradition and the persistent role of the conceptual image.

23. H. Wölfflin, *Principles of Art History* (New York: 1932).

24. Cf. the Reith Lecture by J. Z. Young, "Doubt and Certainty in Science," reprinted in *The Listener,* November 23, 1950. The fallacy of a passive idea of perception is also discussed in detail by E. Brunswik, *Wahrnehmung und Gegenstandswelt* (Vienna: 1934). In its application to art the writings of K. Fiedler contain many valuable hints; cf. also A. Ehrenzweig, loc. cit., for an extreme and challenging presentation of this problem.

25. This may be meant in the rather enigmatic passage on the painter Parrhasius in Pliny's *Natural History,* XXXV, 67, where it is said that "the highest subtlety attainable in painting is to find an outline . . . which should appear

to fold back and to enclose the object so as to give assurance of the parts behind, thus clearly suggesting even what it conceals."

26. Cf. E. Panofsky, "The Codex Huygens and Leonardo da Vinci's Art Theory," *Studies of the Warburg Institute*, XIII (London: 1940), pp. 90 f.

27. Cf. J. V. Schlosser, "*Gespräch von der Bildniskunst*," *Praludien* (Vienna: 1927), where, incidentally, the hobby horse also makes its appearance.

Art and Authenticity

Nelson Goodman

. . . the most tantalizing question of all: If a fake is so expert that even after the most thorough and trustworthy examination its authenticity is still open to doubt, is it or is it not as satisfactory a work of art as if it were unequivocally genuine?

Aline B. Saarinen
New York Times Book Review, July 30, 1961, p. 14.

1. THE PERFECT FAKE

Forgeries of works of art present a nasty practical problem to the collector, the curator, and the art historian, who must often expend taxing amounts of time and energy in determining whether or not particular objects are genuine. But the theoretical problem raised is even more acute. The hardheaded question why there is any aesthetic difference between a deceptive forgery and an original work challenges a basic premise on which the very functions of collector, museum, and art historian depend. A philosopher of art caught without an answer to this question is at least as badly off as a curator of paintings caught taking a Van Meegeren for a Vermeer.

The question is most strikingly illustrated by the case of a given work and a forgery or copy or reproduction of it. Suppose we have before us, on the left, Rembrandt's original painting *Lucretia* and, on the right, a superlative imitation of it. We know from a fully documented history that the painting on the left is the original; and we know from X-ray photographs and microscopic examination and chemical analysis that the painting on the right is a recent fake. Although there are many differences between the two—e.g., in authorship, age, physical and chemical characteristics, and market value— we cannot see any difference between them; and if they are moved while we sleep, we cannot then tell which is which by merely looking at them. Now we are pressed with the question whether there can be any aesthetic difference between the two pictures; and the questioner's tone often intimates that the answer is plainly *no*, that the only differences here are aesthetically irrelevant.

We must begin by inquiring whether the distinction between what can and what cannot be seen in the pictures by "merely looking at them" is entirely clear. We are looking at the pictures, but presumably not "merely looking" at them, when we examine them under a microscope or fluoroscope. Does merely looking, then, mean looking without the use of any instrument? This seems a little unfair to the man who needs glasses to tell a painting from a hippopotamus. But if glasses are permitted at all, how strong may they be, and can we consistently exclude the magnifying glass and the microscope? Again, if incandescent light is permitted, can violet-ray light be ruled out? And even with incandescent light, must it be of medium intensity and from a normal angle, or is a strong raking light permitted? All these cases might be covered by saying that "merely looking" is looking at the pictures without any use of instruments other than those customarily used in looking at things in general. This will cause trouble when we turn, say, to certain miniature illuminations or Assyrian cylinder seals that we can hardly distinguish from the crudest copies without using a strong glass. Furthermore, even in our case of the two pictures, subtle differences of drawing or painting discoverable only with a magnifying glass may still, quite obviously, be aesthetic differences between the pictures. If a powerful microscope is used instead, this is no longer the case; but just how much magnification is permitted? To specify what is meant by "merely looking" at the pictures is thus far from easy; but for the sake of argument,[1] let us suppose that all these difficulties have been resolved and the notion of "merely looking" made clear enough.

Then we must ask who is assumed to be doing the looking. Our questioner does not, I take it, mean to suggest that there is no aesthetic difference between two pictures if at least one person, say a cross-eyed wrestler, can see no difference. The more pertinent question is whether there can be any aesthetic difference if nobody, not even the most skilled expert, can ever tell the pictures apart by merely looking at them. *But notice now that no one can ever ascertain by merely looking at the pictures that no one ever has been or will be able to tell them apart by merely looking at them.* In other words, the question in its present form concedes that no one can ascertain by merely looking at the pictures that there is no aesthetic difference between them. This seems repugnant to our questioner's whole motivation. For if merely looking can never establish that two pictures are aesthetically the same, something that is beyond the reach of any given looking is admitted as constituting an aesthetic difference. And in that case, the reason for not admitting documents and the results of scientific tests becomes very obscure.

The real issue may be more accurately formulated as the question whether there is any aesthetic difference between the two pictures *for me* (or for *x*) if I (or *x*) cannot tell them apart by merely looking at them. But this is not quite right either. For I can never ascertain merely by looking at the pictures that even I shall never be able to see any difference between them. And to concede that something beyond any given looking at the pictures by me may constitute an aesthetic difference between them *for me* is, again, quite at odds with the tacit conviction or suspicion that activates the questioner.

Thus the critical question amounts finally to this: is there any aesthetic difference between the two pictures for *x* at *t*, where *t* is a suitable period of time, if *x* cannot tell them apart by merely looking at them at *t*? Or in other words, can anything that *x* does not discern by merely looking at the pictures at *t* constitute an aesthetic difference between them for *x* at *t*?

2. THE ANSWER

In setting out to answer this question, we must bear clearly in mind that what one can distinguish at any given moment by merely looking depends not only upon native visual acuity but upon practice and training.[2] Americans look pretty much alike to a Chinese who has never looked at many of them. Twins may be indistinguishable to all but their closest relatives and acquaintances. Moreover, only through looking at them when someone has named them for us can we learn to tell Joe from Jim upon merely looking at them. Looking at people or things attentively, with the knowledge of certain presently invisible respects in which they differ, increases our ability to discriminate between them—and between other things or other people—upon merely looking at them. Thus pictures that look just alike to the newsboy come to look quite unlike to him by the time he has become a museum director.

Although I see no difference now between the two pictures in question, I may learn to see a difference between them. I cannot determine now by merely looking at them, or in any other way, that I *shall* be able to learn. But the information that they are very different, that the one is the original and the other the forgery, argues against any inference to the conclusion that I *shall not* be able to learn. And the fact that I may later be able to perceive a distinction between the pictures that I cannot perceive now makes the actual differences between them aesthetically important to me now.

Furthermore, to look at the pictures now with the knowledge that the left one is the original and the other the forgery may help develop the ability to tell which is which later by merely looking at them. Thus, with information not derived from the present or any past looking at the pictures, the present looking may have a quite different bearing upon future lookings from what it would otherwise have. The way the pictures in fact differ constitutes an aesthetic difference between them for me now, because my knowledge of the way they differ bears upon the role of the present looking in training my perceptions to discriminate between these pictures, and between others.

But that is not all. My knowledge of the difference between the two pictures, just because it affects the relationship of the present to future lookings, informs the very character of my present looking. This knowledge instructs me to look at the two pictures differently now, even if what I see is the same. Beyond testifying that I may learn to see a difference, it also indicates to some extent the kind of scrutiny to be applied now, the comparisons and contrasts to be made in imagination, and the relevant associations to be brought to bear. It thereby guides the selection, from my past experience, of items and aspects for use in my present looking. Thus not only later but right now, the unperceived difference between the two pictures is a consideration pertinent to my visual experience with them.

In short, although I cannot tell the pictures apart merely by looking at them now, the fact that the left-hand one is the original and the right-hand one a forgery constitutes an aesthetic difference between them for me now because knowledge of this fact (1) stands as evidence that there may be a difference between them that I can learn to perceive, (2) assigns the present looking a role as training toward such a perceptual discrimination, and (3) makes consequent demands that modify and differentiate my present experience in looking at the two pictures.[3]

Nothing depends here upon my ever actually perceiving or being able to perceive a difference between the two pictures. What informs the nature and use of my present visual experience is not the fact or the assurance that such a perceptual discrimination is within my reach, but evidence that it may be; and such evidence is provided by the known factual differences between the pictures. Thus the pictures differ aesthetically for me now even if no one will ever be able to tell them apart by merely looking at them.

But suppose it could be *proved* that no one ever will be able to see any difference? This is about as reasonable as asking whether, if it can be proved that the market value and yield of a given U.S. bond and one of a certain nearly bankrupt company will always be the same, there is any financial difference between the two bonds. For what sort of proof could be given? One might suppose that if nobody —not even the most skilled expert—has ever been able to see any difference between the pictures, then the conclusion that I shall never be able to is quite safe; but, as in the case of the Van Meegeren forgeries[4] (of which, more later), distinctions not visible to the expert up to a given time may later become manifest even to the observant layman. Or one might think of some delicate scanning device that compares the color of two pictures at every point and registers the slightest discrepancy. What, though, is meant here by "at every point"? At no mathematical point, of course, is there any color at all; and even some physical particles are too small to have color. The scanning device must thus cover at each instant a region big enough to have color but at least as small as any perceptible region. Just how to manage this is puzzling since "perceptible" in the present context means "discernible by merely looking," and thus the line between perceptible and nonperceptible regions seems to depend on the arbitrary line between a magnifying glass and a microscope. If some such line is drawn, we can never be sure that the delicacy of our instruments is superior to the maximal attainable acuity of unaided perception. Indeed, some experimental psychologists are inclined to conclude that every measurable difference in light can sometimes be detected by the naked eye.[5] And there is a further difficulty. Our scanning device will examine color—that is, reflected light. Since reflected light depends partly upon incident light, illumination of every quality, of every intensity, and from every direction must be tried. And for each case, especially since the paintings do not have a plane surface, a complete scanning must be made from every angle. But of course we cannot cover every variation, or even determine a single absolute correspondence, in even one respect. Thus the search for a proof that I shall never be able to see any difference between the two pictures is futile for more than technological reasons.

Yet suppose we are nevertheless pressed with the question whether, if proof *were* given, there would then be any aesthetic difference for me between the pictures. And suppose we answer this farfetched question in the negative. This will still give our questioner no comfort. For the net result would be that if no difference between the pictures can in fact be perceived, then the existence of an aesthetic difference between them will rest entirely upon what is or is not proved by means other than merely looking at them. This hardly supports the contention that there can be no aesthetic difference without a perceptual difference.

Returning from the realm of the ultra-hypothetical, we may be faced with the protest that the vast aesthetic difference thought to obtain between the Rembrandt and the forgery cannot be accounted for in terms of the search for, or even the discovery of, perceptual differences so slight that they can be made out, if at all, only after much experience and long practice. This objection can be dismissed at once; for minute perceptual differences can bear enormous weight. The clues that tell me whether I have caught the eye of someone across the room are almost indiscernible. The actual differences in sound that distinguish a fine from a mediocre performance can be picked out only by the well-trained ear. Extremely subtle changes can alter the whole design, feeling, or expression of a painting. Indeed, the slightest perceptual differences sometimes matter the most aesthetically; gross physical damage to a fresco may be less consequential than slight but smug retouching.

All I have attempted to show, of course, is that the two pictures can differ aesthetically, not that the original is better than the forgery. In our example, the original probably is much the better picture, since Rembrandt paintings are in general much better than copies by unknown painters. But a copy of a Lastman by Rembrandt may well be better than the original. We are not called upon here to make such particular comparative judgments or to formulate canons of aesthetic evaluation. We have fully met the demands of our problem by showing that the fact that we cannot tell our two pictures apart merely by looking at them does not imply that they are aesthetically the same— and thus does not force us to conclude that the forgery is as good as the original.

The example we have been using throughout illustrates a special case of a more general question concerning the aesthetic significance of authenticity. Quite aside from the occurrence of forged duplication, does it matter whether an original work is the product of one or another artist or school or period? Suppose that I can easily tell two pictures apart but cannot tell who painted either except by using some device like X-ray photography. Does the fact that the picture is or is not by Rembrandt make any aesthetic difference? What is involved here is the discrimination not of one picture from another but of the class of Rembrandt paintings from the class of other paintings. My chance of learning to make this discrimination correctly—of discovering projectible characteristics that differentiate Rembrandts in general from non-Rembrandts—depends heavily upon the set of examples available as a basis. Thus the fact that the given picture belongs to the one class or the other is important for me to know in learning how to tell Rembrandt paintings from others. In other words, my present (or future) inability to determine the authorship of the given picture without use of scientific apparatus does not imply that the authorship makes no aesthetic difference to me; for knowledge of the authorship, no matter how obtained, can contribute materially toward developing my ability to determine without such apparatus whether or not any picture, including this one on another occasion, is by Rembrandt. Moreover, where information is such as to be important to me when I have it, it is important to me to have, and thus important to me whether I have it or not.

Incidentally, one rather striking puzzle is readily solved in these terms. When Van Meegeren sold his pictures as Vermeers, he deceived most of the best-qualified experts; and only by his confession was the fraud revealed.[6] Nowadays even the fairly knowing layman is astonished that any competent judge could have taken a Van Meegeren for a Vermeer, so obvious are the differences. What has happened? The general level of aesthetic sensibility has hardly risen so fast that the layman of today sees more acutely than the expert of twenty years ago. Rather, the better information now at hand makes the discrimination easier. Presented with a single unfamiliar picture at a time, the expert had to decide whether it was enough like known Vermeers to be by the same artist. And every time a Van Meegeren was added to the corpus of pictures accepted as Vermeers, the criteria for acceptance were modified thereby; and the mistaking of further Van Meegerens for Vermeers became inevitable. Now, however, not only have the Van Meegerens been subtracted from the precedent-class for Vermeer, but also a precedent-class for Van Meegeren has been established. With these two precedent-classes before us, the characteristic differences become so conspicuous that telling other Van Meegerens from Vermeers offers little difficulty. Yesterday's expert might well have avoided his errors if he had had a few known Van Meegerens handy for comparison. And today's layman who so cleverly spots a Van Meegeren may well be caught taking some quite inferior school-piece for a Vermeer.

In answering the questions raised above, I have not attempted the formidable task of defining "aesthetic" in general,[7] but have simply argued that since the exercise, training, and development of our powers of discriminating among works of art are plainly aesthetic activities, the aesthetic properties of a picture include not only those found by looking at it but also those that determine how it is to be looked at. This rather obvious fact would hardly have needed underlining but for the prevalence of the time-honored Tingle-Immersion theory,[8] which tells us that the proper behavior on encountering a work of art is to strip ourselves of all the vestments of knowledge and experience (since they might blunt the immediacy of our enjoyment), then submerge ourselves completely and gauge the aesthetic potency of the work by the intensity and duration of the resulting tingle. The theory is absurd on the face of it and useless for dealing with any of the important problems of aesthetics; but it has become part of the fabric of our common nonsense.

3. THE UNFAKABLE

A second problem concerning authenticity is raised by the rather curious fact that in music, unlike painting, there is no such thing as a forgery of a known work. There are, indeed, compositions falsely purporting to be by Haydn as there are paintings falsely purporting to be by Rembrandt; but of the *London Symphony*, unlike the *Lucretia*, there can be no forgeries. Haydn's manuscript is no more genuine an instance of the score than is a printed copy off the press this morning, and last night's performance no less genuine than the premiere. Copies of the score may vary in accuracy, but all accurate copies, even if forgeries of Haydn's manuscript, are equally genuine instances of the score. Performances may vary in correctness and quality and even in "authenticity" of a more esoteric kind; but all correct performances are equally genuine instances of the work.[9] In contrast, even the most exact copies of the Rembrandt painting are simply imitations or forgeries, not new instances, of the work. Why this difference between the two arts?

Let us speak of a work of art as *autographic* if and only if the distinction between original and forgery of it is significant; or better, if and only if even the most exact duplication of it does not thereby count as genuine.[10] If a work of art is autographic, we may also call that art autographic. Thus painting is autographic, music nonautographic, or *allographic*. These terms are introduced purely for convenience; nothing is implied concerning the relative individuality of expression demanded by or attainable in these arts. Now the problem before us is to the account for the fact that some arts but not others are autographic.

One notable difference between painting and music is that the composer's work is done when he has written the score, even though the performances are the end-products, while the painter has to finish the picture. No matter how many studies or revisions are made in either case, painting is in this sense a one-stage and music a two-stage art. Is an art autographic, then, if and only if it is one-stage? Counter-examples come readily to mind. In the first place, literature is not autographic though it is one-stage. There is no such thing as a forgery of Gray's *Elegy*. Any accurate copy of the text of a poem or novel is as much the original work as any other. Yet what the writer produces is ultimate; the text is not merely a means to oral readings as a score is a means to performances in music. An unrecited poem is not so forlorn as an unsung song; and most literary works are never read aloud at all. We might try to make literature into a two-stage art by considering the silent readings to be the end-products, or the instances of a work; but then the lookings at a picture and the listenings to a performance would qualify equally as end-products or instances, so that painting as well as literature would be two-stage and music three-stage. In the second place, printmaking is two-stage and yet autographic. The etcher, for example, makes a plate from which impressions are then taken on paper. These prints are the end-products; and although they may differ appreciably from one another, all are instances of the original work. But even the most exact copy produced otherwise than by printing from that plate counts not as an original but as an imitation or forgery.

So far, our results are negative: not all one-stage arts are auto-graphic and not all autographic arts are one-stage. Furthermore, the example of printmaking refutes the unwary assumption that in every autographic art a particular work exists only as a unique object. The line between an autographic and an allographic art does not coincide with that between a singular and a multiple art. About the only positive conclusion we can draw here is that the autographic arts are those that are singular in the earliest stage; etching is singular in its first stage—the plate is unique—and painting in its only stage. But this hardly helps; for the problem of explaining why some arts are singular is much like the problem of explaining why they are auto-graphic.

4. THE REASON

Why, then, can I no more make a forgery of Haydn's symphony or of Gray's poem than I can make an original of Rembrandt's painting or of his etching *Tobit Blind?* Let us suppose that there are various handwritten copies and many editions of a given literary work. Differences between them in style and size of script or type, in color of ink, in kind of paper, in number and layout of pages, in condition, etc., do not matter. All that matters is what may be called *sameness of spelling*: exact correspondence as sequences of letters, spaces, and punctuation marks. Any sequence—even a forgery of the author's manuscript or of a given edition—that so corresponds to a correct copy is itself correct, and nothing is more the original work than is such a correct copy. And since whatever is not an original of the work must fail to meet such an explicit standard of correctness, there can be no deceptive imitation, no forgery, of that work. To verify the spelling or to spell correctly is all that is required to identify an instance of the work or to produce a new instance. In effect, the fact that a literary work is in a definite notation, consisting of certain signs or characters that are to be combined by concatenation, provides the means for distinguishing the properties constitutive of the work from all contingent properties—that is, for fixing the required features and the limits of permissible variation in each. Merely by determining that the copy before us is spelled correctly we can determine that it meets all requirements for the work in question. In painting, on the contrary, with no such alphabet of characters, none of the pictorial properties—none of the properties the picture has as such—is distinguished as constitutive; no such feature can be dismissed as contingent, and no deviation as insignificant. The only way of ascertaining that the *Lucretia* before us is genuine is thus to establish the historical fact that it is the actual object made by Rembrandt. Accordingly, physical identification of the product of the artist's hand, and consequently the conception of forgery of a particular work, assume a significance in painting that they do not have in literature.[11]

What has been said of literary texts obviously applies also to musical scores. The alphabet is different; and the characters in a score, rather than being strung one after the other as in a text, are disposed in a more complex array. Nevertheless, we have a limited set of characters and of positions for them; and correct spelling, in only a slightly expanded sense, is still the sole requirement for a genuine instance of a work. Any false copy is wrongly spelled—has somewhere in place of the right character either another character or an illegible mark that is not a character of the notation in question at all.

But what of performances of music? Music is not autographic in this second stage, either, yet a performance by no means consists of characters from an alphabet. Rather, the constitutive properties demanded of a performance of the symphony are those *prescribed in* the score; and performances that comply with the score may differ appreciably in such musical features as tempo, timbre, phrasing, and expressiveness. To determine compliance requires, indeed, something more than merely knowing the alphabet; it requires the ability to correlate appropriate sounds with the visible signs in the score—to recognize, so to speak, correct pronunciation though without necessarily understanding what is pronounced. The competence required to identify or produce sounds called for by a score increases with the complexity of the composition, but there is nevertheless a theoretically decisive test for compliance; and a performance, whatever its interpretative fidelity and independent merit, has or has not all the constitutive properties of a given work, and is or is not strictly a performance of that work, according as it does or does not pass this test. No historical information concerning the production of the performance can affect the result. Hence deception as to the facts of production is irrelevant, and the notion of a performance that is a forgery of the work is quite empty.

Yet there are forgeries of performances as there are of manuscripts and editions. What makes a performance an instance of a given work is not the same as what makes a performance a premiere, or makes it a performance by a certain musician or upon a Stradivarius violin. Whether a performance has these latter properties is a matter of historical fact; and a performance falsely purporting to have any such property counts as a forgery, not of the musical composition but of a given performance or class of performances.

The comparison between printmaking and music is especially telling. We have already noted that etching, for example, is like music in having two stages and in being multiple in its second stage; but that whereas music is autographic in neither stage, printmaking is autographic in both. Now the situation with respect to the etched plate is clearly the same as with respect to a painting: assurance of genuineness can come only from identification of the actual object produced by the artist. But since the several prints from this plate are all genuine instances of the work, however much they differ in color and amount of ink, quality of impression, kind of paper, etc., one might expect here a full parallel between prints and musical performances. Yet there can be prints that are forgeries of the *Tobit Blind* but not performances that are forgeries of the *London Symphony*. The difference is that in the absence of a notation, not only is there no test of correctness of spelling for a plate but there is no test of compliance with a plate for a print. Comparison of a print with a plate, as of two plates, is no more conclusive than is comparison of two pictures. Minute discrepancies may always go unnoticed; and there is no basis for ruling out any of them as inessential. The only way of ascertaining whether a print is genuine is by finding out whether it was taken from a certain plate.[12] A print falsely purporting to have been so produced is in the full sense a forgery of the work.

Here, as earlier, we must be careful not to confuse genuineness with aesthetic merit. That the distinction between original and forgery is aesthetically important does not, we have seen, imply that the original is superior to the forgery. An original painting may be less rewarding than an inspired copy; a damaged original may have lost most of its former merit; an impression from a badly worn plate may be aesthetically much further removed from an early impression than is a good photographic reproduction. Likewise, an incorrect performance, though therefore not strictly an instance of a given quartet at all, may nevertheless—either because the changes improve what the composer wrote or because of sensitive interpretation—be better than a correct performance.[13] Again, several correct performances of about equal merit may exhibit very different specific aesthetic qualities—power, delicacy, tautness, stodginess, incoherence, etc. Thus even where the constitutive properties of a work are clearly distinguished by means of a notation, they cannot be identified with the aesthetic properties.

Among other arts, sculpture is autographic; cast sculpture is comparable to printmaking while carved sculpture is comparable to painting. Architecture and the drama, on the other hand, are more nearly comparable to music. Any building that conforms to the plans and specifications, any performance of the text of a play in accordance with the stage directions, is as original an instance of the work as any other. But architecture seems to differ from music in that testing for compliance of a building with the specifications requires not that these be pronounced, or transcribed into sound, but that their application be understood. This is true also for the stage directions, as contrasted with the dialogue, of a play. Does this make architecture and the drama less purely allographic arts? Again, an architect's plans seem a good deal like a painter's sketches; and painting is an autographic art. On what grounds can we say that in the one case but not the other a veritable notation is involved? Such questions cannot be answered until we have carried through some rather painstaking analysis.

Since an art seems to be allographic just insofar as it is amenable to notation, the case of the dance is especially interesting. Here we have an art without a traditional notation; and an art where the ways, and even the possibility, of developing an adequate notation are still matters of controversy. Is the search for a notation reasonable in the case of the dance but not in the case of painting? Or, more generally, why is the use of notation appropriate in some arts but not in others? Very briefly and roughly, the answer may be somewhat as follows. Initially, perhaps, all arts are autographic. Where the works are transitory, as in singing and reciting, or require many persons for their production, as in architecture and symphonic music, a notation may be devised in order to transcend the limitations of time and the individual. This involves establishing a distinction between the constitutive and the contingent properties of a work (and in the case of literature, texts have even supplanted oral performances as the primary aesthetic objects). Of course, the notation does not dictate the distinction arbitrarily, but must follow generally—even though it may amend—lines antecedently drawn by the informal classification of performances into works and by practical decisions as to what is prescribed and what is optional. Amenability to notation depends upon a precedent practice that develops only if works of the art in question are commonly either ephemeral or not producible by one person. The dance, like the drama and symphonic and choral music, qualifies on both scores, while painting qualifies on neither.

The general answer to our somewhat slippery second problem of authenticity can be summarized in a few words. A forgery of a work of art is an object falsely purporting to have the history of production requisite for the (or an) original of the work. Where there is a theoretically decisive test for determining that an object has all the constitutive properties of the work in question without determining how or by whom the object was produced, there is no requisite history of production and hence no forgery of any given work. Such a test is provided by a suitable notational system with an articulate set of characters and of relative positions for them. For texts, scores, and perhaps plans, the test is correctness of spelling in this notation; for buildings and performances, the test is compliance with what is correctly spelled. Authority for a notation must be found in an antecedent classification of objects or events into works that cuts across, or admits of a legitimate projection that cuts across, classification by history of production; but definitive identification of works, fully freed from history of production, is achieved only when a notation is established. The allographic art has won its emancipation not by proclamation but by notation.

5. A TASK

The two problems of authenticity I have been discussing are rather special and peripheral questions of aesthetics. Answers to them do not amount to an aesthetic theory or even the beginning of one. But failure to answer them can well be the end of one; and their exploration points the way to more basic problems and principles in the general theory of symbols.

Many matters touched upon here need much more careful study. So far, I have only vaguely described, rather than defined, the relations of compliance and of sameness of spelling. I have not examined the features that distinguish notations or notational languages from other languages and from nonlanguages. And I have not discussed the subtle differences between a score, a script, and a sketch. What is wanted now is a fundamental and thoroughgoing inquiry in the nature and function of notation in the arts.

NOTES

1. And only for the sake of argument—only in order not to obscure the central issue. All talk of mere looking in what follows is to be understood as occurring within the scope of this temporary concession, not as indicating any acceptance of the notion on my part.
2. Germans learning English often cannot, without repeated effort and concentrated attention, hear any differences at all between the vowel sounds in "sup" and "cop." Like effort may sometimes be needed by the native speaker of a language to discern differences in color, etc., that are not marked by his elementary vocabulary. Whether language affects actual sensory discrimination has long been debated among psychologists, anthropologists, and linguists; see the survey of experimentation and controversy in Segall, Campbell, and Herskovits, *The Influence of Culture on Visual Perception* (Indianapolis: Bobbs-Merrill, 1966), pp. 34–48. The issue is unlikely to be resolved without greater clarity in the use of "sensory," "perceptual," and "cognitive," and more care in distinguishing between what a person can do at a given time and what he can learn to do.
3. In saying that a difference *between the pictures* that is thus relevant to my present experience in looking at them constitutes an aesthetic difference between them, I am of course not saying that everything (e.g., drunkenness, snow blindness, twilight) that may cause my experiences of them to differ constitutes such an aesthetic difference. Not every difference in or arising

from how the pictures happen to be looked at counts; only differences in or arising from how they are to be looked at. Concerning the aesthetic, more is said later in this section and in *Languages of Art* VI, 3–6.

4. For a detailed and fully illustrated account, see P. B. Coremans, *Van Meegeren's Faked Vermeers and De Hooghs*, trans. A. Hardy and C. Hutt (Amsterdam: J. M. Meulenhoff, 1949). The story is outlined in Sepp Schüller, *Forgers, Dealers, Experts*, trans. J. Cleugh (New York: G. P. Putnam's Sons, 1960), pp. 95–105.

5. Not surprisingly, since a single quantam of light may excite a retinal receptor. See M. H. Pirenne and F. H. C. Marriott, "The Quantum Theory of Light and the Psycho-Physiology of Vision," in *Psychology*, ed. S. Koch (New York: McGraw-Hill, 1959), Vol. I, p. 290; also Theodore C. Ruch, "Vision," in *Medical Psychology and Biophysics* (Philadelphia: W. B. Saunders, 1960), p. 426.

6. That the forgeries purported to have been painted during a period from which no Vermeers were known made detection more difficult but does not essentially alter the case. Some art historians, on the defensive for their profession, claim that the most perceptive critics suspected the forgeries very early; but actually some of the foremost recognized authorities were completely taken in and for some time even refused to believe Van Meegeren's confession. The reader has a more recent example now before him in the revelation that the famous bronze horse, long exhibited in the Metropolitan Museum and proclaimed as a masterpiece of classical Greek sculpture, is a modern forgery. An official of the museum noticed a seam that apparently neither he nor anyone else had ever seen before, and scientific testing followed. No expert has come forward to claim earlier doubts on aesthetic grounds.

7. I deal with that question in *Languages of Art*, VI.

8. Attributed to Immanuel Tingle and Joseph Immersion (ca. 1800).

9. There may indeed be forgeries of performances. Such forgeries are performances that purport to be by a certain musician, etc.; but these, if in accordance with the score, are nevertheless genuine instances of the work. And what concerns me here is a distinction among the arts that depends upon whether there can be forgeries of works, not upon whether there can be forgeries of instances of works. See further what is said below concerning forgeries of editions of literary works and of musical performances.

10. This is to be taken as a preliminary version of a difference we must seek to formulate more precisely. Much of what follows in this chapter has likewise the character of an exploratory introduction to matters calling for fuller and more detailed inquiry in the later chapters of *Languages of Art*.

11. Such identification does not guarantee that the object possesses the pictorial properties it had originally. Rather, reliance on physical or historical identification is transcended only where we have means of ascertaining that the requisite properties are present.

12. To be original a print must be from a certain plate but need not be printed by the artist. Furthermore, in the case of a woodcut, the artist sometimes only draws upon the block, leaving the cutting to someone else—Holbein's blocks, for example, were usually cut by Lützelberger. Authenticity in an autographic art always depends upon the object's having the requisite, sometimes rather complicated, history of production; but that history does not always include ultimate execution by the original artist.

13. Of course, I am not saying that a correct(ly spelled) performance is correct in any of a number of other usual senses. Nevertheless, the composer or musician is likely to protest indignantly at a refusal to accept a performance with a few wrong notes as an instance of a work; and he surely has ordinary usage on his side. But ordinary usage here points the way to disaster for theory (see *Languages of Art* V, 2).

Minimal Art

Richard Wollheim

If we survey the art situation of recent times, as it has come to take shape over, let us say, the last fifty years, we find that increasingly acceptance has been afforded to a class of objects that, though disparate in many ways—in looks, in intention, in moral impact—have also an identifiable feature or aspect in common. And this might be expressed by saying that they have a minimal art-content: in that either they are to an extreme degree undifferentiated in themselves and therefore possess very low content of any kind, or else the differentiation that they do exhibit, which may in some cases be very considerable, comes not from the artist but from a nonartistic source, like nature or the factory. Examples of the kind of thing I have in mind would be canvases of Reinhardt or (from the other end of the scale) certain combines of Rauschenberg or, perhaps better, the non-"assisted" ready-mades of Marcel Duchamp. The existence of such objects, or rather their acceptance as works of art, is bound to give rise to certain doubts or anxieties; which a robust respect for fashion may fairly permanently suppress but cannot effectively resolve.

In this essay I want to take these doubts and anxieties seriously, or at least some of them, and see if there is anything they show about the abiding nature of art.

In a historic passage Mallarmé describes the terror, the sense of sterility, that the poet experiences when he sits down to his desk, confronts the sheet of paper before him on which his poem is supposed to be composed, and no words come to him. But we might ask, Why could not Mallarmé, after an interval of time, have simply got up from his chair and produced the blank sheet of paper *as* the poem that he sat down to write? Indeed, in support of this, could one imagine anything that was more expressive of, or would be held to exhibit more precisely, the poet's feelings of inner devastation than the virginal paper? The interest for us of such a gesture is, of course, that it would provide us with an extreme instance of what I call Minimal Art.

Now there are probably a lot of reasons any one of us could find for regarding the gesture as unacceptable: that is to say, for refusing to accept *le vide papier* as a work of art. Here I want to concentrate on one. For it has some relevance to the more general problem.

Suppose that Yevtushenko sits down in Moscow and writes on a sheet of paper certain words in a certain order, and what he composes is accepted as a poem; now further suppose that someone in New York, a few weeks later, gets up and reads out those same words in the same order; then we should say that what the person read out in New York was the poem that Yevtushenko wrote in Moscow. Or rather we should say this provided that certain further conditions, which might be called, very roughly, continuity-conditions, were satisfied: that is to say, provided the man read out the words he did read out because Yevtushenko had previously written them down, and that he hadn't quite independently got the idea of conjoining them in Yevtushenko's order, etc.

A poem (one and the same poem) can, then, be written in one place, read out in another, printed in yet another, appear in many copies of the same book, be learnt by generations of children, be studied by critics in different countries: and all this without our having to assume that the poem somehow reproduces itself indefinitely by some process of division or fissure. For the poem, though it is, say, printed on a certain page, is not to be identified with those printed words. The poem enters into all the different occurrences—recitations, inscriptions, printings, punishments, memorizings—not because some common stuff is present on all these occasions, but because of some common structure to which the varied stuff on the different occasions (different paper, different ink, different noises) conforms. It is this structure, which originates with the poet's act of creation, that gives the poem its identity.

Now we can see one overwhelming reason why Mallarmé could not have produced the blank sheet of paper as the poem he had in fact composed. For there is no structure here on the basis of which we could identify later occurrences as occurrences of that poem. We would have no right to say of anything, "Here is Mallarmé's poem."

Alternately, we should have to regard every blank page in the world, or every blank space, or indeed just every blank, as carrying not potentially but actually Mallarmé's poem. It would have to be seen as inscribed in the interstices of every inscription in the world.

And now suppose that Rauschenberg in New York conjoins a bicycle and a wooden culvert, and this combination is accepted as a work of art; and further suppose that someone in Moscow, again after a period of time, also gets hold of a bicycle and a wooden culvert and brings them together in the same way as Rauschenberg did, and (for the sake of argument) exhibits it. Now I think it is evident that no one would say that what had been exhibited in Moscow was the combine that Rauschenberg had constructed in New York. And this would be so, even if something analogous to what I have called the continuity-conditions in the case of Yevtushenko's poem, were satisfied: that is to say, if the Russian artist put the objects together as he did because Rauschenberg had done so first, and he hadn't independently hit on the idea of doing so, etc.

Now all this, it will be appreciated, derives directly from the criteria of identity that we employ for distinguishing works of fine art (not "visual" art, for the criteria are evidently different in the case of, say, engravings or lithographs). What it has nothing to do with are purely artistic or aesthetic considerations. It has, for instance, nothing to do with what we think about the merits of copying: all it relates to is the question whether if copying does issue in works of art, the copy is or isn't an instance of the same work of art as the original.

And the identity of a work of fine art resides in the actual stuff in which it consists.

From which we can see that Mallarmé could, in principle, have got up from his desk and produced the blank sheet of paper as the painting or drawing in which he had been engaged. For then there would have been an actual object that we could have identified as Mallarmé's painting, even though there was nothing to be identified as Mallarmé's poem. The production of the blank sheet of paper as the poem in which he was engaged would find its parallel in the area of the fine arts not in the production of a blank canvas, but in something like the gesturing toward the content of an empty studio.

In philosophical language, a literary work of art is a *type*, of which your copy or my copy or the set of words read out in a particular hall on a particular evening are the various *tokens*: it is a type like the

Union Jack or the Queen of Diamonds, of which the flags that fly at different mastheads and have the same design, or the cards in different packs with the same face, are the tokens.

But what *would* we say about the combine that the Russian Rauschenberg put together in Moscow to the exact specifications of the American Rauschenberg in New York? We have seen so far that we couldn't say that it just is Rauschenberg's combine, in the sense in which the thing read out in New York *is* Yevtushenko's poem. But could we treat it none the less as a work of art: that is to say, as a *new* work of art?

At this historical juncture it seems hard to pronounce definitively on this point. But certainly there would be tremendous resistance to our accepting this suggestion: resistance that we could perhaps break down in this case or that, but not universally I suspect without the total disintegration of our concept of "art" as we have it. The recognition of variants or copies within traditional Western art; the precedent of alien art traditions in which change or stylistic modification has been at a minimum; the parallel existence of etchings and lithographs that come in states and editions—all these provide us with temptations to capitulate, but temptations to which we are unlikely to succumb in any permanent way.

Now it will be apparent from what I have said about types and tokens that the genuine Rauschenberg and the pseudo-Rauschenberg are tokens of the same type—though the type itself is not a work of art. If this is so, then it would seem that our existing concept of a work of art has built into it two propositions, of which the first can be expressed as:

Works of fine art are not types, of which there could be an indefinite numbers of tokens;

and the second as:

There could not be more than one work of fine art that was a token of a given type.

This second proposition needs to be carefully distinguished from another proposition with which it has a great deal in common: i.e.,

> *There could not be a work of fine art that was of a type of*
> *which there was more than one token;*

which, I want to suggest, is clearly false.

For this third proposition would have such sweeping and totally objectionable consequences as that a work of art, once copied, would cease to be a work of art. It is indeed only when this sort of possibility is quite artificially blocked, by, say, a quasiempirical belief in the inimitability of genius, that this Draconian principle could even begin to acquire plausibility.

Yet there are occasions when the more moderate principle seems no less arbitrary in its working; indeed just because of its moderation, it seems, if anything, more arbitrary. In 1917 Marcel Duchamp submitted a urinal as a contribution to an exhibition of art. To many people such a gesture must have seemed totally at variance with their concept of art. But I am not concerned with them. If, however, we confine ourselves to those who found the gesture acceptable, then I want to suggest that what would have seemed quite at variance with *their* concept of art is that accepting the gesture committed them to rejecting in advance any of a similar kind subsequently made. Yet precisely this seems to be the consequence of our principle. By a simple action Duchamp deprived all objects of a certain kind save one of art-quality; and it might seem more arbitrary that he should have been able to do this than that he was able to secure it for that one.

Nor is this particular ready-made of Duchamp's likely to be a unique case. The problem then arises, How are we to delimit the cases where our principle gives rise to anomalies? For unless we can in some way delimit them, we shall find ourselves led back to the Draconian principle that we have already rejected. We shall find ourselves asserting that what was wrong with Duchamp's urinal is that it is one of a type. But this, as we have seen, is not what is wrong with it.

Another and more specific suggestion might be that it is not just that there are other urinals exactly like Duchamp's, but that Duchamp's does not owe its differentiation from them (*it* is a work of art, *they* aren't) to any temporal priority to which it can lay claim. It isn't just that there are other tokens of the same type, but that there are, or very well might be, other tokens that preceded or anticipated it. And this indifference to time-order, respect for which is so carefully enshrined in the "original"-"copy" distinction of traditional thought, serves to single out a whole class of cases where we feel concern about accepting one but no more than one token of a certain type as a work of art.

Consideration of this kind of case suggests another. And this is where, though the facsimile does not in fact antedate the object that is accepted as a work of art, this fact seems to have very little significance. For the art object, or what passes for one, is so readily reproducible. The other tokens that aren't there *could be* with such little disturbance to anything. In such cases the object can't correctly be regarded as one of a stream of identical objects from which it has been arbitrarily abstracted. But there would be no difficulty in imagining such a stream to flow out: the object is a natural tap for its own likenesses.

And possibly there could be other cases where we might be tempted to feel the same kind of reserve. But I shall pause on these two kinds, and it will be apparent, I imagine, why they are of interest to me: for they totally overlap with the two sorts of object that at the beginning of this paper I identified as objects of Minimal Art.

But now, we might ask, why should objects of these two kinds give rise to any peculiar difficulties? Or, to put it another way, is there any common difficulty that we can see as lying in the way of accepting as works of art either artifacts of which there are or are likely to be preexistent facsimiles or highly undifferentiated objects? We don't mind, as we have seen, reproducibility; so why should we mind facile reproducibility? Or is the whole matter, as Koestler once suggested, in a singularly unperceptive essay, just "snobbery"?

I suspect that our principal reason for resisting the claims of Minimal Art is that its objects fail to evince what we have over the centuries come to regard as an essential ingredient in art: work, or manifest effort. And here it is not an issue, as it was in certain Renaissance disputes, of whether the work is insufficiently or excessively banausic, but simply whether it took place at all. Reinhardt or Duchamp, it might be felt, *did* nothing, or not enough.

The connection between art and expression, which has been so elaborately reinforced in the art of the recent past, has of course in turn reinforced the connection between work and art. But I do not think that the former link is necessary for the latter, which quite independently (and I should say, quite rightly) enjoys such prestige in our aesthetic thinking that it is hard to see how objects of Minimal Art can justify their claims to the status of art unless it can be shown that the reason for holding that they inadequately exhibit work is based on too narrow or limited a view of what work is—or more specifically, of what work is as it occurs in the making of a picture.

And my claim, to which the rest of this essay will be devoted, is that this can be done. Indeed the historical significance of the art objects I have been concerned with is largely given by the way in which they force us to reconsider what it is to *make* a work of art: or, to put it linguistically, what is the meaning of the word "work" in the phrase "work of art." In different ways the ready-mades of Duchamp and the canvases of Reinhardt challenge our ordinary conceptions on this subject—and, moreover, challenge them in a way that makes it clear where these conceptions are insensitive or deficient.

The system upon which Marcel Duchamp selected his ready-mades he codified in the theory of *"rendez-vous."* At a certain time, at a certain place, he would chance upon an object, and this object he would submit to the world as a work of art. The confrontation of artist and object was arbitrary, and the creation of art was instantaneous.

Now if we ignore the whimsical, and equally the more disturbed, aspects of these gestures, we can see them as isolating one of the two elements that traditionally constitute the production of an art object, and moreover the one that is often, indeed almost consistently, in ordinary reflection, overlooked in favor of the other. For the production of an art object consists, first of all, in a phase that might be called, perhaps oversimply, "work" *tout court*: that is to say, the putting of paint on canvas, the hacking of stone, the welding of metal elements. (In the next section we shall see that this picture even of the initial phase is too crude; but for the moment it will do.) But the second phase in artistic productivity consists in decision, which, even if it cannot be said to *be* literally work, is that without which work would be meaningless: namely, the decision that the work has gone far enough. Since the first phase is insufficient without the second, the whole process might in a broader sense be called work.

Now in Duchamp's ready-mades or in any form of art that directly depends upon preexistent material for its composition, it is this second phase in the total process of production that is picked out and celebrated in isolation. The isolation is achieved in the starkest fashion: that is, by entrusting the two phases to quite different hands. But, then, even this finds some kind of precedent within traditional art, in the role of the pupil or the *bottega*.

However, what might be objected to in Duchamp's practice, at any rate as we get it in the system of *"rendez-vous,"* is that not merely is there a division of labor between the construction of the object and the decision that the object is in existence, but that the decision taken about the object is not based on the appearance of the object at all. In other words, Duchamp makes a decision like an artist, but the decision that he makes is not like the artist's.

But even here it might be claimed, Duchamp's gesture displays some kind of continuity with traditional or accepted practice: it picks up something that the artist does. For though the artist may make his decision on the basis of what the object looks like, the decision is not fully determined by the look of the object. The artist is always free to go on or to stop, as he pleases, and though we may sometimes criticize the judgment he reaches by saying that it leaves the work still unresolved or alternatively that he has overworked it, the criticism that we make is not purely aesthetic. There enters into it a measure of identification with the artist. To put it another way, when the artist says "That's how I wanted it," in part what he means is "That's how you're going to have it." What I have called Duchamp's whimsical gestures do serve to bring out this "master" aspect in the production of art.

But when we turn to the second kind of object whose acceptance as a work of art I have cited as problematic, the situation becomes more complex. For the challenge that these highly undifferentiated objects present to the conception we ordinarily have of work or effort, as this goes even into what I have identified as the first phase of picture-making, is very searching.

Roughly it might be said that in so far as we think these objects to exhibit to too low a degree the signs of work and on this basis come to dispute their fitness as art, work is conceived somewhat as follows: A man starts with a blank canvas; on this canvas he deposits marks of paint; each mark modifies the look of the canvas; and when this process of modification has gone on long enough, the painter's work is at an end, and the surface of the canvas bears the finished picture. Now of course it will ordinarily be the case that the marks, by and large, differ one from another. But there is in principle the possibility that the marks will be totally repetitive. However, this would naturally be thought to be a mere limiting case of constructivity, and therefore to the extent to which an art object is required to be a *work* of art, the resultant picture, which will be a mere monochrome surface, will be regarded as having a claim to the status of art that is only minimally ahead of the *tabula rasa* it supersedes.

But the question arises whether this account, which is evidently all right as far as it goes, goes far enough. For do we not bring to our perception of art a further notion of work: one that is quite distinct from that which I have set out, that stands indeed in stark contrast to it, and between the two of which there is a fruitful tension? So far I have spoken of constructive work: work that consists in building a picture, in "working it up" from the blank canvas in which it originates into an artifact of some complexity. But now I want to suggest that in our contemplation of art we often envisage another kind of activity as having gone on inside the arena of the painting, which has also made its contribution to the finished state of the object. And this work, which is at once destructive and yet also creative, consists in the dismantling of some image that is fussier or more cluttered than the artist requires.

Perhaps I can clarify this point by considering briefly the notion of "distortion," or at any rate the use to which it is implicitly put even in traditional criticism. For if we take cases inside the historical canon where it is universally agreed that the distortion has occurred and occurred fruitfully—say Mannerist portraiture, or Ingres, or (to come to modern times) *Les Demoiselles d'Avignon*—what do we intend by saying this? Now all we might be thought to mean is that in these works of art there is a discrepancy between the actual image that appears on the canvas and what would have appeared there if an image had been projected on it in accordance with (roughly) the laws of linear perspective. But what I want to suggest now is that in these cases there is a further thought that insinuates itself into our mind, and that is inextricably involved with our appreciation of the object: and that is that the image before us, Parmigianino's or Picasso's, is the result of the partial obliteration or simplifying of a more complex image that enjoyed some kind of shadowy preexistence, and upon which the artist has gone to work. The "preimage," as we might call it, was excessively differentiated, and the artist has dismantled it according to his own inner needs.

My suggestion, now, is that the canvases of Reinhardt exhibit to an ultimate degree this kind of work, which we ordinarily tend to think of as having made some contribution to the object of visual art. Within these canvases the work of destruction has been ruthlessly complete, and any image has been so thoroughly dismantled that no *pentimenti* any longer remain.

But there is still a powerful objection. For it might be said, though there may (or perhaps must) go into the making of a picture work of the kind we have been considering, what reason is there to suppose that such work can legitimately be abstracted from conventional picture-making, and as I have put it, "celebrated in isolation." Now, even if we allow for the hyperbole contained in this last phrase of mine, there is obviously a challenge here. To some degree, it can, I think, be met. Here I can only sketch how.

In conceptual thinking we fragment the world, and we isolate from the continuum of presentation repeated things, categories of object, sorts. We are led to concentrate upon similarities and differences in so far as these are expressed in terms of general characteristics; and this tendency is cemented in us by many of the practical exigencies of life. In the visual arts, however, we escape, or are prised away from, this preoccupation with generality, and we are called upon to concentrate our attention upon individual bits of the world: this canvas, that bit of stone or bronze, some particular sheet of paper scored like this or like that.

It has, over the centuries, been, at any rate within the tradition of the West, a natural concern of the artist to aid our concentration upon a particular object by making the object the unique possessor of certain general characteristics. In other words, by differentiating the work of art to a high degree, the artist made its claim to individuality intuitively more acceptable. For it was now, in an *evident* way, not merely quantitatively but also qualitatively distinct from other objects.

Now this differentiation was, as we have seen, by and large achieved by placing in the object a great deal of what I have called "constructive" work. It was by means of a very large number of nonrepetitive brush-strokes that the highly individuated masterpieces of Van Eyck or Poussin were brought into being. But in the phase I am considering, where work of this kind recedes into the background and the elements of decision or dismantling acquire a new prominence, the claim of the work of art to individual attention comes to rest increasingly upon its mere numerical diversity.

Inevitably a point will be reached where this claim, which is so abstractly couched, can no longer be found acceptable, or even taken seriously. But until then, as we merely move closer into the area of bare uniqueness, we have progressively brought home to us the gravity, the stringency of art's demand that we should look at single objects for and in themselves. A demand that is not fortuitously reminiscent of that involved in a certain conception of love against which Pascal railed: *On n'aime donc jamais personne, mais seulement des qualités. Qu'on ne se moque donc plus de ceux qui se font honorer pour des charges et des offices, car on n'aime personne que pour des qualités empruntées.*

Art and Objecthood

Michael Fried

Edwards's journals frequently explored and tested a meditation he seldom allowed to reach print; if all the world were annihilated, he wrote . . . and a new world were freshly created, though it were to exist in every particular in the same manner as this world, it would not be the same. Therefore, because there is continuity, which is time, "it is certain with me that the world exists anew every moment; that the existence of things every moment ceases and is every moment renewed." The abiding assurance is that "we every moment see the same proof of a God as we should have seen if we had seen Him create the world at first."
—Perry Miller, *Jonathan Edwards*

I

The enterprise known variously as Minimal Art, ABC Art, Primary Structures, and Specific Objects is largely ideological. It seeks to declare and occupy a position—one that can be formulated in words, and in fact has been formulated by some of its leading practitioners. If this distinguishes it from modernist painting and sculpture on the one hand, it also marks an important difference between Minimal Art—or, as I prefer to call it, *literalist* art—and Pop or Op Art on the other. From its inception, literalist art has amounted to something more than an episode in the history of taste. It belongs rather to the history—almost the *natural* history—of sensibility; and it is not an isolated episode but the expression of a general and pervasive condition. Its seriousness is vouched for by the fact that it is in relation both to modernist painting and modernist sculpture that literalist art defines or locates the position it aspires to occupy. (This, I suggest, is what makes what it declares something that deserves to be called a position.) Specifically, literalist art conceives of itself as neither one nor the other; on the contrary, it is motivated by specific reservations, or worse, about both; and it aspires, perhaps not exactly, or not

214

immediately, to displace them, but in any case to establish itself as an independent art on a footing with either.

The literalist case against painting rests mainly on two counts: the relational character of almost all painting; and the ubiquitousness, indeed the virtual inescapability, of pictorial illusion. In Donald Judd's view:

> When you start relating parts, in the first place, you're assuming you have a vague whole—the rectangle of the canvas—and definite parts, which is all screwed up, because you should have a definite *whole* and maybe no parts, or very few.[1]

The more the shape of the support is emphasized, as in recent modernist painting, the tighter the situation becomes:

> The elements inside the rectangle are broad and simple and correspond closely to the rectangle. The shapes and surface are only those that can occur plausibly within and on a rectangular plane. The parts are few and so subordinate to unity as not to be parts in an ordinary sense. A painting is nearly an entity, one thing, and not the indefinable sum of a group of entities and references. The one thing overpowers the earlier painting. It also establishes the rectangle as a definite form; it is no longer a fairly neutral limit. A form can be used only in so many ways. The rectangular plane is given a life span. The simplicity required to emphasize the rectangle limits the arrangements possible within it.

Painting is here seen as an art on the verge of exhaustion, one in which the range of acceptable solutions to a basic problem—how to organize the surface of the picture—is severely restricted. The use of shaped rather than rectangular supports can, from the literalist point of view, merely prolong the agony. The obvious response is to give up working on a single plane in favor of three dimensions. That, moreover, automatically

> gets rid of the problem of illusionism and of literal space, space in and around marks and colors—which is riddance of one of the salient and most objectionable relics of European art. The several limits of painting are no longer present. A work can be as powerful as it can be thought to be. Actual space is intrinsically more powerful and specific than paint on a flat surface.

The literalist attitude toward sculpture is more ambiguous. Judd, for example, seems to think of what he calls Specific Objects as something other than sculpture, while Robert Morris conceives of his own unmistakably literalist work as resuming the lapsed tradition of Constructivist sculpture established by Tatlin, Rodchenko, Gabo, Pevsner, and Vantongerloo. But this and other disagreements are less important than the views Judd and Morris hold in common. Above all they are opposed to sculpture that, like most painting, is "made part by part, by addition, composed" and in which "specific elements . . . separate from the whole, thus setting up relationships within the work." (They would include the work of David Smith and Anthony Caro under this description.) It is worth remarking that the "part-by-part" and "relational" character of most sculpture is associated by Judd with what he calls *anthropomorphism*: "A beam thrusts; a piece of iron follows a gesture; together they form a naturalistic and anthropomorphic image. The space corresponds." Against such "multipart, inflected" sculpture Judd and Morris assert the values of wholeness, singleness, and indivisibility—of a work's being, as nearly as possible, "one thing," a single "Specific Object." Morris devotes considerable attention to "the use of strong gestalt or of unitary-type forms to avoid divisiveness"; while Judd is chiefly interested in the kind of wholeness that can be achieved through the repetition of identical units. The order at work in his pieces, as he once remarked on that in Stella's stripe paintings, "is simply order, like that of continuity, one thing after another." For both Judd and Morris, however, the critical factor is *shape*. Morris's "unitary forms" are polyhedrons that resist being grasped other than as a single shape: the gestalt simply *is* the "constant, known shape." And shape itself is, in his system, "the most important sculptural value." Similarly, speaking of his own work, Judd has remarked that

> the big problem is that anything that is not absolutely plain begins to have parts in some way. The thing is to be able to work and do different things and yet not break up the wholeness that a piece has. To me the piece with the brass and the five verticals is above all *that shape*.

The shape *is* the object: at any rate, what secures the wholeness of the object is the singleness of the shape. It is, I believe, this emphasis on shape that accounts for the impression, which numerous critics have mentioned, that Judd's and Morris's pieces are *hollow*.

II

Shape has also been central to the most important painting of the past several years. In several recent essays[2] I have tried to show how, in the work of Noland, Olitski, and Stella, a conflict has gradually emerged between shape as a fundamental property of objects and shape as a medium of painting. Roughly, the success or failure of a given painting has come to depend on its ability to hold or stamp itself out or compel conviction as shape—that, or somehow to stave off or elude the question of whether or not it does so. Olitski's early spray paintings are the purest example of paintings that either hold or fail to hold as shapes; while in his more recent pictures, as well as in the best of Noland's, and Stella's recent work, the demand that a given picture hold as shape is staved off or eluded in various ways. What is at stake in this conflict is whether the paintings or objects in question are experienced as paintings or as objects: and what decides their identity as *painting* is their confronting of the demand that they hold as shapes. Otherwise they are experienced as nothing more than objects. This can be summed up by saying that modernist painting has come to find it imperative that it defeat or suspend its own objecthood, and that the crucial factor in this undertaking is shape, but shape that must belong to *painting*—it must be pictorial, not, or not merely, literal. Whereas literalist art stakes everything on shape as a given property of objects, if not, indeed, as a kind of object in its own right. It aspires, not to defeat or suspend its own objecthood, but on the contrary to discover and project objecthood as such.

In his essay "Recentness of Sculpture" Clement Greenberg discusses the effect of *presence*, which, from the start, has been associated with literalist work.[3] This comes up in connection with the work of Anne Truitt, an artist Greenberg believes anticipated the literalists (he calls them Minimalists):

> Truitt's art did flirt with the look of non-art, and her 1963 show was the first in which I noticed how this look could confer an effect of *presence*. That presence as achieved through size was aesthetically extraneous, I already knew. That presence as achieved through the look of non-art was likewise aesthetically extraneous, I did not yet know. Truitt's sculpture had this kind of presence but did not *hide* behind it. That sculpture could hide behind it—just as painting did—I found out only after repeated acquaintance with Minimal works of art: Judd's, Morris's,

Andre's, Steiner's, some but not all of Smithson's, some but not all of LeWitt's. Minimal art can also hide behind presence as size: I think of Bladen (though I am not sure whether he is a certified Minimalist) as well as of some of the artists just mentioned.

Presence can be conferred by size or by the look of non-art. Furthermore, what non-art means today, and has meant for several years, is fairly specific. In "After Abstract Expressionism" Greenberg wrote that "a stretched or tacked-up canvas already exists as a picture—though not necessarily as a *successful* one."[4] For that reason, as he remarks in "Recentness of Sculpture," the "look of non-art was no longer available to painting." Instead, "the borderline between art and non-art had to be sought in the three-dimensional, where sculpture was, and where everything material that was not art also was." Greenberg goes on to say:

> The look of machinery is shunned now because it does not go far enough towards the look of non-art, which is presumably an "inert" look that offers the eye a minimum of "interesting" incident—unlike the machine look, which is arty by comparison (and when I think of Tinguely I would agree with this). Still, no matter how simple the object may be, there remains the relations and interrelations of surface, contour, and spatial interval. Minimal works are readable as art, as almost anything is today —including a door, a table, or a blank sheet of paper. . . . Yet it would seem that a kind of art nearer the condition of non-art could not be envisaged or ideated at this moment.

The meaning in this context of "the condition of non-art" is what I have been calling objecthood. It is as though objecthood alone can, in the present circumstances, secure something's identity, if not as non-art, at least as neither painting nor sculpture; or as though a work of art—more accurately, a work of modernist painting or sculpture—were in some essential respect *not an object*.

There is, in any case, a sharp contrast between the literalist espousal of objecthood—almost, it seems, as an art in its own right—and modernist painting's self-imposed imperative that it defeat or suspend its own objecthood through the medium of shape. In fact, from the perspective of recent modernist painting, the literalist position evinces a sensibility not simply alien but antithetical to its own:

as though, from that perspective, the demands of art and the conditions of objecthood are in direct conflict.

Here the question arises: What is it about objecthood as projected and hypostatized by the literalists that makes it, if only from the perspective of recent modernist painting, antithetical to art?

III

The answer I want to propose is this: the literalist espousal of objecthood amounts to nothing other than a plea for a new genre of theatre; and theatre is now the negation of art.

Literalist sensibility is theatrical because, to begin with, it is concerned with the actual circumstances in which the beholder encounters literalist work. Morris makes this explicit. Whereas in previous art "what is to be had from the work is located strictly within [it]," the experience of literalist art is of an object *in a situation*—one that, virtually by definition, *includes the beholder:*

> The better new work takes relationships out of the work and makes them a function of space, light, and the viewer's field of vision. The object is but one of the terms in the newer aesthetic. It is in some way more reflexive because one's awareness of oneself existing in the same space as the work is stronger than in previous work, with its many internal relationships. One is more aware than before that he himself is establishing relationships as he apprehends the object from various positions and under varying conditions of light and spatial context.

Morris believes that this awareness is heightened by "the strength of the constant, known shape, the gestalt," against which the appearance of the piece from different points of view is constantly being compared. It is intensified also by the large scale of much literalist work:

> The awareness of scale is a function of the comparison made between that constant, one's body size, and the object. Space between the subject and the object is implied in such a comparison.

The larger the object the more we are forced to keep our distance from it:

It is this necessary, greater distance of the object in space from our bodies, in order that it be seen at all, that structures the nonpersonal or public mode [which Morris advocates]. However, it is just this distance between object and subject that creates a more extended situation, because physical participation becomes necessary.

The theatricality of Morris's notion of the "nonpersonal or public mode" seems obvious: the largeness of the piece, in conjunction with its nonrelational, unitary character, *distances* the beholder—not just physically but psychically. It is, one might say, precisely this distancing that *makes* the beholder a subject and the piece in question . . . an object. But it does not follow that the larger the piece the more securely its "public" character is established; on the contrary, "beyond a certain size the object can overwhelm and the gigantic scale becomes the loaded term." Morris wants to achieve presence through objecthood, which requires a certain largeness of scale, rather than through size alone. But he is also aware that this distinction is anything but hard and fast:

For the space of the room itself is a structuring factor both in its cubic shape and in terms of the kind of compression different sized and proportioned rooms can effect upon the object-subject terms. That the space of the room becomes of such importance does not mean that an environmental situation is being established. The total space is hopefully altered in certain desired ways by the presence of the object. It is not controlled in the sense of being ordered by an aggregate of objects or by some shaping of the space surrounding the viewer.

The object, not the beholder, must remain the center or focus of the situation; but the situation itself *belongs to* the beholder—it is *his* situation. Or as Morris has remarked, "I wish to emphasize that things are in a space with oneself, rather than . . . [that] one is in a space surrounded by things." Again, there is no clear or hard distinction between the two states of affairs: one is, after all, *always* surrounded by things. But the things that are literalist works of art must somehow *confront* the beholder—they must, one might almost say, be placed not just in his space but in his *way*. None of this, Morris maintains, indicates a lack of interest in the object itself. But the concerns now are for more control of . . . the entire situation. Control is necessary if the variables of object, light, space, body, are to function. The object has not become less important. It has merely become less self-important.

It is, I think, worth remarking that "the entire situation" means exactly that: *all* of it—including, it seems, the beholder's *body*. There is nothing within his field of vision—nothing he takes note of in any way—that, as it were, declares its irrelevance to the situation, and therefore to the experience, in question. On the contrary, for something to be perceived at all is for it to be perceived as part of that situation. Everything counts—not as part of the object, but as part of the situation in which its objecthood is established and on which that objecthood at least partly depends.

IV

Furthermore, the presence of literalist art, which Greenberg was the first to analyze, is basically a theatrical effect or quality—a kind of *stage* presence. It is a function, not just of the obtrusiveness and, often, even aggressiveness of literalist work, but of the special complicity that that work extorts from the beholder. Something is said to have presence when it demands that the beholder take it into account, that he take it *seriously*—and when the fulfillment of that demand consists simply in being *aware* of it and, so to speak, in acting accordingly. (Certain modes of seriousness are closed to the beholder by the work itself, *i.e.*, those established by the finest painting and sculpture of the recent past. But, of course, *those* are hardly modes of seriousness in which most people feel at home, or that they even find tolerable.) Here again the experience of being distanced by the work in question seems crucial: the beholder knows himself to stand in an indeterminate, open-ended—and unexacting—relation *as subject* to the impassive object on the wall or floor. In fact, being distanced by such objects is not, I suggest, entirely unlike being distanced, or crowded, by the silent presence of another *person*; the experience of coming upon literalist objects unexpectedly—for example, in somewhat darkened rooms—can be strongly, if momentarily, disquieting in just this way.

There are three main reasons why this is so. First, the size of much literalist work, as Morris's remarks imply, compares fairly closely with that of the human body. In this context Tony Smith's replies to questions about his six-foot cube, *Die*, are highly suggestive:

> Q: Why didn't you make it larger so that it would loom over the observer?
> A: I was not making a monument.
> Q: Then why didn't you make it smaller so that the observer could see over the top?
> A: I was not making an object.[5]

One way of describing what Smith *was* making might be something like a surrogate person—that is, a kind of *statue*. (This reading finds support in the caption to a photograph of another of Smith's pieces, *The Black Box*, published in the December 1967 issue of *Artforum*, in which Samuel Wagstaff, Jr., presumably with the artist's sanction, observed, "One can see the two-by-fours under the piece, which keep it from appearing like architecture or a monument, and set it off as sculpture." The two-by-fours are, in effect, a rudimentary *pedestal*, and thereby reinforce the statue-like quality of the piece.) Second, the entities or beings encountered in everyday experience in terms that most closely approach the literalist ideals of the nonrelational, the unitary, and the wholistic are *other persons*. Similarly, the literalist predilection for symmetry, and in general for a kind of order that "is simply order . . . one thing after another," is rooted, not, as Judd seems to believe, in new philosophical and scientific principles, whatever he takes these to be, but in *nature*. And third, the apparent hollowness of most literalist work—the quality of having an *inside*— is almost blatantly anthropomorphic. It is, as numerous commentators have remarked approvingly, as though the work in question has an inner, even secret, life—an effect that is perhaps made most explicit in Morris's *Untitled* (1965–66), a large ringlike form in two halves, with fluorescent light glowing from within at the narrow gap between the two. In the same spirit Tony Smith has said, "I'm interested in the inscrutability and mysteriousness of the thing."[6] He has also been quoted as saying:

> More and more I've become interested in pneumatic structures. In these, all of the material is in tension. But it is the character of the form that appeals to me. The biomorphic forms that result from the construction have a dreamlike quality for me, at least like what is said to be a fairly common type of American dream.

Smith's interest in pneumatic structures may seem surprising, but it is consistent both with his own work and with literalist sensibility generally. Pneumatic structures can be described as hollow with a vengeance—the fact that they are not "obdurate, solid masses" (Morris) being *insisted on* instead of taken for granted. And it reveals something, I think, about what hollowness means in literalist art that the forms that result are "biomorphic."

V

I am suggesting, then, that a kind of latent or hidden naturalism, indeed anthropomorphism, lies at the core of literalist theory and practice. The concept of presence all but says as much, though rarely so nakedly as in Tony Smith's statement, "I didn't think of them [i.e., the sculptures he "always" made] as sculptures but as presences of a sort." The latency or hiddenness of the anthropomorphism has been such that the literalists themselves have, as we have seen, felt free to characterize the modernist art they *oppose*, e.g., the sculpture of David Smith and Anthony Caro, as anthropomorphic—a characterization whose teeth, imaginary to begin with, have just been pulled. By the same token, however, what is wrong with literalist work is not that it is anthropomorphic but that the meaning and, equally, the hiddenness of its anthropomorphism are incurably theatrical. (Not all literalist art hides or masks its anthropomorphism; the work of lesser figures like Steiner wears anthropomorphism on its sleeve.) *The crucial distinction that I am proposing so far is between work that is fundamentally theatrical and work that is not.* It is theatricality that, whatever the differences between them, links artists like Bladen and Grosvenor,[7] both of whom have allowed "gigantic scale [to become] the loaded term" (Morris), with other, more restrained figures like Judd, Morris, Andre, McCracken, LeWitt and—despite the *size* of some of his pieces—Tony Smith.[8] And it is in the interest, though not explicitly in the *name*, of theatre that literalist ideology rejects both modernist painting and, at least in the hands of its most distinguished recent practitioners, modernist sculpture.

In this connection Tony Smith's description of a car ride taken at night on the New Jersey Turnpike before it was finished makes compelling reading:

When I was teaching at Cooper Union in the first year or two of the fifties, someone told me how I could get onto the unfinished New Jersey Turnpike. I took three students and drove from somewhere in the Meadows to New Brunswick. It was a dark night and there were no lights or shoulder markers, lines, railings, or anything at all except the dark pavement moving through the landscape of the flats, rimmed by hills in the distance, but punctuated by stacks, towers, fumes, and colored lights. This drive was a revealing experience. The road and much of the landscape was artificial, and yet it couldn't be called a work of art. On the other hand, it did something for me that art had never done. At first I didn't know what it was, but its effect was to liberate me from many of the views I had had about art. It seemed that there had been a reality there that had not had any expression in art.

The experience on the road was something mapped out but not socially recognized. I thought to myself, it ought to be clear that's the end of art. Most painting looks pretty pictorial after that. There is no way you can frame it, you just have to experience it. Later I discovered some abandoned airstrips in Europe —abandoned works, Surrealist landscapes, something that had nothing to do with any function, created worlds without tradition. Artificial landscape without cultural precedent began to dawn on me. There is a drill ground in Nuremberg large enough to accommodate two million men. The entire field is enclosed with high embankments and towers. The concrete approach is three sixteen-inch steps, one above the other, stretching for a mile or so.

What seems to have been revealed to Smith that night was the pictorial nature of painting—even, one might say, the conventional nature of art. And *this* Smith seems to have understood not as laying bare the essence of art, but as announcing its end. In comparison with the unmarked, unlit, all but unstructured turnpike—more precisely, with the turnpike as experienced from within the car, traveling on it—art appears to have struck Smith as almost absurdly small ("All art today is an art of postage stamps," he has said), circumscribed, conventional. . . . There was, he seemed to have felt, no way to "frame" his experience on the road, that is, no way to make sense of it in terms of art, to make *art* of it, at least as art then was. Rather, "you just have to experience it"—as it *happens*, as it merely *is*. (The experience *alone* is what matters.) There is no suggestion that this is problematic in any way. The experience is clearly regarded by Smith as wholly accessible to everyone, not just in principle but in fact, and the question of whether or not one has really *had* it does not arise.

That this appeals to Smith can be seen from his praise of Le Cor-
busier as "more available" than Michelangelo: "The direct and primitive experience of the High Court Building at Chandigarh is like the
Pueblos of the Southwest under a fantastic overhanging cliff. It's
something everyone can understand." It is, I think, hardly necessary
to add that the availability of modernist art is not of this kind, and
that the rightness or relevance of one's conviction about specific
modernist works, a conviction that begins and ends in one's experience of the work itself, is always open to question.

But what *was* Smith's experience on the turnpike? Or to put the
same question another way, if the turnpike, airstrips, and drill ground
are not works of art, what *are* they?—What, indeed, if not empty, or
"abandoned," *situations?* And what was Smith's experience if not the
experience of what I have been calling *theatre?* It is as though the
turnpike, airstrips, and drill ground reveal the theatrical character of
literalist art, only without the object, that is, *without the art itself*—as
though the object is needed only within a *room*[9] (or, perhaps, in
any circumstances less extreme than these). In each of the above
cases the object is, so to speak, *replaced* by something: for example,
on the turnpike by the constant onrush of the road, the simultaneous
recession of new reaches of dark pavement illumined by the onrush-
ing headlights, the sense of the turnpike itself as something enormous,
abandoned, derelict, existing for Smith alone and for those in the car
with him. . . . This last point is important. On the one hand, the
turnpike, airstrips, and drill ground belong to no one; on the other,
the situation established by Smith's presence is in each case felt by
him to be *his*. Moreover, in each case being able to go on and on
indefinitely is of the essence. What replaces the object—what does
the same job of distancing or isolating the beholder, of making him a
subject, that the object did in the closed room—is above all the
endlessness, or objectlessness, of the approach or onrush or perspective. It is the explicitness, that is to say, the sheer persistence, with
which the experience presents itself as directed at him from outside
(on the turnpike from outside the *car*) that simultaneously makes
him a subject—makes him subject—and establishes the experience
itself as something like that of an object, or rather, of objecthood.
No wonder Morris's speculations about how to put literalist work outdoors remain strangely inconclusive:

Why not put the work outdoors and further change the terms?
A real need exists to allow this next step to become practical.
Architecturally designed sculpture courts are not the answer nor

is the placement of work outside cubic architectural forms. Ideally, it is a space, without architecture as background and reference, that would give different terms to work with.

Unless the pieces are set down in a wholly natural context, and Morris does not seem to be advocating this, some sort of artificial but not quite architectural setting must be constructed. What Smith's remarks seem to suggest is that the more effective—meaning effective *as theatre*—the setting is made, the more superfluous the works themselves become.

VI

Smith's account of his experience on the turnpike bears witness to theatre's profound hostility to the arts, and discloses, precisely in the absence of the object and in what takes its place, what might be called the theatricality of objecthood. By the same token, however, the imperative that modernist painting defeat or suspend its objecthood is at bottom the imperative that it *defeat or suspend theatre*. And *this* means that there is a war going on between theatre and modernist painting, between the theatrical and the pictorial—a war that, despite the literalists' explicit rejection of modernist painting and sculpture, is not basically a matter of program and ideology but of experience, conviction, sensibility. (For example, it was a particular experience that *engendered* Smith's conviction that painting—in fact, that the arts as such—were finished.)

The starkness and apparent irreconcilability of this conflict is something new. I remarked earlier that objecthood has become an issue for modernist painting only within the past several years. This, however, is not to say that *before* the present situation came into being, paintings, or sculptures for that matter, simply *were objects*. It would, I think, be closer to the truth to say that they *simply* were not.[10] The risk, even the possibility, of seeing works of art as *nothing more* than objects did not exist. That this possibility began to present itself around 1960 was largely the result of developments within modernist painting. Roughly, the more nearly assimilable to objects certain advanced painting had come to seem, the more the entire history of painting since Manet could be understood—delusively, I believe—as consisting in the progressive (though ultimately inadequate) revelation of its essential objecthood,[11] and the more urgent became the need for modernist painting to make explicit its conventional—specifically, its *pictorial*—essence by defeating or suspending its own objecthood through the medium of shape. The view of modernist painting as tending toward objecthood is implicit in Judd's remark, "The new [i.e., literalist] work obviously resembles sculpture more than it does painting, but it is nearer to painting"; and it is in this view that literalist sensibility in general is grounded. Literalist sensibility is, therefore, a response to the *same* developments that have largely compelled modernist painting to undo its objecthood—more precisely, the same developments *seen differently*, that is, in theatrical terms, by a sensibility *already* theatrical, already (to say the worst) corrupted or perverted by theatre. Similarly, what has compelled modernist painting to defeat or suspend its own objecthood is not just developments internal to itself, but the same general, enveloping, infectious theatricality that corrupted literalist sensibility in the first place and in the grip of which the developments in question—and modernist painting in general—are seen as nothing more than an uncompelling and presenceless kind of theatre. It was the need to break the fingers of this grip that made objecthood an issue for modernist painting.

Objecthood has also become an issue for modernist sculpture. This is true despite the fact that sculpture, being three-dimensional, resembles both ordinary objects and literalist work in a way that painting does not. Almost ten years ago Clement Greenberg summed up what he saw as the emergence of a new sculptural "style," whose master is undoubtedly David Smith, in the following terms:

> To render substance entirely optical, and form, whether pictorial, sculptural, or architectural, as an integral part of ambient space—this brings anti-illusionism full circle. Instead of the illusion of things, we are now offered the illusion of modalities: namely, that matter is incorporeal, weightless, and exists only optically like a mirage.[12]

Since 1960 this development has been carried to a succession of climaxes by the English sculptor Anthony Caro, whose work is far more *specifically* resistant to being seen in terms of objecthood than that of David Smith. A characteristic sculpture by Caro consists, I want to say, in the mutual and naked *juxtaposition* of the *I*-beams, girders, cylinders, lengths of piping, sheet metal, and grill that it comprises rather than in the compound *object* that they compose. The mutual inflection of one element by another, rather than the identity of each, is what is crucial—though of course altering the identity of any element would be at least as drastic as altering its placement.

(The identity of each element matters in somewhat the same way as the fact that it is an *arm*, or *this* arm, that makes a particular gesture; or as the fact that it is *this* word or *this* note and not another that occurs in a particular place in a sentence or melody.) The individual elements bestow significance on one another precisely by virtue of their juxtaposition: it is in this sense, a sense inextricably involved with the concept of meaning, that everything in Caro's art that is worth looking at is in its syntax. Caro's concentration upon syntax amounts, in Greenberg's view, to "an emphasis on abstractness, on radical unlikeness to nature."[13] And Greenberg goes on to remark, "No other sculptor has gone as far from the structural logic of ordinary ponderable things." It is worth emphasizing, however, that this is a function of more than the lowness, openness, part-by-partness, absence of enclosing profiles and centers of interest, unperspicuousness, etc., of Caro's sculptures. Rather they defeat, or allay, objecthood by imitating, not gestures exactly, but the *efficacy* of gesture; like certain music and poetry, they are possessed by the knowledge of the human body and how, in innumerable ways and moods, it makes meaning. It is as though Caro's sculptures essentialize meaningfulness *as such*—as though the possibility of meaning what we say and do *alone* makes his sculpture possible. All this, it is hardly necessary to add, makes Caro's art a fountainhead of antiliteralist and antitheatrical sensibility.

There is another, more general respect in which objecthood has become an issue for the most ambitious recent modernist sculpture and that is in regard to *color*. This is a large and difficult subject, which I cannot hope to do more than touch on here.[14] Briefly, however, color has become problematic for modernist sculpture, not because one senses that it has been *applied*, but because the color of a given sculpture, whether applied or in the natural state of the material, is identical with its surface; and inasmuch as all objects have surface, awareness of the sculpture's surface implies its objecthood—thereby threatening to qualify or mitigate the undermining of objecthood achieved by opticality and, in Caro's pieces, by their syntax as well. It is in this connection, I believe, that a very recent sculpture, *Bunga*, by Jules Olitski ought to be seen. *Bunga* consists of between fifteen and twenty metal tubes, ten feet long and of various diameters, placed upright, riveted together and then sprayed with paint of different colors; the dominant hue is yellow to yellow-orange, but the top and "rear" of the piece are suffused with a deep rose, and close looking reveals flecks and even thin trickles of green and red as well. A rather wide red band has been painted around the top of the piece, while a much thinner band in two different blues (one at the "front" and another at the "rear") circumscribes the very bottom. Obviously, *Bunga* relates intimately to Olitski's spray paintings, especially those of the past year or so, in which he has worked with paint and brush at or near the limits of the support. At the same time, it amounts to something far more than an attempt simply to make or "translate" his paintings into sculptures, namely, an attempt to establish surface—the surface, so to speak, of *painting*—as a medium of sculpture. The use of tubes, each of which one sees, incredibly, as *flat*—that is, flat but *rolled*—makes *Bunga*'s surface more like that of a painting than like that of an object: like painting, and unlike both ordinary objects and other sculpture, *Bunga* is *all* surface. And of course what declares or establishes that surface is color, Olitski's sprayed color.

VII

At this point I want to make a claim that I cannot hope to prove or substantiate but that I believe nevertheless to be true: viz., that theatre and theatricality are at war today, not simply with modernist painting (or modernist painting and sculpture), but with art as such —and to the extent that the different arts can be described as modernist, with modernist sensibility as such. This claim can be broken down into three propositions or theses:

1) *The success, even the survival, of the arts has come increasingly to depend on their ability to defeat theatre.* This is perhaps nowhere more evident than within theatre itself, where the need to defeat what I have been calling theatre has chiefly made itself felt as the need to establish a drastically different relation to its audience. (The relevant texts are, of course, Brecht and Artaud.[15]) For theatre *has* an audience—it *exists for* one—in a way the other arts do not; in fact, this more than anything else is what modernist sensibility finds intolerable in theatre generally. Here it should be remarked that literalist art, too, possesses an audience, though a somewhat special one: that the beholder is confronted by literalist work within a situation that he experiences as *his* means that there is an important sense in which the work in question exists for him *alone*, even if he is not actually alone with the work at the time. It may seem paradoxical to claim both that literalist sensibility aspires to an ideal of "something everyone can understand" (Smith) *and* that literalist art addresses itself to the beholder alone, but the paradox is only apparent. Someone has merely to enter the room in which a literalist work has been placed to *become* that beholder, that audience of one—almost as

though the work in question has been *waiting for* him. And inasmuch as literalist work *depends on* the beholder, is *incomplete* without him, it *has* been waiting for him. And once he is in the room the work refuses, obstinately, to let him alone—which is to say, it refuses to stop confronting him, distancing him, isolating him. (Such isolation is not solitude any more than such confrontation is communion.)

It is the overcoming of theatre that modernist sensibility finds most exalting and that it experiences as the hallmark of high art in our time. There is, however, one art that, by its very nature, *escapes* theatre entirely—the movies.[16] This helps explain why movies in general, including frankly appalling ones, are acceptable to modernist sensibility whereas all but the most successful painting, sculpture, music, and poetry is not. Because cinema escapes theatre—automatically, as it were—it provides a welcome and absorbing refuge to sensibilities at war with theatre and theatricality. At the same time, the automatic, guaranteed character of the refuge—more accurately, the fact that what is provided is a refuge from theatre and not a triumph over it, absorption not conviction—means that the cinema, even at its most experimental, is not a *modernist* art.

2) *Art degenerates as it approaches the condition of theatre.* Theatre is the common denominator that binds a large and seemingly disparate variety of activities to one another, and that distinguishes those activities from the radically different enterprises of the modernist arts. Here as elsewhere the question of value or level is central. For example, a failure to register the enormous difference in quality between, say, the music of Carter and that of Cage or between the paintings of Louis and those of Rauschenberg means that the real distinctions—between music and theatre in the first instance and between painting and theatre in the second—are displaced by the illusion that the barriers between the arts are in the process of crumbling (Cage and Rauschenberg being seen, correctly, as similar) and that the arts themselves are at last sliding towards some kind of final, implosive, hugely desirable synthesis.[17] Whereas in fact the individual arts have never been more explicitly concerned with the conventions that constitute their respective essences.

3) *The concepts of quality and value—and to the extent that these are central to art, the concept of art itself—are meaningful, or wholly meaningful, only within the individual arts. What lies between the arts is theatre.* It is, I think, significant that in their various statements the literalists have largely avoided the issue of value or quality at the same time as they have shown considerable uncertainty as to whether or not what they are making is art. To describe their enter-

prise as an attempt to establish a *new* art does not remove the uncertainty; at most it points to its source. Judd himself has as much as acknowledged the problematic character of the literalist enterprise by his claim, "A work needs only to be interesting." For Judd, as for literalist sensibility generally, all that matters is whether or not a given work is able to elicit and sustain (his) *interest*. Whereas within the modernist arts nothing short of *conviction*—specifically, the conviction that a particular painting or sculpture or poem or piece of music can or cannot support comparison with past work within that art whose quality is not in doubt—matters at all. (Literalist work is often condemned—when it *is* condemned—for being boring. A tougher charge would be that it is merely interesting.)

The interest of a given work resides, in Judd's view, both in its character as a whole and in the sheer *specificity* of the materials of which it is made:

> Most of the work involves new materials, either recent inventions or things not used before in art. . . . Materials vary greatly and are simply materials—formica, aluminum, cold-rolled steel, plexiglas, red and common brass, and so forth. They are specific. If they are used directly, they are more specific. Also, they are usually aggressive. There is an objectivity to the obdurate identity of a material.

Like the shape of the object, the materials do not represent, signify, or allude to anything; they are what they are and nothing more. And what they are is not, strictly speaking, something that is grasped or intuited or recognized or even seen once and for all. Rather, the "obdurate identity" of a specific material, like the wholeness of the shape, is simply stated or given or established at the very outset, if not before the outset; accordingly, the experience of both is one of endlessness, of inexhaustibility, of being able to go on and on letting, for example, the material itself confront one in all its literalness, its "objectivity," its absence of anything beyond itself. In a similar vein Morris has written:

> Characteristic of a gestalt is that once it is established all the information about it, *qua* gestalt, is exhausted. (One does not, for example, seek the gestalt of a gestalt.) . . . One is then both free of the shape and bound to it. Free or released because of the exhaustion of information about it, as shape, and bound to it because it remains constant and indivisible.

The same note is struck by Tony Smith in a statement the first sentence of which I quoted earlier:

> I'm interested in the inscrutability and mysteriousness of the thing. Something obvious on the face of it (like a washng machine or a pump) is of no further interest. A Bennington earthenware jar, for instance, has subtlety of color, largeness of form, a general suggestion of substance, generosity, is calm and reassuring—qualities that take it beyond pure utility. It continues to nourish us time and time again. We can't see it in a second, we continue to read it. There is something absurd in the fact that you can go back to a cube in the same way.

Like Judd's Specific Objects and Morris's gestalts or unitary forms, Smith's cube is *always* of further interest; one never feels that one has come to the end of it; it is inexhaustible. It is inexhaustible, however, not because of any fullness—*that* is the inexhaustibility of art—but because there is nothing there to exhaust. It is endless the way a road might be: if it were circular, for example.

Endlessness, being able to go on and on, even having to go on and on, is central both to the concept of interest and to that of objecthood. In fact, it seems to be the experience that most deeply excites literalist sensibility, and that literalist artists seek to objectify in their work—for example, by the repetition of identical units (Judd's "one thing after another"), which carries the implication that the units in question could be multiplied *ad infinitum*.[18] Smith's account of his experience on the unfinished turnpike records that excitement all but explicitly. Similarly, Morris's claim that in the best new work the beholder is made aware that "he himself is establishing relationships as he apprehends the object from various positions and under varying conditions of light and spatial context" amounts to the claim that the beholder is made aware of the endlessness and inexhaustibility if not of the object itself at any rate of his experience of it. This awareness is further exacerbated by what might be called the *inclusiveness* of his situation, that is, by the fact, remarked earlier, that everything he observes counts as part of that situation and hence is felt to bear in some way that remains undefined on his experience of the object.

Here finally I want to emphasize something that may already have become clear: the experience in question *persists in time*, and the presentment of endlessness that, I have been claiming, is central to literalist art and theory is essentially a presentment of endless, or indefinite, *duration*. Once again Smith's account of his night drive is relevant, as well as his remark, "We can't see it [i.e., the jar and, by implication, the cube] in a second, we continue to read it." Morris, too, has stated explicitly, "The experience of the work necessarily exists in time"—though it would make no difference if he had not. The literalist preoccupation with time—more precisely, with the *duration of the experience*—is, I suggest, paradigmatically theatrical: as though theatre confronts the beholder, and thereby isolates him, with the endlessness not just of objecthood but of *time*; or as though the sense which, at bottom, theatre addresses is a sense of temporality, of time both passing and to come, *simultaneously approaching and receding*, as if apprehended in an infinite perspective . . .[19] This preoccupation marks a profound difference between literalist work and modernist painting and sculpture. It is as though one's experience of the latter *has no* duration—not because one *in fact* experiences a picture by Noland or Olitski or a sculpture by David Smith or Caro in no time at all, but because *at every moment the work itself is wholly manifest*. (This is true of sculpture despite the obvious fact that, being three-dimensional, it can be seen from an infinite number of points of view. One's experience of a Caro is not incomplete, and one's conviction as to its quality is not suspended, simply because one has seen it only from where one is standing. Moreover, in the grip of his best work one's view of the sculpture is, so to speak, *eclipsed* by the sculpture itself—which it is plainly meaningless to speak of as only *partly* present.) It is this continuous and entire presentness, amounting, as it were, to the perpetual creation of itself, that one experiences as a kind of *instantaneousness*: as though if only one were infinitely more acute, a single infinitely brief instant would be long enough to see everything, to experience the work in all its depth and fullness, to be forever convinced by it. (Here it is worth noting that the concept of interest implies temporality in the form of continuing attention directed at the object, whereas the concept of conviction does not.) I want to claim that it is by virtue of their presentness and instantaneousness that modernist painting and sculpture defeat theatre. In fact, I am tempted far beyond my knowledge to suggest that, faced with the need to defeat theatre, it is above all to the condition of painting and sculpture—the condition, that is, of existing in, indeed of secreting or constituting, a continuous and perpetual *present*—that the other contemporary modernist arts, most notably poetry and music, aspire.[20]

VIII

This essay will be read as an attack on certain artists (and critics) and as a defense of others. And of course it is true that the desire to distinguish between what is to me the authentic art of our time and other work, which, whatever the dedication, passion, and intelligence of its creators, seems to me to share certain characteristics associated here with the concepts of literalism and theatre, has largely motivated what I have written. In these last sentences, however, I want to call attention to the utter pervasiveness—the virtual universality—of the sensibility or mode of being that I have characterized as corrupted or perverted by theatre. We are all literalists most or all of our lives. Presentness is grace.

NOTES

1. This was said by Judd in an interview with Bruce Glaser, edited by Lucy R. Lippard and published as "Questions to Stella and Judd," *Art News*, Vol. LXV, No. 5, September 1966. The remarks attributed in the present essay to Judd and Morris have been taken from this interview, from Judd's essay "Specific Objects," *Art Yearbook*, No. 8, 1965, or from Robert Morris's essays, "Notes on Sculpture" and "Notes on Sculpture, Part 2," published in *Artforum*, Vol. IV, No. 6, February 1966, and Vol. 5, No. 2, October 1966, respectively. (I have also taken one remark by Morris from the catalogue to the exhibition "Eight Sculptors: the Ambiguous Image," held at the Walker Art Center, October–December 1966.) I should add that in laying out what seems to me the position Judd and Morris hold in common I have ignored various differences between them, and have used certain remarks in contexts for which they may not have been intended. Moreover, I have not always indicated which of them actually said or wrote a particular phrase; the alternative would have been to litter the text with footnotes.
2. "Shape as Form: Frank Stella's New Paintings," *Artforum*, Vol. V, No. 3, November 1966; "Jules Olitski," the catalogue introduction to an exhibition of his work at the Corcoran Gallery, Washington, D.C., April–June, 1967; and "Ronald Davis: Surface and Illusion," *Artforum*, Vol. V, No. 8, April 1967.
3. Published in the catalogue to the Los Angeles County Museum of Art's exhibition, "American Sculpture of the Sixties." The verb "project" as I have just used it is taken from Greenberg's statement, "The ostensible aim of the Minimalists is to 'project' objects and ensembles of objects that are just nudgeable into art."
4. "After Abstract Expressionism," *Art International*, Vol. VI, No. 8, October

25, 1962, p. 30. The passage from which this has been taken reads as follows:

Under the testing of modernism more and more of the conventions of the art of painting have shown themselves to be dispensable, unessential. But now it has been established, it would seem, that the irreducible essence of pictorial art consists in but two constitutive conventions or norms: flatness and the delimitation of flatness; and that the observance of merely these two norms is enough to create an object that can be experienced as a picture: thus a stretched or tacked-up canvas already exists as a picture—though not necessarily as a *successful* one.

In its broad outline this is undoubtedly correct. There are, however, certain qualifications that can be made.

To begin with, it is not quite enough to say that a bare canvas tacked to a wall is not "necessarily" a successful picture; it would, I think, be less of an exaggeration to say that it is not *conceivably* one. It may be countered that future circumstances might be such as to *make* it a successful painting; but I would argue that, for that to happen, the enterprise of painting would have to change so drastically that nothing more than the name would remain. (It would require a far greater change than that that painting has undergone from Manet to Noland, Olitski, and Stella!) Moreover, seeing something as a painting in the sense that one sees the tacked-up canvas as a painting, and being convinced that a particular work can stand comparison with the painting of the past whose quality is not in doubt, are altogether different experiences: it is, I want to say, as though unless something compels conviction as to its quality it is no more than trivially or nominally a painting. This suggests that flatness and the delimitation of flatness ought not to be thought of as the "irreducible essence of pictorial art" but rather as something like the *minimal conditions for something's being seen as a painting*; and that the crucial question is not what these minimal and, so to speak, timeless conditions are, but rather what, at a given moment, is capable of compelling conviction, of succeeding as painting. This is not to say that painting *has no* essence; it *is* to claim that that essence—i.e., that which compels conviction—is largely determined by, and therefore changes continually in response to, the vital work of the recent past. The essence of painting is not something irreducible. Rather, the task of the modernist painter is to discover those conventions that, at a given moment, *alone* are capable of establishing his work's identity as painting.

Greenberg approaches this position when he adds, "As it seems to me, Newman, Rothko, and Still have swung the self-criticism of modernist painting in a new direction simply by continuing it in its old one. The question now asked through their art is no longer what constitutes art, or the art of painting, as such, but what irreducibly constitutes *good* art as such. Or rather, what is the ultimate source of value or quality in art?" But I would argue that what modernism has meant is that the two questions —What constitutes the art of painting? And what constitutes *good* painting? —are no longer separable; the first disappears, or increasingly tends to disappear, into the second. (I am, of course, taking issue here with the version of modernism put forward in my *Three American Painters*.)

For more on the nature of essence and convention in the modernist arts see my essays on Stella and Olitski mentioned above, as well as Stanley Cavell, "Music Discomposed," and "Rejoinders" to critics of that essay, to be published as part of a symposium by the University of Pittsburgh Press in a volume entitled *Art, Mind and Religion*. Cavell's pieces also appear in *Must We Mean What We Say?*, a book of his essays published by Scribner's in 1969 and reprinted by Cambridge University Press in 1976.

5. Quoted by Morris as the epigraph to his "Notes on Sculpture, Part 2."

6. Except for the Morris epigraph already quoted, all statements by Tony Smith have been taken from Samuel Wagstaff, Jr.'s, "Talking to Tony Smith," *Artforum*, Vol. V, No. 4, December 1966.

7. In the Spring 1966 catalogue to the Primary Structures exhibition at the Jewish Museum, Bladen wrote, "How do you make the inside the outside?" and Grosvenor, "I don't want my work to be thought of as 'large sculpture,' they are ideas that operate in the space between floor and ceiling." The relevance of these statements to what I have adduced as evidence for the theatricality of literalist theory and practice seems obvious.

8. It is theatricality, too, that links all these artists to other figures as disparate as Kaprow, Cornell, Rauschenberg, Oldenburg, Flavin, Smithson, Kienholz, Segal, Samaras, Christo, Kusama . . . the list could go on indefinitely.

9. The concept of a room is, mostly clandestinely, important to literalist art and theory. In fact, it can often be substituted for the word "space" in the latter: something is said to be in my space if it is in the same *room* with me (and if it is placed so that I can hardly fail to notice it).

10. Stanley Cavell has remarked in seminar that for Kant in the *Critique of Judgment* a work of art is not an object. I will take this opportunity to acknowledge the fact that without numerous conversations with Cavell during the past few years, and without what I have learned from him in courses and seminars, the present essay—and not it alone—would have been inconceivable. I want also to express my gratitude and indebtedness to the composer John Harbison, who, together with his wife, the violinist Rosemary Harbison, has given me whatever initiation into modern music I have had, both for that initiation and for numerous insights bearing on the subject of this essay.

11. One way of describing this view might be to say that it draws something like a false inference from the fact that the increasingly explicit acknowledgment of the literal character of the support has been central to the development of modernist painting: namely, that literalness *as such* is an artistic value of supreme importance. In "Shape as Form" I argued that this inference is blind to certain vital considerations; and implied that literalness—more precisely, the literalness of the support—is a value only *within* modernist painting, and then only because it has been *made* one by the history of that enterprise.

12. "The New Sculpture," *Art and Culture*, Boston, 1961, p. 144.

13. This and the following remark are taken from Greenberg's essay, "Anthony Caro," *Arts Yearbook*, No. 8, 1965. Caro's first step in this direction, the elimination of the pedestal, seems in retrospect to have been motivated not by the desire to present his work without artificial aids so much as by the need to undermine its objecthood. His work has revealed the extent to which merely putting something on a pedestal *confirms* it in its object-

hood; though merely removing the pedestal does not in itself undermine objecthood, as literalist work proves.

14. See Greenberg's "Anthony Caro" and the last section of my "Shape as Form" for more, though not a great deal more, about color in sculpture.

15. The need to achieve a new relation to the spectator, which Brecht felt and which he discussed time and again in his writings on theatre, was not simply the result of his Marxism. On the contrary, his discovery of Marx seems to have been in part the discovery of what this relation might be like, what it might mean: "When I read Marx's *Capital* I understood my plays. Naturally I want to see this book widely circulated. It wasn't of course that I found I had unconsciously writtten a whole pile of Marxist plays; but this man Marx was the only spectator for my plays I'd ever come across." (*Brecht on Theater*, edited and translated by John Willett, New York, 1964, pp. 23–24.)

16. Exactly how the movies escape theatre is a beautiful question, and there is no doubt but that a phenomenology of the cinema that concentrated on the similarities and differences between it and the theatre—e.g., that in the movies the actors are not physically present, the film itself is projected *away* from us, the screen is not experienced as a kind of object existing, so to speak, in a specific physical relation to us, etc.—would be extremely rewarding. Cavell, again, has called attention, in conversation, to the sort of *remembering* that goes into giving an account of a movie, and more generally to the nature of the difficulties that are involved in giving such an account.

17. This is the view of Susan Sontag, whose various essays, collected in *Against Interpretation*, amount to perhaps the purest—certainly the most egregious —expression of what I have been calling theatrical sensibility in recent criticism. In this sense they are indeed the "case studies for an aesthetic, a theory of my own sensibility" that she takes them to be. In a characteristic passage Miss Sontag contends:

Art today is a new kind of instrument, an instrument for modifying consciousness and organizing new modes of sensibility. And the means for practicing art have been radically extended. . . . Painters no longer feel themselves confined to canvas and paint, but employ hair, photographs, wax, sand, bicycle tires, their own toothbrushes, and socks. . . . All kinds of conventionally accepted boundaries have thereby been challenged: not just the one between the "scientific" and the "literary-artistic" cultures, or the one between "art" and "non-art"; but also many established distinctions within the world of culture itself—that between form and content, the frivolous and the serious, and (a favorite of literary intellectuals) "high" and "low" culture. (Pp. 296–97)

The truth is that the distinction between the frivolous and the serious becomes more urgent, even absolute, every day, and the enterprises of the modernist arts more purely motivated by the felt need to perpetuate the standards and values of the high art of the past.

18. That is, the *actual* number of such units in a given piece is felt to be arbitrary, and the piece itself—despite the literalist preoccupation with wholistic forms—is seen as a fragment of, or cut into, something infinitely

larger. This is one of the most important differences beween literalist work and modernist painting, which has made itself responsible for its physical limits as never before. Noland's and Olitski's paintings are two obvious, and different, cases in point. It is in this connection, too, that the importance of the painted bands around the bottom and the top of Olitski's sculpture, *Bunga*, becomes clear.

19. The connection between spatial recession and some such experience of temporality—almost as if the first were a kind of natural metaphor for the second—is present in much Surrealist painting (e.g., De Chirico, Dali, Tanguy, Magritte . . .). Moreover, temporality—manifested, for example, as expectation, dread, anxiety, presentiment, memory, nostalgia, stasis—is often the explicit subject of their paintings. There is, in fact, a deep affinity between literalists and Surrealist sensibility (at any rate, as the latter makes itself felt in the work of the above painters), which ought to be noted. Both employ imagery that is at once wholistic and, in a sense, fragmentary, incomplete; both resort to a similar anthropomorphizing of objects or conglomerations of objects (in Surrealism the use of dolls and mannikins makes this explicit); both are capable of achieving remarkable effects of "presence"; and both tend to deploy and isolate objects and persons in *situations*—the closed room and the abandoned artificial landscape are as important to Surrealism as to literalism. (Tony Smith, it will be recalled, described the airstrips, etc., as "Surrealist landscapes.") This affinity can be summed up by saying that Surrealist sensibility, as manifested in the work of certain artists, and literalist sensibility are both *theatrical*. I do not wish, however, to be understood as saying that because they are theatrical, all Surrealist works that share the above characteristics fail as art; a conspicuous example of major work that can be described as theatrical is Giacometti's Surrealist sculpture. On the other hand, it is perhaps not without significance that Smith's supreme example of a Surrealist landscape was the parade ground at Nuremberg.

20. What this means in each art will naturally be different. For example, music's situation is especially difficult in that music shares with theatre the convention, if I may call it that, of duration—a convention that, I am suggesting, has itself become increasingly theatrical. Besides, the physical circumstances of a concert closely resemble those of a theatrical performance. It may have been the desire for something like presentness that, at least to some extent, led Brecht to advocate a nonillusionistic theatre, in which for example the stage lighting would be visible to the audience, in which the actors would not identify with the characters they play but rather would show them forth, and in which temporality itself would be presented in a new way:

Just as the actor no longer has to persuade the audience that it is the author's character and not himself that is standing on the stage, so also he need not pretend that the events taking place on the stage have never been rehearsed, and are now happening for the first and only time. Schiller's distinction is no longer valid: that the rhapsodist has to treat his material as wholly in the past: the mime his, as wholly here and now. It should be apparent all through his performance that 'even at the start and in the middle he knows how it ends' and he must 'thus maintain a calm independence throughout.' He narrates the story of his character by vivid portrayal, always knowing more than it does and treating 'now' and 'here' not as a pretence made possible by the rules of the game but as something to be distinguished from yesterday and some other place, so as to make visible the knotting together of the events. (P. 194)

But just as the exposed lighting Brecht advocates has become merely another kind of theatrical convention (one, moreover, that often plays an important role in the presentation of literalist work, as the installation view of Judd's six-cube piece in the Dwan Gallery shows), it is not clear whether the handling of time Brecht calls for is tantamount to authentic presentness, or merely to another kind of *presence*—i.e., to the presentment of time itself as though it were some sort of literalist object. In poetry the need for presentness manifests itself in the lyric poem; this is a subject that requires its own treatment.

For discussions of theatre relevant to this essay see Cavell's essay on Beckett's *End-Game*, "Ending the Waiting Game," and "The Avoidance of Love: A Reading of King Lear," in *Must We Mean What We Say?*

III. EXPRESSION AND COMMUNICATION

Introduction

One of the more tantalizing ideas in aesthetics since the beginning of the Romantic period has been the notion that art is, or is like, a language. Although it holds a continual fascination for philosophers, this analogy has been merely tantalizing because neither art nor language has yielded to philosophical analysis to a very satisfactory extent. An analogy in which neither term is well enough understood to cast light on the other term is likely to remain suggestive rather than truly fruitful.

The philosophical tradition does contain one lasting monument to the art/language analogy: the expression theory of art, most impressively formulated by Benedetto Croce, R. G. Collingwood, and John Dewey. The expression theory has recently been resurrected from the disrepute into which it had been cast for several decades, and is being reexamined by contemporaary philosophers. This reexamination is proceeding side by side with the exploration of various other ways of conceiving art as expression and communication that make use of the results of our century's deep absorption with language as the primary phenomenon of human life.

The essays here begin with O. K. Bouwsma's classic study of the expression theory of art. Using the method of ordinary language philosophy, Bouwsma remains true to its most basic conviction: that no philosophical position can be easily dismissed as "linguistically confused," and that the confrontation with a philosophical theory is not achieved until one locates the strands of ordinary language which make that philosophical theory seem plausible and natural. In the best tradition of philosophical dialectics, Bouwsma's "diagnostic" method attempts to capture the truth that lies in the original theory, which is in the process "dissolved," a term which has less the connotation of "eliminated" than of "aufgehoben."

241

The remaining two essays apply to a discussion of art the insights gleaned from two modern approaches to language. Leonard B. Meyer discusses music in terms of information theory, in an essay that prefigures what is today known as the semiotic approach to art. Marcia Eaton discusses the interpretation of literary works in terms of J. L. Austin's theory of speech acts, which is proving to have a substantial influence on contemporary literary criticism, judging by the degree to which its terminology has been adapted.

For recent work on the expression theory, Sircello (1) is particularly interesting; see also Benson, Berndtson, E. Casey (1), Garvin, Hospers (1), Tilghman (2), Tormey (2, 4), and Tomas (2). For further applications of speech act theory to the philosophy of art, see particularly Fish and B. Johnson (2); also Ohmann, M. Pratt, Searle (1), B. Smith (1), and Traugott. Another area of interaction between the philosophy of art and the philosophy of language is the topic of metaphor. Metaphor is an intrinsically interesting topic, but of late the idea has also been growing among philosophers that the structure and operation of metaphor may provide a microcosm of the structure and operation of works of art, that works of art might be understood as metaphors "writ large." On the analysis of metaphor, see Beardsley (4), Berggren, Binkley (1), Black, Booth (1), Charlton (2), T. Cohen (2, 4, 5), Davidson, Eaton (3), Goodman (1), Harries (2), Hester, Khatchadourian (5), MacCormac, Mackie, de Man (3), Manns (1), Mew, Sheldon, Sparshott (1), Ushenko (1), and Welsh (2).

The Expression Theory of Art

O. K. Bouwsma

The expression theory of art is, I suppose, the most commonly held of all theories of art. Yet no statement of it seems to satisfy many of those who expound it. And some of us find all statements of it baffling. I propose in what follows to examine it carefully. In order to do this, I want first of all to state the question which gives rise to the theory and then to follow the lead of that question in providing an answer. I am eager to do this without using the language of the expression theory. I intend then to examine the language of that theory in order to discover whether it may reasonably be interpreted to mean what is stated in my answer. In this way I expect to indicate an important ambiguity in the use of the word "expression," but more emphatically to expose confusions in the use of the word "emotion." This then may explain the bafflement.

I

And now I should like to describe the sort of situation out of which by devious turnings the phrase "expression of emotion" may be conceived to arise.

Imagine then two friends who attend a concert together. They go together untroubled. On the way they talk about two girls, about communism and pie on earth, and about a silly joke they once laughed at and now confess to each other that they never understood. They were indeed untroubled, and so they entered the hall. The music begins, the piece ends, the applause intervenes, and the music begins again. Then comes the intermission and time for small talk. Octave, a naive fellow, who loves music, spoke first. "It was lovely, wasn't it? Very sad music, though." Verbo, for that was the other's name, replied: "Yes, it was very sad." But the moment he said this he became uncomfortable. He fidgeted in his seat, looked askance at his

243

friend, but said no more aloud. He blinked, he knitted his brows, and he muttered to himself. "Sad music, indeed! Sad? Sad music?" Then he looked gloomy and shook his head. Just before the conductor returned, he was muttering to himself, "Sad music, crybaby, weeping willows, tear urns, sad grandma, sad, your grandmother!" He was quite upset and horribly confused. Fortunately, about this time the conductor returned and the music began. Verbo was upset but he was a good listener, and he was soon reconciled. Several times he perked up with "There it is again," but music calms, and he listened to the end. The two friends walked home together but their conversation was slow now and troubled. Verbo found no delight in two girls, in pie on earth, or in old jokes. There was a sliver in his happiness. At the corner as he parted with Octave, he looked into the sky, "Twinkling stars, my eye! Sad music, my ear!" and he smiled uncomfortably. He was miserable. And Octave went home, worried about his friend.

So Verbo went home and went to bed. To sleep? No, he couldn't sleep. After four turns on his pillow, he got up, put a record on the phonograph, and hoped. It didn't help. The sentence "Sad, isn't it?" like an imp, sat smiling in the loudspeaker. He shut off the phonograph and paced the floor. He fell asleep, finally, scribbling away at his table, like any other philosopher.

This then is how I should like to consider the use of the phrase "expression of emotion." It may be thought of as arising out of such situations as that I have just described. The use of emotional terms—sad, gay, joyous, calm, restless, hopeful, playful, etc.—in describing music, poems, pictures, etc., is indeed common. So long as such descriptions are accepted and understood in innocence, there will be, of course, no puzzle. But nearly everyone can understand the motives of Verbo's question "How can music be sad?" and of his impulsive "It can't, of course."

Let us now consider two ways in which one may safely escape the expression theory.

Imagine Verbo at his desk, writing. This is what he now writes and this gives him temporary relief. "Every time I hear that music I hear that it's sad. Yet I persist in denying it. I say that it cannot be sad. And now what if I were wrong? If every day I met a frog, and the frog said to me that he was a prince, and that there were crown jewels in his head ('wears yet a precious jewel in his head'), no doubt I should begin by calling him a liar. But the more I'd consider this the more troubled I should be. If I could only believe him, and then treat him like a prince, I'd feel so much better. But perhaps *this* would be more like the case of this music: Suppose I met the frog and every day he said to me, 'I can talk,' and then went on talking and asked me, 'Can I talk?' then what would I do? And that's very much how it is with the music. I hear the music, and there it is again, sad, weeping. It's silly to deny this. See now, how it is? There's a little prince, the soul of a prince, in the frog, and so there's the soul in this music, a princess perhaps. See then how rude I was denying this princess her weeping. Why shouldn't music have a soul too? Why this prejudice in favor of lungs and livers? And it occurs to me that this is precisely how people have talked about music and poems. Art lives, doesn't it? And how did Milton describe a good book? Didn't Shelley pour out his soul? And isn't there soul and spirit in the music? I remember now that the poet Yeats recommended some such thing. There are spirits; the air is full of them. They haunt music, cry in it. They dance in poems, and laugh. Panpsychism for the habitation of all delicacies! So this is how it is, and there is neither joke nor puzzle in this sad music. There's a sad soul in it."

And then it was that Verbo fell asleep. His resistance to the music had melted away as soon as he gave up his curious prejudice in favor of animal bodies, as soon as he saw that chords and tones, like rhymes and rhythms, may sigh and shed invisible tears. Tears without tear glands—oh, I know the vulgar habit! But surely tones may weep. Consider now how reasonable all this is. Verbo is suddenly surprised to discover something which he has always known; namely, that music is sad. And the discovery startles him. Why? Because in connection with this, he thinks of his sister Sandra (Cassie to all who saw her cry). And he knows what her being sad is like. She sobs, she wipes her eyes, and she tells her troubles. Cassie has a soul, of course. So Cassie is sad and the music is sad. So the question for Verbo is, How can the music be like Cassie? and he gives the answer: "Why shouldn't there be a soul of the music, that flits in and flits out (People die too!) and inhabits a sonata for a half-hour? Or why shouldn't there be a whole troupe of them? 'The music is sad' is just like 'Cassie is sad,' after all. And Octave who was not disturbed was quite right for he must have a kind of untroubled belief in spirits. He believes in the frog-prince, in the nymphs in the wood, and in the Psyche of the sonnet."

This then is one way of going to sleep. But there is another one, and it is based upon much the same sort of method. Both accept as the standard meaning for "The music is sad," the meaning of "Cassie is sad." We saw how Verbo came to see that the meaning is the same, and how then it was true in the case of the music. He might however have decided that the meaning certainly was the same, but that as applied to the music it simply made no sense at all, or was plainly false. Souls in sonnets? Don't be silly. There is the story about Parmenides, well known to all readers of Dionoges,[1] which will illustrate the sort of thing I have in mind. According to the story, Parmenides and his finicky friend Zeno once went to a chariot race. The horses and chariots had been whizzing past and the race had been quite exciting. During the third round, at one turn a chariot broke an axle and horse and chariot and rider went through the fence. It was a marvelous exhibition of motion done to a turn at a turn. Parmenides was enjoying himself thoroughly. He clutched at the railing and shouted at the top of his voice, "Go, Buceph! Run!" The race is close. But at about the seventh round, with Buceph now some part of a parasang behind, Parmenides began to consider: "Half the distance in half the time; a quarter of the length of a horse in a quarter of the pace it takes . . ." Suddenly, before the race was half over, Parmenides turned to Zeno. "Zeno," he said, "this is impossible." Zeno, who was ready for his master, retorted, "I quit looking a long time ago." So they left the chariot race, a little embarrassed at their non-existence showing as they walked, but they did not once look back to see how Buceph was doing.

This then is the story about Parmenides. It may be, of course, that this story is not true; it may be one of Dionoges' little jokes. But our concern is not with Parmenides. The point is that it illustrates a certain way of disposing of puzzles. Parmenides has been disciplined to a certain use of such words as "run," "go," "turn," "walk," etc., so that when he is thoughtful and has all his careful wits about him, he never uses those words. He is then fully aware that all forms of motion are impossible. Nevertheless, the eyes are cunning tempters. In any case, as soon as Parmenides reflects, he buries himself in his tight-fitting vocabulary, and shuts out chariots and horses, and Buceph, as well. "Motion is impossible, so what am I doing here? Less than nothing. *N'est pas* is not." This disposition of the puzzle is, of course, open only to very strong men. Not many of those people who believe in the impossibility of motion are capable of leaving a horse race, especially when some fleet favorite is only a few heads behind.

Now something like this was a possibility also for Verbo. When, puzzled as he was, asking "How can that be?" he hit upon the happy solution "Why not?" But he might surely have said, stamping his foot, "It can't be." And in order then to avoid the pain of what can't be, he might have sworn off music altogether. No more concerts, no more records! The more radical decision is in such cases most effective. One can imagine Parmenides, for instance, sitting out the race, with his eyes closed, and every minute blinking and squinting, hoping he'd see nothing. So too Verbo might have continued to listen to music, but before every hearing invigorating his resolution never to say that the music was sad. Success in this latter enterprise is not likely to be successful, and for anyone who has already been puzzled it is almost certainly futile.

We have now noticed two ways in which one may attempt to rid oneself of the puzzle concerning "The music is sad," but incidentally we have also noticed the puzzle. The puzzle is identified with the question, How can music be sad? We have also noticed how easy it is, once having asked the question, to follow it with "Well, it can't." I want now to go on to consider the expression theory in the light of the question, How can it be? In effect, the expression theory is intended to relieve people who are puzzled by music, etc. They listen and they say that the music is sad. They ask, troubled and shaking their heads, How can it be? Then along comes the expression theory. It calms them, saying, "Don't you see that the music expresses sadness and that this is what you mean by its being sad?" The puzzled one may be calmed too, if he isn't careful. In any case, I propose to consider the question "How can it be?" before going on further.

This question, "How can it be?" is apparently then not a question primarily about the music. One listens to the music and hears all that there is to hear. And he is sure that it is sad. Nevertheless, when he notices this and then returns to the music to identify just what is sad in it, he is baffled. If someone, for instance, had said that there is a certain succession of four notes on the flute, in this music, and he now sought to identify them, he could play the music, and when they came along, he would exclaim, "There they are," and that would be just what he aimed at. Or again if someone had said that a certain passage was very painful, and he explained that he meant by this that when it is heard one feels a stinging at one's finger tips, then again one could play the music and wait for the stinging. Neither is it like the question which leaped out of the surprise of the farmer at the birth of his first two-headed calf. He looked, amazed, and exclaimed, "Well, I'll be switched! How can that be?" He bedded the old cow, Janus, tucked in the calf, and went to consult his book. He did not stand muttering, looking at the calf, as Verbo did listening to the record on the phonograph. He took out his great book, *The Cow*, and read the chapter entitled "Two Heads Are Better than One?" He read statistics and something about the incidence of prenatal collusion and decided to keep an eye on collaborators among his herd. And that was all. When now it comes to "The music is sad," there's no such easy relief. What is there to listen for? What statistics are there?

We have noticed before how Verbo settled his difficulty. He did this, but not by examining the music any further. He simply knew that the music was sad, and supplied the invisible tears, the unheard sobs, the soul of the music. If you had asked him to identify the tears, the unheard sobs, the soul of the music, he could have done this. He might have tried, of course, and then he would have been baffled too. But the point is that he tries to think of the sadness of the music in the way in which he thinks of Cassie's sadness. Now we may be ready to explain the predicament, the bafflement. It arises from our trying to understand our use of the sentence "The music is sad" in terms of our uses of other sentences very much like this. So Verbo understands in terms of the sentence "Cassie is sad." One can imagine him saying to himself, "I know what sadness is, of course, having Cassie in the house, so that must be how it is with the music." Happily, as in the case of Parmenides, he thought of only one use, and as with a sharp knife he cut the facts to suit the knife. But suppose now that there are several uses of sentences much like "The music is sad"; what then? Is it like this use or this use or this use? And suppose that sometimes it's like this and at other times like this, and sometimes like both. Suppose further that one is only vaguely aware that this is so, and that one's question "How can that be?" is not stated in such a way as to make this possibility explicit, would it then be any wonder that there is bafflement?

Let us admit then that the use of "The music is sad" is baffling, and that without some exploration, the question "How can that be?" cannot be dealt with. Merely listening to the music will not suffice. We must then explore the uses of other sentences which are or may be similar to this, and we may hope that in this process we may see the expression theory emerge. At any rate, we'll understand what we are about.

II

What now are some of these other types of sentences which might be helpful? Well, here are a few that might serve: "Cassie is sad," "Cassie's dog is sad," "Cassie's book is sad," "Cassie's face is sad." Perhaps, one or the other of these will do.

Though we have already noticed how Verbo came to use "Cassie is sad," I should like to consider that sentence further. Verbo understood this. When, as he remembered so well, the telephone call came and little Cassie answered—she had been waiting for that call—she was hurt. Her voice had broken as she talked, and he knew that the news had been bad. But he did not think she would take it so hard. And when she turned to him and he asked her what the man had said, at first her chin quivered and she didn't speak. Then she moved toward him and fell into his arms, sobbing: "Poor Felicia, poor Felicia!" He stroked her hair and finally, when she was calm, she began to pour out her confidences to him. She loved her cat so; they had been brought up together, had had their milk from the same bottle, and had kept no secrets from each other. And now the veterinary had called to say that she had had another fit. And she burst into tears again. This was some years ago. Cassie is older now.

But this is not the only way in which "Cassie is sad" is used. Verbo had often heard his father and mother remark that it was good that Cassie could cry. They used to quote some grandmother who made a proverb in the family. It went: "Wet pillows are best." She had made this up many years ago when some cousin came to sudden grief. This cousin was just on the verge of planned happiness, when the terrible news came. (Her picture is the third in the album.) She received the news in silence and never spoke of it or referred to it as long as she washed the dishes in her father's house, for, as you may have guessed, she never married. She never cried either. No one ever heard her sniffling in the middle of the night. She expressed no regrets. And she never told cat or mirror anything. Once she asked for a handkerchief, but she said she had a cold. All the family knew what had happened, of course, and everyone was concerned, but there was nothing to do. And so she was in many ways changed. She was drooping, she had no future, and she tried to forget her past. She was not interested. They all referred to her as their sad cousin, and they hoped that she would melt. But she didn't. Yet how can Cassie's cousin be sad if she never cries?

Well, there is a third use of "Cassie is sad." Tonight Cassie, who is eighteen now, quite a young lady, as the neighbors say, goes up to her room with her cat, her big book, and a great bowl of popcorn. She settles into her chair, tells kitty to get down, munches buttery corn, and reads her book. Before very long she is quite absorbed in what she reads and feels pretty bad. Her eyes fill with tears and the words on the page swim in the pool. It's so warm and so sweet and so sad! She would like to read this aloud, it's so wonderful, but she knows how the sadness in her throat would break her words in two. She's so sorry; she's so sad. She raises her eyes, closes them, and revels in a deep-drawn sigh. She takes up a full hand of popcorn and returns to her sadness. She reads on and eats no more corn. If she should sob in corn, she might choke. She does sob once, and quite loud, so that she is startled by it. She doesn't want to be heard sobbing over her book. Five minutes later she lays her book aside, and in a playful mood, twits her cat, pretending she's a little bird. Then, walking like old Mother Hubbard, she goes to the cupboard to get her poor cat a milk.

Cassie is sad, isn't she? Is she? Now that you consider it, she isn't really sad, is she? That cosy chair, that deliberate popcorn, that playing sparrow with her cat, that old Mother Hubbard walk—these are not the manners of a sad girl. She hasn't lost her appetite. Still one can see at once how we come to describe her in this way. Those are not phony tears, and she's as helpless in her sobs and in keeping her voice steady and clear as she was years ago when her dear cat had that fit. And she can, if you are so curious, show you in the book just what made her feel so sad. So you see it is very much like the case in which Cassie was sad. There's an obvious difference, and a similarity too. And now if you balk at this and don't want to say that Cassie in this situation is sad, your objection is intelligible. On the other hand, if Cassie herself laughingly protests, "Oh, yes, I was sad," that will be intelligible too. This then may serve as an illustration of the way in which a puzzle which might become quite serious is fairly easily dealt with. How can Cassie be sad, eating popcorn and playing she's a sparrow?

In order to make this clear, consider Cassie now a grown woman, and an accomplished actress. She now reads that same passage which years ago left her limp as a willow, but her voice is steady and clear, and there are no tears. She understands what she reads and everyone says that she reads it with such feeling—it's so sad!—but there isn't a sign of emotion except for the reading itself, which, as I said, goes along smoothly and controlled even to each breath and syllable. So there are no wet eyes, no drunken voice, and not a sob that isn't in the script. So there. Is she sad? I take it not. The spoken words are not enough. Tears, real tears, a voice that breaks against a word, sighs that happen to one, suffered sobs—when the reading occasions these, then you might say that Cassie was sad. Shall we say, however, that the reading is sad? How can that be? Well, you see, don't you?

Let us now attend to a sentence of a different type: "Cassie's dog is sad." Can a dog be sad? Can a dog hope? Can a dog be disappointed? We know, of course, how a Cartesian would answer. He might very well reply with this question: "Can a locomotive be sad?" Generous, he might allow that a locomotive might look sad, and so give you the benefit of a sad look for your dog. But can a dog be sad? Well, our dog can. Once during the summer when Cassie left her for three weeks, you should have seen her. She wouldn't look at the meatiest bone. She'd hang her head and look up at you as woebegone as a cow. And she'd walk as though her four hearts would break. She didn't cry, of course, and there were no confidences except those touching ones that come by way of petting and snuggling and looking into those wailing eyes. In any case, our dog acted very much like that sad cousin who couldn't cry. She had plenty of reason, much too much, but she kept her wellings-up down. It's clear, in any case, what I mean when I say that our dog was sad. You mustn't expect everything from a sad dog.

So we pass to another type of sentence: "Cassie's book is sad." Well, obviously books don't cry. Books do not remember happier days nor look upon hopes snuffed out. Still, books that are sad must have something to do with sadness, so there must be sadness. We know, of course. Books make people sad. Cassie reads her book and in a few minutes, if she's doing well, she's sad. Not really sad, of course, but there are real tears, and one big sob that almost shook the house. It certainly would be misleading to say that it was imaginary sadness, for the sadness of Cassie isn't imagined by anyone, not even by herself. What she reads, on the other hand, is imaginary. What she reads about never happened. In this respect it's quite different from the case in which she is overwhelmed by the sad news over the telephone. That was not imaginary, and with the tears and sobs there was worry, there was distress. She didn't go twittering about, pretending she was a little bird five minutes after that happened. So a sad book is a book that makes Cassie, for instance, sad. You ask, "Well, what are you crying about?" And she says, "Booh, you just read this." It's true that that is how you will find out, but you may certainly anticipate too that it will be a story about a little boy who died, a brave little boy who had stood up bravely for his father, about a new love and reconciliation come almost too late, about a parting of friends and tender feelings that will die, and so on. At any rate, if this is what it is like, you won't be surprised. It's a sad book.

There is one further sentence to consider: "Cassie's face is sad." The same sort of thing might be said about her speaking, about her walk, about her eyes, etc. There is once again an obvious way of dealing with this. What makes you say her face is sad? Anyone can tell. See those tear stains and those swollen eyes. And those curved lines, they all turn down. Her face is like all those sad faces in simple drawings where with six strokes of my neighbor's pencil I give you "Sad-Eye, the Sorry Man." The sad face is easily marked by these few unmistakable signs. Pull a sad face, or droop one, and then study it. What have you done? In any case, I am supposing that there is another use of "Cassie's face is sad," where this simplicity is absent. Oh, yes, there may be certain lines, but if you now ask, "And is this all you mean by Cassie's face being sad?" the answer may very well be "No." Where then is the sadness? Take a long look and tell me. Cassie, hold still. The sadness is written all over her face, and I can't tell you it's here and not there. The more I look, the more I see it. The sadness in this case is not identified with some gross and simple signs. And you are not likely to find it there in some quick glance. Gaze into that face, leisurely, quietly, gently. It's as though it were composed not of what is sad in all sad faces, but rather of what is sad only in each sad face you've ever known. This sad face is sad but when you try now to tell someone what is sad in it, as you might with the drawing I made, you will have nothing to say. But you may say, "Look, and you will see." It is clear, of course, that when Cassie's face is sad, she need not be sad at all. And certainly when you look as you do, you need not be sad.

We have noticed briefly several types of sentences similar to "The music is sad," and we have seen how in respect to several of these the same sort of puzzling might arise that arose in respect to "The music is sad." We have also seen how in respect to these more obvious cases this puzzling is relieved. The puzzling is relieved by discerning the similarity between the offending use and some other use or uses. And now I should like to ask whether the puzzle concerning "The music is sad" might not also be relieved in some similar fashion. Is there not a use of some type of sentence, familiar and relatively untroubled, which is like the use of "The music is sad"?

We have these types of sentences now ready at our disposal: There are two uses of "Cassie is sad," in the first of which she is concerned about her cat, and in the second of which she is cosy and tearful, reading her book. We have "Cassie's cousin is sad," in which Cassie's cousin has real cause but no tears, and "Cassie's dog is sad," in which her dog is tearless as her cousin, but with a difference of course. You could scarcely say that Fido restrained his tears. Then there were the uses of "Cassie's face is sad" and "Cassie's reading is sad." And, of course, there is the use of "Cassie's book is sad." I am going to take for granted that these uses are also intelligible. Now then is the use of "The music is sad" similar to any of these?

I suppose that if the question is stated in this way, one might go on by pointing out a similarity between it and each one of these other types of sentences. But what we must discover is enough similarity, enough to relieve the puzzle. So the question is, To which use is the use of "The music is sad" most similar? Certainly not to "Cassie is sad (about her cat)," nor to "Cassie's cousin is sad," nor to "Cassie's dog is sad."

There are two analogies that one may hopefully seize upon. The first is this: "Cassie is sad, reading a book," is very much like "Verbo is sad, listening to music." And this first is also very much like "Cassie is sad, hearing the news over the telephone." And just as the first involves "The book is sad," so the second involves "The music is sad," and the third involves "The news is sad." Now let us consider the first. Reading the book is one thing, and feeling sad is quite another, and when you say that the book is sad, you mean by this something like this: When Cassie reads, she feels sad about what she reads. Her feeling sad refers to her tears, her sobs, etc. So too listening to the music and hearing it is one thing, and feeling sad is another, and when you say that the music is sad, you mean that while Verbo listens to the music, he feels sad. And shall we add that he feels sad about it? This might, if you like, refer to something like his half-tears, sub-sobs, etc.

Suppose now we try to relieve Verbo in this way. We say: "Don't you see? 'This music is sad' is like 'The book is sad.' You understand that. That's very much like 'The news is sad.' " Will that satisfy him? I think that if he is very sharp, it won't. He may say: "I can see how 'The book is sad' is like 'The news is sad.' But when it comes to these you can easily point out the disturbance, the weeping, but the music —that's different. Still there might be something." What now bothers him?

I think what bothers him may be explained in this way. When you say that a book is sad, or a certain passage in a book is sad, you may mean one or other or both of two things. You may mean what has already been defined by the analogy above. But you may also mean something else. The following illustration may exhibit this. Imagine Cassie, then, in her big chair, reading, and this is the passage she reads:

"I say this in case we become bad," Alyosha went on, "but there's no reason why we should become bad, is there, boys? Let us be, first and above all, kind, then honest, and let us never forget each other! I say that again. I give you my word, for my part, that I'll never forget one of you. Every face looking at me now I shall remember even for thirty years. Just now Kolya said to Kartashov that he did not care to know whether he exists or not. But I cannot forget that Kartashov exists and that he is blushing now as he did when he discovered the founders of Troy, but is looking at me with his jolly, kind, dear little eyes. Boys, my dear boys, let us all be generous and brave like Ilusha, clever, brave and generous like Kolya (though he will be ever so much cleverer when he grows up), and let us all be as modest, as clever and sweet as Kartashov. But why am I talking about those two! You are all dear to me, boys, from this day forth I have a place in my heart for you all, and I beg you to keep a place in your hearts for me! Well, and who has united us in this kind, good feeling which we shall remember, and intend to re-member all our lives? Who, if not Ilusha, the good boy, the dear boy, precious to us for ever! Let us never forget him. May his memory live for ever in our hearts from this time forth."

Cassie reads this and Cassie cries. Let us call this Cassie's sadness. But is there now any other emotion, any other sadness, present? Well, there may very well be. There may be the Alyosha emotion. Whether that is present, however, depends upon how the passage in question is read. It may be read in such a way, that though Cassie understands all she reads, and so knows about the Alyosha emotion, yet she will miss it. This will be the case if she cries through the reading of it. If she reads the passage well, controlled, clear, unfalteringly, with feel-ing, as we say, which does not mean with crying, then the Alyosha emotion will be present. Otherwise only signs of it will be present. Anyone who has tried to read such a passage well, and who has sometimes failed and sometimes succeeded, will understand what I have in mind. Now then we have distinguished the Cassie emotion and the Alyosha emotion. They may be present together, but only, I think, when the Cassie emotion is relatively weak. And so when someone says that the passage in question is sad, then in order to understand we must ask, Is it sad in the Cassie emotion or is it sad in the Alyosha emotion?

And now we are prepared again to examine the analogy: "The music is sad" is like "The book is sad," where it is sad with the Alyosha emotion. This now eliminates the messiness of tears. What we mean by Alyosha's emotion involves no tears, just as the sadness of the music involves no tears. And this now may remind us of Cassie reading the passage, cool, collected, reading with feeling. But more to the point it suggests the sentence "Cassie's face is sad." For see, when the music is sad, there are no tears, and when the passage is read, well read, there are no tears. And so when I look into this face and find it sad, there are no tears. The sadness in all these cases may be unmistakable, and yet in none of these is there anything to which I might now draw your attention, and say, "That's how I recognize it as sad." Even in the case of the reading, it isn't the sentences, it isn't the subject, that make it sad. The sadness is in the reading. Like a musical score, it too may be played without feeling. And it isn't now as though you both read and have these feelings. There is nothing but the reading, and the feeling is nothing apart from this. Read the passage with and without feeling, and see that the difference consists in a difference in the reading. What baffles in these cases is that when you use the word "sadness" and the phrase "with feeling," you are certain to anticipate sadness and feeling in the ordinary sense. But if the sadness is in the sounds you make, reading or playing, and in the face, once you are forewarned you need no longer anticipate anything else. There is sadness which is heard and sadness which is seen.

This then is my result. "The music is sad" is like "The book is sad," where "The book is sad" is like "The face is sad." But "The music is sad" is sometimes also like "The book is sad," where "The book is sad" is like "The news is sad." If exhibiting these analogies is to be helpful, then, of course, this depends on the intelligibility of such sentences as "The book is sad," "The face is sad," "The news is sad," etc.

III

So far I have tried to do two things. I have tried to state the problem to which the expression theory is addressed, and then I have gone on to work at the solution of that problem in the way in which this statement of the problem itself suggests that it be worked out. In doing this I have sought deliberately to avoid the language of the expression theory.

Here then is the phrase to be studied. The expression theory maintains: "The music is sad" means "The music is the expression of sadness or of a certain sadness." The crucial word is the word "expression." There are now at least two contexts which determine the use of that word, one is the language of emotion, and the other is the language of or about language.

Let us consider first the use of the word "expression" in the language of emotion. In the discussion of the types of sentences above, it will be remembered that Cassie's cousin is sad, but doesn't cry. She does not "express" her emotion. Cassie, on the other hand, carries on, crying, sobbing, and confiding in everyone. She "expresses" her emotion, and the expression of her emotion is tears, noises, talk. That talk is all about her cat, remember. When she reads her book, she carries on in much the same way. In this latter case, there was some question as to whether there was really any emotion. She was so sad, remember, and ate popcorn. But in terms of what we just now said, whether there is emotion or not, there certainly is "expression" of emotion. These tears are just as wet as other tears, and her sobs are just as wet too. So in both cases there is expression of emotion, and in the first case there is emotion, thick as you please, but in the second case, it's not that thick. It appears, then, that you might find it quite natural to say that there is expression of emotion but no emotion, much as you might say that there was the thought of an elephant, but no elephant. This may not seem so strange, however, if we reflect that as in the case of Cassie's cousin, there may be emotion, but no or very little expression of emotion.

In order to probe the further roots of the uses of this phrase, it may be useful to notice that the language of emotion is dominantly the language of water. So many of our associations with the word "emotion" are liquid. See then: Emotions well up. Children and young girls bubble over. There are springs of emotion. A sad person is a deep well. Emotions come in waves; they are like the tides; they ebb and flow. There are floods and "seas of passion." Some people gush; some are turbulent. Anger boils. A man blows up like a boiler. Sorrow overwhelms. The dear girl froze. We all know the theory of humors. In any case, it is easy enough, in this way, to think of a human being as like a reservoir and an ever-flowing pool and stream of emotions. All flow on toward a dam, which may be raised or lowered, and over and through which there is a constant trickle. Behind the dam are many currents, hot, cold, lukewarm, swift, slow, steady, rippling, smooth. And there are many colors. Perhaps we should say that currents are never exhausted and do not altogether trickle away. Emotions, like our thoughts, are funded, ready to be tapped, to be rippled, to be disturbed.

Let us see how the term "expression" fits into this figure. How was it with Cassie's cousin? Well, once there was a clear, smooth-flowing current of affection, and it flowed, trickle, trickle, over the dam in happy anticipation and a chestful of hope's kitchen and linen showers. And suddenly a planet falls, in the form of a letter, into that deep and flowing pool. Commotion follows, waves leap, eddies swirl. The current rushes on to the dam. And what happens? The dam rises.

Cassie's cousin resists, bites her lip, intensifies her fist. She keeps the current back. Her grief is impounded. She does not "express" her emotion. And what happened to Cassie, when she felt so bad about the cat? That's easy. Then too there was a disturbance. The current came down, splashed over the dam which did not rise at all, and it flowed away in a hurly-burly of "Oh! It's awful! My poor kitty!" Cassie let herself go. She "expressed" her emotion.

The use of the word "expression" in the light of this figure is, I take it, clear enough. And the use of the word in this way describes a familiar difference in the way in which good news and bad news may affect us. And now we may ask, And is it something like this that people have in mind when they say that art is the expression of emotion? Certainly something like this, at least part of the time. Consider how Wordsworth wrote about poetry: "Poetry is the spontaneous overflow of powerful emotions." Overflow! This suggests the pool and the dam and the "powerful" current. An emotion, lying quiet, suddenly gets going and goes over. There is spontaneity, of course. No planet falls and no cat is sick. The emotion is unprovoked. There is also the common view that artists are people who are more emotional than other people. They are temperamental. This once again suggests the idea that they have particular need of some overflow. Poetry is a little like blowing off steam. Write poetry or explode!

This isn't all that Wordsworth said about poetry. In the same context he said: "Poetry is emotion recollected in tranquillity." Again this suggests a hiding place of emotion, a place where past heartaches are stored, and may be taken up again, "recollected." We store ideas. We also put away emotions. So we have the pool as we had the pool before in describing Cassie's cousin and Cassie. But now we have something else, "the spontaneous overflow" and the "recollection in tranquillity."

Let us consider this for a moment, again in order to notice the use of the word "expression." Cassie hears bad news and cries. She "expresses" her emotion. The emotion is aroused and out it flows. What now happens in the case of the poet? Ostensibly in his case too emotions are aroused, but they do not flow out. Poets do not cry enough. Emotions are stored up, blocked. Emotions accumulate. And what happens now? Well, one of two things may happen. Emotions may quite suddenly leap up like spray, and find a way out, or again a poet may dip into the pool with his word dipper, and then dip them out. It's as though the emotions come over the dam in little boats (the poems) and the little boats may be used over and over again to carry over new surges. And this too may be described in this way: The poet "expresses" his emotion. Cassie cries. The real incident is sufficient. The poet does not cry. The real incident is not sufficient. He's got to make poems in order to cry. All men must cry. This may seem a bit fantastic, but this sort of fantasy is common in explaining something as old, for instance, as Aristotle's use of the word "catharsis."

The analogy which we have tried to exhibit now is this one: As Cassie "expresses" her emotion at hearing the news, so the poet or reader "expresses" his emotion at reading the poem. The news and the poem arouse or evoke the respective emotions. Now most people who expound the expression theory are not content with this analogy. They say that Cassie merely vents or discharges her emotion. This is not "expression" of emotion. Cassie merely gets rid of her emotion. And what does the poem do? Perhaps in terms of our figure we may say: It ripples it, blows a gentle wind over it, like a bird skimming the water. At any rate the emotion stays. And so the theory seeks a more suitable analogy and finds it conveniently in the language about language.

I should like first to notice certain distinctions which lead to this shift from the first to the second analogy. In the first place poems and music are quite different from the occasions that make Cassie and Cassie's cousin so sad. Tones on a piano and a faithless lover or a dying cat are not much alike, and this is enough to disturb the analogy. But there is also an unmistakable difference in the use of the word "emotion" in the two cases. An "emotion recollected in tranquillity" is, after all, as I suggested before, more like a ripple than like a tempest. It is, accordingly, these distinctions that determine the shift. It may be useful to notice that the general form of the first analogy is retained in the second. For the poem and the music are still conceived as "arousing," as "evoking," the emotion.

The new analogy accordingly is this one: Music "expresses" sadness (art expresses emotion) as sentences "express" ideas. And now, I think, it is easy to see why this analogy should have been seized upon. In the first place so much of art involves symbols, sentences themselves, and representations. There are horses in pictures. It is quite easy then to fall into regarding art as symbolic; that is, as like sentences. And now just as sentences symbolize ideas and serve to evoke them as distinguished from real things, of which ideas are more like shadows, so too music and poems serve to evoke emotions of a peculiar sort, emotions which are like the shadows of real emotions. So this analogy is certainly an improvement. Art is after all an artifice, like sentences, and the emotions involved are related to the real things in much the way that ideas are to real things, faint copies. All this fits in very well with the idea that art is like a dream, a substitute of real life, a vicarious more of what you cannot have, a shadowland.

And now how does this analogy succeed?

Before answering this question, I should like to notice the use of the words "evoking" and "arousing." Sentences "evoke" ideas. As one spieler I know says: "When I read a sentence, an idea pops into my head." Pops! This is something like what, according to the analogy, is meant by sentences "expressing" ideas. I am not interested in criticizing this at this point. I wish only to clarify ideas. Pop! Consider the sentence "The elephant ate a jumbo peanut." If at the moment when you read this sentence you see in your mind's eye a big elephant nuzzling around a huge peanut, this will illustrate what "evoking" is like. The sentence evokes; the idea pops. There is the sentence and there is this unmistakable seeing in your mind's eye. And if this happened, surely you would have got the idea. What I wish to point out is that it is this view, or some similar view of how sentences work, that underlies this present analogy. They "evoke." But the word "evoke" has other contexts. It suggests spirits, witchcraft. The spirit of Samuel appearing at the behest of the witch of Endor is an "evocation." Spiritualistic mediums "evoke" the living spirits of the dead. And the point of this association is that the spirits are waiting, in the second or third canto of Dante's *Comedy*, perhaps, to be called. They are in storage like our ideas, like our emotions. And the word "arouse" is like the word "evoke." Whom do you arouse? The sleeper. And so, sleeping ideas and sleeping emotions lie bedded in that spacious dormitory—hush!—we call the mind. Waiting to be called! And why now have I made a point of this? Because this helps to fill out this analogy by which in particular we are led to use the word "feeling" or "emotion" in the language of the expression theory. The music "evokes," "arouses" feelings.

Now then, do poems and music and pictures evoke emotions as sentences evoke images? I think that they frequently do. Cassie reading her book may be cited as an instance. This seems to me a very common type of experience. It happens at the movies, in reading novels, and even in listening to music. People are moved to tears. If, accordingly, the expression theory were intended merely to describe experience of this sort, I should say, "Very well." In that case there would be no particular puzzle, beyond presenting this analogy clearly. But I, at least, am convinced that this is not all.

The difficulty, then, does not arise concerning experiences of this sort. The puzzle arises and remains most stubbornly where the sadness is dry-eyed. And here the analogy with language seems, at least, to be of no use. Cassie may read the passage with feeling, but without the flicker of an eyelash. And she may listen to sad music as cool and intent as she is gazing at a butterfly. She might say that it was more like watching, fascinated, the pain in a suffering face, herself quite undistressed. Santayana identifies the experience in this way: "Not until I confound the impressions (the music, the sentences) and suffuse the symbols with the emotions they arouse, and find joy and sweetness in the very words I hear, will the expressiveness constitute a beauty."[2] I propose now to study this sentence.

Now notice how curious this is. Once more we have the sentences or the music. And these arouse emotion. This describes Cassie reading her book. So we might expect that Cassie would cry and would sob and so on. But this isn't all. Cassie is confused. Actually she is crying but she thinks the words are crying. She wipes her tears off those words. She sighs but the words heave. The sentence of Santayana suggests that she sees the sentences she reads through her tears and now her tears misserve her much as blue moods or dark glasses do. So Cassie looks through sadness and the sentence is tearful. What a pathetic fallacy! From confusion to suffusion! Are there misplaced emotions? Imagine what this would be like where sentences aroused not emotions but a toothache. And now you confused the toothache with the sentence, and before someone prevented you, you sent the sentence to the dentist.

Nevertheless, Santayana has almost certainly identified an experience that is different from that in which Cassie is sad over her book. We find "joy and sweetness in the very words" we hear. Clearly, too, Santayana has been misled by these words "joy and sweetness." For if there is joy and sweetness, where should these be but where they usually are? Where is joy then and where is sweetness? In the human breast, in the heart ("my heart leaps up when I behold"), in the eye. And if you say this, then indeed there must be some illusion. The sentence is like a mirror that catches and holds what is in the heart. And so artful are poets' sentences that the best readers are the best confused. I want now, however, to suggest that indeed joy and sweetness, and sadness too, are in the very words you hear. But in that case, joy and sweetness must be of the sort that can be in sentences. We must, accordingly, try to figure out what this "joy and sweetness in the very words" is like. For even though, making a mistake, one imagined they were in the words, their being there must make some sense. And Santayana too does not imagine that sentences cry.

Let me return now to the analogy: "The music is sad" is like "The sentence expresses an idea." We saw before how the sentence "The elephant ate a jumbo peanut" might be accompanied by an image and how this was like sentences or music arousing emotions. We want now to see how we might use the phrase "joy and sweetness in the very words." Do we have a meaning for "The idea in the very words you hear." Where is the idea of the elephant eating a jumbo peanut? Suppose we say: "It's in the very words you hear." Have you ever seen, in your mind's eye, that is, an elephant eating a peanut in the very words you hear? A sentence is like a circus tent? I do not suppose that anyone who said that joy and sweetness are in the very words you hear would be likely to say that this was like the way in which you might also see an image in the very sentence which you hear—a bald head in the word "but." I should like in any case to try something different.

I do not intend to abandon the analogy with language yet. Music is expression of emotion as sentences are expression of ideas. But now how do sentences express ideas? We have noticed one way in which sentences do sometimes have meaning. Sentences, however, have been described in many ways. Sentences are like buzzers, like door-bells, like electric switches. Sentences are like mirrors, like maps, like pictures; sentences are like road signs, with arrows pointing the way. And so we might go on to ask, Is music like buzzers, like pictures, like road sign arrows? I do not however intend to do this. It will be noticed that the same analogy by which we have been trying to understand music, art, etc., may serve us also to understand what language is like. The analogy presupposes that we do know something about music, and so turning the analogy to this use may be fruitful. It might show us just how enlightening and how unenlightening the analogy is.

In order to study the analogy between music and the sentence and to try in this way to find out what the sentence is like, I now intend to offer a foolish theory. This may throw into clearer relief what Santayana says. What is understanding a sentence like? Understanding a sentence is speaking the sentence in a certain way. You can tell, listening to yourself talk, that you are understanding the sentence, and so can anyone else who hears you speak. Understanding has its rhythm. So the meaning of the sentence consists in a certain reading of the sentence. If, in this case, a sentence is spoken and not understood by someone, there would be only one thing to do; namely, speak the sentence again. Obviously this account will not do, for there are other ways of clarifying what we mean. Nevertheless, in some cases it may be all that is necessary.

Now notice. If this were what the meaning of a sentence is like, we should see at once what was meant if someone said that the meaning or the idea is in the sentence. For if there is meaning, where could it be but in the sentence, since the sentence is all there is? Of course, it is true that the sentence would have to be spoken and, of course, spoken in some way or other. And with every variation in reading it might then be said to have a different meaning. If anyone asked, "And what does the sentence mean?" expecting you to point to something or to elaborate the matter in gestures or to translate, it would be clear that he quite misunderstood what meaning is like. One might even correct him, saying it is even misleading to say that the meaning is in the sentence, as though it were only a part of the sentence, or tucked away somehow under overlapping syllables. A sentence having meaning in a case like this would be something like a living thing. Here too one might ask, Where is the life in a squirrel and in a geranium? Truly the life is the squirrel and is the geranium, and is no part of either nor tucked away in some hidden fold or tiny vein. And so it is with the sentence, according to our imaginary theory. We might speak of the sentence as like a living thing.

And now let us see whether we have some corresponding use for "The joy and sweetness are in the very words you hear." People do ask about the meaning of poems and even about the meaning of music. Let us first of all say that the meaning is "the joy and sweetness," and the sadness. And where are these? In the very words you hear, and in the music. And now notice that what was admittedly a foolish theory in respect to sentences is not a foolish theory in respect to poems or music. Do you get the poem? Do you get the music? If you do not, pointing, gestures, translations will not help. (Understanding the words is presupposed.) There will be only one thing to do; namely, read the verses again, play the music once more. And what will the joy and sweetness and the sadness be like? They will be like the life in the living thing, not to be distinguished as some one part of the poem or music and not another part, or as some shadow that follows the sounded words or tones. "In the very words you hear," like the squirrel in fur!

I infer now that the analogy between the "joy and sweetness" in words and the meaning in sentences is misleading and is not likely to be helpful. The meaning of sentences is translatable, but the "meaning" of poems, of music, is not. We have seen how this is so. There may, of course, be something in the sounding of all sentences which is analogous to the "joy and sweetness in the very words," but it is not the meaning of those sentences. And now this is an interesting consequence. It makes sense to ask, What does the sentence express? It expresses a meaning, of course, and you may have some way of showing what this is, without using the sentence to do so. But now it makes no sense to ask, What does the poem express? or What does the music express? We may say, if we like, that both are expressive, but we must beware of the analogy with language. And we may prevent the helpless searching in this case, by insisting that they "express" nothing, nothing at all.

And now let us review. My assumption has been that the expression theory is plagued with certain analogies that are not clearly distinguished, and none of which finally is helpful without being misleading. The first analogy is that in terms of which we commonly think of emotions. The second is that in terms of which we think of language, the doorbell view. Besides this there are two different types of experience that arise in connection with art. One of these types may be fairly well described by the analogy with doorbell language. The similarity of our language, however, in respect to both these types of experience, conceals the difference between those two types. Santayana's sentence reveals the agony that follows the recognition of this difference in these types of experience and the attempt to employ the language which describes the one to describe the other. The language requires very interesting translation. My conclusion, accordingly, is this: The analogy drawn from language may be useful in describing one type of experience. It is practically useless in describing the other. Since, then, these two analogies dominate the use of the word "expression," I suggest that, for the sake of clarity and charity, they be abandoned in seeking to describe that "expressiveness" which Santayana says constitutes "a beauty."

If we now abandon these analogies, are we also to abandon the use of the word "expression"? Not unless we please to do so. But we do so at our risk, for these analogies are not easily abandoned. We may, however, fortify our use of this word by considerations such as these. We use the word "expressive" to describe faces. And we use "expressive" in much the same way that we use the phrase "has character." A face that is expressive "has character." But when we now say that a face has character, this may remind us that the letters of the alphabet are characters. Let us suppose for a moment that this is related to "He's a character!" I suppose that he's a character and he has a character do not mean quite the same thing. There are antics in he's a character. Try again: The zigzag line has character and the wavy line has character. Each letter of the alphabet is a character, but also has character. The number tokens, 1 2 3 4 5 6 7 8 9—each has its character. In the same way sounds have character. Let me see whether we can explain this further. You might say that if some dancing master were to arrange a dance for each of the numbers, you might see how a dance for the number one would not do at all for number five. Or again if the numbers were to be dressed in scarves, again a certain color and a certain flimsy material would do for six but would not suit five at all. Now something of the same sort is true of words, and particularly of some. Words have character. I am tempted to say that all these things have their peculiar feel, but this then must be understood on the analogy with touch. If we, for instance, said that all these things have their peculiar feeling, then once again it might be supposed that in connection with them there is a feeling which is aroused by them.

Let your ears and your eyes, perhaps, too, feel these familiar bits of nonsense:

> Hi diddle diddle!
> Fee! fi, fo, fum!
> Intery, mintery.
> Abra ca da bra.

Each has its character. Each is, in this sense, expressive. But to ask now, What is its character or what does it express? is to fall into the pit. You may, of course, experiment to exhibit more clearly just what the character, in each case, is. You may, for instance, contrast the leaping, the stomping, the mincing, the shuffle, with what you get if you change the vowels. Try:

> Ho! doodle doodle!
> Fa, fo, fu, fim!
> Untery, muntery.
> Ay bray cay day bray.

One might also go on to change consonants in order again to exhibit character by giving the words new edges and making their sides steeper or smoothing them down.

I do not intend, in proposing illustrations of this sort, to suggest that art is nonsense and that its character is simple as these syllables are. A face, no doubt may bear the impress, the character, of a life's torment and of its hope and victory. So too words and phrases may come blazing out of the burning past. In art the world is born afresh, but the travail of the artist may have had its beginnings in children's play. My only point is that once the poem is born it has its character as surely as a cry in the night or intery, mintery. And this character is not something that follows it around like a clatter in a man's insides when he reads it. The light of the sun is in the sun, where you see it. So with the character of the poem. Hear the words and do not imagine that in hearing them you gulp a jigger to make yourself foam. Rather suppose that the poem is as hard as marble, ingrained, it may be, with indelible sorrow.

If, accordingly, we now use the sentence "Art is expression," or "Art is expressive," and the use of this sentence is determined by elucidations such as I have just now set out, then, I think that our language may save us from some torture. And this means that we are now prepared to use freely those sentences that the expression theory is commonly inclined to correct. For now, unabashed, we shall say that the music is sad, and we shall not go on to say that this means that the music expresses sadness. For the sadness is to the music rather like the redness to the apple, then it is like the burp to the cider. And above all we shall not, having heard the music or read the poem, ask, What does it express?

IV

And now it's many words ago since we left Verbo and his friend at the corner. Verbo was trying to figure out, you remember, how the music was related to his grandmother. How can music be sad? I suggested then that he was having word trouble, and that it would be necessary to probe his sentences. And so we probed. And now what shall we tell Verbo?

"Verbo," we will say, "the music is sad." And then we will remind him that the geranium is living, and that the sun is light. We will say these things so that he will not look away from the music to discover the sadness of it. Are you looking for the life in the geranium? Are you looking for the light in the sun? As then the life and the light describe the geranium and the sun, so too does sadness describe the music. And then we shall have to go on to tell him about these fearful analogies, and about Santayana's wrestle on the precipice. And about how we cut the ropes! And you may be sure that just as things are going along so well, Verbo will ask, flicking the ashes from his cigarette, "And what about the sadness?"

And now it's time to take the cat out of the bag, for so far all that has been exposed is the bag. The sadness is a quality of what we have already described as the character, the expressive. One piece of music is like and unlike some other pieces of music. These similarities and these differences may be perceived. Now then, we have a class of sad music. But why sad; that is, why use this word? It must be remembered, of course, that the use of this word is not precise. So there may be some pieces of music which are unmistakably sad, and others which shade off in gradations to the point where the question, Is it sad? is not even asked. Suppose we ask our question, Why sad? in respect to the unmistakable cases. Then, perhaps, some such answer as this will do. Sad music has some of the characteristics of people who are sad. It will be slow, not tripping: it will be low, not tinkling. People who are sad move more slowly, and when they speak, they speak softly and low. Associations of this sort may, of course, be multiplied indefinitely. And this now is the kitten in whose interest we made so much fuss about the bag. The kitten has, I think, turned out to be a scrawny little creature, not worth much. But the bag was worth it.

The bag was worth it? What I have in mind is that the identification of music as the expressive, as character, is crucial. That the expressive is sad serves now only to tag the music. It is introspective or, in relation to the music, an aside. It's a judgment that intervenes. Music need not be sad, nor joyous, nor anything else. Aestheticians usually account for this by inventing all sorts of emotions without names, an emotion for every piece of music. Besides, bad music, characterless music, the unexpressive, may be sad in quite the same way that good music may be. This is no objection, of course, to such classifications. I am interested only in clarifying the distinction between our uses of these several sentences.

And now that I have come to see what a thicket of tangle-words I've tried to find my way through, it seems to me that I am echoing such words as years ago I read in Croce, but certainly did not then understand. Perhaps if I read Croce again now I shouldn't understand them either. "Beauty is expression."

NOTES

1. An author of no repute at all, not to be confused with Diogenes.
2. *Sense of Beauty* (1896), p. 149.

Some Remarks on Value and
Greatness in Music

Leonard B. Meyer

As every musician must, I have been concerned with the nature of
value in music and have in moments of impetuous rashness even
asked myself the $64,000 question: What makes music great? In
grappling with these perplexing problems I have changed my mind
many times, testing first this view then that; finding this objection
then another to what I thought at first to be tenable positions. Nor
have I as yet arrived at any fixed opinions or final conclusions.

Indeed, instead of providing positive answers neatly confined to the
area of aesthetics (as I should have preferred), my attempts to
understand the nature of value in music have led to still further
questions as to the nature of value in general and ultimately to the
rarefied realm of metaphysics. Since my ideas on these matters are
still in flux, I shall present neither an explicit theory of value nor a
definitive account of greatness. Rather, in pointing out relationships
and correlations between value in music and value in other areas, I
shall hope to suggest viewpoints and avenues of approach which will
perhaps provide fruitful insights and may later lead to plausible conclusions.

Whatever the difficulties, uncertainties, and hazards may be, the
question "What makes music great?" is one that anyone deeply concerned with his art must attempt at least to answer. And if some
scholars make a point of avoiding such questions altogether as the
positivists do, or throw them into the vast nets of cultural context as
the social scientists have often done, or surreptitiously substitute the
plausibility of technical jargon for basic quesionings as humanists
sometimes do—so much the worse for them. We cannot—nor can
they for all their rationalizations—really escape from the problem of
value.

This is true in two senses. The first is perhaps obvious, yet nonetheless important. We are in fact continually making value judgments both for ourselves and others. As an individual I can listen to and study only a limited number of musical works during my lifetime. I must choose between works, exercising value judgments. As a teacher I decide to use this work for teaching rather than that. And though I may select the work for didactic reasons rather than because I think it is a masterpiece, even as I choose it for this reason I am aware of the distinction between a work which is great in its own terms and one which will serve to illustrate a given point clearly.

The second reason why the problem of value is inescapable for someone concerned with music—or any art for that matter—is that a system or ordering of values is implicit in his account of how and what art communicates. Indeed, as soon as we say it communicates, we introduce values into the discussion. At one time I subscribed to I. A. Richards's statement that "the two pillars upon which a theory of criticism must rest are an account of value and an account of communication."[1] However, it has seemed increasingly clear that these two are as inextricably linked to one another as are means and ends. When you discuss one you are of necessity implying the other. For instance, if your account of musical communication is primarily in terms of the referential and associative states which music can arouse, then your judgments as to value are going to be different from those which would arise out of an account of communication which emphasized the more exclusively intra-musical meanings which I shall call embodied or syntactical. In a sense, then, this paper is an attempt to make explicit the scheme of values implicit in the analysis of musical communication given in *Emotion and Meaning in Music*.[2]

At first it would seem that the problem is not really very difficult. After all there are certain technical criteria for excellence in a piece of music. A good piece of music must have consistency of style: that is, it must employ a unified system of expectations and probabilities; it should possess clarity of basic intent; it should have variety, unity, and all the other categories which are so easy to find after the fact. But these are, I think, only necessary causes. And while they may enable us to distinguish a good or satisfactory piece from a downright bad one, they will not help us very much when we try to discriminate between a pretty good work and a very good one, let alone distinguish the characteristics of greatness.

Indeed the tune "Twinkle, Twinkle, Little Star" possesses style, unity, variety, and so forth. And if we then ask is Bach's B Minor Mass better than "Twinkle, Twinkle"—using *only* these technical categories—we shall, I am afraid, be obliged to answer that they are equally good, adding perhaps, "each in its own way." I shall return to the "each in its own way" argument presently. But for now, it seems to me that, granting listeners who have learned to respond to and understand both works, the statement that these works are equally good is preposterous and false.

Nor are length, size, or complexity *as such* criteria of value, though as we shall see, complexity does have something to do with excellence. Thus some of Brahms's smaller piano pieces are often considered to be better works than, for instance, his Fourth Symphony. And I am sure that each of us can cite instances of this for himself. Perhaps it would be well at this point to turn to particular musical examples to see what we can learn from them.

Because a relatively thorough examination of even two brief pieces would involve a complex and lengthy analysis, I have chosen to discuss, briefly, two fugue subjects: the first by Geminiani, the second by Bach. Since only the themes will be discussed, it should be pointed out that good themes do not necessarily give rise to good total works. And though it is difficult to write a good fugue on a really poor subject, an unprepossessing theme—such as that of Bach's Fugue in C-sharp Minor (W.T.C.,I)—may act as the basis for a very fine work.

Even though it goes against critical canon I intend to treat the themes as entities in their own right, but as themes, not as complete works. For considered in themselves they will serve to raise some of the basic considerations which are involved in value and ultimately in greatness. And these considerations apply with equal force to complete works, even those of the greatest magnitude. In short, reversing the procedure of Plato, who inquired as to the principles of justice in the individual by considering the nature of justice in the State, we shall try to learn something about the value of whole works by considering the nature of value in a small segment.

Here then are the two themes (see page 270). They are certainly not equally good. And at first glance we observe that the Bach theme has more rhythmic and motivic variety, that it covers a larger range, and so forth, than Geminiani's theme. However, there are good themes which lack obvious variety. In any case, it would seem safe to say that variety is a means to an end, not an end in itself.

Looking at these two themes more closely, we see that they are quite similar in their basic melodic structure. Both begin on the fifth degree of the scale, move to the tonic (in the case of the Bach, through the third of the scale), and then skip an octave. This skip

Example 1

creates a structural gap, a sense of incompleteness. We expect that the empty space thus outlined will be filled in, made complete. This melodic incompleteness is complemented by the rhythmic instability of this first musical shape. That is, the first separable musical events in both themes are up-beats which are oriented toward the stability of down-beats.

In a sense the structural gap and the rhythmic up-beats have established musical goals to be reached. We expect the melodic line to descend and ultimately to come to rest on the tonic note, reaching a clear organizing accent in the course of this motion. And so in fact they both do. *But* with crucial differences. The Bach theme moves down slowly with delays and temporary diversions through related harmonic areas. It establishes various levels of melodic activity with various potentials to be realized. Furthermore, these delays are rhythmic as well as melodic (see analysis under Example 1). The Geminiani theme, on the other hand, moves directly—or almost directly—to its goal. The second measure is chromatic and contains a potential for different modes of continuation. Of these the return to the B is certainly the most probable, but only slightly so. However, once the B is reached, the descent to E seems almost inevitable. And when the theme falls to this obvious consequent with neither delay nor diversion, it seems like a blatant platitude, a musical cliché. Nor are there any rhythmic resistances. The initial up-beat perpetuates itself without marked disturbance down to the final note which arrives on the obvious down-beat.

Thus it would seem that in this case at least value has something to do with the activation of a musical impulse having tendencies toward a more or less definite goal and with the temporary resistance or inhibition of these tendencies. The importance of the element of resistance can be made even more apparent if we rewrite the Bach theme in such a way that this element is eliminated.

Example 2

The theme is now as banal as Geminiani's.

From these considerations it follows (1) that a melody or a work which establishes no tendencies, if such can be imagined, will from this point of view (and others are possible) be of no value. Of course, such tendencies need not be powerful at the outset, but may be developed during the course of musical progress. (2) If the most probable goal is reached in the most immediate and direct way, given the stylistic context, the musical event taken in itself will be of little value. And (3) if the goal is never reached or if the tendencies activated become dissipated in the press of overelaborate or irrelevant diversions, then value will tend to be minimal.

The notion that the inhibition of goal-oriented tendencies is related to value is not a new one. Robert Penn Warren writes that "a poem, to be good, must earn itself. It is a motion toward a point of rest, but if it is not a resisted motion, it is a motion of no consequence. For example, a poem which depends upon stock materials and stock responses is simply a toboggan slide, or a fall through space."[3] Dewey's position is quite similar. "Impulsion forever boosted on its forward way would run its course thoughtless, and dead to emotion. . . . The only way it can become aware of its nature and its goal is by obstacles surmounted and means employed."[4]

More recently information theory has developed concepts in which the relationship between resistance and value seems to be implicit. In order to understand how information theory relates to these considerations, it is necessary to examine the nature of goal-tendency processes in more detail.

Musical events take place in a world of stylistic probability. If we hear only a single tone, a great number of different tones could follow it with equal probability. If a sequence of two tones is heard the number of probable consequent tones is somewhat reduced—how much depends upon the tones chosen and the stylistic context—and hence the probability of the remaining alternatives is somewhat increased. As more tones are added and consequently more relationships between tones established, the probabilities of a particular goal become increased. Thus in Bach's theme the probability of any particular tone following the first D is very small, for the number of possible consequents is very large. As the line moves downward through the B-flat and the A, the probabilities of the G become very high and it is the satisfaction of this motion which closes out the first pattern as a musical event. This pattern, after the octave skip, now becomes the unit of motion and becomes the basis for probability estimates on a higher architectonic level. Note that the variety of events in this theme, as well as the delays already noted, make the particular sequence of events seem much less probable than the sequence of events in the Geminiani theme.

Here information theory becomes relevant.[5] It tells us that if a situation is highly organized so that the possible consequents have a high degree of probability, then if the probable occurs, the information communicated by the message (what we have been calling a musical event) is minimal. If, on the other hand, the musical situation is less predictable so that the antecedent-consequent relationship does *not* have a high degree of probability, then the information contained in the musical message will be high. Norbert Wiener has put the matter succinctly: "the more probable the message, the less its information. Clichés, for example, are less illuminating than great poems."[6]

Since resistances, or more generally deviations, are by definition disturbances in the goal-oriented tendencies of a musical impulse, they lower the probability not only of a particular consequent but of the musical event as a whole. In so doing they create or increase information. And it does not seem a rash step to conclude that what creates or increases the information contained in a piece of music increases its value.

(Of course in either linguistic or musical communication a completely random series of stimuli will in all likelihood communicate nothing. For language and music depend upon the existence of an ordered probability system, a stochastic process, which serves to make the several stimuli or events mutually relevant to one another. Thus the probability of any particular musical event depends in part upon the probabilistic character of the style employed. Randomness of choice is limited by the fact of musical style.)

The concepts of information theory suggest that the notion of resistance can be generalized by relating it through probability to uncertainty. For the lower the probability that any particular sequence of events will take place—that is, the lower the probability that the total message will be any particular one—the greater the uncertainty as to what the events and the message will actually be. And also the greater the information contained in the total event. Thus greater uncertainty and greater information go hand in hand.[7]

The relationship between resistance and uncertainty is not difficult to discover. Whenever a tendency is inhibited—or more generally, when deviation takes place—slight though perhaps unconscious uncertainty is experienced. What seemed perhaps so probable that alternative consequents were not considered, now seems less so. For the mind, attempting to account for and understand the import of the deviation, is made aware of the possibility of less probable, alternative consequents.

A distinction must be made between desirable and undesirable uncertainty. Desirable uncertainty is that which arises as a result of the structured probabilities of a musical style. Information is a function of such uncertainty. Undesirable uncertainty arises when the probabilities are not known, either because the listener's habit responses are not relevant to the style (which I have called "cultural noise")[8] or because external interference obscures the structure of the situation in question (i.e., acoustical noise).

It seems further that uncertainty should be distinguished from vagueness, though the distinction is by no means clear-cut. Uncertainty evidently presumes a basic norm of clear probability patterns such that even the ambiguous is felt to be goal-oriented. Vagueness, on the other hand, involves a weakening of the transitive, kinetic character of syntactic relationships and as a result the sense of musical tendency is enervated. When this occurs, attention becomes focused upon the nuances and refinements of phrases, timbres, textures, and the like. And impressionism tends in this respect to be the sensitive projection of the sensuous. We shall return to another aspect of the relationship between value and uncertainty a bit later. Now we must briefly consider the nature of the unexpected, or more particularly, the surprising in relation to information theory.

All deviation involves the less probable. However, because in most cases the less probable grows gradually out of the more probable or because in some cases the musical context is one in which deviation is more or less expected, listeners are as a rule aware of the possibility of deviation. They are set and ready for the less probable, though often unconsciously so. In the case of the unexpected the probability of a given music event seems so high that the possibility of alternative consequent is not considered. It seems as though the message involves a minimum of uncertainty and that, when completed, it will have contained little information. But when at the last moment the improbable abruptly arrives, the listener discovers that his estimates of probability and uncertainty were wrong and that the event or message actually contained more information than it was presumed to contain.

Let us consider these matters in relation to an example from language and in relation to Geminiani's fugue subject. Take the phrase "she is as tall." First off, we can talk about the sequence of sounds in terms of probability, uncertainty, and information. The uncertainty of what will follow the sound "sh" is very high indeed, though clearly some sounds will be less probable than others, given the stylistic context we call English. Thus the sound or "word" *shvin* is highly improbable in an English sentence. But it is not impossible—witness the fact that it has just occurred in one.[9] The uncertainties are reduced and the probabilities increased when the sound "i" (e) arrives. But the pause which actually follows is only one of the possible sequels to the sound "she." The word might have become "sheep." Thus both the sound "i" and the pause add considerable information. And please note that silence is a part of information, musical as well as linguistic.

Now the same kind of analysis is possible for the first event in Geminiani's theme. Considering the notes B and E, for the sake of comparison, as being equivalent to the sound "sh," it is clear that the number of possible consequents is very high. The events could have continued in many different ways, though again some (Example 3a) are more probable, given the stylistic context and the fact that this is the beginning of a work, than others (Example 3b). The high E, like the sound "i" (e), thus adds a great deal of information to the musical message (see Example 1).

The turning of the melodic line downward and the arrival of a

Example 3

clear down-beat—these complement one another—make it clear in retrospect that a musical event has been completed. Had the melodic line not been articulated by a change of motion or had the down-beat been suppressed, the musical event would have been different. That is, just as the sound "she" could have become part of the linguistic event "sheep," so the first three notes of this theme could have become part of the events presented in Example 3, parts c and d.

Of course these events, both the musical and the linguistic ones, exist only on the lowest architectonic level. They cannot stand alone, but are parts of larger wholes. That is, the musical event is part of a syntactical unit we call a theme, the linguistic event part of a syntactical unit we call a sentence or phrase. And these larger units, which are events on higher architectonic levels, are but parts of still larger musical sections or linguistic paragraphs or stanzas. These in turn are parts of whole pieces of music or works of literature.

Turning now to the partial phrase "She is as tall," it is evident that there is one highly probable syntactical consequent. That is, we expect that the phrase will be followed by the word "as" and then by a proper noun or a pronoun. And we would be surprised to find an adjective following either the word "tall" or the words "tall as." For instance, the phrases "she is as tall blue" or "she is as tall as blue" are rather improbable, though not impossible. The first of these alternatives might continue "she is as tall blue lilacs are," and the simile being improbable increases information considerably.

If we take a more probable consequent, "she is as tall as Bill," we have acquired information, but syntactically speaking not very much. Notice incidentally that we actually leave out that part of the construction which is the most probable. That is, we omit the implicit "as Bill *is tall*" because in the context these words contribute no information and hence are unnecessary. Now if we look at the first part of the Geminiani theme we might say, by analogy, that the half-phrase up to the B corresponds to the part-phrase "she is as tall" and that the descent to the E corresponds to the most probable syntactical completion just as the words "as Bill is tall" do. Both completions are obvious and neither is very good. However, this does *not* assert that taken in the context of a larger whole, these phrases might not become part of a meaningful, valuable work.

Before leaving this comparison between musical and linguistic behavior, it might be amusing to construct examples involving the unexpected. Observe, first of all, that since the phrase "she is as tall" is syntactically incomplete, we are alert to the possibility of alternative consequents and that if the word "blue" follows (as in the phrase "she is as tall blue lilacs are"), it seems improbable but in a sense not unexpected. But if we take the phrase "she is as tall as Bill is," we assume our information is complete and are not ready for new information. And so if we add the word "wide" instead of the understood "tall," it is both improbable and unexpected. And the whole message contains more information than we presumed it to contain.

In a similar manner we can add to the Geminiani theme so that what at first seems to be a point of completion ceases to be so and becomes part of an unexpected twist of meaning (Example 4).

Example 4

Notice that not only is information increased in this variant, but that the meaning of the descent from B is in retrospect *literally* different. For its obviousness now seems to have been a means of deception as to the ultimate intent of the theme.

To summarize what we have learned from this excursion into the relationship of information theory to music and to value: first of all, we have found that resistance, or more broadly deviation, is a correlative of information. And since information is valuable—as tautology is not—our hypothesis as to the importance of deviation has received confirmation. Secondly, our inquiry has pointed to a relationship between information and deviation on the one hand, and uncertainty on the other. This implies that uncertainty is somewhat related to value. This apparently paradoxical pairing will be considered presently.

II

Hypotheses gain in plausibility not only through the corroboration of other investigators and through correlation with other fields of inquiry, but also by accounting for facts observed but hitherto unexplained theoretically. Our hypothesis can do this in explaining the difference between primitive music and art music. In so doing it is hoped that another aspect of the relationship between tendency inhibition and value will be revealed.

If we ask, What is the fundamental difference between sophisticated art music and primitive music? (and I do not include under the term "primitive" the highly sophisticated music which so-called primitives often play), then we can point to the fact that primitive music generally employs a smaller repertory of tones, that the distance of these notes from the tonic is smaller, that there is a great deal of repetition, though often slightly varied repetition, and so forth. But these are the symptoms of primitivism in music, not its causes.

The differentia between art music and primitive music lies in speed of tendency gratification. The primitive seeks almost immediate gratification for his tendencies whether these be biological or musical. Nor can he tolerate uncertainty. And it is because distant departures from the certainty and repose of the tonic note and lengthy delays in gratification are insufferable to him that the tonal repertory of the primitive is limited, not because he can't think of other tones. It is not his mentality that is limited, it is his maturity. Note, by the way, that popular music can be distinguished from real jazz on the same basis. For while "pop" music whether of the tin-pan-alley or the Ethelbert Nevin variety makes use of a fairly large repertory of tones, it operates with such conventional clichés that gratification is almost immediate and uncertainty is minimized.

One aspect of maturity both of the individual and of the culture within which a style arises consists then in the willingness to forgo immediate, and perhaps lesser gratification, for the sake of future ultimate gratification. Understood generally, not with reference to any specific musical work, self-imposed tendency-inhibition and the willingness to bear uncertainty are indications of maturity. They are signs, that is, that the animal is becoming a man. And this, I take it, is not without relevance to considerations of value.

"This is all very well and more or less plausible," someone will say, "but in the last analysis isn't music valuable for a variety of reasons rather than just for the rather puritanical ones which you have been hinting at? What of the sensuous pleasure of beautiful sound? What of the ability of music to move us through the deep-seated associations it is able to evoke? Are these without value?"

The problems raised by these questions—that of the relation of pleasure to value and that of the ordering of values—have concerned philosophy from its very beginnings, and I shall not presume to give definite answers to them. What follows must therefore be taken as provisional. At first blush it would seem that we do in fact distinguish between what is *pleasurable* and what is *good*. Indeed the difference between them seems to parallel the distinction drawn above between immediate gratification and delayed gratification. But even as we state it, the distinction breaks down, even linguistically. For delayed gratification too is pleasurable; not only in the sense that it does culminate in ultimate and increased satisfaction, but also in the sense that it involves pleasures related to the conquest of difficulties—to control and power.[10]

Two points should be noted in this connection. In the first place, both immediate gratification and delayed gratification are pleasurable and both are valuable, though they are not necessarily equally valuable. Secondly, value refers to a quality of musical experience. It is inherent neither in the musical object per se nor in the mind of the listener per se. Rather value arises as the result of a transaction, which takes place within an objective tradition, between the musical work and a listener. This being the case, the value of any particular musical experience is a function both of the listener's ability to respond—his having learned the style of the music—and of his mode of response.

Three aspects of musical enjoyment may be distinguished: the sensuous, the associative-characterizing, and the syntactical. And though every piece of music involves all three to some extent, some pieces tend to emphasize one aspect and minimize others. Thus at one end of what is obviously a continuum is the immediate gratification of the sensuous and the exclamatory outburst of uncontrolled, pent-up energy. At the other end of the continuum is the delayed gratification arising out of the perception of and response to the syntactical relationships which shape and mold musical experience, whether intellectual or emotional. The associative may function with either. It may color our sensuous pleasures with the satisfactions of wish-fulfillment. Or it may shape our expectations as to the probabilities of musical progress by characterizing musical events. For just as our estimate of the character of an individual influences our expectations as to his probable behavior, so our estimate of the character of a theme or musical event shapes our expectations as to how it will behave musically. And conversely, the way in which a musical event behaves—involves regular, deviant, or surprising progressions—influences our opinion as to its character. Thus the syntactical and characterizing facets of musical communication are inextricably linked.

The question of the ordering of values still remains. Are the different aspects of musical enjoyment equally valuable? Is a piece of music which appeals primarily to sensuous-associative pleasure as good as one which appeals to syntactical-associative enjoyment? If we put the matter as crudely as possible—if we ask, Is the best arrangement of the best pop tune as good as Beethoven's Ninth Symphony?—then the answer seems easy. But if we put a similar question using less polar works and ask, Is Debussy's *Afternoon of a Faun* as good as the Ninth Symphony? we have qualms about the answer.

At this point some of our social scientist friends, whose blood pressure has been steadily mounting, will throw up their hands in relativistic horror and cry: "You can't do this! You can't compare baked Alaska with roast beef. Each work is good of its kind and there's the end of it." Now granting both that we can enjoy a particular work for a variety of reasons and also that the enjoyment of one kind of music does not preclude the enjoyment of others—that we can enjoy both Debussy and Beethoven—this does not mean that they are equally good. Nor does it mean that all modes of musical enjoyment are equally valuable. In fact, when you come right down to it, the statement that "each is good of its kind" is an evasion of the problem, not a solution of it. And so we are still driven to ask: Are all kinds equally good?

III

To begin the next stage of our inquiry, let us recall an idea brought out in our discussion of the difference between primitive music and sophisticated music. I refer to the observation that willingness to inhibit tendencies and tolerate uncertainties is a sign of maturity. Note, however, that the converse of this is also true. For maturation and individualization are themselves products of the resistances, problems, and uncertainties with which life confronts us. As George Herbert Mead has pointed out, it is only by coming to grips with these difficulties and overcoming them and by making the choices and decisions which each of us must make that the self becomes aware of itself, becomes a self.[11] Only through our encounters with the world, through what we suffer, do we achieve self-realization as particular men and women.

It is because the evaluation of alternative probabilities and the retrospective understanding of the relationships among musical events as they actually occurred leads to self-awareness and individualization that the syntactical response is more valuable than those responses in which the ego is dissolved, losing its identity in voluptuous sensation or in the reverie of daydreams. And for the same reasons works involving deviation and uncertainty are better than those offering more immediate satisfaction. I am not contending that other modes of enjoyment are without value, but rather that they are of a lesser order of value.

The difficulty is that, aside from the most primitive forms of musical-emotional outburst and the most blatant appeals to the sensuous such as one finds in the cheapest pop arrangements, there are no musical works of art in which syntactical relationships do not play a significant rôle. Nor will it do to try to arrange musical works in order of their syntactical vs. their sensuous-associative appeals. For even a work such as Debussy's *Afternoon of a Faun*, which strongly emphasizes the sensuous, is syntactically complex—as complex, for instance, as the first movement of Mozart's famous Piano Sonata in C Major, which is predominantly syntactical.[12]

Thus it would seem that while the contrast between the sensuous-associative and the syntactical may provide a basis for evaluating the responses of listeners, it does not provide a basis for judging the value of most pieces of music. The sensuous-associative is of minor importance in the consideration of value.[13] Music must be evaluated syntactically. And indeed it is so. For who is to say which of two works has greater sensuous appeal or evokes more poignant associations? The matter is by definition completely subjective. And if we ask, Why is Debussy's music superior to that of Delius? the answer lies in the syntactical organization of his music, not in its superior sensuousness.

What then are the determinants of value from the syntactical viewpoint? We noted earlier that complexity, size, and length are not in themselves virtues. For as we all know from sad experience, a large complex work can be pretentious and bombastic, dull and turgid, or a combination of these. Yet insofar as the intricate and subtle interconnections between musical events, whether simultaneous or successive, of a complex work involve considerable resistance and uncertainty—and presumably information—value is thereby created. This viewpoint seems more plausible when we consider that as we become more familiar with a complex work and are therefore better able to comprehend the permutations and interrelations among musical events, our enjoyment is increased. For the information we get out of the work is increased.

Obviously neither information nor complexity refer to the mere accumulation of a heterogeneous variety of events. If the events are to be meaningful, they must arise out of a set of probability relationships, a musical style. Moreover, the capacity of the human mind to perceive and relate patterns to one another and to remember them would appear to limit complexity. For if a work is so complex that the musical events eclipse one another, then value will be diminished. Or, as mentioned earlier, if complexity and length are such that tendencies become dissipated in the course of overelaborate deviations, then meanings will be lost as relationships become obscure. Of course if listeners are unable to remember the musical events, whether because of the magnitude of a work or because it involves stylistic innovations, then the piece of music may seem overcomplex when it is not so. This is why music at first found unintelligible and empty may later become understandable and rewarding.

We have been so conditioned by the nineteenth-century notion that great art is simple that the association of complexity with value is repugnant. Yet, while complexity is not the sufficient cause of value, the implication that the two are in no way related is simply not true. Can one seriously argue that the complexity of Bach's B Minor Mass has nothing to do with its excellence relative to the tune "Twinkle, Twinkle, Little Star"? Or think of some of the masterpieces of Western art: "The Last Judgment" by Michelangelo, Picasso's "Guernica," *The Iliad*, Joyce's *Ulysses*, Mozart's *Jupiter Symphony*, Stravinsky's *Symphony of Psalms*.

Nevertheless one is reluctant. What of a relatively simple but touching work such as Schubert's song, "Das Wandern"? Is it not perfect of its kind? Is it not enchanting precisely *because* of its simplicity? Without arguing the point, it seems probable that the charm of simplicity as such is associative rather than syntactical; that is, its appeal is to childhood, remembered as untroubled and secure. However, a direct, one-to-one correspondence between complexity and value will not stand up. For we are all aware that relatively simple pieces such as some of Schubert's songs or Chopin's preludes are better—more rewarding—than some large and complex works, such as, for instance, Strauss's *Don Quixote*.

This is the case because information is judged not in absolute, but in relative terms. For we evaluate not only the amount of information in a work but also the relationship between the stimulus "input" and the actual informational "output." Evidently the operation of some "principle of psychic economy" makes us compare the ratio of musical means invested to the informational income produced by this investment. Those works are judged good which yield a high return. Those works yielding a low return are found to be pretentious and bombastic.

Musical information is then evaluated both quantitatively and qualitatively. Hence two pieces might, so to speak, yield the same amount of information but not be equally good because one is less elegant and economical than the other. On the other hand, a piece which is somewhat deficient in elegance may be better than a more economical piece because it contains substantially more information and hence provides a richer musical experience.

IV

Musical communication is qualitative not only in this syntactical sense. The content of musical experience is also an important aspect of its quality. With the introduction of "content" we not only leave the concepts of information theory, which is concerned only with the syntactical nature of music, but we also part company from those aestheticians who contend that musical experience is devoid of any content whatsoever. And we move from the consideration of value per se to the consideration of greatness.

For when we talk of greatness, we are dealing with a quality of experience which transcends the syntactical. We are considering another order of value in which self-awareness and individualization arise out of the cosmic uncertainties that pervade human existence; where man's sense of the inadequacy of reason in a capricious and inscrutable universe, his feeling of terrible isolation in a callous and indifferent, if not hostile, nature, and his awareness of his own insignificance and impotence in the face of the magnitude and power of creation, all lead to those ultimate and inescapable questions which Pascal posed when he wrote:

> I see the formidable regions of the universe which enclose me, and I find myself penned in one corner of this vast expanse, without knowing why I am set in this spot rather than another, nor why the little span of life granted me is assigned to this point of time rather than another of the whole eternity which went before or which shall follow after. I see nothing but infinities on every hand, closing me in as if I were an atom or a shadow which lasts but a moment and returns no more. All I know is that I must shortly die, but what I know least of all about is this very death which I cannot escape.[14]

These ultimate uncertainties—and at the same time ultimate realities—of which great music makes us aware result not from syntactical relationships alone, but from the interaction of these with the associative aspect of music. This interaction, at once shaping and characterizing musical experience, gives rise to a profound wonderment—tender, yet awful—at the mystery of existence.[15] And in the very act of sensing this mystery, we attain a new level of consciousness, of individualization. The nature of uncertainty too has changed. It has become a means to an end rather than an end to be suffered.

The reasons for contending that Beethoven's Ninth Symphony is a great work, while Debussy's *Afternoon of a Faun* is only excellent should now be clear.[16] If we ask further about value per se, apart from considerations of greatness, it would seem that the Debussy may be the more elegant work, but the Beethoven is better. On the other hand, *The Afternoon of a Faun* is clearly a better work than the Mozart C Major Piano Sonata. And the greatest works would be those which embody value of the highest order with the most profound—and I use the word without hesitation—content.[17]

In her book, *The Greek Way to Western Civilization*, Edith Hamilton finds that the essence of tragedy springs from the fact of human dignity and she goes on to say that "it is by our power to suffer, above all, that we are of more value than the sparrows."[18] This, I think, carries the insight only part way. Rather it is because tragic suffering, arising out of the ultimate uncertainties of human existence, is able to individualize and purify our wills that we are of more value than the sparrows.

But are not war, poverty, disease, old age, and all other forms of suffering evil? As a general rule they are. For in most cases they lead to the degradation and dissolution of the self. The individual will is lost in the primordial impulses of the group which, as Freud has pointed out, "cannot tolerate any delay between its desires and the fulfillment of what it desires."[19] In short, suffering is regarded as evil because, generally speaking, it brings about a regression toward the immaturity of primitivism.

However, in instances where the individual is able to master it through understanding, as Job did, suffering may ultimately be good. For though, like medical treatment, it is painful, suffering may lead to a higher level of consciousness and a more sensitive, realistic awareness of the nature and meaning of existence. Indeed all maturation, all self-discovery, is in the last analysis more or less painful. And the wonder of great art is this: that through it we can approach this highest level of consciousness and understanding without paying the painful price exacted in real life and without risking the dissolution of the self which real suffering might bring.

One must therefore distinguish between moral values and individual values. Moral values deal with what will probably be good or bad for men taken as a group. Individual values are concerned with experience as it relates to particular men and women. The two should not be confused. For a concern with moral values such as the social sciences exhibit (and their inductive-statistical method makes this all but inevitable) leads to a normative, relativistic view in which values change from culture to culture and from group to group within the culture. A concern with individual values such as one finds in the humanities leads, on the other hand, to a universal view of value, though recognizing that ultimate value-goals may be reached by somewhat different means in different cultures. Indeed it is because the individual dimension of value is universal that, where translation is possible (as it is not in music), one is able to enjoy and value art works of another culture. Lastly, in contending that the ultimate value of art lies in its ability to individualize the self, I am conscious of my opposition to those who, like Plato, Tolstoy, and the Marxists, would make aesthetic value a part of moral value.

It is clear then that our hypothesis as to the relation of resistance and uncertainty to value transcends the realm of aesthetics. For the choice to be made, the question to be asked, is in the final analysis metaphysical. It is this: What is the meaning and purpose of man's existence? And though one's answer can be rationalized and explained—though one can assert that it is through self-realization that man becomes differentiated from the beasts—it cannot be proved. Like an axiom, it must be self-evident.

In closing, I should like to quote from a letter written by a man who suffered greatly and who in so doing came to understand the meaning of suffering. The letter, dated February 14, 1819, two years before he died, is by John Keats.

Man is originally a poor forked creature subject to the same mischances as the beasts of the forest, destined to hardships and disquietude of some kind or other. . . . The common cognomen of this world among the misguided and superstitious is "a vale of tears" from which we are to be redeemed by a certain arbitrary interposition of God and taken to heaven. What a little circumscribed straightened notion! Call the world if you please "the vale of Soul-making." Then you will find out the use of the world. . . . I say *"soul making"*—Soul as distinguished from Intelligence. There may be intelligences or sparks of the divinity in millions—but they are not souls till they acquire identities, till each one is personally itself. . . . How then are Souls made? . . . How but by the medium of a world like this? . . . I will call the *world* a School instituted for the purpose of teaching little children how to read—I will call the *human heart* the *horn book* read in that school—and I will call the *Child able to read*, the Soul made from that *School* and its *horn book*. Do you not see how necessary a World of Pains and troubles is to school an Intelligence and make it a soul? A place where the heart must feel and suffer in a thousand diverse ways. . . . As various as the Lives of Men are—so various become their souls, and thus does God make individual beings.[20]

NOTES

1. I. A. Richards, *Principles of Literary Criticism* (London: Kegan Paul & Co., 1947), p. 25.
2. Leonard B. Meyer, *Emotion and Meaning in Music* (Chicago: The University of Chicago Press, 1956).
3. Robert Penn Warren, "Pure and Impure Poetry," *Kenyon Review*, V (1943), p. 251.
4. John Dewey, *Art as Experience* (New York: Minton, Balch & Co., 1954), p. 59.
5. For a clear discussion of information theory see Warren Weaver, "Recent Contributions to the Mathematical Theory of Communication," *Etc.: A Review of General Semantics*, X (1953), pp. 261–81.
6. Norbert Wiener, *The Human Use of Human Beings* (New York: Doubleday Anchor Books, 1954), p. 21.
7. In part uncertainty is inherent in the nature of the probability process, in part it is intentionally introduced by the composer. See the discussion of Markoff process, systemic uncertainty, and designed uncertainty in Leonard B. Meyer, "Meaning in Music and Information Theory," *JAAC*, XV (1957), pp. 418–19.
8. Ibid., pp. 420–1.
9. This "gimmick"' is borrowed from Weaver, op. cit., p. 267.
10. This does not, of course, assert that all experience is either good or pleasurable. Total quiescence—the absence of any stimulation whatever—is both unpleasant and valueless; as is its opposite, the complete frustration of a strong tendency which can find no substitute outlet. In connection with the former, it would seem that information is a basic need of the mind. See Woodburn Heron, "The Pathology of Boredom," *Scientific American*, CLXXXXVI (Jan. 1957), pp. 52–6.
11. George H. Mead, *Mind, Self and Society* (Chicago: The University of Chicago Press, 1934). See in particular Parts ii and iii.
12. In this connection it should be observed that instrumentation, texture, tempo, and dynamics which are often thought of as contributing most to the sensuous-associative aspect of music may, and in the work of fine composers do, function syntactically.
13. The sensuous-associative may, however, be of importance in accounting for individual musical preferences.

14. Pascal, *Pensées*, trans., H. F. Stewart (New York: Pantheon Books, Inc., 1950), pp. 105–7.
15. What I have been calling "greatness" is clearly related to what some philosophers have distinguished as the "sublime."
16. It seems possible that there is a correspondence between the several aspects of musical communication and the several levels of consciousness; that is, that the sensuous-associative, the syntactical, and the "sublime" give rise to different levels of awareness and individualization.
17. The distinction between *excellence* as syntactical and *greatness* which involves considerations of content makes it clear why we can speak of a "great work" that doesn't quite "come off." For there are works which seek to make us aware of ultimate uncertainties, but which fail in execution. Furthermore, this distinction makes clear the difference between a masterpiece and a great work. Some of Bach's Inventions are masterpieces, but they are not great works.
18. Edith Hamilton, *The Greek Way to Western Civilization* (New York: Mentor Books, 1948), p. 168.
19. Sigmund Freud, *Group Psychology and the Analysis of the Ego* (London: The International Psycho-Analytical Press, 1922), p. 15.
20. John Keats, *Letters*, ed., Maurice Buxton Forman (New York: Oxford University Press, 1935), pp. 335–6.

Liars, Ranters,
and Dramatic Speakers

Marcia M. Eaton

> They [critics] will call upon Shakespeare—they always do—and will quote that hackneyed passage about Art holding the mirror up to Nature, forgetting that this unfortunate aphorism is deliberately said by Hamlet in order to convince the bystanders of his absolute insanity in all art-matters. . . . My dear fellow, whatever you may say, it is merely a dramatic utterance, and no more represents Shakespeare's real views upon art than the speeches of Iago represent his real views upon morals.
>
> Oscar Wilde, *The Decay of Lying*

One of the outstanding shortcomings of arguments offered on both sides of many controversial issues in aesthetics has been a failure to clarify many of the basic concepts that are employed. Frequently one meets with skepticism with regard to such clarification. However, success is the best proof against skepticism, and in this paper I hope to show that elucidation of at least one basic aesthetic concept is, at least in some degree, possible. I shall herein be concerned with one aspect of the nature of a literary work—a literary work as a linguistic object.

I

Elsewhere I have introduced some machinery for dealing with this notion, but for the sake of the self-containment of this paper I shall repeat and enlarge upon it here.[1] Very simply, a linguistic object is a word or group of words. A linguistic action is a conscious action in which a person uses a linguistic object in any of various ways. One possible classification of these various ways in which linguistic objects are used is that which Austin provides in *How to Do Things with Words*. First, there are actions that are "locutionary," in which a

287

person says or writes certain words and in so doing means to refer to certain things. Second, there are "illocutionary" acts, in which the locution is put to such uses as asserting, questioning, commanding, expressing a wish, and so forth. Third, there are "perlocutionary" acts, in which the locution has certain consequences such as persuading, convincing, deceiving, evoking, and so forth.

These classes of linguistic actions (or speech acts, as they are often called) can easily be applied to the actions of writers of literature. When a writer writes down words, sentences, and so forth, he is performing a locutionary act. When he makes assertions, commands, asks questions, and so forth, he is performing illocutionary acts. And, lastly, when a writer produces certain effects on the part of his readers—for example, informing, persuading, or arousing—he is performing perlocutionary acts.

How does a work of literature fit into this scheme? Let us first consider the sentence "Today is Monday." When someone consciously utters this sentence, he is performing a linguistic action, usually that action known as asserting. Likewise when someone writes down that sentence, he is making an assertion, and the written sentence that results is the record or product of his linguistic act of asserting. This product is a linguistic object—a group of written words.

One class of linguistic actions performed by most literary writers is very unusual, that is, quite different from the kind of action ordinarily performed in everyday discourse, both spoken and written. The locutionary and perlocutionary actions of an author are much the same as those of the average language user. But the illocutionary acts that a writer performs vary a great deal from those of the average speaker. The most commonly discussed illocutions are assertions, questions, and commands; so let us consider them. Writers may perform these actions; but often they do not. Rather they are responsible for attributing assertions, questions, commands, and so forth, to others, namely, to *dramatic speakers*. Writing literature may in fact be viewed as putting words into the mouths of dramatic speakers and thus causing *them* to perform certain illocutionary acts.

The notion of a dramatic speaker is not new, though it is often referred to by other terms, for example, "the protagonist." Wellek and Warren discuss a similar notion in their section on author psychology in *Theory of Literature*. Wimsatt and Beardsley characterize such a speaker in the following way: "Even a short lyric poem is dramatic, the response of a speaker (no matter how abstractly conceived) to a situation (no matter how universalized). We ought to impute the thoughts and attitudes of the poem immediately to the dramatic *speaker*, and if to the author at all, only by an act of biographical inference."[2] I am in partial agreement with Wimsatt and Beardsley here. In essence, I take the dramatic speaker to be the person who is saying the words that constitute a literary work.

But who is that person? In drama, the answer to this question is fairly simple. The dramatic speakers are the characters in the play to whom the playwright has attributed the lines. It is not the actor actually saying those lines. For example, in *Hamlet* one dramatic speaker is Hamlet (not Sir Laurence Olivier, Richard Burton, Sir John Gielgud, and so forth), another is Claudius, and so on through the list of characters. No matter who appears in these roles, the dramatic speaker remains constant, as long as the text remains constant.

In novels or short stories the "person" is a bit harder to tie down. Consider the following excerpt, typical of a novel.

> "It's a miracle he has recovered consciousness," the doctor whispered to Raskolnikov.
>
> "What's your opinion?" Raskolnikov asked.
>
> "He won't live long."
>
> "Isn't there any hope at all?"
>
> "Not the slightest. He's at the last gasp. His head's badly injured, too. I could bleed him, I suppose, but it won't be of any use. Sure to die in five or ten minutes."
>
> "In that case, why not bleed him?"
>
> "I might, but I warn you it's absolutely useless!"
>
> Just then more footsteps were heard, the crowd on the landing parted, and a priest, a little grey-haired old man, appeared on the threshold with the Sacrament. A policeman had gone to fetch him soon after the accident. . . .

There are two basic ways of handling such examples. One can treat the statements within quotation marks as statements by various dramatic speakers (Raskolnikov; the doctor), and the remarks not in quotation marks as made by yet another dramatic speaker, namely, the narrator. Or a whole novel may be treated as one long statement by a storyteller, parts of whose remarks are reports of other peoples' utterances. At this point, I see no reason for preferring one of these methods to the other.

The "person" becomes much more difficult to identify when we come to poetry. A poem can, and I believe should, be viewed as a statement or a series of statements in various grammatical moods. To put the matter quite simply, the dramatic speaker is the person making those statements. In poetry such as *Spoon River Anthology,* the speakers are the various people to whom Masters attributes the lines, for example, Fiddler Jones, the village atheist, Carl Hamblin, and so forth. In such a case, the dramatic speaker is akin to those of drama. In other poems, such as Longfellow's "Hiawatha," the dramatic speaker is like the storytelling dramatic speaker of novels. Usually in poetry, however, the dramatic speaker is just an unidentified someone —a person we imagine to be making the statements constituting the poem. As Wimsatt and Beardsley say, we do sometimes by biographical inference equate the writer with the dramatic speaker, but this is by no means necessarily, nor even most frequently, the case.

Any literary work may be the linguistic object that is the record or product of an author's actually asserting, questioning, commanding, wishing, and so forth. But usually it is not. Herein lies one of the characteristics of literature which distinguishes it from other linguistic entities. An author attributes linguistic actions to others; he does not (usually) perform those actions himself. No one would deny that when Shakespeare wrote the words "Get thee to a nunnery," he was performing a linguistic action. But it would be false to say that he, Shakespeare, was himself making a command or a request. Nor do we want to say that when he wrote in one of his sonnets "Why didst thou promise such a beauteous day," he was asking a question.

I call this extraordinary activity, whereby an author attributes linguistic actions to others, namely, dramatic speakers, *translocuting.* A fairly detailed description of this activity of translocuting follows:

Let

L = the act of locuting
I = the act of illocuting
P = the act of perlocuting
T = the act of translocuting
TI = the act of transillocution
TP = the act of transperlocution
TT = the act of transtranslocution
S = an ordinary, nonliterary speaker or writer
A = a literary writer
DS = dramatic speaker

Then,

$$S \xrightarrow[\text{thereby producing}]{\text{locutes}} I \ \& \ (\text{sometimes } P)$$

Sometimes

$$A \xrightarrow[\text{thereby producing}]{\text{locutes}} I \ \& \ (\text{sometimes } P)$$

But usually,

$$A \xrightarrow[\text{thereby producing}]{\text{translocutes}} TI \ \& \ (\text{sometimes } TP \ v \ TT)$$

Or, equivalently,

$$A \xrightarrow[\text{thereby producing}]{\text{translocutes}} [DS \xrightarrow[\text{thereby producing}]{\text{locutes}} I_{DS} \ \& \ (\text{sometimes } P_{DS} \ v \ TT_{DS})]$$

I have included this schema only for the purists among my readers. It sounds and looks much more complicated than it is. In plain language, the above stipulates this: Ordinary (nonliterary) speakers and writers locute, thereby producing illocutions and sometimes perlocutions. Authors and poets and dramatists locute and occasionally thereby produce illocutions and sometimes perlocutions. However, authors, poets, and dramatists more often translocute, thereby producing transillocutions and sometimes transperlocutions and/or transtranslocutions.[3] Or, equivalently, an author, poet, or dramatist translocutes, thereby producing a dramatic speaker who locutes, thereby producing an illocution and sometimes perlocutions and translocutions. Shakespeare translocuted when he wrote "to be or not to be," thereby producing a transillocution, which is equivalent to an illocution on the part of a dramatic speaker.

In passing, it is important to note that literature is not unique in having dramatic speakers as a central element. Advertisements, both visual and audio, have them. For example, when I see a billboard with the words "Winston tastes good like a cigarette should" written on it, I deal with it as I would deal with any linguistic object. Something is being said, and thus it is easy to infer that there is someone doing the saying. We are not apt to treat all advertising speeches as serious remarks made by the adman who wrote them, any more than we attribute all poetic remarks to the poet who made them. Admen translocute most of the time.

It is obvious that central to my analysis of a work of literature is the concept of a dramatic speaker. The concept is vulnerable in the following ways. Adding translocution to Austin's schema would be needlessly multiplying entities if the concept of dramatic speaker were empty. Further, if the concept of a dramatic speaker is beyond un-muddling, then it not only fails to help clarify the notion of a literary work, but does serious harm to that notion in making it more confused and mysterious than it already is. Further, even if unmuddled, it may be useless and/or unnecessary.

Let me begin by defending myself against the accusation of unnecessarily multiplying entities. If such multiplication has taken place, it began long before I put my pen to paper. As I mentioned earlier, it is not my invention. The work of literary critics is full of talk about dramatic speakers, usually referred to in different terms, for example, "the protagonist," "the hero," "the main character," "the title role," and so forth.

But the mere fact that others have used the notion is certainly not grounds, by itself, for continuing that use. There must be positive reasons for the belief in the utility or necessity of such an entity.

Whenever we confront a literary work, we necessarily are aware of the fact that we are dealing with a syntactically and semantically ordered subject. Habits of ordinary discourse cause us to ask, "What is being said here?" and related questions. Further, we know that if something is being said, then there must be someone saying it. We do not always, or even most often, want to assert that the author is the speaker. To do so would be to attribute irrationality, inconsistency, insanity, dishonesty, stupidity, and so forth, to many authors and poets.

Shakespeare is not contemplating suicide when Hamlet says "To be or not to be." This accounts for the introduction of the concept of protagonist, hero, and so forth, in the past. The concept of translocutions further allows us to attribute acts not to writers (thereby avoiding the necessity of making liars or kooks of them) but to the characters whom they create. Thus we are able to put the explanation and interpretation of literature on a par with everyday discourse.

The various problems that the concept of translocution is introduced to elucidate and solve have been dealt with by other philosophers in different ways. Strawson, Austin, and Nowell-Smith, for example, take the line that literature is somehow secondary—parasitic on ordinary discourse. They believe that the statements made in a literary work are "pretend" statements, in some ways underdeveloped or not full-fledged. I shall discuss my reasons for rejecting such a tack below.

Monroe Beardsley has independently arrived at a concept very close to translocutions. He suggests that literature can be dealt with as linguistic works in which illocutions are imitated: "A poem, I suggest, is an imitation of a complex illocutionary act."[4] Obviously, I have great sympathy for his program. But I am put off by the term "imitation." I find its relation to "parasitic" and "secondary" too close for comfort. Again my reasons for this discomfort will become clear later.

This completes my apology for using dramatic speakers and for adding "translocution" to the already overpopulated philosophic vocabulary. The time has come to put them to use, and with the success or failure of this application lies the existence or nonexistence of justification for such an addition.

II

Consider an ordinary, garden-variety speech act. Here a speaker utters (writes) something that is heard (read) and interpreted by a hearer (reader). The literary speech act is very similar to this. Here a writer writes something (namely, the literary work) which is read and interpreted by a reader. However, this literary speech act depends for its existence upon a different, or subspeech, act. This subspeech act consists in a dramatic speaker or group of dramatic speakers making statements which are then read (or heard) and interpreted by a reader.

For practical reasons, the number of things one can do with the utterance made in an ordinary speech act is restricted. However, literary utterances (works) lend themselves to a great variety of activities. One can read a literary work in order to escape, to glean information, to have vicarious experiences, to become sexually aroused, and so on. The list is practically endless. One may read to create, that is, may use the words already written down by someone else, give them a new interpretation, and thus create a new work.[5] However, I am interested only in one general type of activity, which is the act of reading, ordinarily so-called. It is difficult to characterize this activity in any simple way; but essentially it consists of reading some work, X, by some writer, A, because one feels that something interesting is being said in an interesting or aesthetically pleasing way, without any ulterior purpose.

This last kind of activity can itself be subdivided into any number of subactivities. I shall divide it into two main subactivities. (a) A reader, R, may read because he wants to know what A has to say, in the sense of the perlocutions that A is attempting to perform. Here R uses the work, W, to go beyond W; that is, R is interested in W at least in part because he wishes to find out something about A. (b) A reader, $R\emptyset$, reads W because he wants to know what the dramatic speaker is saying. He may do this (1) in light of the work itself or (2) in light of the work plus the larger context of the work, such as historic period, author biography, literary traditions, and so forth. This latter activity approaches the activity described in (a). I have nothing other than intuitions concerning which of these activities or subactivities is the one in which most people most commonly engage. In spite of this I believe that (b:1) is the most aesthetically interesting and relevant of the above.

Thus I shall assume that there are times, and I believe they are frequent, when we want to interpret the actions of a dramatic speaker or group of dramatic speakers. There are problems associated with this activity which the concept of dramatic speakers and translocution can clear up.

I mentioned above that some philosophers have wished to treat the language of literature as "play" language, as language that for some reason or other is secondary to language in its primary use, namely, ordinary, everyday discourse. The motivation behind such a treatment is not difficult to explain. One way of getting at the reasons for relegating literary language to a secondary position is to consider literary language as it is connected to the problem, or cluster of problems, surrounding intention. In general, certain broad types of intentions can be attributed to certain kinds of illocutions. Questions are asked with the intention of someone giving an answer. Commands are given with the intention of someone carrying them out. Assertions are uttered with the intention of informing. In literature, however, this correspondence breaks down. Consider the following examples: In one of Shakespeare's sonnets the dramatic speaker asks the sun this question:

> Why didst thou promise such a beauteous day,
> And make me travel forth without my cloak,
> To let base clouds o'ertake me in my way,
> Hiding thy bravery in their rotten smoke?

No one would believe that the question is meant to be answered, unless he believed that the speaker was insane. In Milton's poem "On Time" the dramatic speaker makes this command:

> Fly envious *Time*, till thou run out thy race,
> Call on the lazy, leaden-stepping hours,
> Whose speed is but the heavy Plummets pace;
> And glut thy self with what thy womb devours. . . .

Certainly the speaker here does not expect his command to be carried out.

Is it possible to make any sense at all out of calling something a command when we know it is not intended to be carried out? Or a question if it is not meant to be answered? It has appeared obvious to some persons that these questions must be given negative replies; and from a negative reply it follows quite naturally that literary commands and questions no longer have the full-fledged quality of ordinary, nonliterary questions and commands. Thus some philosophers have agreed in viewing the use of language in literature as secondary, though their arguments do not necessarily make use of the concept of intention in the manner that I have used it above. In "On Referring" Strawson calls a failure to mention anything or anyone by using a sentence (a frequent occurrence in literature) a "spurious" use of language.[6] Later he changed "spurious" to "secondary." Austin believes that language is used in literature in a "parasitic," "not serious" way. It is not put to its "full normal use."[7] Nowell-Smith gives as Rule 1 of contextual implication the following:

> When a speaker uses a sentence to make a statement, it is contextually implied that he believes it to be true. And, similarly, when he uses it to perform any of the other jobs for which sentences are used, it is contextually implied that he is using it for one of the jobs that it normally does.[8]

This rule, he says, is often broken. But when it is broken, as in literature, language is being put to a secondary or parasitic use.

By calling language as it is used in literature secondary or parasitic, all of these men imply that it is necessary to understand a command, for example, in ordinary conversation (that is, in its primary use) before one can understand its secondary use. None of the men discusses the issue in detail. However, the view that they are getting at is, I believe, something like the following. In language we have the imperative mood, the interrogative mood, and the indicative mood. The primary uses of these moods respectively are commanding, questioning, and asserting. All other uses of these moods are secondary or parasitic—depending in some way upon the primary uses. Similarly, our understanding of the secondary use is dependent upon our understanding of the primary use.

I believe that this view is incorrect. To say that the *primary* uses of the imperative, the interrogative, and the indicative moods are commanding, questioning, and asserting implies that these are their most common uses. This is an empirical claim which no one of the above philosophers proves. And I think there are reasons to believe that such a proof is not forthcoming. Certain conditions must be fulfilled in order for someone to succeed in making a command or assertion or in asking a question. In order for someone to issue a full-fledged command (as opposed to a request, for example), he must have the authority needed and also must intend to be obeyed. In order for someone to make an assertion, he must intend to inform someone of his belief concerning some matter. In order for someone to ask a question, he must intend that someone answer him.[9] A person can command someone to do something without using the imperative mood, assert without using the indicative mood, and question without using the interrogative mood; but ordinarily these linguistic actions are carried out by using the corresponding mood. However, it is probably not the case that these moods are most commonly used for questioning, asserting, or commanding.

Consider the imperative mood. Very rarely does a person have the proper authority needed for the sentence in imperatival form to constitute a command when it is uttered. The imperative mood is more commonly used to voice requests, wishes, and desires or to express feelings. ("Shut the door"; "Turn left at the corner"; "Don't miss the movie at the Orpheum"; and so forth.) Commands are very loosely tied to the imperative mood.

Similarly, although sentences in the indicative mood are tied with greater strength, it is a mistake to say that the primary use of the indicative mood is to assert. The indicative mood is probably used most frequently in polite conversation in which the intention to inform is often, if not usually, absent, or at least in the background. ("It is a nice day"; "My parents are fine"; "I've been very busy lately"; and so forth.)

Questions are more strongly tied to the interrogative mood; that is, the necessary intention of getting someone to give an answer is usually present when someone utters a sentence in this mood. But frequently speakers ask "rhetorical questions" in which such an intention is missing. This is very prevalent in literature.

My reasons for not calling statements in poetry secondary are different from those for not calling statements in novels or plays secondary. Thus I shall first discuss poetry. Some statements that appear in poetry are like commands, assertions, and questions. But the only way in which they are like them is in their mood. Here the similarity ends. It is for this reason that they are not to be called secondary uses at all. They are rather uses of the various grammatical moods that are not unlike uses to which those moods are put in ordinary discourse. For example, "Fly envious Time" is in the imperative mood, but it is certainly not a command. It is nonetheless a perfectly serious, nonparasitic use of the imperative mood. I may go to the window and shout, "Stop raining!" This is one way of expressing my desire that the rain stop. No one would say I was making even a secondary command. Similarly, the imperatival form can be used in poetry to express some wish, desire, or feeling. This is, in fact, how "Fly envious Time" is used. In interpreting this poem, no one would say that the dramatic speaker was commanding time to fly. Rather one would say that the dramatic speaker was expressing his wish that time pass more quickly. The same kind of thing can be said about questions and assertions.

In novels and plays the situation is different. Characters in novels and plays do use the imperative mood to command, the indicative mood to assert, the interrogative mood to question. (This is possible in poetry, but much rarer than in novels and plays.) It is undoubtedly the fictional, "pretend," nature of these media that has led some people to feel the pull toward calling such uses nonserious. When interpreting the action of a novel or a play, we say such things as, "He commanded the troops to retreat"; "He asked the butler where his master was"; "He said (asserted) that the police were outside"; just as we say such things as "He left the room"; "He married the boss's daughter"; "He lived on the moon." The question "Did he really leave the room?" is ambiguous in the same way that "Did he really make a command?" is ambiguous. If we understand the question to assume "in the play or novel," then the answer is yes. But in so far as we are talking about a fictional occurrence the answer is, of course, no. A character in a play or novel who makes a command makes a full-fledged command. It is wrong to talk about secondary or nonserious commands, just as it is wrong to talk about secondary or nonserious marriages.

The important distinction to bear in mind here is the difference between pretending to use and using to pretend. An actor pretends to be someone commanding. Usually he is not someone pretending to command nor is he pretending to be someone pretending to command, although he can do these things too, if the script calls for it. "Is he really commanding?" is a misleading question. Everything an actor does in one sense is a pretense, just as the whole play is a pretense. But questions about particular actions assume the framework of the play. To the question "Did he really tell her to go to a nunnery?" the answer is yes. The phrase "in the play" or "in *Hamlet*" is understood. Similarly, the phrase "in the book" is understood in connection with novels, and the phrase "in the poem" is understood in connection with some types of poetry.

Perhaps a word should be said about pretending. While the following three criteria probably do not constitute necessary and sufficient conditions for "pretending to X," they may nonetheless serve as an approximation of such conditions for the purposes here:

1. A does something, s, which, when he actually does x, can be correctly described as a part of x.
2. s is an important part of x, that is, one of the features of x that distinguishes x from all other acts; but s is not equal to x.
3. A is intentionally refraining from doing some further part of x, which, when added to the distinguishing part, s, will result in success of x, or in A's actually x-ing.

In order to understand these criteria it will be helpful to consider some examples. Suppose A pretends to eat. He chews and swallows. This satisfies 1 and 2. If he chews and swallows air, this also satisfies 3. If A has food in his mouth, he chews, but—by 3—does not swallow. Or A pretends to hit B. He swings his arm in the direction of B (1 and 2) but intentionally fails to make contact with B (3). When an actor is pretending, his pretending consists in pretending to be someone doing something. Most often (that is, in most conventional, as opposed to "happening," dramas) he actually does that thing; what is left out is his really being that person.

In attempting to give an interpretation of a work of literature, reference to the intentions of the dramatic speaker or character is often of help. "Why did he leave the room?" "He wanted to get a revolver." "Why did the captain command his men to go up the hill?" "He wanted to surprise the enemy." "Why did he tell time to fly?" "He wanted to express his desire that time pass more quickly." But employing the notion of dramatic speaker, we are no longer faced with the need to refer to authorial intentions in order to explain at least a great deal of the action, both linguistic and nonlinguistic, of a literary work, and we do this without sacrificing the full-fledged nature of literary language. Relying on material external to a work for the explanation or evaluation of that work has long been a process looked upon unfavorably by various schools of aesthetics. Translocuting and dramatic speakers provide a rationale for doing away with overdependence on referring to things outside of a work.

Thus one of the most fruitful applications of the notions of dramatic speaker and translocution is in connection with the problem of intention. I have elsewhere utilized these concepts in this connection.[10] However, I shall add to my previous treatment of the issue(s) in the section below.

III

In everyday conversation we must know the intentions of the person with whom we are conversing if we are to understand or correctly interpret what he says. Assuming that my views concerning the nature of a literary object are not altogether false, it seems a natural step to say that we must know the intentions of the dramatic speaker if we are to correctly interpret what he says. Surely it is true that we misinterpret a work if we misidentify the dramatic speaker. This misinterpretation could assume gigantic proportions if, for example, we took the lines

> I shall be telling this with a sigh
> Somewhere ages and ages hence:
> Two roads diverged in a wood, and I—
> I took the one less traveled by,
> And that has made all the difference.[11]

to be said by the village prostitute. We also misinterpret a work if we misconstrue that speaker's intentions, for example, interpret the dramatic speaker above to be recommending conformity at all cost.

Change the dramatic speaker and you change the interpretation of that work. Change the intentions of the dramatic speaker and you likewise change the interpretation of the work, just as the interpretation often alters when we misconstrue the intention of a speaker in nonliterary discourse. Of course, we are not always conscious of the fact that we are positing a dramatic speaker and his intentions when we read a literary work. However, it seems to me that the notion does serve as machinery for getting a clearer picture of the nature of a literary work and the interpretation thereof, without being required to involve the writer as a speaker (asserter, questioner, and so forth).

I spoke earlier of the fictional, pretense character of literature which has led persons to deal with literary language as secondary. Plato felt the pull of this feature of literature when he spoke of poets as craftsmen whose end product is "twice-removed" from reality. But one can agree that literature is removed from reality without concluding, as Plato and others have, that poets are liars. The *trans-ing* process, if I may call it that for simplicity's sake, whereby a writer transfers illocutions to dramatic speakers allows for exactly such a stand. As Wilde says, Iago's speeches in no way force us to be critical of Shakespeare's morals. Dramatic speeches are not lies uttered by poets.

Further, just as attention to the trans-ing aspect of literary writing prevents us (without biographical evidence) from identifying the beliefs and moral standards of poets with those of the dramatic speakers whom they create, so it should keep us from some of the pitfalls of some of the doctrines of expressionistic theories of the Collingwood ilk. Consider the following passage:

> It does not, of course, follow that a dramatic writer may not rant in character. The tremendous rant at the end of *The Ascent of F6*, like the Shakespearian ranting on which it is modelled, is done with tongue in cheek. It is not the author who is ranting, but the unbalanced character he depicts; the emotion the author is expressing is the emotion with which he contemplates that character; or rather, the emotion he has towards that secret and disowned part of himself for which the character stands.[12]

Here Collingwood is discussing the theory, T, that x expresses y if and only if P feels y when he writes x. The various shortcomings of this theory have been discussed at length by many philosophers. I wish to show here how the concepts of dramatic speaker and translocution prevent one from ever feeling drawn to such a view.

Collingwood speaks of "ranting in character" and then of "ranting with tongue in cheek" as if they were the same. He goes on to say that it is not the author who is ranting, but the character (dramatic speaker) who is ranting, which is, of course, my view. However, Collingwood then goes on to qualify that position to such an extent that it becomes impossible for me to agree with him. He says that while the author does not express, for example, the anger that Hamlet feels upon seeing his mother and uncle together, he does express the emotion (pity?) that he, Shakespeare, feels upon viewing Hamlet in such a situation. Collingwood then goes the full circle to T, or a revised version of T, by adopting a more or less Freudian view of the artistic process, wherein the writer expresses his neuroses in his work.

What in fact happens, to repeat myself, is that when we read a literary work, we are given a set of translocutions or a set of illocutions made by a dramatic speaker. "Transexpressions," to coin the obvious phrase, are quite different from ordinary expressions of emotion. "Get thee to a nunnery" written by Shakespeare may express Hamlet's anger, but surely it is a mistake to demand the emotions expressed by a dramatic speaker (through his linguistic and nonlinguistic actions) to be felt, even watered-down or controlled, by the author. The trans-ing process removes responsibility for emotions from the author, just as it removes responsibility for beliefs and morals from him. Responsibility can only be established by biographical investigation, which is surely external to a discussion of any given work qua work.

But are the intentions of an author to be left out completely when we read one of his works? Or can those intentions affect the interpretation of his work? There are many different sorts of intentions that an author may have. All linguistic actions are in part the result of certain intentions that the person performing those actions has. Thus far we have spoken of four possible types of actions an author may perform: locutions, illocutions, translocutions, and perlocutions. With each of these classes of linguistic actions a corresponding class of linguistic intentions may be posited. Further, authors have all sorts of intentions to perform nonlinguistic actions. (By a nonlinguistic action I understand an action that could be performed without an explicit use of language.) One kind of nonlinguistic action that an author may intend to perform is a practical action, such as making money, praising one's country, winning the love of a woman, and so forth. Another kind of nonlinguistic action that an author might want to perform is that of expressing his feelings, an act that can be carried out nonlinguistically (by crying or vomiting) as well as linguistically.

As I am in this paper dealing with literature as a linguistic object, I shall limit my discussion to the linguistic intentions of an author. I shall not discuss in detail nonlinguistic intentions. (Suffice it to say that failure to discuss them does not imply belief in their irrelevance or unimportance, but rather a desire to limit the scope of this discussion. Briefly, I believe that the relation between linguistic and nonlinguistic intentions in an author corresponds to the relation of those types of intentions in ordinary speakers and writers.)

How, then, is the author related to a dramatic speaker? The transillocutions that an author performs result in the illocutions of a dramatic speaker. All that we can know about a dramatic speaker comes through the work (or perhaps works) of a writer, so a writer is responsible for the very existence of the dramatic speaker. He is also, of course, responsible for the speeches of a dramatic speaker.

It seems only natural, then, when we are confronted with a problem of interpreting the actions of the dramatic speaker, to seek aid from the person who is responsible for those actions. This is not to say that the intentions of the author are identical with those of the dramatic speaker. Milton did not necessarily intend to express a desire of *his* that time pass more quickly, although there was undoubtedly some thought or feeling that he did want to express, or some feeling that he wished to evoke in his readers when he wrote "Time." The transillocutionary intentions that a writer has result in the illocutions of his dramatic speakers, so we may at times wish to consult the cause to help interpret the effect.

Other linguistic intentions also affect the work. In the first place these directly affect the intentions of the dramatic speaker, that is, are among the causal determinants of the dramatic speaker's intentions. For this reason, knowledge of a poet's intentions may help us to get at the meaning of a poem. Suppose we cannot discover the intentions of the dramatic speaker from the poem itself; for example, there is some ambiguity that even careful reading does not clear up. The intentions of the poet may provide evidence for determining the probable intentions of the dramatic speaker. For example, if the dramatic speaker mentions a dove, I may not be sure whether or not he intends it to have its customary symbolic meaning. If I find out that the poet intended to use religious symbolism, then I have good reason for deciding to interpret the dove as such a symbol.

The objection may be made that the poem is a failure if we cannot know what the intentions of the dramatic speaker are without going outside the poem itself. It is perhaps hard to imagine a work in which we do not have any idea about whether or not a particular symbol is religious without referring to the intentions of the poet. Some persons may feel that a poem is not worth interpreting if the dramatic speaker's intentions are not clear from the work itself. But often we do feel that a poem is worthwhile even if everything, the speaker's intentions included, is not immediately clear;[13] and in such cases knowing the poet's intentions may help us to discover the intentions of the dramatic speaker, thereby placing us in a better position for interpreting the work.

But now let us look at the author's linguistic intentions apart from the dramatic speaker. The locutionary, illocutionary, and perlocutionary intentions of an author are all to be treated as the intentions of a regular speaker using language in a special, though certainly nonsecondary, way. In ordinary conversation it is taken for granted that a speaker's or writer's locutionary intentions are carried out when he utters or writes a sentence. That is, we assume that he has said the words he wanted to say and that those words mean what he thinks they mean. Admittedly, this is sometimes not the case, as with slips of the tongue and typographical errors. But mistakes such as these are generally easily cleared up—usually by asking the speaker what his intentions (locutionary) were. The same holds true for an author. When we are faced with a literary work, we assume that the locutionary intentions of the author have been carried out, for example, that there are not printing errors.

When an author is illocuting himself (rather than transillocuting), his illocutionary intentions affect his action just as do those of the ordinary speaker when he is asserting, commanding, questioning, and so forth. In puzzling cases his illocutionary action can be interpreted by discovering what he intended to do, that is, what kind of illocutionary act he intended to perform—assert, joke, request, and so forth. It is true that an answer to the question "What illocution did you plan to perform?" is more readily available in the case of a regular speaker than it is in the case of an author. But difficulty in obtaining evidence is not to be confused with the uselessness of that evidence.

The same type of thing is to be said concerning the perlocutionary intentions of an author. It must be admitted that simply knowing what consequences an author intended does not insure that those consequences will in fact occur. Suppose a writer is most interested in convincing his readers of something. Will it help to know this? That is, if I know this, will I be convinced? Ordinarily not. Suppose Gerard Manley Hopkins intended to convince me that one should love God when he wrote "Pied Beauty." If I do not believe in God, then no matter how much Hopkins intends that I love Him, I will not be convinced to do so.

Nonetheless, knowing what consequences were intended may help one to understand a work. Knowing the perlocutionary intentions of a writer may, for example, help me to decide whether a particular poem is narrative, didactic, rhetorical, and so forth. I may be able to tell when language is that of exaggeration with the end of persuasion.

That is, I may get a grip on the poem as a whole, and certainly that is one facet of interpretation.

Some critics have carried the use of authorial intentions to an extreme. However, as long as one bears in mind the omnipresence of dramatic speakers and the primacy of translocuting in the activity of writing literature, this use will necessarily be limited. Without authors, there are no dramatic speakers. But once given life, dramatic speakers stand, and speak, by themselves.

NOTES

1. See Marcia Eaton, "Art, Artifacts and Intentions," *American Philosophical Quarterly*, April 1969, and "Good and Correct Interpretations of Literature," *Journal of Aesthetics and Art Criticism*, Winter 1970.
2. W. K. Wimsatt and Monroe C. Beardsley, "The Intentional Fallacy," in *The Verbal Icon* (Lexington, Ky.: University of Kentucky Press, 1954), p. 5.
3. The notion of transtranslocution is simply a device for handling the actions of dramatic speakers when they are poets, authors, and dramatists. For example, in a novel about a novelist, the fictional novelist may translocute due to transtranslocutions on the part of the real novelist.
4. This is from an unpublished article by Monroe C. Beardsley, "The Testability of Interpretation."
5. See Eaton, "Good and Correct Interpretations of Literature," for a discussion of this type of activity.
6. P. F. Strawson, "On Referring," in *Essays in Conceptual Analysis*, ed. Anthony Flew (London: Macmillan & Co., 1956), p. 35.
7. J. L. Austin, *How to Do Things with Words*, ed. J. O. Urmson (Cambridge, Mass.: Harvard University Press, 1962), p. 104.
8. P. H. Nowell-Smith, *Ethics* (Penguin Books, 1954), p. 81.
9. See Austin, *How to Do Things with Words*, for a full treatment of this matter.
10. See Eaton, "Good and Correct Interpretations of Literature."
11. Robert Frost, "The Road Not Taken," from *Mountain Interval* (New York, Henry Holt & Co., 1916).
12. R. G. Collingwood, "Expression in Art," in *Problems in Aesthetics*, ed. Morris Weitz (New York: Macmillan Co., 1959), p. 192.
13. David Nivison has suggested to me an interesting example of a poem (one of Edward Arlington Robinson's), which is widely admired even though its admirers are all rather puzzled about its meaning. It is discussed in Ronald Moran's "Meaning and Value in 'Take Havergal,'" *Colby Library Quarterly*, March 1967.

IV. ART AND KNOWLEDGE

Introduction

Twenty years ago, when the first edition of this anthology was published, the character of the essays in this section would have been very predictable. At that time it was more taken for granted that philosophers knew what knowledge was; even if a satisfactory analysis of the concept of knowledge had yet to be produced, it seemed clear that what needed to be analyzed was that vast organization of empirical data which constitutes modern science. The only philosophical questions of interest were: Granted that science presented us with the paradigm of knowledge, did art provide us with any knowledge at all? And if it did not, how could we justify, or at least explain, the persistent feeling that art is somehow a source of insight?

Today, there is less reliance by philosophers on the maxim that science represents the only or the best form of knowledge. An investigation into the topic of art and knowledge is less likely to involve the application to art of a conception of knowledge determined in its essential details before the investigation, and it is as likely to look to the concept of art for help in clarifying the concept of knowledge as the other way around. The most fundamental form such an investigation can take, for philosophy, is that of an inquiry into the relation between art and *philosophical* knowing. Insofar as the essays in this section take up such inquiries, they reflexively constitute part of their own subject matter. The essays by Danto and de Man fall into this class. The essay by Nelson Goodman is still focused on the relation between art and science, but it attempts to overcome the distinction between cognitive and emotive uses of language, which structured virtually all the earlier work in this area. Thus, it provides a transition to the remainder of the essays in this section.

Paul de Man's "Criticism and Crisis" deserves a word of introduction of its own. The general thrust of Professor de Man's very rich and subtle essay should be understood in relation to Jacques Derrida's complex method of deconstruction (cf. the essays in this volume by Said and Miller). We may (very crudely) summarize Professor de Man this way: Derrida has shown how philosophical texts may be deconstructed, and in so doing he has revealed something about the possibility of philosophical knowledge. Literature, we must now realize, is that form of discourse which deconstructs itself, and is literature precisely to the extent that it does so. If deconstruction is to be the only mode of "knowing" open to us after Derrida, one might then say that literature is that discourse which fulfills the oldest philosophical injunction by knowing itself—*as* literature, which is to say as fiction, as nonrepresentational in the widest sense of the word. This is not meant as an explication of de Man, but only as an attempt to situate his essay in relation to other developments in contemporary criticism.

For background on the general problem of art and knowledge, see Aiken (7), Foss, Kaplan (2), Lewis (2), Miner, Price (1), Raleigh (1), Silvers (3), and Wallach and Walsh (2). Specifically on the work on Paul de Man, see Klein (1). Arthur Danto's essay is one of a group of pieces which have sparked an interest in the idea that a work of art is a work of art not by virtue of any of its perceptible qualities but by virtue of a relational quality, namely, its place within the context of a certain social institution which Professor Danto calls the Artworld. For more on this "institutional theory" of art, see Dickie (1, 3, 7, 9), T. Cohen (6), Mitias, Sclafani (2, 4), and Silvers (2).

Art and Inquiry

Nelson Goodman

A persistent tradition pictures the aesthetic attitude as passive contemplation of the immediately given, direct apprehension of what is presented, uncontaminated by any conceptualization, isolated from all echoes of the past and from all threats and promises of the future, exempt from all enterprise. By purification-rites of disengagement and disinterpretation we are to seek a pristine, unsullied vision of the world. The philosophic faults and aesthetic absurdities of such a view need hardly be recounted until someone seriously goes so far as to maintain that the appropriate aesthetic attitude toward a poem amounts to gazing at the printed page without reading it.

I maintain, on the contrary, that we have to read the painting as well as the poem, and that aesthetic experience is dynamic rather than static. It involves making delicate discriminations and discerning subtle relationships, identifying symbol systems and characters within these systems and what these characters denote and exemplify, interpreting works and reorganizing the world in terms of works and works in terms of the world. Much of our experience and many of our skills are brought to bear and may be transformed by the encounter. The aesthetic 'attitude' is restless, searching, testing—is less attitude than action: creation and re-creation.

What, though, distinguishes such aesthetic activity from other intelligent behavior such as perception, ordinary conduct, and scientific inquiry? One instant answer is that the aesthetic is directed to no practical end, is unconcerned with self-defense or conquest, with acquisition of necessities or luxuries, with prediction and control of nature. But if the aesthetic attitude disowns practical aims, still aimlessness is hardly enough. The aesthetic attitude is inquisitive as contrasted with the acquisitive and self-preservative, but not all nonpractical inquiry is aesthetic. To think of science as motivated ultimately by practical goals, as judged or justified by bridges and bombs and the control of nature, is to confuse science with technology.

Science seeks knowledge without regard to practical consequences, and is concerned with prediction not as a guide for behavior but as a test of truth. Disinterested inquiry embraces both scientific and aesthetic experience.

Attempts are often made to distinguish the aesthetic in terms of immediate pleasure, but troubles arise and multiply here. Obviously, sheer quantity or intensity of pleasure cannot be the criterion. That a picture or poem provides more pleasure than does a proof is by no means clear; and some human activities unrelated to any of these provide enough more pleasure to render insignificant any differences in amount or degree among various types of inquiry. The claim that aesthetic pleasure is of a different and superior *quality* is by now too transparent a dodge to be taken seriously.

The inevitable next suggestion—that aesthetic experience is distinguished not by pleasure at all but by a special aesthetic emotion—can be dropped on the waste-pile of "dormitive virtue" explanations.

This clears the way for the sophisticated theory that what counts is not pleasure yielded but pleasure 'objectified', pleasure read into the object as a property thereof. Apart from images of some grotesque process of transfusion, what can this mean? To consider the pleasure as possessed rather than occasioned by the object—to say in effect that the object is pleased—may amount to saying that the object expresses the pleasure. But since some aesthetic objects are sad—express sadness rather than pleasure—this comes nowhere near distinguishing in general between aesthetic and nonaesthetic objects or experience.

Some of these difficulties are diminished and others obscured if we speak of satisfaction rather than pleasure. "Satisfaction" is colorless enough to pass in contexts where "pleasure" is ludicrous, hazy enough to blur counter-instances, and flexible enough to tolerate convenient vacillation in interpretation. Thus we may hope to lessen the temptation to conjure up a special quality or kind of feeling or to indulge in mumbo-jumbo about objectification. Nevertheless, satisfaction pretty plainly fails to distinguish aesthetic from non-aesthetic objects and experiences. Not only does some scientific inquiry yield much satisfaction, but some aesthetic objects and experiences yield none. Music and our listening, pictures and our looking, do not fluctuate between aesthetic and non-aesthetic as the playing or painting varies from exalted to excruciating. Being aesthetic does not exclude being unsatisfactory or being aesthetically bad.

The distinguishing feature, some say, is not satisfaction secured but satisfaction sought: in science, satisfaction is a mere by-product of inquiry; in art, inquiry is a mere means for obtaining satisfaction. The difference is held to be neither in process performed nor in satisfaction enjoyed but in attitude maintained. On this view the scientific *aim* is knowledge, the aesthetic *aim* satisfaction.

But how cleanly can these aims be separated? Does the scholar seek knowledge or the satisfaction of knowing? Obtaining knowledge and satifying curiosity are so much the same that trying to do either without trying to do the other surely demands a precarious poise. And anyone who does manage to seek the satisfaction without seeking the knowledge will pretty surely get neither, while on the other hand abstention from all anticipation of satisfaction is unlikely to stimulate research. One may indeed be so absorbed in working on a problem as never to think of the satisfaction to be had from solving it; or one may dwell so fondly on the delights of finding a solution as to take no steps toward arriving at one. But if the latter attitude is aesthetic, aesthetic understanding of anything is foredoomed. And I cannot see that these tenuous, ephemeral, and idiosyncratic states of mind mark any significant difference between the aesthetic and the scientific.

Failure to arrive at an acceptable formulation in terms of pleasure or satisfaction, yielded or 'objectified' or anticipated, will hardly dislodge the conviction that the distinction between the scientific and the aesthetic is somehow rooted in the difference between knowing and feeling, between the cognitive and the emotive. This latter deeply entrenched dichotomy is in itself dubious on many grounds, and its application here becomes especially puzzling when aesthetic and scientific experience alike are seen to be fundamentally cognitive in character. But we do not easily part with the idea that art is in some way or other more emotive than is science.

The shift from pleasure or satisfaction to emotion-in-general softens some of the crudities of the hedonistic formulas but leaves us with trouble enough. Paintings and concerts, and the viewing and hearing of them, need not arouse emotion, any more than they need give satisfaction, to be aesthetic; and anticipated emotion is no better criterion than anticipated satisfaction. If the aesthetic is characteristically emotive in some way, we have yet to say in what way.

Any picture of aesthetic experience as a sort of emotional bath or orgy is plainly preposterous. The emotions involved tend to be muted and oblique as compared, for example, with the fear or sorrow or depression or exultation that arises from actual battle or bereavement or defeat or victory, and are not in general keener than the excitement or despair or elation that accompanies scientific exploration and discovery. What the inert spectator feels falls far short of what the characters portrayed on the stage feel, and even of what he himself would feel on witnessing real-life events. And if he leaps on the stage to participate, his response can no longer be called aesthetic. That art is concerned with simulated emotions suggests, as does the copy theory of representation, that art is a poor substitute for reality; that art is imitation, and aesthetic experience a pacifier that only partly compensates for lack of direct acquaintance and contact with the Real.

Often the emotions involved in aesthetic experience are not only somewhat tempered but also reversed in polarity. We welcome some works that arouse emotions we normally shun. Negative emotions of fear, hatred, disgust may become positive when occasioned by a play or painting. The problem of tragedy and the paradox of ugliness are made to order for ancient and modern Freudians, and the opportunity has not been neglected. Tragedy is said to have the effect of purging us of pent-up and hidden negative emotions, or of injecting measured doses of the killed virus to prevent or mitigate the ravages of an actual attack. Art becomes not only palliative but therapeutic, providing both a substitute for good reality and a safeguard against bad reality. Theatres and museums function as adjuncts to Departments of Public Health.

Again, even among works of art and aesthetic experiences of evident excellence, the emotive component varies widely—from, say, a late Rembrandt to a late Mondrian, or from a Brahms to a Webern quartet. The Mondrian and the Webern are not obviously more emotive than Newton's or Einstein's laws; and a line between emotive and cognitive is less likely to mark off the aesthetic neatly from the scientific than to mark off some aesthetic objects and experiences from others.

All these troubles revive the temptation to posit a special aesthetic emotion or feeling or a special coloration of other emotions occurring in aesthetic experience. This special emotion or coloring may be intense when other emotions are feeble, may be positive when they are negative, and may occur in experience of the most intellectual art and yet be lacking in the most stirring scientific study. All difficulties are resolved—by begging the question. No doubt aesthetic emotions have the property that makes them aesthetic. No doubt things that burn are combustible. The theory of aesthetic phlogiston explains everything and nothing.

Thus two stubborn problems still confront us. First, despite our conviction that aesthetic experience is *some*how emotive rather than cognitive, the failure of formulae in terms of either yielded or anticipated emotions has left us with no way of saying *how*. Second, despite our recognition that emotion in aesthetic experience tends to be denatured and often even inverted, the obvious futility of explanations in terms of a special secretion of the aesthetic glands leaves us without any way of saying *why*. Perhaps the answer to the second question will be found in the answer to the first; perhaps emotion in aesthetic experience behaves as it does because of the role it plays.

Most of the troubles that have been plaguing us can, I have suggested, be blamed on the domineering dichotomy between the cognitive and the emotive. On the one side, we put sensation, perception, inference, conjecture, all nerveless inspection and investigation, fact, and truth; on the other, pleasure, pain, interest, satisfaction, disappointment, all brainless affective response, liking, and loathing. This pretty effectively keeps us from seeing that in aesthetic experience the *emotions function cognitively*. The work of art is apprehended through the feelings as well as through the senses. Emotional numbness disables here as definitely if not as completely as blindness or deafness. Nor are the feelings used exclusively for exploring the emotional content of a work. To some extent, we may feel how a painting looks as we may see how it feels. The actor or dancer—or the spectator—sometimes notes and remembers the feeling of a movement rather than its pattern, insofar as the two can be distinguished at all. Emotion in aesthetic experience is a means of discerning what properties a work has and expresses.

To say this is to invite hot denunciation for cold over-intellectualization; but rather than aesthetic experience being here deprived of emotions, the understanding is being endowed with them. The fact that emotions participate in cognition no more implies that they are not felt than the fact that vision helps us discover properties of objects implies that color-sensations do not occur. Indeed, emotions must be felt—that is, must occur, as sensations must—if they are to be used cognitively. Cognitive use involves discriminating and relating them in order to gauge and grasp the work and integrate it with the rest of our experience and the world. If this is the opposite of passive absorption in sensations and emotions, it by no means amounts to cancelling them. Yet it explains the modifications that emotions may undergo in aesthetic experience.

In the first place, a context of inquiry rather than of indulgence or incitement may result in a characteristic displacement of emotion. The psychological, physiological, and physical setting is different. A dollar earned, a dollar saved, a dollar spent, is still a dollar; affection eventuating in slavery, in frustration, in illumination, is still affection;

but in neither case are all three quite the same. Emotions are not so insular as to be untouched by their environment, but cognitive use neither creates new emotions nor imparts to ordinary emotions some magic additive.

Furthermore the frequent disparity between the emotion felt and the emotive content thereby discovered in the object is now readily understood. Pity on the stage may induce pity in the spectator; but greed may arouse disgust, and courage admiration. So may a white house look white at noon, but red at sunset; and a globe looks round from any angle. Sensory and emotive experiences are related in complex ways to the properties of objects. Also, emotions function cognitively not as separate items but in combination with one another and with other means of knowing. Perception, conception, and feeling intermingle and interact; and an alloy often resists analysis into emotive and non-emotive components. The same pain (or is it the same?) tells of ice or fire. Are anger and indignation different feelings or the same feeling under different circumstances? And does awareness of the overall difference arise from or lead to awareness of the difference in circumstances? The answers do not matter here; for I am not resting anything on the distinction between emotion and other elements in knowing but rather insisting that emotion belongs with them. What does matter is that the comparisons, contrasts, and organization involved in the cognitive process often affect the participating emotions. Some may be intensified, as colors are against a complementary ground, or pointed up by subtle rhyming; others may be softened, as are sounds in a louder context. And some emotions may emerge as properties of the orchestrated whole, belonging like the shape of an eggshell to none of the lesser parts.

Again, negative emotions obviously function cognitively quite as well as positive ones. The horror and revulsion we may feel at *Macbeth* are not lesser means of understanding than the amusement and delight we may find in *Pygmalion*. We are not called upon to suppose that somehow—say by catharsis—the revulsion is transformed into delight, or to explain why the most forbidding portrait is as legitimately aesthetic as the most appealing one; for pleasantness in an emotion is no more a condition for cognitive functioning than is redness in a color-sensation. In aesthetic experience, emotion positive or negative is a mode of sensitivity to a work. The problem of tragedy and the paradox of ugliness evaporate.

Equally plainly, quantity or intensity of emotion is no measure of its cognitive efficacy. A faint emotion may be as informative as an overwhelming one; and finding that a work expresses little or no emotion can be as significant aesthetically as finding that it expresses much. This is overlooked by all attempts to distinguish the aesthetic in terms of amount or degree of emotion.

Although many puzzles are thus resolved and the role of emotion in aesthetic experience clarified, we are still left without a way of distinguishing aesthetic from all other experience. Cognitive employment of the emotions is neither present in every aesthetic, nor absent from every non-aesthetic, experience. We have already noted that some works of art have little or no emotive content, and that even where the emotive content is appreciable, it may sometimes be apprehended by non-emotive means. In daily life, classification of things by feeling is often more vital than classification by other properties: we are likely to be better off if we are skilled in fearing, wanting, braving, or distrusting the right things, animate or inanimate, than if we perceive only their shapes, sizes, weights, etc. And the importance of discernment by feeling does not vanish when the motivation becomes theoretic rather than practical. The zoologist, psychologist, sociologist, even when his aims are purely theoretic, legitimately employs emotion in his investigations. Indeed, in any science, while the requisite objectivity forbids wishful thinking, prejudicial reading of evidence, rejection of unwanted results, avoidance of ominous lines of inquiry, it does not forbid the use of feeling in exploration and discovery, the impetus of inspiration and curiosity, or the cues given by excitement over intriguing problems and promising hypotheses. And the more we discuss these matters, the more we come to realize that emotions are not so clearly differentiated or so sharply separable from other elements in cognition that the distinction can provide a firm basis for answering any moot question.

Repeated failure to find a neat formula for sorting experiences into aesthetic and non-aesthetic, in rough conformity with rough usage, suggests the need for a less simple-minded approach. Perhaps no single, simple, significant feature neatly marks off all arts from all sciences and technologies, or all aesthetic from all scientific and practical experience. In some respects, certain arts may be less like others than like some sciences and technologies; and the traditional classification of objects and activities into the aesthetic and the non-aesthetic may be more harmful than helpful.

Aesthetic and scientific activity alike, I have suggested, consist to a large extent of symbol processing: of inventing, applying, interpreting, transforming, manipulating, symbols and symbol systems. Thus what is called for is a grounded and circumstantial investigation of the most important features of likeness and difference among symbol systems in general, both linguistic and non-linguistic—a study of systems of description, representation, mapping, diagramming, exemplification, expression, and formal notation. Occasional earlier efforts toward a general theory of symbols have been at best fragmentary and at worst infected with serious fallacies and confusions, such as that so-called iconic signs can be distinguished from others on the basis of resemblance to what they stand for, that languages differ from pictures in being more artificial or conventional, and that the difference between analog and digital systems has something to do with analogy and digits.

I cannot now undertake to outline a more systematic investigation into the general theory of symbols, or even to make clear some of its results. I can only try to give you some inkling of what I mean. Some of the features that seem to me to constitute important distinctions among types of symbol systems are these:

(1) *Syntactic density*, depending not upon the internal structure of symbols but on the number of symbols and the nature of their ordering in an entire scheme—a feature that distinguishes representational systems from the articulate systems of languages and notations;

(2) *Semantic density*, depending upon the number of reference-classes and the nature of their ordering under a given symbol system—a feature that distinguishes ordinary languages from notational systems such as that of music;

(3) *Exemplification*, reference running not from a label to what it denotes but from a sample to label denoting it—a feature that distinguishes expression from representation and description; and

(4) *Relative syntactic repleteness*, depending on the comprehensiveness of the set of features that are constitutive of the characters of the scheme—a feature that distinguishes pictures from graphic diagrams. I list these without any adequate explanation and without any attempt to justify their choice, merely in order to suggest the kind of characteristics of symbol systems that seems to me relevant.

Taken severally, these features are neither necessary nor sufficient for aesthetic experience. Each cuts across the usual boundary between the aesthetic and the non-aesthetic, and effects some interesting new alliances and alienations. Pictorial representation, for example, is like the symbol system involved in gauging weights or temperatures in being both syntactically and semantically dense; literary expression and geological sampling share the property of being syntactically less replete. Yet while any of the four symptoms may be absent from aesthetic or present in non-aesthetic experience, they probably tend to be present, or present in higher degree, in aesthetic experience. If they are *severally* neither sufficient nor necessary for aesthetic experience, they may be *conjunctively* sufficient and *disjunctively* necessary; perhaps, that is, an experience is aesthetic if it has all these attributes and only if it has at least one of them.

I am not claiming that this proposal conforms faithfully to ordinary usage. Presystematic usage of "aesthetic" and "non-aesthetic" is even less clearly established by practice, and more seriously infected with inept theorizing, than in the case of most terms. Rather I am suggesting that we have here an appropriate use for some badly abused terms. Density, repleteness, and exemplification, then, are earmarks of the aesthetic; articulateness, attenuation, and denotation are earmarks of the non-aesthetic. A vague and yet harsh dichotomy of experiences gives way to a sorting of features, elements, and processes. Classification of a totality as aesthetic or non-aesthetic counts for less than identification of its aesthetic and non-aesthetic aspects. Phases of a decidedly aesthetic compound may be utterly non-aesthetic; for example, a score and its mere reading may be devoid of all aesthetic aspects. On the other hand, aesthetic features may predominate in the delicate qualitative and quantitative discrimination required in testing some scientific hypotheses. Art and science are not altogether alien.

The distinction here drawn between the aesthetic and the non-aesthetic is independent of all considerations of aesthetic value. That is as it should be. An abominable performance of the *London Symphony* is as aesthetic as a superb one; and Piero's *Risen Christ* is no more aesthetic but only better than a hack's. The symptoms of the aesthetic are not marks of merit; and a characterization of the aesthetic neither requires nor provides a definition of aesthetic excellence.

Folklore has it that the good picture is pretty. At the next higher level, "pretty" is replaced by "beautiful", since the best pictures are often obviously not pretty. But again, many of them are in the most obvious sense ugly. If the beautiful excludes the ugly, beauty is no measure of aesthetic merit; but if the beautiful may be ugly, then "beauty" becomes only an alternative and misleading word for aesthetic merit.

Little more light is shed by the dictum that while science is judged by its truth, art is judged by the satisfaction it gives. Many of the objections urged earlier against satisfaction, yielded or anticipated, as a distinguishing feature of the aesthetic weigh also against satisfaction as a criterion of aesthetic merit: satisfaction cannot be identified with pleasure, and positing a special aesthetic feeling begs the question. We are left with the unhelpful formula that what is aesthetically good is aesthetically satisfactory. The question is what makes a work good or satisfactory.

Being satisfactory is in general relative to function and purpose. A good furnace heats the house to the required temperature evenly, economically, quietly, and safely. A good scientific theory accounts for the relevant facts clearly and simply. We have seen that works of art or their instances perform one or more among certain symbol functions: representation, description, exemplification, expression. The question what constitutes effective symbolization of any of these kinds raises in turn the question what purpose such symbolization serves.

An answer sometimes given is that exercise of the symbolic faculties beyond immediate need has the more remote practical purpose of developing our abilities and techniques to cope with future contingencies. Aesthetic experience becomes a gymnasium workout, pictures and symphonies the bar-bells and punching bags we use in strengthening our intellectual muscles. Art equips us for survival, conquest, and gain. And it channels surplus energy away from destructive outlets. It makes the scientist more acute, the merchant more astute, and clears the streets of juvenile delinquents. Art, long derided as the idle amusement of the guilty leisure class, is acclaimed as a universal servant of mankind. This is a comforting view for those who must reconcile aesthetic inclinations with a conviction that all value reduces to practical utility.

More lighthearted and perhaps more simple-minded is the almost opposite answer: that symbolization is an irresponsible propensity of man, that he goes on symbolizing beyond immediate necessity just for the joy of it or because he cannot stop. In aesthetic experience, he is a puppy cavorting or a well-digger who digs doggedly on after finding enough water. Art is not practical but playful or compulsive. Dogs bark because they are canine, men symbolize because they are human; and dogs go on barking and men go on symbolizing when there is no practical need just because they cannot stop and because it is such fun.

A third answer, bypassing the issue over practicality versus fun, points to communication as the purpose of symbolizing. Man is a social animal, communication is a requisite for social intercourse, and symbols are media of communication. Works of art are messages conveying facts, thoughts, and feelings; and their study belongs to the obstreperous and omnivorous new growth called 'communications theory'. Art depends upon and helps sustain society—exists because, and helps insure that, no man is an island.

Each of these explanations—in terms of gymnastics, play, or conversation—distends and distorts a partial truth. Exercise of the symbolizing skills may somewhat improve practical proficiency; the cryptographic character of symbol invention and interpretation does give them the fascination of a game; and symbols are indispensable to communication. But the lawyer or admiral improving his professional competence by hours in museums, the cavorting puppy, the neurotic well-digger, and the woman on the telephone do not, separately or together, give the whole picture. What all three miss is that the drive is curiosity and the aim enlightenment. Use of symbols beyond immediate need is for the sake of understanding, not practice; what compels is the urge to know, what delights is discovery, and communication is secondary to the apprehension and formulation of what is to be communicated. The primary purpose is cognition in and for itself; the practicality, pleasure, compulsion, and communicative utility all depend upon this.

Symbolization, then, is to be judged fundamentally by how well it serves the cognitive purpose: by the delicacy of its discriminations and the aptness of its allusions; by the way it works in grasping, exploring, and informing the world; by how it analyzes, sorts, orders, and organizes; by how it participates in the making, manipulation, retention, and transformation of knowledge. Considerations of simplicity and subtlety, power and precision, scope and selectivity, familiarity and freshness, are all relevant and often contend with one another; their weighting is relative to our interests, our information, and our inquiry.

So much for the cognitive efficacy of symbolization in general, but what of aesthetic excellence in particular? Distinguishing between the aesthetic and the meritorious cuts both ways. If excellence is not required of the aesthetic, neither is the excellence appropriate to aesthetic objects confined to them. Rather, the general excellence just sketched becomes aesthetic when exhibited by aesthetic objects; that is, aesthetic merit is such excellence in any symbolic functioning that, by its particular constellation of attributes, qualifies as aesthetic. This subsumption of aesthetic under cognitive excellence calls for one more reminder that the cognitive, while contrasted with both the practical and the passive, does not exclude the sensory or the emotive, that what we know through art is felt in our bones and nerves and muscles as well as grasped by our minds, that all the sensitivity and responsiveness of the organism participates in the invention and interpretation of symbols.

The problem of ugliness dissolves; for pleasure and prettiness neither define nor measure either the aesthetic experience or the work of art. The pleasantness or unpleasantness of a symbol does not determine its general cognitive efficacy or its specifically aesthetic merit. *Macbeth* and the Goya *Witches' Sabbath* no more call for apology than do *Pygmalion* and the Botticelli *Venus*.

The dynamics of taste, often embarrassing to those who seek inflexible standards of immutable excellence, also become readily understandable. After a time and for a time, the finest painting may pall and the greatest music madden. A work may be successively offensive, fascinating, comfortable, and boring. These are the vicissitudes of the vehicles and instruments of knowledge. We focus upon frontiers; the peak of interest in a symbol tends to occur at the time of revelation, somewhere midway in the passage from the obscure to the obvious. But there is endurance and renewal, too. Discoveries become available knowledge only when preserved in accessible form; the trenchant and laden symbol does not become worthless when it becomes familiar, but is incorporated in the base for further exploration. And where there is density in the symbol system, familiarity is never complete and final; another look may always disclose significant new subtleties. Moreover, what we read from and learn through a symbol varies with what we bring to it. Not only do we discover the world through our symbols but we understand and reappraise our symbols progressively in the light of our growing experience. Both the dynamics and the durability of aesthetic value are natural consequences of its cognitive character.

Like considerations explain the relevance to aesthetic merit of experience remote from the work. What a Manet or Monet or Cézanne does to our subsequent seeing of the world is as pertinent to their appraisal as is any direct confrontation. How our lookings at pictures and our listenings to music inform what we encounter later and elsewhere is integral to them as cognitive. The absurd and awkward myth of the insularity of aesthetic experience can be scrapped.

The role of theme and variation—common in architecture and other arts as well as in music—also becomes intelligible. Establishment and modification of motifs, abstraction and elaboration of patterns, differentiation and interrelation of modes of transformation, all are processes of constructive search; and the measures applicable are not those of passive enjoyment but those of cognitive efficacy: delicacy of discrimination, power of integration, and justice of proportion between recognition and discovery. Indeed, one typical way of advancing knowledge is by progressive variation upon a theme. Among modern composers, theme and variation along with all recognizable pattern is sometimes scorned, and maximum unpredictability is the declared aim; but as C. I. Lewis pointed out, complete irregularity is inconceivable—if no sequence is ever repeated in a given composition, that fact in itself constitutes a notable regularity.

Aesthetic merit, however, is by no means my main concern, and I am somewhat uncomfortable about having arrived at an incipient definition of what is often confusingly called 'beauty'. Excessive concentration on the question of excellence has been responsible, I think, for constriction and distortion of aesthetic inquiry. To say that a work of art is good or even to say how good it is does not after all provide much information, does not tell us whether the work is evocative, robust, vibrant, or exquisitely designed, and still less what are its salient specific qualities of color, shape, or sound. Moreover works of art are not racehorses, and picking a winner is not the primary goal. Conceiving of aesthetic experience as a form of understanding results both in resolving and in devaluing the question of aesthetic value.

In saying that aesthetic experience is cognitive experience distinguished by the dominance of certain symbolic characteristics and judged by standards of cognitive efficacy, have I overlooked the sharpest contrast: that in science, unlike art, the ultimate test is truth? Do not the two domains differ most drastically in that truth means all for the one, nothing for the other?

Despite rife doctrine, truth by itself matters very little in science. We can generate volumes of dependable truths at will so long as we are unconcerned with their importance; the multiplication tables are inexhaustible, and empirical truths abound. Scientific hypotheses, however true, are worthless unless they meet minimal demands of scope or specificity imposed by our inquiry, unless they effect some telling analysis or synthesis, unless they raise or answer significant questions. Truth is not enough; it is at most a necessary condition. But even this concedes too much; the noblest scientific laws are seldom quite true. Minor discrepancies are overridden in the interest of breadth or power or simplicity. Science denies its data as the statesman denies his constituents—within the limits of prudence.

Yet neither is truth one among competing criteria involved in the rating of scientific hypotheses. Given any assemblage of evidence, countless alternative hypotheses conform to it. We cannot choose among them on grounds of truth; for we have no direct access to their truth. Rather we judge them by such features as their simplicity and strength. These criteria are not supplemental to truth but applied hopefully as a means for arriving at the nearest approximation to truth that is compatible with our other interests.

Does this leave us with the cardinal residual difference that truth—though not enough, not necessary, and not a touchstone for choosing among hypotheses—is nevertheless a consideration relevant in science but not in art? Even so meek a formulation suggests too strong a contrast. Truth of a hypothesis after all is a matter of fit—fit with a body of theory, and fit of hypothesis and theory to the data at hand and the facts to be encountered. And as Philipp Frank liked to remind us, goodness of fit takes a two-way adjustment—of theory to facts and of facts to theory—with the double aim of comfort and a new look. But such fitness, such aptness in conforming to and reforming our knowledge and our world, is equally relevant for the aesthetic symbol. Truth and its aesthetic counterpart amount to appropriateness under different names. If we speak of hypotheses but not of works of art as true, that is because we reserve the terms "true" and "false" for symbols in sentential form. I do not say this difference is negligible, but it is specific rather than generic, a difference in field of application rather than in formula, and marks no schism between the scientific and the aesthetic.

None of this is directed toward obliterating the distinction between art and science. Declarations of indissoluble unity—whether of the sciences, the arts, the arts and sciences together, or of mankind—tend anyway to focus attention upon the differences. What I am stressing is that the affinities here are deeper, and the significant differentia other, than is often supposed. The difference between art and science is not that between feeling and fact, intuition and inference, delight and deliberation, synthesis and analysis, sensation and cerebration, concreteness and abstraction, passion and action, mediacy and immediacy, or truth and beauty, but rather a difference in domination of certain specific characteristics of symbols.

The implications of this reconception may go beyond philosophy. We hear a good deal about how the aptitudes and training needed for the arts and for the sciences contrast or even conflict with one another. Earnest and elaborate efforts to devise and test means of finding and fostering aesthetic abilities are always being initiated. But none of this talk or these trials can come to much without an adequate conceptual framework for designing crucial experiments and interpreting their results. Once the arts and sciences are seen to involve working with—inventing, applying, reading, transforming, manipulating—symbol systems that agree and differ in certain specific ways, we can perhaps undertake pointed psychological investigation of how the pertinent skills inhibit or enhance one another; and the outcome might well call for changes in educational technology. Our preliminary study suggests, for example, that some processes requisite for a science are less akin to each other than to some requisite for an art. But let us forego foregone conclusions. Firm and usable results are as far off as badly needed; and the time has come in this field for the false truism and the plangent platitude to give way to the elementary experiment and the hesitant hypothesis.

Whatever consequences might eventually be forthcoming for psychology or education would in any case count as by-products of the theoretical inquiry. The prior aim is to take some steps towards a systematic study of symbols and symbol systems and the ways they function in our perceptions and actions and arts and sciences, and thus in the creation and comprehension of our worlds.

To the memory of Rudolph Wittkower

Artworks and Real Things*

Arthur C. Danto

The children imitating the cormorants,
Are more wonderful
Than the real cormorants.

Issa

Painting relates to both art and life . . .
(I try to work in that gap between the two).

Rauschenberg

From philosophers bred to expect a certain stylistic austerity, I beg indulgence for what may strike them as an intolerable wildness in the following paper. It is a philosophical reflection on New York painting from circa 1961 to circa 1969, and a certain wildness in the subject may explain the wildness I apologize for in its treatment. Explain but not excuse, I will be told: the properties of the subject treated of need never penetrate the treatment itself; Freud's papers on sexuality are exemplarily unarousing, papers in logic are not logical *merely* in consequence of their subject. But in a way the paper is part of its own subject, since it becomes an artwork at the end. Perhaps the final creation in the period it treats of. Perhaps the final artwork in the history of art!

I

Rauschenberg's self-consciously characterized activity exemplifies an ancient task imposed generically upon artists in consequence of an

* This paper was read in an earlier version at a conference on the philosophy of art at the University of Illinois at Chicago Circle. I am grateful to Professor George Dickie for having invited it. For prodromal reflections on much the same topic, see my paper "The Artworld," in *Journal of Philosophy*, vol. 61 (1964), pp. 571–584.

322

alienating criticism by Plato of art as such. Art allegedly stands at a certain invidious remove from reality, so that in fabricating those entities whose production defines their essence, artists are contaminated at the outset with a kind of ontological inferiority. They bear, as well, the stigma of a moral reprobation, for with their productions they charm the souls of artlovers with shadows of shadows. Finally, speaking as a precocious therapist as well as a true philistine, Plato insinuates that art is a sort of perversion, a substitute, deflected, compensatory activity engaged in by those who are impotent to *be* what as a *pis-aller* they *imitate*. Stunned by this triple indictment into a quest for redemption, artists have sought a way towards ontological promotion, which means of course collapsing the space between reality and art. That there should, by Rauschenberg's testimony, still remain an insulating vacuity between the two which even *he* has failed to drain of emptiness, stimulates a question regarding the philosophical suitability of the task.

To treat as a defect exactly what makes a certain thing or activity possible and valuable is almost a formula for generating platonic philosophy, and in the case of art an argument may be mounted to show that its possibility and value is logically tied up with putting reality at a distance. It was, for example, an astonishing discovery that representations of barbaric rites need *themselves* no more be barbaric than representations of any *x* whatever need have the properties of *x*-hood. By *imitating* practices it was *horrifying* to engage in (Nietzsche), the Greeks spontaneously put such practices at a distance and invented civilization in the process; for civilization consists in the awareness of media as media and hence of reality as reality. So just those who gave birth to tragedy defeated an insupportable reality by putting between themselves and it a spiritualizing distance it is typical of Plato to find demeaning. It may be granted that this achievement creates the major problem of representational art, which is sufficiently to resemble the realities it denotes that identification of it as a representation of the latter is possible, while remaining sufficiently different that confusion of the two is difficult. Aristotle, who explains the pleasure men take in art through the pleasure they take in imitations, is clearly aware that the pleasure in question (which is intellectual) logically presupposes the knowledge that it *is* an imitation and not the real thing it resembles and denotes. We may take (a minor) pleasure in a man imitating a crow-call of a sort we do not commonly take in crow-calls themselves, but this pleasure is rooted in cognition: we must know enough of crow-calls to know that these are what the man is imitating (and not, say, giraffe-calls), and must know that he and not crows is the provenance of the caws. One further condition for pleasure is this, that the man *is* imitating and not just an unfortunate crow-boy, afflicted from birth with a crowish pharynx. These crucial asymmetries need not be purchased at the price of decreased verisimilitude, and it is not unreasonable to insist upon a perfect acoustical indiscernibility between true and sham crow-calls, so that the uninformed in matters of art might—like an overhearing crow, in fact—be deluded and adopt attitudes appropriate to the reality of crows. The knowledge upon which artistic pleasure (in contrast with *aesthetic* pleasure) depends is thus external to and at right angles to the sounds themselves, since they concern the causes and conditions of the sounds and their relation to the real world. So the option is always available to the mimetic artist to rub away all differences between artworks and real things providing he is assured that the audience has a clear grasp of the distances.

It was in the exercise of this option, for example, that Euripides undertook the abolition of the chorus, inasmuch as *real* confrontation, *real* frenzies of jealousy commonly transpire without benefit of the ubiquitous, nosy, and largely disapproving chorus inexplicably (to *him*) deemed necessary for the action to get on by his predecessors. And in a similar spirit of realism, the stony edifying heroes of the past are replaced by plain folks, and their cosmic suffering with the commonplace heartpains of such (for example) as us. So there *was* some basis for the wonder of his contemporary, Socrates (who may, considering his Egyptolatry in the *Laws*, have been disapproving not so much of art as of *realistic* art in the *Republic*), as to what the *point* of drama any longer could be: if we *have* the real thing, of what service is an idle iteration of it? And so he created a dilemma by looking inversely at the cognitive relations Aristotle subsequently rectified: either there is going to be a discrepancy, and mimesis fails, or art succeeds in erasing the discrepancy, in which case it just *is* reality, a roundabout way of getting what we already *have*. And, as one of his successors has elegantly phrased it: "one of the damned things is enough." Art fails if it is indiscernible from reality, and it equally if oppositely fails if it is not.

We are all familiar enough with one attempt to escape this dilemma, which consists in locating art in whatever makes for the discrepancies between reality and imitations of it. Euripides, it is argued, went in just the wrong direction. Let us instead make objects which are *insistently* art by virtue of the fact that no one can mistake

them for reality. So the disfiguring conventions abolished in the name
of reality become reintroduced in the name of art, and one settles for
perhaps a self-conscious woodenness, a deliberate archaism, an op-
eratic falseness so marked and underscored that it must be apparent
to any audience that illusion could never have been our intent. *Non*-
imitativeness becomes the criterion of art, the more artificial and the
less imitative in consequence, the purer the art in question. But a
fresh dilemma awaits at the other end of the inevitable route, namely
that non-imitativeness is *also* the criterion of reality, so the more
purely art things become, the closer they verge on reality, and *pure*
art collapses into pure *reality*. Well, this may after all be the route to
ontological promotion, but the other side of the dilemma asks what
makes us want to call *art* what by common consent is reality? So in
order to preserve a distinction, we reverse directions, hardly with a
light heart since the same dilemma, we recall, awaits us at the other
end. And there seems, on the face of it, only one available way to
escape the unedifying shuttle from dilemma to dilemma, which is to
make non-imitations which are radically distinct from all heretofore
existing real things. Like Rauschenberg's stuffed goat garlanded with
a tire! It is with such unentrenched objects, like combines and emeru-
bies, that the abysses between life and art are to be filled!

There remains then only the nagging question of whether all unentrenched objects are to be reckoned artworks, e.g., consider the first
can-opener. *I* know of an object indiscernible from what happen to be
our routine can-openers, which *is* an artwork:

> The single starkness of its short, ugly, ominous blade-like ex-
> tremity, embodying aggressiveness and masculinity, contrast
> formally as well as symbolically with the frivolous diminishing
> helix, which swings freely (but upon a fixed enslaving axis!)
> and is pure, helpless femininity. The two motifs are symbioti-
> cally sustained in a single, powerful composition, no less uni-
> versal and hopeful for its miniature scale and commonplace
> material.
> [*Gazette des beaux arts*, vol. 14, no. 6, pp. 430–431. My
> translation]

As an artwork, of course, it has the elusive defining properties of
artworks, significant form *compris*. In virtue of its indiscernibility
from the domestic utensil, then, one might think it uncouth if not

unintelligible to withhold predication of significant form to the latter, merely on grounds of conspicuous *Zuhandenheit* (one *could* open cans with the work the critic of the *Gazette* was so stirred by) or large numbers. For it would be startling that two things should have the same shape and yet one have and the other lack significant form. Or it would be were we to forget for an inadvertent moment the existence of a Polynesian language in which the sentence "Beans are high in protein," indiscernible acoustically from the English sentence "Beans are high in protein" actually means, in its own language, what "Motherhood is sacred" means in English. And it induces profound filial sentiments when audited by native speakers though hardly that with us. So perhaps significant form is supervenient upon a semantical reading, itself a weak function of language affiliation which mere inscriptional congruity happens to underdetermine? The question is suitably rhetorical at this point, for my concern is that the logical intersection of the non-imitative and the non-entrenched may as easily be peopled with artworks as by real things, and *may* in fact have pairs of indiscernible objects, one an artwork and one not. In view of this possibility, we must avert our eyes from the objects themselves in a counter-phenomenological turn—*Von den Sachen selbst!*—and see whatever it is, which clearly does *not* meet the eye, which keeps art and reality from leaking hopelessly into one another's territory. Only so can we escape the dilemma of Socrates, which has generated so much art-history through the misunderstandings it epitomizes and encourages.

II

Borges merits credit for, amongst other things, having discovered the Pierre Menard Phenomenon: two art-objects, in this instance two fragments of the *Quixote*, which though verbally indiscriminable have radically non-overlapping and incompatible *artistic* properties. The art-works in question stand to their common physical embodiment in something like the relationship in which a set of isomers may stand to a common molecular formula, which then underdetermines and hence fails to explain the differences in their chemical reactions. The difference, of course, is given by the way the elements recorded in the formula are put together. Of the two *Quixotes*, for example, one is "more subtle" and the other "more clumsy" than its counterpart. That of Cervantes is the more coarse: it "opposes to the fiction of chivalry the tawdry provincial reality of his country." Menard's ("On the other hand . . ." !) selects for *its* reality "the land of Carmen during the century of Lepanto and Lope de Vega." Menard's work is an oblique condemnation of *Salammbô*, which Cervantes' could hardly have been. Though visibly identical, one is almost incomparably richer than the other and, Borges writes, "The contrast in style is also vivid. The archaic style of Menard—quite foreign, after all—suffers from a certain affectation. Not so that of his forerunner, who handles with ease the current Spanish of his time." Menard, were he to have *completed* his *Quixote*, would have had the task of creating at least one character in excess of Cervantes': the author of the (so-called in Menard's but *not* so-called in Cervantes') "Autobiographical Fragment." And so on. Menard's work was *his*, not a copy nor an accidentally congruent achievement of the sort involved in the discovery that the painters of Jupiter are making (there being no question here of cultural diffusion) flat works using the primary colors and staggeringly like Mondrians, but rather a fresh, in its own way remarkable creation. A mere copy would have no *literary* value at all, but would be merely an exercise in facsimilitation, and a *forgery* of so well known a work would be a fiasco. It is a precondition for the Menard phenomenon that author and audience alike know (not the original but) the *other* Quixote. But Menard's is not a quotation either, as it were, for quotations in this sense *merely* resemble the expressions they denote without having *any* of the artistically relevant properties of the latter: *quotations* cannot be scintillating, original, profound, searching, or whatever what is quoted may be. There are, indeed, theories of quotation according to which they lack *any* semantical structure, which their originals seldom lack. So a *quotation* of the Quixote (*either* Quixote) would be artistically null though quite superimposable upon its original. Quotations, in fact, are striking examples of objects indiscernible from originals which are not artworks though the latter are. Copies (in general) lack the properties of the originals they denote and resemble. A copy of a cow is not a cow, a copy of an artwork is not an artwork.

Quotations are entities difficult to locate ontologically, like reflections and shadows, being neither artworks nor real things, inasmuch as they are parasitic upon reality, and have in particular that degree of derivedness assigned by Plato to artworks as class. So though a copy —or quotation—of an artwork is logically excluded from the class of artworks, it raises too many special questions to be taken as our specific example of an entity indiscernible from an artwork though not one. But it is not difficult to generate less intricate examples.

Consider, for the moment, *neckties*, which have begun to work their way into the artworld, e.g., Jim Dine's *Universal Tie*, John Duff's *Tie Piece*, etc. Suppose Picasso exhibits now a tie, painted uniform blue in order to reject any touch of *le peinture* as decisively as the Strozzi altarpiece rejects, as an act of artistic will, giottesque perspective. One says: my child could do *that*. Well, true enough, there is nothing beyond infantile capability here: so let a child, with his stilted deliberateness, color one of his father's ties an all over blue, no brushstrokes 'to make it nice.' I would hesitate to predict a magnificent future in art for this child on the basis of his having caused the existence of something indistinguishable from something created by the greatest master of modern times. I would go further, and say that he has not produced an artwork. For something prevents *his* object from entering the artworld, as it prevents from entering that world those confections by a would-be van Meegeren of Montmartre who sees at once the Picasso tie as a chance for clever forgery. Three such objects would give rise to one of those marvelous Shakespearean plots, of confused twins and mistaken identities, a possibility not a joking one for Kahnwieler (or was it Kootz?) who takes all the necessary precautions. *In spite of which,* let us suppose, the ties get mixed up, and the child's tie hangs to this very day in the Museum of the Municipality of Talloir. Picasso, of course, disputes its authenticity, and refuses to sign it (in fact he signs the forgery). The original was confiscated by the Ministry of Counterfacts. I look forward to the time when a doctoral candidate under Professor Theodore Reff straightens out the attributions by counting threads, though the status of a forgery with an authentic signature remains for philosophers of art to settle. Professor Goodman has an intriguing argument that sooner or later differences are bound to turn up, that what looks identically similar today will look artistically so diverse tomorrow that men will wonder how the case I have described would ever have arisen. Well, sufficient unto the day may be the similarities thereof: tomorrow's differentiations would appear *whichever* of the three ties were to hang in the museum, and I am inclined to feel that any seen differences will ultimately be used to reenforce the attribution, right or wrong, which is the accepted one. But that leaves still unsettled the ontological questions, besides generating a kind of absurdity of connoisseurship by bringing into the aesthetics of this order of object the refined peering appropriate, say, to Poussin or Morandi or Cézanne. None of whom, though clearly not for reasons of artistic ineptitude, would have been able to make an artwork out of a painted tie. So it isn't just that Picasso happens to be an *artist* that makes the difference in the cases at hand. But the further reasons are interesting.

For one thing, there would have been no room in the artworld of Cézanne's time for a painted necktie. Not everything can be an artwork at every time: the artworld must be ready for it. Much as not every line which is *witty* in a given context can be witty in all. Pliny tells of a contest between rival painters, the first drawing a straight line; the second drawing, in a different color, a line *within* that line; the first drawing an ultimately fine line within this. One does not ordinarily think of lines as having sides, but with each inscribed line, a space exists between its edges and the edges of the containing line, so that the result would be like five very thin strips of color. Nested lines, each making space where none was believed possible, shows remarkable steadiness of hand and eye, and bears witness to the singular prowess of Parahesios and his rival here. And the object was a wonder in its time. But not an artwork! No more than the famous free-hand circle of Giotto. But I could see exactly such an object turning up on Madison Avenue today, a synthesis, perhaps, of Barnett Newman and Frank Stella. Such an object in the time of Parahesios would have *merely* been a set-piece of draughtsmanly control. So it is not even as though, on the Berkeleyan assumption that only artworks can anticipate artworks, Parahesios were a predecessor of the contemporary painter of fine stripes. Parahesios could not have modified his perception of art, nor that of his times, to accommodate his *tour de main* as an artistic achievement. But Picasso's artworld was ready to receive, at Picasso's hand, a necktie: for he had made a chimpanzee out of a toy, a bull out of a bicycle seat, a goat out of a basket, a venus out of a gas-jet: so why not a *tie out of a tie*? It had room not only in the artworld, but in the corpus of the artist, in a way in which the identical object, from the hands of Cézanne, would have had room for neither. Cézanne could only have made a mountain out of paint, in the received and traditional manner of such transformations. He did not have the option even of making paint out of paint, in the later manner of the Abstract Expressionists.

But while these considerations serve to show that the identical object could, in one art-historical context be an artwork and in another one not, the problem remains of moving from *posse ad esse*. What, apart from the possibility, makes it actually a work of art in the context of late Picasso? And what makes then the differences between what Picasso did and his contemporaries, the child and the forger, did? Only when the world was ready for "Necktie" could the comedy of mistaken identities have transpired, and while it is easy to see how, given the sharp and exact resemblances, an artwork which was a necktie should have been confused with a necktie which was not an artwork, the task of explicating the differences remains.

One way to see the matter is this: Picasso *used* the necktie to *make a statement*, the forger employed the necktie to copy what Picasso made a statement with, but made *no* statement by means of his. And this would be true even were he inspired by van Meegeren to invent, say, a rose-colored necktie to fill a gap in Picasso's development. The child and Cézanne are simply making noise. Their objects have no location in the history of art. Part at least of what Picasso's statement is about is art, and art had not developed appropriately by the time of Cézanne for such a statement to have been intelligible, nor can the child in question have sufficiently internalized the history and theory of art to make a statement, much less *this* statement, by means of the painted necktie. At least the right relations hold between the four objects to enable a distinction structurally of a piece with that between statement, echo, and noise to be made. And though a real enough object—a hand-painted tie!—Picasso's work stands at just the right remove from reality for it to *be* a statement, indeed a statement in part about reality and art sufficiently penetrating to enable its own enfranchisement into the world of art. It enters at a phase of art-history when the consciousness of the difference between reality and art is part of what makes the difference between art and reality.

III

Testamorbida is a playwright who deals in Found Drama. Disgusted with theatricality, he has run through the tiresome post-Pirandello devices for washing the boundaries away between life and art, and has sickened of the contrived atmospheres of happenings. Nothing is going to be real enough save reality. So he declares his latest play to have been everything that happened in the life of a family in Astoria between last Saturday and tonight, the family in question having been picked by throwing a dart at the map of the town. How natural are the actors! They have no need to overcome the distance from their roles by stanislaviskyian exercise, since they *are* what they play. Or 'play.' The author 'ends' the play by fiat at eleven-ten (curtain), and has the after-theater party with friends at the West End Bar. No reviews, there was no audience, there was just one 'performance.' For all the 'actors' know, it was an ordinary evening, pizza and television, hair put up in rollers, a wrong number and a toothache. All that makes this slice of life an artwork is the declaration that it is so, plus the meta-artistic vocabulary: 'actor,' 'dialogue,' 'natural,' 'beginning,' 'end.' And perhaps the title, which may be as descriptive as you please, viz., "What a Family in Astoria Did . . .".

Titles are borne by artworks, interestingly enough, though not by things indiscernible from them which are *not* artworks, e.g., another period in the life of that or any family in Astoria or anywhere. Even 'Untitled' is a kind of title: non-artworks are not entitled even to be untitled. Cézanne's hand-painted necktie may bear a label, say at the Cézanne House, along with other memorabilia, but 'Cézanne's Necktie' is not its title ('Cézanne's Necktie' could be the title of Picasso's tie if it were painted in just the color of the Louvre's *Vase Bleu*). Noblemen have titles too. 'Title' has the ring of status, of something which can be conferred. It has, indeed, enough of the ring of legality to suggest that 'artwork'—perhaps like 'person!'—is after all an ascriptive term rather than a descriptive—or exclusively descriptive —one.

Ascriptivity, as I understand it, is a property of predicates when they attach to objects in the light of certain conventions, and which apply less on the basis of certain necessary and sufficient conditions than of certain defeating conditions not holding. 'Person' is defeasible, for example, through such avenues as minority, subcompetence, disenfranchisement, financial responsibility and liability, and the like. A corporation can consist of a single person, who is not identical with the corporation in question, and the distinction between that person and the corporation he belongs to is perhaps enough like the distinction between an artwork and the physical object it consists in but is not identical with that we can think of artworks in terms of privileges, exemptions, rights, and the like. Thus artworks, which happen to contain neckties, are entitled to hang in museums, in a way in which neckties indiscernible from the former are not. They have, again, a certain peer-group which their indiscernible but plebeian counterparts do not. The blue necktie which is an artwork belongs with the Cowper-Niccolini Madonna and the Cathedral of Laon, while the necktie just like it which is not an artwork belongs just with the collars and cufflinks of banal haberdashery, somewhat *abîmé* by blue-paint. The blue necktie, indeed, is in the museum and in the collection, but its counterparts, though they can be geometrically in the museum, are there only in the way sofas and palm-trees typically are. There is, in fact, a kind of *In-der-Pinakothek-sein* not so awfully different from the *In-der-Welt-sein* which pertains to persons in contrast with things. A necktie which is an artwork differs from one which is not like a person differs from a body: metaphysically, it takes two sets of predicates amazingly similar to the P- and M-predicates which *persons* take on a well-known theory of P. F. Strawson's: no accident, perhaps, if 'person' too is an ascriptive predicate. The blue necktie, thus, which is an artwork, is *by* Picasso, whereas its counterpart is not *by* Cézanne even though he put the paint on it. And so forth. So let us try this out for a moment, stressing here the defeating conditions, less to strike a blow against Testamorbida than to see what kind of thing it is that can be subject to defeat of this order. I shall mention only two defeating conditions as enough for our purposes, though hardly exhausting the list. Indeed, were art to evolve, new defeating conditions would emerge.

(1) *Fakes*. If illusion were the aim after all of art, then there would be just exactly the same triumph in getting Stendhal to swoon at a fake Guido Reni as causing birds to peck at painted grapes. There is, I believe, no stigma attached to painting pictures of pictures: Burliuk once told me that, since artists paint the things they love and since *he* loved *pictures*, he saw no obstacle to painting pictures of pictures, viz., of Hogarth's *Shrimp Girl*. It *happens* that Burliuk remained himself, his picture of the *Shrimp Girl* deviating from the *Shrimp Girl* roughly as he differed from Hogarth. He was not, on the other hand, pretending the *Shrimp Girl* was *his* any more than he was pretending that Westhampton, which he also and in the same spirit painted pictures of, was *his*: what was *his* was the painting, a statement in paint which denoted the *Shrimp Girl* as his seascapes denoted glimpses of Westhampton: so we are distanced as much from the one motif as from the other, admiring in both cases the vehicle. Well, a man might love his own paintings as much as he loves those of others, so what was to have prevented Burliuk from painting, say, his *Portrait of Leda*? This is not a case of *copying* the latter, so that we have two copies of the same painting: it is explicitly a painting *of* a painting, a different thing altogether, though it might exactly enough resemble a copy. A copy is defective, for example, insofar as it deviates from the original, but the question of deviation is simply irrelevant if it is a painting of a painting: much as we do not expect the artist to use chlorophyl in depicting trees. Now, if deviation is irrelevant, so is non-deviation. A copy is, indeed, just like a quotation, showing what we are to respond to rather than being what we are to respond to: whereas a painting of a painting is something *to* which we respond. Artists who repeat themselves, the Pierre Menard phenomenon notwithstanding, raise some remarkable questions. Schumann's last composition was based on a theme he claimed was dictated to him by angels in his sleep, but was *in fact* the slow

movement of his own recently published Violin Concerto. (Is it an accident that Schumann was working on a book of quotations at the time of his *Zusammenbruch*?) Robert Desnos's *Dernier Poème à Youki* (*"J'ai tant rêvé de toi que tu perds ta réalité . . ."*) is simply, according to Mary Ann Caws, "a retranslation into French of the rough and truncated translation into Czech" of his earlier and famous poem addressed to the actress Yvonne George: but was Desnos delirious when he addressed this poem, at his death, to Youki (or did he confuse Youki and Yvonne) or think it was a new poem or what? (I mention Schumann and Desnos in case someone thinks Goodman's distinction of one- and two-stage arts has any bearing). Repetitions are maddening.

A fake pretends to be a statement but is not one. It lacks the required relation to the artist. That we should mistake a fake for a real work (or *vice versa*) does not matter. Once we discover that it is a fake, it loses its stature as an artwork because it loses its structure as a statement. It at best retains a certain interest as a decorative object. Insofar as being a fake is a defeating condition, it is analytical to the concept of an artwork that it be "original". Which does not entail that it need or cannot be derivative, imitative, influenced, 'in the manner of,' or whatever. We are not required to invent a language in order to make a statement. Being an original means that the work must in a deep sense originate with the artist we believe to have done it.

(2) *Non-artistic provenance.* It is analytically true that artworks can only be *by* artists, so that an object, however much (or exactly) it may resemble an artwork is not *by* whoever is responsible for its existence, unless he is an artist. But "artist" is as ascriptive a term as "artwork," and in fact "by" is as ascriptive as either. Since, after all, not everything whose existence we owe to artists are *by* him. Consider the customs inspector who bears the stings of past and recent *gaffes* by his peers and decides to take no chances: a certain piece of polished brass—in fact the bushing for a submarine—is declared an artwork. But *his* so calling it that no more makes it an artwork than someone in the same métier calling an object near of morphic kin to it *not* an artwork made the latter *not* be one. What injustice, then, if an artist decides to exhibit the bushing as a found object.

Douaniers, children, chimpanzees, counterfeiters: tracing an object to any of these defeats it as an artwork, demotes it to the status of a mere real object. Hence the logical irrelevance of the claim that a child, a chimpanzee, a forger or, *à la rigueur*, a customs inspector could *do* any of them. The mere object perhaps does not lie outside their powers. But as an artwork it does. Much in the way in which not everyone who can say the words "I pronounce you man and wife" can marry people, nor who can pronounce the words "Thirty days or thirty dollars" can *sentence* a man. So the question of whether an object is *by* someone, and how one is qualified to make artworks out of real things, are of a piece with the question of whether it is an artwork.

The moment something is considered an artwork, it becomes subject to an *interpretation*. It owes its existence as an artwork to this, and when its claim to art is defeated, it loses its interpretation and becomes a mere thing. The interpretation is in some measure a function of the artistic context of the work: it means something different depending upon its art-historical location, its antecedents, and the like. And as an artwork, finally, it acquires a structure which an object photographically similar to it is simply disqualified from sustaining if it is a real thing. Art exists in an atmosphere of interpretation and an artwork is thus a vehicle of interpretation. The space between art and reality is like the space between language and reality partly because art *is* a language of sorts, in the sense at least that an artwork says something, and so presupposes a body of sayers and interpreters who are in position, who define what being in position is, to interpret an object. There is no art without those who speak the language of the artworld, and who know enough of the difference between artworks and real things to recognize that calling an artwork a real thing *is* an interpretation of it, and one which depends for its point and appreciation on the contrast between the artworld and the real-world. And it is exactly with reference to this that the defeating conditions for ascription of "artwork" are to be understood. If this is so, then ontological promotion of art is hardly to be looked for. It is a logical impossibility. Or nearly so: for there is one further move to reckon with.

IV

Much as philosophy has come to be increasingly its own subject, has turned reflexively inward onto itself, so art has done, having become increasingly its own (and only) subject: like the Absolute of Hegel, which finally achieved congruence with itself by becoming self-contemplative in the respect that *what* it contemplates is itself in contemplation. Rosenberg thus reads the canvas as an arena in which a real action occurs when an artist (but *nota bene: only* when an *artist*) makes a wipe of paint upon it: a stroke. To appreciate that the boundaries have been crossed, we must read the stroke as saying, in effect, about itself, that it *is* a stroke and not a representation of anything. Which the indiscernible strokes made by housepainters cannot *begin* to say, though it is true that they are strokes and not representations. In perhaps the subtlest suite of paintings in our time, such strokes—fat, ropy, expressionist—have been read with a deadly literalness of their makers' or the latter's ideologues' intention as (mere) real things, and made the subject of paintings as much as if they were apples, by Roy Lichtenstein. These are paintings *of* brush strokes. And Lichtenstein's paintings say, about themselves, at least this: that they *are* not but only represent brush strokes, and yet they are art. The boundaries between reality and art as much inform these works as they did the initial impulses of the Abstract Expressionists they impale. The boundaries between art and reality, indeed, become *internal* to art itself. And this is a revolution. For when one is able to bring within oneself what separates oneself from the world, viz., as when Berkeley brings the brain into the mind, the distinction between mind and brain now standing as a distinction within the mind itself, everything is profoundly altered. And in a curious way, the Platonic challenge has been met. Not by promoting art but by demoting reality, conquering it in the sense that when a line is engulfed, what lies on both sides of that line is engulfed as well. To incorporate one's own boundaries in an act of spiritual topology is to transcend those boundaries, like turning oneself inside out and taking one's external environment in as now part of oneself.

I would like briefly to note two consequences of this. The first is that it has been a profoundly disorienting maneuver, increasingly felt as the categories which pertain to art suddenly pertain to what we always believed contrasted essentially with art. Politics becomes a form of theater, clothing a kind of costume, human relations a kind of role, life a game. We interpret ourselves and our gestures as we once interpreted artworks. We look for meanings and unities, we become players in a play.

The other consequence is more interesting. The relationship between reality and art has traditionally been the province of philosophy, since the latter is analytically concerned with relations between the world and its representations, the space between representation and life. By bringing within itself what it had traditionally been regarded as logically apart from, art transforms itself into philosophy, in effect. The distinction between philosophy of art and art itself is no longer tenable, and by a curious, astounding magic we have been made over into contributors to a field we had always believed it our task merely to analyze from without.

Criticism and Crisis

Paul de Man

When the French poet Stéphane Mallarmé visited Oxford in 1894 to deliver a lecture entitled *La Musique et les lettres* and dealing with the state of French poetry at the time, he exclaimed, with mock sensationalism:

"I am indeed bringing you news. The most surprising news ever. Nothing like it ever happened before. They have tampered with the rules of verse . . . *On a touché au vers*" (Pléiade ed., 643).

In 1970, one might well feel tempted to echo Mallarmé's words, this time with regard not to poetry, but to literary criticism. *On a touché à la critique.* . . . Well-established rules and conventions that governed the discipline of criticism and made it a cornerstone of the intellectual establishment have been so badly tampered with that the entire edifice threatens to collapse. One is tempted to speak of recent developments in Continental criticism in terms of *crisis*. To confine oneself for the moment to purely outward symptoms, the crisis-aspect of the situation is apparent, for instance, in the incredible swiftness with which often conflicting tendencies succeed each other, condemning to immediate obsolescence what might have appeared as the extreme point of avant-gardisme briefly before. Rarely has the dangerous word "new" been used so freely; a few years ago, for very different reasons, there used to be in Paris a *Nouvelle Nouvelle Revue Française*, but today almost every new book that appears inaugurates a new kind of nouvelle nouvelle critique. It is hard to keep up with the names and the trends that succeed each other with bewildering rapidity. Not much more than ten years ago, names such as those of Bachelard, Sartre, Blanchot, or Poulet seemed to be those of daring pioneers, and younger men such as Jean-Pierre Richard or Jean Starobinski proudly considered themselves as continuators of the novel approaches that originated with their immediate predecessors. At that time, the main auxiliary discipline for literary criticism

337

was undoubtedly philosophy. At the Sorbonne, which then as now saw its role primarily as one of conservation and even reaction, the theses considered too bold and experimental ·to be handled by the chairs of literature would quite naturally find their home among the philosophers. These philosophers were themselves engaged in working out a difficult synthesis between the vitalism of Bergson and the phenomenological method of Husserl; this tendency proved quite congenial to the combined use of the categories of sensation, consciousness and temporality that is prevalent among the literary critics of this group. Today, very little remains, at least on the surface, of this cooperation between phenomenology and literary criticism. Philosophy, in the classical form of which phenomenology was, in France, the most recent manifestation, is out of fashion and has been replaced by the social sciences.

But it is by no means clear which one of the social sciences has taken its place, and the hapless and impatient new new critic is hard put deciding in which discipline he should invest his reading time. For a while, after Lucien Goldman's theses on the sociology of Jansenism in the seventeenth century, it seemed as if sociology was in the lead, and the name of Lukács was being mentioned in Parisian intellectual circles with the same awe that used to surround the figures of Kierkegaard and Hegel a few years earlier. But then Lévi-Strauss' *Tristes tropiques* appeared, and anthropology definitely edged out sociology as the main concern of the literary critic. Hardly had he mastered the difficult terminology of tribal intersubjectivity when linguistics appeared over the horizon with an even more formidable technical jargon. And with the somewhat subterranean influence of Jacques Lacan, psychoanalysis has made a comeback, giving rise to a neo-Freudian rebirth that seems to be quite germane to the concerns of several critics.

This sudden expansion of literary studies outside their own province and into the realm of the social sciences was perhaps long overdue. What is nowadays labeled "structuralism" in France is, on a superficial level, nothing but an attempt to formulate a general methodology of the sciences of man. Literary studies and literary criticism naturally play a certain part in this inquiry. There is nothing particularly new or crisis-like about this. Such attempts to situate literary studies in relation to the social sciences are a commonplace of nineteenth-century thought, from Hegel to Taine and Dilthey. What seems crisis-like is, among outer signs, the sense of urgency, the impatient competitiveness with which the various disciplines vie for leadership.

What interest can this Gallic turbulence have for literary studies in America? The irony of Mallarmé's situation at his Oxford lecture was that his English listeners had little awareness of the emergency by which he claimed to be so disturbed. English prosody had not waited for some rather disreputable foreigners to start tampering with verse; free and blank verse were nothing very new in the country of Shakespeare and Milton, and English literary people thought of the alexandrine as the base supporting the column of the Spenserian stanza rather than as a way of life. They probably had difficulty understanding the rhetoric of crisis that Mallarmé was using, with an ironic slant that would not have been lost in Paris, but that certainly baffled his foreign audience. Similarly, speaking of a crisis in criticism in the United States today, one is likely to appear equally out of tone. Because American criticism is more eclectic, less plagued than its European counterpart by ideology, it is very open to impulses from abroad but less likely to experience them with the same crisis-like intensity. We have some difficulty taking seriously the polemical violence with which methodological issues are being debated in Paris. We can invoke the authority of the best historians to point out that what was considered a crisis in the past often turns out to be a mere ripple, that changes first experienced as upheavals tend to become absorbed in the continuity of much slower movements as soon as the temporal perspective broadens.

This kind of pragmatic common sense is admirable, up to the point where it lures the mind into self-satisfied complacency and puts it irrevocably to sleep. It can always be shown, on all levels of experience, that what other people experience as a crisis is perhaps not even a change; such observations depend to a very large extent on the standpoint of the observer. Historical "changes" are not like changes in nature, and the vocabulary of change and movement as it applies to historical process is a mere metaphor, not devoid of meaning, but without an objective correlative that can unambiguously be pointed to in empirical reality, as when we speak of a change in the weather or a change in a biological organism. No set of arguments, no enumeration of symptoms will ever prove that the present effervescence surrounding literary criticism is in fact a crisis that, for better or worse, is reshaping the critical consciousness of a generation. It remains relevant, however, that these people are experiencing it as a crisis and that they are constantly using the language of crisis in referring to what is taking place. We must take this into account when reflecting on the predicament of others as a preliminary before returning to ourselves.

Again, Mallarmé's text of his Oxford lecture, very closely linked to another prose text of his that was written a little later on the same subject and is entitled *Crise de vers,* can give us a useful hint. Apparently, in these texts, Mallarmé is speaking about the experiments in prosody undertaken by a group of younger poets who call themselves (often without his direct encouragement) his disciples, and whom he designates by name: Henri de Régnier, Moréas, Vielé-Griffin, Gustave Kahn, Charles Morice, Emile Verhaeren, Dujardin, Albert Mockel, and so on. And he pretends to believe that their partial rejection of traditional verse, in favor of free verse forms that he calls "polymorphic," represents a major crisis, the kind of apocalyptic tempest that often reappears as a central symbol in much of his own later poetry. It is obvious, for any historian of French literature, that Mallarmé exaggerates the importance of what is happening around him, to the point of appearing completely misled, not only in the eyes of his more phlegmatic British audience, but in the eyes of future historians as well. The poets he mentions are hardly remembered today, and certainly not praised for the explosive renovation with which Mallarmé seems to credit them. Moreover, one can rightly point out that Mallarmé not only overstates their importance, but that he seems to be blind to the forces within his own time that were indeed to have a lasting effect: he makes only a passing reference to Laforgue, who is somewhat incongruously linked with Henri de Régnier, but fails to mention Rimbaud. In short, Mallarmé seems to be entirely mystified into over-evaluating his own private circle of friends, and his use of the term "crisis" seems to be inspired by propaganda rather than by insight.

It does not take too attentive a reading of the text, however, to show that Mallarmé is in fact well aware of the relative triviality of what his disciples are taking so seriously. He is using them as a screen, a pretext to talk about something that concerns him much more; namely, his own experiments with poetic language. That is what he is referring to when he describes the contemporary condition of poetry as follows: "Orage, lustral; et dans des bouleversements, tout à l'acquit de la génération, récente, l'acte d'écrire se scruta jusqu'en l'origine. Très avant, au moins, quant au point, je le formule;—à savoir s'il y a lieu d'écrire." Freely translated and considerably flattened by filling in the elliptic syntax this becomes: "A tempest cleared the air: the new generation deserves credit for bringing this about. The act of writing scrutinized itself to the point of reflecting on its own origin, or, at any rate, far enough to reach the point where it could ask whether it is necessary for this act to take place." It matters little whether the "recent" generation to which Mallarmé refers indicates his younger disciples or his own contemporaries such as Verlaine, Villiers or even potentially Rimbaud. We know with certainty that something crisis-like was taking place at that moment, making practices and assumptions problematic that had been taken for granted.

We have, to a large extent, lost interest in the actual event that Mallarmé was describing as a crisis, but we have not at all lost interest in a text that pretends to designate a crisis when it is, in fact, itself the crisis to which it refers. For here, as in all of Mallarmé's later prose and poetic works, the act of writing reflects indeed upon its own origin and opens up a cycle of questions that none of his real successors have been allowed to forget. We can speak of crisis when a "separation" takes place, by self-reflection, between what, in literature, is in conformity with the original intent and what has irrevocably fallen away from this source. Our question in relation to contemporary criticism then becomes: Is criticism indeed engaged in scrutinizing itself to the point of reflecting on its own origin? Is it asking whether it is necessary for the act of criticism to take place?

The matter is still further complicated by the fact that such scrutiny defines, in effect, the act of criticism itself. Even in its most naïve form, that of evaluation, the critical act is concerned with conformity to origin or specificity: when we say of art that it is good or bad, we are in fact judging a certain degree of conformity to an original intent called artistic. We imply that bad art is barely art at all; good art, on the contrary, comes close to our preconceived and implicit notion of what art ought to be. For that reason, the notion of crisis and that of criticism are very closely linked, so much so that one could state that all true criticism occurs in the mode of crisis. To speak of a crisis of criticism is then, to some degree, redundant. In periods that are not periods of crisis, or in individuals bent on avoiding crisis at all cost, there can be all kinds of approaches to literature: historical, philological, psychological, etc., but there can be no criticism. For such periods or individuals will never put the act of writing into question by relating it to its specific intent. The Continental criticism of today is doing just that, and it therefore deserves to be called genuine literary criticism. It will become clear, I hope, that this is not to be considered as an evaluative but as a purely descriptive statement.

Whether authentic criticism is a liability or an asset to literary studies as a whole remains an open question. One thing, however, is certain; namely, that literary studies cannot possibly refuse to take cognizance of its existence. It would be as if historians refused to acknowledge the existence of wars because they threaten to interfere with the serenity that is indispensable to an orderly pursuit of their discipline.

The trend in Continental criticism, whether it derives its language from sociology, psychoanalysis, ethnology, linguistics, or even from certain forms of philosophy, can be quickly summarized: it represents a methodologically motivated attack on the notion that a literary or poetic consciousness is in any way a privileged consciousness, whose use of language can pretend to escape, to some degree, from the duplicity, the confusion, the untruth that we take for granted in the everyday use of language. We know that our entire social language is an intricate system of rhetorical devices designed to escape from the direct expression of desires that are, in the fullest sense of the term, unnameable—not because they are ethically shameful (for this would make the problem a very simple one), but because unmediated expression is a philosophical impossibility. And we know that the individual who chose to ignore this fundamental convention would be slated either for crucifixion, if he were aware, or, if he were naïve, destined to the total ridicule accorded such heroes as Candide and all other fools in fiction or in life. The contemporary contribution to this age-old problem comes by way of a rephrasing of the problem that develops when a consciousness gets involved in interpreting another consciousness, the basic pattern from which there can be no escape in the social sciences (if there is to be such a thing). Lévi-Strauss, for instance, starts out from the need to protect anthropologists engaged in the study of a so-called "primitive" society from the error made by earlier positivistic anthropologists when they projected upon this society assumptions that remained nonconsciously determined by the inhibitions and shortcomings of their own social situation. Prior to making any valid statement about a distant society, the observing subject must be as clear as possible about his attitude towards his own. He will soon discover, however, that the only way in which he can accomplish this self-demystification is by a (comparative) study of his own social self as it engages in the observation of others, and by becoming aware of the pattern of distortions that this situation necessarily implies. The observation and interpretation of others is always also a means of leading to the observation of the self; true anthropological knowledge (in the ethnological as well as in the philosophical, Kantian sense of the term) can only become worthy of

being called knowledge when this alternating process of mutual interpretation between the two subjects has run its course. Numerous
complications arise, because the observing subject is no more constant than the observed, and each time the observer actually succeeds
in interpreting his subject he changes it, and changes it all the more as
his interpretation comes closer to the truth. But every change of the
observed subject requires a subsequent change in the observer, and
the oscillating process seems to be endless. Worse, as the oscillation
gains in intensity and in truth, it becomes less and less clear who is in
fact doing the observing and who is being observed. Both parties tend
to fuse into a single subject as the original distance between them
disappears. The gravity of this development will at once be clear if I
allow myself to shift, for a brief moment, from the anthropological to
the psychoanalytical or political model. In the case of a genuine
analysis of the psyche, it means that it would no longer be clear who
is analyzing and who is being analyzed; consequently the highly embarrassing question arises, who should be paying whom. And on a
political level, the equally distressing question as to who should be
exploiting whom, is bound to arise.

The need to safeguard reason from what might become a dangerous *vertige*, a dizziness of the mind caught in an infinite regression,
prompts a return to a more rational methodology. The fallacy of a
finite and single interpretation derives from the postulate of a privileged observer; this leads, in turn, to the endless oscillation of an
intersubjective demystification. As an escape from this predicament,
one can propose a radical relativism that operates from the most
empirically specific to the most loftily general level of human behavior. There are no longer any standpoints that can a priori be
considered privileged, no structure that functions validly as a model
for other structures, no postulate of ontological hierarchy that can
serve as an organizing principle from which particular structures derive in the manner in which a deity can be said to engender man and
the world. All structures are, in a sense, equally fallacious and are
therefore called myths. But no myth ever has sufficient coherence not
to flow back into neighboring myths or even has an identity strong
enough to stand out by itself without an arbitrary act of interpretation
that defines it. The relative unity of traditional myths always depends
on the existence of a privileged point of view to which the method
itself denies any status of authenticity. "Contrary to philosophical
reflection, which claims to return to the source," writes Claude Lévi-
Strauss in *Le Cru et le cuit,* "the reflective activities involved in the
structural study of myths deal with light rays that issue from a virtual

focal point. . . ." The method aims at preventing this virtual focus from being made into a *real* source of light. The analogy with optics is perhaps misleading, for in literature everything hinges on the existential status of the focal point; and the problem is more complex when it involves the disappearance of the self as a constitutive subject.

These remarks have made the transition from anthropology to the field of language and, finally, of literature. In the act of anthropological intersubjective interpretation, a fundamental discrepancy always prevents the observer from coinciding fully with the consciousness he is observing. The same discrepancy exists in everyday language, in the impossibility of making the actual expression coincide with what has to be expressed, of making the actual sign coincide with what it signifies. It is the distinctive privilege of language to be able to hide meaning behind a misleading sign, as when we hide rage or hatred behind a smile. But it is the distinctive curse of all language, as soon as any kind of interpersonal relation is involved, that it is forced to act this way. The simplest of wishes cannot express itself without hiding behind a screen of language that constitutes a world of intricate intersubjective relationships, all of them potentially inauthentic. In the everyday language of communication, there is no a priori privileged position of sign over meaning or of meaning over sign; the act of interpretation will always again have to establish this relation for the particular case at hand. The interpretation of everyday language is a Sisyphean task, a task without end and without progress, for the other is always free to make what he wants differ from what he says he wants. The methodology of structural anthropology and that of post-Saussurian linguistics thus share the common problem of a built-in discrepancy within the intersubjective relationship. As Lévi-Strauss, in order to protect the rationality of his science, had to come to the conclusion of a myth without an author, so the linguists have to conceive of a meta-language without speaker in order to remain rational.

Literature, presumably, is a form of language, and one can argue that all other art forms, including music, are in fact proto-literary languages. This, indeed, was Mallarmé's thesis in his Oxford lecture, as it is Lévi-Strauss' when he states that the language of music, as a language without speaker, comes closest to being the kind of meta-language of which the linguists are dreaming. If the radical position suggested by Lévi-Strauss is to stand, if the question of structure can only be asked from a point of view that is not that of a privileged subject, then it becomes imperative to show that literature constitutes no exception, that its language is in no sense privileged in terms of unity and truth over everyday forms of language. The task of structuralist literary critics then becomes quite clear: in order to eliminate the constitutive subject, they have to show that the discrepancy between sign and meaning (*signifiant* and *signifié*) prevails in literature in the same manner as in everyday language.

Some contemporary critics have more or less consciously been doing this. Practical criticism, in France and in the United States, functions more and more as a demystification of the belief that literature is a privileged language. The dominant strategy consists of showing that certain claims to authenticity attributed to literature are in fact expressions of a desire that, like all desires, falls prey to the duplicities of expression. The so-called "idealism" of literature is then shown to be an idolatry, a fascination with a false image that mimics the presumed attributes of authenticity when it is in fact just the hollow mask with which a frustrated, defeated consciousness tries to cover up its own negativity.

Perhaps the most specific example of this strategy is the use made by structuralist critics of the historical term "romantic"; the example also has the virtue of revealing the historical scheme within which they are operating, and which is not always openly stated. The fallacy of the belief that, in the language of poetry, sign and meaning can coincide, or at least be related to each other in the free and harmonious balance that we call beauty, is said to be a specifically romantic delusion. The unity of appearance (sign) and idea (meaning)—to use the terminology that one finds indeed among the theoreticians of romanticism when they speak of *Schein* and *Idee*—is said to be a romantic myth embodied in the recurrent topos of the "Beautiful Soul." The *schöne Seele*, a predominant theme of pietistic origin in eighteenth- and nineteenth-century literature, functions indeed as the *figura* of a privileged kind of language. Its outward appearance receives its beauty from an inner glow (or *feu sacré*) to which it is so finely attuned that, far from hiding it from sight, it gives it just the right balance of opacity and transparency, thus allowing the holy fire to shine without burning. The romantic imagination embodies this figure at times in the shape of a person, feminine, masculine or hermaphrodite, and seems to suggest that it exists as an actual, empirical subject: one thinks, for instance, of Rousseau's Julie, of Hölderlin's Diotima, or of the beautiful soul that appears in Hegel's *Phenomenology of the Spirit* and in Goethe's *Wilhelm Meister*.

At this point, it is an irresistible temptation for the demystifying critic, from Voltaire down to the present, to demonstrate that this person, this actual subject, becomes ludicrous when it is transplanted in the fallen world of our facticity. The beautiful soul can be shown to spring from fantasies by means of which the writer sublimates his own shortcomings; it suffices to remove the entity for a moment from the fictional world in which it exists to make it appear even more ridiculous than Candide. Some authors, writing in the wake of the romantic myth, have been well aware of this. One can see how certain developments in nineteenth-century realism, the ironic treatment of the Rousseauistic figure by Stendhal, of the quixotic figure by Flaubert, or of the "poetic" figure by Proust, can be interpreted as a gradual demystification of romantic idealism. This leads to a historical scheme in which romanticism represents, so to speak, the point of maximum delusion in our recent past, whereas the nineteenth and twentieth centuries represent a gradual emerging from this aberration, culminating in the breakthrough of the last decades that inaugurates a new form of insight and lucidity, a cure from the agony of the romantic disease. Refining on what may appear too crude in such a historical scheme, some modern critics transpose this movement within the consciousness of a single writer and show how the development of a novelist can best be understood as a successive process of mystifications and partial demystifications. The process does not necessarily move in one single direction, from delusion to insight; there can be an intricate play of relapses and momentary recoveries. All the same, the fundamental movement of the literary mind espouses the pattern of a demystifying consciousness; literature finally comes into its own, and becomes authentic, when it discovers that the exalted status it claimed for its language was a myth. The function of the critic then naturally becomes coextensive with the intent at demystification that is more or less consciously present in the mind of the author.

This scheme is powerful and cogent, powerful enough, in fact, to go to the root of the matter and consequently to cause a crisis. To reject it convincingly would require elaborate argument. My remarks are meant to indicate some reasons, however, for considering the conception of literature (or literary criticism) as demystification the most dangerous myth of all, while granting that it forces us, in Mallarmé's terms, to scrutinize the act of writing "jusqu'en l'origine."

For reasons of economy, my starting point will have to be oblique, for in the language of polemics the crooked path often travels faster than the straight one. We must ask ourselves if there is not a recurrent epistemological structure that characterizes all statements made in the mood and the rhetoric of crisis. Let me take an example from philosophy. On May 7 and May 10 of 1935, Edmund Husserl, the founder of phenomenology, delivered in Vienna two lectures entitled "Philosophy and the Crisis of European Humanity"; the title was later changed to "The Crisis of European Humanity and Philosophy," to stress the priority of the concept of crisis as Husserl's main concern. The lectures are the first version of what was to become Husserl's most important later work, the treatise entitled *The Crisis of the European Sciences and Transcendental Phenomenology*, now the sixth volume of the complete works edited by Walter Biemel. In these various titles, two words remain constant: the word "crisis" and the word "European"; it is in the interaction of these two concepts that the epistemological structure of the crisis-statement is fully revealed.

Reading this text with the hindsight that stems from more than thirty years of turbulent history, it strikes one as both prophetic and tragic. Much of what is being stated seems relevant today. It is not by a mere freak of language that the key word "demythification" (*Entmythisierung*), that was destined to have such an important career, appears in the text (VI.340.4), although the context in which the term is used, designating what takes place when the superior theoretical man observes the inferior natural man, is highly revealing. There is a very modern note in Husserl's description of philosophy as a process by means of which naïve assumptions are made accessible to consciousness by an act of critical self-understanding. Husserl conceived of philosophy primarily as a self-interpretation by means of which we eliminate what he calls *Selbstverhülltheit*, the tendency of the self to hide from the light it can cast on itself. The universality of philosophical knowledge stems from a persistently reflective attitude that can take philosophy itself for its theme. He describes philosophy as a prolegomenon to a new kind of praxis, a "universal critique of all life and all the goals of life, of all the man-created cultural systems and achievements" and, consequently, "a criticism of man himself (*Kritik der Menschheit selbst*) and of the values by which he is consciously or pre-consciously being governed."

Alerted by this convincing appeal to self-critical vigilance, Husserl's listeners and his present-day readers may well be tempted to turn this philosophical criticism on Husserl's own text, especially on the numerous sections in which philosophy is said to be the historical privilege of European man. Husserl speaks repeatedly of non-European cultures as primitive, prescientific and prephilosophical, myth-dominated and congenitally incapable of the disinterested distance without which there can be no philosophical meditation. This, although by his own definition philosophy, as unrestricted reflection upon the self, necessarily tends toward a universality that finds its concrete, geographical correlative in the formation of supratribal, supernational communities such as, for instance, Europe. Why this geographical expansion should have chosen to stop, once and forever, at the Atlantic Ocean and at the Caucasus, Husserl does not say. No one could be more open to Lévi-Strauss' criticism of the mystified anthropologist than Husserl when he warns us, with the noblest of intentions, that we should not assume a potential for philosophical attitudes in non-European cultures. The privileged viewpoint of the post-Hellenic, European consciousness is never for a moment put into question; the crucial, determining examination on which depends Husserl's right to call himself, by his own terms, a philosopher, is in fact never undertaken. As a European, it seems that Husserl escapes from the necessary self-criticism that is prior to all philosophical truth about the self. He is committing precisely the mistake that Rousseau did not commit when he carefully avoided giving his concept of natural man, the basis of his anthropology, any empirical status whatever. Husserl's claim to European supremacy hardly stands in need of criticism today. Since we are speaking of a man of superior good will, it suffices to point to the pathos of such a claim at a moment when Europe was about to destroy itself as center in the name of its unwarranted claim to be the center.

The point, however, transcends the personal situation. Speaking in what was in fact a state of urgent personal and political crisis about a more general form of crisis, Husserl's text reveals with striking clarity the structure of all crisis-determined statements. It establishes an important truth: the fact that philosophical knowledge can only come into being when it is turned back upon itself. But it immediately proceeds, in the very same text, to do the opposite. The rhetoric of crisis states its own truth in the mode of error. It is itself radically blind to the light it emits. It could be shown that the same is true of Mallarmé's *Crise de vers,* which served as our original starting point —although it would be a great deal more complex to demonstrate the self-mystification of as ironical a man as Mallarmé than of as admirably honest a man as Husserl.

Our question, rather, is the following: How does this pattern of self-mystification that accompanies the experience of crisis apply to literary criticism? Husserl was demonstrating the urgent philosophical necessity of putting the privileged European standpoint into question, but remained himself entirely blind to this necessity, behaving in the most unphilosophical way possible at the very moment when he rightly understood the primacy of philosophical over empirical knowledge. He was, in fact, stating the privileged status of philosophy as an authentic language, but withdrawing at once from the demands of this authenticity as it applied to himself. Similarly, demystifying critics are in fact asserting the privileged status of literature as an authentic language, but withdrawing from the implications by cutting themselves off from the source from which they receive their insight.

For the statement about language, that sign and meaning can never coincide, is what is precisely taken for granted in the kind of language we call literary. Literature, unlike everyday language, begins on the far side of this knowledge; it is the only form of language free from the fallacy of unmediated expression. All of us know this, although we know it in the misleading way of a wishful assertion of the opposite. Yet the truth emerges in the foreknowledge we possess of the true nature of literature when we refer to it as *fiction*. All literatures, including the literature of Greece, have always designated themselves as existing in the mode of fiction; in the *Iliad*, when we first encounter Helen, it is as the emblem of the narrator weaving the actual war into the tapestry of a fictional object. Her beauty prefigures the beauty of all future narratives as entities that point to their own fictional nature. The self-reflecting mirror-effect by means of which a work of fiction asserts, by its very existence, its separation from empirical reality, its divergence, as a sign, from a meaning that depends for its existence on the constitutive activity of this sign, characterizes the work of literature in its essence. It is always against the explicit assertion of the writer that readers degrade the fiction by confusing it with a reality from which it has forever taken leave. "Le pays des chimères est en ce monde le seul digne d'être habité," Rousseau has Julie write, "et tel est le néant des choses humaines qu'hors l'Etre existant par lui-même, il n'y a rien de beau que ce qui n'est pas" (*La Nouvelle Heloïse,* Pléiade ed. II, 693). One entirely misunderstands this assertion of the priority of fiction over reality, of imagination over perception, if one considers it as the compensatory expression of a shortcoming, of a deficient sense of reality. It is attributed to a fictional character who knows all there is to know of human happiness and who is about to face death with Socratic equanimity. It transcends the notion of a nostalgia or a desire, since it discovers desire as a fundamental pattern of being that discards any possibility of satisfaction. Elsewhere, Rousseau speaks in similar terms of the nothingness of fiction (*le néant de mes chimères*): "If all my dreams had turned into reality, I would still remain unsatisfied: I would have kept on dreaming, imagining, desiring. In myself, I found an unexplainable void that nothing could have filled; a longing of the heart towards another kind of fulfillment of which I could not conceive but of which I nevertheless felt the attraction" (Letter to Malesherbes, Pléiade ed. I, 1140).

These texts can be called romantic, and I have purposely chosen them within the period and the author that many consider the most deluded of all. But one hesitates to use terms such as nostalgia or desire to designate this kind of consciousness, for all nostalgia or desire is desire of something or for someone; here, the consciousness does not result from the absence of something, but consists of the presence of a nothingness. Poetic language names this void with ever-renewed understanding and, like Rousseau's longing, it never tires of naming it again. This persistent naming is what we call literature. In the same manner that the poetic lyric originates in moments of tranquility, in the absence of actual emotions, and then proceeds to invent fictional emotions to create the illusion of recollection, the work of fiction invents fictional subjects to create the illusion of the reality of others. But the fiction is not myth, for it knows and names itself as fiction. It is not a demystification, it is demystified from the start. When modern critics think they are demystifying literature, they are in fact being demystified by it; but since this necessarily occurs in the form of a crisis, they are blind to what takes place within themselves. At the moment that they claim to do away with literature, literature is everywhere; what they call anthropology, linguistics, psychoanalysis is nothing but literature reappearing, like the Hydra's head, in the very spot where it had supposedly been suppressed. The human mind will go through amazing feats of distortion to avoid facing "the nothingness of human matters." In order not to see that the failure lies in the nature of things, one chooses to locate it in the individual, "romantic" subject, and thus retreats behind a historical scheme which, apocalyptic as it may sound, is basically reassuring and bland.

Lévi-Strauss had to give up the notion of subject to safeguard reason. The subject, he said, in fact, is a "foyer virtuel," a mere hypothesis posited by the scientists to give consistency to the behavior of entities. The metaphor in his statement that "the reflective activities [of the structuralists] deal with light that issues from a virtual focal point . . ." stems from the elementary laws of optical refraction. The image is all the more striking since it plays on the confusion between the imaginary loci of the physicist and the *fictional* entities that occur in literary language. The virtual focus is a quasi-objective structure posited to give rational integrity to a process that exists independently of the self. The subject merely fills in, with the dotted line of geometrical construction, what natural reason had not bothered to make explicit; it has a passive and unproblematic role. The "virtual focus" is, strictly speaking, a nothing, but its nothingness concerns us very little, since a mere act of reason suffices to give it a mode of being that leaves the rational order unchallenged. The same is not true of the imaginary source of fiction. Here the human self has experienced the void within itself and the invented fiction, far from filling the void, asserts itself as pure nothingness, *our* nothingness stated and restated by a subject that is the agent of its own instability. Lévi-Strauss' suppression of the subject is perfectly legitimate as an attempt to protect the scientific status of ethnology; by the same token, however, it leads directly into the larger question of the ontological status of the self. From this point on, a philosophical anthropology would be inconceivable without the consideration of literature as a primary source of knowledge.

V. PSYCHOLOGY AND AESTHETICS

Introduction

"Psychology" in this section must be read as meaning "psychoanalysis," despite the fact that psychoanalysis has scant standing among philosophers, having come off somewhat badly in regard to the question of its "scientific" status. Our justification for this narrowing of focus is that psychoanalysis, whether scientific or not, is the only psychological school which has deeply affected our perception and interpretation of works of art. Perhaps this is because psychoanalysis is itself less a science than a method of reading and interpreting, in which dreams, jokes, slips of the tongue, are all treated as texts. It is certainly noteworthy that psychoanalysis draws so many of its key concepts from the world of literature—Oedipus, Narcissus, Sade. It seems that psychoanalysis has been on an intimate footing with literature since its very beginning, and this intimacy has manifested itself in the almost compulsive way in which psychoanalysis has been drawn to the analysis of literary and artistic productions. The results of the ocean of "analytic criticism," which psychoanalysis seems to be unable to stop itself from producing, have been admittedly meager. This situation has led some contemporary psychoanalytic critics to reflect back on the inner necessity of literature's relationship to psychoanalysis, and to make use of both psychoanalytic and literary texts in the course of this reflection. The results of such an endeavor are interesting, not only from the standpoint of the analytic critic, but to the critic generally, as emblematic of the relation of literature to criticism in all of its varieties; and to the philosopher generally, as emblematic of the type of reflective self-criticism that philosophy itself must engage in.

The major essay in this section is Jacques Lacan's "Seminar on 'The Purloined Letter,' " the understanding of which requires a short summary of Lacan's thought with a view toward clarifying the key Lacanian terms, *Imaginary* and *Symbolic*. This short summary can be most easily presented in the form of a developmental scenario or myth in which we follow a newborn child through these two realms.

For Lacan, the human child is born as an "un-whole," incomplete and living in a state of free-floating "lack." The child in this first state has no self or other; this stage is strictly ineffable and inaccessible to discourse. In a sense, therefore, the child possesses neither lack nor wholeness; the "lack" in question will become meaningful only later through deferred action.

At a certain point around six to eight months, the child begins to notice and react to its mirror image. This "mirror stage" is emblematic for Lacan of a more general psychological development which institutes for the child a dialectic of self and other. The child recognizes itself for the first time, but as something not itself; the subject is first constituted as radically alienated from itself. The identification of oneself with an image of bodily wholeness which is yet separate from oneself converts *lack* into *desire*, specifically, a desire to regain the undifferentiated state of the premirror stage, which now presents itself as a lost paradise of wholeness in which self and other were indistinguishable.

The stage of this narcissistic desire for complete self-presence is what Lacan calls the *Imaginary*. The child's narcissism finds its expression in its dyadic relation to its mother. The child fulfills its desire by imagining itself the sole, complete object of its mother's desire (i.e., it imagines itself as the phallus, a functional term for Lacan signifying the object of desire, not the biological organ). The child fills the lack in its mother (as she fills the lack in it) by *becoming* the object of its mother's desire. Fusing its mother and itself in this way, the child achieves its dream of unity by presenting itself as a blank, a nothing. The child is a self, but not yet a full-fledged subject, in this period of imaginary possession.

The fact of sexual difference presents the greatest threat to the fulfillment of this desire for an order which reflects the self's imagined wholeness. The child denies the mother's lack of a phallus by being the phallus for her, thus denying her castration (and by extension, its own). It should be particularly noted here again that castration and loss of the phallus in no way refer in Lacan's vocabulary to loss of a bodily part, but refer to the inevitable separation of the human being from the object of his desire. Desire first constitutes itself as an attempt to *re*gain a unity of self and object of desire which in fact never existed.

The irruption of the institutor of difference, the Law of the Father, into the closed circuit of mother and child blocks the child's self-communion and creates the triangular Oedipal situation which separates mother and child. The triangle centers on the castration complex, that experience of lack which affirms (sexual) difference. Successful passage through the Oedipal crisis requires that the child identify with the father as he who "has" the phallus. This represents a castration to the extent that it forbids identification of the child with its mother. It also opens the way for the resolution of the Oedipal complex by allowing the infant to constitute itself as possessor of the phallus—to take on its identity as a sexed subject within the order of the *Symbolic*. As opposed to the realm of the Imaginary, which is constituted by the dual relation of mother and child, the Symbolic is a field preexisting any individual who may be inserted into it. It is the field of the Other and it is in this field that the subject is constituted in alienation. The lost maternal object becomes unconscious, and this determines the mode of all future desire. The Oedipal relation opens into absence, difference, the unconscious—the subject must accept absence, refuse to deny difference, become alienated in the intersubjective circuit of exchange imposed by unconscious desire. The Oedipal passage from Imaginary to Symbolic is the transgression of the metaphorics of wholeness and self-presence by difference, articulation—in a word, "textuality."

This short summary hardly begins to suggest the range of Lacan's difficult thought on these matters; it is only meant as an explication of some crucial terms, and to place the reader in a position to begin to read Lacan. Lacan's piece is followed by two others which develop his ideas and extend the range of their application to literature. Jeffrey Mehlman's article was written specifically as an explication of Lacan on Poe; for more such direct explication, see Felman (2). Stephen Melville's article, published here for the first time, attempts to situate Lacan within the larger context of the literary critical community while drawing some very important morals concerning the nature of both psychoanalysis and criticism.

For more on Lacan as a theorist, see Lemaire. The recent structuralist-oriented approach to psychoanalytic criticism exists in exemplary form in Felman (3); Irwin also provides a provocative application of Lacanian ideas. Other important explorations of this area are Brenkman (2), Brooks, A. Cohen, Derrida (11), Gallop, Jameson (1), B. Johnson (1), and Sibony. Part of the reawakening interest in psychoanalytic approaches to literature has been an increased tendency to read Freudian texts themselves using the techniques of psychoanalytic criticism. Stephen Melville's article here bears on this issue; see also Carroll, Cixous, Derrida (5), Hertz, Mehlman (2), and Weber, plus the special issue of the journal *Dia-*

critics, Vol. 9, #1 (Spring 1979) devoted to the general topic "The Tropology of Freud." The older psychoanalytic criticism, closer in orientation to American ego psychology, is best represented by Crews and Holland; see also Faber, Fraiberg, Heller, S. Hyman, E. Jones, Kazin, Kohut, Kris, Lesser, Lee, Marcuse, Marotti, Spector, and Trilling (1). A very powerful variant of this older Freudian criticism has been developed in a long series of works by Harold Bloom.

The pieces by Lacan, Mehlman, and Melville form a closely inter-related set; the fourth piece included here, that by Kenneth Burke, stands somewhat apart. Kenneth Burke himself has always stood somewhat apart, and his work on Freud is not assimilable to any of the recognized Freudian "schools." Burke was probably the first critic of note to take Freud seriously while *not* being already committed to the truth of psychoanalysis as an epistemological discipline. He was thus the first person to discern certain possibilities in Freud which both critics and psychoanalysts have only recently begun to exploit. Therefore, there is a real sense in which we have only just begun to catch up with Kenneth Burke.

Freud—and the Analysis of Poetry

Kenneth Burke

The reading of Freud I find suggestive almost to the point of bewilderment. Accordingly, what I should like most to do would be simply to take representative excerpts from his work, copy them out, and write glosses upon them. Very often these glosses would be straight extensions of his own thinking. At other times they would be attempts to characterize his strategy of presentation with reference to interpretative method in general. And, finally, the Freudian perspective was developed primarily to chart a psychiatric field rather than an aesthetic one; but since we are here considering the analogous features of these two fields rather than their important differences, there would be glosses attempting to suggest how far the literary critic should go along with Freud and what extra-Freudian material he would have to add. Such a desire to write an article on Freud in the margin of his books must for practical reasons here remain a frustrated desire. An article such as this must condense by generalization, which requires me to slight the most stimulating factor of all—the detailed articulacy in which he embodies his extraordinary frankness.

Freud's frankness is no less remarkable by reason of the fact that he had perfected a method for being frank. He could say humble, even humiliating, things about himself and us because he had changed the rules somewhat and could make capital of observations that others, with vested interests of a different sort, would feel called upon to suppress by dictatorial decree. Or we might say that what for him could fall within the benign category of observation could for them fall only within its malign counterpart, spying.

Yet though honesty is, in Freud, methodologically made easier, it is by no means honesty made easy. And Freud's own accounts of his own dreams show how poignantly he felt at times the "disgrace" of his occupation. There are doubtless many thinkers whose strange device might be *ecclesia super cloacam*. What more fitting place to erect one's church than above a sewer! One might even say that sewers are what churches are for. But usually this is done by laying all the stress upon the ecclesia and its beauty. So that, even when the man's work fails to be completed for him as a social act, by the approval of his group, he has the conviction of its intrinsic beauty to give him courage and solace.

But to think of Freud, during the formative years of his doctrine, confronting something like repugnance among his colleagues, and even, as his dreams show, in his own eyes, is to think of such heroism as Unamuno found in Don Quixote; and if Don Quixote risked the social judgment of ridicule, he still had the consolatory thought that his imaginings were beautiful, stressing the ecclesia aspect, whereas Freud's theories bound him to a more drastic self-ostracizing act— the charting of the relations between ecclesia and cloaca that forced him to analyze the cloaca itself. Hence, his work was with the confessional as cathartic, purgative; this haruspicy required an inspection of the entrails; it was, bluntly, an interpretative sculpting of excrement, with beauty replaced by a science of the grotesque.

Confronting this, Freud does nonetheless advance to erect a structure which, if it lacks beauty, has astounding ingeniousness and fancy. It is full of paradoxes, of leaps across gaps, of vistas—much more so than the work of many a modern poet who sought for nothing else but these and had no search for accuracy to motivate his work. These qualities alone would make it unlikely that readers literarily inclined could fail to be attracted, even while repelled. Nor can one miss in it the profound charitableness that is missing in so many modern writers who, likewise concerned with the cloaca, become efficiently concerned with nothing else, and make of their work pure indictment, pure oath, pure striking-down, pure spitting-upon, pure kill.

True, this man, who taught us so much about father-rejection and who ironically himself became so frequently the rejected father in the works of his schismatic disciples, does finally descend to quarrelsomeness, despite himself, when recounting the history of the psychoanalytic movement. But, over the great course of his work, it is the matter of human rescue that he is concerned with—not the matter of vengeance. On a few occasions, let us say, he is surprised into vengefulness. But the very essence of his studies, even at their most forbidding moments (in fact, precisely at those moments), is charitableness, a concern with salvation. To borrow an excellent meaningful pun from Trigant Burrow, this salvation is approached not in terms of religious hospitality but rather in terms of secular hospitalization. Yet it is the spirit of Freud; it is what Freud's courage is for.

Perhaps, therefore, the most fitting thing for a writer to do, particularly in view of the fact that Freud is now among the highly honored class—the exiles from Nazi Germany (how accurate those fellows are! how they seem, with almost 100 per cent efficiency, to have weeded out their greatest citizens!)—perhaps the most fitting thing to do would be simply to attempt an article of the "homage to Freud" sort and call it a day.

However, my job here cannot be confined to that. I have been commissioned to consider the bearing of Freud's theories upon literary criticism. And these theories were not designed primarily for literary criticism at all but were rather a perspective that, developed for the charting of a nonaesthetic field, was able (by reason of its scope) to migrate into the aesthetic field. The margin of overlap was this: The acts of the neurotic are symbolic acts. Hence insofar as both the neurotic act and the poetic act share this property in common, they may share a terminological chart in common. But insofar as they deviate, terminology likewise must deviate. And this deviation is a fact that literary criticism must explicitly consider.

As for the glosses on the interpretative strategy in general, they would be of this sort: For one thing, they would concern a distinction between what I should call an essentializing mode of interpretation and a mode that stresses proportion of ingredients. The tendency in Freud is toward the first of these. That is, if one found a complex of, let us say, seven ingredients in a man's motivation, the Freudian tendency would be to take one of these as the essence of the motivation and to consider the other six as sublimated variants. We could imagine, for instance, manifestations of sexual impotence accompanying a conflict in one's relations with his familiars and one's relations at the office. The proportional strategy would involve the study of these three as a cluster. The motivation would be synonymous with the interrelationships among them. But the essentializing strategy would, in Freud's case, place the emphasis upon the sexual manifestation, as causal ancestor of the other two.

This essentializing strategy is linked with a normal ideal of science: to "explain the complex in terms of the simple." This ideal almost vows one to select one or another motive from a cluster and interpret the others in terms of it. The naive proponent of economic determinism, for instance, would select the quarrel at the office as the essential motive, and would treat the quarrel with familiars and the sexual impotence as mere results of this. Now, I don't see how you can possibly explain the complex in terms of the simple without having your very success used as a charge against you. When you get through, all that your opponent need say is: "But you have explained the complex in terms of the simple—and the simple is precisely what the complex is not."

Perhaps the faith philosophers, as against the reason philosophers, did not have to encounter a paradox at this point. Not that they avoided paradoxes, for I think they must always cheat when trying to explain how evil can exist in a world created by an all-powerful and wholly good Creator. But at least they did not have to confront the complexity-simplicity difficulty, since their theological reductions referred to a ground in God, who was simultaneously the ultimately complex and the ultimately simple. Naturalistic strategies lack this convenient "out"—hence their explanations are simplifications, and every simplification is an oversimplification.[1]

It is possible that the literary critic, taking communication as his basic category, may avoid this particular paradox (communication thereby being a kind of attenuated God term). You can reduce everything to communication—yet communication is extremely complex. But, in any case, communication is by no means the basic category of Freud. The sexual wish, or libido, is the basic category; and the complex forms of communication that we see in a highly alembicated philosophy would be mere sublimations of this.

A writer deprived of Freud's clinical experience would be a fool to question the value of his category as a way of analyzing the motives of the class of neurotics Freud encountered. There is a pronouncedly individualistic element in any technique of salvation (my toothache being alas! my private property), and even those beset by a pandemic of sin or microbes will enter heaven or get discharged from the hospital one by one; and the especially elaborate process of diagnosis involved in Freudian analysis even to this day makes it more available to those suffering from the ills of preoccupation and leisure than to those suffering from the ills of occupation and unemployment (with people generally tending to be only as mentally sick as they can afford to be). This state of affairs makes it all the more likely that the typical psychoanalytic patient would have primarily private sexual motivations behind his difficulties. (Did not Henry James say that sex is something about which we think a great deal when we are not thinking about anything else?)[2] Furthermore, I believe that studies of artistic imagery, outside the strict pale of psychoanalytic emphasis, will bear out Freud's brilliant speculations as to the sexual puns, the double-entendres, lurking behind the most unlikely façades. If a man acquires a method of thinking about everything else, for instance, during the sexual deprivations and rigors of adolescence, this cure may well take on the qualities of the disease; and insofar as he continues with this same method in adult years, though his life has since become sexually less exacting, such modes as incipient homosexuality or masturbation may very well be informatively interwoven in the strands of his thought and be discoverable by inspection of the underlying imagery or patterns in this thought.

Indeed, there are only a few fundamental bodily idioms—and why should it not be likely that an attitude, no matter how complex its ideational expression, could only be completed by a channelization within its corresponding gestures? That is, the details of experience behind A's dejection may be vastly different from the details of experience behind B's dejection, yet both A and B may fall into the same bodily posture in expressing their dejection. And in an era like ours, coming at the end of a long individualistic emphasis, where we frequently find expressed an attitude of complete independence, of total, uncompromising self-reliance, this expression would not reach its fulfillment in choreography except in the act of "practical narcissism" (that is, the only wholly independent person would be the one who practiced self-abuse and really meant it).

But it may be noticed that we have here tended to consider mind-body relations from an interactive point of view rather than a materialistic one (which would take the body as the essence of the act and the mentation as the sublimation).

Freud himself, interestingly enough, was originally nearer to this view (necessary, as I hope to show later, for specifically literary purposes) than he later became. Freud explicitly resisted the study of motivation by way of symbols. He distinguished his own mode of analysis from the symbolic by laying the stress upon free association. That is, he would begin the analysis of a neurosis without any preconceived notion as to the absolute meaning of any image that the patient might reveal in the account of a dream. His procedure involved the breaking down of the dream into a set of fragments, with the analyst then inducing the patient to improvise associations on each of these fragments in turn. And afterward, by charting recurrent themes, he would arrive at the crux of the patient's conflict.

Others (particularly Stekel), however, proposed a great short cut here. They offered an absolute content for various items of imagery. For instance, in Stekel's dictionary of symbols, which has the absoluteness of an old-fashioned dream-book, the right-hand path equals the road to righteousness, the left-hand path equals the road to crime, in anybody's dreams (in Lenin's presumably, as well as the Pope's). Sisters are breasts and brothers are buttocks. "The luggage of a traveller is the burden of sin by which one is oppressed," etc. Freud criticizes these on the basis of his own clinical experiences—and whereas he had reservations against specific equations, and rightly treats the method as antithetical to his own contribution, he decides that a high percentage of Stekel's purely intuitive hunches were corroborated. And after warning that such a gift as Stekel's is often evidence of paranoia, he decides that normal persons may also occasionally be capable of it.

Its lure as efficiency is understandable. And, indeed, if we revert to the matter of luggage, for instance, does it not immediately give us insight into a remark of André Gide, who is a specialist in the portrayal of scrupulous criminals, who has developed a stylistic trick for calling to seduction in the accents of evangelism, and who advises that one should learn to "travel light"?

But the trouble with short cuts is that they deny us a chance to take longer routes. With them, the essentializing strategy takes a momentous step forward. You have next but to essentialize your short cuts in turn (a short cut atop a short cut), and you get the sexual emphasis of Freud, the all-embracing ego compensation of Adler, or Rank's master-emphasis upon the birth trauma, etc.

Freud himself fluctuates in his search for essence. At some places you find him proclaiming the all-importance of the sexual, at other places you find him indignantly denying that his psychology is a pansexual one at all, and at still other places you get something halfway between the two, via the concept of the libido, which embraces a spectrum from phallus to philanthropy.

The important matter for our purposes is to suggest that the examination of a poetic work's internal organization would bring us nearer to a variant of the typically Freudian free-association method than to the purely symbolic method toward which he subsequently gravitated.[3]

The critic should adopt a variant of the free-association method. One obviously cannot invite an author, especially a dead author, to oblige him by telling what the author thinks of when the critic isolates some detail or other for improvisation. But the critic can note the context of imagery and ideas in which an image takes its place. He can also note, by such analysis, the kinds of evaluations surrounding the image of a crossing; for instance, is it an escape from or a return to an evil or a good, etc.? Thus finally, by noting the ways in which this crossing behaves, what subsidiary imagery accompanies it, what kind of event it grows out of, what kind of event grows out of it, what altered rhythmic and tonal effects characterize it, etc., one grasps its significance as motivation. And there is no essential motive offered here. The motive of the work is equated with the structure of interrelationships within the work itself.

"But there is more to a work of art than that." I hear this objection being raised. And I agree with it. And I wonder whether we could properly consider the matter in this wise:

For convenience using the word "poem" to cover any complete, made artistic product, let us divide this artifact (the invention, creation, formation, poetic construct) in accordance with three modes of analysis: dream, prayer, chart.

The psychoanalysis of Freud and of the schools stemming from Freud has brought forward an astoundingly fertile range of observations that give us insight into the poem as dream. There is opened up before us a sometimes almost terrifying glimpse into the ways in which we may, while overtly doing one thing, be covertly doing another. Yet, there is nothing mystical or even unusual about this. I may, for instance, consciously place my elbow upon the table. Yet at the same time I am clearly unconscious of the exact distance between my elbow and my nose. Or, if that analogy seems like cheating, let us try another: I may be unconscious of the way in which a painter friend, observant of my postures, would find the particular position of my arm characteristic of me.

Or let us similarly try to take the terror out of infantile regression. Insofar as I speak the same language that I learned as a child, every time I speak there is, within my speech, an ingredient of regression to the infantile level. Regression, we might say, is a function of progression. Where the progression has been a development by evolution or continuity of growth (as were one to have learned to speak and think in English as a child, and still spoke and thought in English) rather than by revolution or discontinuity of growth (as were one to have learned German in childhood, to have moved elsewhere at an early age, and since become so at home in English that he could not even understand a mature conversation in the language of his childhood), the archaic and the now would be identical. You could say, indifferently, either that the speech is regression or that it is not regression. But were the man who had forgot the language of his childhood to begin speaking nothing but this early language (under a sudden agitation or as the result of some steady pressure), we should have the kind of regression that goes formally by this name in psychoanalytic nomenclature.

The ideal growth, I suppose—the growth without elements of alienation, discontinuity, homelessness—is that wherein regression is natural. We might sloganize it as "the adult a child matured." Growth has here been simply a successive adding of cells—the growth of the chambered nautilus. But there is also the growth of the adult who, "when he became a man, put away childish things." This is the growth of the crab, that grows by abandoning one room and taking on another. It produces moments of crisis. It makes for philosophies of emancipation and enlightenment, where one gets a jolt and is "awakened from the sleep of dogma" (and alas! in leaving his profound "Asiatic slumber," he risks getting in exchange more than mere wakefulness, more than the eternal vigilance that is the price of liberty—he may get wakefulness plus, i.e., insomnia).

There are, in short, critical points (or, in the Hegel-Marx vocabulary, changes of quantity leading to changes of quality) where the process of growth or change converts a previous circle of protection into a circle of confinement. The first such revolution may well be, for the human individual, a purely biological one—the change at birth when the fetus, heretofore enjoying a larval existence in the womb, being fed on manna from the placenta, so outgrows this circle of protection that the benign protection becomes a malign circle of confinement, whereat it must burst forth into a different kind of world—a world of locomotion, aggression, competition, hunt. The mother, it is true, may have already been living in such a world; but the fetus was in a world within this world—in a monastery—a world such as is lived in by "coupon clippers," who get their dividends as the result of sharp economic combat but who may, so long as the payments are regular, devote themselves to thoughts and diseases far "beyond" these harsh material operations.

In the private life of the individual there may be many subsequent jolts of a less purely biological nature, as with the death of some one person who had become pivotal to this individual's mental economy. But whatever these unique variants may be, there is again a universal variant at adolescence, when radical changes in the glandular structure of the body make this body a correspondingly altered environment for the mind, requiring a corresponding change in our perspective, our structure of interpretations, meanings, values, purposes, and inhibitions, if we are to take it properly into account.

In the informative period of childhood our experiences are strongly personalized. Our attitudes take shape with respect to distinct people who have roles, even animals and objects being vessels of character. Increasingly, however, we begin to glimpse a world of abstract relationships, of functions understood solely through the medium of symbols in books. Even such real things as Tibet and Eskimos and Napoleon are for us, who have not been to Tibet, or lived with Eskimos, or fought under Napoleon, but a structure of signs. In a sense, it could be said that we learn these signs flat. We must start from scratch. There is no tradition in them; they are pure present. For though they have been handed down by tradition, we can read meaning into them only insofar as we can project or extend them out of our own experience. We may, through being burned a little, understand the signs for being burned a lot—it is in this sense that the coaching of interpretation could be called traditional. But we cannot understand the signs for being burned a lot until we have in our own flat experience, here and now, been burned a little.

Out of what can these extensions possibly be drawn? Only out of the informative years of childhood. Psychoanalysis talks of purposive forgetting. Yet purposive forgetting is the only way of remembering. One learns the meaning of "table," "book," "father," "mother," "mustn't," by forgetting the contexts in which these words were used. The Darwinian ancestry (locating the individual in his feudal line of descent from the ape) is matched in Freud by a still more striking causal ancestry that we might sloganize as "the child is father to the man."[4]

As we grow up, new meanings must either be engrafted upon old meanings (being to that extent *double-entendres*) or they must be new starts (hence, involving problems of dissociation).

In the study of the poem as dream we find revealed the ways in which the poetic organization takes shape under these necessities. Revise Freud's terms, if you will. But nothing is done by simply trying to refute them or to tie them into knots. One may complain at this procedure, for instance: Freud characterizes the dream as the fulfillment of a wish; an opponent shows him a dream of frustration, and he answers: "But the dreamer wishes to be frustrated." You may demur at that, pointing out that Freud has developed a "heads I win, tails you lose" mode of discourse here. But I maintain that, in doing so, you have contributed nothing. For there are people whose values are askew, for whom frustration itself is a kind of grotesque ambition. If you would, accordingly, propose to chart this field by offering better terms, by all means do so. But better terms are the only kind of refutation here that is worth the trouble. Similarly, one may be unhappy with the concept of ambivalence, which allows pretty much of an open season on explanations (though the specific filling-out may provide a better case for the explanation than appears in this key term itself). But, again, nothing but an alternative explanation is worth the effort of discussion here. Freud's terminology is a dictionary, a lexicon for charting a vastly complex and hitherto largely uncharted field. You can't refute a dictionary. The only profitable answer to a dictionary is another one.

A profitable answer to Freud's treatment of the Oedipus complex, for instance, was Malinowski's study of its variants in a matriarchal society.[5] Here we get at once a corroboration and a refutation of the Freudian doctrine. It is corroborated in that the same general patterns of enmity are revealed; it is refuted in that these patterns are shown not to be innate but to take shape with relation to the difference in family structure itself, with corresponding difference in roles.

Freud's overemphasis upon the patriarchal pattern (an assumption of its absoluteness that is responsible for the Freudian tendency to underrate greatly the economic factors influencing the relationships of persons or roles) is a prejudicial factor that must be discounted, even when treating the poem as dream. Though totemistic religion, for instance, flourished with matriarchal patterns, Freud treats even this in patriarchal terms. And I submit that this emphasis will conceal from us, to a large degree, what is going on in art. (We are still confining ourselves to the dream level—the level at which Freudian co-ordinates come closest to the charting of the logic of poetic structure.)

In the literature of transitional eras, for instance, we find an especial profusion of rebirth rituals, where the poet is making the symbolic passes that will endow him with a new identity. Now, imagine him trying to do a very thorough job of this reidentification. To be completely reborn, he would have to change his very lineage itself. He would have to revise not only his present but also his past. (Ancestry and cause are forever becoming intermingled—the thing is that from which it came—cause is *Ur-sache*, etc.) And could a personalized past be properly confined to a descent through the father, when it is the *mater* that is *semper certa*? Totemism, when not interpreted with Freud's patriarchal bias, may possibly provide us with the necessary cue here. Totemism, as Freud himself reminds us, was a magical device whereby the members of a group were identified with one another by the sharing of the same substance (a process often completed by the ritualistic eating of this substance, though it might, for this very reason, be prohibited on less festive occasions). And it is to the mother that the basic informative experiences of eating are related.

So, all told, even in strongly patriarchal societies (and much more so in a society like ours, where theories of sexual equality, with a corresponding confusion in sexual differentiation along occupational lines, have radically broken the symmetry of pure patriarchalism), would there not be a tendency for rebirth rituals to be completed by symbolizations of matricide and without derivation from competitive, monopolistic ingredients at all?[6]

To consider explicitly a bit of political dreaming, is not Hitler's doctrine of Aryanism something analogous to the adoption of a new totemic line? Has he not voted himself a new identity and, in keeping with a bastardized variant of the strategy of materialistic science, rounded this out by laying claim to a distinct blood stream? What the Pope is saying, benignly, in proclaiming the Hebrew prophets as the spiritual ancestors of Catholicism, Hitler is saying malignly in proclaiming for himself a lineage totally distinct.

Freud, working within the patriarchal perspective, has explained how such thinking becomes tied up with persecution. The paranoid, he says, assigns his imagined persecutor the role of rejected father. This persecutor is all-powerful, as the father seems to the child. He is responsible for every imagined machination (as the Jews, in Hitler's scheme, become the universal devil-function, the leading brains behind every "plot"). Advancing from this brilliant insight, it is not hard to understand why, once Hitler's fantasies are implemented by the vast resources of a nation, the "persecutor" becomes the persecuted.

The point I am trying to bring out is that this assigning of a new lineage to one's self (as would be necessary, in assigning one's self a new identity) could not be complete were it confined to symbolic patricide. There must also be ingredients of symbolic matricide intermingled here (with the phenomena of totemism giving cause to believe that the ritualistic slaying of the maternal relationship may draw upon an even deeper level than the ritualistic slaying of the paternal relationship). Lineage itself is charted after the metaphor of the family tree, which is, to be sure, patriarchalized in Western heraldry, though we get a different quality in the tree of life. MacLeish, in his period of aesthetic negativism, likens the sound of good verse to the ring of the ax in the tree, and if I may mention an early story of my own, "In Quest of Olympus," a rebirth fantasy, it begins by the felling of a tree, followed by the quick change from child to adult, or, within the conventions of the fiction, the change from tiny "Treep" to gigantic "Arjk"; and though, for a long time, under the influence of the Freudian patriarchal emphasis, I tended to consider such trees as fathers, I later felt compelled to make them ambigously parents. The symbolic structure of Peter Blume's painting, "The Eternal City," almost forces me to assign the tree, in that instance, to a purely maternal category, since the rejected father is pictured in the repellent phalluslike figure of Mussolini, leaving only the feminine role for the luxuriant tree that, by my interpretation of the picture, rounds out the lineage (with the dishonored Christ and the beggar-woman as vessels of the past lineage, and the lewd Mussolini and the impersonal tree as vessels of the new lineage, which I should interpret on the nonpolitical level as saying that sexuality is welcomed, but as a problem, while home is relegated to the world of the impersonal, abstract, observed).

From another point of view we may consider the sacrifice of gods, or of kings, as stylistic modes for dignifying human concerns (a kind of neo-euhemerism). In his stimulating study of the ritual drama, *The Hero*, Lord Raglan overstresses, it seems to me, the notion that these dramas appealed purely as spectacles. Would it not be more likely that the fate of the sacrificial king was also the fate of the audience, in stylizied form, dignified, "writ large"? Thus, their engrossment in the drama would not be merely that of watching a parade, or of utilitarian belief that the ritual would insure rainfall, crops, fertility, a good year, etc.; but, also, the stages of the hero's journey would chart the stages of their journey (as an Elizabethan play about royalty was not merely an opportunity for the pit to get a glimpse of high life, a living newspaper on the doings of society, but a dignification or memorializing of their own concerns, translated into the idiom then currently accepted as the proper language of magnification).[7]

But though we may want to introduce minor revisions in the Freudian perspective here, I submit that we should take Freud's key terms, "condensation" and "displacement," as the over-all categories for the analysis of the poem as dream. The terms are really two different approaches to the same phenomenon. Condensation, we might say, deals with the respects in which house in a dream may be more than house, or house plus. And displacement deals with the way in which house may be other than house, or house minus. (Perhaps we should say, more accurately, minus house.)

One can understand the resistance to both of these emphases. They leave no opportunity for a house to be purely and simply a house—and whatever we may feel about it as regards dreams, it is a very disturbing state of affairs when transferred to the realm of art. We must acknowledge, however, that the house in a poem is, when judged purely and simply as a house, a very flimsy structure for protection against wind and rain. So there seems to be some justice in retaining the Freudian terms when trying to decide what is going on in poetry. As Freud fills them out, the justification becomes stronger. The ways in which grammatical rules are violated, for instance; the dream's ways of enacting conjunctions, of solving arguments by club offers of mutually contradictory assertions; the importance of both concomitances and discontinuities for interpretative purposes (the phenomena of either association or dissociation, as you prefer, revealed with greatest clarity in the *lapsus linguae*); the conversion of an expression into its corresponding act (as were one, at a time when "over the fence is out" was an expression in vogue, to apply this comment upon some act by following the dream of this act by a dreamed incident of a ball going over a fence); and, above all, the notion that the optative is in dreams, as often in poetry and essay, presented in the indicative (a Freudian observation fertile to the neopositivists' critique of language)—the pliancy and ingenuity of Freud's researches here make entrancing reading, and continually provide insights that can be carried over, *mutatis mutandis*, to the operations of poetry. Perhaps we might sloganize the point thus: Insofar as art contains a surrealist ingredient (and all art contains some of this ingredient), psychoanalytic co-ordinates are required to explain the logic of its structure.

Perhaps we might take some of the pain from the notions of condensation and displacement (with the tendency of one event to become the synecdochic representative of some other event in the same cluster) by imagining a hypothetical case of authorship. A novelist, let us say, is trying to build up for us a sense of secrecy. He is picturing a conspiracy, yet he was never himself quite this kind of conspirator. Might not this novelist draw upon whatever kinds of conspiracy he himself had experientially known (as for instance where he to draft for this purpose memories of his participation in some childhood bund)? If this were so, an objective breakdown of the imagery with which he surrounded the conspiratorial events in his novel would reveal this contributory ingredient. You would not have to read your interpretation into it. It would be objectively, structurally, there, and could be pointed to by scissorwork. For instance, the novelist might explicitly state that, when joining the conspiracy, the hero recalled some incident of his childhood. Or the adult conspirators would, at strategic points, be explicitly likened by the novelist to children, etc. A statement about the ingredients of the work's motivation would thus be identical with a statement about the work's structure—a statement as to what goes with what in the work itself. Thus, in Coleridge's "The Eolian Harp," you do not have to interpret the poet's communion with the universe as an affront to his wife; the poet himself explicitly apologizes to her for it. Also, it is an objectively citable fact that imagery of noon goes with this apology. If, then, we look at other poems by Coleridge, noting the part played by the Sun at noon in the punishments of the guilt-laden Ancient Mariner, along with the fact that the situation of the narrator's confession involves the detention of a wedding guest from the marriage feast, plus the fact that a preference for church as against marriage is explicitly stated at the end of the poem, we begin to see a motivational cluster emerging. It is obvious that such structural interrelationships cannot be wholly conscious, since they are generalizations about acts that can only be made inductively and statistically after the acts have been accumulated. (This applies as much to the acts of a single poem as to the acts of many poems. We may find a theme emerging in one work that attains fruition in that same work—the ambiguities of its implications where it first emerges attaining explication in the same integer. Or its full character may not be developed until a later work. In its ambiguous emergent form it is a synecdochic representative of the form it later assumes when it comes to fruition in either the same work or in another one.)

However, though the synecdochic process (whereby something does service for the other members of its same cluster or as the foreshadowing of itself in a later development) cannot be wholly conscious, the dream is not all dream. We might say, in fact, that the Freudian analysis of art was handicapped by the aesthetic of the period—an aesthetic shared even by those who would have considered themselves greatly at odds with Freud and who were, in contrast with his delving into the unbeautiful, concerned with beauty only. This was the aesthetic that placed the emphasis wholly upon the function of self-expression. The artist had a number—some unique character or identity—and his art was the externalizing of this inwardness. The general Schopenhauerian trend contributed to this. Von Hartmann's *Philosophy of the Unconscious* has reinforced the same pattern. This version of voluntaristic processes, as connected with current theories of emancipation, resulted in a picture of the dark, unconscious drive calling for the artist to "out with it." The necessary function of the Freudian secular confessional, as a preparatory step to redemption, gave further strength to the same picture. Add the "complex in terms of the simple" strategy (with its variants —higher in terms of lower, normal as a mere attenuation of the abnormal, civilized as the primitive sublimated); add the war of the generations (which was considered as a kind of absolute rather than as a by-product of other factors, for those who hated the idea of class war took in its stead either the war of the generations or the war of the sexes)—and you get a picture that almost automatically places the emphasis upon art as utterance, as the naming of one's number, as a blurting-out, as catharsis by secretion.

I suggested two other broad categories for the analysis of poetic organization: prayer and chart.

Prayer would enter the Freudian picture insofar as it concerns the optative. But prayer does not stop at that. Prayer is also an act of communion. Hence, the concept of prayer, as extended to cover also secular forms of petition, moves us into the corresponding area of communication in general. We might say that, whereas the expressionistic emphasis reveals the ways in which the poet with an attitude embodies it in appropriate gesture, communication deals with the choice of gesture for the inducement of corresponding attitudes. Sensory imagery has this same communicative function, inviting the reader, within the limits of the fiction at least, to make himself over in the image of the imagery.

Considering the poem from this point of view, we begin with the incantatory elements in art, the ways of leading in or leading on the hypothetical audience X to which the poem, as a medium, is addressed (though this hypothetical audience X be nothing more concrete, as regards social relations, than a critical aspect of the poet's own personality). Even Freud's dream had a censor; but the poet's censor is still more exacting, as his shapings and revisions are made for the purpose of forestalling resistances (be those an essay reader's resistances to arguments and evidence or the novel reader's resistance to developments of narrative or character). We move here into the sphere of rhetoric (reader-writer relationships, an aspect of art that Freud explicitly impinges upon only to a degree in his analysis of wit), with the notion of address being most evident in oration and letter, less so in drama, and least in the lyric. Roughly, I should say that the slightest presence of revision is per se indication of a poet's feeling that his work is addressed (if only, as Mead might say, the address of an "I" to its "me").

Here would enter consideration of formal devices, ways of pointing up and fulfilling expectations, of living up to a contract with the reader (as Wordsworth and Coleridge might put it), of easing by transition or sharpening by ellipsis; in short, all that falls within the sphere of incantation, imprecation, exhortation, inducement, weaving and releasing of spells; matters of style and form, of meter and rhythm, as contributing to these results; and thence to the conventions and social values that the poet draws upon in forming the appropriate recipes for the roles of protagonist and antagonist, into which the total agon is analytically broken down, with subsidiary roles polarized about one or the other of the two agonists tapering off to form a region of overlap between the two principles—the ground of the agon. Here, as the reverse of prayer, would come also invective, indictment, oath. And the gestures might well be tracked down eventually to choices far closer to bodily pantomime than is revealed on the level of social evaluation alone (as were a poet, seeking the gestures appropriate for the conveying of a social negativeness, to draw finally upon imagery of disgust, and perhaps even, at felicitous moments, to select his speech by playing up the very consonants that come nearest to the enacting of repulsion).

As to the poem as chart: the Freudian emphasis upon the pun brings it about that something can be only insofar as it is something else. But, aside from these ambiguities, there is also a statement's value as being exactly what it is. Perhaps we could best indicate what we mean by speaking of the poem as chart if we called it the poet's contribution to an informal dictionary. As with proverbs, he finds some experience or relationship typical, or recurrent, or significant enough for him to need a word for it. Except that his way of defining the word is not to use purely conceptual terms, as in a formal dictionary, but to show how his vision behaves, with appropriate attitudes. In this, again, it is like the proverb that does not merely name but names vindictively, or plaintively, or promisingly, or consolingly, etc. His namings need not be new ones. Often they are but memorializings of an experience long recognized.

But, essentially, they are enactments, with every form of expression being capable of treatment as the efficient extension of one aspect or another of ritual drama (so that even the scientific essay would have its measure of choreography, its pedestrian pace itself being analyzed as gesture or incantation, its polysyllables being as style the mimetics of a distinct monasticism, etc.). And this observation, whereby we have willy-nilly slipped back into the former subject, the symbolic act as prayer, leads us to observe that the three aspects of the poem, here proposed, are not elements that can be isolated in the poem itself, with one line revealing the "dream," another the "prayer," and a third the "chart." They merely suggest three convenient modes in which to approach the task of analysis.[8]

The primary category, for the explicit purposes of literary criticism, would thus seem to me to be that of communication rather than that of wish, with its disguises, frustrations, and fulfillments. Wishes themselves, in fact, become from this point of view analyzable as purposes that get their shape from the poet's perspective in general (while this perspective is in turn shaped by the collective medium of communication). The choice of communication also has the advantage, from the sociological point of view, that it resists the Freudian tendency to overplay the psychological factor (as the total medium of communication is not merely that of words, colors, forms, etc., or of the values and conventions with which these are endowed, but also the productive materials, co-operative resources, property rights, authorities, and their various bottle-necks which figure in the total act of human conversation).[9]

To sum up: I should say that, for the explicit purposes of literary criticism, we should require more emphasis than the Freudian structure gives, (1) to the proportional strategy as against the essentializing one, (2) to matriarchal symbolizations as against the Freudian patriarchal bias, (3) to poem as prayer and chart, as against simply the poem as dream.

But I fully recognize that, once the ingenious and complex structure has been erected, nearly anyone can turn up with proposals that it be given a little more of this, a little less of that, a pinch of so-and-so, etc. And I recognize that, above all, we owe an enormous debt of gratitude to the man who, by his insight, his energy, and his remarkably keen powers of articulation, made such tinkering possible. It is almost fabulous to think that, after so many centuries of the family, it is only now that this central factor in our social organization has attained its counterpart in an organized critique of the family and of the ways in which the informative experience with familiar roles may be carried over, or "metaphored," into the experience with extra-familiar roles, giving these latter, insofar as they are, or are felt to be, analogous with the former, a structure of interpretations and attitudes borrowed from the former. And insofar as poets, like everyone else, are regularly involved in such informative familiar relationships, long before any but a few rudimentary bodily gestures are available for communicative use (with their first use unquestionably being the purely self-expressive one), the child is indeed the adult poet's father, as he is the father of us all (if not so in essence, then at least as regards an important predisposing factor "to look out for"). And thence we get to Freud's brilliant documentation of this ancestry, as it affects the maintenance of a continuity in the growing personality.

Only if we eliminate biography entirely as a relevant fact about poetic organization can we eliminate the importance of the psychoanalyst's search for universal patterns of biography (as revealed in the search for basic myths which recur in new guises as a theme with variations); and we can eliminate biography as a relevant fact about poetic organization only if we consider the work of art as if it were written neither by people nor for people, involving neither inducements nor resistances.[10] Such can be done, but the cost is tremendous insofar as the critic considers it his task to disclose the poem's eventfulness.

However, this is decidedly not the same thing as saying that "we cannot appreciate the poem without knowing about its relation to the poet's life as an individual." Rather, it is equivalent to saying: "We cannot understand a poem's structure without understanding the function of that structure. And to understand its function we must understand its purpose." To be sure, there are respects in which the poem, as purpose, is doing things for the poet that it is doing for no one else. For instance, I think it can be shown by analysis of the imagery in Coleridge's "Mystery Poems" that one of the battles being fought there is an attempt to get self-redemption by the poet's striving for the vicarious or ritualistic redemption of his drug. It is obvious that this aspect of the equational structure is private and would best merit discussion when one is discussing the strategy of one man in its particularities. Readers in general will respond only to the sense of guilt, which was sharpened for Coleridge by his particular burden of addiction, but which may be sharpened for each reader by totally different particularities of experience. But if you do not discuss the poem's structure as a function of symbolic redemption at all (as a kind of private-enterprise Mass, with important ingredients of a black Mass), the observations you make about its structure are much more likely to be gratuitious and arbitrary (quite as only the most felicitous of observers could relevantly describe the distribution of men and postures in a football game if he had no knowledge of the game's purpose and did not discuss its formations as oppositional tactics for the carrying-out of this purpose, but treated the spectacle simply as the manifestation of a desire to instruct and amuse).

Thus, in the case of "The Ancient Mariner," knowledge of Coleridge's personal problems may enlighten us as to the particular burdens that the Pilot's boy ("who now doth crazy go") took upon himself as scapegoat for the poet alone. But his appearance in the poem cannot be understood at all, except in superficial terms of the interesting or the picturesque, if we do not grasp his function as a scapegoat of some sort—a victimized vessel for drawing off the most malign aspects of the curse that afflicts the "greybeard loon" whose cure had been effected under the dubious aegis of moonlight. And I believe that such a functional approach is the only one that can lead into a profitable analysis of a poem's structure even on the purely technical level.

I remember how, for instance, I had pondered for years the reference to the "silly buckets" filled with curative rain. I noted the epithet as surprising, picturesque, and interesting. I knew that it was doing something, but I wasn't quite sure what. But as soon as I looked upon the Pilot's boy as a scapegoat, I saw that the word *silly* was a technical foreshadowing of the fate that befell this figure in the poem. The structure itself became more apparent: the "loon"-atic Mariner begins his cure from drought under the aegis of a moon that causes a silly rain, thence by synecdoche to silly buckets, and the most malignant features of this problematic cure are transferred to the Pilot's boy who now doth crazy go. Now, if you want to confine your observations to the one poem, you have a structural-functional-technical analysis of some important relationships within the poem itself. If you wish to trail the matter farther afield, into the equational structure of other work by Coleridge, you can back your interpretation of the moon by such reference as that to "moon-blasted madness," which gives you increased authority to discern lunatic ingredients in the lunar. His letters, where he talks of his addiction in imagery like that of the "Mystery Poems" and contemplates entering an insane asylum for a cure, entitle you to begin looking for traces of the drug as an ingredient in the redemptive problem. His letters also explicitly place the drug in the same cluster with the serpent; hence, we begin to discern what is going on when the Mariner transubstantiates the water snakes, in removing them from the category of the loathsome and accursed to the category of the blessed and beautiful. So much should be enough for the moment. Since the poem is constructed about an opposition between punishments under the aegis of the sun and cure under the aegis of the moon, one could proceed in other works to disclose the two sets of equations clustered about these two principles. Indeed, even in "The Ancient Mariner" itself we get a momentous cue, as the sun is explicitly said to be "like God's own head."[11] But, for the moment, all I would maintain is that, if we had but this one poem by Coleridge, and knew not one other thing about him, we could not get an insight into its structure until we began with an awareness of its function as a symbolic redemptive process.

I can imagine a time when the psychological picture will be so well-known and taken into account—when we shall have gone so far beyond Freud's initial concerns—that a reference to the polymorphous perverse of the infantile, for instance, will seem far too general—a mere first approximation. Everyone provides an instance of the polymorphous perverse, in attenuated form, at a moment of hesitancy; caught in the trackless maze of an unresolved, and even undefined, conflict, he regresses along this channel and that, in a formless experimentation that "tries anything and everything, somewhat." And insofar as his puzzle is resolved into pace, and steady rhythms of a progressive way out are established, there is always the likelihood that this solution will maintain continuity with the past of the poet's personality by a covert drawing upon analogies with this past. Hence the poet or speculator, no matter how new the characters with which he is now concerned, will give them somewhat the roles of past characters; whereat I see nothing unusual about the thought that a mature and highly complex philosophy might be so organized as to be surrogate for, let us say, a kind of adult breastfeeding—or, in those more concerned with alienation, a kind of adult weaning. Such categories do not by any means encompass the totality of a communicative structure; but they are part of it, and the imagery and transitions of the poem itself cannot disclose their full logic until such factors are taken into account.

However, I have spoken of pace. And perhaps I might conclude with some words on the bearing that the Freudian technique has upon the matter of pace. The Freudian procedure is primarily designed to break down a rhythm grown obsessive, to confront the systematic pieties of the patient's misery with systematic impieties of the clinic.[12] But the emphasis here is more upon the breaking of a malign rhythm than upon the upbuilding of a benign one. There is no place in this technique for examining the available resources whereby the adoption of total dramatic enactment may lead to correspondingly proper attitude. There is no talk of games, of dance, of manual and physical actions, of historical role, as a "way in" to this new upbuilding. The sedentary patient is given a sedentary cure. The theory of rhythms—work rhythms, dance rhythms, march rhythms—

is no explicit part of this scheme, which is primarily designed to break old rhythms rather than to establish new ones.

The establishing of a new pace, beyond the smashing of the old puzzle, would involve a rounded philosophy of the drama. Freud, since his subject is conflict, hovers continually about the edges of such a philosophy; yet it is not dialectical enough. For this reason Marxists properly resent his theories, even though one could, by culling incidental sentences from his works, fit him comfortably into the Marxist perspective. But the Marxists are wrong, I think, in resenting him as an irrationalist, for there is nothing more rational than the systematic recognition of irrational and nonrational factors. And I should say that both Freudians and Marxists are wrong insofar as they cannot put their theories together, by an over-all theory of drama itself (as they should be able to do, since Freud gives us the material of the closet drama, and Marx the material of the problem play, the one treated in terms of personal conflicts, the other in terms of public conflicts).

The approach would require explicitly the analysis of role: salvation via change or purification of identity (purification in either the moral or chemical sense); different typical relationships between individual and group (as charted attitudinally in proverbs, and in complex works treated as sophisticated variants);   modes of acceptance, rejection, self-acceptance, rejection of rejection[13] ("the enemies of my enemies are my friends"); transitional disembodiment as intermediate step between old self and new self (the spirituality of Shelley and of the Freudian cure itself); monasticism in the development of methods that fix a transitional or otherworldly stage, thereby making the evanescent itself into a kind of permanency—with all these modes of enactment finally employing, as part of the gesture idiom, the responses of the body itself as actor. (If one sought to employ Freud, as is, for the analysis of the poem, one would find almost nothing on poetic posture or pantomime, tonality, the significance of different styles and rhythmic patterns, nothing of this behaviorism.) Such, it seems to me, would be necessary, and much more in that direction, before we could so extend Freud's perspective that it revealed the major events going on in art.

But such revisions would by no means be anti-Freudian. They would be the kind of extensions required by reason of the fact that the symbolic act of art, whatever its analogies with the symbolic act of neurosis, also has important divergencies from the symbolic act of neurosis. They would be extensions designed to take into account the full play of communicative and realistic ingredients that comprise so large an aspect of poetic structure.

NOTES

1. The essentializing strategy has its function when dealing with classes of items; the proportional one is for dealing with an item in its uniqueness. By isolating the matter of voluntarism, we put Freud in a line or class with Augustine. By isolating the matter of his concern with a distinction between unconscious and conscious, we may put him in a line with Leibnitz's distinction between perception and apperception. Or we could link him with the Spinozistic *conatus* and the Schopenhauerian will. Or, as a rationalist, he falls into the bin with Aquinas (who is himself most conveniently isolated as a rationalist if you employ the essentializing as against the proportional strategy, stressing what he added rather than what he retained). Many arguments seem to hinge about the fact that there is an unverbalized disagreement as to the choice between these strategies. The same man, for instance, who might employ the essentializing strategy in proclaiming Aquinas as a rationalist, taking as the significant factor in Aquinas's philosophy his additions to rationalism rather than considering this as an ingredient in a faith philosophy, might object to the bracketing of Aquinas and Freud (here shifting to the proportional strategy, as he pointed out the totally different materials with which Aquinas surrounded his rational principle).

2. We may distinguish between public and universal motives. Insofar as one acts in a certain way because of his connection with a business or party, he would act from a public motive. His need of response to a new glandular stimulation at adolescence, on the other hand, would arise regardless of social values, and in that sense would be at once private and universal. The particular forms in which he expressed this need would, of course, be channelized in accordance with public or social factors.

3. Perhaps, to avoid confusion, I should call attention to the fact that symbolic in this context is being used differently by me from its use in the expression "symbolic action." If a man crosses a street, it is a practical act. If he writes a book about crossings—crossing streets, bridges, oceans, etc.—that is a symbolic act. Symbolic, as used in the restricted sense (in contrast with free association), would refer to the imputation of an absolute meaning to a crossing, a meaning that I might impute even before reading the book in question. Against this, I should maintain: One can never know what a crossing means, in a specific book, until he has studied its tie-up with other imagery in that particular book.

4. Maybe the kind of forgetting that is revealed by psychoanalysis could, within this frame, be better characterized as an incomplete forgetting. That is, whereas "table," for instance, acquires an absolute and emotionally neutral meaning as a name merely for a class of objects, by a merging of all the contexts involving the presence of a table a table becomes symbolic, or a *double-entendre*, or more than table, when some particular informative context is more important than the others. That is, when "table," as used by

the poet, has overtones of, let us say, *one* table at which his mother worked when he was a child. In this way the table, its food, and the cloth may become surrogates for the mother, her breasts, and her apron. And incest awe may become merged with "mustn't touch" injunctions, stemming from attempts to keep the child from meddling with the objects on the table. In a dream play by Edmund Wilson, *The Crime in the Whistler Room*, there are two worlds of plot, with the characters belonging in the one world looking upon those in the other as dead, and the hero of this living world taking a dream shape as werewolf. The worlds switch back and forth, depending upon the presence or removal of a gate-leg table. In this instance I think we should not be far wrong in attributing some such content as the above to the table when considering it as a fulcrum upon which the structure of the plot is swung.

5. It is wrong, I think, to consider Freud's general picture as that of an individual psychology. Adler's start from the concept of ego compensation fits this description par excellence. But Freud's is a family psychology. He has offered a critique of the family, though it is the family of a neopatriarch. It is interesting to watch Freud, in his *Group Psychology and the Analysis of the Ego*, frankly shifting between the primacy of group psychology and the primacy of individual psychology, changing his mind as he debates with himself in public and leaves in his pages the record of his fluctuations, frankly stated as such. Finally, he compromises by leaving both, drawing individual psychology from the role of the monopolistic father, and group psychology from the roles of the sons, deprived of sexual gratification by the monopolistic father, and banded together for their mutual benefit. But note that the whole picture is that of a family, albeit of a family in which the woman is a mere passive object of male wealth.

6. Or you might put it this way: Rebirth would require a killing of the old self. Such symbolic suicide, to be complete, would require a snapping of the total ancestral line (as being an integral aspect of one's identity). Hence, a tendency for the emancipatory crime to become sexually ambivalent. Freud's patriarchal emphasis leads to an overstress upon father-rejection as a basic cause rather than as a by-product of conversion (the Kierkegaard earthquake, that was accompanied by a changed attitude toward his father). Suicide, to be thorough, would have to go farther, and the phenomena of identity revealed in totemism might require the introduction of matricidal ingredients also. Freud himself, toward the end of *Totem and Taboo*, gives us an opening wedge by stating frankly, "In this evolution I am at a loss to indicate the place of the great maternal deities who perhaps everywhere preceded the paternal deities." This same patriarchal emphasis also reinforces the Freudian tendency to treat social love as a mere sublimation of balked male sexual appetite, whereas a more matriarchal concern, with the Madonna and Child relationship, would suggest a place for affection as a primary biological motivation. Not even a naturalistic account of motivation would necessarily require reinforcement from the debunking strategy (in accordance with which the real motives would be incipient perversions, and social motives as we know them would be but their appearances, or censored disguise).

7. Might not the sacrificial figure (as parent, king, or god) also at times derive from no resistance or vindictiveness whatsoever, but be the recipient of the burden simply through "having stronger shoulders, better able to bear it"?

And might the choice of guilty scapegoats (such as a bad father) be but a secondary development for accommodating this socialization of a loss to the patterns of legality?

8. Dream has its opposite, nightmare; prayer has its opposite, oath. Charts merely vary—in scope and relevance. In "Kubla Khan," automatically composed during an opium dream, the dream ingredient is uppermost. In "The Ancient Mariner," the prayer ingredient is uppermost. In "Dejection" and "The Pains of Sleep," the chart ingredient is uppermost: here Coleridge is explicitly discussing his situation.

9. I have since come to realize that "communication" is itself but a technical species of "love," hence always lurks about the edges of the Freudian "Libido."

10. Those who stress form of this sort, as against content, usually feel that they are concerned with judgments of excellence as against judgments of the merely representative. Yet, just as a content category such as the Oedipus complex is neutral, i.e., includes both good and bad examples of its kind, so does a form category, such as sonnet or iambic pentameter, include both good and bad examples of its kind. In fact, though categories or classifications may be employed for evaluative purposes, they should be of themselves nonevaluative. "Apples" is a neutral, nonevaluative class, including firm apples and rotten ones. Categories that are in themselves evaluative are merely circular arguments—disguised ways of saying "this is good because it is good." The orthodox strategy of disguise is to break the statement into two parts, such as: "This is good because it has form; and form is good." The lure behind the feeling that the miracle of evaluation can be replaced by a codified scientific routine of evaluation seems to get its backing from the hope that concept of quality can be matched by a number. The terms missing may be revealed by a diagram, thus:

Quantity	Number
Weight	Pound
Length	Foot
Duration	Hour
Quality	( )
Excellence	( )
Inferiority	( )

Often the strategy of concealment is accomplished by an ambiguity, as the critic sometimes uses the term "poetry" to designate good poetry, and sometimes uses it to designate "poetry, any poetry, good, bad, or indifferent." I do, however, strongly sympathize with the formalists, as against the sociologists, when the sociologist treats poetry simply as a kind of haphazard sociological survey—a report about world conditions that often shows commendable intuitive insight but is handicapped by a poor methodology of research and controls.

11. That's not the whole story. A few lines later the sun becomes "No bigger than the Moon." And earlier, the Mariner's disclosure that he killed the Albatross had emerged from a description of "Moon-shine." Thus not only the cure, but also the offense and the avenger, have moony ingredients.

12. There are styles of cure, shifting from age to age, because each novelty becomes a commonplace, so that the patient integrates his conflict with the in-

gredients of the old cure itself, thus making them part of his obsession. Hence, the need for a new method of jolting. Thus, I should imagine that a patient who had got into difficulties after mastering the Freudian technique would present the most obstinate problems for a Freudian cure. He would require some step beyond Freud. The same observation would apply to shifting styles in poetry and philosophy, when considered as cures, as the filling of a need.

13. I am indebted to Norbert Gutermann for the term "self-acceptance" and to William S. Knickerbocker for the term "rejection of rejection."

Seminar on "The Purloined Letter"

Jacques Lacan

TRANSLATOR'S PREFACE

If "psychoanalytic criticism" is an effort to bring analytic categories to bear in the solution of critical problems, Lacan's text is certainly not an example of that discipline. One has the feeling that, on the contrary, in the confrontation between analysis and literature, the former's role for Lacan is not to solve but to open up a new kind of textual problem. The Poe text then is in many ways a pretext, an exemplary occasion for Lacan to complicate the question of *Beyond the Pleasure Principle*. It is indeed a "purloined letter."

The crux of the problem is in the ambiguity of the term *letter* in Lacan's analysis. It may mean either typographical character or epistle. Why?

(a) As typographical character, the letter is a unit of signification without any meaning in itself. In this it resembles the "memory trace," which for Freud is never the image of an event, but a term which takes on meaning only through its differential opposition to other traces. It is a particular arrangement of "frayings." The striking image of this situation in the tale is that we never know the *contents* of the crucial letter. Here then is a psychoanalysis indifferent to deep meanings, concerned more with a latent organization of the manifest than a latent meaning beneath it. In its refusal to accord any "positive" status to linguistic phenomena, this might be viewed as Lacan's Saussurean side (see text note 24).

(b) As epistle, the letter allows Lacan to play on the intersubjective relations which expropriate the individual. ("To whom does a letter belong?") It is Lévi-Strauss (and Mauss) who are no doubt at the source of this effort to think of the Oedipus complex in terms of a structure of *exchange* crucial to the "fixation" of unconscious "memory traces."

These losses—of the plenitude of meaning and the security of (self-)

382

possession—are thus the principal modes of the Lacanian *askesis* in this parable of analysis. To which we may add a third: that of metalanguage. By which we mean: (1) that the Prefect is already repeating the "events" he recounts at the moment he pretends to view them objectively; (2) even Dupin (as analyst) is trapped in the phantasmatic circuit (repetitive structure, mobile scenario . . .) at the moment of his rage against the Minister. The difference between the Prefect (trapped in his transference) and Dupin (counteracting the countertransference) is that the latter is intermittently aware of his loss.

In translating the text, we found that a large measure of its difficulty was a function of Lacan's idiosyncratic use of prepositions. As a result, the reader has to play with various possibilities of subordination in a number of sentences in order to determine the "proper" one(s). For better or worse, in English we have (necessarily) chosen to normalize the use of prepositions. We have thus occasionally been obliged to chart a course through Lacan's labyrinth rather than reproduce that labyrinth whole. There has no doubt been a concomitant loss (in syntactical richness) and gain (in clarity).

The notes we have added to the text (signed "Trans.") are, on the whole, explanations of allusions or clarifications of particularly oblique points.

This text was orginally written in 1956 and—along with an introductory postface—is the opening text of the *Ecrits*.

—J.M.

Und ween es uns glückt,
Und ween es sich schickt,
So sind es Gedanken.

Our inquiry has led us to the point of recognizing that the repetition automatism (*Wiederholungszwang*) finds its basis in what we have called the *insistence* of the signifying chain.[1] We have elaborated that notion itself as a correlate of the *ex-sistence* (or: eccentric place) in which we must necessarily locate the subject of the unconscious if we are to take Freud's discovery seriously.[2] As is known, it is in the realm of experience inaugurated by psychoanalysis that we may grasp along what imaginary lines the human organism, in the most intimate recesses of its being, manifests its capture in a *symbolic* dimension.[3]

The lesson of this seminar is intended to maintain that these imaginary incidences, far from representing the essence of our experience, reveal only what in it remains inconsistent unless they are related to the symbolic chain which binds and orients them.

We realize, of course, the importance of these imaginary impregnations (*Prägung*) in those partializations of the symbolic alternative which give the symbolic chain its appearance. But we maintain that it is the specific law of that chain which governs those psychoanalytic effects that are decisive for the subject: such as foreclosure (*Verwerfung*), repression (*Verdrängung*), denial (*Verneinung*) itself—specifying with appropriate emphasis that these effects follow so faithfully the displacement (*Entstellung*) of the signifier that imaginary factors, despite their inertia, figure only as shadows and reflections in the process.[4]

But this emphasis would be lavished in vain, if it served, in your opinion, only to abstract a general type from phenomena whose particularity in our work would remain the essential thing for you, and whose original arrangement could be broken up only artificially.

Which is why we have decided to illustrate for you today the truth which may be drawn from that moment in Freud's thought under study—namely, that it is the symbolic order which is constitutive for the subject—by demonstrating in a story the decisive orientation which the subject receives from the itinerary of a signifier.[5]

It is that truth, let us note, which makes the very existence of fiction possible. And in that case, a fable is as appropriate as any other narrative for bringing it to light—at the risk of having the fable's coherence put to the test in the process. Aside from that reservation, a fictive tale even has the advantage of manifesting symbolic necessity more purely to the extent that we may believe its conception arbitrary.

Which is why, without seeking any further, we have chosen our example from the very story in which the dialectic of the game of even or odd—from whose study we have but recently profited—occurs.[6] It is, no doubt, no accident that this tale revealed itself propitious to pursuing a course of inquiry which had already found support in it.

As you know, we are talking about the tale which Baudelaire translated under the title: *La lettre volée*. At first reading, we may distinguish a drama, its narration, and the conditions of that narration.

We see quickly enough, moreover, that these components are necessary and that they could not have escaped the intentions of whoever composed them.

The narration, in fact, doubles the drama with a commentary without which no *mise en scène* would be possible. Let us say that the action would remain, properly speaking, invisible from the pit—aside from the fact that the dialogue would be expressly and by dramatic necessity devoid of whatever meaning it might have for an audience: —in other words, nothing of the drama could be grasped, neither seen nor heard, without, dare we say, the twilighting which the narration, in each scene, casts on the point of view that one of the actors had while performing it.

There are two scenes, the first of which we shall straightway designate the primal scene, and by no means inadvertently, since the second may be considered its repetition in the very sense we are considering today.

The primal scene is thus performed, we are told, in the royal *boudoir*, so that we suspect that the person of the highest rank, called the "exalted personage," who is alone there when she receives a letter, is the Queen. This feeling is confirmed by the embarrassment into which she is plunged by the entry of the other exalted personage, of whom we have already been told prior to this account that the knowledge he might have of the letter in question would jeopardize for the lady nothing less than her honor and safety. Any doubt that he is in fact the King is promptly dissipated in the course of the scene which begins with the entry of the Minister D. . . . At that moment, in fact, the Queen can do no better than to play on the King's inattentiveness by leaving the letter on the table "face down, address uppermost." It does not, however, escape the Minister's lynx eye, nor does he fail to notice the Queen's distress and thus to fathom her secret. From then on everything transpires like clockwork. After dealing in his customary manner with the business of the day, the Minister draws from his pocket a letter similar in appearance to the one in his view, and, having pretended to read it, he places it next to the other. A bit more conversation to amuse the royal company, whereupon, without flinching once, he seizes the embarrassing letter, making off with it, as the Queen, on whom none of his maneuver has been lost, remains unable to intervene for fear of attracting the attention of her royal spouse, close at her side at that very moment.

Everything might then have transpired unseen by a hypothetical spectator of an operation in which nobody falters, and whose *quo-*

tient is that the Minister has filched from the Queen her letter and that—an even more important result than the first—the Queen knows that he now has it, and by no means innocently.

A *remainder* that no analyst will neglect, trained as he is to retain whatever is significant, without always knowing what to do with it: the letter, abandoned by the Minister, and which the Queen's hand is now free to roll into a ball.

Second scene: in the Minister's office. It is in his hotel, and we know—from the account the Prefect of police has given Dupin, whose specific genius for solving enigmas Poe introduces here for the second time—that the police, returning there as soon as the Minister's habitual, nightly absences allow them to, have searched the hotel and its surroundings from top to bottom for the last eighteen months. In vain,—although everyone can deduce from the situation that the Minister keeps the letter within reach.

Dupin calls on the Minister. The latter receives him with studied nonchalance, affecting in his conversation romantic *ennui*. Meanwhile Dupin, whom this pretense does not deceive, his eyes protected by green glasses, proceeds to inspect the premises. When his glance catches a rather crumpled piece of paper—apparently thrust carelessly in a division of an ugly pasteboard card-rack, hanging gaudily from the middle of the mantelpiece—he already knows that he's found what he's looking for. His conviction is re-enforced by the very details which seem to contradict the description he has of the stolen letter, with the exception of the format, which remains the same.

Whereupon he has but to withdraw, after "forgetting" his snuff-box on the table, in order to return the following day to reclaim it—armed with a facsimile of the letter in its present state. As an incident in the street, prepared for the proper moment, draws the Minister to the window, Dupin in turn seizes the opportunity to snatch the letter while substituting the imitation, and has only to maintain the appearances of a normal exit.

Here as well all has transpired, if not without noise, at least without all commotion. The quotient of the operation is that the Minister no longer has the letter, but, far from suspecting that Dupin is the culprit who has ravished it from him, knows nothing of it. Moreover, what he is left with is far from insignificant for what follows. We shall return to what brought Dupin to inscribe a message on his counterfeit letter. Whatever the case, the Minister, when he tries to make use of it, will be able to read these words, written so that he may recognize Dupin's hand: ". . . *Un dessein si funeste / S'il n'est digne d'Atreé est digne de Thyeste*," whose source, Dupin tells us, is Crébillon's *Atreé*.[7]

Need we emphasize the similarity of these two sequences? Yes, for the resemblance we have in mind is not a simple collection of traits chosen only in order to delete their difference. And it would not be enough to retain those common traits at the expense of the others for the slightest truth to result. It is rather the intersubjectivity in which the two actions are motivated that we wish to bring into relief, as well as the three terms through which it structures them.[8]

The special status of these terms results from their corresponding simultaneously to the three logical moments through which the decision is precipitated and the three places it assigns to the subjects among whom it constitutes a choice.

That decision is reached in a glance's time.[9] For the maneuvers which follow, however stealthily they prolong it, add nothing to that glance, nor does the deferring of the deed in the second scene break the unity of that moment.

This glance presupposes two others, which it embraces in its vision of the breach left in their fallacious complementarity, anticipating in it the occasion for larceny afforded by that exposure. Thus three moments, structuring three glances, borne by three subjects, incarnated each time by different characters.

The first is a glance that sees nothing: the King and the police.

The second, a glance which sees that the first sees nothing and deludes itself as to the secrecy of what it hides: the Queen, then the Minister.

The third sees that the first two glances leave what should be hidden exposed to whomever would seize it: the Minister, and finally Dupin.

In order to grasp in its unity the intersubjective complex thus described, we would willingly seek a model in the technique legendarily attributed to the ostrich attempting to shield itself from danger; for that technique might ultimately be qualified as political, divided as it here is among three partners: the second believing itself invisible because the first has its head stuck in the ground, and all the while letting the third calmly pluck its rear; we need only enrich its proverbial denomination by a letter, producing *la politique de l'autruiche*, for the ostrich itself to take on forever a new meaning.[10]

Given the intersubjective modulus of the repetitive action, it remains to recognize in it a *repetition automatism* in the sense that interests us in Freud's text.

The plurality of subjects, of course, can be no objection for those who are long accustomed to the perspectives summarized by our formula: *the unconscious is the discourse of the Other*.[11] And we will not recall now what the notion of the *immixture of subjects*, recently introduced in our re-analysis of the dream of Irma's injection, adds to the discussion.

What interests us today is the manner in which the subjects relay each other in their displacement during the intersubjective repetition.

We shall see that their displacement is determined by the place which a pure signifier—the purloined letter—comes to occupy in their trio. And that is what will confirm for us its status as repetition automatism.

It does not, however, seem excessive, before pursuing this line of inquiry, to ask whether the thrust of the tale and the interest we bring to it—to the extent that they coincide—do not lie elsewhere.

May we view as simply a rationalization (in our gruff jargon) the fact that the story is told to us as a police mystery?

In truth, we should be right in judging that fact highly dubious as soon as we note that everything which warrants such mystery concerning a crime or offense—its nature and motives, instruments and execution; the procedure used to discover the author, and the means employed to convict him—is carefully eliminated here at the start of each episode.

The act of deceit is, in fact, from the beginning as clearly known as the intrigues of the culprit and their effects on his victim. The problem, as exposed to us, is limited to the search for and restitution of the object of the deceit, and it seems rather intentional that the solution is already obtained when it is explained to us. Is *that* how we are kept in suspense? Whatever credit we may accord the conventions of a genre for provoking a specific interest in the reader, we should not forget that "the Dupin tale," this the second to appear, is a prototype, and that even if the genre were established in the first, it is still a little early for the author to play on a convention.[12]

It would, however, be equally excessive to reduce the whole thing to a fable whose moral would be that in order to shield from inquisitive eyes one of those correspondences whose secrecy is sometimes necessary to conjugal peace, it suffices to leave the crucial letters lying about on one's table, even though the meaningful side be turned face down. For that would be a hoax which, for our part, we would never recommend anyone try, lest he be gravely disappointed in his hopes.

Might there then be no mystery other than, concerning the Prefect, an incompetence issuing in failure—were it not perhaps, concerning Dupin, a certain dissonance we hesitate to acknowledge between, on the one hand, the admittedly penetrating, though, in their generality, not always quite relevant remarks with which he introduces us to his method and, on the other, the manner in which he in fact intervenes.

Were we to pursue this sense of mystification a bit further we might soon begin to wonder whether, from that initial scene which only the rank of the protagonists saves from vaudeville, to the fall into ridicule which seems to await the Minister at the end, it is not this impression that everyone is being duped which makes for our pleasure.

And we would be all the more inclined to think so in that we would recognize in that surmise, along with those of you who read us, the definition we once gave in passing of the modern hero, "whom ludicrous exploits exalt in circumstances of utter confusion."[13]

But are we ourselves not taken in by the imposing presence of the amateur detective, prototype of a latter-day swashbuckler, as yet safe from the insipidity of our contemporary *superman?*

A trick . . . sufficient for us to discern in this tale, on the contrary, so perfect a verisimilitude that it may be said that truth here reveals its fictive arrangement.

For such indeed is the direction in which the principles of that verisimilitude lead us. Entering into its strategy, we indeed perceive a new drama we may call complementary to the first, in so far as the latter was what is termed a play without words whereas the interest of the second plays on the properties of speech.[14]

If it is indeed clear that each of the two scenes of the real drama is narrated in the course of a different dialogue, it is only through access to those notions set forth in our teaching that one may recognize that it is not thus simply to augment the charm of the exposition, but that the dialogues themselves, in the opposite use they make of the powers of speech, take on a tension which makes of them a different drama, one which our vocabulary will distinguish from the first as persisting in the symbolic order.

The first dialogue—between the Prefect of police and Dupin—is played as between a deaf man and one who hears. That is, it presents the real complexity of what is ordinarily simplified, with the most confused results, in the notion of communication.

This example demonstrates indeed how an act of communication may give the impression at which theorists too often stop: of allowing in its transmission but a single meaning, as though the highly significant commentary into which he who understands integrates it, could, because unperceived by him who does not understand, be considered null.

It remains that if only the dialogue's meaning as a report is retained, its verisimilitude may appear to depend on a guarantee of exactitude. But here dialogue may be more fertile than seems, if we demonstrate its tactics: as shall be seen by focusing on the recounting of our first scene.

For the double and even triple subjective filter through which that scene comes to us: a narration by Dupin's friend and associate (henceforth to be called the general narrator of the story)—of the account by which the Prefect reveals to Dupin—the report the Queen gave him of it, is not merely the consequence of a fortuitous arrangement.

If indeed the extremity to which the original narrator is reduced precludes her altering any of the events, it would be wrong to believe that the Prefect is empowered to lend her his voice in this case only by that lack of imagination on which he has, dare we say, the patent.

The fact that the message is thus re-transmitted assures us of what may by no means be taken for granted: that it belongs to the dimension of language.

Those who are here know our remarks on the subject, specifically those illustrated by the counter case of the so-called language of bees: in which a linguist[15] can see only a simple signaling of the location of objects, in other words: only an imaginary function more differentiated than others.

We emphasize that such a form of communication is not absent in man, however evanescent a naturally given object may be for him, split as it is in its submission to symbols.

Something equivalent may no doubt be grasped in the communion established between two persons in their hatred of a common object: except that the meeting is possible only over a single object, defined by those traits in the individual each of the two resist.

But such communication is not transmissible in symbolic form. It may be maintained only in the relation with the object. In such a manner it may bring together an indefinite number of subjects in a common "ideal": the communication of one subject with another within the crowd thus constituted will nonetheless remain irreducibly mediated by an ineffable relation.[16]

This digression is not only a recollection of principles distantly addressed to those who impute to us a neglect of non-verbal communication: in determining the scope of what speech repeats, it prepares the question of what symptoms repeat.

Thus the indirect telling sifts out the linguistic dimension, and the general narrator, by duplicating it, "hypothetically" adds nothing to it. But its role in the second dialogue is entirely different.

For the latter will be opposed to the first like those poles we have distinguished elsewhere in language and which are opposed like word to speech.

Which is to say that a transition is made here from the domain of exactitude to the register of truth. Now that register, we dare think we needn't come back to this, is situated entirely elsewhere, strictly speaking at the very foundation of intersubjectivity. It is located there where the subject can grasp nothing but the very subjectivity which constitutes an Other as absolute. We shall be satisfied here to indicate its place by evoking the dialogue which seems to us to merit its attribution as a Jewish joke by that state of privation through which the relation of signifier to speech appears in the entreaty which brings the dialogue to a close: "Why are you lying to me?" one character shouts breathlessly. "Yes, why do you lie to me saying you're going to Cracow so I should believe you're going to Lemberg, when in reality you *are* going to Cracow?"[17]

We might be prompted to ask a similar question by the torrent of logical impasses, eristic enigmas, paradoxes and even jests presented to us as an introduction to Dupin's method if the fact that they were confided to us by a would-be disciple did not endow them with a new dimension through that act of delegation. Such is the unmistakable magic of legacies: the witness's fidelity is the cowl which blinds and lays to rest all criticism of his testimony.

What could be more convincing, moreover, than the gesture of laying one's cards face up on the table? So much so that we are momentarily persuaded that the magician has in fact demonstrated, as he promised, how his trick was performed, whereas he has only renewed it in still purer form: at which point we fathom the measure of the supremacy of the signifier in the subject.

Such is Dupin's maneuver when he starts with the story of the child prodigy who takes in all his friends at the game of even and odd with his trick of identifying with the opponent, concerning which we have nevertheless shown that it cannot reach the first level of theoretical elaboration, namely intersubjective alternation, without immediately stumbling on the buttress of its recurrence.[18]

We are all the same treated—so much smoke in our eyes—to the names of La Rochefoucauld, La Bruyère, Machiavelli and Campanella, whose renown, by this time, would seem but futile when confronted with the child's prowess.

Followed by Chamfort, whose maxim that "it is a safe wager that every public idea, every accepted convention is foolish, since it suits the greatest number," will no doubt satisfy all who think they escape its law, that is, precisely, the greatest number. That Dupin accuses the French of deception for applying the word *analysis* to algebra will hardly threaten our pride since, moreover, the freeing of that term for other uses ought by no means to provoke a psychoanalyst to intervene and claim his rights. And there he goes making philological remarks which should positively delight any lovers of Latin: when he recalls without deigning to say any more that "*ambitus* doesn't mean ambition, *religio*, religion, *homines honesti*, honest men," who among you would not take pleasure in remembering . . . what those words mean to anyone familiar with Cicero and Lucretius. No doubt Poe is having a good time. . . .

But a suspicion occurs to us: might not this parade of erudition be destined to reveal to us the key words of our drama? Is not the magician repeating his trick before our eyes, without deceiving us this time about divulging his secret, but pressing his wager to the point of really explaining it to us without us seeing a thing. *That* would be the summit of the illusionist's art: through one of his fictive creations to *truly delude us*.

And is it not such effects which justify our referring, without malice, to a number of imaginary heroes as real characters?

As well, when we are open to hearing the way in which Martin Heidegger discloses to us in the word *aletheia* the play of truth, we rediscover a secret to which truth has always initiated her lovers, and through which they learn that it is in hiding that she offers herself to them *most truly*.

Thus even if Dupin's comments did not defy us so blatantly to believe in them, we should still have to make that attempt against the opposite temptation.

Let us track down [*dépistons*] his footprints there where they elude [*dépiste*] us.[19] And first of all in the criticism by which he explains the Prefect's lack of success. We already saw it surface in those furtive gibes the Prefect, in the first conversation, failed to heed, seeing in them only a pretext for hilarity. That it is, as Dupin insinuates, because a problem is too simple, indeed too evident, that it may appear obscure, will never have any more bearing for him than a vigorous rub of the rib cage.

Everything is arranged to induce in us a sense of the character's imbecility. Which is powerfully articulated by the fact that he and his confederates never conceive of anything beyond what an ordinary rogue might imagine for hiding an object—that is, precisely the all too well known series of extraordinary hiding places: which are promptly catalogued for us, from hidden desk drawers to removable table tops, from the detachable cushions of chairs to their hollowed-out legs, from the reverse side of mirrors to the "thickness" of book bindings.

After which, a moment of derision at the Prefect's error in deducing that because the Minister is a poet, he is not far from being mad, an error, it is argued, which would consist, but this is hardly negligible, simply in a false distribution of the middle term, since it is far from following from the fact that all madmen are poets.

Yes indeed. But we ourselves are left in the dark as to the poet's superiority in the art of concealment—even if he be a mathematician to boot—since our pursuit is suddenly thwarted, dragged as we are into a thicket of bad arguments directed against the reasoning of mathematicians, who never, so far as I know, showed such devotion to their formulae as to identify them with reason itself. At least, let us testify that unlike what seems to be Poe's experience, it occasionally befalls us—with our friend Riguet, whose presence here is a guarantee that our incursions into combinatory analysis are not leading us astray—to hazard such serious deviations (virtual blasphemies, according to Poe) as to cast into doubt that "x^2 plus px is perhaps not absolutely equal to q," without ever—here we give the lie to Poe—having had to fend off any unexpected attack.

Is not so much intelligence being exercised then simply to divert our own from what had been indicated earlier as given, namely, that the police have looked *everywhere*: which we were to understand—vis-à-vis the area in which the police, not without reason, assumed the letter might be found—in terms of a (no doubt theoretical) exhaustion of space, but concerning which the tale's piquancy depends on our accepting it literally: the division of the entire volume into numbered "compartments," which was the principle governing the operation, being presented to us as so precise that "the fiftieth part of a line," it is said, could not escape the probing of the investigators. Have we not then the right to ask how it happened that the letter was not found *anywhere*, or rather to observe that all we have been told of a more far-ranging conception of concealment does not explain, in all rigor, that the letter escaped detection, since the area combed did in fact contain it, as Dupin's discovery eventually proves.

Must a letter then, of all objects, be endowed with the property of *nullibiety*: to use a term which the thesaurus known as *Roget* picks up from the semiotic utopia of Bishop Wilkins?[20]

It is evident ("a little *too* self-evident")[21] that between *letter* and *place* exist relations for which no French word has quite the extension of the English adjective: *odd. Bizarre,* by which Baudelaire regularly translates it, is only approximate. Let us say that these relations are . . . *singuliers*, for they are the very ones maintained with place by the *signifier*.

You realize, of course, that our intention is not to turn them into "subtle" relations, nor is our aim to confuse letter with spirit, even if we receive the former by pneumatic dispatch, and that we readily admit that one kills whereas the other quickens, insofar as the signifier—you perhaps begin to understand—materializes the agency of death.[22] But if it is first of all on the materiality of the signifier that we have insisted, that materiality is *odd* [*singulière*] in many ways, the first of which is not to admit partition. Cut a letter in small pieces, and it remains the letter it is—and this in a completely different sense than *Gestalttheorie* would account for with the dormant vitalism informing its notion of the whole.[23]

Language delivers its judgment to whomever knows how to hear it: through the usage of the article as partitive particle. It is there that spirit—if spirit be living meaning—appears, no less oddly, as more available for quantification than its letter. To begin with meaning itself, which bears our saying: a speech rich with meaning ["plein *de* signification"], just as we recognize a measure of intention ["de l'intention"] in an act, or deplore that there is no more love ["plus *d'amour*"]; or store up hatred ["*de la* haine"] and expend devotion ["*du* dévouement"], and so much infatuation ["tant *d'*infatuation"] is easily reconciled to the fact that there will always be ass ["*de la* cuisse"] for sale and brawling ["*du* rififi"] among men.

But as for the letter—be it taken as typographical character, epistle, or what makes a man of letters—we will say that what is said is to be understood *to the letter* [à la lettre], that *a letter* [*une lettre*] awaits you at the post office, or even that you are acquainted with letters [*que vous avez des lettres*]—never that there is *letter* [de la lettre] anywhere, whatever the context, even to designate overdue mail.

For the signifier is a unit in its very uniqueness, being by nature symbol only of an absence. Which is why we cannot say of the purloined letter that, like other objects, it must be *or* not be in a particular place but that unlike them it will be *and* not be where it is, wherever it goes.[24]

Let us, in fact, look more closely at what happens to the police. We are spared nothing concerning the procedures used in searching the area submitted to their investigation: from the division of that space into compartments from which the slightest bulk could not escape detection, to needles probing upholstery, and, in the impossibility of sounding wood with a tap, to a microscope exposing the waste of any drilling at the surface of its hollow, indeed the infinitesimal gaping of the slightest abyss. As the network tightens to the point that, not satisfied with shaking the pages of books, the police take to counting them, do we not see space itself shed its leaves like a letter?

But the detectives have so immutable a notion of the real that they fail to notice that their search tends to transform it into its object. A trait by which they would be able to distinguish that object from all others.

This would no doubt be too much to ask them, not because of their lack of insight but rather because of ours. For their imbecility is neither of the individual nor the corporative variety; its source is subjective. It is the realist's imbecility, which does not pause to observe that nothing, however deep in the bowels of the earth a hand may seek to ensconce it, will ever be hidden there, since another hand can always retrieve it, and that what is hidden is never but what is *missing from its place,* as the call slip puts it when speaking of a volume lost in a library. And even if the book be on an adjacent shelf or in the next slot, it would be hidden there, however visibly it may appear. For it can *literally* be said that something is missing from its place only of what can change it: the symbolic. For the real, whatever upheaval we subject it to, is always in its place; it carries it glued to its heel, ignorant of what might exile it from it.

And, to return to our cops, who took the letter from the place where it was hidden, how could they have seized the letter? In what they turned between their fingers what did they hold but what *did not answer* to their description. "A letter, a litter": in Joyce's circle, they played on the homophony of the two words in English.[25] Nor does the seeming bit of refuse the police are now handling reveal its other nature for being but half torn. A different seal on a stamp of another color, the mark of a different handwriting in the superscription are here the most inviolable modes of concealment. And if they stop at the reverse side of the letter, on which, as is known, the recipient's address was written in that period, it is because the letter has for them no other side but its reverse.

What indeed might they find on its observe? Its message, as is often said to our cybernetic joy? . . . But does it not occur to us that this message has already reached its recipient and has even been left with her, since the insignificant scrap of paper now represents it no less well than the original note.

If we could admit that a letter has completed its destiny after fulfilling its function, the ceremony of returning letters would be a less common close to the extinction of the fires of love's feasts. The signifier is not functional. And the mobilization of the elegant society whose frolics we are following would as well have no meaning if the letter itself were content with having one. For it would hardly be an adequate means of keeping it secret to inform a squad of cops of its existence.

We might even admit that the letter has an entirely different (if no more urgent) meaning for the Queen than the one understood by the Minister. The sequence of events would not be noticeably affected, not even if it were strictly incomprehensible to an uninformed reader.

For it is certainly not so for everybody, since, as the Prefect pompously assures us, to everyone's derision, "the disclosure of the document to a third person, who shall be nameless" (that name which leaps to the eye like the pig's tail twixt the teeth of old Ubu), "would bring in question the honor of a personage of most exalted station, indeed that the honor and peace of the illustrious personage are so jeopardized."

In that case, it is not only the meaning but the text of the message which it would be dangerous to place in circulation, and all the more so to the extent that it might appear harmless, since the risks of an indiscretion unintentionally commited by one of the letter's holders would thus be increased.

Nothing then can redeem the police's position, and nothing would be changed by improving their "culture." *Scripta manent*: in vain would they learn from a *de luxe*-edition humanism the proverbial lesson which *verba volant* concludes. May it but please heaven that writings remain, as is rather the case with spoken words: for the indelible debt of the latter impregnates our acts with its transferences.

Writings scatter to the winds blank checks in an insane charge.[26] And were they not such flying leaves, there would be no purloined letters.[27]

But what of it? For a purloined letter to exist, we may ask, to whom does a letter belong? We stressed a moment ago the oddity implicit in returning a letter to him who had but recently given wing to its burning pledge. And we generally deem unbecoming such premature publications as the one by which the Chevalier d'Éon put several of his correspondents in a rather pitiful position.

Might a letter on which the sender retains certain rights then not quite belong to the person to whom it is addressed? or might it be that the latter was never the real receiver?

Let's take a look: we shall find illumination in what at first seems to obscure matters: the fact that the tale leaves us in virtually total ignorance of the sender, no less than of the contents, of the letter. We are told only that the Minister immediately recognized the handwriting of the address and only incidentally, in a discussion of the Minister's camouflage, is it said that the original seal bore the ducal arms of the S . . . family. As for the letter's bearing, we know only the dangers it entails should it come into the hands of a specific third party, and that its possession has allowed the Minister to "wield, to a very dangerous extent, for political purposes," the power it assures him over the interested party. But all this tells us nothing of the message it conveys.

Love letter or conspiratorial letter, letter of betrayal or letter of mission, letter of summons or letter of distress, we are assured of but one thing: the Queen must not bring it to the knowledge of her lord and master.

Now these terms, far from bearing the nuance of discredit they have in *bourgeois* comedy, take on a certain prominence through allusion to her sovereign, to whom she is bound by pledge of faith, and doubly so, since her role as spouse does not relieve her of her duties as subject, but rather elevates her to the guardianship of what royalty according to law incarnates of power: and which is called legitimacy.

From then on, to whatever vicissitudes the Queen may choose to subject the letter, it remains that the letter is the symbol of a pact, and that, even should the recipient not assume the pact, the existence of the letter situates her in a symbolic chain foreign to the one which constitutes her faith. This incompatibility is proven by the fact that the possession of the letter is impossible to bring forward publicly as legitimate, and that in order to have that possession respected, the Queen can invoke but her right to privacy, whose privilege is based on the honor that possession violates.

For she who incarnates the figure of grace and sovereignty cannot welcome even a private communication without power being concerned, and she cannot avail herself of secrecy in relation to the sovereign without becoming clandestine.

From then on, the responsibility of the author of the letter takes second place to that of its holder: for the offense to majesty is compounded by *high treason*.

We say: the *holder* and not the *possessor*. For it becomes clear that the addressee's proprietorship of the letter may be no less debatable than that of anyone else into whose hands it comes, for nothing concerning the existence of the letter can return to good order without the person whose prerogatives it infringes upon having to pronounce judgment on it.

All of this, however, does not imply that because the letter's secrecy is indefensible, the betrayal of that secret would in any sense be honorable. The *honesti homines*, decent people, will not get off so easily. There is more than one *religio*, and it is not slated for tomorrow that sacred ties shall cease to rend us in two. As for *ambitus*: a detour, we see, is not always inspired by ambition. For if we are taking one here, by no means is it stolen (the word is apt), since, to lay our cards on the table, we have borrowed Baudelaire's title in order to stress not, as is incorrectly claimed, the conventional nature of the signifier, but rather its priority in relation to the signified.[28] It remains, nevertheless, that Baudelaire, despite his devotion, betrayed Poe by translating as "la lettre volée" (the stolen letter) his title: the purloined letter, a title containing a word rare enough for us to find it easier to define its etymology than its usage.

To purloin, says the Oxford dictionary, is an Anglo-French word, that is: composed of the prefix *pur-*, found in *purpose, purchase, purport,* and of the Old French word: *loing, loigner, longé*. We recognize in the first element the Latin *pro-*, as opposed to *ante*, in so far as it presupposes a rear in front of which it is borne, possibly as its warrant, indeed even as its pledge (whereas *ante* goes forth to confront what it encounters). As for the second, an old French word: *loigner*, a verb attributing place *au loing* (or, still in use, *longé*), it does not mean *au loin* (far off), but *au long de* (alongside); it is a question then of *putting aside*, or, to invoke a familiar expression which plays on the two meanings: *mettre à gauche* (to put to the left; to put amiss).

Thus we are confirmed in our detour by the very object which draws us on into it: for we are quite simply dealing with a letter which has been diverted from its path; one whose course has been *prolonged* (etymologically, the word of the title), or, to revert to the language of the post office, a *letter in sufferance*.[29]

Here then, *simple and odd,* as we are told on the very first page, reduced to its simplest expression, is the singularity of the letter, which as the title indicates, is the *true subject* of the tale: since it can be diverted, it must have a course *which is proper to it*: the trait by which its incidence as signifier is affirmed. For we have learned to conceive of the signifier as sustaining itself only in a displacement comparable to that found in electric news strips or in the rotating memories of our machines-that-think-like men, this because of the alternating operation which is its principle, requiring it to leave its place, even though it returns to it by a circular path.[30]

This is indeed what happens in the repetition automatism. What Freud teaches us in the text we are commenting on is that the subject must pass through the channels of the symbolic, but what is illustrated here is more gripping still: it is not only the subject, but the subjects, grasped in their intersubjectivity, who line up, in other words our ostriches, to whom we here return, and who, more docile than sheep, model their very being on the moment of the signifying chain which traverses them.

If what Freud discovered and rediscovers with a perpetually increasing sense of shock has a meaning, it is that the displacement of the signifier determines the subjects in their acts, in their destiny, in their refusals, in their blindnesses, in their end and in their fate, their innate gifts and social acquisitions notwithstanding, without regard for character or sex, and that, willingly or not, everything that might be considered the stuff of psychology, kit and caboodle, will follow the path of the signifier.

Here we are, in fact, yet again at the crossroads at which we had left our drama and its round with the question of the way in which the subjects replace each other in it. Our fable is so constructed as to show that it is the letter and its diversion which governs their entries and roles. If *it* be "in sufferance," *they* shall endure the pain. Should they pass beneath its shadow, they become its reflection. Falling in possession of the letter—admirable ambiguity of language—its meaning possesses them.

So we are shown by the hero of the drama in the repetition of the very situation which his daring brought to a head, a first time, to his triumph. If he now succumbs to it, it is because he has shifted to the second position in the triad in which he was initially third, as well as the thief—and this by virtue of the object of his theft.

For if it is, now as before, a question of protecting the letter from inquisitive eyes, he can do nothing but employ the same technique he himself has already foiled: leave it in the open? And we may properly doubt that he knows what he is thus doing, when we see him immediately captivated by a dual relationship in which we find all the traits of a mimetic lure or of an animal feigning death, and, trapped in the typically imaginary situation of seeing that he is not seen, misconstrue the real situation in which he is seen not seeing.[31]

And what does he fail to see? Precisely the symbolic situation which he himself was so well able to see, and in which he is now seen seeing himself not being seen.

The Minister acts as a man who realizes that the police's search is his own defence, since we are told he allows them total access by his absences: he nonetheless fails to recognize that outside of that search he is no longer defended.

This is the very *autruicherie* whose artisan he was, if we may allow our monster to proliferate, but it cannot be by sheer stupidity that he now comes to be its dupe.[32]

For in playing the part of the one who hides, he is obliged to don the role of the Queen, and even the attributes of femininity and shadow, so propitious to the act of concealing.

Not that we are reducing the hoary couple of *Yin* and *Yang* to the elementary opposition of dark and light. For its precise use involves what is blinding in a flash of light, no less than the shimmering shadows exploit in order not to lose their prey.

Here sign and being, marvelously asunder, reveal which is victorious when they come into conflict. A man man enough to defy to the point of scorn a lady's fearsome ire undergoes to the point of metamorphosis the curse of the sign he has dispossessed her of.

For this sign is indeed that of woman, in so far as she invests her very being therein, founding it outside the law, which subsumes her nevertheless, originarily, in a position of signifier, nay, of fetish.[33] In order to be worthy of the power of that sign she has but to remain immobile in its shadow, thus finding, moreover, like the Queen, that simulation of mastery in inactivity that the Minister's "lynx eye" alone was able to penetrate.

This stolen sign—here then is man in its possession: sinister in that such possession may be sustained only through the honor it defies, cursed in calling him who sustains it to punishment or crime, each of which shatters his vassalage to the Law.

There must be in this sign a singular *noli me tangere* for its possession, like the Socratic sting ray, to benumb its man to the point of making him fall into what appears clearly in his case to be a state of idleness.[34]

For in noting, as the narrator does as early as the first dialogue, that with the letter's use its power disappears, we perceive that this remark, strictly speaking, concerns precisely its use for ends of power —and at the same time that such a use is obligatory for the Minister.

To be unable to rid himself of it, the Minister indeed must not know what else to do with the letter. For that use places him in so total a dependence on the letter as such, that in the long run it no longer involves the letter at all.

We mean that for that use truly to involve the letter, the Minister, who, after all, would be so authorized by his service to his master the King, might present to the Queen respectful admonitions, even were he to assure their sequel by appropriate precautions—or initiate an action against the author of the letter, concerning whom, the fact that he remains outside the story's focus reveals the extent to which it is not guilt and blame which are in question here, but rather that sign of contradiction and scandal constituted by the letter, in the sense in which the Gospel says that it must come regardless of the anguish of whomever serves as its bearer—or even submit the letter as evidence in a dossier to a "third person" qualified to determine whether it would issue in a Star Chamber for the Queen or the Minister's disgrace.

We will not know why the Minister does not resort to any of these uses, and it is fitting that we don't, since the effect of this non-use alone concerns us; it suffices for us to know that the way in which the letter was acquired would pose no obstacle to any of them.

For it is clear that if the use of the letter, independent of its meaning, is obligatory for the Minister, its use for ends of power can only be potential, since it cannot become actual without vanishing in the process—but in that case the letter exists as a means of power only through the final assignations of the pure signifier, namely: by prolonging its diversion, making it reach whomever it may concern through a supplementary transfer, that is, by an additional act of treason whose effects the letter's gravity makes it difficult to predict—or indeed by destroying the letter, the only sure means, as Dupin divulges at the start, of being rid of what is destined by nature to signify the annulment of what it signifies.

The ascendancy which the Minister derives from the situation is thus not a function of the letter, but, whether he knows it or not, of the role it constitutes for him. And the Prefect's remarks indeed present him as someone "who dares all things," which is commented upon significantly: "those unbecoming as well as those becoming a man," words whose pungency escapes Baudelaire when he translates: "ce qui est indigne d'un homme aussi bien que ce qui est digne de lui" (those unbecoming a man as well as those becoming him). For in its original form, the appraisal is far more appropriate to what might concern a woman.

This allows us to see the imaginary import of the character, that is, the narcissistic relation in which the Minister is engaged, this time, no doubt, without knowing it. It is indicated as well as early as the second page of the English text by one of the narrator's remarks, whose form is worth savoring: the Minister's ascendancy, we are told, "would depend upon the robber's knowledge of the loser's knowledge of the robber." Words whose importance the author underscores by having Dupin repeat them literally after the narration of the scene of the theft of the letter. Here again we may say that Baudelaire is imprecise in his language in having one ask, the other confirm, in these words: "Le voleur sait-il? . . ." (Does the robber know?), then: "Le voleur sait . . ." (the robber knows). What? "que la personne volée connaît son voleur" (that the loser knows his robber).

For what matters to the robber is not only that the said person knows who robbed her, but rather with what kind of a robber she is dealing; for she believes him capable of anything, which should be understood as her having conferred upon him the position that no one is in fact capable of assuming, since it is imaginary, that of absolute master.

In truth, it is a position of absolute weakness, but not for the person of whom we are expected to believe so. The proof is not only that the Queen dares to call the police. For she is only conforming to her displacement to the next slot in the arrangement of the initial triad in trusting to the very blindness required to occupy that place: "No more sagacious agent could, I suppose," Dupin notes ironically, "be desired or even imagined." No, if she has taken that step, it is less out of being "driven to despair," as we are told, than in assuming the charge of an impatience best imputed to a specular mirage.

For the Minister is kept quite busy confining himself to the idleness which is presently his lot. The Minister, in point of fact, is not *altogether* mad.[35] That's a remark made by the Prefect, whose every word is gold: it is true that the gold of his words flows only for Dupin and will continue to flow to the amount of the fifty thousand francs worth it will cost him by the metal standard of the day, though not without leaving him a margin of profit. The Minister then is not *altogether* mad in his insane stagnation, and that is why he will behave according to the mode of neurosis. Like the man who withdrew to an island to forget, what? he forgot—so the Minister, through not making use of the letter, comes to forget it. As is expressed by the persistence of his conduct. But the letter, no more than the neurotic's unconscious, does not forget him. It forgets him so little that it transforms him more and more in the image of her who offered it to his capture, so that he now will surrender it, following her example, to a similar capture.

The features of that transformation are noted, and in a form so characteristic in their apparent gratuitousness that they might validly be compared to the return of the repressed.

Thus we first learn that the Minister in turn has *turned the letter over,* not, of course, as in the Queen's hasty gesture, but, more assiduously, as one turns a garment inside out. So he must procede, according to the methods of the day for folding and sealing a letter, in order to free the virgin space on which to inscribe a new address.[36]

That address becomes his own. Whether it be in his hand or another, it will appear in an extremely delicate feminine script, and, the seal changing from the red of passion to the black of its mirrors, he will imprint his stamp upon it. This oddity of a letter marked with the recipient's stamp is all the more striking in its conception, since, though forcefully articulated in the text, it is not even mentioned by Dupin in the discussion he devotes to the identification of the letter.

Whether that omission be intentional or involuntary, it will surprise in the economy of a work whose meticulous rigor is evident. But in either case it is significant that the letter which the Minister, in point of fact, addresses to himself is a letter from a woman: as though this were a phase he had to pass through out of a natural affinity of the signifier.

Thus the aura of apathy, verging at times on an affectation of effeminacy; the display of an *ennui* bordering on disgust in his conversation; the mood the author of the philosophy of furniture[37] can elicit from virtually impalpable details (like that of the musical instrument on the table), everything seems intended for a character, all of whose utterances have revealed the most virile traits, to exude the oddest *odor di femina* when he appears.

Dupin does not fail to stress that this is an artifice, describing behind the bogus finery the vigilance of a beast of prey ready to spring. But that this is the very effect of the unconscious in the precise sense that we teach that the unconscious means that man is inhabited by the signifier: could we find a more beautiful image of it than the one Poe himself forges to help us appreciate Dupin's exploit? For with this aim in mind, he refers to those toponymical inscriptions which a geographical map, lest it remain mute, superimposes on its design, and which may become the object of a guessing game: who can find the name chosen by a partner?—noting immediately that the name most likely to foil a beginner will be one which, in large letters spaced out widely across the map, discloses, often without an eye pausing to notice it, the name of an entire country. . . .

Just so does the purloined letter, like an immense female body, stretch out across the Minister's office when Dupin enters. But just so does he already expect to find it, and has only, with his eyes veiled by green lenses, to undress that huge body.

And that is why without needing any more than being able to listen in at the door of Professor Freud, he will go straight to the spot in which lies and lives what that body is designed to hide, in a gorgeous center caught in a glimpse, nay, to the very place seducers name Sant' Angelo's Castle in their innocent illusion of controlling the City from within in. Look! between the cheeks of the fireplace, there's the object already in reach of a hand the ravisher has but to extend. . . . The question of deciding whether he seizes it above the mantelpiece as Baudelaire translates, or beneath it, as in the original text, may be abandoned without harm to the inferences of those whose profession is grilling.[38]

Were the effectiveness of symbols[39] to cease there, would it mean that the symbolic debt would as well be extinguished? Even if we could believe so, we would be advised of the contrary by two episodes which we may all the less dismiss as secondary in that they seem, at first sight, to clash with the rest of the work.

First of all, there's the business of Dupin's remuneration, which, far from being a closing *pirouette*, has been present from the beginning in the rather un-self-conscious question he asks the Prefect about the amount of the reward promised him, and whose enormousness, the Prefect, however reticent he may be about the precise figure, does not dream of hiding from him, even returning later on to refer to its increase.

The fact that Dupin had been previously presented to us as a virtual pauper in his ethereal shelter ought rather to lead us to reflect on the deal he makes out of delivering the letter, promptly assured as it is by the check-book he produces. We do not regard it as negligible that the unequivocal hint through which he introduces the matter is a "story attributed to the character, as famous as it was excentric," Baudelaire tells us, of an English doctor named Abernethy, in which a rich miser, hoping to sponge upon him for a medical opinion, is sharply told not to take medicine, but to take advice.

Do we not in fact feel concerned with good reason when for Dupin what is perhaps at stake is his withdrawal from the symbolic circuit of the letter—we who become the emissaries of all the purloined letters which at least for a time remain in sufferance with us in the transference. And is it not the responsibility their transference entails which we neutralize by equating it with the signifier most destructive of all signification, namely: money.

But that's not all. The profit Dupin so nimbly extracts from his exploit, if its purpose is to allow him to withdraw his stakes from the game, makes all the more paradoxical, even shocking, the partisan attack, the underhanded blow, he suddenly permits himself to launch against the Minister, whose insolent prestige, after all, would seem to have been sufficiently deflated by the trick Dupin has just played on him.

We have already quoted the atrocious lines Dupin claims he could not help dedicating, in his counterfeit letter, to the moment in which the Minister, enraged by the inevitable defiance of the Queen, will think he is demolishing her and will plunge into the abyss: *facilis descensus Averni*,[40] he waxes sententious, adding that the Minister cannot fail to recognize his handwriting, all of which, since depriving of any danger a merciless act of infamy, would seem, concerning a figure who is not without merit, a triumph without glory, and the rancor he invokes, stemming from an evil turn done him at Vienna (at the Congress?) only adds an additional bit of blackness to the whole.[41]

Let us consider, however, more closely this explosion of feeling, and more specifically the moment it occurs in a sequence of acts whose success depends on so cool a head.

It comes just after the moment in which the decisive act of identifying the letter having been accomplished, it may be said that Dupin already *has* the letter as much as if he had seized it, without, however, as yet being in a position to rid himself of it.

He is thus, in fact, fully participant in the intersubjective triad, and, as such, in the median position previously occupied by the Queen and the Minister. Will he, in showing himself to be above it, reveal to us at the same time the author's intentions?

If he has succeeded in returning the letter to its proper course, it remains for him to make it arrive at its address. And that address is in the place previously occupied by the King, since it is there that it would re-enter the order of the Law.

As we have seen, neither the King nor the Police who replaced him in that position were able to read the letter because that *place entailed blindness*.

Rex et augur, the legendary, archaic quality of the words seems to resound only to impress us with the absurdity of applying them to a man. And the figures of history, for some time now, hardly encourages us to do so. It is not natural for man to bear alone the weight of the highest of signifiers. And the place he occupies as soon as he dons it may be equally apt to become the symbol of the most outrageous imbecility.[42]

Let us say that the King here is invested with the equivocation natural to the sacred, with the imbecility which prizes none other than the Subject.[43]

That is what will give their meaning to the characters who will follow him in his place. Not that the police should be regarded as constitutionally illiterate, and we know the role of pikes planted on the *campus* in the birth of the State. But the police who exercise their functions here are plainly marked by the forms of liberalism, that is, by those imposed on them by masters on the whole indifferent to eliminating their indiscreet tendencies. Which is why on occasion words are not minced as to what is expected of them: "*Sutor ne ultra crepidam*, just take care of your crooks.[44] We'll even give you scientific means to do it with. That will help you not to think of truths you'd be better off leaving in the dark."[45]

We know that the relief which results from such prudent principles shall have lasted in history but a morning's time, that already the march of destiny is everywhere bringing back—a sequel to a just aspiration to freedom's reign—an interest in those who trouble it with their crimes, which occasionally goes so far as to forge its proofs. It may even be observed that this practice, which was always well received to the extent that it was exercised only in favor of the greatest number, comes to be authenticated in public confessions of forgery by the very ones who might very well object to it: the most recent manifestation of the pre-eminence of the signifier over the subject.

It remains, nevertheless, that a police record has always been the object of a certain reserve, of which we have difficulty understanding that it amply transcends the guild of historians.

It is by dint of this vanishing credit that Dupin's intended delivery of the letter to the Prefect of police will diminish its import. What now remains of the signifier when, already relieved of its message for the Queen, it is now invalidated in its text as soon as it leaves the Minister's hands?

It remains for it now only to answer that very question, of what remains of a signifier when it has no more signification. But this is the same question asked of it by the person Dupin now finds in the spot marked by blindness.

For that is indeed the question which has led the Minister there, if he be the gambler we are told and which his act sufficiently indicates.

For the gambler's passion is nothing but that question asked of the signifier, figured by the *automaton* of chance.

"What are you, figure of the die I turn over in your encounter (*tychē*) with my fortune?[46] Nothing, if not that presence of death which makes of human life a reprieve obtained from morning to morning in the name of meanings whose sign is your crook. Thus did Scheherazade for a thousand and one nights, and thus have I done for eighteen months, suffering the ascendancy of this sign at the cost of a dizzying series of fraudulent turns at the game of even or odd."

So it is that Dupin, *from the place he now occupies,* cannot help feeling a rage of manifestly feminine nature against him who poses such a question. The prestigious image in which the poet's inventiveness and the mathematician's rigor joined up with the serenity of the dandy and the elegance of the cheat suddenly becomes, for the very person who invited us to savor it, the true *monstrum horrendum*, for such are his words, "an unprincipled man of genius."

It is here that the origin of that horror betrays itself, and he who experiences it has no need to declare himself (in a most unexpected manner) "a partisan of the lady" in order to reveal it to us: it is known that ladies detest calling principles into question, for their charms owe much to the mystery of the signifier.

Which is why Dupin will at last turn toward us the medusoid face of the signifier nothing but whose obverse anyone except the Queen has/been able to read. The commonplace of the quotation is fitting for the oracle that face bears in its grimace, as is also its source in tragedy: ". . . *Un destin si funeste, / S'il n'est digne d' Atrée, est digne de Thyeste.*"[47]

So runs the signifier's answer, above and beyond all significations: "You think you act when I stir you at the mercy of the bonds through which I knot your desires. Thus do they grow in force and multiply in objects, bringing you back to the fragmentation of your shattered childhood. So be it: such will be your feast until the return of the stone guest I shall be for you since you call me forth."

Or, to return to a more moderate tone, let us say, as in the quip with which—along with some of you who had followed us to the Zurich Congress last year—we rendered homage to the local password, the signifier's answer to whomever interrogates it is: "Eat your Dasein."

Is that then what awaits the Minister at a rendez-vous with destiny? Dupin assures us of it, but we have already learned not to be too credulous of his diversions.

No doubt the brazen creature is here reduced to the state of blindness which is man's in relation to the letters on the wall that dictate his destiny. But what effect, in calling him to confront them, may we expect from the sole provocations of the Queen, on a man like him? Love or hatred. The former is blind and will make him lay down his arms. The latter is lucid, but will awaken his suspicions. But if he is truly the gambler we are told he is, he will consult his cards a final time before laying them down and, upon reading his hand, will leave the table in time to avoid disgrace.[48]

Is that all, and shall we believe we have deciphered Dupin's real strategy above and beyond the imaginary tricks with which he was obliged to deceive us? No doubt, yes, for if "any point requiring reflection," as Dupin states at the start, is "examined to best purpose in the dark," we may now easily read its solution in broad daylight. It was already implicit and easy to derive from the title of our tale, according to the very formula we have long submitted to your discretion: in which the sender, we tell you, receives from the receiver his own message in reverse form. Thus it is that what the "purloined letter," nay, the "letter in sufferance" means is that a letter always arrives at its destination.

Translated by Jeffrey Mehlman

NOTES

1. The translation of repetition *automatism*—rather than *compulsion*—is indicative of Lacan's speculative effort to reinterpret Freudian "over-determination" in terms of the laws of probability. (Chance is *automaton*, a "cause not revealed to human thought," in Aristotle's *Physics*.) Whence the importance assumed by the Minister's passion for gambling later in Lacan's analysis. Cf. *Ecrits*, pp. 41–61.—TRANS.
2. Cf. Heidegger, *Von Wesen der Wahrheit*. Freedom, in this essay, is perceived as an "ex-posure." *Dasein* exists, stands out "into the disclosure of what is." It is Dasein's "ex-sistent in-sistence" which preserves the disclosure of beings. —TRANS.
3. For more on the meanings Lacan attributes to the terms *imaginary* and *symbolic*, see the entries in Laplanche and Pontalis, *The Language of Psychoanalysis*, New York, 1973.—TRANS.
4. For the notion of *foreclosure*, the defense mechanism specific to psychosis, see the entry from *The Language of Psychoanalysis*.—TRANS.
5. For more on the notion of the signifier, and its relation to the Freudian "memory trace," see J. Mehlman, "The 'Floating Signifier': From Lévi-Strauss to Lacan," *Yale French Studies*, No. 48 (1973). —TRANS.

6. Lacan's analysis of the guessing game in Poe's tale entails demonstrating the insufficiency of an *imaginary* identification with the opponent as opposed to the *symbolic* process of an identification with his "reasoning." See *Ecrits*, p. 59. —TRANS.

7. "So infamous a scheme,/ If not worthy of Atreus, is worthy of Thyestes." The lines from Atreus's monologue in Act V, Scene V of Crébillon's play refer to his plan to avenge himself by serving his brother the blood of the latter's own son to drink. —TRANS.

8. This intersubjective setting which coordinates three terms is plainly the Oedipal situation. The illusory security of the initial *dyad* (King and Queen in the first sequence) will be shattered by the introduction of a *third* term. —TRANS.

9. The necessary reference here may be found in "Le Temps logique et l'Assertion de la certitude anticipée," *Ecrits*, p. 197.

10. *La Politique de l'autruiche* condenses ostrich (*autruche*), other people (*autrui*), and (the politics of) Austria (*Autriche*). —TRANS.

11. Such would be the crux of the Oedipus complex: the assumption of a desire which is originally another's, and which, in its displacements, is perpetually other than "itself." —TRANS.

12. The first "Dupin tale" was "The Murders in the Rue Morgue." —TRANS.

13. Cf. "Fonction et champ de la parole et du langage" in *Ecrits*. Translated by A. Wilden, *The Language of the Self*, Baltimore, 1968.

14. The complete understanding of what follows presupposes a rereading of the short and easily available text of "The Purloined Letter."

15. Cf. Emile Benveniste, "Communication animale et langage humain," *Diogene*, No. 1, and our address in Rome, *Ecrits*, p. 178.

16. For the notion of *ego ideal*, see Freud, *Group Psychology and the Analysis of the Ego*. —TRANS.

17. Freud comments on the joke in *Jokes and Their Relation to the Unconscious*, New York, 1960, p. 115: "But the more serious substance of the joke is what determines the truth. . . . Is it the truth if we describe things as they are without troubling to consider how our hearer will understand what we say? . . . I think that jokes of that kind are sufficiently different from the rest to be given a special position: What they are attacking is not a person or an institution but the certainty of our knowledge itself, one of our speculative possessions." Lacan's text may be regarded as a commentary on Freud's statement, an examination of the corrosive effect of the demands of an intersubjective situation on any naive notion of "truth." —TRANS.

18. Cf. *Ecrits*, p. 58. "But what will happen at the following step (of the game) when the opponent, realizing that I am sufficiently clever to follow him in his move, will show his own cleverness by realizing that it is by playing the fool that he has the best chance to deceive me? From then on my reasoning is invalidated, since it can only be repeated in an indefinite oscillation . . ."

19. We should like to present again to M. Benveniste the question of the antithetical sense of (primal or other) words after the magisterial rectification he brought to the erroneous philological path on which Freud engaged it (cf. *La Psychanalyse*, vol. 1, pp. 5–16). For we think that the problem remains intact once the instance of the signifier has been

evolved. Bloch and Von Wartburg date at 1875 the first appearance of the meaning of the term *dépister* in the second use we make of it in our sentence.

20. The very one to which Jorge Luis Borges, in works which harmonize so well with the phylum of our subject, has accorded an importance which others have reduced to its proper proportions. Cf. *Les Temps modernes*, June–July 1955, pp. 2135–36, and October 1955, pp. 574–75.

21. Underlined by the author.

22. The reference is to the "death instinct," whose "death," we should note, lies entirely in its diacritical opposition to the "life" of a naive vitalism or naturalism. As such, it may be compared with the logical moment in Lévi-Strauss's thought whereby "nature" exceeds, supplements, and symbolizes itself: the prohibition of incest. —TRANS.

23. This is so true that philosophers, in those hackneyed examples with which they argue on the basis of the single and the multiple, will not use to the same purpose a simple sheet of white paper ripped in the middle and a broken circle, indeed a shattered vase, not to mention a cut worm.

24. Cf. Saussure, *Cours de linguistique generale*, Paris, 1969, p. 166: "The preceding amounts to saying that *in language there are only differences*. Even more: a difference presupposes in general positive terms between which it is established, but in language there are only differences *without positive terms*." —TRANS.

25. Cf. *Our Examination Round his Factification for Incamination of Work in Progress*, Shakespeare & Co., 12 rue de l'Odéon, Paris, 1929.

26. The original sentence presents an exemplary difficulty in translation: "Les écrits emportent au vent les traites en blanc d'une cavalerie folle." The blank (bank) drafts (or transfers) are not delivered to their rightful recipients (the sense of *de cavalerie, de complaisance*). That is: in analysis, one finds absurd symbolic debts being paid to the "wrong" persons. At the same time, the mad, driven quality of the payment is latent in *traite*, which might also refer to the day's trip of an insane cavalry. In our translation, we have displaced the "switch-word"—joining the financial and equestrian series—from *traite* to *charge*.—TRANS.

27. *Flying leaves* (also fly-sheets) and *purloined letters*—*feuilles volantes* and *lettres volées*—employ different meanings of the same word in French. —TRANS.

28. See the discussion of Lévi-Strauss's statement—"the signifier precedes and determines the signified" in "The 'Floating Signifier': From Lévi-Strauss to Lacan." —TRANS.

29. We revive this archaism (for the French: *lettre en souffrance*). The sense is a letter held up in the course of delivery. In French, of course, *en souffrance* means in a state of suffering as well. —TRANS.

30. See *Ecrits*, p. 59: ". . . it is not unthinkable that a modern computer, by discovering the sentence which modulates without his knowing it and over a long period of time the choices of a subject, would win beyond any normal proportion at the game of even and odd . . ."

31. See the entry on *imaginary* in *The Language of Psychoanalysis*.—TRANS.

32. *Autruicherie* condenses, in addition to the previous terms, deception (*tricherie*). Do we not find in Lacan's proliferating "monster" something of the *proton pseudos*, the "first lie" of Freud's 1895 *Project*: the persistent illusion which seems to structure the mental life of the patient? —TRANS.

33. The fetish, as replacement for the missing maternal phallus, at once masks and reveals the scandal of sexual difference. As such it is the analytic object *par excellence*. The female temptation to exhibitionism, understood as a desire to *be* the (*maternal*) phallus, is thus tantamount to being a fetish. —TRANS.

34. See Plato's *Meno*: "Socrates, . . . at this moment I feel you are exercising magic and witchcraft upon me and positively laying me under your spell until I am just a mass of helplessness. If I may be flippant, I think that not only in outward appearance but in other respects as well you are like the flat sting ray that one meets in the sea. Whenever anyone comes into contact with it, it numbs him, and that is the sort of thing you are doing to me now . . ." —TRANS.

35. Baudelaire translates Poe's "*altogether* a fool" as "*absolument* fou." In opting for Baudelaire, Lacan is enabled to allude to the realm of psychosis. —TRANS.

36. We felt obliged to demonstrate the procedure to an audience with a letter from the period concerning M. de Chateaubriand and his search for a secretary. We were amused to find that M. de Chateaubriand completed the first version of his recently restored memoirs in the very month of November 1841 in which the purloined letter appeared in *Chamber's Journal*. Might M. de Chateaubriand's devotion to the power he decries and the honor which that devotion bespeaks in him (the *gift* had not yet been invented), place him in the category to which we will later see the Minister assigned: among men of genius with or without principles?

37. Poe is the author of an essay with this title.

38. And even to the cook herself. —J. L.
    The paragraph might be read as follows: analysis, in its violation of the imaginary integrity of the ego, finds its fantasmic equivalent in rape (or castration). But whether that "rape" takes place from in front or from behind (above or below the mantelpiece) is, in fact, a question of interest for policemen and not analysts. Implicit in the statement is an attack on those who have become wed to the ideology of "maturational development" (libidinal stages et al.) in Freud (i.e., the ego psychologists). —TRANS.

39. The allusion is to Lévi-Strauss's article of the same title ("L'efficacité symbolique") in *L'Anthropologie structurale*.

40. Virgil's line reads: *facilis descensus Averno*.

41. Cf. Corneille, *Le Cid* (II, 2): "A vaincre sans péril, on triomphe sans gloire." (To vanquish without danger is to triumph without glory). —TRANS.

42. We recall the witty couplet attributed before his fall to the most recent in date to have rallied Candide's meeting in Venice: "Il n'est plus aujourd'hui que cinq rois sur la terre,/ Les quatre rois des cartes et le roi d'Angleterre." (There are only five kings left on earth: four kings of cards and the king of England.)

43. For the antithesis of the "sacred," see Freud's "The Antithetical Sense of Primal Words." The idiom *tenir à* in this sentence means both to prize and to be a function of. The two senses—King and/as Subject—are implicit in Freud's frequent allusions to "His majesty the Ego." —TRANS.

44. From Pliny, 35, 10, 35: "A cobbler not beyond his sole . . ." —TRANS.

45. This proposal was openly presented by a noble Lord speaking to the Upper Chamber in which his dignity earned him a place.

46. We note the fundamental opposition Aristotle makes between the two terms recalled here in the conceptual analysis of chance he gives in his *Physics*. Many discussions would be illuminated by a knowledge of it.

47. Lacan misquotes Crébillon (as well as Poe and Baudelaire) here by writing *destin* (destiny) instead of *dessein* (scheme). As a result he is free to pursue his remarkable development on the tragic Don Juan ("multiply in objects . . . stone guest"). —TRANS.

48. Thus nothing shall (have) happen(ed)—the final turn in Lacan's theater of lack. Yet within the simplicity of that empty present the most violent of (pre-)Oedipal dramas—Atreus, Thyestes—shall silently have played itself out. —TRANS.

Poe Pourri: Lacan's Purloined Letter

Jeffrey Mehlman

*Demander un livre de famille
à Edgar Poe!*

Baudelaire

However disoriented the American reader may have been by the publication (in 1966) of Jacques Lacan's *Écrits*, by their hermeticism, collective length, and outrageous eclecticism, there is one aspect of Lacan's corpus which must have struck our hypothetical reader as alarmingly familiar: the privileged position accorded to the work of Edgar Allan Poe. For to note that Lacan's monumental call to a rereading of Freud begins with an analysis of "The Purloined Letter" is, no doubt, to situate him in that (presumably mystified) tradition of French fascination with Poe which has long been a pretext for eloquent condescension on the part of Anglo-American men of letters. The argument is well known: Baudelaire, Mallarmé, and Valéry, in their inability, as Huxley has it, to "appreciate those finer shades of vulgarity that ruin Poe for us," have forged an imaginary Poe, which it is the duty of Anglo-Saxon common sense to resist.[1] To quote Huxley again: "we can only say, with due respect, that Baudelaire, Mallarmé, and Valéry are wrong, and that Poe is not one of our major poets."[2] But already Valéry, in his comments on *Eureka*, was less interested in the poetry, less taken in by Poe's "walloping dactylic," than appreciative of a kind of speculative enterprise. Once again, the Anglo-American, T. S. Eliot this time, would set matters straight with a rapid allusion to Poe's "lack of qualification in philosophy, theology, or natural science."[3] The transition from literature "proper" (Baudelaire and Mallarmé) to cosmology (Valéry) might then lead one to suspect that Lacan's reading of Freud with Poe is but the latest repetition of a familiar scenario: the (would-be) French

413

genius affirming his intellectual eminence through a deluded idealization of Poe.

The situation appears even more inauspicious when one recalls what it is that Eliot et al. have prided themselves on rejecting in Poe. The Virginian's interest in cryptograms and cyphers, puzzles and labyrinths, is characteristic, writes Eliot, of the "intellect of a highly gifted person before puberty."[4] Now this mystifying cult of intelligence, of course, finds its principle incarnation in the figure of the enigmatic French "analyst," Dupin. One begins wondering then to what extent the French, in idealizing Poe, have not quite simply fallen for Poe's deluded idealization of Gallic genius. More specifically, and worse yet: from Eliot's point of view, in taking Lacan's text seriously, our task in this essay, might we not *at best* be lapsing into Poe's delusion? As the play of mirrors proliferates, we approach a first intimation of what Eliot may have meant when he claimed that "one cannot be sure that one's own writings have *not* been influenced by Poe."[5]

Our very attempt to write on Lacan's Poe is thus fraught with the danger that we may lapse into the repetitive and viciously circular project hypothesized above. Yet no sooner have we sketched out the specular structure of that peril than we may state that the *subject* of Lacan's analysis of Poe is simultaneously the irreducibility of that danger and the precarious means by which it may be circumvented. Our first paradoxical task will consist in that demonstration: of how a reading of Lacan on Poe may be our best guide in avoiding the pitfalls entailed by a reading of Lacan on Poe.

For what interests the Frenchman in "The Purloined Letter," and what allows him to treat the tale as a parable of psychoanalysis, is a structure of repetition which exceeds and disrupts the sterile, specular repetition which we have alluded to earlier. Without recounting Poe's plot, we may recall for the reader its principal moments by citing Lacan's delineation of the three *positions*, each incarnated by a specific quality of vision, in that intersubjective structure: "The first [instance] is a glance that sees nothing: the King and the police. The second, a glance which sees that the first sees nothing and deludes itself as to the secrecy of what it hides: the Queen, then the Minister. The third sees that the first two glances leave what should be hidden exposed to whomever would seize it: the Minister, and finally, Dupin"[6] (p. 387). Before indicating more precisely the function of each of these instances, we should stress that what is at stake is a homology among differential relations rather than an analogy between independent terms: the situation of the Minister, for instance

—who moves from the third to the second slot in the structure— vitiates any comprehension of what is recurring in terms of an analysis of individual characters per se.

What then of the three positions? The first, occupied initially by the King and subsequently by the police, is a position which "entails blindness" (p. 405). It is occupied by the naive realist or empiricist whose blindness is a function of his perpetual search for a "real object," when what is at stake and in play is a repetitive *structure*. Needless to say, this refusal to take into account structural realities has a political dimension—whence the King and the police—and will serve Lacan implicitly in his oblique critique of American ego psychology. For the notion of therapy as a (genital) adaptation to external reality is plainly complicitous with the philosophical naivete Lacan scorns as the "realist's imbecility."

If the first position denotes a deluded objectivity, the second, for Lacan, entails an equally deluded subjectivism. For both the Queen and then the Minister betray a false sense of security—or power—in their misguided sentiment that their most *intimate* secret or possession remains inviolate. Thus the Minister, for example, "in seeing that he is not seen, misconstrues the real situation in which he is seen not seeing" (p. 400). Such are the ruses of narcissism, of any pretention to *possess* (i.e., to master consciously) the letter. Now Lacan is particularly eloquent on the transformation observed in the tale as the Minister shifts from the third to the second position. Since his power depends on his *not using* the letter, he is gradually paralyzed, effeminized by its possession. "A man man enough to defy to the point of scorn a lady's fearsome ire undergoes to the point of metamorphosis the curse of the sign he has dispossessed her of" (p. 400). As the Minister takes on the traits of his victim, lapses into an "insane stagnation," he becomes one of "those wrecked by (a) success," which, given its depressing results, can best be described as manic.

But is not the structure of the Minister's predicament, in its play of specular reflections, precisely that which we posited in our introduction? Between, on the one hand, the French idealizing an American's (Poe's) idealization of the French (Dupin) and, on the other, the Minister, addressing the disguised letter to himself in a feminine script and placing his own seal upon it, a common narcissism may be intuited.

What then of the third position, occupied first by the Minister, then by Dupin? It is for Lacan above all the locus of substitution of letter for letter, the precarious instance through which the structure perpetuates itself in a process of *exchange*. The force of whoever manages to coincide with that process lies in the capacity to affirm a radical kind of instability. Thus the movement of Lacan's version would consist in the erosion and disruption of a sterile, viciously circular form of repetition (the second position) by a more surprising and liberating form of structural repetition. Such would be the irruption of the unconscious in and against the logic of identity of a narcissistically constituted ego.

The tertiary instance, which, for Lacan, will serve as a figure for the psychoanalytic endeavor, is an odd combination of triviality and violence. On the one hand, our commentator deliberately underlines the apparent insignificance of replacing one tattered piece of paper (whose contents are never known) by another. The very marginality of the act takes on a strange centrality. On the other hand, when Lacan metaphorizes his interpretation of Dupin's theft of the letter, the image employed is one of rape. The *odor di femina* exuded by the Minister in his newly effeminized state gives way to the following remarkable development:

> Just so does the purloined letter, like an immense female body, stretch out across the Minister's office when Dupin enters. But just so does he already expect to find it, and has only, with his eyes veiled by green lenses, to undress that huge body. And that is why without needing any more than being able to listen in at the door of Professor Freud, he will go straight to the spot in which lies and lives what that body is designed to hide, in a gorgeous center caught in a glimpse, nay, to the very place seducers name Sant' Angelo's Castle in their innocent illusion of controlling the City from within it. Look! between the cheeks of the fireplace, there's the object already in reach of a hand the ravisher has but to extend . . . The question of deciding whether he seizes it above the mantelpiece as Baudelaire translates, or beneath it, as in the original text, may be abandoned without harm to the inferences of those whose profession is grilling [p. 404].

We may interpret as follows: in its violation of the imaginary integrity of the ego, psychoanalysis finds its metaphoric (phantasmatic) equivalent in rape. But precisely to the extent that such "rape" consists in the insistence of a certain uncontrolled metaphoricity we may be more inclined to speak of the violence of such metaphoricity than of any "metaphors of violence" (or rape).

The status of "rape" in Freud's own theoretical development may help clarify matters. Historians of Freud's thought are agreed that a turning point in his work comes with the abandonment of the theory of infantile seduction, according to which hysterical symptoms are the result of an act of sexual violence (seduction or rape) performed by an adult upon the subject in his childhood. For a variety of reasons, Freud writes to Fliess, in a celebrated letter of September 21, 1897: "Let me tell you straight away the great secret which has been slowly dawning on me in recent months. I no longer believe in my *neurotica*."[7] We should do well to insist on three aspects of this turning point. *First*, its fruitfulness: for the shift of focus from a primal *event* to a structuring *fantasy* marks Freud's entry into the "psychical reality" which is the specific medium of psychoanalysis. *Second*, its violence: for it would be difficult to overestimate the apparent havoc that the disappearance of a grounding event exercised in Freud's thought. The loss of faith in the ontological status of an original act of violence is itself sufficiently violent to sweep away what had functioned as Freud's ultimate certainties and to transform the very ground of psychoanalysis. *Third*, its instability: for there is an oddly liberating form of weakness in this turning-point (whence the remarkable ambivalence of the letter to Fliess: "It is curious that I feel not in the least disgraced, though the occasion might seem to require it. Certainly I shall not tell it in Gath, or publish it in the streets of Askalon, in the land of the Philistines—but between ourselves I have a feeling more of triumph than of defeat [which cannot be right]").[8] It is as though what had been lost were an illusory possession weighing Freud down, as though the analytic moment were not one of any speculative *acquisition*, but rather of expropriation.

Now it is precisely this violence, instability, and analytic fruitfulness which are *repeated* in Lacan's reading of Dupin's theft of the letter. We have already commented on Lacan's imagery of rape and the disruption of narcissistic integrity which it entails. The fruitfulness associated with the third position concerns the fact that it is the instance in the structure most alive to the structurality of the structure, congruent with that process of *exchange* of signs which assures the structure's perpetuation or repetition. To coincide with that moment, we have suggested, is to accede to the dimension permitting maximum comprehension.

But the specificity of Lacan's analysis of "The Purloined Letter" comes into greatest relief when we analyze the *instability* of Dupin's theft. For it will be recalled that the inevitable result of purloining the letter is to pass from the third to the second position, from the sheer process of substitution to a state of possession or narcissistic mastery.

Such, for example, was the Minister's fate: to be wrecked by his success. And such as well will be Lacan's reading of the danger facing Dupin as soon as he has seized the letter: to be possessed by it. The interpretative problem concerns the "rage of a manifestly feminine nature" betrayed by Dupin's substitute letter. For that letter, bearing a devastating quotation from Crébillon's *Atrée*, betrays a surprisingly impassioned desire for vengeance on the part of so calculating a "rationalist." The problem is compounded by Dupin's unexpected insistence on prompt and ample remuneration from the Prefect for delivery of the letter; for Dupin, after all, had previously been presented as a somewhat otherworldly creature, living in relative indifference to monetary concerns. Lacan's elegant solution to the dilemma is: (1) to view the expression of *blind* rage as a function of Dupin's entry into the (second) position previously occupied by the Queen and the Minister; and (2) to treat the question of Dupin's remuneration above all as the "analyst's" effort to rid himself of the letter. In psychoanalytic terms, the insistence on *exchanging* the letter for money is thus tantamount to the analyst's undoing the effects of the countertransference and freeing himself from the phantasmatic circuit whose power over him the venom of the counterfeit letter betrays. It should, moreover, be clear that to the extent that there is a locus of power in Lacan's version of the tale, it is not in the intellectual strength of the master-analyst Dupin, but rather in the persistence of a structure whose mode of existence is the erosion of just such an imaginary autonomy. We are far from Poe as adolescent idealizer of otherworldly genius—Eliot's criticism—in the Frenchman's reading.

The notion of a discovery so tenuous or unstable in its essence that its very consolidation is equivalent to its loss is odd indeed. And yet within the history of Freud's metapsychology, it may be demonstrated that the crucial category of the "pleasure principle" is subject to the same vicissitudes as Dupin (and the Minister). For at the inception of psychoanalysis (1895), the pleasure principle is characterized by a tendency toward total discharge of energy. And that "total discharge" had as its empirical referent the total evacuation of affect from representation to representation in hysterical symptoms and dreams, or the condensations and displacements of unconscious (i.e., "primary process") thinking. For such is the metapsychological reality which finds its emblem in the substitution of letter for letter in Lacan's version of "The Purloined Letter." Such "absolute discharge," moreover, is opposed to a stasis of libidinal energy, which is clearly the matrix of what will later be conceptualized as the ego. Now with the consolidation of psychoanalytic theory, contemporaneous with the emergence of ego psychology, we find Freud writing one of his most paradoxical texts: *Beyond the Pleasure Principle* (1920). But what precisely is "beyond the pleasure principle" in that work is a principle of "absolute discharge of energy," thematized in terms of the "death instinct," and identical in structure to . . . "the pleasure principle." At the same time, the pleasure principle, and sexuality generally, are reinscribed as part of a counterveiling force: Eros. But Eros, the metapsychological function perpetually constructing larger and larger libidinal units, is, in its structure, a reincarnation of the narcissistic *stasis* known as the ego. Thus, though the structure of the theory remains identical at twenty-five years distance, it would appear that the "pleasure principle" itself has changed positions in the structure. It is as though for what was radical in the pleasure principle to be retained, it had to be lost and rediscovered as other than itself (as the "death instinct"). But, of course, that very radicalism is the condition of the discovery: the structural role of repetition in/as difference. The "pleasure principle," like the "purloined letter," "will and will not be where it is—wherever it goes."

But what of our own effort in this essay? If the position presented in this reading of "The Purloined Letter" concerning the status of texts is to be taken seriously, what might it mean for a reading of Lacan's text? For if the analyst's maxim that "there is no metalanguage" has any consequence, it must lie in the inevitability of posing that question. To what extent must the "Seminar on 'The Purloined Letter'" be read as a "purloined letter"? Until now, we have been concerned with rendering explicit the structure and implications of a remarkably difficult and rhetorically scandalous text. Such a move might find its emblem in the Minister's (or Dupin's) theft (i.e., acquisition) of the letter. Were we, however, to pursue such an effort at appropriation, at clarifying the myriad details of Lacan's problematic "seminar," an undeniable gain in comprehension would no doubt ensue,[9] but at the risk of reifying—or, worse yet, of monumentalizing —a text whose whole force, if we are to take seriously the theory of textuality it articulates, should lie in its capacity for displacement, in an instability which finds its symbol, in the tale, in that furtive *substitution* of apparently insignificant pieces of crumpled paper. Ultimately, the question we must ask is what critical move might correspond to Dupin's success in ridding himself of the letter, and what textual gains might accrue from that loss.

The analysis which follows is an oblique response to those questions, an effort to see the power of Lacan's text less in any statement it makes than in its disseminating force, its deconstructive capacity to work in and on other texts, to transform them by bringing into relief their own virtual strengths and weaknesses. Already, we have seen the vicissitudes of the "pleasure principle" in the history of Freud's thought repeat the destiny of the Minister (or Dupin) once they have appropriated the letter. But the "Seminar" may be *lost* to even greater profit in a crucial text whose situation in Freud's *corpus* may be recalled by Lacan's version of Poe. For like the "Seminar," "The Uncanny" is written in the margins of *Beyond the Pleasure Principle,* is implicitly concerned with the repetition compulsion, and is pursued through a speculative reading of a short story (Hoffmann's "The Sand-Man"[10]*). It is to the role of that reading in the general economy of "The Uncanny"[11]† that we shall direct our attention. For it is in the *contamination* of Freud's reading of Hoffmann by Lacan's reading of Poe (and *vice versa*) that a certain liberating *decomposition*, alluded to in our title, will reveal its insistence.

The entirety of "The Uncanny" functions under the sign of marginality. The phenomenon of the uncanny would appear to be the most peripheral region of a domain (aesthetics) which is itself peripheral in relation to psychoanalysis. And indeed, Freud's reading of "The Sand-Man" seems less an effort to embrace the entirety of the tale in any global interpretation than progressively to eliminate from his focus all but that insistent margin of the text which he will define as "uncanny." A convenient approach to Freud's reading will thus be a delineation of those segments of the text from which he successively diverts his attention.

There is one important character in "The Sand-Man" to whom Freud pays no attention at all. The object of this first elimination is Nathanael's *fiancée* Klara. Klara is the voice of *Heimlichkeit*, of a certain realism or clarity (whence the name) exercised out of a fidelity to "the true, external world" (S.M., p. 101). Now what is odd is that in discouraging Nathanael from what she takes to be purely subjective fantasies, Klara adopts voluntaristic accents that are not without recalling that side of Freud himself which we associate with ego psychology: "If our mind is firm enough and adequately fortified by the joys of life to be able to recognize alien and hostile influences as such, and to proceed tranquilly along the path of our own choosing

---

* Abbreviated here as S.M.
† Abbreviated here as Unc.

and propensities, then this mysterious power will perish in its futile attempt to assume a shape that is supposed to be a reflection of ourselves" (S.M., p. 102). If then Freud chose not to comment on Klara, it was not because her position was not imaginatively available to him, but rather because of its irrelevance to any comprehension of the "uncanny" as Freud was attempting to articulate it. *Tentatively* then, we may say that Freud's elimination of Klara from consideration parallels Lacan's critique of those emblems of naive empiricism (and the therapeutic attitude complicitous with it)—the King and the Police—in "The Purloined Letter."

A second potential focus in "The Sand-Man," which Freud will eventually eliminate, is the doll Olympia. Inheriting the example of Olympia from his predecessor in investigating "the uncanny," E. Jentsch, Freud will attempt to show that there is a level of the story more essentially uncanny than that concerning the doll. Jentsch had chosen as a quintessential instance of the uncanny those moments in a story in which the reader is left in uncertainty whether a particular figure is a human being or an automaton. For Freud, however, Olympia becomes the pretext less for any discussion of intellectual uncertainty than for an elaboration of a permanent narcissistic instance in the subject.

> Now Spalanzani's otherwise incomprehensible statement that the optician has stolen Nathanael's eyes so as to set them in the doll becomes significant and supplies fresh evidence for the identity of Olympia and Nathanael. Olympia is, as it were, a dissociated complex of Nathanael's which confronts him as a person, and Nathanael's enslavement to this complex is expressed in his senseless obsessive love for Olympia. We may with justice call such love narcissistic . . . [Unc., p. 138].

But what are the principal characteristics of this relation? In commenting on the structure of narcissism, Freud has recourse to the writings of Rank on the "double." Now it is of the essence of the "double" to be an instrument of self-defeat for the subject, an illusory defence for fending off "the power of death." For, "from having been an assurance of immortality, he [the double] becomes the ghastly harbinger of death" (Unc., p. 141). The structure of the "double" then is that of a vicious circle or *tourniquet* (Sartre): an unreal victory which is but the means of a devastating defeat. Moreover, despite his efforts to situate the phenomenon of the "double" *geneti-*

cally, in terms of a "primary narcissism," Freud finds himself increasingly obliged to posit such doubling as potentially a permanent function of the ego. Thus: "the idea of the *double* does not disappear with the passing of the primary narcissism, for it can receive fresh meaning from the later stages of development of the ego" (Unc., p. 141). Thus, what is at stake here begins to take on the appearance of a structural instance rather than a genetic phase. And in the case of "The Sand-Man," the positive (manic) and negative (depressive) phases of the vicious circle are, respectively, the *idealization* of Olympia's beauty and the (psychotic) *dismemberment* of her (lifeless) body. But beyond the specific terms of the conflict, it is the viciously circular structure of narcissism that interests us here and produces the air of paralysis or immobility which dominates Nathanael's relation with Olympia. To quote Hoffmann: "he scarcely even left his window and, almost without interruption, gazed into her room . . ." (S.M., p. 113).

The reader has perhaps observed that in delineating the principal characteristics of Olympia as she functions in "The Uncanny," we have simultaneously reproduced the structure of the second position in Lacan's reading of "The Purloined Letter." Specifically: the vicious circularity of Nathanael's relation with Olympia finds its counterpart in the Minister's pretense to an absolute mastery (through possession of the letter) which is in fact a form of enslavement. The effect of this tourniquet is to reduce the Minister to an odd form of immobility: "There must be in this sign a singular *noli me tangere* for its possession, like the Socratic sting ray, to benumb its man to the point of making him fall into what appears clearly, in his case, to be a case of idleness" (p. 400). Finally, just as Olympia was interpreted as a narcissistic identification of Nathanael, so too do we find the Minister, effeminized by the possession of the letter, taking on the characteristics of the lady from whom he stole it. The situations in Poe and in Hoffmann are, of course, remarkably dissimilar, but it is precisely because the repetition referred to is insistent *through* that difference that the emerging coherence of our parallelism carries conviction. In view of the relation between Olympia (Hoffmann-Freud) and the second position of Lacan's structure, we may suggest that the relation established between Klara and Lacan's initial position already appears less tentative.

But our repetitive series takes on even greater coherence in view of the fact that "Olympia" functions in "The Uncanny" above all in diacritical opposition to a separate textual function which exceeds it and whose insistence it might have masked.

> But I cannot think . . . that the theme of the doll, Olympia, who is to all appearances a living being, is by any means the only element to be held responsible for the quite unparalleled atmosphere of uncanniness which the story evokes; or, indeed, that it is the most important among them . . . The main theme of the story is, on the contrary, something different, something which gives its name to the story, and which is *always re-introduced* at the critical moment: it is the theme of the Sand-Man who tears out children's eyes [Unc., p. 121].

That statement, positing a mode of repetition *different* from that of narcissistic "doubling," may be profitably juxtaposed with a footnote which Freud appends to his discussion of the fundamentally narcissistic nature of man's capacity for "self-observation," of the fact that a faculty exists "which is able to treat the rest of the ego like an object" (Unc., p. 142).

> I cannot help thinking that when poets complain that two souls dwell within the human breast, and when popular psychologists talk of the splitting of the ego in an individual, they have some notion of this division (which relates to the sphere of ego psychology) between the critical faculty and the rest of the ego, and not of the antithesis discovered by psychoanalysis between the ego and what is unconscious and repressed [Unc., p. 142].

The footnote is admirable in its explicit refusal of those facile assimilations of literary and psychoanalytic texts, which have become the principal technique of "psychoanalytic literary criticism." But its interest for us lies in the fact that the essence of psychoanalysis itself is here homologous with "the most important" source of "uncanniness" in "The Sand-Man." We begin to see what centrality Freud may be tempted to attribute to the marginal phenomenon of the "uncanny," why indeed "psychoanalysis . . . has itself become uncanny."

In "The Uncanny" then, "popular psychologists" and "poets," like Jentsch and, for that matter, Nathanael-Olympia "themselves," are all lured into a position whose structure is narcissistic in an effort to blot out an ill-defined threat, whose menace may well lie in its capacity for radical displacement: i.e., its refusal to be contained by any of the ontological domains ("fiction," "reality," "theory," "life") implied by Freud's categories. That threat, in the essay, bears the name "castration." What are its properties? "Castration," first of all, is inseparable from a series of repetitions-in-difference: first the lawyer

Coppelius, then the optician Coppola. It will be noted that it is only when dealing with this variety of (Oedipal) repetition that Freud finds himself analysing those grotesque puns which were, after all, at the heart of *Die Traumdeutung*: "Coppolla=crucible, connecting it with the chemical operations that caused the father's death; and also with *coppo*=eye-socket . . ." (Unc., p. 136).

The notion of "castration," of course, entails the removal of a precious organ, and the Sand-Man does indeed "tear out" children's eyes. But the story presents a second, more subtle facet of the process whereby the body's integrity is subverted. For Coppola is an optician, a vendor of "spectacles." "Castration" would then seem to involve both a loss of the natural organ and its replacement by a *prosthetic* device, a *supplement*, which Coppola himself refers to as the organ itself: "fine eyes, beautiful eyes" (Unc., p. 134). The *loss* of the organ thus entails as well its *replacement* by a simulacrum apt to pass itself off as that which it symbolizes. This operation will interest us later on when we turn to the relationship between the *heimlich* and the *unheimlich*.

There is, of course, as well an obvious objection to be made against any interpretation of "The Sand-Man" in terms of castration (in a surgical sense): the organ in question is not the penis, but the eye. Freud would counter that point by invoking "psychoanalytic experience." "A study of dreams, phantasies and myths has taught us that a morbid anxiety connected with the eyes and with going blind is often enough a substitute for the dread of castration" (Unc., p. 137). And yet in articulating his position, Freud follows a curious line of argument:

We may try to reject the derivation of fears about the eye from the fear of castration on rationalistic grounds, and say that so precious an organ as the eye should be guarded by a proportionate dread; indeed, we might go further and say that *the fear of castration itself contains no other significance and no deeper secret than a justifiable dread of this kind*. But this view does not account adequately for the substitutive relation between the eye and the male member which is seen to exist in dreams and myths and phantasies; nor can it dispel the impression one gains that it is the threat of being castrated in especial which excites a peculiarly violent and obscure emotion, and that this emotion is what *first* gives the idea of losing other organs its intense colouring [Unc., p. 138; my emphasis].

The conclusion is clearly that behind the fear of losing the eye is a dread of a loss of a more *primal* organ: the penis. And yet in rejecting the common-sense point of view that the loss of the visual *function* is in itself sufficient cause for terror, Freud rejects as well the notion that what is at stake in "castration" is loss of a biological (sexual) function. Thus the eye may replace the penis, but the penis is somehow already separated from itself, since fear of castration is not fear of loss of the penis. The substitution—and hence repetition —were already at work *in the beginning*. Whereby the very notion of an origin is eroded.

We may now return to Lacan's reading of Poe, and specifically to the *third* position in the structure. Our earlier analysis had led us to see in Lacan's metaphor of violence (Dupin's theft as rape) an allusion to a certain violence of metaphoricity or substitution as it disrupted the assurances of narcissistic consciousness. The analogous instance in "The Uncanny" is "castration," the structuring moment of *triangular* (Oedipal) sexuality. The importance attached to the irrelevance of the crime or *event* alluded to in the "purloined letter" finds its counterpart in the erosion of the primacy of the "primal" (phallic) organ. In both cases, what is at stake and in play is the sheer movement of substitution or repetition in difference of unconscious structure.

A brief examination of Freud's analysis of the "uncanny" in its relation to other crucial concepts in his writings, in isolation from the analysis of "The Sand-Man," will confirm these results. An initial thesis, which might be abstracted from Freud's comments, is: what is uncanny about the uncanny is that *anything* may be uncanny. For what is at stake is not a specific content but a capacity for a thing to be repeated as other than itself. In Freud's words: "The uncanny is in reality nothing new or foreign, but something familiar and old established in the mind that has been estranged only by the process of repression" (Unc., p. 148). If we search for the harmonics of these statements in Freud's work, we necessarily encounter the difficult concepts of *pansexuality* and *anaclisis*.[12] *Pansexuality* should, no doubt, be understood not as any simplistic explanation of every phenomenon by a sexual substratum, but rather as Freud's discovery that *any* function (be it corporeal or intellectual) may be sexualized. (The *pan* thus corresponds to the *anything* of our thesis.) The prototype of that process of sexualization is delineated in the *Three Contributions to the Theory of Sex* as the *anaclisis* (German: *Anlehnung*; French: *étayage*) of the oral drive (German: *Trieb*; French: *pulsion*) on the instinct of hunger: in the course of ingesting milk, the infant experiences a "marginal pleasure" at the contact of lips on the (mother's) breast; unconscious sexuality will consist in the (hallucinatory) repetition of this fantasy of a pleasure in exchange which itself lies entirely in its *deviation* from the satisfaction of the natural function (ingestion of food). But in its structure, this process of *deviation*, whereby unconscious sexuality is generated, is homologous with that movement of *estrangement* whereby the canny recurs as uncanny. And, to return to "The Sand-Man," we find a similar process whereby perception—the very model of unmediated contact between subject and object—is displaced or perverted by the interposition of Coppola's prosthetic spectacles. In each case, an apparently naive relation between subject and object becomes alienated in a circuit of exchange. And between the fantasied repetition of that circuit and the sheer fact of repression, we are hard put to distinguish.

A second thesis: what is uncanny about the uncanny is that its first occurrence is a recurrence. The attentive reader of Freud will sense in such a situation important harmonics with the crucial motif of *Nachtraglichkeit*, the temporal mode whereby the sexual "trauma" takes on traumatic significance only *after the event* with its oblique recurrence. We need not pursue our discussion of the parallel between the structure of repetition in "The Uncanny" and in *Nachtraglichkeit* here. Suffice it to say that to the extent that in the structure of the "uncanny" we have seen *intersect* the concept of *Anlehnung* (wherein Freud elaborates a difficult genesis of sexuality) and that of *Nachtraglichkeit* (wherein he simultaneously erodes the very notion of an origin), we may claim that writing "The Uncanny" is Freud's way of reaffirming, in displaced form, his discovery of the an-archical nature of unconscious sexuality.

It is a discovery which is perpetually—and necessarily—escaping Freud. Which is to say that the ultimate relevance of Lacan's maxim that "there is no metalanguage" concerns the constant threat of repression to which the discovery of the fact of repression is itself exposed. In terms of Freud's analysis of "The Sand-Man," that repression, I would suggest, takes the specific form of obliterating the distinction between the second and third positions in the structure which (after Lacan) we have elaborated. Two examples will suffice. Concerning *repetition*: simultaneous with the effort to articulate a *third* realm beyond the specular dualisms of narcissism is an unmistakable pressure in the text to merge narcissistic repetition and the repetition in/as difference of the unconscious as common manifestations of an "archaic mode of thought." Concerning *threats to bodily unity*: here too there is a tendency to fuse the psychotic fragmentation or splitting of Olympia with the more subtle displacement—or supplementing—of unity in "castration." (Freud: "Coppelius, after sparing Nathanael's eyes, has screwed off his arms and legs as an experiment [. . .] This singular feature . . . introduces a new castration equivalent . . ." [Unc., p. 139]). In view of this pressure to obliterate the distinction between positions in "The Uncanny," we are thus tempted to suggest that one sense of Lacan's intervention in analyzing Poe is to render explicit a dimension in Freud which was threatened with being lost.

What is at stake in that (potential) loss becomes clearer when we return to Freud's discussion of the "uncanny" as that which renders irrelevant the distinction between reality and fiction. For that characteristic of the "uncanny" is open to two different interpretations, each of which is solidary with a different concept of the uncanny. A first version of the uncanny involves the surprising discovery that "primitive beliefs we have surmounted seem once more to be confirmed" (Unc., p. 157). Now though such a revelation—that the presumably fictive is in fact true—*appears* to deny the pertinence of the distinction reality/fiction, ultimately it is dependent on a "reality-testing": the ability to affirm the (unexpected) truth of a belief. There is thus a hidden *telos* in this version of the uncanny: the perfect coincidence of subject (repository of fiction) and object (representative of reality). A second version of the uncanny entails nothing but the reactivation of "repressed infantile complexes" (electively, the castration complex). In such a case, the opposition reality/fiction is reduced to minimal pertinence; the sheer repetition of the "complex" is sufficient to evoke the "uncanny" regardless of any question of belief. Eventually, as though the essay itself were a competition for priority between the two versions, Freud, in the final pages, describes the second concept ("the class which proceeds from repressed complexes") as "the more irrefragable" and "the more durable" of the two (Unc., p. 161).

But what are we to make of that move? In order to come to terms with it, we shall call into play the argument of one of the central studies of Freud's thought to have emerged in France in recent years: Jean Laplanche's *Vie et mort en psychanalyse* (Flammarion, 1970). The remarkable result of Laplanche's scrupulous study of Freud's terminology is the discovery that corresponding to each of a series of crucial Freudian terms—in a way which Freud plainly does not control—there are two different concepts at work. We find, on the one hand, a version of each notion suited to a biological, genetic, adaptative, or functional scheme, and, on the other, one which finds its place in the context of an articulation of the specific modes of negativity (censorship, repetition, displacement . . .) of a transmissible unconscious structure. A specific example will offer some clarification. We have already had the occasion to discuss the meaning of *Anlehnung* (anaclisis) in the *Three Contributions*, where it functions as the ideal moment whereby the sexual drive (*Trieb*) achieves independence from the instinctual function and affirms its "end" as the perpetual reactivation of a fantasy whose object (e.g., breast) is *displaced* from the natural (instinctual) object (milk). On the other hand, *anaclisis*, in the "Introduction to Narcissism," functions in a more familiar sense. In opposition to "narcissistic object choice," "anaclitic object choice" entails a selection of the love object modeled (not on the self, but) on the object of the instinct of self-conservation (essentially, the mother). We thus find *Anlehnung* (in the first instance) of the sexual *drive* on the *instinct* and (in the second) of the *subject* on the *object*. The first points toward the repetition of a fantasy of exchange in opposition to any natural satisfaction; the second presents a sexuality solidary with a biological functionalism.

The situation of *Anlehnung* is but an example of the simultaneity in Freud's text of two mutually exclusive conceptual schemes struggling, as it were, for domination of a single terminological apparatus. One is teleologically oriented toward a fusion—or successful integration—of subject and object; the other articulates the bizarre rhetoric of a structure of exchange in which subject and object are together alienated. It may already be intuited that the crux of Freud's discovery, of the fact of dynamic repression, is linked to the second of these schemes. The persistence of the first then—of that which Freud (at his most radical) must think again—manifests the tendency in Freud's own texts to repress his own discovery (of the fact of repression). That tendency, triumphant in the United States, has been institutionalized as psychoanalytic ego psychology. It is in this context, moreover, that the empirical impossibility of the "death instinct" finds its place . . . as the return of the repressed. In the view we are articulating, the "death instinct" (which is consequently an *anti*-instinct) would constitute Freud's unwitting *re*-discovery of the unconscious. For, as we have suggested above, this radical principle of repetition is itself, in its structure, the repetition of what, in the *Project* of 1895, had been called the "principle of neuronic inertia" and, later on, the "pleasure principle." And whatever the biological fantasia accompanying the hypothesis of the death instinct, what the "absolute discharge of energy" which characterizes each of these instances originally referred to (in 1895) was the total evacuation of affect from representation in symptoms and dreams: i.e., the fact of unconscious displacement and condensation or primary process thinking.

We may return now to "The Uncanny," a text written virtually at the same time as *Beyond the Pleasure Principle*. For what is striking in that shorter text, it may now be seen, is that Freud consciously presents both conceptual schemes as rival interpretations of the uncanny. The first concerns "surmounted" modes of thought finding unexpected confirmation in reality: i.e., a successful integration of subject and object. The second entails the reactivation of the culminating phase of the structuring (Oedipal) instance of human desire: the castration complex. It is perhaps because Freud is dealing with a subject (the uncanny) as apparently *peripheral* to psychoanalysis "proper" that the latent conflict which structures the whole of metapsychology—grossly: a rivalry between "structuralist" and "functionalist" schemes to invest a single terminology—can find so condensed a formulation in this brief text. The fact, moreover, that the second version is eventually described as the "more durable" or "irrefragable" of the two confirms our reading of *Beyond the Pleasure Principle* as an unwitting rediscovery of the very crux of psychoanalysis. Therein would lie the remarkable "nodality" of "The Uncanny," its status as a microcosm of Freud's thought, and therein as well lies the uncanny appropriateness of Lacan's introducing his *Écrits* with a strategic repetition of Freud's effort in "Das Unheimliche."

Having successfully *lost* Lacan's text in Freud's, having (hopefully) demonstrated the deconstructive force which a certain *pourrissement de Poe* may take on in "The Uncanny," we may perhaps have given the impression that our subject has been entirely intrapsychoanalytic. Which is why we shall conclude by demonstrating briefly the interpretative role which our observations may play within a "purely literary" text: the poetry of Mallarmé.

Has it ever been observed that the question Freud was constrained to ask at a turning point in the history of psychoanalysis—whether the seduction scenes on which his entire theory was predicated were fantasies—is the subject of *L'après-midi d'un faune*? For Freud, too, like the waking Sicilian faun, might well have asked: *Aimai-je un rêve*? Have I invested everything in a fantasy? Our question, however perverse, will seem less arbitrary when we examine the precise circumstances of the alleged rape (and its failure) in Mallarmé:

> Mon crime, c'est d'avoir, gai de vaincre ces peurs
> Traîtresses, divisé la touffe échevelée
> De baisers que les dieux gardaient si bein mêlée:
> Car, à peine j'allais cacher un rire ardent
> Sous les replis heureux d'une seule (gardant
> Par un doigt simple, afin que sa candeur de plume
> Se teignît a l'émoi de sa soeur qui s'allume
> La petite, naïve et ne rougissant pas:)
> Que de mes bras, défaits par de vagues trépas,
> Cette proie à jamais ingrate se délivre
> Sans pitié du sanglot dont j'étais encore ivre.[13]

At first sight then, the rape appears to fail because of the faun's gluttony; it is when separating the *two* nymphs he desires that they together escape. And yet the act of dividing two sisters has curiously oblique resonances in Mallarmé's poetry. One thinks in particular of "Sainte," an evocation of a stained-glass window by the poet at the very moment in which one image of Saint Cecilia (with viola and book) is transformed into another (her finger appearing to stroke an imaginary harp formed by the angel's wing in the background):

> A ce vitrage d'ostensoir
> Que frôle une harpe par l'Ange
> Formée avec son vol du soir
> Pour la délicate phalange
>
> Du doigt que, sans le vieux santal
> Ni le vieux livre, elle balance
> Sur le plumage instrumental . . .[14]

Thus the motif of dividing a creature from her "sister" (in both poems) is supplemented by the odd repetition of finger pressed to feather (*candeur de plume, vol du soir*) in each case. The precision of the superimposition is matched only by the grotesque difference between the texts. For the absurdity of the link we have established may be appreciated in the suggestion that if, at some level, what is at stake in the two poems is identical, then (again, at a level which remains problematic) what is occurring in the apparently pious scene in the stained-glass window is . . . rape.

That window or partition, of course, has manifold incarnations in Mallarmé: as the glass pane of "Les Fenêtres," the frozen surface of the lake in the swan sonnet, or, for that matter, "Le Tombeau d'Edgar Poe." Each partition, dividing subject from the object of its desire, is, by implication, the scene of a process of substitution which, in the case of "Sainte" finds a limited and intended illustration, but which, in the case of such skewed repetitions as the one we have indicated between "Sainte" and "L'Après-midi d'un faune," is so oblique—and unmotivated—as to throw into question any intentionality, to divide not only the subject of the poem but the subjectivity of the poet *from itself*. It is as though the apparent piety of the scene in "Sainte" and the apparent lasciviousness of the anecdote in "L'Après-midi d'un faune" were pretexts for a more fundamental process of repetition we are hard put to locate in any subject.

At this juncture, we would reverse the direction of our parallel and say not that a "rape" is taking place "in" the stained-glass window, but that what is ultimately violated in "L'Après-midi" is the faun's faith in the ontological status of the object of his rape. Which is to say that the deconstruction of Mallarmé's text (and the faun's dream) consists in the demonstration of the metaphorical structure of what is assumed to be real, the affirmation of a process of substitution or exchange which Lacan, it will be recalled, in "analyzing" Dupin's substitution of letter for letter, metaphorized as rape.

The series of associations—instrument, feather, finger, window, etc.—to which we have only alluded in our invocation of Mallarmé recurs in a text which we are tempted to call Mallarmé's version of "Das Unheimliche:" "Le Démon de l'Analogie." The poet, obsessed by a "meaningless" sentence: *La Pénultième est morte,* wanders anxiously through the streets of Paris, accumulating mental images (of instruments, wings, palms, etc.) strangely associated with the "absurd phrase." Finally, he comes across an antique dealer's shop *window*, through which, to his shock, he sees displayed the very iconography of his obsession. "Je m'enfuis, bizarre, personne condamnée à porter probablement le detuil de l'inexplicable Pénultième."[15] The coincidence between subjective fantasy and objective reality will no doubt recall one mode of the "uncanny" in Freud—or that situation in which the Minister gains *possession* of his *object* in Lacan. And yet there is an element in *excess* of that coincidence which remains "inexplicable" and delivers the poet over to a dimension he calls *bizarre. Bizarre,* Lacan reminds us in his "Seminar," is Baudelaire's translation of Poe's word *odd*, concerning the relation between letter and place. Better, writes Lacan, render it as *singulier*, no doubt his translation of *unheimlich*. But what is *bizarre* (*odd, singulier*) is the inexplicable phrase: *La Pénultième est morte*. We would suggest that in this death which ensues before the end we find a pendant to Freud's uncanny, which begins with its *recurrence*. Between that erosion of beginning and that displacement of end, constituting the space in which both subject and object are alienated, is the sheer process of substitution or exchange, the brute fact of repetition as difference, whose insistence, through Freud, Hoffmann, Lacan, Poe, and Mallarmé, we have attempted to induce.

NOTES

1. Aldous Huxley, "Vulgarity in Literature," 1930, reprinted in *The Recognition of Edgar Allan Poe*, ed. E. W. Carlson (Ann Arbor, 1966), p. 161.
2. Ibid., p. 160.
3. T. S. Eliot, "From Poe to Valery," 1948, reprinted in Carlson, op. cit., p. 218.
4. Ibid., p. 212.
5. Ibid., p. 205.
6. Page references are to the translation of the "Seminar on 'The Purloined Letter'" in this volume; originally published in *Yale French Studies*, 48 (1973).
7. Sigmund Freud, *The Origins of Psychoanalysis*, ed. M. Bonaparte, A. Freud, E. Kris (New York, 1954).
8. Ibid., p. 217.
9. I have in fact pursued such an effort in the introduction and notes to the aforementioned translation of the "Seminar."
10. "The Sand-Man" in *Tales of E.T.A. Hoffmann*, trans. Kent and Knight (Chicago, 1969).
11. Sigmund Freud, "The Uncanny," in *On Creativity and the Unconscious* (New York, 1958).
12. The ensuing comments on *pansexuality*, *anaclisis*, and *Nachtraglichkeit* are based on the analyses in Chapters I and II of Jean Laplanche, *Vie et Mort en pyschanalyse* (Paris, 1970); in English, *Life and Death in Psychoanalysis*, trans. J. Mehlman (Baltimore, 1976).
13. My crime is to have parted, in elation
    From conquering those treacherous fears, the tangled
    Tuft of kisses the gods kept so well mingled:
    Hardly was I about to hide a flushed
    Laugh in one girl's glad creases (holding hushed
    With a mere finger, that her feathered whiteness
    Might catch the fever of her sister's brightness,
    The little one, free from all guilt or lying:)
    When from my arms, loosed by some sort of dying,
    That quarry, evermore ungrateful, stole
    Away, heedless of sobs I reeled with still.

    Translation by Keith Bosley, from *Mallarmé: The Poems* (New York, 1977).
14. On this monstrance window, brushed
    By a harp the Angel made

When his wings at evening rushed
For delicately joined

Fingers which, old sandalwood
Old book gone, are poised to dance
On her instrument, feathered . . .

Translation by Keith Bosley.

15. "I fled, *bizarre*, one probably condemned to wear mourning for the inexplicable Penultimate." Translation by Keith Bosley, except that the key word *bizarre* has been left untranslated.

Psychoanalysis Demands a Mind

Stephen Melville

The notion of a psychoanalytic literary criticism appears to be all but coeval with the notion of psychoanalysis itself.[1] Further, this possibility seems to have been always implicitly double: involving, on the one hand, the obvious ability of psychoanalysis itself to find and illustrate its own truths through literary reference (and this can be said to cover everything from the passing reference to Oedipus or Hamlet within the Freudian text to some of the most sophisticated modern analyses of literary works); and, on the other hand, the vision of something that would be—somehow—a more critically adequate "psychoanalysis of the text" (whether conceived simply as the analysis of fictional characters apart from any reference to an author or in terms of some more elaborate approach to the form and language of the text).

Over the past several decades the latter vision has taken something of a beating. In particular, two of the foremost practitioners of psychoanalytic criticism have found themselves obliged to give it up as a genuine possibility for literary criticism.[2] Throughout this essay I will be concerned with the problems that drove Frederick Crews and Norman Holland, in very different ways, to this conclusion. I shall approach these problems through Holland's assertion that "psychoanalysis demands a mind."[3] This apparently self-evident truth has acquired a certain independence from its rather restrained initial context and become the statement that is understood to rule out in advance any literary critical "psychoanalysis of the text."

This review of Holland's assertion is not simply a hypothetical exercise aiming at the merely formal reinstatement of an empty possibility; there is work being done now that can be measured only against the criteria implicit in the notion of a psychoanalysis of the text (and, in another sense, there has always been work done that can only be so measured and has in fact been so measured: which is to say that a part of what is at stake here is a certain reappropriation of the history of psychoanalytic criticism). The spelling out of these criteria at a theoretical level is accordingly a matter of some interest.

—Psychoanalysis demands a mind.

The phrase I have taken for a title is the central node in a discursive structure, the critical analysis of which aims toward the theoretical articulation of such criteria. The structure I will lay out is one the reader is asked to recognize as in some sense adequate to the ways in which we talk—with greater or lesser sophistication—about a cluster of issues surrounding psychoanalytic criticism. Such a recognition will almost certainly be hedged with reservations—and is properly so hedged; it is a part of the thesis advanced here that the ways in which we are disposed to talk about the history and structure of psychoanalytic criticism will be, crucially, less than adequate to the real strength of that history and practice.

In a sense, this essay is an attempt to spell out what in our ordinary recognitions of psychoanalysis and its possibilities for literary criticism we can explicitly acknowledge and what we cannot; and if there are acknowledgments we cannot make, we are called upon to review our ordinary understanding so as to find our way to what we do want to say. There is, then, a circularity to the project. The argument roughly runs: if our ordinary understanding of psychoanalysis is such as to generate a picture of psychoanalytic criticism that falls apart in certain specifiable ways, then that collapse itself can point back toward a revision of psychoanalysis. It is important to note that the enterprise is revisionary and not revolutionary—so that if on the one hand there is something that looks like a call for a new psychoanalytic criticism at work here (and of course there is), there is on the other hand (and less explicitly) a counterimpulse toward the acknowledgment of the power psychoanalytic criticism has shown itself capable of throughout its history.

The argument leans upon two exemplary readings of Henry James's *The Turn of the Screw*.[4] The two readings discussed were chosen precisely because they are exemplary; the ways in which they are incommensurable will be so obvious as to need no further comment. I should, however, like to emphasize that the examples were chosen for the clarity of their contrast, and not in an attempt to do justice to the larger history of psychoanalytic criticism or even the larger psychoanalytic literature on *The Turn of the Screw*. Their work is merely one of enabling recognition.

Finally, this essay has, in effect, attached itself to certain remarks by Norman Holland, and has done so at three points. These attach-

ments seem to me inevitable, but not wholly just; and I should therefore like to be as explicit as possible in advance about the nature of
these points.

—The proposition that "psychoanalysis demands a mind" is one
that Holland wrote down, and it therefore has to be attributed to him;
but what matters about this proposition is that it seems to have so
resonated with an entire set of tacit understandings about psychoanalysis that it has been easily detached from its initial (and modest)
context to become the slogan that is analyzed here. Holland's "responsibility" for this statement is at best indirect—so that what I will
refer to from time to time as "Holland's proposition" is, one could
say, less what Holland wrote than that structure, floating loosely
somewhere between Holland and his readers, in which Holland's sentence has an overwhelming obviousness that lets it escape the particular text through which it emerged.

—Holland's version of the history of psychoanalytic criticism is
here taken over uncritically from time to time. It seems to me that in
this history Holland himself is responding directly to the consequences of the (independent) proposition that "psychoanalysis
demands a mind" and that the history is organized by those consequences. It is a history that would exclude the possibility of a
"psychoanalysis of the text." There is, of course, work within that
history which outraces the terms of my critique—but this is work that
outraces the terms by which that history is organized as well: this is
one statement of the problem of recognition and acknowledgment
that is always near the center here.

—Holland is ultimately led to introduce a new version of psychoanalytic criticism, "reader response criticism." One of the goals of
this essay is to be able to account for the possibility of this move—
which is not to say that it will offer in any sense a justification of
Holland's understanding of what such criticism looks like. My claim
is rather that the possibility of grasping psychoanalytic criticism as a
"reader response" criticism is inscribed within psychoanalysis itself in
a way that is precisely blocked by Holland's formulation of the history of psychoanalytic criticism. It is only by clearing away the implicit recognitions at work behind Holland's history that one comes to
be able to acknowledge the way in which psychoanalytic criticism can
be (has always been) a form of reader response criticism.

—Psychoanalysis demands a mind.

There are senses in which I will want to say this is exactly right;
but most of these senses are Lacanian, and depend upon a parsing of

"demand" to which I will turn later.[5] For the time being I should like to oppose to this formulation another: psychoanalysis poses a mind. The first part of this essay will be devoted to disentangling these two formulations from one another within the structure of psychoanalytic criticism; this disentangling will, in its turn, lead on into psychoanalysis itself, and thence back to questions of psychoanalytic criticism. The overall movement is loosely helical, with the stakes raised and the complexity increased in each repetition.

—Psychoanalysis demands a mind.

In Holland's 1961 essay the argument this statement has been taken to embody is only implicit, subsumed under the author's impulse toward his reader response program, but its sense is clear enough. The assertion operates to compel recognition of the only two possibilities open to a would-be psychoanalytic criticism. Only a mind can anchor the truth of a psychoanalytic interpretation, and in literature there are only two minds available—the author's and the reader's. Each is a legitimate object of psychoanalytic knowledge, and any attempt at psychoanalytic criticism, whatever its intent, must —if pushed—end by appealing to one or the other in order finally to ground its claims. Thus, for example, the attempt to analyze the governess in *The Turn of the Screw* must (and in Edmund Wilson's revisions of his initial thesis, does) become an analysis of James himself if it is seriously challenged.

Holland's remark is, of course, intended to help justify the "natural" choice of the reader's mind as the obvious and most accessible mind for psychoanalytic criticism. But this "reader response" criticism has been criticized, I think correctly, as being essentially reader-analysis (and so, I would say, merely psychological) at its most direct and obvious level; if it is pushed for some more properly literary critical justification, it is hard to see what more it can do than reverse its field and appeal to an analysis of the author after all.[6] It would appear that literary critical interest in psychoanalysis returns us always to the author's side of Holland's choice, and I will focus on that side of the alternative here.[7]

Edmund Wilson's celebrated interpretation of *The Turn of the Screw* has already put in a brief appearance. I now want to make more systematic and paradigmatic use of it. It is, of course, naive by the standards of contemporary psychoanalytic criticism; it is also— no doubt in part because of its naiveté—a singularly clear example of the way in which the demand for mind works within psychoanalytic criticism. What we want to see is the "necessity" by which Wilson finds himself pushed to appeal to James's mind.

Wilson takes it from the outset that there is a truth behind the text, and that this truth can be psychoanalytically known: it is apparent through and beneath *The Turn of the Screw*. His reading is offered with considerable directness: "This story . . . perhaps conceals another horror behind the ostensible one. . . . The theory is, then, that the governess who is made to tell the story is a neurotic case of sex repression, and that the ghosts are not real ghosts but hallucinations of the governess."[8] There is, then, visible through the text, a second narrative that is truer than the more apparent one—so much truer that by the end of his presentation Wilson is wondering how what now seems so obvious could have ever been missed. The argument for the reading is essentially a restatement of the given narrative in such a way that the Freudian reading is in fact obvious. Wilson, as it were, paraphrases in light of the truth. Such a paraphrase is all that is necessary; it allows us to recognize the truths we know from psychoanalysis. So, for example, Wilson has only to write: "Observe, also, from the Freudian point of view, the significance of the governess' interest in the little girl's pieces of wood and of the fact that the male apparition first takes shape on a tower and the female apparition on a lake."[9] Given the proper point of view, the rest is merely a matter of seeing; Wilson needs no more than: Observe. Recognize.

There is, however, a level at which a need for argument does emerge: the one narrative does not slide wholly and smoothly behind the other, and, as a result, certain cruxes are engendered. These are not the (usually vague) "incoherences" that are traditionally taken to call forth and license a psychoanalytic interpretation; these are artifacts of that interpretation—for example, if the ghosts are to be understood as hallucinatory, how is the governess able to describe them so that another person (Mrs. Grose) can recognize and name them? This is a point to which the psychoanalytic claim to know the truth of the text feels compelled to respond (as if in "real life"), and much energy has in fact been expended on this point (among others). But if a "realistic" answer to this objection cannot be found, then the analysis takes a step back: not only is the governess self-deceived, but Henry James is as well. There is nothing wrong with the interpretation as given—it was just attributed to the wrong mind. This slide is, in principle, uncontrollable[10]—it is an effect of displacement of a crux that is instituted by the determination of the psychoanalytic truth of the text—and Wilson, in the chain of postscripts attached to the original essay, has oscillated between the two positions. In general, there is relatively little variation in the meanings assigned to the various scenes or incidents of the text within the large psychoanalytic literature on *The Turn of the Screw*, but there is considerable diversity in the location of the "mind" to which these meanings are to be attributed—the governess, the children, various versions of "Henry James" (as the disappointed playwright, as subject to "vastations," as repeating a paternal injury . . .). What we need to see here is that the "mind" is demanded by the truth claims of the analysis, and that the satisfaction of this demand only creates new difficulties.

The salient features of Wilson's interpretation are features it shares with the larger tradition of psychoanalytic criticism and may be summed up as follows:

1. The enterprise is knowing and veridical; it seeks to know the truth of the text.

2. This truth lies "behind" or "beneath" the text, which becomes an occlusive rhetorical screen, an obstacle, to be gotten through or past in the search for truth.

3. This truth is immediately and nonproblematically recognizable once one knows to look for it. It is a truth guaranteed by the science of psychoanalysis.

4. Because the truth found in the literary text is psychoanalytic, it has to be attributed to a mind—but once the field of truth is cut free of the rhetorical screen of the text there is no principle by which the location of the relevant mind can be determined.

5. The relevant mind is then constructed through another narrative—"the real story"—which comes to take up the place and fill in the blanks of the text that was initially to be interpreted.

6. But the location of this mind is unstable and immediately reversible into another mind and another "real story"—that of the author—the blanks of which are now filled in by the text.

The peculiar structural lability at work here is hardly captured by the statement that psychoanalysis demands a mind. It seems more nearly accurate to say that a mind is imposed by the exigencies of psychoanalytic interpretation and its claim to truth; and that it is a necessary concomitant of this that the mind imposed cannot then be positioned, so that the imposition of mind results in an oscillatory framing effect in which either the text serves only to frame the mind within it or the text serves only to display the mind by which it is framed (and here one may perhaps glimpse something of the way in which a sort of reader response criticism is inscribed also within this system). So that one is tempted to say that the psychoanalytic demand for mind is at once a posing and deposing of that mind.[11] It should be clear that we are dealing with a system of mutual implication that can be entered in several different ways. What matters is to see how the system of truth, mind, and narrative is put to work when one undertakes to know a text psychoanalytically.

—Psychoanalysis (de)poses a mind.

The simple slogan I set out to oppose to Holland's demand turns out to carry within itself a certain complexity—and, in fact, all the complexity I will shortly want to redispose within the statement that psychoanalysis demands a mind. It should be remarked that we have come to this pass by following out what appeared to be one side of a choice, but that our recovered slogan does not allow the easy distinction between two types of psychoanalytic criticism—one of "minds" and one of "texts"—set up at the outset. Rather, it restores a measure of real duplicity to the double possibility I have claimed to be always involved in the notion of psychoanalytic criticism. We can say that one effect of Holland's proposition has been to break that duplicity into a simpler and more absolute relation of mutual exeriority, so that any attempt (like the present) to reestablish the possibility of what appears therein as a "psychoanalysis of the text" in opposition to a psychoanalytic knowledge of relevant minds is inevitably an attack upon the choice itself. The difference between the two is no longer a matter of epistemology or objectivity, but one of acknowledgment—of the way in which one comes to grips with the psychoanalytic posing of mind in literary criticism.[12]—Just as this essay is an attempt to acknowledge the assertion that psychoanalysis demands a mind.

What we want, obviously, is to find a way to approach the literary work such that it no longer serves only to display—to be, variously, the internal or external frame for—the truth of psychoanalysis. (More exactly: we want to find a way of understanding psychoanalytic criticism that will allow us to acknowledge the strength we have always recognized in good psychoanalytic criticism—that is, criticism that is more or other than an illustration of psychoanalytic truth. Our issue is not "methodological.") I am suggesting that Wilson makes a certain kind of mistake—a failure of recognition, a mistake about what it is that he is doing—with the result that he is, finally, unable to do what he wants to do. (This formulation is intended to have psychoanalytic overtones; the question then is, Can Wilson's version of psychoanalysis let us hear these overtones? or, Is this a mistake like getting the truth about X wrong, and so correctable simply by getting it right?) The activity of psychoanalytic criticism, I want to say, is one that poses a mind in a way that is ineluctably problematic; and this problem is one on which the possibility of psychoanalytic criticism turns.[13]

The central problem for psychoanalytic criticism on this view is not "reductionism" in opposition to "non-reductionism" (Crews is quite right about the inevitability of reduction), but of the acknowledgment of that reduction—the explicit posing of that logic by which psychoanalytic interpretation both poses and deposes a mind. It should be clear that what I call "acknowledgment" is not simple, consisting both in an appropriation or recognition of oneself and in a contestation of that identification (and here too there are psychoanalytic overtones that are not wholly comprehensible to a psychoanalysis that sees itself as knowing the truth about minds).[14] An essay that would attempt this sort of acknowledgment[15] can look like an attack on the possibility of any psychoanalytic criticism whatsoever at least as much as it can look like a piece of psychoanalytic criticism. And it is certainly part of what I am arguing here that this is the way psychoanalytic criticism should look. In the long run I will want to take this even further: if psychoanalytic criticism can look like this, it is because psychoanalysis itself is not what it is taken to be in the construction of a relation of mutual exteriority between the psychoanalysis of minds and the psychoanalysis of texts.

Shoshana Felman's "Turning the Screw of Interpretation" is organized by a complex system of acknowledgments—of *The Turn of the Screw*, of the critical history it has generated, and of the situation of psychoanalysis in the literary work; this is, I believe, what makes it compelling criticism. Here I can consider only briefly one relatively minor moment of the essay.

We have already paused over this moment in Wilson's reading: Flora's "phallic" play with the two pieces of wood that she assembles into a little sailboat. No doubt more recent psychoanalytic criticism would want to spell things out more fully here, but it—no more than Wilson—would have no serious problems about what a phallus is— what and how it might mean. It belongs to the psychoanalytic truth we bring to and find in the text (as Felman puts it, it is an answer and not a question). It deserves notice that Wilson does not even have to say outright that he is talking about a phallus—let alone give some explanation of it.[16] At a basic rhetorical level, Wilson can do this only because he knows that we know, simply by "observing," what this is all about.

The scene comes up several times in Felman's essay, but centrally in her section VII ("A Child Is Killed"). She is led to consider it on this occasion because it seems to be a sort of actualization within the reality of the story of one of the text's leading metaphors for the governess herself. Insofar as she is determined to make sense and stay in control of her situation, the governess is repeatedly figured as the helmsman of a boat; and it is thus unsurprising that this appearance of a boat decides her search for a single meaning behind the children[17]—Flora's screwing of one stick into another is the one thing she finds about which there can be no ambiguity, a pure epistemological moment and breakthrough to the truth. (It is the crux of the story she is interpreting precisely analogous to that single, crucial scene that would not allow of a Freudian double reading so sought after by the anti-Freudian interpreters of The Turn of the Screw; in all three instances—Freudian, anti-Freudian, and that of the governess—the emergence of such a crux is an artifact of a certain problematic imputation of truth to the story.)

As Felman explores the textual web in which this boat and its phallic mast figure—a web that ties together metaphors of helmsman and tiller, the death of little Miles, an allusion to the title, an inevitable evocation of the Master, and so on—we begin to see that what matters is not that the mast is a phallic symbol ("long-hard-vertical"), but that what we recognize as a phallus is recognized as such because of the way it functions as a particular node in the rhetorical structure of the text. The risk we run in simply calling the mast a phallus is thinking that with this we have said something, that we have managed to abstract some transparently meaningful truth from the occlusive rhetoric of the text.[18]

To put this another way: it is as true (and no more true) in literature as it is in life that sometimes a cigar is just a cigar, so if you are to persuade me that our friend Jacques is smoking his phallus, you are going to have to do something more than describe its shape; you are going to have to show how it functions for him. If we accept Flora's mast as phallic, it is only the way in which it belongs to the ("merely") rhetorical web of the text that can tell us what "phallic" means here—and, further, this meaning may be one from which we cannot exempt ourselves as neutral and exterior knowers.[19] To recognize how this phallus means is to be called upon to recognize also how we stand behind the governess as she watches Flora and say our "She knows! She knows!" in chorus with her.

"Knowledge"—knowledge as what one sees through to, behind the screen of the merely given—is precisely what is at stake in The Turn of the Screw[20]; and we have to acknowledge explicitly that we can make our claim to psychoanalytic knowledge of the real narrative only by failing the simplest and most obvious reading of these stakes. We can see the phallus as clear and untroubled meaning, the simple truth of a certain scene, only if we have already denied everything in the text that argues the impossibility and, eventually, the tragedy of this seeing. On the simplest reading of the text, this sort of seeing, this impulse toward naming, kills. Perhaps more pointedly, we can say that this activity is revealed as fetishistic, clinging to the meaning and identity of the phallus in the face of a world in which that kind of simplicity must be surrendered. And this fetishism can be recognized in the governess only on the condition that we acknowledge it in our (psychoanalytically knowing) selves as well.

All of this is an attempt, following Felman, to show something of the way in which psychoanalysis itself is staked in the text it would read—to suggest that every piece of psychoanalytic criticism is as much a rereading of Freud across the literary text as it is a reading of the text itself. And it is important to see that this is as true of Wilson as it is of Felman—the issue I want to set between them is whether and how this fact is to be acknowledged, and what this means about how we are going to have to understand the assertion that psychoanalysis demands a mind.

To this point I have treated the phallus as one example among others, but implicit within that treatment is its repetition at a higher level. The phallus here is not simply one example among others, but the privileged example for psychoanalytic criticism insofar as psychoanalysis sees the literary text as a vehicle for the articulation and illustration of the pre-existent truths of the science. It is, in effect, the example of examples.

With this assertion I am, however, moving toward a more abstract and Lacanian use of the word "phallus," a use that assumes a certain willingness to return to Freud—a willingness that may not be forthcoming from many of those currently interested in psychoanalysis. While I am not saying that the only criticism I am willing to count as psychoanalytic is criticism that hunts out *phalloi* (roughly, Holland's phase 1), I am trying to point to a function within any psychoanalytic criticism whatsoever, which—in one or another critical instance—may be variously filled by the penis, or the devouring mother, or the narcissistic wound; and this function, within a strictly Freudian perspective, must be recognized as phallic—that is, as one by which the critic protects himself and his integrity, the exterior neutrality of his knowing, from the fact and presence of the other[21]—just as the claim to be the phallus and a concomitant denial of castration function as the guarantee of the inviolability and integrity of the narcissistic or Imaginary (Lacan's term) child in the face of Oedipus. This sort of guarantee of the self in its radical autonomy or of knowledge in its radical exteriority is, however, achieved only at a certain cost: Freud's little patient[22] had "an anxious susceptibility against either of his little toes being touched"; and Wilson, in like manner, can safeguard the truth of his example only by displacing the textual ambiguity by which he was initially troubled through the various cruxes engendered by his analysis and into the question of the mind under analysis. So that we begin by knowing the truth and end by finding ourselves caught up in a chain of oscillations that will not allow us to know where we have found this truth.

But if we can see this, we can see also that the central question can no longer be presented as bearing merely upon the application of psychoanalysis to literature (this restriction already collapsed with the calling into question of the distinction between a psychoanalysis of minds and a psychoanalysis of texts in literary criticism); the question about psychoanalytic criticism is a question about psychoanalysis itself—about the way in which truth and knowledge, demand and desire, articulate themselves around the phallus. And a part of what this question is going to have to understand is what it means that psychoanalysis can come to this sort of problematic recognition of itself in (can be called into question by) the literary text. The general assertions toward which I am tending should be fairly clear: psychoanalysis cannot exempt itself from itself; the analyst cannot simply know; the inscription of an auto-analysis into the historical foundations of psychoanalysis is not simply accidental.[23] The suggestion is that psychoanalysis is founded upon and finds its sense in a dialectic of self and other that cannot be confined to the merely objective, but which rebounds upon and determines the inner theoretical structure of the discipline itself. At this very general level, the claim is that psychoanalysis cannot find its truth out there, in the world, except by passing through a moment in which it places itself at risk—and that this can be accomplished only through an other, through and across which psychoanalysis comes to acknowledge itself. And all this moves toward envisioning a relation between psychoanalysis and literature that is possessed of a greater necessity than we are used to assuming (a relation that might, for example, let us begin to see something of why so many psychoanalytic concepts find their first articulation through literary "examples" [like Oedipus]: examples possessed of that sort of foundational power, that ability to forge self-recognition, are examples that are no longer accidental and exterior to the field; they are comments on the structure of the field itself—

there is nothing obvious about the ways in which truth, knowledge, and recognition are at work in Freud dreaming Sophocles).

—Psychoanalysis demands a mind.

This is then not a statement about the conditions to which psychoanalytic criticism must answer; it is the position of a problem within psychoanalysis itself. We have come to the point of recognizing that there is nothing simple or obvious about what this statement means, and that it cannot be accepted uncritically and apart from some psychoanalytic parsing of "demand."

I would suggest that Jacques Lacan has become important for psychoanalysis and for psychoanalytic criticism in part because he offers a way of coming to grips with "what psychoanalysis demands." Lacan's relevance to literary criticism is usually taken to reside in his central claim that the Unconscious is structured as a language. This does seem to reopen the possibility of a "psychoanalysis of the text," but the claim itself is comprehensible only on the basis of Lacan's radical reconstruction of psychoanalysis as a discipline, the truth of which lies in its adherence to its object (the Unconscious)—and not as a "science." The vision of psychoanalysis that emerges from this rethinking is one that does not easily tolerate the distinction of a "psychoanalysis of texts" from a "psychoanalysis of minds," and so determines the limits of any "application" of Lacan's theses to the literary object. (As I have indicated earlier [note 16], it is not clear that Lacan himself understands this as fully as he might.)

In the following pages I want to explore how Lacan lets us come to grips with our psychoanalytic demand—that is, I will explore the way in which psychoanalysis finds its claim to objectivity from within a dialectic of demand and desire. This elucidation of demand will be developed from an essay entitled "The Signification of the Phallus."[24] The linkage of the notions of demand and of the phallus has been throughout our implicit guiding thread and is now our explicit object. Along the way we shall reencounter, and place, the central Lacanian claim about the linguistic structure of the Unconscious.

I would suggest that, for the most part, we operate with an implicit picture of psychoanalysis that recognizes "desire" as a central theoretical term (and practical issue) which is understood to be directly connected to a biology of needs (to such an extent that there is no theoretically marked difference between desire and need: they name equally the working of the "sexual instinct"). It is because the analysand has a problem at the level of desire/need that he or she may be (incidentally) described as "demanding"—but "demand" itself is not the sort of term that stands in need of any theoretical clarification; it functions only "adjectivally."

The Lacanian picture I will present insists, in contrast, on the necessity for a detailed theoretical articulation of the three terms, "need," "demand," and "desire"; the stakes here are not simply clarity or some specious rigor, but the autonomy and disciplinary standing of psychoanalysis itself. From this position, what is profoundly problematic in the more or less ordinary understanding I have sketched above is its willingness to understand psychoanalysis as either ultimately biological or nonproblematically independent of biology. The problem here is that the simple assertion of the autonomy of psychoanalysis (the assertion that a reduction to biology simply will not happen) leaves that reduction in principle possible and enforces an understanding of the root concepts of psychoanalysis as metaphors for a biological reality. What is needed is a way of spelling out both how psychoanalysis depends upon biology in order to found itself and how psychoanalysis thereby founds itself as other than biological.[25] And this entails a construal of sexuality in psychoanalysis as something other than, but related to, the biological business of mating and reproduction—that is, we are going to need the distinction, registered in Freud's German, between "instinct" and the motive of sexuality, "drive." In general, we are going to refer to "instinct" and "need" together as answering to the biological roots of psychoanalysis in opposition to the more properly psychoanalytic notions of "drive" and "desire"; "demand" will be the term through which this distinction is to be negotiated.

The three terms constitute less a progression (as if in attaining to "desire" one left "need" somehow behind) than the tying of an essential knot (and, as we will see, also the untying of a knot). This knottedness will end by guiding our reinterpretation of the received notions of sexual development and its stages—oral, anal, phallic, genital—as well. Very roughly, we are going to be saying that human being is the sort of being (being that speaks) whose needs can emerge only through demands which already surpass the objects of need, and for whom the object of demand necessarily reemerges as the articulated object of desire—but (and here is the knot) also one for whom demand and need are only fully distinguished from the standpoint of desire (which is then the untying of the knottedness of demand and need). The Lacanian *topos* with which we are concerned here is that of the location of the subject of desire in the splitting of demand (gnomically notated by Lacan as $\$ \lozenge D$), and the concomitant emergence of a sexual drive that is propped up "anaclitically" on the logic of instinct and need.[26]

Lacan's explanation takes the form of a highly abstract pseudo-Hegelian dialectic, which I will here intercalate with what I hope will prove to be a usefully concrete description.

In general: "That which is . . . alienated in needs constitutes an *Urverdrängung* (primal repression), an inability, it is supposed, to be articulated in demand, but it re-appears in something it gives rise to that presents itself in man as desire (*das Begehren*)." (I have elided in this citation a "thus" to which we will return in considering the signification of the phallus; in so doing I have flattened out a complex structure so as to make it more amenable to narrative presentation, at a certain cost in accuracy.)

If a child cries out for its mother's presence, how can it do so except by crying out to her and to her implication in language and sense? For a being that speaks a cry—like silence—can no longer be brute, innocent, insignificant, total—so the infant's cry for presence is always already necessarily a cry for the mother's breast or for her holding it or for her changing it; and when she does these things, what has become of the child's demand insofar as it surpasses the need through or upon which it was articulated? The breast the mother gives it satisfies its need for nurturance, but at the same time marks out as well the shadowed outline of that other and irreal breast that would answer to the radicality of the child's demand for nothing more than its mother's absolute presence to it, her fulfillment of it insofar as it is not whole. The child's entanglement in need and demand conceals and reveals an inchoate and inarticulate recognition of the way in which to be human is to be always somewhat less-than-whole, to be involved essentially with an other for the very terms in which one would make one's self present to oneself. (Lacan: "In any case, man cannot aim at being whole [the 'total personality' is another of the deviant premises of modern psychotherapy], while ever the play of displacement and condensation to which he is doomed in the exercise of his functions marks his relation as a subject to the signifier.") What the child demands is a radical presence that is invariably absent and is marked as such precisely through the mother's satisfaction of its needs. ("Demand in itself bears on something other than the satisfactions it calls for. It is demand of a presence or of an absence—which is what is manifested in the primordial relation to the mother, pregnant with that Other to be situated *within* the needs that it can satisfy. Demand constitutes the Other as already possessing the 'privilege' of satisfying needs, that is to say, the power of depriving them of that alone by which they are satisfied.")

Nothing that the mother can give the child when the child cries out for her can satisfy that for which it is crying insofar as it is crying out beyond its needs (and this nothing that she can give it will be her love). But everything she does give it reduces the child's demand to need(s), and it is left with its (surpassing) demand—which then gives itself always and necessarily as sheerly gratuitous. ("In this way, demand annuls [*aufhebt*] the particularity of everything that can be granted by transmuting it into a proof of love, and the very satisfactions that it obtains for need are reduced [*sich erniedrigt*] to the level of being no more than the crushing of the demand for love . . .") The child's demand can become more than gratuitous only by reasserting its particularity at a "higher" level—now not the breast the mother can give the child, but that other breast that counts for it, that is capable of bearing the weight of the child's meaning and self—for it is finally the self that is at stake in the child's demand for radical presence.

This other breast through which the child would be whole and present to itself is the breast that is (in the place of) the object of desire. Lacan thus arrives at his statement of desire:

> It is necessary, then, that the particularity thus abolished should reappear *beyond* demand. . . . By a reversal that is not simply the negation of the negation, the power of pure loss emerges from the residue of an obliteration. For the unconditional element of demand, desire substitutes the "absolute" condition: this condition unties the knot of that element in the proof of love that is resistant to the satisfaction of a need. Thus desire is neither the appetite for satisfaction, nor the demand for love, but the difference that results from the subtraction of the first from the second, the phenomenon of their splitting (*Spaltung*).

This rearticulation of objects beyond the objects of need is conceivable only within an order of signification; and this point returns us to the "thus" elided at the beginning of this discussion—the "thus" that marks the passage from the blankness of demand into the signification of desire.

Signification is that wherein we are inscribed from the outset—an order of language and society by which we are named and in which it is not possible to name our self as if out of some prior and proper self. It is because there is no way to human being except through this inscription that there is a limit we can assign to the biology of instinct and need. Being human—being the being that speaks—is always already a break with the simplicity of instinct. Feeding, evacuating, mating . . . all these acts count for us by counting for us—by the ways in which they are precisely not natural but traversed and constituted by a web of signification.

With this we are approaching once again the way in which need inevitably entails a demand that escapes or surpasses its point of articulation—so that if I am at your breast, I nurse not only at the breast that is there, but also at that other which is not; and so mark myself—my lips, my mouth—as also that place where I would be my self: an erotogenic zone appears as the significant inscription of a site for the attainment of a totality of self. My "oral fantasies" are the stage on which I play myself as whole.

The emergence of the articulated particularity of desire and my accession to it (acknowledgment of it) is (in a certain sense) the surrender of these stages through an acceptance of the fact of castration. Herein lies the psychoanalytic privilege of the phallus as that which is at once the summation of my fantasies (the ultimate locus of my claim to totality) and something other than (mere) fantasy—the signifier through which the possibility and necessity of signification itself are realized for me. The phallus is not mine and cannot ground my claims to integral identity and self-presence; it is that through which sexuality as such (that is to say as other than instinctive) is articulated within the larger socio-linguistic ("Symbolic") order. So that when I play myself on this stage, I can end only by finding that this stage is not mine to play upon—and that no stage ever was. Lacan describes the phallus as "a signifier intended to designate as a whole the effects of the signified, in that the signifier conditions them by its presence as a signifier"—which is to say, among other things, that it sets in motion a logic of deferred action that radically transforms the apparently linear development we are accustomed to assume in Freud's accounts of sexuality. Something of the complexity involved here is reflected in our own initial suspension of the "thus" in offering a general statement of the dialectic of need, demand, and desire.

We are discussing what appears, under one light, as a submission of the child to the priority of language and society as it opens the order of signification or of filiation and alliance—a priority that is classically marked by the intervention of the father in the closed and fantastic world of mother and child.[27] But this submission also unravels the complicity of need and demand so as to allow the re-emergence of particularity and objectivity beyond demand and as desire. This "submission" is also an act of acknowledgment, a coming to terms with the conditions of selfhood and objectivity—conditions which found them as (properly) problematic.

—Psychoanalysis demands a mind.

My gloss upon Lacan, for all its brevity and abstraction, has, I hope, at least served to point toward what it might mean to say that "psychoanalysis demands a mind" once it is recognized that such an assertion cannot not read itself: either the psychoanalytic demand for mind remains locked in a fantasy of autonomy and inviolability that it cannot articulate, or it must acknowledge itself as a desire for that which, in principle, always exists elsewhere and beyond, not subject to any simple subsumption under the identity of psychoanalysis; psychoanalytic criticism can either insist upon finding itself and only itself in its literary other, or it can admit its implication in and dependence upon a larger universe of critical discourse.

About psychoanalysis and psychoanalytic criticism I will want then to say the following:

—Psychoanalysis as a discipline is complexly structured, at once epistemologically unconstrained and radically self-critical—or: always capable of reducing a text to its psychoanalytic truth and always subject to its own dismantling by the text it would (simply) know.

—Literature is not simply and accidentally connected to psychoanalysis as a projection or illustration of psychoanalytic knowledge and truth; psychoanalytic literary criticism is a necessary moment within psychoanalytic self-understanding and self-criticism.

—Psychoanalytic criticism, whatever its particular "methodological" stance, will always be a form of "phallus-hunting" (this is part of what it means for psychoanalysis to demand a mind); but a criticism that would maintain itself purely as this demand will inevitably fail to understand—to pose—itself, and so end by losing itself and its object as it were behind its own back.

—A psychoanalytic criticism that would acknowledge both itself and its literary object will, in certain respects, look like an anti-psychoanalytic criticism—precisely because it holds itself in the self-critical limits of the discipline.

—Such criticism will also look like a peculiar mode of reader response criticism—not Holland's mode, since it will have no use for the first person and will not depend upon clinically tested reader-subjects. The impulse to it is perhaps nonetheless captured in Holland's description of his own program: "We express and re-create ourselves in our interpretations—that we have always done—but now we can do it understandingly."[28] But when we say this now, what we mean is that psychoanalysis facing the text is already a reader facing the text. Psychoanalysis can demand a mind because psychoanalysis itself is structured as a person: in this knot all the senses I have attributed to "psychoanalysis demands a mind" meet and find what unity, propriety, and self-presence are there to be found.

The consequences of this position are not immediately clear, nor are they easy to bear, and some elucidation of them seems in order. To say that psychoanalysis is like a person is to say, among other things, that it is prone to misunderstand itself, to make mistakes, to go astray even as it takes itself to be true to itself, to lose track of what and how it means—and that all of this is as if proper to what psychoanalysis is ("when it is true to itself"). Or it means that the project of constructing an understanding of psychoanalysis that would be exempt from such error or that would be able to guarantee itself against the predations of time and accident is one that invariably entails some loss of the "proper" content of psychoanalysis— and this is to say that such "predations" are not "predations" in the way we usually mean.[29]

It is possible to read this essay—and no doubt it will be so read— as a championing of something new and Lacanian against something old and "traditional." It would be foolish of me to claim that this is not going on here, but it should be pointed out that this opposition is subsumed under a problematic of recognition and acknowledgment that precludes any radical dismissal or exclusion of "the traditional" —and that precludes as well any final rest within the presumptive truth of Lacan's reading of psychoanalysis. Rather, what I am claiming as a strength of Lacan's rereading of Freud is its ability to pose its own problematic openness to, for example, Derrida's critique of it. If one were to ask whether the position taken here is Lacanian or Derridean,[30] I could only respond that a part of the meaning of "psychoanalysis demands a mind" is that persons and positions are not connected that way—or that psychoanalytic theory is not decidable that way, insisting instead precisely in the possibility of such controversies—even as it insists in the controversy between Lacan and "the tradition." The difficulties here are the difficulties proper to that which would deploy itself in the field of language and desire not as a knowledge of the self but as criticism of the self; they are inscribed within the irreducible tension at work in the psychoanalytic demand for mind.

NOTES

1. I will want, in the end, to say "*is* coeval with the notion of psychoanalysis itself"—but this needs some preparation.

2. I refer here especially to Frederick Crews, "Reductionism and its Discontents," *Critical Inquiry*, vol. 1, no. 3; and Norman Holland, "Literary Interpretation and Three Phases of Psychoanalysis," *Critical Inquiry*, vol. 3, no. 2.

3. The reference is to "The Next New Criticism," *The Nation*, vol. 192 (April 22, 1961)—but the statement is interesting only insofar as, shorn of its context, it has become, in others' hands, a club with which to beat back a certain type of problem.

4. The first of these is Edmund Wilson's famous paper, "The Ambiguity of Henry James," which can be found in Gerald Willen (ed.), *A Casebook on Henry James's The Turn of the Screw* (New York: Thomas Y. Crowell Co., 1960, pp. 115–153). The second is Shoshana Felman's long essay, "Turning the Screw of Interpretation," in *Yale French Studies*, no. 55/56 (*Literature and Psychoanalysis: The Question of Reading: Otherwise*), pp. 94–207.

5. There is one obvious sense to this statement that is to be suspended for a while, and that is the straightforward "clinical" and "scientific" sense the statement would seem to have for psychoanalysis proper. There is another sense the rightness of which must unfortunately be stressed—a sense that opposes "mind" to "institutional orthodoxy."

6. Crews (*op. cit.*) is very good on these points; he seems particularly sensitive to the structural lability I am pointing to here. I would claim that this lability is a direct reflection and consequence of the sorts of problems that I will be raising through Wilson's essay on James.

7. Crews's remark is to the point: ". . . Holland seems to me to be forgetting the entire rc˙ ,on d'être of critical activity. We don't go to criticism to discover Seymour's identity theme, or Holland's, or Frank Kermode's, or anyone else's. We go to criticism because we hope to learn more about literature than we could have figured out for ourselves." *Op. cit.*, p. 554. All the same, there is something about the impulse to reader response that needs to be accounted for and to which I will return at the end of this article.

8. Wilson, *op. cit.*, p. 115.

9. Wilson, p. 117.

10. That such an oscillation is in fact necessary may not be readily apparent; it might seem (traditionally has seemed) that the slide to the author's mind is inevitable, but that there is nothing that would compel a slide back into the fiction. In part this involves an argument about what literary criticism is, and it may be taken as a measure of Wilson's literary critical integrity that he insists on the return to the fiction when (in 1959) he can see his way

to it. But the central point here is that the slide to the author's mind is itself already a slide into further narrative and can (and will) be criticized as such if the "diagnosis" is contested. Here again the "reading" can be saved only by a retreat back into the text; if my reading of "James" is shown to be "wrong" or profoundly problematic, I save myself by insisting on the dynamics I have found in the text, but now reassign them, after all, to the governess . . . The necessity inheres in the controversies that follow from a certain assumption about the divisibility of minds and texts, an assumption that is being contested here.

11. In the recent essay "Coming into One's Own" (in Goeffrey Hartman, ed., *Psychoanalysis and the Question of the Text*, Baltimore: Johns Hopkins, 1979) Jacques Derrida has been led to an interestingly parallel assertion in reading *Beyond the Pleasure Principle:* "The auto-biography of *writing* at once posits and deposes, in the same motion, the psychoanalytic movement" (p. 120). I take it that Derrida and I are, roughly, working at different ends of the same problem—a problem that can be described as that of psychoanalytic closure and self-mastery.

12. An impulse to reader response criticism is inscribed here insofar as it is an attempt to come to grips with the posing of the psychoanalyst's mind in literary criticism.

13. This means that there is no question of doing away with "Wilsonian" analyses; such analyses are necessary. But not sufficient.

14. I should state that my thinking about and use of "acknowledgment" derives much from reading Stanley Cavell's *Must We Mean What We Say?* (Cambridge: Cambridge University Press, 1976) and his more recent *The Claim of Reason: Wittgenstein, Skepticism, Morality, and Tragedy* (Oxford: Oxford University Press, 1979). I would, nonetheless, not want to claim to be using it in his sense; at best I may be moving toward that sense.

15. I refer here in particular to Felman's "Turning the Screw of Interpretation."

16. In many ways Jacques Lacan is the hero of my argument, but—as Lorna Gladstone has pointed out to me—he is able to employ exactly the same rhetorical maneuver in his seminar on Poe's "The Purloined Letter." That his reading of Freud may be enabling for literary criticism does not mean that his readings are necessarily paradigmatic for criticism. Derrida's critique of Lacan can be said to begin from the disparity between Lacan's analytic sophistication and his critical naiveté.

17. Felman, *op. cit.*, pp. 161–177; pages 169–174 are especially to the point.

18. A parallel point has been made frequently by phenomenologically inclined psychoanalysts. See for example Jacob Needleman's statement in his introduction to the work of the analyst and literary critic Ludwig Binswanger, *Being-in-the-World* (New York: Harper & Row, 1968): "If knife is said to be symbol of the phallus, understanding of the patient falls short if it is not further asked: What does the phallus mean to the individual? The full phenomenal meaning of the knife in the world of the patient must be laid forth before the analyst can understand what phallus means to the patient. In psychoanalysis, however, the question is: What does the knife mean? And the answer, the phallus, presupposes that all meaning-direction emanates from a biological need. This ignores the possibility that these biological needs are themselves enmeshed in a larger meaning-matrix and, therefore, themselves point to something beyond themselves. It also, if the analyst is

not careful, presupposes a *fixed* notion of what phallus means to any individual" (p. 74). From a Lacanian point of view, the problem with this formulation is its too easy assumption of a simple opposition between "meaning" and "biology."

19. Here again we can catch a glimpse of the way in which something like a reader response criticism seems to haunt the field of psychoanalytic criticism.

20. This point I take to stand free of any psychoanalytic interpretation; it is given in James's initial idea of a ghost story for the jaded, a ghost story that would chill its audience despite that audience's knowledge of such stories. It seems to me important that a psychoanalytic criticism should be able to make this sort of contact with more traditional critical modes (even if only to contest them).

21. Here again we touch upon an impulse to something that would be a reader response criticism: "This third phase is not a retreat to subjectivity. It is a giving up the illusion that I can only understand reality (or a text) by keeping myself out." (Holland, "Three Phases . . . ," p. 231.)

22. The case is from "Splitting of the Ego in the Defensive Process" as given in *Sexuality and the Psychology of Love* (New York: Collier Books, 1963, pp. 220–223.). It will be found in volume 23, p. 271 ff. of the standard edition.

23. These remarks intend to point toward the difficult but nonetheless clear privilege that must be accorded to the Freudian text within psychoanalysis. There is something proper to psychoanalysis that makes it "personal" in a way that physics, say, is not. Derrida's "Coming into One's Own" is very much concerned with this matter, although from a somewhat different angle; we might remark Derrida's description of the Freud of *Beyond the Pleasure Principle* "producing the institution of his desire, making it the start of his own genealogy, making the tribunal and the legal tradition his heritage, his to delegate, his legacy, *his own*" (p. 116).

24. The citations will be drawn from Alan Sheridan's (partial) translation of Lacan's *Ecrits* (New York: W. W. Norton & Co., 1977, pp. 281–291). The essay will be found on pp. 685–95 of the French text (Seuil, 1966).

25. On this general topic Jean Laplanche's *Life and Death in Psychoanalysis* (Baltimore: Johns Hopkins, 1976) is both important and useful.

26. This "splitting" of demand is directly reflected in the double framing by the literary text of the mind demanded as discussed on page 439 above.

27. The exact status of the classical triad of momma, poppa, and baby is a matter of continuing and politically significant controversy. The controversy is not settled but may be suspended for the space of this essay by remarking that it can be reformulated in terms of logical places and the disruption of what would be a closed binary system by a third element. This is, I think, a legitimate begging of a question I hope to address elsewhere.

28. Holland, "Three Phases . . . ," p. 233.

29. Here, for the last time, I direct the reader toward Derrida's writings on Freud and on Lacan—"The Purveyor of Truth" (*Yale French Studies*, no. 52: *Graphesis: Perspectives in Literature and Philosophy*); "Coming into One's Own"; and "Speculations—on Freud," *Oxford Literary Review* vol. 3 no. 2. (These two texts have now appeared as sections of a much longer essay on *Beyond the Pleasure Principle* entitled "Speculer—sur Freud." This piece, along with several other essays on psychoanalysis, appears in

Derrida's *La Carte Postale: de Socrate à Freud et au-delà* (Paris: Aubier-Flammarion, 1980).

30. The position taken here has certain affinities as well with that of Nicholas Abraham and Maria Torok in "The Shell and the Kernel," *Diacritics* vol. 9 no. 1 (Spring 1979) and Derrida's introduction to it, "Me—Psychoanalysis."

I would like to acknowledge the help and support of the various Chicago Gnu critics.

VI. AESTHETICS AS A PHILOSOPHICAL DISCIPLINE

Introduction

The renaissance of aesthetics in contemporary Anglo-American philosophy began with the attempt to use the methods of linguistic analysis on both the problems of traditional aesthetics and the texts which those problems had generated. In the essays by W. E. Kennick and Guy Sircello, we can trace the evolution of this attempt. In the essay by Kennick, the logical analysis of arguments tends to separate itself from the diagnosis of the human impulses which give rise to those arguments. The analysis of *what* traditional philosophers have said is separated from the account of *why* they have said what said. In the later piece by Guy Sircello, we find a heightened awareness of the degree to which the judgment of the ordinary language philosopher on *what* is said entails a confrontation with the "form of life" in which the statement in question is embedded. Sircello exhibits the realization that "ordinary language" is not a *kind* of language opposed to "philosophical language," and that the obligation of the ordinary language philosopher is precisely to discover the ways in which philosophical language can be ordinary language.

The two remaining essays represent what seem to the editors to be potentially the two most fruitful approaches to aesthetics and the philosophy of art today, not least insofar as they do not merely illustrate a method, but do so in a way that gives shape and focus to the field as a whole. The essay by J. Hillis Miller provides an introduction both to the method of deconstruction and the problem of textuality and reading, while the essay by Stanley Cavell uses the methods of ordinary language philosophy and delineates the problem of modernism in the arts. It would be useless to try to summarize these two very substantial pieces; to the extent that the problems of textuality and of modernity (if indeed they are two distinct problems) inhabit the heart of philosophy as a whole, this anthology may

457

be said to close with two meditations on philosophy as an aesthetical discipline.

For more on the debate over the impact of linguistic analysis on the attempt to produce a definition of art, a debate which connects the essays by Kennick and Sircello, see Bond, Brown, Carney, Gallie, Mandelbaum, Margolis (7), Passmore, Sclafani (3), Tollefson, and Zerbey. On the method of deconstruction and its impact on criticism and philosophy, see (besides the writers Professor Miller mentions, especially Derrida) particularly Bass, Donato, Felman (1), Hartman (4, 5), B. Johnson (1), and Klein (2); see also Abel, Barthes, Borinsky, Culler, Michaels, Nelson, Riddel, Said, Shell, Spivak, Rowe, and Ryan. Rorty provides a lucid introduction to Derrida from the standpoint of analytic philosophy, while Abrams and Booth (2) provide a somewhat more critical account. Professor Cavell's essay deals in part with the issue of the concept of intention in works of art; this issue has its origin in Wimsatt and Beardsley (2) and may be followed up in Cioffi, R. Freedman, Hancher (2), Hungerland (1), Kemp, Kuhns (2), Lang (3), Romo, Savile (2), and Skinner. Concerns close to those of Professor Cavell are treated in Bates, Fried, and Rothman.

Does Traditional Aesthetics Rest on a Mistake?

W. E. Kennick

It rests, I think, on at least two of them, and the purpose of this paper is to explore the claim that it does.

By "traditional aesthetics" I mean that familiar philosophical discipline which concerns itself with trying to answer such questions as the following: What is Art? What is Beauty? What is the Aesthetic Experience? What is the Creative Act? What are the criteria of Aesthetic Judgment and Taste? What is the function of Criticism? To be sure, there are others, like: Are the aesthetic object and the work of art the same? or, Does art have any cognitive content?—but these questions are commonly taken to be subordinate to those of the first group, which might be called the "basic questions" of traditional aesthetics.

1. *The Basic Questions as Requests for Definitions.* If someone asks me "What is helium?" I can reply: "It's a gas" or "It's a chemical element" or "It's a gaseous element, inert and colorless, whose atomic number is 2, and whose atomic weight is 4.003." A number of replies will do, depending upon whom I am talking to, the aim of his question, and so on. It is a pretty straightforward business; we get answers to such questions every day from dictionaries, encyclopedias, and technical manuals.

Now someone asks me "What is Space?" or "What is Man?" or "What is Religion?" or "What is Art?" His question is of the same form as the question "What is helium?" but how vastly different! There is something very puzzling about these questions; they cannot be answered readily by appealing to dictionaries, encyclopedias, or technical manuals. They are philosophical questions, we say, giving our puzzlement a name, although we should not think of calling "What is helium?" a philosophical question. Yet we expect something of the same sort of answer to both of them. There's the rub.

We say that questions like "What is Space?" or "What is Art?"

are requests for information about the nature or essence of Space or
of Art. We could say that "What is helium?" is a request for information about the nature or essence of helium, but we rarely, if ever, do;
although we do use questions like "What is helium?" as analogues of
questions like "What is Space?" to show the sort of reply we are
looking for. What we want, we say, is a definition of Space or of Art,
for as Plato and Aristotle taught us long ago, "definition is the formula of the essence." So, just as the traditional metaphysicians have
long sought for the nature or essence of Space and of Time, of
Reality and of Change, the traditional aesthetician has sought for the
essence of Art and of Beauty, of the Aesthetic Experience and the
Creative Act. Most of the basic questions of traditional aesthetics are
requests for definitions; hence the familiar formulae that constitute
the results of traditional aesthetic inquiry: "Art is Expression"
(Croce), "Art is Significant Form" (Clive Bell), "Beauty is Pleasure
Objectified" (Santayana), and so on. Given these definitions we are
supposed to know what Art is or what Beauty is, just as we are
supposed to know what helium is if someone tells us that it is a
chemical element, gaseous, inert, and colorless, with an atomic number of 2 and an atomic weight of 4.003. F. J. E. Woodbridge once
remarked that metaphysics searches for the nature of reality and finds
it by definition. We might say that traditional aesthetics searches for
the nature of Art or Beauty and finds it by definition.

But why should it be so difficult to discern the essence of Art or
Beauty? Why should it take so much argument to establish or defend
such formulae as "Art is Expression"? And once we have arrived at
such formulae or have been given them in answer to our question,
why should they be so dissatisfying?

To come closer to an answer to these questions, we must look at
what it is the aesthetician expects of a definition of Art or Beauty. De
Witt Parker has stated with unusual clarity the "assumption" of the
aesthetician in asking and answering such questions as "What is
Art?;" at the beginning of his essay on "The Nature of Art" (note the
title) he says:

> The assumption underlying every philosophy of art is the
> existence of some *common nature* present in all the arts, despite
> their differences in form and content; something the *same* in
> painting and sculpture; in poetry and drama; in music and arch-
> itecture. Every single work of art, it is admitted, has a unique
> flavor, a *je ne sais quoi* which makes it incomparable with every
> other work; nevertheless, there is some mark or set of marks

which, if it applies to any work of art, applies to *all* works of art, *and to nothing else*—a common denominator, so to say, which constitutes the definition of art, and serves to separate . . . the field of art from other fields of human culture.[1]

What we are after, it should be clear, is what the traditional logic texts call a "definition *per genus et differentiam*" of Art and Beauty.

2. *The Assumption Questioned; the First Mistake.* The assumption that, despite their differences, all works of art must possess some common nature, some distinctive set of characteristics which serves to separate Art from everything else, a set of necessary and sufficient conditions for their being works of art at all, is both natural and disquieting, and constitutes what I consider to be the first mistake on which traditional aesthetics rests. It is natural, because, after all, we do use the word "art" to refer to a large number of very different things—pictures and poems and musical compositions and sculptures and vases and a host of other things; and yet the word is one word. Surely, we are inclined to say, there must be something common to them all or we should not call them by the same name. *Unum nomen; unum nominatum.*

Yet the assumption is disquieting when we come to search for the common nature which we suppose all works of art to possess. It is so elusive. We ought to be able to read a poem by Donne or by Keats, a novel by George Eliot or Joseph Conrad, or a play by Sophocles or Shakespeare, to listen to Mozart and Stravinsky, and to look at the pictures of Giotto and Cezanne and the Chinese masters and *see* what Art is. But when we look we do not see what Art is. So we are inclined to suppose that its essence must be something hidden, something that only an aesthetican can see, like the sounds that only a dog can hear, or else, as Parker, for example, supposes, that it must be something very complex, involving many characteristics (op. cit., p. 93). This explains why an adequate definition of Art is so hard to arrive at, why it is so much harder to answer questions like "What is Art?" than it is to answer questions like "What is helium?" Perhaps this also explains why there is a Philosophy of Art when there is no Philosophy of Helium?

But this explanation will not do. It will not do, that is, to suppose simply that the essence or nature of Art is elusive, very hard to detect, or very complex. It suggests that what we are faced with is a problem of scrutinizing, that what we have to do is to look long and hard at works of art, examine them carefully and diligently and, *voila*! we shall *see*. But no amount of looking and scrutinizing gives us what we want. All we see is this poem and that play, this picture and that statue, or some feature of them that catches our attention; and if we find some resemblances between poems or plays or pictures, or even between persons *and* pictures, pictures *and* musical compositions, these rememblances quickly disappear when we turn to other poems and plays and pictures. That is why in aesthetics it is best not to look at too many works of art and why, incidentally, aesthetics is best taught without concrete examples; a few will do. We can readily believe that we have seen the essence of Art when we have selected our examples properly; but when we range farther afield we lose it.

Despite the temptation to think that if we look long enough and hard enough at works of art we shall find the common denominator in question, after all the fruitless scrutinizing that has already been done, it is still more tempting to think that we are looking for something that is not there, like looking for the equator or the line on the spectrum that separates orange from red. No wonder that in aesthetics we soon begin to feel the frustration of St. Augustine when he asked himself "What is Time?" "If I am not asked, I know; if I am asked, I know not." Something must be wrong.

What is wrong, as I see it, has nothing to do with the nature or essence of Art at all; that is, there is neither anything mysterious nor anything complicated about works of art which makes the task of answering the question "What is Art?" so difficult. Like St. Augustine with Time, we do know quite well what Art is; it is only when someone asks us that we do not know. The trouble lies not in the works of art themselves but in the concept of Art. The word "art," unlike the word "helium," has a complicated variety of uses, what is nowadays called a complex "logic." It is not a word coined in the laboratory or the studio to name something that has hitherto escaped our attention; nor is it a relatively simple term of common parlance like "star" or "tree" which names something with which we are all quite familiar. As Professor Kristeller has shown us,[2] it is a word with a long, involved, and interesting history; a complicated concept indeed, but not for the reasons which the aestheticians suppose. Any good dictionary will indicate some of its many meanings, some of the variety of uses which the word "art" has; but no dictionary will give us the kind of formula which the aestheticians seek. That is why we suppose that the nature of Art is a philosophical problem and why there is a Philosophy of Art but no Philosophy of Helium. It is the complicated concepts like those of Space, Time, Reality, Change, Art, Knowledge, and so on that baffle us. Dictionaries and their definitions are of use in making short shrift of questions of the form

"What is X?" only in relatively simple and comparatively trivial cases; in the hard and more interesting cases they are frustrating and disappointing.

Doubtless there is an answer to this, and it might run somewhat as follows: "We know that the word 'Art' has a variety of uses in English. Most commonly it is used to refer to pictures alone; when we visit an art museum or consult an art critic, we expect to see pictures or to hear pictures talked about. We say that painting, painting pictures, *not* painting houses or fences, is *an* art, that cooking and sewing and basket-weaving, book-binding and selling are *arts*, but only some pictures do we call *works* of art, and rarely do we refer to dishes or garments or baskets as works of art, except honorifically. We speak of the liberal arts and the industrial arts and the art of war. But all of this is beside the point. As aestheticians we are interested only in what are sometimes called the "fine arts," or what Collingwood calls "art proper"—works of art. Surely all of these have something in common, else how should we be able to separate those paintings and drawings and poems and plays, musical compositions and buildings which are works of art from those which are not?"

To answer the last question first and make a long story short: we are able to separate those objects which are works of art from those which are not, because we know English; that is, we know how correctly to use the word "art" and to apply the phrase "work of art." To borrow a statement from Dr. Waismann and change it to meet my own needs, "If anyone is able to use the word 'art' or the phrase 'work of art' correctly in all sorts of contexts and on the right sort of occasions, he knows 'what art is,' and no formula in the world can make him wiser."[3] "Art proper" is simply what is properly called "art." The "correctly" and "properly" here have nothing to do with any "common nature" or "common denominator" of all works of art; they have merely to do with the rules that govern the actual and commonly accepted usage of the word "art."

Imagine a very large warehouse filled with all sorts of things— pictures of every description, musical scores for symphonies and dances and hymns, machines, tools, boats, houses, churches and temples, statues, vases, books of poetry and of prose, furniture and clothing, newspapers, postage stamps, flowers, trees, stones, musical instruments. Now we instruct someone to enter the warehouse and bring out all the works of art it contains. He will be able to do this with reasonable success, despite the fact that, as even the aestheticians must admit, he possesses no satisfactory definition of Art in terms of some common denominator, because no such definition has yet been found. Now imagine the same person sent into the ware-house to bring out all objects with Significant Form, or all objects of Expression. He would rightly be baffled; he knows a work of art when he sees one, but he has little or no idea what to look for when he is told to bring an object that possesses Significant Form.

To be sure, there are many occasions on which we are not sure whether something is a work of art or not; that is, we are not sure whether to call a given drawing or musical composition a work of art or not. Are "Nearer my God to Thee" and the political cartoons of Mr. Low works of art? But this merely reflects the systematic vague-ness of the concepts in question, or what Dr. Waismann on another occasion has called their "open texture"; a vagueness, note, which the definitions of the aestheticians do nothing at all to remove. On such occasions we can, of course, tighten the texture, remove some of the vagueness, by making a decision, drawing a line; and perhaps curators and purchasing committees of art museums are sometimes forced for obvious practical reasons to do this. But in doing so, they and we are not discovering anything about Art.

We do know what art is when no one asks us what it is; that is, we know quite well how to use the word "art" and the phrase "work of art" correctly. And when someone asks us what art is, we do *not* know; that is, we are at a loss to produce any simple formula, or any complex one, which will neatly exhibit the logic of this word and this phrase. It is the compulsion to reduce the complexity of aesthetic concepts to simplicity, neatness, and order that moves the aestheti-cian to make his first mistake, to ask "What is Art?" and to expect to find an answer like the answer that can be given to "What is helium?"

What I have said about Art in this section applies, *mutatis mutan-dis*, to Beauty, the Aesthetic Experience, the Creative Act, and all of the other entities with which traditional aesthetics concerns itself.

Where there is no mystery, there is no need for removing a mys-tery, and certainly none for inventing one.

3. *Common Denominators and Similarities.* Is the search for common characteristics among works of art, then, a fool's errand? That depends upon what we expect to find. If we expect to find some common denominator in Parker's sense, we are bound to be disap-pointed. We shall get ourselves enmeshed in unnecessary difficulties, and the definitions which we hope will free us from the net will be specious at best. If we say "Art is Significant Form" we may feel momentarily enlightened; but when we come to reflect upon what we mean by "significant form" we shall find ourselves entangled again. For the notion of Significant Form is clearly more obscure than is

that of Art or Beauty, as the example of the warehouse above amply illustrates; the same holds for Expression, Intuition, Representation, and the other favored candidates of the aestheticians. Nor will it do to say, as Professor Munro does,[4] that "art is skill in providing stimuli to satisfactory aesthetic experience." This has merely a scientific *sound*, and this sound is about as close as the effort to make aesthetics scientific comes to science. The notion of aesthetic experience is fraught with the same difficulties as the notion of art. To put it dogmatically, there is no such thing as *the* Aesthetic Experience; different sorts of experiences are properly referred to as aesthetic. Do not say they must all be contemplative. Does that really help at all?

There is, however, a fruitful and enlightening search for similarities and resemblances in art which the search for the common denominator sometimes furthers, the search for what, to torture a phrase of Wittgenstein's, we can call "family resemblances." When we squint we can sometimes see features of an object which otherwise we should miss. So in aesthetics, when we narrow our view, when in the search for the common denominator we carefully select our examples and restrict our sight, we may not see what we are looking for, but we may see something of more interest and importance. The simplifying formulae of the aestheticians are not to be scrapped merely because they fail to do what they are designed to do. What fails to do one thing may do another. The mistake of the aestheticians can be turned to advantage. The suspicion that aesthetics is not nonsense is often justified. For the idea that there is a unity among the arts, properly employed, can lead to the uncovering of similarities which, when noticed, enrich our commerce with art. Croce's supposed discovery that Art is Expression calls our attention to, among other things, an interesting feature of some, if not all, works of art, namely, their indifference to the distinction between the real and the unreal.

Or, to take examples from critics, when F. R. Leavis says of Crabbe, "His art is that of the short-story writer,"[5] and when Professor Stechow compares the fourth movement of Schumann's "Rhenish" Symphony with certain features of the Cologne Cathedral,[6] we have something of interest and importance. Our attention is refocused on certain works, and we see them in a new light. One of the offices of creative criticism, as of creative aesthetics, is the finding and pointing out of precisely such similarities.

4. *Aesthetic Theories Reconsidered.* Philosophical mistakes are rarely downright howlers; they have a point. What I have said is, I think, correct, but it neglects an important facet of the quest for essences, a by-product of that search, so to speak, which we should

not ignore. An aesthetic theory, by which I mean a systematic answer to such questions as "What is Art?" "What is Beauty?" and the like, frequently does something quite other than what it sets out to do. The assumption underlying traditional aesthetics, as Parker states it in the passage quoted above, is wrong, and I hope I have shown why it is wrong. It does not follow from this, however, that aesthetic theories are wholly without point, that they are merely mistaken, that formulae like "Art is Significant Form" are worthless, useless, or meaningless. They do serve a purpose, but their purpose is not that which Parker assigns them. Considered in context, in the historical or personal context, for example, they are frequently seen to have a point which has nothing to do with the philosophical excuses that are made for them.

Take Bell's famous dictum that "Art is Significant Form." It does not help us to understand what art is at all, and to that extent it is a failure; its shortcomings in this direction have been exposed on numerous occasions. It is easy to beat Bell down; he is so vulnerable. But when we stop to consider that he was an Englishman and when he wrote his book on art (1914) and what the taste of the English was like then and of his association with Roger Fry, the statement that "Art is Significant Form" loses some of its mystifying sound. It has a *point*. Not the point that Bell thinks it has, for Bell was also looking for the common denominator; another point. We might put it this way. The taste of Edwardian Englishmen in art was restricted to what we pejoratively call the "academic." Subject-matter was of prime importance to them—portraits of eminent persons, landscapes with or without cows, genre scenes, pictures of fox hunts, and the rest. Bell had seen the paintings of Cézanne, Matisse, and Picasso, and he was quick to see that subject-matter was not of prime importance in them, that the value of the paintings did not rest on realism or sentimental associations. It rested on what? Well "significant form"; lines and colors and patterns and harmonies that stir apart from associations evoked by subject-matter. He found also that he could look at other paintings, older paintings, paintings by the Venetian and Dutch masters, for example, and at vases and carpets and sculptures in the same way he looked at Cézanne. He found such looking rewarding, exciting. But when he turned to the pictures of the academicians, the thrill disappeared; they could not be looked at profitably in this way. What was more natural, then, than that he should announce his discovery by saying "Art *is* Significant Form"? He *had* discovered something for himself. Not the essence of Art, as the philosophers would have it, although he thought that this is what he found, but *a new way of looking at pictures*. He wanted to share his discovery with others and to reform English taste. *Here* is the point of his dictum; "Art is Significant Form" is a slogan, the epitome of a platform of aesthetic reform. It has work to do. Not the work which the philosophers assign it, but a work of teaching people a new way of looking at pictures.

When we blow the dust of philosophic cant away from aesthetic theories and look at them in this way, they take on an importance which otherwise they seem to lack. Read Aristotle's *Poetics*, not as a philosophical exercise in definition, but as instruction in one way to read tragic poetry, and it takes on a new life. Many of the other dicta of the aestheticians can also be examined in this light. We know that as definitions they will not do; but as instruments of instruction or reform they will do. Perhaps that is why they have had more real weight with practicing critics than they have had with philosophers. The critics have caught the point, where the philosophers, misguided from the start by a foolish preoccupation with definition, have missed it.

5. *Aesthetics and Criticism; the Second Mistake.* One of the prime reasons for the aesthetician's search for definitions of Art, Beauty, and the rest, is his supposition that unless we know what Art or Beauty is, we cannot say what good art or beautiful art is. Put it in the form of an assumption: Criticism presupposes Aesthetic Theory. This assumption contains the second mistake on which traditional aesthetics rests, namely, the view that responsible criticism is impossible without standards or criteria universally applicable to all works of art. The second mistake is in this way closely related to the first.

To see more clearly how this assumption operates, we can turn to a recent book by Mr. Harold Osborne,[7] *Aesthetics and Criticism*. Osborne believes that "a theory of the nature of artistic excellence is implicit in every critical assertion which is other than autobiographical record," and he thinks that "until the theory has been made explicit the criticism is without meaning" (p. 3). By a "theory of the nature of artistic excellence" Osborne means a theory of the nature of Beauty (p. 3).

Osborne examines several theories of the nature of Beauty and finds them all wanting. His moves against them are instructive. Take, for example, his move against a version of the Realistic Theory in Chapter V, that theory holding that artistic excellence consists in "truth to life"—or so Osborne states it. He correctly notes that practicing critics have rarely insisted that verisimilitude is a necessary condition of artistic excellence, and we should all agree that it is not.

"But," says Osborne, "if correspondence with real or possible actuality is not a necessary condition of artistic excellence, then most certainly it is not and cannot be of itself an *artistic* virtue, or an aesthetic merit, in those works of literature where it happens to occur" (p. 93). This is a curious argument. It seems to contain a glaring non sequitur. But what leads Osborne from his protasis to his conclusion is the assumption that the only acceptable reason offerable for a critical judgment of a work of art is one framed in terms of a characteristic which all works of art, *qua* works of art, must possess. Since we admit that not all works of art must possess truth to life or verisimilitude, we cannot use their adventitious possession of this property as a reason for praising, judging, or commending them as works of art.

Now surely this is mistaken. We can agree that correspondence with real or possible actuality, whatever that may mean, is not a *necessary* condition of artistic excellence; that is, it is *not* necessary that it appear among the reasons offerable for the judgment that a given work of art is good or beautiful. But it does not follow that therefore it does not and cannot appear as *a* reason for such a judgment. We can and do praise works of art, *as* works of art, whatever the force of that is, for a variety of reasons, and not always the same variety. Oborne's reply here is that in doing so we are being "illogical and inconsistent." Attacking the users of the Hedonistic Criterion, he says, "In so far as he [the critic] also uses other criteria [than the hedonistic one] for grading and assessing works of art, he is being illogical and inconsistent with himself whenever he does introduce the hedonistic—or emotional—assumption" (p.139). But why? There is nothing whatever illogical or inconsistent about praising, grading, or judging a work of art for more than one reason, unless we assume with Osborne that one and only one reason is offerable on pain of inconsistency, which is clearly not the case in art or anywhere else.

Osborne, true to the assumptions of traditional aesthetics, is looking for that condition which is both necessary and sufficient for artistic excellence or merit. His own candidate for that condition is what he calls "configurational coherence." But if anything pointed were needed to convince us of the emptiness of the search, it is the unintelligibility of Osborne's account of "beauty as configuration." If what I have said above about the concepts of Art and Beauty is true, we should not be surprised by this. For "art" and "beauty" do not name one and only one substance and attribute respectively; no wonder we cannot find the one thing they name or render intelligible the felt discovery that they do name one thing. We can *make* each of them name one thing if we wish. But why should we bother? We get along very well with them as they are.

6. *Ethics and Criticism; the Second Mistake Again.* "But surely," someone will say, "this cannot be the whole story. We can and do say that this work of art, this picture, for example, is better than that, or that this is a good one and that one is not. Do we not presuppose certain standards or criteria when we make such judgments? And isn't this really all that Osborne and other aestheticians have in mind when they insist that criticism presupposes aesthetic theory? They are looking for the standards of critical judgment and taste in the nature of art, just as many moralists have looked for the standards of right conduct in the nature of man. They may be looking in the wrong place, but clearly they are right in assuming that there must be something to find."

My reply is this: they are not looking in the wrong place so much as they are looking for the wrong thing. The bases of responsible criticism are indeed to be found *in* the work of art and nowhere else, but this in no way implies that critical judgments presuppose any canons, rules, standards, or criteria applicable to all works of art.

When we say that a certain knife is a good knife, we have in mind certain features of the knife, or of knives in general, which we believe will substantiate or support this claim: the sharpness of the blade, the sturdiness of the handle, the durability of the metal, the way it fits the hand, and so on. There are a number of such considerations, all of which refer to characteristics of the knife and not to our feelings about or attitudes toward it, which may be said to constitute the criteria of a good knife. Special criteria may be adduced for fishing knives as opposed to butcher knives, and so on, but this does not affect the issue in question. Note first that there is no definite or exhaustively specifiable list of criteria in common and universal employment; it does not make sense to ask how many there are or whether we have considered them all. But there are generally accepted criteria with which we are all familiar which we use to support our judgments, though in cases of special instruments or implements, like ophthalmoscopes, only specialists are acquainted with the criteria. Secondly, note how the criteria are related to the purposes or functions of knives, to the uses to which we put them, the demands we make upon them. "Knife," we might say, is a function-word, a word that names something which is usually defined by its function or functions. The criteria, we can say loosely, are derivable from the definition. This second consideration has led some aestheticians to look for the standards of taste and criticism in the function of art.

Now take apples. They have, of course, no function. We use them, we do things with them—eat them, use them for decoration, feed them to pigs, press cider from them, and so on—but none of these things can be said to constitute the function of an apple. Depending, however, on how we use them or what we use them for, we can frame lists of criteria similar to the lists for knives. The best apples for decoration are not always the best for eating, nor are the best for making pies always the best for making cider. Now take mathematicians. A mathematician, unless he is assigned a particular work to do, again has no function. There are certain things a mathematician does, however, and in terms of these we can again frame criteria for judging, praising, grading, and commending mathematicians. Finally, take men in general. We often praise a man, *as* a man, as opposed to as a plumber or a mathematician, and we call this sort of praise moral praise. Here again, we have criteria for assessing the moral worth of men, although, theological considerations aside, we do not frame them in terms of man's function, purpose, or task, even if some moralists, like Aristotle, have tried to frame them in terms of man's end. But we make demands on men, moral demands on all men, and our criteria reflect these demands.

Let us turn now to art. The question we have to raise is this: Are critical judgments of pictures and poems logically symmetrical to the sorts of judgments we have been considering? I think they are not, or not entirely. Not because they are somehow more subjective or unreliable than other value judgments (this issue is as false as an issue can be!), but because the pattern of justification and support which is appropriate to them is of a different sort. Any critical judgment, to be justified, must be supported by reasons; this goes without saying, for this is what "justification" means. But must the reasons offerable and acceptable in cases of critical appraisal be of the same order or type as those offerable and acceptable in cases of instruments, implements, useful objects, professional services, jobs, offices, or moral conduct? In particular, must there be any general rules, standards, criteria, canons, or laws applicable to all works of art by which alone such critical appraisals can be supported? I think not.

In the first place, we should note that only a man corrupted by aesthetics would think of judging a work of art *as* a work of art in general, as opposed to as this poem, that picture, or this symphony. There is some truth in the contention that the notions of Art and Work of Art are special aestheticians' concepts. This follows quite naturally from the absence of any distinguishing feature or features common to all works of art as such, and from the absence of any single demand or set of demands which we make on all works of art as such. Despite the occasional claim that it has, Art has no function or purpose, in the sense in which knives and ophthalmoscopes have function, and this is an insight to be gained from the "art for art's sake" position. This does not mean that we cannot use individual works of art for special purposes; we can and do. We can use novels and poems and symphonies to put us to sleep or wake us up; we can use pictures to cover spots on the wall, vases to hold flowers, and sculptures for paper weights or door stops. This is what lends point to the distinction between judging something *as* a work of art and judging it *as* a sedative, stimulant, or paper weight; but we cannot conclude from this that Art has some special function or purpose in addition to the purposes to which it can be put.

Similarly there is no one thing which we *do* with all works of art: some we hang, some we play, some we perform, some we read; some we look at, some we listen to, some we analyze, some we contemplate, and so on. There is no special aesthetic use of works of art, even though it may make sense, and even be true, to say that a person who uses a statue as a door stop is not using it as a work of art; he is not doing one of the things we normally do with works of art; he is not treating it properly, we might say. But the proper treatment of works of art varies from time to time and from place to place. It was quite proper for a cave man to hurl his spear at the drawing of a bison, just as it was quite proper for the Egyptians to seal up paintings and sculptures in a tomb. Such treatment does not render the object thus treated not a work of art. The attempt to define Art in terms of what we do with certain objects is as doomed as any other. From this and the first consideration it follows that there is no way by which we can derive the criteria of taste and criticism from the function of art or from its use.

The remaining parallel is with moral appraisal, and this is the most interesting of them all. It has been, and perhaps still is, a common view among philosophers that Beauty and Goodness are two species of the same genus, namely, Value, and that therefore there are at least two classes of value judgments, namely, moral judgments and aesthetic judgments. For this reason there is a tendency further to suppose that there is a logical symmetry between the two. But the supposition of symmetry is a mistake, and I am led to suspect that it does little but harm to suppose that Beauty and Goodness are two species of the same genus at all. There are clearly certain similarities between the two, that is, between the logic of statements of the form "This is good" and the logic of statements of the form "This is beautiful"—they are used in many of the same ways—but this must not blind us to the differences. Criticisms suffer from a very natural comparison with ethics.

Moral appraisal is like the other forms of appraisal, in this respect; it expresses a desire for uniformity. It is when we are interested in uniformity of size, milk producing capacity, conduct, and so on, that standards or criteria become so important. We maintain standards in products and in workmanship; we enforce them, hold ourselves up to them, teach them to our children, insist on them, and so on, all for the sake of a certain uniformity. In morals we *are* interested in uniformity, at least in what we expect men not to do; that is one reason why rules and laws are necessary and why they play such an important rôle in moral appraisal. But in art, unless, like Plato, we wish to be legislators and to require something of art, demand that it perform a specified educational and social service, we are not as a rule interested in uniformity. Some critics and aestheticians are, of course, interested in uniformity—uniformity in the works of art themselves or uniformity in our approach to them. For them it is quite natural to demand criteria. For them it is also quite natural to formulate theories of Art and Beauty. Remember what we said about aesthetic theories above: the definitions in which they issue are often slogans of reform. As such they are also often devices for the encouragement of uniformity. But this merely betrays the persuasive character of many aesthetic theories, and the peculiar legislative posture of some critics and aestheticians is no warrant for the assumption that the criteria in question are necessary for responsible criticism. Nor should it blind us to the fact that we do quite well without them. Criticism has in no way been hampered by the absence of generally applicable canons and norms, and where such norms have been proposed they have either, like the notorious Unities in the case of tragedy, been shown to be absurd, or else, like the requirements of balance, harmony, and unity in variety, they have been so general, equivocal, and empty as to be useless in critical practice. Ordinarily we feel no constraint in praising one novel for its verisimilitude, another for its humour, and still another for its plot or characterization. We remark on the richness of Van Gogh's impasto, but we do not find it a fault in a Chinese scroll painting that it is flat and smooth. Botticelli's lyric grace in his glory, but Giotto and Chardin are not to be condemned because their poetry is of another order. The merits of Keats and Shelley are not those of Donne and Herbert. And why should Shakespeare and Aeschylus be measured by the same rod? Different works of art are, or may be, praiseworthy or blameworthy for different reasons, and not always the same reasons. A quality that is praiseworthy in one painting may be blameworthy in another; realism is not always a virtue, but this does not mean that it is not sometimes a virtue.[8]

Mr. Hampshire has put the reaason why the criteria sought by the aestheticians are so "elusive" and why the parallel with ethics is a mistake in this way: "A work of art," he says, "is gratuitous. It is not *essentially* the answer to a question or the solution of a presented problem" (op. cit., p. 162). There is no one problem being solved or question answered by all poems, all pictures, all symphonies, let alone all works of art. If we set a number of people to doing the same thing, we can rate them on how well they do it. We have, or can frame, a criterion. But not all artists are doing the same thing— solving the same problem, answering the same question, playing the same game, running the same race. Some of them may be, we do group artists together by "schools," and in other ways, to indicate precisely this kind of similarity; but only in so far as they are does it make sense to compare and appraise them on the same points. It is no criticism of Dickens that he did not write like Henry James. Writing a novel or a lyric poem may, in some interesting respects, be like playing a game or solving a problem, we in fact speak of artists as solving problems. But it is also different; so that if we wish to retain the analogy we must call attention to the differences by saying that not all poets or novelists are playing the *same* game, solving the *same* problems. There is indeed a certain gratuitousness in art which destroys the parallelism or symmetry between moral and aesthetic appraisal.

But there is also a gratuitousness in aesthetic criticism. Moral appraisal like legal judgment, is a practical necessity; aesthetic appraisal is not. That is why the claim that in art it is all a matter of taste is tolerable, even if it is false, when this sounds so shocking in morals. We can live side by side in peace and amity with those whose tastes differ quite radically from our own; similar differences in moral standards are more serious. And yet, of course, aesthetic criticism is not merely a matter of taste, if by taste we mean unreasoned preferences. Taste does play an important part in the differences among critical appraisals, but we are clearly not satisfied when, in answer to our question "Why is it good?" or "What's good about it?," we are told "It's good because I like it." Mrs. Knight correctly notes that "my *liking* a picture is never a criterion of its goodness" (op. cit., p. 154). That is, my liking a picture is no reason for its *being* good, though it may be a reason for my *saying* that it is good.

But if it is not all a matter of liking and disliking, why is it that a certain feature is a virtue in a given work of art? If someone tells me that a certain work of art is good for such and such reasons, how can I tell whether the reasons he offers are good reasons or not, or even if they are relevant? These questions are not easily answered, for in practice we adduce many considerations for saying that a work of art is good or that a certain feature of it is a virtue. I will make no attempt to canvass these considerations but will close with some observations on a logical feature of the problem.

We are confronted, I think, with a problem that is really two problems: there is the problem of saying why a given work of art is good or bad, and there is the problem of saying why our reasons are good or bad, or even relevant. We may praise a picture, say, for its subtle balance, color contrast, and draughtsmanship; this is saying why the picture is good. We may now go on to raise the more "philosophical" question of what makes balance, or this sort of color contrast, or this kind of draughtsmanship an artistic virtue. The first sort of question, the question of why the work of art is good or bad, is decided by appeal to the "good-making characteristics" or "criterion-characters" of the work of art in question, that is, by an appeal to certain objectively discriminable characteristics of the work under discussion. These characteristics are many and various; there is a large variety of reasons offerable for a work of art's being a good or bad work of art. The second sort of question, the question of the worth or relevance of the reasons offered in answer to the first question, is settled by appeal either to custom or to decision. In this respect aesthetic criticism is very like moral appraisal. We either simply praise what is customarily praised and condemn what is customarily condemned or we *decide* what the criteria shall be. This does not mean that the criteria, that is, the reasons offerable for a work of art's being good or bad, are arbitrary. There may be plenty of reasons why one feature is a "criterion-character" and another is not. Part of the reason may be psychological, part sociological, part metaphysical, or even religious and ethical. Only an aesthete ignores, or tries to ignore, the many relations of a poem or picture to life and concentrates on what are called the purely "formal" values of the work at hand; but in doing so he *determines* what he will accept as a reason for a work of art's being good or bad. That a work of art assists the cause of the proletariat in the class struggle *is* a reason for its being a good work of art to a convinced Marxist, but it is not a reason, let alone a good reason, to the bourgeois aesthete. That a picture contains nude figures is a reason, to the puritan and the prude, for condemning it, though no enlightened man can be brought to accept it. Thus morals and politics and religion do enter into our critical judgments, even when we claim that they should not.

I noted above that there is no one use which we make of all works of art, nor is there any one demand or set of demands which we make on them. This is, I think, important, and serves to explain, at least in part, the actual relativity of aesthetic criteria. What one age looks for in painting or in literature, another age may neglect. What one group demands, another forbids. We are not always consistent in even our own demands on art, and I can see no reason why we should be. We can be interested in works of art for many reasons, and some of these reasons may be more decisive at one time or in one set of circumstances than they are at another time or in another set of circumstances. This affects the very logic of critical appraisal by determining the relevance and merit of the reasons we offer for our judgments. We are well aware of the fact that the estimate of a given poet or painter changes from period to period. El Greco's or Shakespeare's reputation has not always been what it is, and no one should be surprised if it should change in the future. But if we examine the reasons that have been offered for the different estimates, we find that they too are different. Different reasons are persuasive at different times and in different contexts. The same explanation is operative: the needs and interests that art gratifies are different from time to time and, to a lesser extent perhaps, from person to person. But as the needs and interests vary, so also will the criteria and the weight we place on them. This is a vicious relativism only to those who are morally disposed to insist on the uniformity of taste.

Summary: I have tried to show (1) that the search for essences in aesthetics is a mistake, arising from the failure to appreciate the complex but not mysterious logic of such words and phrases as "art," "beauty," "the aesthetic experience," and so on. But (2) although the characteristics common to all works of art are the object of a fool's errand, the search for similarities in sometimes very different works of art can be profitably pursued, and this search is occasionally stimulated by the formulae of the aestheticians. (3) Although the definitions of the aestheticians are useless for the role usually assigned to them, we must not ignore the live purpose they frequently serve as slogans in the effort to change taste and as instruments for opening up new avenues of appreciation. (4) If the search for the common denominator of all works of art is abandoned, abandoned with it must be the attempt to derive the criteria of critical appreciation and appraisal from the nature of art. (5) Traditional aesthetics mistakenly supposes that responsible criticism is impossible without a set of rules, canons, or standards applicable to all works of art. This supposition arises from an uncritical assimilation of the pattern of critical appraisal to that of appraisal in other areas, particularly morals, and from a failure to appreciate the gratuitousness of art and the manner in which reasons are operative in the justification of critical judgments.

NOTES

1. De Witt H. Parker, "The Nature of Art," *Revue Internationale de Philosophie*, July 1939, p. 684; reprinted in E. Vivas and M. Krieger, eds., *The Problems of Aesthetics* (New York, 1953), p. 90. Italics mine.
2. P. O. Kristeller, "The Modern System of the Arts: A Study in the History of Aesthetics," *Journal of the History of Ideas*, xii (1951), pp. 496–527; xiii (1952), pp. 17–46.
3. See F. Waismann, "Analytic-Synthetic II," *Analysis*, 11 (1950), p. 27.
4. Thomas Munro, *The Arts and Their Interrelations* (New York, 1949), p. 108.
5. F. R. Leavis, *Revaluation: Tradition and Development in English Poetry* (London, 1936), p. 125.
6. Wolfgang Stechow, "Problems of Structure in Some Relations Between the Visual Arts and Music," *The Journal of Aesthetics and Art Criticism*, xi (1953), p. 325.
7. Routledge and Kegan Paul Ltd., London, 1955.
8. I owe much in this section to Helen Knight's "The Use of 'Good' in Aesthetic Judgments," *Aesthetics and Language*, William Elton ed. (Oxford, 1954), pp. 147 ff., and to Stuart Hampshire's "Logis and Appreciation," ibid., pp. 161 ff.

Arguing about "Art"

Guy Sircello

In a scientific era philosophy is at a disadvantage. For, unlike the sciences, it seems never to get "results," which, once established, provide the foundation for further progress. This situation often gives nonphilosophers a reason to reject the philosophical enterprise altogether or, at least, a rationalization for their distaste for philosophy. To philosophers, however, it merely provides another subject matter; they philosophize about philosophy in order to understand its inconclusiveness. The philosophy of art is no different in this respect from the rest of philosophy. A rather large number of philosophers—and philosophically inclined artists and critics—have worked out their respective theories about, for example, the nature of art. But the only results have been that there are as many theories as there are theoreticians, that most of them conflict with most of the rest, and that none of them has won the day. The philosopher of art is forced to wonder what there is about philosophical inquiries into the nature of art that produces this situation.

Because of the work of Wittgenstein and his heirs, philosophy at present has some sophisticated tools that are well designed precisely for this sort of inquiry. For it is essentially an inquiry into how high-level discourse about art functions, how such language is used. One of the first principles of such an inquiry is, and ought to be, "look and see." But the Wittgensteinian philosophical legacy is very complicated. It also contains a tendency to debunk what has traditionally gone by the name "philosophy." This tendency has sometimes been expressed in the view that traditional philosophy has been guilty of "mistakes," particularly in the use of language, and that it has, therefore, been led to pose inherently insoluble problems. This view is strongly represented in contemporary philosophy of art. W. E. Kennick's paper "Does Traditional Aesthetics Rest on a Mistake?" has been an influential application of this line of criticism to the old question of the definition of art.[1] It embodies a viewpoint often

477

assumed in recent discussions on the nature of discourse proposing to define "art."

Adherence to Kennick's general view has, I believe, stood in the way of the proper application of the Wittgensteinian principle "look and see." Philosophers have not been able to look carefully and see clearly what is going on when writers propound conflicting theories concerning the nature of art. For this reason it is important to subject Kennick's own critique to critical examination. Such an examination is the business of the first section of this paper. I hope to make clear not only that Kennick's critique of "traditional aesthetics" is based upon false presuppositions but also to show how those presuppositions have been especially vicious in preventing philosophers from seeing the conflicts between theories of art in a correct light.[2]

I

Kennick's understanding of one of the "mistakes" made by "traditional aesthetics" rests already upon an interpretation of traditional aesthetics. According to that interpretation, traditional aestheticians "assume" that all works of art have "some common nature, some distinctive set of characteristics which serves to separate art from everything else." Now Kennick gives no justification for this sweeping general interpretation, which is surprising in a philosopher who, it will turn out, is squeamish about generalizations in the philosophy of art. Perhaps he believes his point too obviously true to need documentation. But is it so clear that all traditional aestheticians have made the assumption that Kennick alleges in view of the fact that it is not very clear what it is, after all, to make such an assumption? But surely, you say, we cavil to balk at this stage of Kennick's argument. And you are probably right. What Kennick means is fairly clear and probably true, at least for the majority of cases of "traditional aesthetics." Most writers on the philosophy of art make, or very strongly imply, statements of the form "(All) Art is (essentially) P." And such statements would seem to be analyzable in terms of statements of the form "Works of art share an essential property (or set of essential properties), and it is (they are) P." It is the first clause of this statement-form that Kennick believes is wrong.

It is wrong, argues Kennick, because (a) we know how to apply the term "art" in English by virtue of knowing the language rules governing the term; (b) these rules of application determine a single class of entities, which are central cases of art; and (c) when inspected in an unbiased way, these entities reveal no common and unique properties. Now, whereas (a) is, generally speaking, true, (b) is not. Consequently, the truth of (c), which depends upon (b), is not determinable, and Kennick's whole critique of traditional aesthetics, which rests upon (c), is ill founded. In arguing these points, I shall assume that Kennick's argument does not turn essentially on peculiarities of the English language or any other particular language. I shall assume, with Kennick, that the English term "art" is translatable into other languages and that the rules governing the application of "art" determine the same class of entities as the rules governing the application of all translations of the term "art."

Let us consider the implications of Kennick's assumption (b) for the situation in which there is disagreement about whether a thing is a work of art. Of course, such a disagreement can arise when two persons do not agree on what properties are truly ascribable to a thing. Thus, for example, there might be a disagreement about whether Turner's *Shade and Darkness: The Evening of the Deluge* is a work of art or not. Yet it might be that that disagreement would disappear if there could be agreement on whether the Turner is a *picture* or not. But to one person it clearly is a picture, and to the other it is not; the latter cannot recognize any objects in it—it looks like nothing but paint messed onto a canvas. This sort of disagreement will not allow us to test Kennick's assumption, however. We must imagine a disagreement concerning whether a thing is properly called art or not under the condition that there are no disagreements concerning any properties of the thing in question. In such a situation, one of the following states of affairs must obtain if Kennick's thesis (b) is correct. Either (1) one or both of the persons disagreeing must be using the term "art" incorrectly or (2) the thing in question is one with respect to which the term "art" is "systematically vague." A term is systematically vague, according to Kennick, in virtue of there being individuals to which "we are not sure" whether the term is applicable or not. Kennick's formulation makes it appear as if the systematic vagueness of a term depended simply upon "our" uncertainty, but Kennick, I am sure, does not mean that. The concept can be made clearer in terms of the indeterminacy of the rules governing the application of a term. A term is systematically vague if there are individuals to which the term may be either applied or denied without being (linguistically) incorrect. Such individuals, then, are "marginal cases" of the concept designated by the term. I take it that this interpretation of "systematic vagueness" and "marginal case" is one that Kennick intends in his article.

We can readily imagine disagreements concerning whether a thing (or a sort of thing) is art in which (a) one or more of the persons disagreeing are incorrectly applying (or refusing to apply) the term "art" or (b) the thing about which there is disagreement is a marginal case of art. For example, imagine two school girls of about eight years of age (and as precocious, prissy, and self-important as you please). One day Pamela announces to Patricia that she is going to be an artist because she can draw so well. Patricia retorts that *she* is going to be an artist too; she is going to write poems (she *loves* poems). Pamela, with victory in her voice, says that Patricia can't be an artist by writing poems: "Poems aren't art." "Poems can too be art," says Patricia. "My daddy says people who write poems and even stories are artists with words." But Pamela comes back with the crushing blow: "Oh, no, art is what we do in school, like drawing and painting and cutting and pasting." Who is right, here? We have no hesitation in saying Patricia is right and Pamela wrong. The reason is fairly clear. Pamela does not know all the ways in which the term "art" can be properly applied. She has a typical grammar-school notion of "art"; the term is hardly ever used by that age group to cover anything but the products of those activities which fill the time in a school day called "art period."

Imagine another case now in which Pamela has heard her mother say admiringly to her father, who is a fine cabinetmaker, "It's a work of art, John!" One day, in "art period," Patricia volunteers the information that *her* father is an artist (a portrait painter, as it turns out). Not to be outdone, and remembering what her mother has so often said, Pamela asserts that *her* father is an artist, too. Patricia challenges her: "He is not; he just makes furniture, and furniture isn't art!" Whereupon there follows a dispute of the "Is too!"—"Is not!" variety. In this situation, however, neither child is right; but neither is clearly wrong either. For both girls show that they are unaware of the marginal status of furniture in the realm of art. Furniture in general is no more clearly art than it is *not* art. The girls' disagreement in this situation, therefore, is as understandable as their dispute is pointless.

The two situations sketched above illustrate the only possibilities that are allowable under Kennick's assumptions when disagreements occur over the applicability of the term "art." There are, however, considerably more interesting and important disagreements than those between Pamela and Patricia. Despite the fact that the art theories of Tolstoy and Clive Bell are both "emotivist" theories, they are clearly very far apart. For the "emotion" that Bell calls aesthetic is a rarefied sort of response that Tolstoy would not even regard as aesthetically relevant. Moreover, the feelings that Tolstoy has in mind when he speaks of the communication of feeling in art are what Bell thinks of as aesthetically irrelevant. Because of this disagreement it is plausible to suppose that there are some things that Tolstoy would, with no hesitation, call art and that Bell would deny are art. Let us take as an example a crooning lullaby made up entirely of soothing nonsense syllables. Let us further imagine that the lullaby is invented at bedtime one night by a not particularly musical mother and is then forgotten. And let us also suppose that there is some clear communication of feeling when the mother sings her lullaby: the child basks in the mother's tenderness and love and falls contentedly to sleep. Now, for Tolstoy a lullaby of such a description clearly qualifies as art. Indeed, he sometimes refers to lullabies as paradigms of art. Bell, on the other hand, might very well not regard our hypothetical lullaby as art at all. To be sure, there is a problem here concerning how Bell would *perceive* the song. On his own admission, Bell was unmusical and could not readily perceive "significant form" in music. He was convinced, however, that it was there; and insofar as a thing evinces significant form, for him, it is art. However, in order to generate a disagreement between Tolstoy and Bell it is not necessary for us to suppose our hypothetical lullaby to be totally without "formal" interest. And that is fortunate, for it is unclear what such a lullaby would be like due to the vagueness of Bell's notion of form, especially as it is applicable to music. All that we need to assume about the hypothetical lullaby is that both Tolstoy and Bell *agree* that it is without (significant) formal interest and that it is indeed a means by which certain feelings are communicated. The hypothetical lullaby is meant to show simply that there are cases in which such an assumption is plausible. It is virtually certain that Tolstoy and Bell would disagree about whether a lullaby of the proposed sort would qualify as art.

Let us take another case of disagreement about whether a thing is art or not. In an essay "Art, Popular Art and the Illusion of the Folk," André Malraux draws a distinction between the arts of high culture and the popular arts of an urbanized society.[3] The conclusion of his essay is that the popular arts are not arts at all, not even inferior arts; they are "anti-arts." What we must assume, of course, is that when Malraux refers to the popular arts using the term "art," he means something like "so-called arts." That is, we must assume, in order to make Malraux's discourse consistent, that he uses the term "art" to refer to the popular arts only because some persons have done so. But whatever the complexities of Malraux's use of the term "art" may be, one thing is clear: Were he sent into Professor Kennick's imaginary warehouse in order to bring out everything in it that falls under the concept "art," Malraux would bring out the *Mona Lisa*, copies of *Hamlet*, and the score of Beethoven's Ninth Symphony, but he would leave the Beatles albums, Mickey Spillane novels, and Superman comic books inside. The same test applied to Tolstoy, however, would very likely result in the Shakespeare, the Beethoven, and the Da Vinci being left in the warehouse; for Tolstoy would consider them to be "counterfeit art." Now the logic of the term "counterfeit art" is not clear; but it is not unreasonable to suppose that the concept "counterfeit art" works like "counterfeit dollar bills." Just as counterfeit dollar bills are not dollar bills, counterfeit art is not art. There is, hence, a rather wide discrepancy between the way that Malraux applies "art" and the way Tolstoy does. Furthermore, it is reasonable to suppose that the discrepancy between Malraux and Tolstoy would not be due to any disagreement concerning the *properties* of the Shakespearean play, the Beethoven symphony, and the Da Vinci portrait; for it is easy to believe that Malraux and Tolstoy could agree that the latter works do have some abstract *meaning* (Malraux's criterion) and also that they do not "infect" us with some common human feeling (Tolstoy's criterion).

The critic Leslie Fiedler has written a defense of comic books.[4] In his essay Fiedler refers to comic books as a sort of art, and there are not even any implied quotation marks around "art" when he so uses it. There is, thus, a clear disagreement between Fiedler and Malraux in the way they use (or would use) the term "art." It is fairly clear that the disagreement is not (or would not be) due to the fact that the two men believe comic books to have different properties. Fiedler might well admit that comic books are purely sensationalistic and that they lack any redeeming element of "significance" in Malraux's sense. For he says that the comics remain close to the impulsive and "subliminal" life and that there is in them an "aboriginal violence." It is quite reasonable, then, to suppose that there exists between Fiedler and Malraux a third disagreement concerning the proper application of the term "art."[5]

One of the two ways, allowed by Kennick's position, of explaining the disagreements just described is to suppose that some or all of the men involved are (or were) using the term "art," or its equivalent in Russian or French, incorrectly. Yet, if they are using the term incorrectly, it is not because they, like Pamela and Patricia, do not know enough about how "art" is (or is to be) applied. To suppose so would be ludicrous; that is the last way we would think of to explain their disagreements. But in the situations involving the young girls it is a perfectly natural explanation. Pamela and Patricia are quite young; they are at the beginning of their formal education; and there is much, we naturally and justifiably assume, that they do not know about their native tongue. On the other hand, Clive Bell et al. were (or are) mature, well-educated, and articulate men. If we are going to maintain that Bell, Tolstoy, Malraux, and/or Fiedler are using "art" incorrectly, we are obliged, then, to account for this fact in some other way. An obvious alternative is that they are deliberately using "art" incorrectly in order to serve some special purpose. Professor Kennick's suggestion, made in another place, is that theoreticians who use the term "art" incorrectly do so because they are, in effect, making recommendations to *change* the way the term is applied.[6] I am not interested in pursuing this hypothesis here, however; nor am I interested in pursuing any rival hypothesis. Rather, I shall try to confront head-on the thesis that generates such hypotheses, namely, the thesis that at least some of the above distinguished men are incorrectly applying the term "art."

Now to say that a use of any term is incorrect presupposes the existence of a standard which, however implicit, can, if need be, be brought out into the open. Against what standard can Bell's, Tolstoy's, Malraux's, and Fiedler's varied uses of "art" be measured? In the case of Pamela and Patricia the standard is obvious: The use of "art" by persons with considerably more maturity, education, and general verbal expertise than they. But, obviously that standard will not do when the usage of persons who are mature, educated, and articulate is itself at issue.

We must, therefore, try to discover a group of standard-makers who have not been touched by the possibly incorrect applications of "art" found in or implied by the work of Bell, Tolstoy, Malraux, or Fiedler. Notice, however, the predicament that this restriction puts us in. On the one hand, we need the most educated persons, those with the widest experience in their language, to serve as standard-makers. On the other hand, we need persons who have not been exposed to the sorts of controversies that Bell, Tolstoy, Malraux, and Fiedler are engaged in, for precisely these controversies pose our problem. An obvious way out of the predicament is to find some "middle" group, that is, those who are sophisticated with respect to their language but are naive with respect to the controversies surrounding "art." And such persons are easily enough described if not so easily found. We simply need a group of bright, verbally gifted, extensively read adolescents, say, who happen to have been on a reading program that contained no serious discussion of the arts.

It should be clear, however, that such a description of our standard-makers is inadequate. For we still want to know what particular uses of "art" these standard-makers have been exposed to. If the range of uses is no more extensive than that with which Pamela and Patricia are familiar, it is clearly insufficient. But what other uses need they be familiar with? Have our standard-makers ever encountered an application of the term "art" to a comic book? If so, have they thereby been exposed to an "incorrect" use and become "biased" as a result? If not, is their knowledge of the term "art" and its uses inadequate? Have they never heard *Hamlet* spoken of as phony, fake, or counterfeit art? If not, is their knowledge of the use of the term "art" deficient? Or if so, have they been tainted by some "incorrect" use of the term? In other words, it is unclear what we must build into the standard-makers against whose uses of "art" the disagreements among Bell, Tolstoy, Malraux, and Fiedler are to be settled. And we cannot become clear on the matter until we have already determined who among Bell, Tolstoy, Malraux, and Fiedler are applying "art" correctly and who are not. But if that is so, then there is no way of determining who is right in the disagreements described above. Furthermore, the same is true with respect to any disagreement concerning the application of "art" among any serious, mature, educated, and articulate persons. I want to emphasize, however, that these consequences in no way deprive us *in general* of any way of determining whether a person is using the term "art" incorrectly. As the Pamela-Patricia situation showed, it is sometimes perfectly possible to locate a misuse of the term. In the latter case, however, we were able to invoke the rather vague and gross standard of "mature, educated speakers" because the discriminations we had to make were not very subtle. But when it comes to deciding who is "correct" and who "incorrect" among the likes of Bell, Tolstoy, Malraux, and Fiedler, we have need of a far more finely calibrated measuring stick.

Thus it is that one of the consequuences of Kennick's position is untenable. For it commits us to there being, in certain situations, an incorrect use of the term "art" without there being any way of identifying that incorrect use. Anyone maintaining Kennick's position is forced, therefore, to accept the only other possible way of explaining disagreements of the sort described above, namely, that those disagreements are due to the systematic vagueness of the concept "art." Unfortunately, this alternative is equally embarrassing to Kennick's position, but for different reasons. For, on the basis of what we can reasonably believe about the extent of disagreements about art, the conclusion seems inescapable that the term "art" is systematically vague with respect to *every* individual to which it is permissible (linguistically speaking) to apply it. There is nothing, it seems, to which our language permits us to apply the term "art" to which it is *not* permissible, as far as the rules of language are concerned, to deny the term "art." Put in yet another way, there are no "central cases" of art determinable by the rules of application of the term "art." We might say, paradoxically, that *all* cases of art are "marginal" (though strictly speaking, of course, there are no marginal cases either).

The argument in support of this claim is that the history of art and aesthetics, especially in modern times, shows that there is nothing that has been seriously maintained to be art that has not also been seriously maintained not to be art. One has only to think, on the one hand, of Tolstoy denying that the works of Shakespeare and Beethoven are art and, on the other, of contemporary "conceptual" artist Mike Heizer calling his ditch in Nevada a work of art. To some rigorists this argument may seem "merely empirical." And it is true, of course, that it would not be "contradictory" to assert that there is a work of art that could not be denied, on pain of language misuse, to be a work of art. Nevertheless, it is incumbent upon anyone who thinks that a "merely empirical" argument is not good enough in this case to bring forth something (real or hypothetical) of which it could not be denied, on pain of *misuse of language*, that it is art. It takes no special perspicacity to see that for anything brought forth, there would be some serious, mature, educated, and articulate theoretician of art whose position would entail (and who would accept the entailment) that that thing is not art.

The embarrassment to Kennick's argument of the above point is that it deprives that argument of a crucial step. As shown above, Kennick's argument depends upon there being a class of individuals to which the term "art" is applicable and to which it cannot, on pain of linguistic misuse, be denied. It depends, that is, upon the existence of a class of linguistically determined central cases of art.[7] Unable to make this crucial step, Kennick's critique of "traditional aesthetics" falters, for it is against this alleged class of "indubitable" art objects that Kennick measures traditional theories of art and finds them wanting. Whatever the class of "objects" that Kennick might have in mind when he criticizes traditional aesthetics, it has no more sanction in terms of linguistic rules than any different class that we can suppose Tolstoy, Bell, Malraux, Fiedler, or any other "traditional aesthetician" to have had in mind.

But are we, after all, pressed to this consequence? Let us go back a few paces in the argument. Remember that in asserting that Pamela was using "art" incorrectly, we used as a standard of correctness the body of mature, educated, and articulate speakers of the language. When we were required by Kennick's assumption to find a standard of correctness to mediate the disagreements between Bell and Tolstoy, Tolstoy and Malraux, and Malraux and Fiedler, however, Kennick's position began to weaken. But can we not question the necessity, after all, of discovering some *standard* by which to gauge correct and incorrect usage? Perhaps our mistake was in looking so hard for what we did not even need. Consider, after all, what the respective objects of those disagreements were: (1) an impromptu, formally nondescript croon that could not even be called "amateurish"; (2) a Shakespearean play, a Beethoven symphony, a Da Vinci portrait; and (3) comic books such as *Superman* and *Captain Marvel*. Must we go *searching* for a "standard" in order to "locate" these sorts of things properly under the rubric "art"? Are we not forgetting what we know already? Are we not immediately and without further investigation willing to acknowledge that the mother's croon and the comic books occupy the margins of the realm of art, whereas the Shakespeare, the Beethoven, and the Da Vinci are in the center? And if we thus admit that we know, does it not become clear that it is Tolstoy, and only Tolstoy, out of the above foursome who is doing violence to the concept of art? For he alone is denying that things that lie in the center of the realm of art are art. And, indeed, such a judgment on Tolstoy is common. Tolstoy's view has been seen as perverse or crazy; it is certainly idiosyncratic. Surely this is the reasonable conclusion, the conclusion of common sense or at least of an educated and cultivated sort of common sense, which is the only relevant sort in this situation. When we come to our senses, then, and forswear sophistries, we realize that there is indeed a center to the concept of art. And it is no doubt this center which Kennick has in mind when he criticizes "traditional aesthetics." Furthermore, he is very likely right in his main contention that the class of things that are art, on this determination, share no distinguishing property or set of properties.

It is easy to be swept along by this tide of common sense. What, however, have we shown? Notice that when we appealed to common sense in the paragraph above, we did so in order to determine what were *linguistically* correct and incorrect applications of the term "art." By the end of the paragraph, however, we were determining, by the exercise of our common sense, what is and what is not art. Common sense tells us that Tolstoy is wrong in excluding what he does from the realm of art, perhaps. But does it tell us that Tolstoy, in so doing, is using the term "art" (or its Russian equivalent) incorrectly? It is the latter point which is at issue. My argument with Kennick up to now has not been, after all, that the class of objects he uses in his critique is not the class of what is, reasonably speaking, art. My argument has been with his attempt to justify that class in terms of the *correct use of the term "art."* And it is that attempt which has not been vindicated by the preceding appeal to common-sense reasonability.

One reason that that appeal might seem to establish more than it does is that it is phrased in terms of the notions of "center" and "margins." I was, however, deliberately playing upon an ambiguity in these terms. For these terms can have a purely linguistic sense, as I indicated earlier in this paper. But they can also have a "phenomenological" sense. Phenomenologically considered, a "central case" of art is (roughly) what clearly and indubitably appears to a person to be art. Correspondingly, a "marginal case" is what does not clearly and indubitably appear to be art but what does not clearly and indubitably appear not to be art. What the above appeal to common sense argued was that works of Shakespeare, Beethoven, and Da Vinci clearly and indubitably appear to a reasonable person of cultivated common sense to be art and that Superman comics and the mother's croon appear *to such a person* neither to be clearly and indubitably art nor to be clearly and indubitably not art.

The discovery that there are no *linguistically determined* central cases of art has undercut a fundamental assumption of Kennick's whole approach. The way that Kennick sees the traditional problem of the definition of art is that theoreticians are seeking a formula that is adequate to an antecedently given class of art "objects" and that is the same for every (reasonable) theoretician of art. And the existence of such a class of objects is implied by one of the very conditions of reasonable discourse about art, namely, the language rules governing the term "art." But since we now know that the use of language in reasoning about art does not commit anyone to the existence of a determinate class of art objects antecedent to any theoretical formulation of the nature of art, disagreements among theories of art may now be seen in a light different from the one Kennick puts on them. Whereas Kennick's presupposition leads him to see conflicting theories of art simply as conflicting statements about a common class of objects, it is now possible to see conflicting theories or definitions of art as conflicting ways of determining what belongs and what does not belong to the class of art objects.

Of course, it is not necessary in every disagreement about the nature of art that the latter be the root of the conflict. It is surely conceivable that two aestheticians agree perfectly on the members of the class of art objects yet differ in their theories. It is quite plausible, however, that the most striking and apparently irreconcilable disagreements about the nature of art, such as, for example, that between Clive Bell and Tolstoy, are founded upon disagreements about what things should *count* as art. Furthermore, it is quite clear that some disagreements, such as the one between Malraux and Fiedler, are explicitly disagreements about what should count as art and are only implicitly disagreements about the nature of art. In any case, it does seem true that the most troublesome, and therefore most interesting, arguments about art are those in which what is at stake is what is to be included in, and what excluded from, the domain of art.

If the latter is true, however, Kennick's critical stance, now bereft of its linguistic foundations, is no longer in a position to arbitrate controversies about art. Rather, since that critique itself depends upon a determination of what is inside and what is outside (and what is on the borders) of the realm of art, it itself appears now to be only another participant in the running battle about art. Kennick's confidence in the rules of language in resolving disputes about art is not only misplaced, therefore, but it has prevented him from seeing his own part in those disputes and thereby from seeing what is ultimately at stake in those disputes.

II

What, then, is at stake in controversies about what is and what is not art? In order to answer the question, let us see what sort of support we can discover for Kennick's own position (or what we can reconstruct as Kennick's position) on this issue. For, as I indicated earlier, there is a definite reasonability to Kennick's position even though that reasonability does not rest upon the grounds Kennick supposes. Therefore, it is still an open question whether the assumptions concerning what is and what is not art that are behind Kennick's critique are correct. And if they are, then Kennick will have been right, in spite of himself, concerning at least the incorrectness (if not the mistakenness) of a great deal of "traditional aesthetics." Our subsidiary question, then, is whether the way of determining the class of art objects implied by Kennick's critique is the *only* "reasonable" or, perhaps, the *most* "reasonable" way of determining that class.

Let us first be clear about what I take Kennick's implicit position on this matter to be. It is a position, remember, that takes the works of Shakespeare, Da Vinci, and Beethoven to be clear and indisputable cases of art, that places the mother's formless lullaby and comic books on the very edge of the realm of art. To fill in the position a bit more, we can reasonably suppose that it places the music of the Beatles and of Frank Sinatra rather closer to the center than comic books, and the folk songs and dances of Yugoslavia closer still. A number of plausible reasons can be offered for this general way of laying out the realm of art:

1. Most university-educated persons who have an interest in the arts would probably agree with it.
2. It includes most if not all of what is "traditionally" called art without at the same time rejecting out of hand contemporary developments in popular art forms and avant-garde movements.
3. It is an accommodating position in that it can allow at least a partial sort of truth to more tendentious theories of art put forth by artists themselves.
4. It does not take an extreme, exclusivistic, or shockingly idiosyncratic point of view on art. (This is simply a corollary of reasons 1, 2, and 3).

These reasons are not only plausible reasons, but they are, I think, the *strongest possible* reasons that can be given for the position.

It is not the case, however, that philosophers, critics, and artists maintaining quite different positions have *no* reasons for their stands. Tolstoy, for example, has reasons for excluding the works of Shakespeare and Beethoven from the realm of art:

1. They are too sophisticated and are, therefore, inaccessible to most men.
2. They are, moreover, obscure and not easily understood.
3. They are related most immediately to other works of art rather than to genuine and universal emotions of the artists.
4. As a result of 1, 2, and 3 they are not means of communicating basic human emotions among men.

We may suppose that Clive Bell, too, would have had reasons for rejecting the hypothesized lullaby as art:

1. It is virtually without form.
2. Its appeal is exclusively to the "merely human" feelings of affection, tenderness, comfort, and so forth.

André Malraux, likewise, has his reasons for rejecting comic books and relegating them to the sphere of antiart:

1. They embody no "cosmic" meanings.
2. They do not exhibit a sense of universal "values."
3. They appeal to the baser elements in man, to his purely sensual instincts and his sensationalistic interests.

Leslie Fiedler, on the other hand, apparently does not even think of comic books as *marginal* cases of art. For him, they are as truly art as *Oedipus Rex* and *Macbeth*. He evidently agrees with Malraux that the comics are related to the "lower" aspects of human nature. Ultimately, however, his justification for calling the comics art is, as I read him, that they give us back a true, if distressing, reflection of human nature. Man is, for Fiedler, at least as dark, violent, and brutal as he is benevolent, idealistic, and spiritual. We might bring forth many more "points of view" of the above sorts without altering the result. *All* of the views would be reasonable, at least in the sense that their proponents have what they consider *reasons* for believing as they do.

The obvious next step is to inquire whether any of these reasons can be rejected as inadequate reasons, bad reasons, or, finally, as being no reasons at all. The answer, obviously, is: Yes, they can—all of them. What possible bearing does a respect for traditional uses of the term "art" or for the uses of that term by an academically molded "common man" have on what is "truly" art when compared to the presence of "spiritual value" in a work? Clearly, none. Or what possible relevance can the communication of unsophisticated feelings among unsophisticated people have for the essence of art to a person struck by the exalted and sublime emotions aroused by significant forms? Again, none. Or what difference does it make that Superman comics do not project "spiritual values" if they do present the awful and bloody truth about human nature? The answer is: None.

But surely, you say, we were not inquiring whether these various reasons could (or would) be rejected by persons holding some competing position. We wanted to know if any of them could be rejected as "inherently" bad reasons. We can at least imagine what clear cases of "inherently" bad reasons would be. They would be clear cases of *irrelevant* reasons. Suppose, for example, that *Hamlet* were excluded from the class of art works because the word "Hamlet" has fewer than seven letters, or that Beethoven's Ninth Symphony were excluded because it consists of more than ten notes. It is, I submit, impossible to imagine any seriously argued (or taken) position entailing those consequences. Even Tolstoy's position, which is often labeled "crazy" or "preposterous," is not *so* crazy or preposterous. Tolstoy's position is still taken seriously by persons interested in philosophical problems of art. But so is Bell's, and Malraux's, and Fiedler's. So is Kennick's. None of their reasons can be rejected out of hand as clear cases of bad reasons.

Let us then restrict our discussion only to those competing points of view whose reasons are taken seriously by the community of persons interested in the philosophy of art. The area of possible disagreement does not thereby become smaller by a single jot. Only the probability of mediating the disagreements seems considerably reduced. For if *none* of the reasons listed above is "inherently" inadequate, yet if *all* of them are insufficient from some competing point of view, there are no winners, even if there are no losers. Every reason is a reasonable reason but also a bad one, no one more so than the rest. Are these "reasons," then, nothing but a sham? Are they nothing but the mere mask of rational discourse where there can be no reality of it because there is no way of separating the true from the false? We must see them in that light if we insist that a reason operate only to prove a conclusion and if we suppose that the relevant "conclusions" in these situations take the forms "*x* is art," "*x* is not art," and "perhaps *x* is art, on the one hand, and perhaps it is not art, on the other."

But reasons operate in different ways. Reasons operate to ground assertions but also to justify actions. Suppose that *T* always walks home from school on the south side of the boulevard but *V* always walks home on the north side. Now they might not have any particular reasons for doing so, but they might also have quite definite reason. *T*'s reason might be that there is a vicious and dangerous dog living on the north side whose owners are not overscrupulous about securing it in their yard. *V*'s reasons, on the other hand, are that there is a profusion of flowers in bloom the year around on the north side and that their fragrance fills the air. Moreover, he says, trees line the sidewalk and the sunlight filtering through their foliage makes wonderful patterns on the ground. Now let us suppose that T admits all that V says about the *beauties* of the north side and that V admits all that T says about the *dangers* of the north side. For T, those beauties do not constitute good enough reasons for walking on the north side; and for V, those dangers are not sufficient reason for walking on the south side.

Three points need emphasis in this situation. (1) From an "objective" point of view the different actions of T and V are equally reasonable. Their reasons are not bad by virtue of being clearly irrelevant as might be the following: that the south side is nearer to Guatemala. Nor are they bad reasons by virtue of describing either side falsely. (2) On the other hand, for T, V's reasons are insufficient and for V, T's reasons are insufficient. (3) Most importantly, the reasons that T and V give serve to put their respective actions in a certain light. Knowing T's reasons (and, of course, knowing them to be his true reasons), we are able to see T's habitual behavior as a sign of T's fearfulness and general timidity. Similarly, V's habitual behavior can be seen as a sign of his aesthetic sensibility. The reasons of T and V thus do not function to *convince* anyone, least of all one another, of the universal correctness of walking home either on the north side or the south side. (They might, of course, persuade someone of the advisability of doing one or the other by pointing out the dangers of the dog or the beauties of the trees; but that is an incidental thing.) What these reasons necessarily do is to lend a sort of character to actions that, in themselves and devoid of such justifying reasons, would be without particular significance.

Let us, then, view the reasons that Tolstoy, Bell, Malraux, Fiedler, and Kennick give (or which may be given on their behalf) not so much as relating to *what* they assert or imply about whether a thing is art or not but rather as relating to their "acts" of asserting (or implying) that a thing is or is not art. If we do so, those reasons can be seen as functioning much as the reasons T and V give for their actions. In particular, those reasons allow us to see the various inclusions and exclusions from the realm of art in a certain light. These points of view, like the habitual actions of T and V, take on certain "characters" in virtue of those reasons. Thus, knowing the reasons given above for what I have called Kennick's position, we may characterize that position in a range of ways: moderate, liberal, tolerant, blandly inoffensive, wishy-washy, and so forth. Of course, these characterizations are not synonymous. Which one chooses might depend upon, among other things, whether one agrees with the position, or whether or not one finds it admirable. Note, however, that the same is true of characterizing T's and V's actions. V might see T's action as a sign of timidity, but another might see it as a sign of prudence or good sense. It is certainly not the case that the reasons for a point of view completely or uniquely determine the "character" of that point of view. Those reasons do, however, lend it some character or other. And the *range*, at least, of possible characterizations of a position is delimited by the reasons given for it. Thus, no one could reasonably call Kennick's point of view extravagant any more than one could call T's action bold on the basis of their respective reasons.

Similarly, the position of Clive Bell with respect to items like our hypothetical lullaby can be plausibly described as elitist, snobbish, intellectualistic, coldly inhuman, or possibly all of them together. On the other hand, Tolstoy's way of separating art from nonart might be thought of as extreme, radical, antiestablishmentarian, possibly sentimental, or perhaps mystical, depending upon the position with which one contrasts it. Again, Malraux's emphasis on the spiritual and the cosmic in art can be seen as snobbish, overly grave and long-faced, or perhaps as stuffy or pompous. On the other hand, Fiedler's inclusion of comic books in the domain of art *for the reasons that he gives* might show him to be hard-headed and realistic. Of course, a person with Malraux's general position might see Fiedler's stand as vulgar, base, or perverse.

The use of reasons in justifying a position on what art is and on what art is not is neither pointless nor deceptive. Such reasons do not, however, establish the "truth" of a position. For, conceived now not as a set of assertions and their implications but as a pattern of "action," these positions are neither true nor false. They have, instead, certain "expressive characters" signifying attitudes or personal traits.

III

It appears that one of two conclusions is forced upon us concerning disagreements over what is and what is not art. We might conclude that they are not disagreements at all. They are simply manifestations of different attitudes or personal traits. On the other hand, one can say that these apparent disagreements are genuine disagreements, but that they are simply not disagreements about the nature of some "external" subject matter. They are, rather, disagreements about what character or attitude one ought to have. Thus, *T* and *V* do not disagree in any respect concerning the nature of the north and south side of the boulevard. But they do disagree about how one ought to behave towards those facts.

In either case, however, the philosopher of art need no longer concern himself with the question of the nature of art. It is certainly not the case that a philosopher of art can expect to define art in the "traditional" sense of formulating the distinguishing characteristics of a class of things that are art. But if I am right, a philosopher of art cannot even perform the "negative" task of criticizing the definitions of others from some "position" of his own. For, in either case, the philosopher would be simply displaying some attitude or other, some personal trait or other. To do so might be revealing, but it would hardly be enlightening. Moreover, if there are no "real" disagreements between various "positions" on art, then no one needs the philosopher's special insight into the truth to mediate them. And if the disagreements only concern what *attitudes* to take or what personal traits to develop, the philosopher appears to have no competence in settling such disputes. It seems that there is nothing more for a philosopher to say about what art is than what I have already said.

Is philosophy of art dead? It seems so—but I am not totally convinced. And yet if it is not dead, it is dying. If it is to revive, it may well be that it must begin to ask questions that it has been unfashionable to ask for decades. If I am right in my claim that any serious and reasoned determination of what is art and what is not is to project some attitude or personal characteristic, then the suggestion is that if philosophy is to have any role in this activity, it will be to determine which attitude or which character it is *best* to have. If the philosopher can no longer ask, "Whose theory is true—Tolstoy's or Bell's?" perhaps he must ask, "Whose view is better—Tolstoy's sentimental one or Bell's aloof and intellectualistic one?" The philosophical question with respect to art would be analogous to the question "Is it better to be timid and fearful like *T* or aesthetically gratified like *V*?" It may also be that from asking which is "better" the philosopher may progress to seeking the "best." And the quest may issue in—a theory of art!—but this time with a difference. The difference would be that it would be more completely justified, that is, that whatever attitude it projected would itself be justified as the "best" attitude.

All this sounds hopelessly naive. It is likely, after all, that a philosopher could never in principle *argue* such a point convincingly, thoroughly, and, above all, with discipline. It is not at all clear what would even be *relevant* in such an argument. For there has been almost no progress on these sorts of issues since Plato, who did treat them seriously—and philosophically. The real question, therefore, is whether it is worth *trying* to revive this Platonic conception of philosophy at least with respect to the very limited question "What is art?" I think it is, and for two reasons. First, the only alternative is for philosophy to abandon the question altogether, which would be to abandon so-called theoretical discussion about art to arationality. Second, the prospect of such a revival opens up more exciting vistas than the philosophy of art has seen for some time.

NOTES

1. W. E. Kennick, "Does Traditional Aesthetics Rest on a Mistake?," *Mind* 67 (1958):317–34. Reprinted in *Collected Papers on Aesthetics*, ed. Cyril Barrett (Oxford: Blackwell, 1965), pp. 1–21.
2. I want it to be clear that I am focusing on Professor Kennick's paper solely because of what I take to be its influence and general significance. I do not know if that paper still represents Kennick's view. If it does not, however, the fact should not render my critique pointless.
3. André Malraux, "Art, Popular Art and the Illusion of the Folk," reprinted in *Modern Culture and the Arts*, ed. James B. Hall and Barry Ulanov (New York: McGraw-Hill, 1967), pp. 29–38.
4. Leslie Fiedler, "The Comics: Middle Against Both Ends," reprinted in *Modern Culture and the Arts*, pp. 526–38.
5. It may bother some readers that I am dismissing too easily the very real possibilities that Bell and Tolstoy, Tolstoy and Malraux, and Malraux and Fiedler are actually disagreeing about the *properties* that the aforementioned works have. This, of course, remains a live possibility precisely because the key properties—having significant form, being communicative of feeling, having abstract meaning, etc.—are so vague. My point in choosing the pairs of theoreticians that I did, however, was to be able to isolate kinds of "works" with respect to which a disagreement over their properties would seem unlikely so that I could then claim to have bona-fide examples of disagreements "purely" in the application of the term "art." Now it is enough for my purposes if it is merely *quite likely* that the disagreements described above are disagreements solely in the application of "art." For I shall go on to show that the consequences that should follow from such a likelihood, if we grant Kennick's position, are *not in the least likely* or even plausible.
6. W. E. Kennick, ed., *Art and Philosophy* (New York: St. Martin's, 1964), p. 89.
7. Note that nothing in my arguments thus far precludes the possibility that there are central cases of art that are *not* determined by linguistic rules. In

such cases, of course, the notion of "central case" would have to be understood in a way somewhat different from the way it has generally been understood in the Wittgensteinian tradition. Later on, I introduce such an "unorthodox" notion of "central case" and of its correlative concept, "marginal case."

In Memory of William K. Wimsatt (1907–1975)

Stevens' Rock and Criticism as Cure

J. Hillis Miller

> It is not enough to cover the rock with leaves.
> We must be cured of it by a cure of the ground
> Or a cure of ourselves, that is equal to a cure
>
> Of the ground, a cure beyond forgetfulness.
> > —Stevens, "The Rock"

A "cure of the ground"? What can this mean? "Progress," Stevens says in the "Adagia," "is a movement through changes of terminology." "Rock," "ground," and even "forgetfulness" readers of Stevens will be able to interpret from other poems by him, from works in his immediate tradition, the tradition of Whitman and Emerson, or from the common language of poetry and metaphysics. Such readers will remember, among other rocks in Stevens, "this tufted rock/ Massively rising high and bare" in "How to Live. What to Do," the Leibnizian "thought-like Monadnocks" of "This Solitude of Cataracts," the rocky mountain of "Chocorua to Its Neighbor," the rock of "The Poem that Took the Place of a Mountain," "The exact rock where his inexactnesses/ Would discover, at last, the view toward which they had edged," and that ecstatic meridian rock of "Credences of Summer":

> The rock cannot be broken: It is the truth.
> It rises from land and sea and covers them.
> It is a mountain half way green and then,
> The other immeasurable half, such rock
> As placid air becomes.

Forgetfulness, or its converse, memory, is also a motif found elsewhere in Stevens, inextricably entwined with the theme of time, as in

497

"The Owl in the Sarcophagus," where the fleeting present moment, the presence of the present, "the mother of us all," cries in her vanishing, "Keep you, keep you, I am gone, oh keep you as/ My memory."

"Ground" too is a common word in Stevens. To follow it through his poetry is to observe its modulation from the everyday use of it as the solid earth we stand on ("The jar was round upon the ground"), to ground as background upon which a figure appears, to the more "metaphysical" use of the term as meaning "foundation," "basis," "source," "mind", or "consciousness," "reason," "measure." The rock "is the habitation of the whole,/ Its strength and measure," "the main of things, the mind," in short, a Monadnock. Ground and rock are apparently not the same, since a cure of the ground is necessary to cure us of the rock, though what the difference is between ground and rock remains, at this point, something still to be interrogated. The means of this interrogation, however, as of the investigation of "forgetfulness," would, it seems, be the familiar one of following these words in their interplay with other words as they gradually weave together in a single grand intertextual system, a polyphonic harmony of many notes, "The Whole of Harmonium," as Stevens wanted to call his *Collected Poems*.

What, then, of "cure"? It has little resonance in philosophic or poetic tradition and, according to the *Concordance to the Poetry of Wallace Stevens*, the word is used only once, in a more or less unpregnant way, prior to its decidedly pregnant use in "The Poem as Icon," the middle of the three sections of "The Rock." "The Poem as Icon" is in fact partly a meditation on the multiple senses, "the new senses in the engenderings of sense," of the word "cure," in its relation to certain other terms and figures. The word thereafter disappears from the poetic canon, not even being used in the third poem of "The Rock," though it does appear in the "Adagia": "Poetry is a health"; "Poetry is a cure of the mind." In formulations of the workings of intertextuality—the weavings of word with word, of figure and figure, in the canon of a writer, or of that canon in relation to tradition—the theorist would need to allow for the emergence of a word which is played with, turned this way and that, mated or copulated with other words, used as an indispensable means of that progress which takes place through changes of terminology, and then dropped.

To think of the whole work of a writer as being based on a permanent ground in an underlying system or code of terms, conceptual, figurative, "symbolic," mythical, or narrative, is an error, just as it is an error to suggest, as I. A. Richards does in his admirable *How to*

Read a Page, that there may be in our Western languages a finite set of key words of multiple sense whose mastery would give approximate mastery of Western thought and literature. The repertoire of such words, uncanny with antithetical and irreconcilable meanings, is very large, finite still (there are only so many words in the *OED*), but virtually inexhaustible. Any poet's vocabulary is to some degree irreducibly idiosyncratic. The most unexpected words, for example "cure," may become momentarily nodes, at once fixed rock and treacherous abyss of doubled and redoubled meanings, around or over which the thought of the poet momentarily swirls or weaves its web. Such words are not the equivalents or substitutes for other terms. Each has its own proper laws and so may not be made an example of some general law. Such words may not be translated, thereby made transparent, dispensed with, evaporated, sublimated. They remain stubbornly heterogeneous, unassimilable, impervious to dialectical elation (*Aufhebung*), rocks in the stream, though the rock is air. The vocabulary of a poet is not a gathering or a closed system, but a dispersal, a scattering.

What, then, of "cure"? The first section of "The Rock," "Seventy Years Later," is, at least until the last two stanzas, as bleak and cold a poem as any Stevens wrote. It is a poem about forgetting. The old man of seventy has forgotten not the illusions of his past but the affective warmth of those illusions, "the life these lived in the mind." When that warmth goes, the illusions come to be seen as illusions and so are undermined, annihilated. Not only are their validity and vitality rejected, their very existence is denied: "The sounds of the guitar/ Were not and are not. Absurd. The words spoken/ Were not and are not." "Absurd": from *ab*, away, an intensive here, and *surdus*, deaf, inaudible, insufferable to the ear. The sounds of the guitar, those for example played by Stevens' man with the blue guitar, were not only an inharmonious jangling masking as harmony, they did not even exist at the time, were inaudible when they most seemed audible. They did not exist because they were pure fiction, based on nothingness. A surd in mathematics is a sum containing one or more irrational roots of numbers. (The square root of two is an irrational number. There is a square root of two, but it is not a number that can be expressed as an integer or as a finite fraction, not a number that can be expressed "rationally.") A surd in phonetics is a voiceless sound in speech, that is to say, a sound with no base in the vibration of the vocal chords. The original root of the word surd, *swer*, means to buzz or whisper, as in "susurration" or "swirl." The Latin *surdus* was chosen in medieval mathematics to translate an Arabic term which was itself a translation of the Greek *alogos*, speechless, word-less, inexpressible, irrational, groundless.

The first six stanzas of "Seventy Years Later" record a radical act of forgetting. This disremembering annihilates everything that seemed most vital in the poet's past, most solidly grounded. It annihilates it by uprooting it, by seeing its roots as non-existent, "alogical." Then in the final three stanzas the dismantled illusion is put together again. Though the base may be "nothingness," this nothingness contains a "métier," a craftsmanlike power of working, "a vital asumption." It contains a desire for illusion so great that the leaves come and cover that high rock of air, as the lilacs bloom in the spring, cleansing blindness, bringing sight again to birth, and so starting the cycle of illusion over again. Blindness is parallel to the deafness of "absurd," and the power of seeing again is here replaced and implicitly figured by "a birth of sight." The lilacs satisfy sight. They fill the eye, as the sounds of the guitar filled the ear, saturated it, so hiding the "perma-nent cold" at the base, "the dominant blank, the unapproachable," as he calls it in "An Ordinary Evening in New Haven." A cure of ourselves equal to a cure of the ground would make us sound, heal us of our deafness, our absurdity. Then we could hear again the sounds of the guitar, as springtime makes us see again, like a blindness cured, or scoured.

The cure of the ground called for in the beginning of the second poem of "The Rock," "The Poem as Icon," must be a "cure beyond forgetfulness." It must be a cure not subject to the periodic cycles of annihilation revealing the illusion to be illusion and so negating it. Or, perhaps, it must be a cure which reaches beyond forgetfulness, that repression which disables present affirmations. Such repression has caused us to forget the something lacking in earlier satisfactions, something missing even when we "lived in the houses of mothers." To remove this repression would, perhaps, make it possible to get to something solid that lies beneath, or to make something solid beneath that is not based on a forgetting and so vulnerable to forgetting. After the cure we would live in a permanent state of illusion known as illusion, therefore "beyond forgetfulness." This illusion would be known in such a way that the abyss, the *Abgrund*, would appear as the truth of the ground, without undermining the illusion, so that the illusion might never be forgotten. Or does Stevens mean that the cure beyond forgetfulness would permanently cover or solidify the abyss? Then the illusion might never again be scoured away and the abyss never again be seen: "the poem makes meanings of the rock,/ Of such mixed motion and such imagery/ That its barrenness becomes a thousand things/ And so exists no more." The undecidable oscillation among these alternatives is expressed in Stevens' often-cited adage: "The final belief is to believe in a fiction, which you know to be a fiction, there being nothing else."

A similar oscillation (but what is the status of similarity here?) is expressed in the relation between rock and ground. Ground and rock are each the base of the other. The rock is the truth, but the rock is air, nothingness, and so must be grounded on something solid beneath it. The ground, on the other hand, is itself not ground. It is an abyss, the groundless, while the rock remains visible in the air as "the gray particular of man's life/ The stone from which he rises, up—and —ho,/ The step to the bleaker depths of his descents. . . ." The rock is the solid of the ground, the ground the base of the rock, in a perpetual reversal, interchange, doubling, or abyssing, what Stevens elsewhere calls, "an insolid billowing of the solid" ("Reality Is an Activity of the Most August Imagination").

The cure of the ground would be a caring for the ground, a securing of it, making it solid, as one cures a fiberglass hull by drying it carefully. At the same time the cure of the ground must be an effacing of it, making it vanish as a medicine cures a man of a disease by taking it away, making him sound again, or as an infatuated man is cured of a dangerous illusion. "Cure" comes from Latin *cura*, care, as in "curate" or "a cure of souls." The word "scour," which I used above, has the same root. A cure of the ground would scour it clean, revealing the bedrock beneath. Such a curing would be at the same time—according to an absolute meaning of the word, with a different root, Middle English *cuuve*, cover, conceal, protect—a caring for the ground by hiding it. Stevens might even have known (why should he not have known?) the word "curiologic," which means, according to the *OED*, "of or pertaining to that form of hieroglyphic writing in which objects are represented by pictures, and not by symbolic characters." The root here is neither *cura* nor *cuuve*, but the Greek *kuriologia*, the use of literal expressions, speaking literally, from *kurios*, as an adjective: regular, proper; as a noun: lord, master. A curiological cure of the ground would find proper names for that ground, make a mimetic icon of it, copy it exactly, appropriate it, master it. The cure of the ground proposed in the poem is the poem itself. The poem is an icon, at once a "copy of the sun" and a figure of the ground, though the relation of sun and ground remains to be established. The icon (image, figure, resemblance) at once creates the ground, names it "properly," reveals it, and covers it over. The poem annihilates the rock, takes the place of it, and replaces it with its own self-sufficient fiction, the leaves, blossom, and fruit which come to cover the high rock. At that point its barrenness has become a thousand things and so exists no more.

The multiple meanings of the word "cure," like the meanings of all the key words and figures in "The Rock," are incompatible, irreconcilable. They may not be organized into a logical or dialectical structure but remain stubbornly heterogeneous. They may not be followed, etymologically, to a single root which will unify or explain them, explicate them by implicating them in a single source. They may not be folded together in a unified structure, as of leaves, blossom, and fruit from one stem. The origin rather is bifurcated, even trifurcated, a forking root which leads the searcher for the ground of the word into labyrinthine wanderings in the forest of words. The meaning of the passages in "The Rock" turning on the word "cure" oscillates painfully within the reader's mind. However hard he tries to fix the word in a single sense it remains indeterminable, uncannily resisting his attempts to end its movement. Cover the abyss, or open it up, or find the bottom, the ground of the rock, and make it a solid base on which to build—which is it? How could it be all three at once? Yet it is impossible to decide which one it is. To choose one is to be led to the others and so to be led by the words of the poem into a blind alley of thought.

Since it is a question here of the abyss of the absurd and of the grounding or filling of that abyss, one may borrow from the French an untranslatable name for this enigma of the nameless, this impasse of language: *mise en abyme*. *Abyme* is an older variant of modern French *abîme*, from late Latin *abyssus*, from Greek *abussos*, without bottom. The circumflexed î, an i deprived of its head or dot and given a hat or tent instead, indicates a dropped s. This is then dropped in turn to be replaced by a y, *i grec*, Greek i. In fact the late Latin y was an equivalent both for Greek u, *upsilon*, "bare u," and for the y, or u with a tail, that is, an i sound, as in French *ici*. The Greek u, which became Roman y, is only one of the two letters derived from the Phoenician *waw*, which itself was derived from v. The other descendant is f, Greek *digamma*, "double gamma." The *gamma* is of course also y-shaped. The word *abyme* is itself a *mise en abyme*, hiding and revealing the hollow of the u by the masculine addition of the tail, but leaving no sign of the absent s. The word contains dropped letter behind dropped letter, in a labyrinth of interchanges figured by the doubling shape of the y: a path leading to a fork, Hercules at the crossroads, or Theseus at one of the infinitely repeating branches of the Daedalian labyrinth, to which I shall return.

Mise en abyme is a term in heraldry meaning a shield which has in its center (*abyme*) a smaller image of the same shield, and so, by implication, ad infinitum, with ever smaller and smaller shields receding toward the central point. The nearest equivalent in English language of heraldry is the admirably suggestive term "escutcheon of pretense." The arms to which a knight pretends to have a claim are *mise en abyme* on his own shield. As in the case of a bend sinister, the implication is of a possible illegitimacy, some break in the genetic line of filiation. I have, in *The Form of Victorian Fiction*, called this structure "the Quaker Oats box effect." To name it or to give examples of it is not to create a concept, a general structure which all the examples illustrate, since it is precisely a question, in this case, of what has no concept, no literal name. Therefore it can only be "figured," each time differently, and by analogies which are not symmetrical with one another. What is the meaning of the terms "figure," "icon," "analogy" here if there is no literal name on which they are based? Here, in any case, from Michel Leiris's autobiography, *L'âge d'homme* (1939), is a splendid "example" of a *mise en abyme*:

> I owe my first precise contact with the notion of infinity to a box of cocoa of Dutch manufacture, raw material (*matière première*) for my breakfasts. One side of this box was decorated with an image representing a peasant girl with a lace headdress who held in her left hand an identical box decorated with the same image and, pink and fresh, offered it with a smile. I remained seized with a sort of vertigo in imagining that infinite series of an identical image reproducing a limitless number of times the same young Dutch girl, who, theoretically getting smaller and smaller without ever disappearing, looked at me with a mocking air and showed me her own effigy painted on a cocoa box identical to the one on which she herself was painted.

The paradox of the *mise en abyme* is the following: without the production of some schema, some "icon," there can be no glimpse of the abyss, no vertigo of the underlying nothingness. Any such schema, however, both opens the chasm, creates it or reveals it, and at the same time fills it up, covers it over by naming it, gives the groundless a ground, the bottomless a bottom. Any such schema almost instantaneously becomes a trivial mechanism, an artifice. It becomes something merely made, confected, therefore all-too-human and rational. Examples would include the Daedalian labyrinth, product, after all, of a human artificer, however "fabulous," and the

Borgesian labyrinths of words, products of a visible manipulation of verbal effects. Another "example" is the cunning wordplay of Stevens' "The Rock," with its sagacious and somewhat covert use of the full etymological complexity of a word like "cure." If Stevens is right to say that "poetry must be irrational" and that "poetry must resist the intelligence almost successfully," then the moment when the intelligence triumphs over the poem, encompassing its *mise en abyme* with human reason, is the moment of the poem's failure, its resolution into a rational paradigm. The *mise en abyme* must constantly begin again. "The Rock" is, accordingly, a running *mise en abyme*. The poem repeatedly takes some apparently simple word, a word not noticeably technical or tricky ("found," "exclaiming," "ground," or "cure") and plays with each word in turn, placing it in a context of surrounding words so that it gives way beneath its multiplying contradictory meanings and reveals a chasm below, a chasm which the word, for example the word "cure," cures in all senses of the word.

There are other ways, however, in which "The Rock" is a *mise en abyme*. One is the sequence of phrases in apposition. This is a constant feature of Stevens' poetic procedure: "The blooming and the musk/ Were being alive, an incessant being alive,/ A particular of being, that gross universe"; "They bud the whitest eye, the pallidest sprout,/ New senses in the engenderings of sense,/ The desire to be at the end of distances,/ The body quickened and the mind in root." The relation among the elements in such a series is undecidable, abyssed. Since the phrases often have the same syntactical pattern and are objects of the same verb (most often the verb "to be"), it seems as if they must be equivalents of one another, or at least figures for one another, but can "eye," "sprout," "senses," "desire," "body," and "mind" really be equivalent? Perhaps the phrases form a progression, a gradual approximation through incremental repetition ("being alive, an incessant being alive"), reaching closer and closer to the desired meaning in what Stevens in "An Ordinary Evening in New Haven" calls "the edgings and inchings of final form"? Perhaps each new phrase cancels the previous one? Sometimes the parallel in syntax is misleading, as when the phrase "that gross universe" is placed in apposition with the subsidiary word "being" in the phrase before, rather than with the apparently parallel word "particular." The sequence plays with various incongruent senses and grammatical functions of the word "being." Sometimes the established syntactical pattern misleads the reader into interpreting the grammar incorrectly or at any rate leads him into a fork in the labyrinth where he cannot decide which path to take, as when the parallelism of "And yet the leaves, if they broke into bud,/ If they broke into bloom, if they bore fruit,/ And if we ate the incipient colorings/ Of their fresh culls might be a cure of the ground" makes "colorings" appear to be simultaneously the object of "ate" and the subject of "might be," which it cannot, logically, be. The actual subject of "might be" is "leaves," three lines above. The phrase seems alogical, absurd, with no root in a single sense.

Such sequences, with their tantalizing half-parallelisms and asymmetrical analogies, with their suggestions that the series might continue indefinitely without exhausting itself or "getting it right," are *mises en abyme*. They are like those nursery rhymes which work by variation and incremental repetition, such as "The House That Jack Built." John Ruskin, in the twenty-third letter of *Fors Clavigera* (1872), compares "The House That Jack Built" to the Daedalian maze: "the gradual involution of the ballad, and the necessity of clearmindedness as well as clear utterance on the part of its singer, is a pretty vocal imitation of the deepening labyrinth." Like Stevens' sequences of phrases in apposition, "The House That Jack Built" turns back on itself, a snake with its tail in its mouth, or a snake almost succeeding in getting its tail in its mouth. Just as "that gross universe" comments on or defines the word "being," which has been the theme varied in the sequence of phrases in Stevens' sentence until then, so the *mise en abyme* of the potentially endlessly mounting series in "The House That Jack Built" is broken when "the farmer sowing his corn" is reached, since that corn is presumably the source of the malt that lay in the house that Jack built. This takes the listener back to the second item in the sequence and so makes the infinitely receding series, the labyrinth within the house that Jack built, an infinitely rotating circle instead. In the same way the diminishing sequence described in the passage from Leiris quoted above is blocked by the end which turns back to remind the reader that the "first" girl is herself an image painted on a box. The series, moreover, is asymmetrically balanced by a second paragraph describing the multiplying of erotic reflections in facing mirrors: "I am not far from believing that there was mixed in this first notion of infinity, acquired at about the age of ten (?), an element of a distinctly disturbing sort: the hallucinatory and genuinely ungraspable character of the young Dutch girl, repeated to infinity as libertine visions can be indefinitely multiplied by means of a carefully constructed play of mirrors in a boudoir."

This structure of not quite congruent parallelism is characteristic of all forms of the *mise en abyme*. This is one of the ways it keeps

open the chasm while filling it, resists the intelligence almost successfully. An admirable example of this asymmetry is that cartoon by
Charles Addams showing the receding reflections in doubled mirrors
of a man in a barber chair, facing frontwards, then backwards, then
frontwards again, in endless recession. One figure in the midst of the
sequence, five images back into the mirror's depths, is a wolfman with
fangs and a hairy face. The wolfman is the terrifying item which is
part of the series but does not fit it, though he is neither its beginning,
nor its end, nor its base. Another more complex example of the
mirror as *mise en abyme* is Thomas Hardy's admirable poem "The
Pedigree." As Ruskin astutely saw, "Jack's ghostly labyrinth [mean-
ing the mythical Daedalian maze, with its Charles Addams monster
as inhabitant] has set the pattern of almost everything linear and complex, since."

Characteristic of such structures is some play with the figure of
container and contained or with an inside/outside opposition which
reverses itself. Inside becomes outside, outside inside, dissolving the
polarity. The house that Jack built contains all the elements in the
nursery rhyme, though they are mostly outside the house. As Ruskin
suggests, the cunning artifice of the poem is the house itself, just as
the Daedalian labyrinth is at once an enclosure and a place of endless
wandering. A labyrinth is a desert turned inside out. In a similar way
the passage from Leiris's autobiography turns on the cocoa box
which is a container of the *matière première* of the child's breakfast,
while the girl who offers the box is also offering herself, in a troubling
erotic abyssing which is another characteristic of the *mise en abyme*.
Eating and sex are interchanged, as also in "The Rock," which has in
its first section an embrace at noon at the edge of a field and moves
on to the image of curing the ground and curing ourselves by eating
the fruit grown from the rock. That eating, with its disturbing Mil-
tonic and Biblical echoes, is also a transgression, with erotic and
Satanic overtones. These involve seeing and knowing, in various punning ways, knowledge of the whole and of the base of the whole by
incorporation of a synecdochic part: "in the day ye eat thereof then
your eyes shall be opened, and ye shall be as gods, knowing good and
evil" (Genesis, 3:5); "They bear their fruit so that the year is
known,/ As if its understanding was brown skin,/ The honey in its
pulp, the final found,/ The plenty of the year and of the world." Like
the passage from Leiris, "The Rock" contains a complicated play on
the figure of container and contained, a version of what Kenneth
Burke calls "the paradox of substance." The rock is the base from
which things rise up, therefore it is outside. At the same time it is the

habitation of the whole, that in which space and all the contents of space are contained. This enigmatic structure is repeated by the houses of mothers, by the sun, the fruit, and by the poem itself. To read the poem or to eat the fruit is to incorporate the whole as it is contained in the part, to incorporate even the ground of that whole, and so to become oneself whole, sound, cured, knowing all in a final "found."

The *mise en abyme* is likely also to contain some puzzling play with the intertwined notions of representation, on the one hand, and, on the other, figure, metaphor. The girl on the cocoa box offers smilingly a picture of herself, an image, an effigy, but she is herself only an image. The image within an image tends both to affirm the literal reality of the outside image and to undermine it, as in another, more recent, *New Yorker* cartoon showing a middle-aged couple watching on television a representation of themselves watching a televised picture of themselves watching television, and so on. In "The Rock" this aporia of representation enters by way of the contradictory meanings of the word "icon," as it has already entered more obscurely in the word "shadow" in the first section. The poem as icon is both curiological, a mimetic copy of the whole, and at the same time a figure, similitude, or metaphor of it. It is an icon in both senses, in an undecidable play between literal and figurative. This baffling interchange between proper and improper uses of language, in a bewildering multiplication of different chains of figurative terminology superimposed, juxtaposed, interwoven, is a final form of *mise en abyme* in the poem.

"The Rock" contains at least four distinct linguistic "scenes," repertoires of terms adding up to a distinct pattern. The poem is like one of those paintings by Tchelitchew that are simultaneous representations of several different objects, superimposed or interwoven, or it is like one of those children's puzzles in which the trick is to see the five monkeys hidden in the tree, or, more grotesquely, the sailboats in the vegetable garden. The poem contains a scene of love, even a love story: "the meaning at noon at the edge of the field . . . , an embrace between one desperate clod/ And another"; "as a man loves, as he lives in love." The poem presents a geometrical diagram. This diagram is described and analyzed with appropriate mathematical and logical terminology: "absurd," "invention," "assertion," "a theorem proposed," "design," "assumption," "figuration," "predicate," "root," "point A/ In a perspective that begins again/ At B," "adduce." The poem presents in addition a natural scene, the rock which in the turn of the seasons and in the diurnal warmth of the rising and setting sun is covered with leaves, blossoms, and fruit. Man shares in this natural cycle as he eats of the fruit, or as he becomes himself a natural body rooted in the ground, his eye growing in power like the sprouting eye of a potato: "They bud the whitest eye, the pallidest sprout,/ New senses in the engenderings of sense." "The Rock," finally, describes and analyzes itself. It presents a theory of poetry, with an appropriate terminology—"icon," "copy," "figuration," "imagery," and so on.

The question, it would seem, is which of these scenes is the literal subject of the poem, the real base of which the others are illustrative figures. This question is unanswerable. Each scene is both literal and metaphorical, both the ground of the poem and a figure on that ground, both that which the poem is centrally about and a resource of terminology used figuratively to describe something other than itself, in a fathomless *mise en abyme*. The structure of each scene separately and of all four in their relation is precisely a dramatization, or articulation, or iconic projection of the uncanny relation, neither polar opposition, nor hierarchy, nor genetic filiation, between figurative and literal.

In one sense the description of all four of the scenes is entirely literal. They are icons in the sense of being mimetic pictures of things which—for most practical purposes and for those living within the terminology of English or American communities—are supposed to exist as independent objects. There really are rocks, leaves, flowers, fruit, and the seasons of the year. A man and a woman have no doubt met in the "real world" at the edge of a field at noon to embrace. This may well be an autobiographical reference to some episode in the old poet's past. There really are geometrical diagrams with points A and B, theorems, and so on. A poem's self-referentiality is just that, a form of reference or mimesis, as "realistic" as a description of the weather.

On the other hand, no reader of "The Rock" can remain long under the illusion that it is a poem about the weather or indeed a poem about geometry or about love or about poetry. When the reader focuses on any one of these scenes, it emerges in full mimetic vividness, as the chain of words describing it is culled out of the mesh of other words in the poem, but at the same time the reader sees that it cannot be copied, made into an icon, without the use of terms drawn from the other scenes, as the embrace at noon at the edge of the field is, mathematically, "a theorem proposed between the two." Simultaneously, each scene, though it must borrow names from the others to name itself, becomes itself a resource of figurative language for the other scenes: the leaves bud, blossom, and fruit "as a man loves, as he lives in love." Each scene is both ground and design on that ground, both literal and figurative, icon in both senses of the word, in an oscillation which forms and reforms itself with each word, phrase, or image throughout the poem. As the reader tries to rest on each element in the poem or on a chain of elements forming a single scene, as he seeks a solid literal ground which is the curiological basis of the other figurative meanings, that element or chain gives way, becomes itself a verbal fiction, an illusion, an icon (in the sense of similitude and not in the sense of mimetic copy). The element becomes an *Abgrund*, not a *Grund*. The reader is forced then to shift sideways again seeking to find somewhere else in the poem the solid ground of that figure, seeking, and failing or falling, and seeking again.

Another way to put this is to say that the reader can make sense of the poem by assuming any one of the scenes to be the literal ground on the basis of which the others are defined as analogical, figurative, iconic. By that definition, however, the base, when examined, must be defined as itself analogical. That which must necessarily be taken as literal in order to define the figurative is itself figurative, and so the distinction breaks down. In order for the fruit, man, lovers, poem, and geometric design to be defined as figurative, the leftover term, the sun in its turnings, must be taken as literal. If, however, fruit, man, poem, and so on are figurative, so is the sun, since it is, like the others, an icon of the ground. Analogy cannot be defined except with the use of analogies. The defined enters into and so contaminates the definer, annulling the validity of the definition. Figure must always be defined figuratively. There is always a remainder, something alogical left over which does not fit any logical scheme of interpretation. Something has to be left out, assumed to be marginal, in order to make a completely coherent interpretation. The word "cull" in the poem carries this ambiguity. A cull (from *colligere*, to gather) is a fruit chosen, collected, or separated out from the rest, but chosen because it does not fit. A cull is imperfect or inferior. The act of differentiation establishes the criteria of fitness or perfection. Without the culling out of the culls there can be no gathering of what is left as examples of a uniform grade. The figurative, as in the example I have just given, in fact defines the literal rather than the other way around. Whichever scene is taken as figurative implicitly defines some scene as literal, but that scene, when it is looked at directly, turns out to be itself clearly figurative. The reader must then seek the literal base elsewhere, in a constant lateral transfer with no resting place in the unequivocally literal, the mimetic, the "exact rock," cured at last.

Each of the scenes in "The Rock" is, as a "particular of being," the equivalent of all the others. Each holds an equivalent status as simultaneously both figure and ground, in a chain of chains which is articulated in the poem around the verb "to be": "The fiction of the leaves is the icon/ Of the poem, the figuration of blessedness,/ And the icon is the man." "This is the cure/ Of leaves and of the ground and of ourselves./ His words are both the icon and the man." Extending these chains of equivalence, or linking them together, one would get the following affirmation: the icon is the man is the poem is the fruit is the sun is a theorem or geometrical design is the relation of love is . . . the rock.

The structure of each of these scenes is the same. It is in fact the traditional metaphysical structure of *aletheia*, the appearance of something visible out of the abyss of truth. Truth is, for Stevens too, evasive, veiled, feminine, and dwells at the bottom of a well. The revelation or unveiling of what has been hidden brings the truth momentarily into the open, out of Lethean forgetfulness, and displays it. This revelation expands to become a container of the whole or means of appropriating the whole, and then instantaneously hides the abyss or ground. It quickly becomes a fiction, an illusion, something hollowed out, a mere "rind" or "cull," something that never was, and so vanishes. The lovers appear at noon and create a relation between one another, a theorem which makes them "Two figures in a nature of the sun,/ In the sun's design of its own happiness." A geometrical design is an appropriation of space which appears in the open. Fruit grows out of the leaves and blossoms which come and cover the high rock. That fruit encompasses the whole year and becomes "the final found,/ The plenty of the year and of the world." The fruit is a gathering of the whole, a cull. To eat the fruit would be to possess the whole and so to cure the ground. It would be to understand it, in the etymological sense of reaching the base and standing there, in a "final found," with a multiple pun on "found" as discovery, invention, and foundation. The man in turn grows like the fruit. His maturing is a birth and extension of sight, "new senses in the engenderings of sense." These allow him to encompass space. This equivalence of seeing and symbol making goes back, in Stevens' case, to Emerson, as in the formulation of Charles Sanders Peirce: "The symbol may, with Emerson's Sphynx, say to man, 'Of thine eye I am the eyebeam.'" All the symbols or icons of the poem are a means of seeing, an extension of sight, "like a blindness cleaned." The poem itself rises as an icon which is the equivalent of the leaves, blossom, and fruit, and so cures the ground.

The reader is tempted to arrange these items in some kind of hierarchy. Surely, he thinks, one item in the series is the base of the others, grounding the sequence and putting a stop to the discomfort of their oscillation. No doubt the prime candidate for such a base or head appears to be the self, the self of the poet or speaker, the self in general of each individual included in the collective "we" of the poem. One wants to find in the poem a personal voice and a personal drama, the voice and drama of Stevens himself in old age. The experience of reading the poem would then have the security and enclosure of an intersubjective relation. In such a relation my self as reader would respond through the words to the self of the poet and communicate with him, beyond the grave. After all, does not the poem assert that "a cure of ourselves" would be "equal to a cure/ Of the ground, a cure beyond forgetfulness"? The affirmative substitutions and translations of "The Poem as Icon" seem to come to rest in the ecstatic certainty of a poem which would found and be founded on the solid rock of the self, the man's words being the man and rooting him:

> This is the cure
> Of leaves and of the ground and of ourselves.
> His words are both the icon and the man.

The poem's many echoes of its immediately preceding American tradition, the Whitman of "Song of Myself," the Emerson of "Experience," would seem to confirm this priority of the self over the other icons of the poem. In Whitman there is the same return to the self as the base of all experience, and the same universalization of the self to enclose all events, things, and persons, as the reader is tempted to find in "The Rock." It is surely in honor of Whitman that Stevens chooses to have lilacs come and bloom, like a blindness cleaned, to cover the high rock. Stevens' leaves grow up from chthonic depths, as signs, like the inscribed leaves of a book, just as do Whitman's leaves of grass: "I bequeath myself to the dirt to grow from the grass I love"; "Or I guess the grass is itself a child, the produced babe of the vegetation,/ Or I guess it is a uniform hieroglyphic." The equivalence, in Stevens' poem, between the leaves covering the rock, the man, and the poem as icon is sanctioned by Whitman. Whitman's pun on leaves as the leaves of a book surfaces most when Stevens says, "The fiction of the leaves is the icon/ Of the poem." Whitman's "Song of Myself," moreover, like Stevens' "The Rock," is governed by the repeated movement of *aletheia*, the appearance from the dark ground of some "particular of being" which manifests itself in the sunlight. "I find," says Whitman, "I incorporate gneiss, coal, long-threaded moss, fruits, grains, esculent roots." Rocks and earth are part of these figures of descent and return in Whitman's song of himself: "the mica on the side of the rock," a shining from the depths, "the plutonic rocks" which "send in vain their old heat against [his] approach," "voluptuous cool-breath'd earth," "earth of departed sunset." There is even a striking anticipation of Stevens' embrace of two desperate clods at the edge of the field at noon in Whitman's: "I believe the soggy clods shall become lovers and lamps."

From Whitman the reader moves back one further step to Whitman's immediate precursor, Emerson. The sequence forms its own *mise en abyme* of successive influence and misinterpretation, from Emerson to Whitman to Stevens. For Emerson, in "Experience," the strong affirming self is the bedrock fiction beneath which one cannot and should not go. The self is the one power remaining when all else has been peeled off and cast away, like dead husks. Though the self is illusion too, it is an illusion which constantly reforms itself, however often it is expelled. It is the bleak truth which is the source of all power, as if nothingness contained a vital métier forming a base for all practical purposes as solid as the divine rock. Such a self would be a substance in the etymological sense, a ground on which all the experiences or affirmations of the self may be based. Once again the governing figure is that of descent and ascent again into solar prominence:

The great and crescive self, rooted in absolute nature, supplants all relative existence and ruins the kingdom of mortal friendships and love. Marriage (in what is called the spiritual world) is impossible, because of the inequality between every subject and every object. The subject is the receiver of Godhead, and at every comparison must feel his being enhanced by that cryptic might. Though not in energy, yet by presence, this magazine of substance cannot be otherwise than felt; nor can any force of intellect attribute to the object the proper deity which sleeps or wakes forever in every subject. . . . We cannot say too little of our constitutional necessity of seeing things under private aspects or saturated with our humours. And yet is the God native of these bleak rocks. That need makes in morals the capital virtue of self-trust. We must hold hard to this poverty, however scandalous, and by more vigorous self-recoveries, after the sallies of action, possess our axis more firmly. The life of truth is cold and so far mournful; but it is not the slave of tears, contritions and perturbations. It does not attempt another's work, nor adopt another's facts. It is a main lesson of wisdom to know your own from another's. . . . [I]n the solitude to which every man is always returning, he has a sanity and revelations which in his passage into new worlds he will carry with him. Never mind the ridicule, never mind the defeat; up again old heart?—it seems to say—there is victory yet for all justice; and the true romance which the world exists to realize will be the transformation of genius into practical power.

This ringing affirmation, central in the American tradition of the strong self, makes the scandalous poverty of that self a radiating power and of its fictive and perspectival insubstantiality a godlike rock. Stevens' "The Rock," on the other hand, in spite of its discovery of a cure of the ground in the equivalence of self, leaves, ground, and rock, is a thorough deconstruction of the Emersonian bedrock self. Stevens' poem, in one of its aspects, is an interpretation of Emerson and Whitman which undermines their apparent affirmations (though of course both Emerson and Whitman had, each in his own way, already annihilated his own seemingly solid grounding). Stevens' poem, in any case, further hollows Emerson and Whitman out, gives their key figures and terms one final twist that shatters the structure based on them and shows it to have been baseless. For Stevens, Emerson's bleak rocks are no beginning below or before which one could not go. The self, for him, is deprived of its status as ground by being shown to be a figure on that ground. The self has the same status as the other elements with which it is equated. The self exists, but in the same fragile and groundless way as fruit, sun, poem, and geometrical diagram. It exists as icon, as image, as figure for the underlying nothing. The self is not the rock but an insubstantial substitute for the absent rock, something that was not, and is not, absurd. Moreover, the self is not the base of the sequence. It is only one link in a chain. This link has the same status as the others in the sense that it is inscribed in a horizontal series of displacements. In this series each item depends on the others for its definition and therefore for its existence. The self, for Stevens, is generated by this play of linguistic substitutions, vanishing itself if they vanish, depending for its illusory existence on figurative borrowings from them: "His *words* are both the icon and the man" (my italics).

Moreover, there is a significant difference between Stevens' use of the collective "we" and Emerson's. When Emerson says, "We must hold hard to this poverty," he means something not too different from Whitman's, "I incorporate gneiss, coal," or from his, "We also ascend dazzling and tremendous as the sun,/ We found our own O my soul in the calm and cool of the daybreak." For both Emerson and Whitman, each self must affirm itself, if not in isolation, then as the axis of all, the incorporator of all: "I am large, I contain multitudes." One of the crucial moments of Emerson's "Experience" is his rejection of any confrontation of another, or equal relation to another, even in love. The other can only be an image or icon of the self and so not its equal. All doubling or imaging must be rejected as introducing chaos into the spherical and all-inclusive unity of the self. Subject can only marry object, that is, not something its equal or fellow but something which can be devoured, wholly mastered: "There will be the same gulf between every me and thee as between the original and the picture. The universe is the bride of the soul. . . . Life will be imaged, but cannot be divided nor doubled. Any invasion of its unity would be chaos. The soul is not twin-born but the only begotten, and though revealing itself as child in time, child in appearance, is of a fatal and universal power, admitting no co-life."

Who, in contraast, is the "we" of Stevens' "The Rock," the we of whom the first two lines say, "It is an illusion that we were ever alive,/ Lived in the houses of mothers . . ."? Husband and wife? Poetic "we"? A general collective first person plural standing for all men and women together, all old folk of seventy? There is a bleak impersonality of tone and locution in Stevens' poem which forbids thinking of it or feeling it as the autobiographical statement of a recognizable person, the man Wallace Stevens, vice president of the Hartford Accident and Indemnity Company, author of *Harmonium*. This is thematized in the way the personal self in the poem dissolves into a plural self, all mankind and womankind, the "ourselves" of "a cure of ourselves," and that "ourselves" into a collective impersonal consciousness, "the main of things, the mind," "the starting point of the human and the end," and that mind, beyond any personality, into the rock, and the rock into nothingness. Self in the sense of individual personality is one of the major illusions dissolved by the poem. This dissolution, paradoxically, takes place not by a movement into a more and more vacuous solipsism, as is sometimes said to be Stevens' fate as a poet, but precisely by incorporating that doubling of self and other which Emerson so resolutely, and by the necessity of his genuinely solipsistic definition of the strong self, rejects. Stevens is more open to the existence of others, more in need of them, and so, in the end, vulnerable, as Emerson and Whitman are not, to an abyssing or dissolution of the self. This dissolution comes through the doubling of the self or through its attempt to found itself on a relation to another. For Stevens the self-enclosed sphere of the self is broken. It is thereby engulfed in the chasm of its own bifurcation. This conflict between an attempted self-subsistent enclosure and the doubling, breaking apart, and abyssing of that enclosure may be seen in all the chief scenes of "The Rock."

All four scenes takes the form, or attempt to take the form, of a rounded, unified whole which is soundly based. Poem, fruit, sun, geometrical diagram or logical system, single man rooted in the earth, child enclosed in the house of his mother, lovers embraced at noon— all strive to take that form. Each of these figures, however, divides itself by a scission both horizontal and vertical and so becomes not an enclosed finite figure but a *mise en abyme*. The geometrical design appears at first to be a closed logical system based on solid predicates which may secure the proposition of theorems generating figures in the sun's design of its own happiness. Such figures would satisfy the desire to be at the end of distances. This closed figure, alas, turns into an infinitely repeating series, like that cartoon by Charles Addams, with the rock, "that which is near," functioning not as a base but as "point A/ In a perspective that begins again/ At B." Starting at A, motivated by the desire to be at the end of distances, one reaches on a line toward the horizon point B. At B the receding perspective begins again, and so on, ad infinitum, without ever reaching the end of distances. No solid starting place exists, but only an arbitrary beginning which constantly begins again at points B, C, D, and so on, and there is no reaching the horizon. This endlessly receding geometrical figure is asymmetrically balanced, in "Forms of the Rock in a Night-Hymn," by the figure of the rock as "The starting point of the human and the end,/ That in which space itself is contained, the gate/ To the enclosure." Which figure can be built on the rock? The question is unanswerable. The circumscribed design constantly turns into the labyrinthine *mise en abyme*, as the enclosure of the last lines is abyssed by their opening into the alternations of day and night, night with its midnight-minting fragrances exhaling or coining chasms of darkness.

The same transformation deconstructs the human scene of the poem. To "live in the houses of mothers" rather than in the masculine labyrinth of the house that Jack built was to dwell in a warm embracing enclosure which at the same time allowed an idyllic openness and freedom of movement. In the houses of mothers, says Stev-

ens, we children "arranged ourselves/ By our own motions in a freedom of air." The doubling of that relation in the meeting of lovers at
noon at the edge of the field produced a schism which in retrospect
undermines both scenes and makes them like a perspective starting at
A that begins again at B. If the *mise en abyme* has something uncanny about it, one can also often detect in it, as in the passage cited
above from Leiris or in the present poem, a shadowy psychodrama
involving the differences of the sexes and of generations, the prohibition against incest, and narcissistic mirroring. In one version of the
myth of Narcissus he is in love with his twin sister, who dies, and who
is searched for, vainly and fatally, in the mirror image. The doubling
of brother and sister or of any man and woman of the same generation is the embrace of two desperate clods, detached bits of the
substantial earth beneath, trying to recover a lost unity, trying to
make a global whole which would encompass space in a theorem
proposed between the two. This theorem would generate a finite diagram, a closed logical system, in a warm house: "Ah, love, let us be
true/ To one another!" Let us recover together what we had in the
houses of mothers but have lost. Once the division has occurred,
however, and it has always already occurred, the chasm between self
and other remains unfilled.

The desire to be at the end of distances can never be satisfied. The
division perpetuates itself in whatever expedients are chosen to close
or cure the wound. In "a fantastic consciousness" I face my sister
self, that other desperate clod. I see in her a substitute for the lost
mother, but the failure of that substitution reminds me that the
mother was herself the abyss I have forgotten. The warmth in the
mother's house was an illusion, something that never was. Her house
stands "rigid in rigid emptiness." My narcissistic relation to my double of the other sex is an affective movement seeking to find a bedrock for the self or in the self. It discovers only a perspective that
begins again at B, a perpetually receding horizon. Stevens dismantles
Emerson by insisting on the doubling or imaging of the self in the
other, by making the self, against Emerson's prohibition, twin-born, a
schismatic or schizoid "we." The relation to my mirror image doubles
my relation, across a generation gap, to my mother and reveals that
relation too to have been an empty image, an icon of nothing. Though
it seemed an enclosure, solidly based, it was already the abyss, since
there was something missing which was suppressed or veiled. This
absence has now been revealed in the annihilating, after the fact, both
of that warm enclosure and of the security of its repetition in the
embrace at noon at the edge of the field. Both the relation to the

mother and the relation to the beloved are the experience of a perpetual distance, desire, dissatisfaction, an "emptiness that would be
filled" ("An Ordinary Evening in New Haven"). They are figures,
not realities, "Two figures in a nature of the sun,/ In the sun's design
of its own happiness."

Perhaps, then, if the self, for Stevens, is no Emersonian or Whit-
manian rock, a solid foundation may be found in that which is
imaged by the self in its doublings, that is, in the sun's rising and
setting, in the sequence of the seasons, in that univeral manifestation
of permanence in change of which Whitman said, "there are millions
of suns left." Poem, man, lovers, fruit, geometric figure are all helio-
tropic, "copies of the sun," "figures" or "shadows" cast by the sun.
The poem is the sun. The fruit is a little sun, a mango. Both the man
alone and the man in relation to his beloved are suns or figures in the
sun. The poem is governed, like so many of Stevens' poems, by the
annual and diurnal movements of the sun, as it shifts with the seasons, causing them, and as it rises and sets each day, appearing like
man from the ground and disappearing into the rock, that "stone
from which he rises, up—and—ho,/ The step to the bleaker depths of
his descents."

Is the sun, then, the literal, of which all the other icons are figures,
the bedrock which supports and validates them? No, the sun is the
figure par excellence, both in Western tradition generally and in Stevens' work as a whole. The sun is that which cannot be looked at
directly but is the source of all seeing, the designer of the figures of its
happiness. The sun is the visible, invisible figure for the invisible and
unnamable, for the base of the intelligible, "the main of things, the
mind." The sun is the traditional icon for being, for the good, for the
real, in short, for the rock. The rock in turn is a figure for the ground,
and vice versa, in a perpetual displacement.

If the structure of the various scenes in "The Rock" is a repetition
of the act of manifestation, it is also a deconstruction of that structure. The rhetorical name for this is catachresis. Catachresis is the
violent, forced, or abusive use of a word to name something which
has no literal name. The word also means, in music, a harsh or
unconventional dissonance, a surd. Examples of catachresis are table
"leg" and mother "tongue." Such a word is neither literal, since a
table leg is not truly a leg, nor speech a tongue, nor figurative, since it
is not a substitute for some proper word. (The Romance word for
tongue, *lingua, lengua, langue*, is folded into the apparently literal
word "language.") Catachresis explodes the distinction between literal and figurative on which the analysis of tropes is based and so

leads the "science" of rhetoric to destroy itself as science, as clear and distinct knowledge of truth. (See Jacques Derrida's "La mythologie blanche," *Marges*, for the best discussion of catachresis, including an identification of its relation to the solar trajectory.)

"The Rock" seems to be based on the notion of a name which would be an icon for the hidden truth, the figure for a covert literal. All the terms in the poem, however, are at once literal and figurative. Each is a catachresis. According to the logic of a theory of language which bases meaning on the solid referentiality of literal names for visible physical objects, open to the light of the sun, the referent of a catachresis does not exist, was not, and is not, absurd. Each term in "The Rock," including "rock" and "ground," is a catachresis for something which has not, cannot have, a proper name. That something is the abyss, the *Abgrund* or *Ungrund*, the chasm, the blank, the unapproachable, of which the poem, in all the ways I have identified, is a *mise en abyme*. The cure of the ground in a curiological picturing, which Stevens says we *must* have, remains necessarily a future imperative. This imperative can never be fulfilled. To name the abyss is to cover it, to make a fiction or icon of it, a likeness which is no likeness. What is a likeness of the sun? Of what is the sun a likeness?

All the catachreses in the poem reform the fiction of the referential, the illusion that the terms of the poem refer literally to something that exists, some physical rock or ground, some psychological entity, even some metaphysically existing nothing, the "nothing that is." In fact they refer to the blind spot, the perpetually absent, the sun when it is below the horizon, "grounded." For this invisible sun, as Aristotle said, there is no name and therefore no substance, no *logos*. The sun in its risings and settings is alogical, the father of all *mises en abyme*. The word "sun" itself is deprived thereby of full propriety. It is a catachresis, since the word cannot be based on a full perception by the senses of what it names. Since all referentiality in language is a fiction, the aboriginal trope or turning away from the abyss, the blind spot, the referentiality of language is its fall, its unconquerable penchant toward fiction. All words are initially catachreses. The distinction between literal and figurative is an alogical deduction or bifurcation from that primal misnaming. The fiction of the literal or proper is therefore the supreme fiction. All poetry and all language are *mises en abyme*, since all language is based on catachresis. The continuity of Western thought on this point and Stevens' congruity with that tradition in his use of the rising and setting sun as the prime "example" of the iconic structure which disarticulates itself is indicated by the applicability to "The Rock" of a passage in Aristotle's

Topics: "he who has stated that it is a property of the sun to be 'the brightest star that moves above the earth' has employed in the property something of a kind which is comprehensible only by sensation, namely 'moving above the earth'; and so the property of the sun would not have been correctly assigned, for it will not be manifest, when the sun sets, whether it is still moving above the earth, because sensation then fails us" (V, 3, 131B).

Where is the sun after it sets, disappears into the ground? It becomes the ground, vanishes into the rock, where sensation fails us and where blindness is substituted once more for sight and insight. Of that blind spot nothing "true" or "proper" can be said, and so we must be silent, deaf and dumb, absurd. The end of Stevens' poem is a brilliant illustration or expression (darkness made visible, silence given speech) of this doubleness of the sun, its visibility and invisibility as the *mise en abyme* of the rock. Like the poem, the man, and the fruit, the sun rises from the rock as its visible embodiment or icon, while the rock is a night-sun, shining with its fragrant black light on what "night illumines." The rock as "the habitation of the whole" encloses the sun and all things under the sun. The rock, though it may appear to be the literal of which all else is a figure, is itself another catachresis. At the farthest or deepest point of the *mise en abyme*, at the end of the poem, the perspective begins again with a further glimpse, a seeing which is no seeing, into the chasm of night. The rock is

> The starting point of the human and the end,
> That in which space itself is contained, the gate
> To the enclosure, day, the things illumined
>
> By day, night and that which night illumines,
> Night and its midnight-minting fragrances,
> Night's hymn of the rock, as in a vivid sleep.

"As in a vivid sleep"! The final quiet displacement by way of the "as" to another figure expresses once more and for the last time the cadence which has governed the poem. Like a voice of the voiceless, or like an ability to hear the soundless, the absurd, or the mute, or like a seeing, with "blindness cleaned," of what can be only illusion, a vivid sleep is an oxymoron. It is a sleep which is yet acutely conscious, though a consciousness not grounded in sensation. A vivid sleep is a clear consciousness of nothing, as night's hymn of the rock is darkness visible. That hymn is the final icon or figuration of blessedness, the last appearance of religious terminology in the poem. These terms, like the other chains of terms, are another, perhaps even the most powerful or violent, catachresis. This hymn creates what it praises in the very act of naming it. It creates what it worships in the abusive displacements that figure forth that which has no proper name, and so has only a figurative or poetical existence. "After one has abandoned a belief in God, poetry is that essence which takes its place as life's redemption"; "God and the imagination are one" ("Adagia").

Beginning with the word "cure" in "The Rock" the interpreter is led further and further into a labyrinth of branching connections going back through Whitman and Emerson to Milton, to the Bible, to Aristotle, and behind him into the forking pathways of our Indo-European family of languages. Stevens' poem is an abyss and the filling of the abyss, a chasm and a chasmy production of icons of the chasm, inexhaustible to interpretation. Its textual richness opens abyss beneath abyss, beneath each deep a deeper deep, as the reader interrogates its elements and lets each question generate an answer which is another question in its turn. Each question opens another distance, a perspective begun at A which begins again at B, without ever reaching any closer to the constantly receding horizon. Such a poem is incapable of being encompassed in a single logical formulation. It calls forth potentially endless commentaries, each one of which, like this essay, can only formulate and reformulate its *mise en abyme*.

II

"O Socrates, make music and work at it."
—*Phaedo*, 60e

As the reader drowns under the ever-accumulating flood of criticism, he is justified in asking, why is there criticism rather than silent admiration? If every literary text performs already its own self-interpretation, which means its own self-dismantling, why is there any need for criticism? A poem, for example Stevens' "The Rock," is entirely self-sufficient. It does not need to have one word added to it. Why does it nevertheless call forth so many supplementary words? The publication, in any given year, of an apparently ungovernable multiplicity of critical texts raises the question of the validity of the whole enterprise. Why must there be literary criticism at all, or at any rate more literary criticism? Don't we have enough already? What ineluctable necessity in literature makes it generate unending oceans of commentary, wave after wave covering the primary textual rocks, hiding them, washing them, uncovering them again, but leaving them, after all, just as they were?

The answer to these questions, insofar as there is an answer, is provided by the formulation of the questions themselves, as well as by what can be seen in such a poem as "The Rock." If that poem is a continuous *mise en abyme*, forming and reforming itself around words or images—"icon," "rock," "cure," and so on—which both name the "alogical" and cover it over, criticism is a continuation of that activity of the poem. If the poem is a cure of the ground which never succeeds, criticism is a yielding to the temptation to try once more for the "cure beyond forgetfulness," and then once more, and once beyond that, in an ever-renewed, ever-unsuccessful attempt to "get it right," to name things by their right names. As Stevens says, "They will get it straight one day at the Sorbonne," and when "I call you by name, my green, my fluent mundo,/ You will have stopped revolving except in crystal" ("Notes Toward a Supreme Fiction"). They never get it right, however, neither in poetry nor in the criticism of poetry, neither at the Sorbonne nor in generations of ordinary evenings in New Haven. The work continues, and the world keeps fluently turning, never called by name, never fixed in a definitive formulation. The critic cannot by any means get outside the text, escape from the blind alleys of language he finds in the work. He can only rephrase them in other, allotropic terms. The critical text prolongs, extends, reveals, covers, in short, cures, the literary text in the same way that the literary text attempts to cure the ground. If poetry is the impossible possible cure of the ground, criticism is the impossible possible cure of literature.

A recognition of the incorporation of the work of criticism into the unending activity of poetry itself seems especially to characterize criticism today. Literature, however, has always performed its own *mise en abyme*, though it has usually been misunderstood as doing the opposite. It has often been interpreted as establishing a ground in consciousness, in the poem as self-contained object, in nature, or in some metaphysical base. Literature therefore needs to be prolonged in criticism. The activity of deconstruction already performed and then hidden in the work must be performed again in criticism. It can be performed, however, only in such a way as to be misunderstood in its turn, like the work itself, so that it has to be done over, and then again. If a work of literature must be read in order to come into existence as a work of literature, and if, as Charles Sanders Peirce said, the only interpretation of one sign is another sign, then criticism is the allegory or putting otherwise of the act of reading. This response of new sign generated by old sign continues interminably as long as the work is read.

What, then, can be said to be special in the present moment in criticism? Each such moment tends to feel itself to be a turning point, an instant of crisis, a crossroads, a time when important new developments are taking place or are about to take place. A recent announcement of a new institute of criticism and theory speaks of our time as "a period of crisis for the humanistic disciplines and of concurrent excitement (and attendant confusion) in the area of critical theory." No doubt this is true, though the odds are strongly against 1976 being as important in literary criticism as, say, 1798. Moreover, it can always be demonstrated that the apparent novelty of any new development in criticism is the renewal of an insight which has been found and lost and found again repeatedly through all the centuries of literary study since the first Homeric and Biblical commentaries. The novelty of any "new criticism" is not in its intrinsic insights or techniques but rather in the "accidents" of its expression, though how can "accident" here be distinguished from "substance"? The novelty of an innovative criticism, nevertheless, is in large part in its institutionalization, in the mode of its insertion into the teaching or reading of literature at a given historical moment, rather than in any absolute originality of terminology or insight.

A distinctive feature of English and American literary criticism today is its progressive naturalization, appropriation, or accommodation of recent continental criticism. Much, though by no means all, of our current criticism in English would be impossible without the continental "influence," meaning primarily, at the moment, so-called structuralism. Structuralism, however, can in no way be described in a single coherent paradigm. It divides and subdivides into warring sects, Saussurians, Barthesians, Marxists, Foucaultians, Lacanians, Lévi-Straussians, Derridaists, and so on. No critic would accept a lumping of his work with that of the others. Nevertheless, some paths in this labyrinth may be mapped.

The "new turn" in criticism, which is a return of the old, is characterized by a focus on language as the central problematic of literary study. This focus determines a breaking down of barriers and a putting in question of grounds, even of the apparently solid basis of new linguistic theory. This rediscovery of an often hidden center of gravity in literature might be called the linguistic moment. This moment may have such moment or momentum that it prolongs and expands itself to attract into orbit around its mass all the other themes and features of a given work. These become planets around its solar focus, the other focus being that nameless *abyme* with which language can never coincide. This breaking of barriers and questioning of grounds involves a return to the explicit study of rhetoric. Rhetoric means in this case the investigation of figures of speech rather than the study of the art of persuasion, though the notion of persuasion is still present in a more ambiguous displaced form, as the idea of production, or of function, or of performance. The new turn in criticism involves an interrogation of the notion of the self-enclosed literary work and of the idea that any work has a fixed, identifiable meaning. The literary work is seen in various ways as open and unpredictably productive. The reading of a poem is part of the poem. This reading is productive in its turn. It produces multiple interpretations, further language about the poem's language, in an interminable activity without necessary closure.

The boundaries between literature and criticism are broken down in this activity, not because the critic arrogates to himself some vague right to be "poetical" in his writing, but because he recognizes it as his doom not to be able to be anything else. The critic is not able by any "method" or strategy of analysis to "reduce" the language of the work to clear and distinct ideas. He is forced at best to repeat the work's contradictions in a different form. The work is seen as heterogeneous, dialogical rather than monological. It has at least two apparent grounds, centers, foci, or *logoi*, and is therefore incapable of being encompassed in any single coherent or homogeneous interpretation. Any reading can be shown to be a misreading on evidence drawn from the text itself. Moreover, any literary text, with more or less explicitness or clarity, already reads or misreads itself. The "deconstruction" which the text performs on itself and which the critic repeats is not of the superstructure of the work but of the ground on which it stands, whether that ground is history, or the social world, or the solid, extra-linguistic world of "objects," or the givenness of the generative self of the writer, his "consciousness."

If the literary work is within itself open, heterogeneous, a dialogue of conflicting voices, it is also seen as open to other texts, permeable to them, permeated by them. A literary text is not a thing in itself, "organically unified," but a relation to other texts which are relations in their turn. The study of literature is therefore a study of intertextuality, as in the recent work of Harold Bloom, or, in a different way, in that of Geoffrey Hartman. The relation between text and precursor text is devious, problematic, never a matter of direct cause and effect. For this, as for other reasons, such criticism puts in question the traditional notions of literary history as a sequence of self-enclosed "periods," each with its intrinsic characteristics: motifs, genres, ideologies, and so on. It also brings into question the traditional study of "sources."

The boundaries, finally, between literary texts and other kinds of texts are also perforated or dismantled. If insights or methods developed in psychology, anthropology, philosophy, and linguistics are appropriated by literary criticism, linguistics, on the other hand, broadens out imperialistically to redefine all of those disciplines. The founding or fathering texts of these disciplines are reinterpreted according to new notions about language, as Freud is reread in the light of modern linguistics by the school of Jacques Lacan. Lacanian psychoanalysis becomes in its turn the basis of a kind of literary criticism. From the point of view of literary criticism, this blurring of traditional boundaries means that a "philosophical" or "psychological" text, a work by Hegel, say, or one by Freud, is to be read in the same way as a "literary" text. This is done, for example, by Jacques Derrida in his reading of Plato in "La pharmacie de Platon" or in his reading of Hegel in *Glas*. It is done in Edward Said's interpretation, in *Beginnings*, of Freud's *Die Traumdeutung* as a narrative text like a novel.

These assumptions about literature are sufficiently different from the traditional assumptions of much literary study in England and America as to take some time to be assimilated. In time they will be naturalized, tested, challenged, refuted, and perhaps ultimately in some form institutionalized in courses, curricula, and the programs of "departments" in our colleges and universities. This give and take will no doubt characterize literary study, in the United States at least, during the coming years, though with how much giving and how much taking remains to be seen.

Already a clear distinction can be drawn, among critics influenced by these new developments, between what might be called, to conflate two terminologies, Socratic, theoretical, or canny critics, on the one hand, and Apollonian/Dionysian, tragic, or uncanny critics, on the other. Socratic critics are those who are lulled by the promise of a rational ordering of literary study on the basis of solid advances in scientific knowledge about language. They are likely to speak of themselves as "scientists" and to group their collective enterprise under some term like "the human sciences." The human sciences—it has a reassuringly logical, progressive, quantifiable sound, "canny" in the sense of shrewd or practical. Such an enterprise is represented by the discipline called "semiotics," or by new work in the exploration and exploitation of rhetorical terms. Included would be aspects of the work of Gérard Genette, Roland Barthes, and Roman Jakobson, as well as that of scholars like A. J. Greimas, Tzvetan Todorov, Cesare Brandi, and Jean-Claude Coquet. Jonathan Culler's *Structuralist Poetics* is a canny and wholesomely skeptical introduction to the work of much critics.

For the most part these critics share the Socratic penchant, what Nietzsche defined as "the unshakable faith that thought, using the thread of logic (*an den Leitfaden der Kausalität*), can penetrate the deepest abysses of being, and that thought is capable not only of knowing but even of correcting (*corrigiren*) it" (*The Birth of Tragedy*, 15). Here is another meaning for "cure." Socratic or scientific criticism, criticism by what Nietzsche calls *theoretischen Menschen*, criticism as cure, would be not only a penetration of the ground but also its correction, its straightening out. The inheritors today of the Socratic faith would believe in the possibility of a structuralist-inspired criticism as a rational and rationalizable activity, with agreed-upon rules of procedure, given facts, and measurable results. This would be a discipline bringing literature out into the sunlight in a "happy positivism." Such an appropriation of the recent turn in criticism would have the attractive quality of easily leading to institution-alizing in textbooks, courses, curricula, all the paraphernalia of an established academic discipline.

Opposed to these are the critics who might be called "uncanny." Though they have been inspired by the same climate of thought as the Socratic critics and though their work would also be impossible without modern linguistics, the "feel" or atmosphere of their writing is quite different from that of a critic like Culler, with his brisk common sense and his reassuring notions of "literary competence" and the acquisition of "conventions," his hope that all right-thinking people might agree on the meaning of a lyric or a novel, or at any rate share a "universe of discourse" in which they could talk about it. "Uncanny" critics would include, each in his own way, a new group of critics gathered at Yale: Harold Bloom, Paul de Man, and Geoffrey Hartman. Jacques Derrida teaches a seminar early each fall at Yale and so may be included among the Yale group. These critics may be taken by a convenient synecdoche as "examples" of criticism as the uncanny, but there are of course others, for example Derrida's associates in France, Sarah Kofman, Philippe Lacoue-Labarthe, Jean-Luc Nancy, Bernard Pautrat (essays by all of whom are gathered in their new book, *Mimesis*). The American critic Edward Said admirably explores an uncanny topic in *Beginnings*.

These critics are not tragic or Dionysian in the sense that their work is wildly orgiastic or irrational. No critic could be more rigorously sane and rational, Apollonian, in his procedure, for example, than Paul de Man. One feature of Derrida's criticism is a patient and minutely philological "explication de texte." Nevertheless, the thread of logic leads in both cases into regions which are alogical, absurd. This might find a fit emblem not only in the *polemos* of Apollo and Dionysus but also in the marriage of Dionysus to Ariadne. The work of these critics is in one way or another a labyrinthine attempt to escape from the labyrinth of words, an attempt guided not only by the Apollonian thread of logic but by Ariadne's thread as she might be imagined to have rescued it from the too rational and betraying Theseus, or to have incarnated it in herself as the clue to an escape from the abyss by a cure of the ground. As Ruskin says, in *Fors Clavigera*, "The question seems not at all to have been about getting in; but getting *out* again. The clue, at all events, could be helpful only after you had carried it in; and if the spider, or other monster in midweb, ate you, the help in your clue, for return, would be insignificant. So that this thread of Ariadne's implied that even victory over the monster would be vain, unless you could disentangle yourself from his web also."

Ariadne's thread, then, is another *mise en abyme*, both a mapping of the abyss and an attempted escape from it, criticism as cure. This escape can never succeed, since the thread is itself the interminable production of more labyrinth. What would be outside the labyrinth? More labyrinth, the labyrinth, for example, of the story of Ariadne, which is by no means over with the triumphant escape of Theseus from the maze. According to Ruskin, the traditional labyrinth is "composed of a single path or track, coiled, and recoiled, on itself," and "the word 'Labyrinth' properly means 'rope-walk,' or 'coil-of-rope-walk,' its first syllable being probably also the same as our English name 'Laura,' 'the path.' " This is, apparently, a false, but suggestively false, etymology. At the center, "midweb," of Ruskin's image is no male minotaur, but a female spider. The labyrinth is spun from the spider's belly, and Arachne is here conflated with Ariadne. Far from providing a benign escape from the maze, Ariadne's thread makes the labyrinth, is the labyrinth. The interpretation or solving of the puzzles of the textual web only adds more filaments to the web. One can never escape from the labyrinth because the activity of escaping makes more labyrinth, the thread of a linear narrative or story. Criticism is the production of more thread to embroider the texture or textile already there. This thread is like the filament of ink which flows from the pen of the writer, keeping him in the web but suspending him also over the chasm, the blank page that thin line hides. In one version of Ariadne's story she is said to have hanged herself with her thread in despair after being abandoned by Theseus.

In a different way in each case, the work of the uncanny critics, however reasonable or sane their apparent procedure, reaches a point where it resists the intelligence almost successfully. At this point it no longer quite makes rational sense, and the reader has the uncomfortable feeling that he cannot quite hold what is being said in his mind or make it all fit. Sooner or later there is the encounter with an "aporia" or impasse. The bottom drops out, or there is an "abyssing," an insight one can almost grasp or recognize as part of the familiar landscape of the mind, but not quite, as though the mental eye could not quite bring the material into lucid focus. This "abyssmal" discomfort is no doubt the reason why the work of these critics sometimes encounters such hostility from Socratic reviewers and readers. In fact the moment when logic fails in their work is the moment of their deepest penetration into the actual nature of literary language, or of language as such. It is also the place where Socratic procedures will ultimately lead, if they are carried far enough. The center of the work of the uncanny critics is in one way or another a formulation of this experience which momentarily and not wholly successfully rationalizes it, puts it in an image, a figure, a narrative, or a myth. Here, however, the distinction between story, concept, and image breaks down, at the vanishing point where each turns into something other than itself, concept into the alogical, figure into catachresis, narrative into ironical allegory.

In Paul de Man's essays, for example (example in what sense?), there is a sober and painstaking movement through a given text or set of citations. This leads rather suddenly, usually at the end of the essay, to an aporia, a formulation which is itself, necessarily, paradoxical or self-contradictory. The Apollonian here reaches its limits and becomes uncanny, without ceasing for all that to be coolly rational in its tone, keeping its balance over the abyss. De Man might be called "the master of the aporia," though this would be an oxymoron, since the aporia, like the chasm it opens, cannot, in fact, be mastered. "This complication," to give one example of this, in de Man's analysis of Nietzsche's deconstruction of the principle of identity, "is characteristic for all deconstructive discourse: the deconstruction states the fallacy of reference in a necessarily referential mode. . . . The differentiation between performative and constative language (which Nietzsche anticipates) is undecidable; the deconstruction leading from one model to the other is irreversible, but it always remains suspended, regardless of how often it is repeated. . . . The aporia between performative and constative language is merely a version of the aporia between trope and persuasion that both generates and paralyzes rhetoric and thus gives it the appearance of a history."

In Harold Bloom's case, for example in *Kabbalah and Criticism*, there is the lucid, learned, patient presentation of a systematic terminology, or rather a terminology drawn simultaneously from three or four different language systems, that of somewhat esoteric Greek philosophy (*clinamen, tessera,* etc.), that of Freudian psychology (anxiety, repression, etc.), that of Kabbalah (*tikkun, Zimzum,* etc.), and that of classical rhetoric (synecdoche, hyperbole, metalepsis, etc.). The presentation is so reasonable, so genuinely learned, and so sane in tone, that it is with something of a start that the reader wakes up to realize what outrageous demands are being made on him. Can he adopt such a wildly eclectic vocabulary? *Tikkun? Zimzum? Clinamen?* Transumption? *Nachträglichkeit? Sefirot?* Can he really be expected to make practical use of such terms? Moreover, if the central insight of Bloom's new work is into the rhetorical and figurative relations of intertextuality, into the way each sign or text is a misreading or verbal swerving from a previous sign or text and calls forth new signs or texts which are misinterpretations in their turn, this insight is with difficulty reconciled with his repeatedly affirmed Emersonian desire to maintain the "bedrock" priority of the strong self as the motivating momentum in this dynamic play of sign with sign, text with text. The conflicting demands of sign and self in his criticism form a blind alley, a bifurcated root in his thinking. This double source cannot be synthesized into a logical or dialectical totality. Bloom's self-contradiction is generative rather than paralyzing, however, as is proven by the admirable essays on the major poets of the Romantic tradition in *Poetry and Repression: Revisionism from Blake to Stevens.* The cogs and levers in Bloom's "machine for criticism" proliferate inexhaustibly, six terms becoming twenty-four, the six original ratios becoming in his most recent work doubled again in twelve *topoi* or crossings. The machine, nevertheless, works. It keeps working perhaps through its own constant autodestruction and triumphant hyperbolic replication. It works to produce splendid essays of interpretation (or misinterpretation, misprision, since all strong reading, for Bloom, must be misreading). After Bloom's work we shall never be able to read Shelley or Browning, Tennyson or Stevens, in the same way again. They are changed by being shown to have made their poetry out of changes, anamorphoses of their precursors.

In Geoffrey Hartman's case there is an increasing tendency to puns and to wordplayfulness. As he says in his essay on Derrida's *Glas*, "I must pun as I must sneeze." This wordplay is carried on, in all Hartman's books from *The Unmediated Vision* to *The Fate of Reading*, for the sake of an interrogation of the *logos*, the ground or *Grund* at the base of all wordplay. The question, for him, is not so much of the fate of reading as of the fate of poetry. It is a question of the vitality of words, their rootedness, the question whether poetry can survive in a post-enlightenment culture. The danger, for Hartman, as he puts it in "False Themes and Gentle Minds," one of the key essays in *Beyond Formalism*, is an uprooting of poetry such as that of "eighteenth century topographical fancies with their personification mania": "Romance loses its shadow, its genuine darkness: nothing remains of the drama of liberation whereby ingenium is born from genius, psyche from persona, and the spirit of poetry from the grave clothes of Romance." True poetry must be like Milton's *L'Allegro* and *Il Penseroso*, which "show a mind moving from one position to another and projecting an image of its freedom against a darker, demonic ground. Poetry, like religion, purifies that ground: it cannot leave it." On the other hand, the danger is that this return from that differentiation, which leads one word to another in endless punning permutation, will reach not a vital source, the ground of puns, but an undifferentiated blur, a meaningless Blouaugh!, like the roar of William Carlos Williams' sea-elephant. Hartman's essay on Gerard Manley Hopkins in *Beyond Formalism* argues that Hopkins' ways with words "evoke the tendency of semantic distinctions to fall back into a phonemic ground of identity. There is, in other words, a linguistic indifference against which language contends, and contends successfully, by diacritical or differential means." Hartman is caught in the aporia of these two irreconcilable models, whose incompatibility both motivates his criticism and prevents it from becoming clear, wholly enlightened. Hovering between a need for the clarifying distinctions of wordplay and a need for the "rich, dark nothing" of the chthonic ground, a ground which may or may not (such uncertainty is the curse of enlightenment) be a vital source, a source in any case both desired and feared, stretched in this double bind, Hartman's criticism conducts its testing of the ground and its covering of the ground, its mode of criticism as cure.

If Paul de Man is the master, no master, of the aporia, Jacques Derrida is, as Geoffrey Hartman calls him, a "boa-deconstructor." His prodigious effort in the disarticulation of the major texts of Western metaphysics, philosophical and literary, might, however, be more aptly figured in the sinuous emblem of some slenderer and more insinuating serpent than a snake that crushes. Deconstruction as a mode of interpretation works by a careful and circumspect entering of each textual labyrinth. The critic feels his way from figure to figure, from concept to concept, from mythical motif to mythical motif, in a repetition which is in no sense a parody. It employs, nevertheless, the subversive power present in even the most exact and unironical doubling. The deconstructive critic seeks to find, by this process of retracing, the element in the system studied which is alogical, the thread in the text in question which will unravel it all, or the loose stone which will pull down the whole building. The deconstruction, rather, annihilates the ground on which the building stands by showing that the text has already annihilated that ground, knowingly or unknowingly. Deconstruction is not a dismantling of the structure of a text but a demonstration that it has already dismantled itself. Its apparently solid ground is no rock but thin air.

The uncanny moment in Derrida's criticism, the vacant place at the non-center around which all his work is organized, is the formulation and reformulation of this non-existence of the ground out of which the whole textual structure seems to rise like the pleasure dome of Kubla Khan. Derrida has shown marvelous fecundity in finding or inventing new terms to express this generative non-source, absence, forking, or scattering beneath all appearances of presence: *le supplément, le pharmakon, la différance, l'hymen, la dissémination, la marge, le cadre, la signature*, and so on. Each of these both is and is not concept, figure, and infolded narrative. No one of them may be made the ground of its own textual structure, for example, of a discipline of critical studies. Each is eccentric, like all genuine terms, for example those bizarre terms used by Bloom. Of all these critical terms in Derrida's work one could say what he says of *la dissémination* in "La double séance," his essay on Mallarmé:

> In spite of appearances, the endless work of condensation and displacement does not lead us finally back to dissemination as an ultimate signification, or a first truth. . . . According to a schema which we have experienced with the word "between" (*entre*), the quasi "meaning" of dissemination is the impossible return to the rejoined, reattached unity of a meaning, the closed-off way to such a *reflection* [in the sense of veering back]. Is dissemination nevertheless the *loss* of such a truth, the *negative* interdict against reaching such a signification? Far from allow-

ing in this way the supposition that a virgin substance preceded
or surveys it from above, dispersing or obstructing itself in a
secondary negativity, dissemination *affirms* the always already
divided generation of meaning. . . . No more than castration can
dissemination, which entails, "inscribes," reprojects it, become
an original, central, or ultimate signification, the proper place of
the truth. It represents on the contrary the affirmation of that
non-origin, the empty and remarkable place of a hundred
blanks to which one cannot give meaning, multiplying to infinity
supplementary marks and games of substitution.

In *Positions*, Derrida provides a commentary on "hundred blanks"
(*cent blancs*) by making it one link in a chain generating a complicated multiple pun. It is a phrase, like the word "cure" in Stevens'
poem, which is a node or knot of irreconcilable or undecidable meanings: *sens blanc, sang blanc, sans blanc, cent blancs, semblant*. Such
words, says Derrida, "are not *atoms*, but points of economic condensation, necessary stations along the way for a large number of
marks, for somewhat more effervescent crucibles. Then their effects
not only turn back on themselves through a sort of closed self-excitation, they spread themselves in a chain over the theoretical and practical whole of a text, each time in a different way." These proliferating
supplements and substitutions are the other possible words, none
equivalents of one another, which may express the chasm of the
alogical, each time in a different way. Each term has its own systematic play of concepts and figures folded into it, incompatible with
the self-excitation of any other word.

De Man, Bloom, Hartman, and Derrida, then, come together in the
way their criticism is an interrogation of the ground of literature, not
just of its intrinsic structure. They come together also in the way the
criticism of each, in a different manner each time, is uncanny, cannot
be encompassed in a rational or logical formulation, and resists the
intelligence of its readers. They differ greatly, however, in their modes
of uncanniness and in their attitudes toward their own insights. Even
so, their criticism seems at the opposite pole from that of the canny
critics, the semioticians or structuralists, diagram- and system-
makers, seekers for a sound scientific base for literary study.

The most uncanny moment of all, however, in this developing
polarity among critics today, is the moment when the apparent opposites reverse themselves, the Socratic becoming uncanny, the
uncanny, canny, sometimes all too shrewdly rational. Recognition of
this movement of reversal or exchange is the second climax of *The*

Birth of Tragedy, the first being the insight into the interchangeability of the Apollonian and the Dionysian in tragic art, according to the formulation that, in tragedy, "Dionysus speaks the language of Apollo; and Apollo, finally, the language of Dionysus" (*Dionysus redet die Sprache des Apollo, Apollo aber schliesslich die Sprache Dionysus*). If tragedy is this fraternal union (*Bruderbund*), a union which is also a constant brother-murder, Socratic or scientific thought seems at first the escape from all such paradoxes into the clear light of logical insight. Insight, however, becomes blindness when it reaches its limits, and science turns back into tragic art, the art of the abyss, the alogical. "This sublime metaphysical illusion," says Nietzsche, the illusion, that is, that science can penetrate and correct or "cure" the deepest abysses of being, "accompanies science as an instinct, and leads science again and again to its limits (*zu ihren Grenzen*), at which it must turn into art—*which is really the aim of this mechanism*" (*auf welche es eigentlich, bei diesem Mechanismus, abgesehen ist*).

Such a reversal is occurring or has already occurred in a number of ways within the Socratic penchant of contemporary criticism. It has occurred most strikingly, perhaps, in the way the rational and reassuringly "scientific" study of tropes by present-day rhetoricians—though it depends fundamentally on an initially clear distinction between literal and figurative uses of language, and on clear distinctions among the tropes—ends by putting these distinctions in question and so undermines its own ground. This movement is clear in the best of such critics, for example in Gérard Genette's three volumes of *Figures*. His admirable "Métonymie chez Proust," in *Figures III*, aims to build itself on Roman Jakobson's firm distinction between metonymy and metaphor and even to show them working harmoniously to make *A la recherche du temps perdu* possible: "For it is metaphor which recovers lost time, but it is metonymy which reanimates it, and puts it in motion again: which returns it to itself and to its true 'essence,' which is its proper fleeting away and its proper Research. Here then, here alone—by metaphor, but *in* metonymy— here begins Narrative." But, as Genette's essay has shown, almost in spite of itself, if metaphor is so dependent on the accidental contiguities of metonymy, then the apparent continuity both of the text of *A la recherche* and of Marcel's life fragment irreparably and become mere juxtapositions of broken shards. The "true" insight of Genette's essay, skirted, avoided, circled around with averted eyes, but unmistakably brought to the surface nevertheless, is the exact opposite of its happy claim that metonymy can be a form of cohesion and therefore a support of metaphor, as Paul de Man has obliquely demonstrated, in "Proust et l'allégorie de la lecture," in *Mouvements premiers*. In fact the same contamination of the substantial similarities of metonymy by the external contingencies of metonymy had already undone the clear distinction between metaphor and metonymy in the precursor texts for Genette's essay, Roman Jakobson's brilliant and influential "Two Aspects of Language and Two Types of Aphasic Disturbances," in *Fundamentals of Language*, and "Linguistics and Poetics," in *Style in Language*. A flash of self-subverting genius in the later essay, aided by an aphorism from Goethe, *Alles Vergängliche ist nur ein Gleichnis* ("Anything transient is but a likeness"), breaks down the polarity between the two figures on which the genuinely productive insights (for example into the role of metonymy in realistic fiction) were based: "In poetry where similarity is superinduced upon contiguity, any metonymy is slightly metaphorical and any metaphor has a metonymical tint." The word "slightly" here has the same force as in the phrase "slightly pregnant." It echoes backward to unravel the whole theoretical basis of the essay on aphasia.

If the uncanny turn of current criticism is partly the moment when "the human sciences" reach their limits and become absurd, the fact that this moment recurs is also uncanny. Criticism repeats or reformulates again and again "the same" blind alley, like Freud in "Das Unheimliche" finding himself repeatedly coming back to the bordello section of that Italian town, however hard he tried to escape it. Any "Socratic" method in criticism, if carried far enough (not very far, actually), reaches its limits and subverts itself. The emblem for this might be that recurrent dream Socrates describes in the *Phaedo*. The dream brought an injunction which implicitly challenged Socrates' lifelong commitment to reason and logical thought. " 'O Socrates,' it said, 'make music and work at it' " (*O Sokrates, ephe, mousiken poiei kai ergathon*).

Examples of this reversal abound in modern criticism. The New Criticism discovered irony and the irresolvable ambiguities of figure. These discoveries subverted, at least implicitly, its presupposition that a poem is a self-contained "object," an organic unity. The criticism of Georges Poulet, basing itself on the assumption of the irreducible priority and "givenness" of the self, of the presence of consciousness to itself, ends by recognizing in consciousness a fathomless chasm. It ends also in recognizing that any stability or coherence in the self is an effect of language. The self is a linguistic construction rather than being the given, the rock, a solid *point de départ*. A similar self-subversion occurs from the other direction in structuralism. In this case, however, it is not the symmetrically opposite discovery that consciousness is the base of language, but rather the discovery that language is not a base. This is the moment of the self-deconstruction of rhetoric. The study of tropes looks at first like a safely scientific, rational, or logical discipline, but it still leads to the abyss, as it did for the old rhetoricians in the endless baroque, though entirely justifiable, proliferation of names for different figures of speech. More fundamentally, the study of rhetoric leads to the abyss by destroying, through its own theoretical procedures, its own basic axiom. Broadening itself imperialistically to take in other disciplines (philosophy, anthropology, literary criticism, psychology), rhetoric ultimately encounters, within itself, the problems it was meant to solve. Nietzsche expressed this aporia of Socratism or scientism in a brilliant passage in the fifteenth section of *The Birth of Tragedy*. The passage matches the double structure of the "cure of ground" in Stevens' "The Rock":

> But science [*Wissenschaft*], spurred by its powerful illusion, speeds irresistibly towards its limits [*bis zu ihren Grenzen*], where its optimism, concealed in the essence of logic, suffers shipwreck [*scheitert*]. For the periphery of the circle of science [*des Kreises der Wissenschaft*] has an infinite number of points; and while there is no telling how this circle could ever be surveyed completely, noble and gifted men nevertheless reach, e'er half their time [*noch vor der Mitte seines Daseins*] and inevitably, such boundary points [*Grenzpunkte*] on the periphery from which one gazes at what defies illumination. When they see to their horror how logic coils up at these boundaries and finally bites its own tail—suddenly the new form of insight breaks through, *tragic insight*, which, merely to be endured, needs art as a protection and remedy [*als Schutz und Heilmittel*].

If the canny becomes the uncanny and deconstructs itself, the uncanny is also in perpetual danger of becoming Apollonian in a bad sense. Nietzsche also anticipated this moment of reversal. *The Birth of Tragedy* is often erroneously read as granting superior authenticity to the Dionysian, to music, to the irrational, to the formless, which are supposed to be closer to the eternal stream of the underlying universal will. There are passages which seem unequivocally to support such a reading. In fact, however, this error is at crucial moments deconstructed by the text itself. If science is the illusion that seeks to "correct" the abyss, straighten it out, make it solid or rigid, or if science attempts to heal the wound of the abyss, with the suggestion of a sexual absence that must be repaired or filled by some prosthesis, the Apollonian art which intervenes when science fails and recoils in horror from its glimpse of an unfillable, incurable, incorrigible abyss, is no less an illusion than science itself. No less an illusion too is that image of a formless will flowing beneath the forms of both science and of Apollonian beauty. In one extraordinary passage of *The Birth of Tragedy*, the book expresses its own aporia. The terminology of the underlying chaos, of the universal will, "the eternal life beyond all phenomena," on which the book as a whole has been based, the source of the validation of "unconscious Dionysiac wisdom," is rejected as being as much an illusion as the "lies from the features of nature" which are the basis of Apollonian healing and "triumph over the suffering inherent in life." Socratic logic, Apollonian plastic form, and Dionysian music—all three are illusions, and Nietzsche's book becomes itself a *mise en abyme*, the self-subversion of the distinctions on which it seems to be solidly founded. If all three of these "panaceas" are illusions, what then is the will, the "insatiable will" which the passage posits in order to define all veils of the will as illusions? Is it not an illusion too, the third or Buddhistic illusion that the stream flows on beneath all phenomena? The passage, one can see, destroys its own terminology:

It is an eternal phenomenon: the insatiable will always finds a way [*ein Mittel*] to detain its creatures in life and compel them to live on, by means of an illusion spread over things. One is chained by the Socratic love of knowledge and the delusion of being able thereby to heal the eternal wound of existence [*die ewige Wunde des Daseins heilen zu können*]; another is ensnared by art's seductive veil of beauty fluttering before his eyes; still another by the metaphysical comfort that beneath the whirl of phenomena eternal life flows on indestructibly—to say nothing of the more vulgar and almost more powerful illusions which the will always has at hand. These three stages of illusion are actually designed only for the more nobly formed natures, who actually feel profoundly the weight and burden of existence, and must be deluded by exquisite stimulants [*ausgesuchte Reizmittel*] into forgetfulness of their displeasure [*Unlust*]. All that we call culture is made up of these stimulants: and, according to the proportion of the ingredients, we have either a dominantly *Socratic* or *artistic* or *tragic* culture;

or, if historical exemplifications are permitted, there is either an Alexandrian or a Hellenic or a Buddhistic culture.

The *mise en abyme* of uncanny criticism, for example in the passage by Nietzsche just cited or in those present-day critics of the uncanny I have discussed, is not the abyss itself in the sense of some direct representation of the truth of things, as Dionysian music may seem to be in *The Birth of Tragedy*. There is no "truth of things," as such, to be represented. The *mise en abyme* of uncanny criticism is rather the ordering of the abyss, the blank, *cent blancs*, its formulation in one or another terminology or figure. Any such formulation, whether it is called "the Dionysian," "the uncanny," "allegory," *"la dissémination,"* "the aporia," *"la differance,"* "decentering," "deconstruction," "double bind," "cure," *"mise en abyme,"* "transumption," "the voice of the shuttle," "signature," or whatever, can quickly become, like any other critical word, a dead terminology able to be coldly manipulated by epigones, mere leaves covering the ground rather than a means of insight into it. The critics of the uncanny must be exceedingly nimble, as de Man, Hartman, Derrida, and Bloom in their different ways conspicuously are, in order to keep their insights from becoming pseudo-scientific machines for the unfolding (explication), or dismantling (deconstruction), of literary texts. This uncanny and yet wholly inevitable reversal of the Apollonian into the Dionysian and of the tragic into the Socratic, the Socratic into the tragic again, like a Möbius strip which has two sides but only one side, is the inner drama or warfare of current literary criticism. The task of criticism in the immediate future should be the further exploration, as much by practical essays of interpretation as by theoretical speculation, of this coming and going in quest and in questioning of the ground.

Music Discomposed

Stanley Cavell

I

It is widespread opinion that aesthetics, as we think of it, became a subject, and acquired its name, just over two hundred years ago; which would make it the youngest of the principal branches of philosophy. Nothing further seems to be agreed about it, not even whether it is one subject, nor if so, what it should include, nor whether it has the right name, nor what the name should be taken to mean, nor whether given its problems, philosophers are particularly suited to venture them. Various reasons for these doubts suggest themselves: (1) The problems of composers, painters, poets, novelists, sculptors, architects . . . are internal to the procedures of each, and nothing general enough to apply to all could be of interest to any. One cannot, I think, or ought not, miss the truth of that claim, even while one feels that its truth needs correct placement. There *are* people recognizable as artists, and all produce works which we acknowledge, in some sense, to call for and warrant certain kinds of experience. (2) There is an established activity and a recognizable class of persons whose established task it is to discuss the arts, namely the criticism and the critics of literature, painting, music. . . . This fact faces two ways: One way, it suggests that there *is* something importantly common to the arts, namely, that they all require, or tolerate, such an activity; and that itself may incite philosophical reflection. Another way, it suggests that only someone competent as a critic of art is competent to speak of art at all, at least from the point of view of the experience which goes into it or which is to be found in it, so that an aesthetician incapable of producing criticism is simply incapable of recognizing and relevantly describing the objects of his discourse. (3) It is not clear what the data of the subject shall be. The enterprise of epistemologists, however paradoxical its conclusions have been, begins and continues with examples and procedures common to all men; and moral philosophers of every taste agree in appealing to the experience, the concepts, and the conflicts all men share. But upon what, or whom, does the aesthetician focus? On the artist? On the work he produces? On what the artist says about his work? On what critics say about it? On the audience it acquires?

One familiar resolution of these questions has been to commend the artist's remarks, and his audience's responses, to the attention of psychologists or sociologists, confining philosophy's attention to "the object itself." The plausibility of this resolution has strong sources. There is the distinction established in the philosophy of science according to which the philosopher's concern is confined to the "context of justification" of a theory, its "context of discovery" yielding, at best, to history and psychology. There is the decisive accomplishment, in literary criticism, of the New Critics, whose formalist program called for, and depended upon, minute attention concentrated on the poem itself. There is, finally, the realization on the part of anyone who knows what art is that many of the responses directed to works of art are irrelevant to them as art and that the artist's intention is *always* irrelevant—it no more counts toward the success or failure of a work of art that the artist intended something other than is *there*, than it counts, when the referee is counting over a boxer, that the boxer had intended to duck.

I cannot accept such a resolution, for three main sorts of reasons: (1) The fact that the criticism of art may, and even must, be formal (in the sense suggested) implies nothing whatever about what the content of aesthetics may or must be. Kant's aesthetics is, I take it, supposed to be formal, but that does not deter Kant from introducing intention (anyway, "purposiveness") and a certain kind of response ("disinterested pleasure") in determining the grounds on which anything is to count as art. And such books as *The Birth of Tragedy* and *What Is Art?* rely fundamentally on characterizing the experience of the artist and of his audience, and I am more sure that Nietzsche (for all his reputedly unsound philology) and Tolstoy (for all his late craziness) know what art is than I know what philosophy or psychology are, or ought to be. (2) The denial of the relevance of the artists' intention is likely not to record the simple, fundamental fact that what an artist meant cannot alter what he has or has not accomplished, but to imply a philosophical *theory* according to which the artist's intention is something in his mind while the work of art is something out of his mind, and so the closest connection there could be between them is one of causation, about which, to be sure, only a psychologist or biographer could care. But I am far less sure that any such philosophical theory is correct than I am that when I experience a work of art I feel that I am *meant* to notice one thing and not another, that the placement of a note or rhyme or line has a *purpose*, and that certain works are perfectly realized, or contrived, or meretricious. . . . (3) Nothing could be commoner among critics of art than to ask *why* the thing is as it is, and characteristically to put this question, for example, in the form "Why does Shakespeare follow the murder of Duncan with a scene which begins with the sound of knocking?", or "Why does Beethoven put in a bar of rest in the last line of the fourth Bagatelle (Op. 126)?" The best critic is the one who knows best where to ask this question, and how to get an answer; but surely he doesn't feel it necessary, or desirable even were it possible, to get in touch with the artist to find out the answer. The philosopher may, because of his theory, explain that such questions are misleadingly phrased, and that they really refer to the object itself, not to Shakespeare or Beethoven. But who is misled, and about what? An alternative procedure, and I think sounder, would be to accept the critic's question as perfectly appropriate—as, so to speak, a philosophical datum—and then to look for a philosophical explanation which can accommodate that fact. Of course, not just *any* critic's response can be so taken. And this suggests a further methodological principle in philosophizing about art. It seems obvious enough that in setting out to speak about the arts one begins with a rough canon of the objects to be spoken about. It seems to me equally necessary, in appealing to the criticism of art for philosophical data, that one begin with a rough canon of criticism which is not then repudiated in the philosophy to follow.

Confusion prescribes caution, even if the confusion is private and of one's own making. Accordingly, I restrict my discussion here primarily to one art, music; and within that art primarily to one period, since the second World War; and within that period to some characteristic remarks made by theorists of music about the *avant garde* composers who regard themselves as the natural successors to the work of Schoenberg's greatest pupil, Anton Webern. Though narrow in resource, however, my motives will seem extremely pretentious, because I am going to raise a number of large questions about art and philosophy and ways they bear on one another. Let me therefore say plainly that I do not suppose myself to have *shown* anything at all; that what I set down I mean merely as suggestions; and that I am often not sure that they are philosophically relevant. They are the result, at best, of a clash between what I felt missing in the philosophical procedures I have some confidence in, and what I feel present and significant in some recent art.

II

I believe it is true to say that modernist art—roughly, the art of one's own generation—has not become a problem for the philosophy contemporary with it (in England and America anyway); and perhaps that is typical of the aesthetics of any period. I do not wish to insist upon a particular significance in that fact, but I am inclined to believe that there is decisive significance in it. For example, it mars the picture according to which aesthetics stands to art or to criticism as the philosophy of, say, physics stands to physics; for no one, I take it, could claim competence at the philosophy of physics who was not immediately concerned with the physics current in his time. One may reply that this is merely a function of the differences between science and art—the one progressing, outmoding, or summarizing its past, the other not. I would not find that reply very satisfactory, for two related reasons: (1) It obscures more than it reveals. It is not clear what it is about science which allows it to "progress" or, put another way, what it is which is called "progress" in science (for example, it does not progress evenly),[1] moreover, the succession of styles of art, though doubtless it will not simply constitute progress, nevertheless seems not to be mere succession either. Art critics and historians (not to mention artists) will often say that the art of one generation has "solved a problem" inherited from its parent generation; and it seems right to say that there is progress during *certain* stretches of art and with respect to certain developments within them (say the developments leading up to the establishment of sonata form, or to the control of perspective, or to the novel of the nineteenth century). Moreover, the succession of art styles is *irreversible*, which may be as important a component of the concept of progress as the component of superiority. And a new style not merely replaces an older one, it may change the significance of any earlier style; I do not think this is merely a matter of changing taste but a matter also of changing the *look*, as it were, of past art, changing the ways it can be described, outmoding some, bringing some to new light—one may even want to say, it can change what the past *is*, however against the grain that sounds. A generation or so ago, "Debussy" referred to music of a certain ethereal mood, satisfying a taste for refined sweetness or poignance; today it refers to solutions for avoiding tonality: I find I waver between thinking of that as a word altering its meaning and thinking of it as referring to an altered object. (2) Critics, on whom the philosopher may rely for his data, *are* typically concerned with the art of their time, and what they find it relevant to say about the art of any period will be molded by that concern. If I do not share those concerns, do I understand what the critic means? Virtually every writer I have read on the subject of non-tonal music will at some point, whether he likes it or not, compare this music explicitly with tonal music; a critic like Georg Lukacs will begin a book by comparing (unfavorably) Bourgeois Modernism with the Bourgeois Realism of the nineteenth century; Clement Greenberg will write, "From Giotto to Courbet, the painter's first task had been to hollow out an illusion of three-dimensional space on a flat surface. . . . This spatial illusion or rather the sense of it, is what we may miss [in Modernism] even more than we do the images that used to fill it." Now, do I understand these comparisons if I do not share their experience of the modern? I do not mean merely that I shall not then understand what they say about modern art; I mean that I shall not then understand what they see in traditional art: I feel I am *missing* something about art altogether, something, moreover, which an earlier critic could not give me.

III

The writing I have begun studying, and upon which I base my observations, occurs largely in two sets of professional periodicals: *Die Reihe*, whose first issue appeared in 1955; and *Perspectives of New Music*, starting in 1962.[2] Both were created in direct response to "the general problems relating to the composition of music in our time," as the prefatory note to *Die Reihe*'s first number puts it. Opening these periodicals, and allowing time to adapt to the cross-glare of new terms, symbols invented for the occasion, graphs, charts, some equations . . . several general characteristics begin to emerge as fairly common to their contents. There is, first, an obsession with *newness* itself, every other article taking some position about whether the novelty of the new music is radical, or less than it seems, whether it is aberrant or irreversible, whether it is the end of music as an art, or a reconception which will bring it new life. None, that I recall, raises the issue as a problem to be investigated, but as the cause of hope or despair or fury or elation. It is characteristic to find, in one and the same article, analyses of the most intimidating technicality and arcane apparatus, combined or ended with a mild or protracted cough of philosophy (e.g., "The new music aspires to Being, not to Becoming"). If criticism has as its impulse and excuse the opening of access between the artist and his audience, giving voice to the legitimate claims of both, then there is small criticism in these pages—although there is a continuous reference to the *fact* that artist and audience are out of touch, and a frequent willingness to assign blame to one or the other of them. One is reminded that while the history of literary criticism is a part of the history of literature, and while the history of visual art is written by theorists and connoisseurs of art for whom an effort at accurate phenomenology can be as natural as the deciphering of iconography, histories of music contain virtually no criticism or assessment of their objects, but concentrate on details of its notation or its instruments or the occasions of its performance. The serious attempt to articulate a *response* to a piece of music, where more than reverie, has characteristically stimulated mathematics or metaphysics —as though music has never quite become one of the facts of life, but shunts between an overwhelming directness and an overweening mystery. Is this because music, as we know it, is the newest of the great arts and just has not had the time to learn how to criticize itself; or because it inherently resists verbal transcriptions? (Both have been said, as both are said in accounting for the lack of a canon of criticism about the cinema.) Whatever the cause, the absence of humane music criticism (of course there were isolated instances) seems particularly striking against the fact that music has, among the arts, the most, perhaps the only, systematic and precise vocabulary for the description and analysis of its objects. Somehow that possession must itself be a liability; as though one now undertook to criticize a poem or novel armed with complete control of medieval rhetoric but ignorant of the modes of criticism developed in the past two centuries.

A final general fact about the writing in these periodicals is its concentration on the composer and his problems; a great many of the articles are produced by composers themselves, sometimes directly about, sometimes indirectly, their own music. Professor Paul Oskar Kristeller, in his review of the writing about the arts produced from Plato to Kant, notices in his final reflections that such writing has typically proceeded, and its categories and style thereby formed, from the spectator's or amateur's point of view.[3] Does the presence of these new journals of music indicate that the artist is, some place, finally getting the attention he deserves? But one can scarcely imagine a serious journal contributed to by major poets, novelists, or painters devoted to the problems of the making of poems and novels and paintings, nor that any such artist would find it useful if somehow it appeared. It might even be regarded by them as unseemly to wash these problems in public, and at best it distracts from the job of getting on with real work. Magazines are for interviews or for publishing one's work and having others write about it. Why is it not regarded as unseemly or distracting by composers? Perhaps it is. Then what necessity overrides a more usual artistic reticence? Perhaps it is an awareness that the problems composers face now are no longer merely private but are the problems of their art in general, "the general problems relating to the composition of music in our time." (This is likely to seem at once unmentionably obvious to composers and unintelligible to spectators, which is itself perhaps a measure of the problems of composition in our time.) This further suggests, as in the case of ordinary learned journals, the emergence of a new universal style or mode of procedure, implying an unparalleled dispersal of those who must inescapably be affected by one another's work. Painting still grows, as it always has, in particular cities; apprenticeship and imitation are still parts of its daily life. Writers do not share the severe burden of modernism which serious musicians and painters and sculptors have recognized for generations: a writer can still work with the words we all share, more or less, and have to share; he still, therefore, has an audience with the chance of responding to the way *he* can share the words more than more or less. My impression is that serious composers have, and feel they have, all but lost their audience, and that the essential reason for this (apart, for example, from the economics and politics of getting performances) has to do with crises in the internal, and apparently irreversible, developments within their own artistic procedures. This is what I meant by "the burden of modernism": the procedures and problems it now seems necessary to composers to employ and confront to make a work of art at all *themselves* insure that their work will not be comprehensible to an audience.

This comes closer to registering the dissonant and unresolved emotion in the pages to which I refer. They are prompted by efforts to communicate with an audience lost, and to compose an artistic community in disarray—efforts which only the art itself can accomplish. So the very existence of such periodicals suggests that they cannot succeed.

But here a difference of animus in these two periodicals becomes essential. *Die Reihe* began first, with an issue on electronic music, and its general tone is one of self-congratulation and eagerness for the future, whether it contains art and composers and performers or not. *Perspectives* began publication seven years later (and lean years or fat, seven years in our period may contain an artistic generation); and for a variety of reasons its tone is different. It is committed to much of the same music, shares some of the same writers, but the American publication is quite old world in its frequent concern with tradition and the artist and the performer, and in its absence of belief that progress is assured by having *more* sounds and rhythms, etc., available for exploitation. Whatever the exact pattern of rancors and rites in these pages, the sense of conflict is unmistakable, and the air is of men fighting for their artistic lives. Perhaps, then, their theories and analyses are not addressed to an audience of spectators, but as has been suggested about their music itself, to one another. The communications often include artistic manifestos, with declarations of freedom and promises for the future. But unlike other manifestos, they are not meant to be personal; they do not take a position against an establishment, for they represent the establishment; a young composer, therefore, seems confronted not by one or another group of artists but by one or another official philosophy, and his artistic future may therefore seem to depend not on finding his own conviction but on choosing the right doctrine. Sometimes they sound like the dispassionate analyses and reports assembled in professional scientific and academic journals. But unlike those journals they are not organs of professional societies with fairly clear requirements for membership and universally shared criteria for establishing competence, even eminence, within them. One comes to realize that these professionals themselves do not quite know who is and who is not rightly included among their peers, whose work counts and whose does not. No wonder then, that we outsiders do not know. And one result clearly communicated by these periodicals is that there is no obvious way to find out.

What they suggest is that the possibility of fraudulence, and the experience of fraudulence, is endemic in the experience of contemporary music; that its full impact, even its immediate relevance, depends upon a willingness to trust the object, knowing that the time spent with its difficulties may be betrayed. I do not see how anyone who has experienced modern art can have avoided such experiences, and not just in the case of music. Is Pop Art art? Are canvases with a few stripes or chevrons on them art? Are the novels of Raymond Roussel or Alian Robbe-Grillet? Are art movies? A familiar answer is that time will tell. But my question is: *What* will time tell? That certain departures in art-like pursuits have become established (among certain audiences, in textbooks, on walls, in college courses); that *someone* is treating them with the respect due, we feel, to art;

that one no longer has the right to question their status? But in waiting for time to tell that, we miss what the present tells—that the dangers of fraudulence, and of trust, are essential to the experience of art. If anything in this paper should count as a thesis, that is my thesis. And it is meant quite generally. Contemporary music is only the clearest case of something common to modernism as a whole, and modernism only makes explicit and bare what has always been true of art. (That is almost a definition of modernism, not to say its purpose.) Aesthetics has so far been the aesthetics of the classics, which is as if we investigated the problem of other minds by using as examples our experience of *great* men or *dead* men. In emphasizing the experiences of fraudulence and trust as essential to the experience of art, I am in effect claiming that the answer to the question "What is art?" will in part be an answer which explains why it is we treat certain objects, or how we *can* treat certain objects, in ways normally reserved for treating persons.

Both Tolstoy's *What Is Art?* and Nietzsche's *Birth of Tragedy* begin from an experience of the fraudulence of the art of their time. However obscure Nietzsche's invocation of Apollo and Dionysus and however simplistic Tolstoy's appeal to the artist's sincerity and the audience's "infection," their use of these concepts is to specify the genuine in art in opposition to specific modes of fraudulence, and their meaning is a function of that opposition. Moreover, they agree closely on what those modes of fraudulence are: in particular, a debased Naturalism's heaping up of random realistic detail, and a debased Romanticism's substitution of the stimulation and exacerbation of feeling in place of its artistic control and release; and in both, the constant search for "effects."

IV

How can fraudulent art be exposed? Not, as in the case of a forgery or counterfeit, by comparing it with the genuine article, for there *is* no genuine article of the right kind. Perhaps it helps to say: If we call it a matter of comparing something with the genuine article, we have to add (1) that what counts as the genuine article, is not *given*, but itself requires critical determination; and (2) that what needs to be exposed is not that a work is a *copy*. (That of course *may* be an issue, and that *may* be an issue of forgery. Showing fraudulence is more like showing something is imitation—not: *an* imitation. The emphasis is not on copying a *particular* object, as in forgery and counterfeit, but on producing *the effect* of the genuine, or having some of its properties.) Again, unlike the cases of forgery and counterfeit, there is no one feature, or definite set of features, which may be described in technical handbooks, and no specific tests by which its fraudulence can be detected and exposed. Other frauds and imposters, like forgers and counterfeiters, admit *clear* outcomes, conclude in dramatic discoveries—the imposter is unmasked at the ball, you find the counterfeiters working over their press, the forger is caught signing another man's name, or he confesses. There are no such proofs possible for the assertion that the art accepted by a public is fraudulent; the artist himself may not know; and the critic may be shown up, not merely as incompetent, nor unjust in accusing the wrong man, but as taking others in (or out); that is, as an imposter.

The only exposure of false art lies in recognizing something about the object itself, but something whose recognition requires exactly the same capacity as recognizing the genuine article. It is a capacity not insured by understanding the language in which it is composed, and yet we may not understand what is said; nor insured by the healthy functioning of the senses, though we may be told we do not *see* or that we fail to *hear* something; nor insured by the aptness of our logical powers, though what we may have missed was the object's consistency or the way one thing followed from another. We may have missed its tone, or neglected an allusion or a cross current, or failed to see its point altogether; or the object may not have established its tone, or buried the allusion too far, or be confused in its point. You often do not know which is on trial, the object or the viewer: modern art did not invent this dilemma, it merely insists upon it. The critic will have to *get* us to see, or hear or realize or notice; help us to appreciate the tone; convey the current; point to a connection; show how to take the thing in. . . . What this getting, helping, conveying, and pointing consist in will be shown in the specific ways the critic accomplishes them, or fails to accomplish them. Sometimes you can say he is exposing an object to us (in its fraudulence, or genuineness); sometimes you can say he is exposing us to the object. (The latter is, one should add, not always a matter of noticing fine differences by exercising taste; sometimes it is a matter of admitting the lowest common emotion.) Accordingly, the critic's anger is sometimes directed at an object, sometimes at its audience, often at both. But sometimes, one supposes, it is produced by the frustrations inherent in his profession. He is part detective, part lawyer, part judge, in a country in which crimes and deeds of glory look alike, and in which the public not only, therefore, confuses one with the other, but does not know that one or the other has been committed; not because the news has not got out, but because what counts as the one or the other cannot be defined until it happens; and when it has happened there is no sure way he can get the news out; and no way at all without risking something like a glory or a crime of his own.

One line of investigation here would be to ask: Why does the assertion "You have to *hear* it!" mean what it does? Why is its sense conveyed with a word which emphasizes the function of a sense organ, and in the form of an imperative? The combination is itself striking. One cannot be commanded to hear a sound, though one can be commanded to listen to it, or for it. Perhaps the question is: How does it happen that the *achievement* or *result* of using a sense organ comes to be thought of as the *activity* of that organ—as though the aesthetic experience had the form not merely of a continuous effort (e.g., listening) but of a continuous achievement (e.g., hearing).

Why—on pain of what—must I hear it; what consequence befalls me if I don't? One answer might be: Well, then I wouldn't hear it—which at least says that there is no point to the hearing beyond itself; it is worth doing in itself. Another answer might be: Then I wouldn't *know* it (what it is about, what it is, what's happening, what is *there*). And what that seems to say is that works of art are objects of the sort that can only be *known in sensing*. It is not, as in the case of ordinary material objects, that I know *because* I see, or that seeing is *how* I know (as opposed, for example, to being told, or figuring it out). It is rather, one may wish to say, that *what* I know is what I see; or even: seeing *feels* like knowing. ("Seeing the point" conveys this sense, but in ordinary cases of seeing the point, once it's seen it's known, or understood; about works of art one may wish to say that they require a continuous seeing of the point.) Or one may even say: In such cases, knowing functions like an organ of sense. (The religious, or mystical, resonance of this phrase, while not deliberate, is welcome. For religious experience is subject to distrust on the same grounds as aesthetic experience is: by those to whom it is foreign, on the ground that its claims must be false; by those to whom it is familiar, on the ground that its quality must be tested.)

Another way one might try to capture the idea is by saying: Such objects are only *known by feeling*, or *in* feeling. This is not the same as saying that the object expresses feeling, or that the aesthetic response consists in a feeling of some sort. Those are, or may be, bits of a theory about the aesthetic experience and its object; whereas what I am trying to describe, or the descriptions I am trying to hit on, would at best serve as data for a theory. What the expression "known by feeling" suggests are facts (or experiences) such as these: (1) What

I know, when I've *seen* or *heard* something is, one may wish to say, not a matter of *merely* knowing it. But what more is it? Well, as the words say, it is a matter of *seeing* it. But one could also say that it is not a matter of *merely* seeing it. But what more is it? Perhaps "merely knowing" should be compared with "not really knowing": "You don't really know what it's like to be a Negro"; "You don't really know how your remark made her feel"; "You don't really know what I mean when I say that Schnabel's slow movements give the impression not of slowness but of infinite length." You merely say the words. The issue in each case is: What would *express* this knowledge? It is not that my knowledge will be real, or more than *mere* knowledge, when I acquire a particular feeling, or come to see something. For the issue can also be said to be: What would express the acquisition of that feeling, or show that you have seen the thing? And the answer might be that I now *know* something I didn't know before. (2) "Knowing by feeling" is not like "knowing by touching"; that is, it is not a case of providing the *basis* for a claim to know. But one could say that feeling functions as a touchstone: the mark left on the stone is out of the sight of others, but the result is one of knowledge, or has the form of knowledge—it is directed to an object, the object has been tested, the result is one of conviction. This seems to me to suggest why one is anxious to communicate the experience of such objects. It is not merely that I want to tell you how it is with me, how I feel, in order to find sympathy or to be left alone, or for any other of the reasons for which one reveals one's feelings. It's rather that I want to tell you something I've seen, or heard, or realized, or come to understand, for the reasons for which *such* things are communicated (because it is news, about a world we share, or could). Only I find that I can't *tell* you; and that makes it all the more urgent to tell you. I want to tell you because the knowledge, unshared, is a burden—not, perhaps, the way having a secret can be a burden, or being misunderstood; a little more like the way, perhaps, not being believed is a burden, or not being trusted. It matters that others know what I see, in a way it does not matter whether they know my tastes. It matters, there is a burden, because unless I can tell what I know, there is a suggestion (and to myself as well) that I do *not* know. But I *do*— what I see is *that* (pointing to the object). But for that to communicate, you have to see it too. Describing one's experience of art is itself a form of art; the burden of describing it is like the burden of producing it. Art is often praised because it brings men together. But it also separates them.

The list of figures whose art Tolstoy dismisses as fraudulent or irrelevant or bad, is, of course, unacceptably crazy: most of Beethoven, all of Brahms and Wagner; Michelangelo, Renoir; the Greek dramatists, Dante, Shakespeare, Milton, Goethe, Ibsen, Tolstoy. . . . But the sanity of his procedure is this: it confronts the fact that we often do not find, and have never found, works we would include in a canon of works of art to be of importance or relevance to us. And the implication is that apart from this we cannot know that they are art, or what makes them art. One could say: objects so canonized do not exist for us. This strikes Tolstoy as crazy—as though we were to say we know that there are other minds because other people have told us there are.

V

But I was discussing some writing now current about the new music. Perhaps I can say more clearly why it leads, or has led me, to these various considerations by looking at three concepts which recur in it over and over—the concepts of composition, improvisation, and chance.

The reason for their currency can be put, roughly, this way. The innovations of Schoenberg (and Bartok and Stravinsky) were necessitated by a crisis of composition growing out of the increasing chromaticism of the nineteenth century which finally overwhelmed efforts to organize music within the established assumptions of tonality. Schoenberg's solution was the development of the twelve-tone system which, in effect, sought to overcome this destructiveness of chromaticism by accepting it totally, searching for ways to organize a rigidly recurrent total chromatic in its own terms. History aside, what is essential is that no assumption is any longer to be made about how compositional centers or junctures could be established—e.g., by establishing the "dominant" of a key—and the problem was one of discovering what, in such a situation, could be heard as serving the structural functions tonality used to provide. Schoenberg's twelve-tone "rows" and the operations upon them which constitute his system, were orderings and operations upon pitches (or, more exactly, upon the familiar twelve classes of pitches). About 1950, composers were led to consider that variables of musical material other than its pitches could also be subjected to serial ordering and its Schoenbergian transformations—variables of rhythm, duration, density, timbre, dynamics, and so on. But now, given initial series of pitches, rhythms, timbres, dynamics, etc., together with a plot of the transformations each is to undergo, and a piece is written or, rather, determined; it is, so it is said, totally organized. What remains is simply to translate the rules into the notes and values they determine and see what we've got. Whether what such procedures produce is music or not, they certainly produced philosophy. And it is characteristic of this philosophy to appeal to the concepts of composition, chance, and improvisation.

The motives or necessities for these concepts are not always the same. In the writing of John Cage, chance is explicitly meant to *replace* traditional notions of art and composition; the radical ceding of the composer's control of his material is seen to provide a profounder freedom and perception than mere art, for all its searches, had found. In the defense of "total organization," on the contrary, chance and improvisation are meant to *preserve* the concepts of art and composition for music; to explain how, although the composer exercises choice only over the initial conditions of his work, the determinism to which he then yields his power itself creates the spontaneity and surprise associated with the experience of art; and either (a) because it produces combinations which are unforeseen, or (b) because it includes directions which leave the performer free to choose, i.e., to improvise. It is scarcely unusual for an awareness of determinism to stir philosophical speculation about the possibilities of freedom and choice and responsibility. But whereas the more usual motivation has been to preserve responsibility in the face of determinism, these new views wish to preserve choice by foregoing responsibility (for everything but the act of "choosing").

Let us listen to one such view, from Ernst Krenek, who was for years a faithful disciple of Schoenberg and who has emerged as an important spokesman for total organization.

Generally and traditionally "inspiration" is held in great respect as the most distinguished source of the creative process in art. It should be remembered that inspiration by definition is closely related to chance, for it is the very thing that cannot be controlled, manufactured or premeditated in any way. It is what falls into the mind (according to the German term *Einfall*) unsolicited, unprepared, unrehearsed, coming from nowhere. This obviously answers the definition of chance as "the absence of any known reason why an event should turn out one way rather than another." Actually the composer has come to distrust his inspiration because it is not really as innocent as it was supposed to be, but rather conditioned by a tremendous body of recollection, tradition, training, and experience. In order to avoid the dictations of such ghosts, he prefers to set up an impersonal mechanism which will furnish, according to premeditated patterns, unpredictable situations . . . the creative act takes place in an area in which it has so far been entirely unsuspected, namely in setting up the serial statements. . . . What happens afterwards is predetermined by the selection of the mechanism, but not premeditated except as an unconscious result of the predetermined operations. The unexpected happens by necessity. The surprise is built in.[4]

This is not serious, but it is meant; and it is symptomatic—the way it is symptomatic that early in Krenek's paper he suggests that the twelve-tone technique "appears to be a special, or limiting, case of serial music, similar to an interpretation of Newtonian mechanics as a limiting expression of the Special Theory of Relativity, which in turn has been explained as a limiting expression of that General Theory." (Note the scientific caution of "appears to be.") The vision of our entire body of recollection, tradition, training, and experience as so many ghosts *could* be serious. It was serious, in their various ways, for Kierkegaard, Marx, Nietzsche, Emerson, Ibsen, Freud, and for most of the major poets and novelists of the past hundred years. It is not merely a modern problem; it is, one could say, the problem of modernism, the attempt in every work to do what has never been done, because what is known is known to be insufficient, or worse. It is an old theme of tragedy that we will be responsible for our actions beyond anything we bargain for, and it is the prudence of morality to have provided us with excuses and virtues against that time. Krenek turns this theme into the comedy of making choices whose consequences we accept as the very embodiment of our will and sensibility although we cannot, in principle, see our responsibility in them. He says that "the composer has come to distrust his inspiration," but he obviously does not mean what those words convey—that the composer (like, say, Luther or Lincoln) is gripped by an idea which is causing him an agony of doubt. What in fact Krenek has come to distrust is the composer's capacity to feel any idea as his own. In denying tradition, Krenek is a Romantic, but with no respect or hope for the individual's resources; and in the reliance on rules, he is a

Classicist, but with no respect or hope for his culture's inventory of conventions.

It is less my wish here to detail the failings or to trace the symptoms in such philosophizing as Krenek's, than it is to note simply that theorizing of this kind is characteristic of the writing about new music —alternating, as was suggested, with purely technical accounts of the procedures used in producing the work. For this fact in itself suggests: (1) that such works cannot be *criticized*, as traditional art is criticized, but must be defended, or rejected, as art altogether; and (2) that such work would not exist but for the philosophy. That, in turn, suggests that the activity going into the production, or consumption, of such products cannot be satisfied by the art it yields, but only in a philosophy which seems to give justification and importance to the activity of producing it. I am not suggesting that such activity is in fact unimportant, nor that it can in no way be justified, but only that such philosophizing as Krenek's does not justify it and must not be used to protect it against aesthetic assessment. (Cage's theorizing, which I find often quite charming, is exempt from such strictures, because he clearly believes that the work it produces is no more important than the theory is, and that it is not justified by the theory, but, as it were, illustrates the theory. That his work is performed as music—rather than a kind of paratheater or parareligious exercise— is only another sign of the confusions of the age. I do not speak of his music explicitly meant to accompany the dance.)

I have suggested that it is significant not only *that* philosophy should occur in these ways, but also that it should take the content it has. I want now to ask why it is that the concepts of chance and improvisation should occur at all in discussing composition; what might they be used to explain?

VI

What is composition, what is it to compose? It seems all right to say, "It is to make something, an object of a particular sort." The question then is, "What sort?" One direction of reply would be, "An object of art." And what we need to know is just what an object of art is. Suppose we give a minimal answer: "It is an object in which human beings will or can take an interest, one which will or can absorb or involve them." But we can be absorbed by lots of things people make: toys, puzzles, riddles, scandals. . . . Still, something is said, because not *everything* people make is an object of this sort. It is a problem, an artistic problem—an experimental problem, one could say—to discover what will have the capacity to absorb us the way art does. Could someone be interested and become absorbed in a pin, or a crumpled handkerchief? Suppose someone did. Shall we say, "It's a matter of taste"? We might dismiss him as mad (or suppose he is pretending), or, alternatively, ask ourselves what he can possibly be *seeing in* it. That these *are* our alternatives is what I wish to emphasize. The situation demands an explanation, the way watching someone listening intently to Mozart, or working a puzzle, or, for that matter, watching a game of baseball, does not. The forced choice between the two responses—"He's mad" (or pretending, or on some drug, etc.) or else "What's in it?"—are the imperative choices we have when confronted with a new development in art. (A revolutionary development in science is different: not because the new move can initially be proved to be valid—perhaps it can't, in the way we suppose that happens—but because it is easier, for the professional community, to spot cranks and frauds in science than in art; and because if what the innovator does is valid, then it is *eo ipso* valid for the rest of the professional community, *in their own work*, and as it stands, as well.) But objects of art not merely interest and absorb, they move us; we are not merely involved with them, but concerned with them, and care about them; we treat them in special ways, invest them with a value which normal people otherwise reserve only for other people—*and* with the same kind of scorn and outrage. They *mean* something to us, not just the way statements do, but the way people do. People devote their lives, sometimes sacrifice them, to producing such objects just in order that they will have such consequences; and we do not think they are mad for doing so. We approach such objects not merely because they are interesting in themselves, but because they are felt as made by someone—and so we use such categories as intention, personal style, feeling, dishonesty, authority, inventiveness, profundity, meretriciousness, etc., in speaking of them. The category of intention is as inescapable (or escapable with the same consequences) in speaking of objects of art as in speaking of what human beings say and do: without it, we would not understand what they are. They are, in a word, not works of nature but of *art* (i.e., of act, talent, skill). Only the concept of intention does not function, as elsewhere, as a term of excuse or justification. We follow the progress of a piece the way we follow what someone is saying or doing. Not, however, to see how it will come out, nor to learn something specific, but to see what *it* says, to see what someone has been able to make out of these materials. A work of art does not express some particular intention (as statements do), nor achieve particular goals (the way technological skill and moral action do), but, one may say, celebrates the fact that men can intend their lives at all (if you like, that they are free to choose), and that their actions are coherent and effective at all in the scene of indifferent nature and determined society. This is what I understand Kant to have seen when he said of works of art that they embody "purposiveness without purpose."

Such remarks are what occur to me in speaking of compositions as objects *composed*. The concepts of chance and of improvision have natural roles in such a view: the capacities for improvising and for taking and seizing chances are virtues common to the activity leading to a composition. It suggests itself, in fact, that these are two of the virtues necessary to act coherently and successfully at all. I use "virtue" in what I take to be Plato's and Aristotle's sense: a capacity by virtue of which one is able to act successfully, to follow the distance from an impulse and intention through to its realization. Courage and temperance are virtues because human actions move precariously from desire and intention into the world, and one's course of action will meet dangers or distractions which, apart from courage and temperance, will thwart their realization. A world in which you could get what you want merely by wishing would not only contain no beggars, but no human activity. The success of an action is threatened in other familiar ways: by the lack of preparation or foresight; by the failure of the most convenient resources, natural or social, for implementing the action (a weapon, a bridge, a shelter, an extra pair of hands); and by a lack of knowledge about the best course to take, or way to proceed. To survive the former threats will require ingenuity and resourcefulness, the capacity for improvisation; to overcome the last will demand the willingness and capacity to take and to seize chances.

Within the world of art one makes one's own dangers, takes one's own chances—and one speaks of its objects at such moments in terms of tension, problem, imbalance, necessity, shock, surprise. . . . And within this world one takes and exploits these chances, finding, through danger, an unsuspected security—and so one speaks of fulfillment, calm, release, sublimity, vision. . . . Within it, also, the means of achieving one's purposes cannot lie at hand, ready-made. The means themselves have inevitably to be fashioned for *that* danger, and for *that* release—and so one speaks of inventiveness, resourcefulness, or else of imitativeness, obviousness, academicism. The *way* one escapes or succeeds is, in art, as important as the success itself; indeed, the way constitutes the success—and so the means that are fashioned are spoken of as masterful, elegant, subtle, profound. . . .

I said: in art, the chances you take are your own. But of course you are inviting others to take them with you. And since they are, nevertheless, your own, and your invitation is based not on power or authority, but on attraction and promise, your invitation incurs the most exacting of obligations: that *every* risk must be shown worthwhile, and every infliction of tension lead to a resolution, and every demand on attention and passion be satisfied—that risks those who trust you can't have known they would take, will be found to yield value they can't have known existed. The creation of art, being human conduct which affects others, has the commitments any conduct has. It escapes morality; not, however, in escaping commitment, but in being free to choose only those commitments it wishes to incur. In this way art plays with one of man's fates, the fate of being accountable for everything you do and are, intended or not. It frees us to sing and dance, gives us actions to perform whose consequences, commitments, and liabilities are discharged in the act itself. The price for freedom in this choice of commitment and accountability is that of an exactitude in meeting those commitments and discharging those accounts which no mere morality can impose. You cede the possibilities of excuse, explanation, or justification for your failures; and the cost of failure is not remorse and recompense, but the loss of coherence altogether.

The concept of improvisation, unlike the concept of chance, is one which has established and familiar uses in the practice of music theorists and historians. An ethnomusicologist will have recourse to the concept as a way of accounting for the creation-cum-performance of the music of cultures, or classes, which have no functionaries we would think of as composers, and no objects we would think of as embodying the intention to art; and within the realm of composed (written) music, improvisation is, until recent times, recognized as explicitly called for at certain sharply marked incidents of a performance—in the awarding of cadenzas, in the opportunities of ornamentation, in the realization of figured bass. In such uses, the concept has little explanatory power, but seems merely to name events which one knows, as matters of historical fact (that is, as facts independent of anything a critic would have to discover by an analysis or interpretation of the musical material as an aesthetic phenomenon), not to have been composed.

My use of the concept is far more general. I mean it to refer to certain qualities of music generally. Perhaps what I am getting at can be brought out this way. In listening to a great deal of music, particularly to the time of Beethoven, it would, I want to suggest, be possible to imagine that it was being improvised. Its mere complexity, or a certain kind of complexity, would be no obstacle. (Bach, we are told, was capable of improvising double fugues on any given subjects.) I do not suggest that a chorus or a symphony orchestra can be imagined to be improvising its music; on the contrary, a group improvisation itself has a particular *sound*. On the other hand I do not wish to restrict the sense of improvisation to the performance of one player either. It may help to say: One can hear, in the music in question, how the composition is *related* to, or could grow in familiar ways, from a process of improvisation; as though the parts meted out by the composer were re-enactments, or dramatizations, of successes his improvisations had discovered—given the finish and permanence the occasion deserves and the public demands, but containing essentially only such discoveries. If this could be granted, a further suggestion becomes possible. Somewhere in the development of Beethoven, this ceases to be imaginable. (I do not include *all* music after Beethoven. Chopin and Liszt clearly seem improvisatory, in the sense intended; so do Brahms Intermezzi, but not Brahms Symphonies; early Stravinsky, perhaps, but not recent Stravinsky.)

Why might such a phenomenon occur? It is, obviously enough, within contexts fully defined by shared formulas that the possibility of full, explicit improvisation traditionally exists—whether one thinks of the great epics of literature (whose "oral-formulaic" character is established), or of ancient Chinese painting, or of Eastern music, or of the theater of the Commedia dell'Arte, or jazz. If it seems a paradox that the reliance on formula should allow the fullest release of spontaneity, that must have less to do with the relation of these phenomena than with recent revolutions in our aesthetic requirements. The suggestion, however, is this. The context in which we can hear music as improvisatory is one in which the language it employs, its conventions, are familiar or obvious enough (whether because simple or because they permit of a total mastery or perspicuity) that at no point are we or the performer in doubt about our location or goal; there are solutions to every problem, permitting the exercise of familiar forms of resourcefulness; a mistake is clearly recognizable as such, and may even present a chance to be seized; and just as the general range of chances is circumscribed, so there is a preparation for every chance, and if not an inspired one, then a formula for one. But in the late experience of Beethoven, it is as if our freedom to act no longer depends on the possibility of spontaneity; improvising to fit a *given* lack or need is no longer enough. The entire enterprise of action and of communication has become problematic. The problem is no longer how to do what you want, but to know what would satisfy you. We could also say: Convention as a whole is now looked upon not as a firm inheritance from the past, but as a continuing improvisation in the face of problems we no longer understand. Nothing we now have to say, no *personal* utterance, has its meaning conveyed in the conventions and formulas we now share. In a time of slogans, sponsored messages, ideologies, psychological warfare, mass projects, where words have lost touch with their sources or objects, and in a phonographic culture where music is for dreaming, or for kissing, or for taking a shower, or for having your teeth drilled, our choices seem to be those of silence, or nihilism (the denial of the value of shared meaning altogether), or statements so personal as to form the possibility of communication without the support of convention—perhaps to become the source of new convention. And then, of course, they are most likely to fail even to seem to communicate. Such, at any rate, are the choices which the modern works of art I know seem to me to have made. I should say that the attempt to re-invent convention is the alternative I take Schoenberg and Stravinsky and Bartok to have taken; whereas in their total organization, Krenek and Stockhausen have chosen nihilism.

VII

The sketches I have given of possible roles of improvisation and chance in describing composition obviously do not fit their use in the ideology of the new music; they may, however, help understand what that ideology is. When a contemporary theorist appeals to *chance*, he obviously is not appealing to its associations with taking and seizing chances, with risks and opportunities. The point of the appeal is not to call attention to the act of composition, but to deny that act; to deny that what he offers is composed. His concept is singular, with no existing plural; it functions not as an explanation for particular actions but as a metaphysical principle which supervises his life and work as a whole. The invocation of chance is like an earlier artist's invocation of the muse, and serves the same purpose: to indicate that his work comes not from *him*, but *through* him—its validity or authority is not a function of his own powers or intentions. Speaking for the muse, however, was to give voice to what all men share, or all would hear; speaking through chance forgoes a voice altogether—there is nothing to say. (That is, of course, by now a cliché of popular modernism.) This way of forgoing composition may perhaps usefully be compared with the way it is forgone in modernist painting. The contemporary English sculptor Anthony Caro is reported to have said: "I do not compose." Whatever he meant by that, it seems to have clear relevance to the painting of abstract expressionism and what comes after.[5] If you look at a Pollock drip painting or at a canvas consisting of eight parallel stripes of paint, and what you are looking for is *composition* (matters of balance, form, reference among the parts, etc.), the result is absurdly trivial: a child could do it; I could do it. The question, therefore, if it is art, must be: How is this to be seen? What is the painter doing? The problem, one could say, is not one of escaping inspiration, but of determining how a man could be inspired to do *this*, why he feels *this* necessary or satisfactory, how he can *mean* this. Suppose you conclude that he cannot. Then that will mean, I am suggesting, that you conclude that this is not art, and this man is not an artist; that in failing to mean what he's done, he is fraudulent. But how do you know?

In remarking the junctures at which composers have traditionally called for improvisation (cadenzas, figured bass, etc.), I might have put that by saying that the composer is at these junctures leaving something open to the performer. It is obvious that throughout the first decades of this century composers became more and more explicit in their notations and directions, leaving less and less open to the performer. One reason for allowing improvisation in the new music has been described as returning *some* area of freedom to the performer in the midst of specifications so complex and frequent (each note may have a different tempo, dynamic marking, and direction for attack, at extreme rates of speed) that it is arguable they have become unrealizable in practice. Does this use of "something left open" suggest that we have an idea of some notation which may be "complete," closing all alternatives save one to the performer? And is the best case of "leaving nothing open" one in which the composer codes his music directly into his "performer," thus obviating any need for an intermediary between him and his audience? What would be the significance of this displacement? A composer might be relieved that at least he would no longer have to suffer bad performances, and one might imagine a gain in having all performances uniform. But perhaps what would happen is that there would, for music made that way, no longer be anything we should call a "performance"; the concept would have no use there, anymore than it has for seeing movies. (One goes to see Garbo's performance as Camille, but not to see a performance of [the movie] *Camille*.)

Perhaps, then, one would go to "soundings," "first plays," and "re-runs" of pieces of music. And then other musical institutions would radically change, e.g., those of apprenticeship, of conservatories, of what it is one studies and practices to become a composer. Would we then go on calling such people composers? But of course everything depends upon just what we are imagining his procedures to be. If, for example, he proceeds only so far as Krenek's "initial choices" and accepts whatever then results, I think we would not; but if, even if he begins that way, we believe that he has in some way tested the result on himself, with a view to satisfying himself—even if we do not know, or he does not know, what the source of satisfaction is—then perhaps we would. If we would not, would this suggest that the concept of a composition is essentially related to the concept of a performance? What it suggests is that it is not clear what is and is not essentially connected to the concept of music.

I do not, however, hesitate, having reminded myself of what the notion of improvisation suggests, to say that what is called for in a piece such as Stockhausen's *Pianostück Elf* (where nineteen frag-ments are to be selected from, in varying orders, depending upon certain decisions of the performer) is not improvisation. (The main reason, I think, for my withholding of the concept, is that nothing counts as the *goal* of a performance.) To call it improvisation is to substitute for the real satisfactions of improvisation a dream of spontaneity—to match the dream of organization it is meant to complement; as Krenek's fantasy of physics substitutes for the real satisfaction of knowledge. It also, since improvisation implies shared conventions, supposes that you can create a living community at a moment's notice. A similar point occurs when such a work is praised, as it has been, on the ground that it is graphically lovely. It is, I think, quite pretty to look at, but so is a Chopin or Bach or medieval manuscript graphically satisfying. To rest one's hope for organization on such an admittedly pleasant quality is to suppose that you can become a visual artist inadvertently. It expresses the same contempt for the artistic process as calling something musically organized (let alone totally organized) on grounds unrelated to any way in which it is, or is meant to be, heard.

VIII

Why, instead of philosophy, didn't music made in these ways pro-duce laughter and hostility? It did, of course, and does. But the response couldn't end there, because nobody could *prove* it wasn't music. Of course not, because it is not clear that the notion of "proving it is (or is not) music" is even intelligible, which means that it is not fully intelligible to say that nobody could do what it describes. (*What* can't anybody do here?) My suggestion is only that some composers would have had the remarkable feeling that their lives depended on performing this indescribable task. Why? Because those productions themselves seemed to prove something, namely, that music (or whatever it is) produced in those ways was indistinguishable from, or close enough to music produced in traditional ways—by composers, that is, artists, from their inspiration and technique, both painfully acquired, and out of genuine need—to be confused with it, and therewith certain to replace it. (It's just as good, and so much easier to make.) And it seemed to prove that the detractors of modernism were right all along: whatever artists and aestheticians may have said about the internal and coherent development of the art, it all turns out to have arrived at pure mechanism, it has no *musical* significance, a child could do it. This, or something like it, had been said about Beethoven, about Stravinsky, and doubtless about every *avant garde* in the history of the arts. Only no child ever *did* it before, and *some* people obviously did find it musically significant. Saint-Saëns stormed out of the first performance of *The Rite of Spring*. But Ravel and serious young composers stayed and were convinced. But now a child *has* done it, or might as well have, and a child could understand it as well as anyone else—you prove he couldn't. It is, I take it, significant about modernism and its "permanent revolution" that its audience recurrently tells itself the famous stories of riots and walkouts and outrages that have marked its history. It is as though the *impulse* to shout fraud and storm out is always present, but fear of the possible consequence overmasters the impulse. Remember Saint-Saëns: He said the Emperor had no clothes, and then history stripped him naked. The philistine audience cannot afford to admit the new; the *avant garde* audience cannot afford not to. This bankruptcy means that both are at the mercy of their tastes, or fears, and that no artist can test his work either by their rejection or by their acceptance.

These may or may not exhaust all the audiences there are, but they certainly do not include all the people there are. This suggests that genuine responses to art are to be sought in individuals alone, as the choice or affinity for a canon of art and a canon of criticism must be made by individuals alone; and that these individuals have no audience to belong in as sanctioning, and as sharing the responsibility for, the partiality they show for the work of individual artists and particular critics. (As the faithful auditor of God is perhaps no longer to be expected, and cannot receive sanction, through membership in a congregation.) This suggests one way of putting the modern predicament of audience: taste now appears as partialness.

This is the point at which Nietzsche's perception outdistances Tolstoy's. Tolstoy called for sincerity from the artist and infection from his audience; he despised taste just because it revealed, and concealed, the loss of our *appetite* for life and consequently for art that matters. But he would not face the possible cost of the artist's radical, unconventionalized sincerity—that his work may become uninfectious, and even (and even deliberately) unappetizing, forced to defeat the commonality which was to be art's high function, in order to remain art at all (art in exactly the sense Tolstoy meant, directed from and to genuine need). Nietzsche became the unbalanced ledger of that cost, whereas Tolstoy apparently let himself imagine that we could simply *stop* our reliance on taste once we were told that it was blocking us to satisfaction—and not merely in art. What modern artists realize, rather, is that taste must be *defeated*, and indeed that this can be accomplished by nothing less powerful than art itself. One may see in this the essential moral motive of modern art. Or put it this way: What looks like "breaking with tradition" in the successions of art is not really that; or is that only after the fact, looking historically or critically; or is that only as a result not as a motive: the unheard of appearance of the modern in art is an effort not to break, but to keep faith with, tradition. It is perhaps fully true of Pop Art that its motive is to break with the tradition of painting and sculpture; and the result is not that the tradition is broken, but that these works are irrelevant to that tradition, i.e., they are not paintings, whatever their pleasures. (Where history has cunning, it is sometimes ironic, but sometimes just.)

IX

I said earlier that the periodicals about music which we were discussing were trying to do what only the art of music itself could do. But maybe it just is a fact about modern art that coming to care about it demands coming to care about the problems in producing it. Whatever painting may be about, modernist painting is about *painting*, about what it means to use a limited two-dimensional surface in ways establishing the coherence and interest we demand of art. Whatever music can do, modern music is concerned with the making of music, with what is required to gain the movement and the stability on which its power depends. The problems of composition are no longer irrelevant to the audience of art when the solution to a compositional problem has become identical with the aesthetic result itself.

In this situation, criticism stands, or could, or should stand, in an altered relation to the art it serves. At any time it is subordinate to that art, and expendable once the experience of an art or period or departure is established. But in the modern situation it seems inevitable, even, one might say, internal, to the experience of art. One evidence of what I have in mind is the ease with which a new departure catches phrases which not merely free new response, but join in the creation of that response; moreover, the phrases do not cease to matter once the response is established, but seem required in order that the response be sustained. New theater is "absurd"; new painting is "action"; Pop Art exists "between life and art"; in serial music "chance occurs by necessity." Often one does not know whether interest is elicited and sustained primarily by the object or by what can be said about the object. My suggestion is not that this is bad, but that it is definitive of a modernist situation. Perhaps it would be nicer if composers could not think, and felt no need to open their mouths except to sing—if, so to say, art did not present problems. But it does, and they do, and the consequent danger is that the words, because inescapable, will usurp motivation altogether, no longer tested by the results they enable. I think this has already happened in the phrases I cited a moment ago, and this suggests that a central importance of criticism has become to protect its art against criticism. Not just from bad criticism, but from the critical impulse altogether, which no longer knows its place, perhaps because it no longer has *a* place. In a Classical Age, criticism is confident enough to prescribe to its art without moralism and its consequent bad conscience. In a Romantic Age, art is exuberant enough to escape criticism without the loss of conscience—appealing, as it were, to its public directly. In a Modern Age, both that confidence and that appeal are gone, and are to be re-established, if at all, together, and in confusion.

If we say it is a gain to criticism, and to art, when we know that criticism must not be prescriptive (e.g., tell artists what they ought to produce), then we should also recognize that this injunction is *clear* only when we already accept an object as genuine art and a man as an authentic artist. But the modernist situation forces an awareness of the *difficulty* in avoiding prescription, and indeed of the ways in which criticism, and art itself, are ineluctably prescriptive—art, because its successes garner imitations, not just because there are always those who want success at any price, but because of the very authority which has gone into the success; criticism, not because the critic cannot avoid prescriptive utterances, but because the terms in which he defines his response themselves define which objects are and which are not relevant to his response. When, therefore, artists are unmoored from tradition, from taste, from audience, from their own past achievement; when, that is, they are brought to rely most intimately on the critic, if only the critic in themselves; then the terms in which they have learned to accept criticism will come to dictate the terms in which they will look for success: apart from these, nothing will count as successful because nothing will be evaluable, nothing have a chance of validity. Here the artist's survival depends upon his constantly eluding, and constantly assembling, his critical powers.

A certain use of mathematical-logical descriptions of tone-row occurrences is only the clearest case of these difficulties, as it is also the case which most clearly shows the force of the aesthetically and intellectually irrelevant in establishing a reigning criticism—in this case, the force of a fearful scientism, an intellectual chic which is at once intimidating and derivative, and in general the substitution of precision for accuracy. This is hardly unusual, and it should go without saying that not *all* uses of such techniques are irrelevant, and that they represent an indispensable moment in coming to understand contemporary music. The issue is simply this: we know that criticism ought to come only after the fact of art, but we cannot *insure* that it will come only after the fact. What is to be hoped for is that criticism learn to criticize itself, as art does, distrusting its own success.

This is particularly urgent, or perhaps particularly clear, in the case of music, because, as suggested, the absence of a strong tradition of criticism leaves this art especially vulnerable to whatever criticism becomes established, and because the recent establishment of criticism is peculiarly invulnerable to control (because of its technicalities, its scientific chic . . .). But if it is not technicality as such which is to be shunned, only, so to speak, its counterfeit, how do you tell? The moral is again, as it is in the case of the art itself: you cannot tell from outside; and the expense in getting inside is a matter for each man to go over. And again, this strict economy is not new to modern art, but only forced by it. Nor do I wish to impugn all music made with attention to "total organization," but only to dislodge the idea that what makes it legitimate is a philosophical theory—though such a theory may be needed in helping to understand the individual artistic success which alone would make it legitimate. It may be, given the velocity of our history, that the music and the theory of music illustrated in the recent work of Krenek is by now, five years later, already repudiated—not perhaps theoretically, but in fact, in the practice of those who constitute the musical world. What would this show? One may find that it shows such worries as have been expressed in this essay to be unfounded; that the fraudulent in art and the ideological in criticism will not defeat the practice of the real thing. At least they won't have this time; but that means that certain composers have in the meantime gone on writing, not only against the normal odds of art, but against the hope that the very concept of art will not be forgotten. That a few composers might, because of this distraction and discouragement, cease trying to write, is doubtless to be expected in a difficult period. But it is not unthinkable that next time all on whom the art relies will succumb to that distraction and discouragement. I do not absolutely deny, even in the face of powerful evidence, that in the end the truth will out. I insist merely that philosophy ought to help it out. Nor have I wished to suggest that the recognition of the "possibility of fraudulence" manifests itself as a permanent suspicion of all works giving themselves out as compositions or paintings or poems. . . . One *can* achieve unshakable justified faith in one's capacity to tell. I have wanted only to say that *that* is what one will have achieved. If someone supposes that that leaves us in a hopelessly irrational position, he is perhaps supposing a particular view of faith, and a limited horizon of hope.[6]

X

I have spoken of the *necessities* of the problems faced by artists, of the *irreversibility* of the sequence of art styles, of the difficulties in a contemporary artist's continuing to *believe* in his work, or *mean* it. And I said it was the artist's need to maintain his own belief that forced him to give up—to the extent and in the way he has given up—the belief and response of his audience. This is reflected in literature as well, but differently. I do not mean, what I take to be obvious enough, that modern poetry often takes the making of poetry and the difficulties of poetry in the modern age, as its subject matter. What I have in mind is best exemplified in the modern theater. The fact that the language the literary artist uses does communicate directly with his audience—in ways the contemporary "languages" of painting and music do not—was earlier taken as an advantage to the literary artist. But it is also his liability. A writer like Samuel Beckett does *not* want what is communicated easily to be what he communicates—it is not what he means. So his effort is not to find belief from his audience, but to defeat it, so that his meaning *has* to be searched for. Similarly, modern dramatists do not *rely* on their audiences, but *deny* them. Suppose an audience is thought of as "those present whom the actors ignore." Then to stop ignoring them, to recognize them explicitly, speak *to* them, insist on the fact *that* this is acting and this is a theater, functions to remove the status of *audience* from "those out there who were ignored." Modern dramatists (e.g., Beckett, Genet, Brecht) can be distinguished by the various ways in which they deny the existences of audiences—as if they are saying: what is meant cannot be understood from that position.

But why not? Why, to raise the question in a more familiar form, can't one still write like Mozart? The question makes the obscurities and withdrawals and unappealingness of modern art seem *willful*—which is another *fact* of the experience of that art. But what is the answer to that question? One answer might be: Lots of people have written like Mozart, people whose names only libraries know; and Mozart wasn't one of them. Another answer might be: Beethoven wrote like Mozart, until he became Beethoven. Another: If Mozart were alive, he wouldn't either. Or even: the best composers do write as Mozart did (and as Bach and Beethoven and Brahms did), though not perhaps with his special fluency or lucidity. But by now that question is losing its grip, one is no longer sure what it is one was asking, nor whether these answers mean anything (which seems the appropriate consequence of looking for a simple relation between past and present). A final answer I have wanted to give is: No one *does* now write that way. But perhaps *somebody* does, living at the edge of an obscure wood, by candlelight, with a wig on. What would our response to him be? We wouldn't take him seriously as an artist? Nobody could mean such music now, be sincere in making it? And yet I've been insisting that we can no longer be sure that any artist is sincere—we haven't convention or technique or appeal to go on any longer: *anyone* could fake it. And this means that modern art, if and where it exists, *forces* the issue of sincerity, depriving the artist and his audience of every measure except absolute attention to one's experience and absolute honesty in expressing it. This is what I meant in saying that it lays bare the condition of art altogether. And of course it runs its own risks of failure, as art within established traditions does.

This will seem an unattractive critical situation to be left with. Don't we know that ". . . the goodness or badness of poetry has nothing to do with sincerity. . . . The worst love poetry of adolescents is the most sincere"?[7] But I am suggesting that we may not know what sincerity is (nor what adolescence is). The adolescent, I suppose it is assumed, has strong feelings, and perhaps some of them can be described as feelings of sincerity, which, perhaps, he attaches to the words in his poetry. Does all that make the words, his utterance in the poem, sincere? Will he, for example, *stand by them*, later, when *those* feelings are gone? Suppose he does; that will not, of course, prove that his poetry is worthwhile, nor even that it is poetry. But I haven't suggested that sincerity proves anything in particular—it can prove madness or evil as well as purity or authenticity. What I have suggested is that it shows what kind of stake the stake in modern art is, that it helps explain why one's reactions to it can be so violent, why for the modern artist the difference between artistic success and failure can be so uncompromising. The task of the modern artist, as of the modern man, is to find something he can be sincere and serious in; something he can mean. And he may not at all.

Have my claims about the artist and his audience been based on hearsay, or real evidence, or really upon the work itself? But now the "work itself" becomes a heightened philosophical concept, not a neutral description. My claims do not rest upon works of art themselves, apart from their relations to how such works are made and the reasons for which they are made, and considering that some are sincere and some counterfeit. . . . But my claim is that to know such things is to know what a work of art is—they are, if one may say so, part of its grammar. And, of course, I may be taken in.

NOTES

1. See Thomas S. Kuhn, *The Structure of Scientific Revolutions* (Chicago: University of Chicago Press, 1962).
2. *Die Reihe*, Theodore Presser Co., Bryn Mawr, Pennsylvania, in association with Universal Edition. *Perspectives of New Music*, Princeton University Press.
3. "The Modern System of the Arts," reprinted in *Renaissance Thought II* (New York, 1965), p. 225.
4. "Extents and Limits of Serial Techniques," *Musical Quarterly*, XLVI, 1960, pp. 228–229.

5. Reported by Michael Fried (who showed me its significance) in an article on Caro in *The Lugano Review*, 1965. See, in addition, his *Three American Painters*, the catalog essay for an exhibition of the work of Noland, Olitski, and Stella, at the Fogg Museum, in the spring of 1965; and his "Jules Olitski's New Paintings," *Artforum*, November 1965.
6. The addition of this paragraph is only the main, not the only, point at which a reading by the composer John Harbison caused modification or expansion of what I had written.
7. René Wellek, *A History of Modern Criticism*, Vol. II (New Haven: Yale University Press, 1955), p. 137.

BIBLIOGRAPHY

Journal Abbreviations

AJP	*Australasian Journal of Philosophy*	*MLN*	*Modern Language Notes*
APQ	*American Philosophical Quarterly*	*NLH*	*New Literary History*
		PAS	*Proceedings of the Aristotelian Society*
BJA	*British Journal of Aesthetics*	*PE*	*Philosophical Exchange*
CI	*Critical Inquiry*	*PERS*	*The Personalist*
GR	*Georgia Review*	*PHIL*	*Philosophy*
JAAC	*Journal of Aesthetics and Art Criticism*	*PPR*	*Philosophy and Phenomenological Research*
JHI	*Journal of the History of Ideas*	*PQ*	*Philosophical Quarterly*
		PR	*Philosophical Review*
JP	*Journal of Philosophy*	*PS*	*Philosophical Studies*
JPS	*Journal of Philosophical Studies*	*RM*	*Review of Metaphysics*
		YFS	*Yale French Studies*

Abel, Lionel. "Jacques Derrida: His *'Difference'* with Metaphysics." *Salmagundi*, No. 25 (1974).

Abrams, M. H. "The Deconstructive Angel." *CI*, 3 (1977).

Ackerman, James S. "A Theory of Style." *JAAC*, 20 (1962).

Aiken, Henry D. (1) "The Aesthetic Relevance of Artists' Intentions." *JP*, 52 (1955).

———. (2) "The Aesthetic Relevance of Belief." *JAAC*, 9 (1951).

———. (3) "Art as Expression and Surface." *JAAC*, 4 (1945).

———. (4) "The Concept of Relevance in Aesthetics." *JAAC*, 6 (1947).

———. (5) "Criteria for an Adequate Aesthetics." *JAAC*, 7 (1948).

———. (6) "A Pluralistic Analysis of Aesthetic Value." *PR*, 59 (1950).

———. (7) "Some Notes Concerning the Aesthetic and the Cognitive." *JAAC*, 13 (1955).

Aldrich, Virgil. (1) "Art and the Human Form." *JAAC*, 29 (1972).

———. (2) "Back to Aesthetic Experience." *JAAC*, 24 (1966).

———. (3) "Beauty as Feeling." *Kenyon Review*, 1 (1939).

———. (4) *Philosophy of Art*. Englewood Cliffs, N.J., 1963.

———. (5) "Pictorial Meaning and Picture Thinking." *Keyon Review*, 5 (1943).

———. (6) "Pictorial Meaning, Picture-Thinking, and Wittgenstein's Theory of Aspects." *Mind*, 67 (1958).

———. (7) "Picture Space." *PR*, 67 (1958).

———. (8) "Pictures and Persons—An Analogy." *RM*, 28 (1975).

Allen, Neil W., and Joel Snyder. "Photography, Vision and Representation." *CI*, 2 (1975).

Ames, Van Meter. (1) "Art for Art's Sake Again?" *JAAC*, 33 (1975).

————. (2) "Is It Art?" *JAAC*, 30 (1971).

Amyx, Clifford. "The Iconic Sign in Aesthetics." *JP*, 6 (1947).

Arnheim, Rudolf. (1) *Art and Visual Perception*. Berkeley and Los Angeles, 1954; new edition, 1974.

————. (2) *Film As Art*. Berkeley and Los Angeles, 1957.

————. (3) "Gestalt and Art." *JAAC*, 2 (1943).

————. (4) "The Gestalt Theory of Expression." *PR*, 56 (1949).

————. (5) "On the Nature of Photography." *CI*, 1 (1974).

————. (6) "The Priority of Expression." *JAAC*, 8 (1949).

————. (7) "The Robin and the Saint: On the Twofold Nature of the Artistic Image." *JAAC*, 18 (1959).

————. (8) "A Stricture on Space and Time." *CI*, 4 (1978).

————. (9) *Towards a Psychology of Art*. New York and London, 1966.

Arvon, Henri. *Marxist Aesthetics*. Ithaca, N.Y., 1973.

Aschenbrenner, Karl. (1) "Aesthetic Theory—Conflict and Conciliation." *JAAC*, 18 (1959).

————. (2) "Critical Reasoning." *JP*, 57 (1960).

————. (3) "The Philosopher's Interest in Art." *JAE*, 5 (1969).

Ashmore, Jerome. "The Artist's Adequation." *Man and World*, 5 (1970).

Auerbach, Eric. *Mimesis*. Princeton, 1953.

Bach, K. "Part of What a Picture Is." *BJA*, 10 (1970).

Bachrach, Jay. (1) "Richard Wollheim and the Work of Art." *JAAC*, 32 (1973).

————. (2) "Type and Token and the Identification of the Work of Art." *PPR*, 31 (1973).

Ballard, E. G. "In Defense of Symbolic Aesthetics." *JAAC*, 12 (1953).

Barnes, Albert. *The Art in Painting*. New York, 1937.

Barthes, Roland. (1) *Critical Essays*. Evanston, Ill., 1972.

————. (2) "An Introduction to the Structural Analysis of Narrative." *NLH*, 6 (1975).

————. (3) *Writing Degree Zero*. London, 1967.

Bartlett, Ethel M. *Types of Aesthetic Judgment*. London, 1937.

Bartlett, F. C. "Types of Imagination." *JPS*, 3 (1928).

Bass, Alan. " 'Literature'/Literature." *MLN*, 87 (1972).

Bates, Stanley. "Tolstoy Evaluated: Tolstoy's Theory of Art." In *Aesthetics: A Critical Anthology*, edited by George Dickie and Richard Sclafani. New York, 1977.

Battcock, Gregory. *Why Art*. New York, 1977.

Battin, M. P. (1) "On the Creation of Art." *JAAC*, 23 (1965).

————. (2) "On the Generality of Critical Reasons." *JP*, 59 (1962).

————. (3) "Representation and Presentation: A Reply to Professor Dickie." *JP*, 58 (1961).

Baxandall, Lee. (1) *Marxism and Aesthetics*. New York, 1968.

————. (2) ed., *Radical Perspectives in the Arts*. Baltimore, 1972.

Bazin, Andre. *What is Cinema?* Berkeley and Los Angeles, 1967.

Bell, Clive. *Art*. New York, 1958.

Beardsley, Monroe. (1) "Aesthetic Experience Regained." *JAAC*,   (1969).

————. (2) "The Aesthetic Point of View." In *Perspectives in Education, Religion, and the Arts*, edited by Howard E. Kiefer and Milton K. Munitz. Albany, 1970.

————. (3) *Aesthetics: Problems in the Philosophy of Criticism*. New York, 1958.

————. (4) "Metaphor and Falsity." *JAAC*, 35 (1976).

————. (5) "Modes of Interpretation." *JHI*, 32 (1971).

————. (6) "The Philosophy of Literature." In *Aesthetics: A Critical Anthology*, edited by George Dickie and Richard Sclafani. New York, 1977.

————. (7) *The Possibility of Criticism*. Philadelphia, 1970.

————. (8) "What is an Aesthetic Quality?" *Theoria*, 39 (1973).

Bedford, Errol. "Seeing Paintings." *PAS*, Supp. 40 (1966).

Beloff, John. "Creative Thinking in Art and Science." *BJA*, 10 (1976).

Benson, John. "Emotion and Expression." *PR*, 76 (1967).

Berggren, Douglas. "The Use and Abuse of Metaphor." *RM*, 16 (1962–63).

Berleant, Arnold. (1) *The Aesthetic Field*. Springfield, Ill., 1971.

————. (2) "The Verbal Presence: An Aesthetics of Literary Performance." *JAAC*, 31 (1973).

Berndtson, Arthur. *Art, Expression, and Beauty*. New York, 1969.

Binkley, Timothy. (1) "On the Truth and Probity of Metaphor." *JAAC*, 33 (1974).

————. (2) "Piece: Contra Aesthetics." *JAAC*, 35 (1977).

Black, Max. "Metaphor." *PAS*, 55 (1954–55).

Blanshard, Frances. *Retreat from Likeness in the Theory of Painting*. New York, 1949.

Bloom, Harold. (1) *The Anxiety of Influence*. Oxford, 1973.

————. (2) *Figures of Capable Imagination*. New York, 1976.

————. (3) *Kabbalah and Criticism*. New York, 1975.

————. (4) *A Map of Misreading*. Oxford, 1975.

————. (5) *Poetry and Repression*. New Haven, 1976.

————. (6) *The Ringers in the Tower*. Chicago, 1971.

————. (7) *Wallace Stevens: The Poems of Our Climate*. Ithaca, 1977.

Boas, George. "The Problem of Meaning in the Arts." *University of California Publications in Philosophy*, 25 (1950).

Booth, Wayne C. (1) "Metaphor as Rhetoric: The Problem of Evaluation." *CI*, 5 (1978).

————. (2) "Preserving the Exemplar, or How Not to Dig Our Own Graves." *CI*, 3 (1977).

————. (3) *The Rhetoric of Fiction*. Chicago, 1961.

————. (4) *A Rhetoric of Irony*. Chicago, 1974.

Bond, E. J. "The Essential Nature of Art." *APQ*, 12 (1975).

Borinsky, Alicia. "Repetition, Museums, Libraries: Jorge Luis Borges." *Glyph 2* (1977).

Brenkman, John (1) "Narcissus in the Text." *GR*, 30 (1976).

————. (2) "The Other and the One: Psychoanalysis, Reading, *The Symposium*." *YFS*, 55/56 (1978).

Brion, Marcel. "Abstract Art." *Diogenes*, 24 (1958).

Brooks, Peter. (1) "The Aesthetics of Astonishment." *GR*, 30 (1976).

————. (2) "Freud's Masterplot: Questions of Narrative." *YFS*, 55/56 (1978).

Brown, Lee. (1) "Definitions and Art Theory." *JAAC*, 27 (1969).

————. (2) "Traditional Aesthetics Revisited." *JAAC*, 29 (1971).

Brownell, Baker. *Art is Action*. New York, 1939.

Brunius, Teddy. "The Uses of Works of Art." *JAAC*, 22 (1963).

Burke, Kenneth. (1) *Counter-Statement*. New York, 1931.

————. (2) *A Grammar of Motives*. New York, 1945.

————. (3) *Language as Symbolic Action*. Berkeley and Los Angeles, 1966.

————. (4) *Philosophy of Literary Form*. Baton Rouge, La., 1941; third edition, rev., Berkeley and Los Angeles, 1973.

————. (5) *A Rhetoric of Motives*. New York, 1950.

Butler, Christopher. "What is a Literary Work?" *NLH*, 5 (1973–74).

Capitan, William. "On Unity in Poems." *Monist*, 50 (1966).

Carney, James. "Defining Art." *BJA*, 15 (1975).

Carrier, David. (1) "Greenberg, Fried and Philosophy: American-Type Formalism." In *Aesthetics: A Critical Anthology*, edited by George Dickie and Richard Sclafani. New York, 1977.

————. (2) "A Reading of Goodman on Representation." *Monist*, 58 (1974).

Carritt, E. F. "Art Without Form?" *PHIL*, 16 (1941).

Carroll, David. "Freud and the Myth of the Origin." *NLH*, 6 (1975).

Carter, Curtis L. (1) "The Concept of Psychical Disturbance." *PERS*, 52 (1971).

————. (2) "Langer and Hofstader on Painting and Language: A Critique." *JAAC*, 32 (1974).

Cary, Joyce. *Art and Reality*. New York, 1958.

Casebier, Allan. (1) "The Alleged Special Logic for Aesthetic Terms." *JAAC*, 31 (1973).

————. (2) "The Concept of Aesthetic Distances." *PERS*, 52 (1971).

Casey, Edward. (1) "Expression and Communication in Art." *JAAC*, 29 (1971).

————. (2) "Imagination and Repetition in Literature: A Reassessment." *YFS*, 52 (1975).

Casey, John. *The Language of Criticism*. London, 1966.

Cavell, M. "Taste and the Moral Senses." *JAAC*, 34 (1975).

Cavell, Stanley. (1) "Existentialism and Analytic Philosophy." *Daedalus*, 93 (1964).

————. (2) "Leopards in Connecticut." *GR*, 30 (1976).

————. (3) "More of the World Viewed." *GR*, 28 (1974).

————. (4) *Must We Mean What We Say?* New York, 1969.

————. (5) *The Senses of Walden*. New York, 1972.

————. (6) *The World Viewed*. New York, 1971.

Caws, Peter. "The Ontology of Criticism." *Semiotext(e)*, 1 (1975).

Chalmers, F. Graeme. "The Study of Art in a Cultural Context." *JAAC*, 32 (1973).

Charlton, W. (1) *Aesthetics: An Introduction*. London, 1970.

————. (2) "Living and Dead Metaphors." *BJA*, 15 (1975).

Chattersee, Margaret. "Some Philosophical Problems Arising in the Arts." *JAAC*, 27 (1969).

Child, Arthur. "The Social-Historical Relativity of Esthetic Value." *PR*, 53 (1944).

Chipp, Herschel B. (ed.) *Theories of Modern Art: A Source Book by Artists and Critics*. Berkeley and Los Angeles, 1968.

Cioffi, Frank. "Intention and Interpretation in Criticism." *PAS*, 64 (1963–64).

Clark, Robert C. "Total Control and Chance in Music: A Philosophical Analysis." *JAAC*, 28 (1970).

Clement, W. C. "Quality Orders." *Mind*, 65 (1956).

Cohen, Alain. "Proust and the President Schreber: A Theory of Primal Quotation or *For a Psychoanalysis of (-desire-in) Philosophy*." *YFS*, 52 (1975).

Cohen, Marshall. (1) "Aesthetic Essence." In *Philosophy in America*, edited by Max Black. London, 1962.

————. (2) "Appearance and the Aesthetic Attitude." *JP*, 56 (1959).

————. (3) "Lear and Nature." *PE*, 2 (1970).

————. (4) "Notes on Modernist Art." *NLH*, 3 (1971).

Cohen, Ted. (1) "Aesthetic/Non-Aesthetic and the Concept of Taste: A Critique of Sibley's Position." *Theoria*, 39 (1973).

————. (2) "Figurative Speech and Figurative Acts." *JP*, 72 (1975).

————. (3) "Illocutions and Perlocutions." *Foundations of Language*, 9 (1973).

————. (4) "Metaphor and the Cultivation of Intimacy." *CI*, 5 (1978).

————. (5) "Notes on Metaphor." *JAAC*, 34 (1976).

————. (6) "The Possibility of Art: Remarks on a Proposal by Dickie," *PR*, 82 (1973).

Coker, Wilson. *Music and Meaning: A Theoretical Introduction to Musical Aesthetics*. New York, 1972.

Coleman, Francis J. (1) "A Few Observations on Fictional Discourse." In *Language and Aesthetics*, edited by Benjamin Tilghman. Lawrence, Kans., 1973.

————. (2) "Is Aesthetic Pleasure a Myth?" *JAAC*, 29 (1971).

————. (3) "On 'Knowing that a Work of Art is Good.'" In *Contemporary Aesthetics*, edited by Francis J. Coleman. New York, 1968.

————. (4) "A Phenomenology of Aesthetic Reasoning." *JAAC*, 25 (1966).

Courtney, Richard. "Imagination and the Dramatic Act: Comments on Sartre, Ryle, and Furlong." *JAAC*, 30 (1972).

Cowie, Peter. *Antonioni, Bergman, Renais*. New York, 1963.

Crane, R. S., ed. (1) *Critics and Criticism: Ancient and Modern*. Chicago, 1952.

————. (2) *The Languages of Criticism and the Structure of Poetry*. Toronto, 1953.

————. (3) *Principles of Literary History*. Chicago, 1967.

Crawford, Donald. "Causes, Reasons and Aesthetic Objectivity." *APQ*, 8 (1971).

Crews, Frederick. *Out of My System*. Oxford, 1975.

Crossley, D. J. "The Aesthetic Attitude: Back in Gear with Bullough." *PERS*, 56 (1975).

Culler, Jonathan. *Structuralist Poetics: Structuralism, Linguistics, and the Study of Literature*. Ithaca, N.Y., 1975.

Danto, Arthur. (1) "Artworks and Real Things." *Theoria*, 39 (1973).

————. (2) "The Artworld." *JP*, 61 (1964).

————. (3) "The Transfiguration of the Commonplace." *JAAC*, 33 (1974).

Davidson, Donald. "What Metaphors Mean." *CI*, 5 (1978).

Dawson, Sheila. "Distancing as an Aesthetic Principle." *AJP*, 39 (1961).

Derrida, Jacques. (1) "Differance." In *Speech and Phenomena and Other Essays*.

————. (2) "The Ends of Man." *PPR*, 30 (1969).

————. (3) "Form and Meaning: A Note on the Phenomenology of Language." In *Speech and Phenomena and Other Essays*.

————. (4) "Fors: The Anglish Words of Nicolas Abraham and Maria Torok." *GR*, 31 (1977).

————. (5) "Freud and the Scene of Writing." *YFS*, 48 (1972).

————. (6) "A Hegelianism Without Reserves: From Restricted to General Economy." *Semiotext(e)*, 2 (1976).

————. (7) "Limited, Inc." *Glyph 2* (1977).

————. (8) *Of Grammatology*. Baltimore, 1976.

————. (9) "*Ousia* and *Gramme*: A Note to a Footnote in *Being and Time*."

In *Phenomenology in Perspective*, edited by F. Joseph Smith. The Hague, 1970.

———. (10) "Positions." *Diacritics*, 2 (1972) and 3 (1973).

———. (11) "The Purveyor of Truth." *YFS*, 52 (1975).

———. (12) "The Question of Style" (abridged version). In *The New Nietzsche*, edited by David Allison. New York, 1977.

———. (13) "Signature Event Context." *Glyph 1* (1977).

———. (14) *Speech and Phenomena and Other Essays*. Evanston, Ill., 1973.

———. (15) "Structure, Sign and Play in the Discourse of the Human Sciences." In *The Structuralist Controversy: The Languages of Criticism and the Sciences of Man*, edited by Richard Macksey and Eugenio Donato. Baltimore, 1972 (1970).

———. (16) "The Supplement of Coppula: Philosophy *Before* Linguistics." *GR*, 30 (1976).

———. (17) "The White Mythology." *NLH*, 6 (1974).

Dessoir, Max. *Aesthetics and Theory of Art*. Detroit, 1970.

Detweiler, Robert. "The Moment of Death in Modern Fiction." *Contemporary Literature*, 13 (1972).

Devereaux, Daniel. "Artifacts, Natural Objects, and Works of Art." *Analysis*, 37 (1977).

Dikie, George. (1) "The Actuality of Art: Remarks on Criticisms by Cohen." *PERS*, 58 (1977).

———. (2) *Aesthetics: An Introduction*. Indianapolis, 1971.

———. (3) *Art and the Aesthetic: An Institutional Analysis*. Ithaca, N.Y., 1975.

———. (4) "Art Narrowly and Broadly Speaking." *APQ*, 5 (1968).

———. (5) "Attitude and Object: Aldrich on the Aesthetic." *JAAC*, 25 (1966).

———. (6) "Beardsley's Phantom Aesthetic Experience." *JP*, 62 (1965).

———. (7) "Defining Art." *APQ*, 6 (1969).

———. (8) "Design and Subject Matter: Fusion and Confusion." *JP*, 58 (1961).

———. (9) "The Institutional Conception of Art." In *Language and Aesthetics*, edited by Benjamin Tilghman. Lawrence, Kans., 1973.

———. (10) "Is Psychology Relevant to Aesthetics?" *PR*, 71 (1962).

———. (11) "The Myth of the Aesthetic Attitude." *APQ*, 1 (1964).

———. (12) "Psychical Distance: In a Fog at Sea." *BJA*, 13 (1973).

———. (14) "Taste and Attitude: The Origin of the Aesthetic." *Theoria*, 39 (1973).

Diffey, T. J. "Morality and Literary Criticism." *JAAC*, 33 (1975).

Donato, Eugenio. (1) "The Idioms of the Text: Notes on the Language of Philosophy and the Fictions of Literature." *Glyph 2* (1977).

———. (2) "Of Structuralism and Literature." *MLN*, 82 (1967).

Donovan, Josephine. "Feminism and Aesthetics." *CI*, 3 (1977).

Ducasse, C. J. (1) "Some Questions in Aesthetics." *Monist*, 42 (1932).

———. (2) "What Has Beauty to do with Art?" *JP*, 25 (1928).

Dufrenne, Mikel. *The Phenomenology of Aesthetic Experience*. Evanston, Ill., 1973.

Dutton, Denis. "Plausibility and Aesthetic Interpretation." *Canadian Journal of Philosophy*, 7 (1977).

Eagleton, Terry. (1) *Criticism and Ideology*. London, 1976.

———. (2) *Marxism and Literary Criticism*. Berkeley and Los Angeles, 1976.

Earle, William. "Revolt Against Realism in the Films." *JAAC*, 27 (1968).

Eaton, Marcia. (1) "Art, Artifacts and Intentions." *APQ*, 2 (1965).

————. (2) "Good and Correct Interpretations of Literature." *JAAC*, 29 (1970).

————. (3) "Metaphor and the Causal Theory of Expression." *PERS*, 58 (1977).

Edie, James. "The Problem of Enactment." *JAAC*, 29 (1970).

Eisenstein, Sergei. *Film Form: Essays in Film Theory*. New York, 1949.

Ellis, John M. *The Theory of Literary Criticism*. Berkeley and Los Angeles, 1974.

Eshleman, Martin. "Aesthetic Experience, the Aesthetic Object and Criticism." *Monist* 50 (1966).

Faber, M. D. *The Design Within: Psychoanalytic Approaches to Shakespeare*. New York, 1970.

Falk, B. "Portraits and Persons." *PAS*, 75 (1974–75).

Fell, H. Granville. "The Validity of Fakes as Works of Art." *The Connoisseur*, 117–118 (1946).

Felman, Shoshana. (1) "Madness and Philosophy *or* Literature's Reason." *YFS*, 52 (1975).

————. (2) "On Reading Poetry: Reflections on the Limits and Possibilities of Psychoanalytic Approaches." In *The Literary Freud: Mechanisms of Defense and the Poetic Will*, edited by Joseph H. Smith, M.D., New Haven, 1980.

————. (3) "Turning the Screw of Interpretation." *YFS*, 55/56 (1978).

Fiedler, Conrad. *On Judging Works of Visual Art*. Berkeley and Los Angeles, 1949.

Fish, Stanley. (1) "Facts and Fictions." *CI*, 1 (1975).

————. (2) "How Ordinary is Ordinary Language?" *NLH*, 5 (1973–74).

————. (3) "How to do Things with Austin and Searle: Speech Act Theory and Literary Criticism." *MLN*, 91 (1976).

————. (4) "Normal Circumstances, Literal Language, Direct Speech Acts, the Ordinary, the Everyday, the Obvious, What Goes Without Saying, and Other Special Cases." *CI*, 4 (1978).

Fisher, Philip. "The Future's Past." *NLH*, 6 (1975).

Foss, Lawrence. "Art as Cognitive: Beyond Scientific Realism." *Philosophical Studies*, 38 (1964).

Fraiberg, Louis. "Freud's Writings on Art." *International Journal of Psychoanalysis*, 37 (1956).

Frank, Paul L. "Historical or Stylistic Periods?" *JAAC*, 13 (1955).

Freedman, Marcia P. "The Myth of the Aesthetic Predicate." *JAAC*, 27 (1968).

Freedman, Ralph. "Intentionality and the Literary Object." *Contemporary Literature*, 17 (1976).

Fried, Michael. (1) "Art and Objecthood." *Artforum*, 5 (1967).

————. (2) "The Beholder in Courbet." *Glyph 4* (1978).

————. (3) "Manet's Sources." *Artforum*, 7 (1969).

————. (4) *Morris Louis*. New York, 1971.

————. (5) "New Work by Anthony Caro." *Artforum*, 5 (1967).

————. (6) "Shape as Form: Frank Stella's New Paintings." *Artforum*, 5 (1966).

————. (7) *Three American Painters*. Cambridge, Mass., 1965.

————. (8) "Thomas Couture and the Theatricalization of Action in 19th-Century French Painting." *Artforum*, 8 (1970).

————. (9) "Toward a Supreme Fiction: Genre and Beholder in the Art Criticism of Diderot and His Contemporaries." *NLH*, 6 (1975).

Friedrich, Carl. "Style as the Principle of Historical Interpretation." *JAAC*, 14 (1955).
Frye, Northrup. (1) *The Anatomy of Criticism*. Princeton, 1957.
————. (2) *The Critical Path: An Essay on the Social Context of Literary Citicism*. Bloomington, Ind., 1971.
————. (3) *Spiritus Mundi*. Bloomington, Ind., 1976.
————. (4) *The Stubborn Structure*. Ithaca, N.Y., 1970.
————. (5) *The Well-Tempered Critic*. Bloomington, Ind., 1963.
Gadamer, Hans-Georg. (1) *Philosophical Hermeneutics*. Berkeley and Los Angeles, 1976.
————. (2) *Truth and Method*. New York, 1975.
Gale, George. "Are Some Aesthetic Judgments Empirically True?" *APQ*, 12 (1975).
Gale, Richard. "The Fictive Use of Language." *PHIL*, 46 (1971).
Gallie, W. B. (1) "Art as an Essentially Contested Concept." *PQ*, 6 (1956).
————. (2) "The Function of Philosophical Aesthetics." *Mind*, 57 (1948).
Gallop, Jane. "The Ladies' Man." *Diacritics*, 6 (1976).
Gardner, Howard. "The Development of Sensitivity to Artistic Styles." *JAAC*, 29 (1970).
Garvin, Lucius. "Emotivism, Expression, and Symbolic Meaning." *JP*. 55 (1958).
Gass, William. (1) "Carrots, Noses, Snow, Roses, Roses." *JP*, 73 (1976).
————. (2) *Fiction and the Figures of Life*. New York, 1970.
————. (3) *On Being Blue*. Boston, 1976.
Gilman, Eric. "The Use of Moral Concepts in Literary Criticism." *PHIL*, 41 (1966).
Gombrich, E. H. (1) *Art and Illusion*. London, 1962.
————. (2) "The Evidence of Images." In *Interpretation: Theory and Practice*, edited by Charles Singleton. Baltimore, 1969.
————. (3) *Meditations on a Hobby Horse*. London, 1963.
————. (4) "Mirror and Map: Theories of Pictorial Representation." *Philosophical Transactions of the Royal Society of London*, 270 (1975).
————. (5) "The Museum: Past, Present and Future." *CI*, 3 (1976).
————. (6) "The Sky is the Limit." In *Studies in Perception: Essays in Honor of J. J. Gibson*, edited by R. B. Macleod and H. L. Pick, Jr. Ithaca, N.Y., 1974.
————. (7) "The What and the How: Perspectival Representation and the Phenomenal World." In *Logic and Art: Essays in Honor of Nelson Goodman*, edited by R. Rudner and I. Scheffler. Indianapolis, 1972.
Gombrich, E. H. and Quentin Bell. "Canons and Values in the Visual Arts: A Correspondence." *CI*, 2 (1976).
Gombrich, E. H., Julian Hochberg, and Max Black. *Art, Perception and Reality*. Baltimore, 1972.
Goodman, Nelson. (1) *Languages of Art*. Indianapolis, 1968.
————. (2) "On Some Questions Concerning Notation." *Monist*, 58 (1974).
————. (3) "On Reconceiving Cognition." *Monist*, 58 (1974).
————. (4) *Problems and Projects*. Indianapolis, 1972.
————. (5) "The Status of Style." *CI*, 1 (1975).
Gotshalk, D. W. (1) "Art and Beauty." *Monist*, 41 (1931).
————. (2) *Art and the Social Order*. Chicago, 1947.
————. (3) "Aesthetic Expression." *JAAC*, 13 (1954).
————. (4) "A Next Step for Aesthetics." *JAAC*, 18 (1959).

Granrose, John. "Pragmatic Justification in Aesthetics." *JAAC*, 30 (1972).

Green, Theodore M. *The Arts and the Art of Criticism*. Princeton, 1940.

Greenberg, Clement. (1) "After Abstract Expressionism." *Art International*, 6 (1962).

———. (2) *Art and Culture*. Boston, 1961.

———. (3) "Counter Avant-Garde." *Art International*, 15 (1971).

———. (4) "Louis and Noland." *Art International*, 4 (1960).

———. (5) "Modernist Painting." *Art and Literature*, 4 (1954). Reprinted in *The New Art*, edited by Gregory Battcock, New York, 1966.

———. (6) "The Necessity of Formalism." *NLH*, 3 (1971).

———. (7) "Poetry of Vision." *Artforum*, 6 (1968).

———. (8) "Post-Painterly Abstraction." *Art International*, 8 (1964).

———. (9) "The Recentness of Sculpture." *Art International*, 11 (1967).

Greene, Gordon K. "For Whom and Why Does a Composer Prepare a Score." *JAAC*, 32 (1974).

Grossman, Morris. "Art and Morality." *JAAC*, 31 (1973).

Hancher, Michael. (1) "The Science of Interpretation and the Art of Interpretation." *MLN*, 85 (1970).

———. (2) "Three Kinds of Intention." *MLN*, 87 (1972).

Hanke, John. "Can Representational Works of Art Be Physical Objects?" *Journal of Value Inquiry*, 10 (1976).

Harlow, Barbara. "Realignment: Alois Riegl's Image of Late Roman Art Industry." *Glyph 3* (1978).

Harre, R. "Quasi-Aesthetic Appraisals." *PHIL*, 33 (1958).

Harries, Karsten. (1) *The Meaning of Modern Art*. Evanston, Ill., 1968.

———. (2) "Metaphor and Transcendence." *CI*, 5 (1978).

Harrison, A. "Poetic Ambiguity." *Analysis*, 23 (1962).

Harrison, Bernard. "Some Uses of 'Good' in Criticism." *Mind*, 69 (1960).

Hartman, Gregory. (1) "The Aesthetics of Complicity." *GR*, 28 (1974).

———. (2) *Beyond Formalism*. New Haven, 1970.

———. (3) *The Fate of Reading*. Chicago, 1975.

———. (4) "Monsieur Texte: On Jacques Derrida, His *Glas*." *GR*, 29 (1975).

———. (5) "Monsieur Texte II: Epiphony in Echoland." *GR*, 30 (1976).

Hauser, Arnold. *The Philosophy of Art History*. New York, 1959.

Haydon, Glenn. *On the Meaning of Music*. Washington, D.C., 1948.

Heidegger, Martin. *Poetry, Language, Thought*. New York, 1971.

Hein, Hilde. "Performance as an Aesthetic Category." *JAAC*, 28 (1970).

Heller, Eric. "The Dismantling of a Marionette Theater; or, Psychology and the Misinterpretation of Literature." *CI*, 4 (1978).

Henze, Donald F. (1) "Is the Work of Art a Construct?" *JP*, 52 (1955).

———. (2) "The Work of Art." *JP*, 54 (1957).

Hermerén, Goren. (1) "Intention and Interpretation in Literary Criticism." *NLH*, 7 (1975).

———. (2) *Representation and Meaning in the Visual Arts*. Lund, 1969.

Hernandi, Paul. "Literary Theory: A Compass for Critics." *CI*, 3 (1976).

Herrmann, Rolf-Dieter. "How a European Views the *Journal of Aesthetics and Art Criticism*," *JAAC*, 29 (1970).

Hertz, Niel. "Freud and the Sandman." In *Textual Strategies: Criticism in the Wake of Structuralism*, edited by Josué Harari. Ithaca, N.Y., 1979.

Hester, Marcus. "Metaphor and Aspect Seeing." *JAAC*, 25 (1966).

Heyl, B. C. (1) "Aesthetic Truth Reconsidered." *JAAC*, 8 (1950).

————. (2) "Relativism Again." *JAAC*, 5 (1946).

Hiler, Hilaire. *Why Abstract?* New York, 1945.

Hinton, J. M. "Perception and Identification." *PR*, 76 (1967).

Hirsch, E. D. (1) *The Aims of Interpretation*. Chicago, 1976.

————. (2) *Validity in Interpretation*. New Haven, 1967.

Hofstader, Albert. "On the Grounds of Esthetic Judgment." *JP*, 54 (1957).

Holland, Norman. (1) *The Dynamics of Literary Response*. New York, 1968.

————. (2) *Five Readers Reading*. New Haven, 1975.

————. (3) "Freud and the Poet's Eye." *Literature and Psychology*, 11 (1961).

————. (4) "Human Identity." *CI*, 4 (1978).

————. (5) "Literary Interpretation and Three Phases of Psychoanalysis." *CI*, 3 (1976).

————. (6) *Poems in Persons: An Introduction to the Psychoanalysis of Literature*. New York, 1973.

————. (7) *Psychoanalysis and Shakespeare*. New York, 1966.

Holquist, Michael. "Whodunit and Other Questions: Metaphysical Detective Stories in Post-War Fiction." *NLH*, 3 (1971).

Hospers, John. (1) "The Concept of Artistic Expression." *PAS*, 55 (1954–55).

————. (2) "Implied Truths in Literature." *JAAC*, 19 (1960).

————. (3) *Meaning and Truth in the Arts*. Chapel Hill, N.C., 1946.

Howard, V. A. (1) "On Musical Quotation." *Monist*, 58 (1974).

————. (2) "On Representational Music." *Nous*, 6 (1972).

Howell, Robert. "The Logical Structure of Pictorial Representation." *Theoria*, 40 (1974).

Howes, F. *Music and Its Meanings*. London, 1958.

Hoy, David. (1) *The Critical Circle: Literature and History in Contemporary Hermeneutics*. Berkeley and Los Angeles, 1978.

————. (2) "Literary History: Paradigm or Paradox?" *YFS*, 52 (1975).

Hungerland, Isabel C. (1) "The Concept of Intention in Art Criticism." *JP*, 52 (1955).

————. (2) "Contextual Implication." *Inquiry*, 4 (1960).

————. (3) "Iconic Signs and Expressiveness." *JAAC*, 3 (1944).

————. (4) "The Logic of Aesthetic Concepts." *Proceedings and Addresses of the APA*, 36 (1962–63).

————. (5) "Once Again, Aesthetic and Non-Aesthetic." *JAAC*, 26 (1968).

Hyman, Lawrence W. "Literature and Morality in Contemporary Criticism." *JAAC*, 29 (1971).

Hyman, Stanley. "Freud and the Climate of Tragedy." *Partisan Review*, 23 (1956).

Ingarden, Roman. (1) "Aesthetic Experience and Aesthetic Object." *PPR*, 21 (1966).

————. (2) "Artistic and Aesthetic Values." *BJA*, 4 (1964).

————. (3) *The Cognition of the Literary Work of Art*. Evanston, Ill., 1973.

————. (4) *The Literary Work of Art*. Evanston, Ill., 1973.

Irwin, John T. *Doubling and Incest/ Repetition and Revenge: A Speculative Reading of Faulkner*. Baltimore, 1975.

Isenberg, Arnold. *Aesthetics and the Theory of Criticism*. Chicago, 1973.

Iser, Wolgang. (1) "Indeterminacy and the Reader's Response in Prose Fiction." In *Aspects of Narrative: Selected Papers of the English Institute*, edited by J. Hillis Miller. New York, 1971.

———. (2) "The Reading Process: A Phenomenological Approach." *NLH*, 3 (1972).

———. (3) "The Reality of Fiction." *NLH*, 7 (1975).

Jameson, Frederic. (1) "Imaginary and Symbolic in Lacan: Marxism, Psychoanalysis, Psychoanalytic Criticism and the Problem of the Subject." *YFS*, 55/56 (1978).

———. (2) *Marxism and Form*. Princeton, 1971.

———. (3) *The Prison-House of Language: A Critical Account of Structuralism and Russian Formalism*. Princeton, 1972.

———. (4) "The Symbolic Inference; or, Kenneth Burke and Ideological Analysis." *CI*, 4 (1978).

Jauss, Hans Robert. (1) "The Idealist Embarrassment: Observations on Marxist Aesthetics." *NLH*, 7 (1975).

Jenkins, Iredell. (1) "The Aesthetic Object." *RM*, 11 (1957).

———. (2) *Art and the Human Enterprise*. Cambridge, Mass., 1958.

Jessup, Bertram. (1) "Aesthetic Size." *JAAC*, 9 (1950).

———. (2) "Meaning Range in the Work of Art." *JAAC*, 12 (1954).

Johnson, Barbara. (1) "The Frame of Reference: Poe, Lacan, Derrida." *YFS*, 55/56 (1978).

———. (2) "Poetry and Performative Speech." *YFS*, 54 (1977).

Johnson, Ellen. *Modern Art and the Object*. London and New York, 1976.

Johnson, Martin. *Art and Scientific Thought*. London, 1944.

Jones, Ernest. *Hamlet and Oedipus*. New York, 1949.

Jones, Peter. (1) *Philosophy and the Novel*. Oxford, 1975.

———. (2) "Works of Art and Their Availability-for-Use." *BJA*, 11 (1971).

Kadish, Mortimer R. (1) "The Evidence for Esthetic Judgment." *JP*, 54 (1957).

———. (2) *Reason and Controversy in the Arts*. Columbus, Ohio, 1968.

Kaelin, Eugene. *An Existentialist Aesthetic*. Madison, Wis., 1962.

Kallen, Horace M. (1) *Art and Freedom*. New York, 1942.

———. (2) "Beauty and Use." *PR*, 48 (1939).

Kaplan, Abraham. (1) "On the So-Called Crisis in Criticism." *JAAC*, 8 (1948).

———. (2) "Referential Meaning in the Arts." *JAAC*, 12 (1954).

Kaufmann, Walter. *Tragedy and Philosophy*. Garden City, N.Y., 1969.

Kavolis, V. "Aesthetic Education in Civilizational Perspective." *Journal of Aesthetic Education*, 9 (1975).

Kemp, John. "The Work of Art and the Artist's Intentions." *BJA*, 4 (1964).

Kennick, W. E. (1) "Art and the Ineffable." *JP*, 58 (1961).

———. (2) "Does Traditional Aesthetics Rest on a Mistake?" *Mind*, 67 (1958).

Kermode, Frank. "The Structure of Fiction." *MLN*, 84 (1969).

Kernan, Alvin. "The Idea of Literature." *NLH*, 5 (1973–74).

Khatchadourian, Haig. (1) "Art-Names and Aesthetic Judgments." *PHIL*, 36 (1961).

———. (2) *The Concept of Art*. New York, 1971.

———. (3) "Family Resemblances and the Classification of Works of Art." *JAAC*, 28 (1969).

———. (4) "Is It Art? Is It Good Art?" *Anais Do VIII Congresso Interamericano De Filosofía E V Da Sociedad Interamericana De Filosofía*, 3 (1974).

———. (5) "Metaphor." *BJA*, 8 (1968).

Kivy, Peter. (1) "Aesthetics and Rationality." *JAAC*, 34 (1975).

———. (2) "Aesthetic Aspects and Aesthetic Qualities." *JP*, 65 (1968).

————. (3) *Speaking of Art*. The Hague, 1973.

Kjørup, Soren. "George Inness and the Battle at Hastings; or, Doing Things with Pictures." *Monist*, 58 (1974).

Klein, Richard. (1) "The Blindness of Hyperboles, The Ellipses of Insight." *Diacritics*, 3 (1973).

————. (2) "Prolegomena to Derrida." *Diacritics*, 2 (1972).

Knight, Helen. "The Use of 'Good' in Aesthetic Judgments." *PAS*, 36 (1949).

Kogan. J. "Dialectics of the Aesthetic Experience." *PPR*, 35 (1975).

Kohut, Heinz. "Psychoanalysis and the Interpretation of Literature." *CI*, 4 (1978).

Kolnai, Aurel. "Aesthetic and Moral Experience: The Five Contrasts." *BJA*, 11 (1971).

Kolodny, Anette. (1) "The Feminist as Literary Critic." *CI*, 2 (1976).

————. (2) "Some Notes on Defining a 'Feminist Literary Criticism.' " *CI*, 2 (1975).

Kracauer, Sigfried. *Theory of Film*. New York, 1960.

Krieger, Murray. *Theory of Criticism: A Tradition and Its System*. Baltimore, 1977.

Kris, Ernst. *Psychoanalytic Explorations in Literature*. London, 1953.

Kristeller, Paul O. "The Modern System of the Arts." *JHI*, 12 (1951) and 13 (1952).

Kuhns, Richard. (1) "Art Structures." *JAAC*, 19 (1960).

————. (2) "Criticism and the Problem of Intention." *JP*, 57 (1960).

————. (3) *Structures of Experience*. New York, 1970.

Kupperman, J. (1) "Art and Aesthetic Experience." *BJA*, 15 (1975).

————. (2) "Reasons in Support of Evaluations of Works of Art." *Monist*, 50 (1966).

Lacan, Jacques. (1) "Desire and the Interpretation of Desire in *Hamlet*." *YFS*, 55/56 (1978).

————. (2) *Ecrits: A Selection*. New York, 1977.

————. (3) *The Four Fundamental Concepts of Psychoanalysis*. New York, 1978.

————. (4) *The Language of the Self* (with Notes and Commentary by Anthony Wilden). Baltimore, 1968.

————. (5) "Seminar on 'The Purloined Letter.' " *YFS*, 48 (1972).

Lackey, Douglas P. "Reflections on Cavell's Ontology of Film." *JAAC*, 32 (1973).

Lang, Berel. (1) *Art and Inquiry*. Detroit, 1976.

————. (2) "The Form of Aesthetics." *JAAC*, 27 (1968).

————. (3) "The Intentional Fallacy Revisited." *BJA*, 14 (1974),

————. (4) "A Note on the Location of Paintings." *JAAC*, 31 (1972).

————. (5) "Style as Instrument, Style as Person." *CI*, 4 (1978).

Laszlo, Ervin. "Affect and Expression in Music." *JAAC*, 27 (1965).

Lee, Harry B. (1) "The Creative Imagination." *Psychoanalytic Quarterly*, 18 (1949).

————. (2) "On the Esthetic States of Mind." *Psychiatry*, 10 (1947).

Lemaire, Anika. *Jacques Lacan*. London, 1977.

Lesser, Simon. *Fiction and the Unconscious*. New York, 1957.

Lewis, David. (1) "Percepts and Color Mosaics in Visual Experience." *PR*, 75 (1966).

————. (2) "Truth in Fiction." *APQ*, 15 (1978).

Lind, Richard. "Must the Critic Be Correct?" *JAAC*, 35 (1977).

Lindgren, Ernest. *The Art of Film*. New York, 1963.

Lipman, Matthew. (1) "The Aesthetic Experience of the Body." *JAAC*, 15 (1957).

———. (2) "Critical Description and the Analysis of Causes and Effects." *Journal of Value Inquiry*, 10 (1976).

———. (3) "Definition and Status in Aesthetics." *Philosophical Forum*, 7 (1975).

———. (4) *What Happens in Art*. New York, 1967.

Logan, J. F. "More on Aesthetic Concepts." *JAAC*, 25 (1967).

Loreau, Max. "Premises for a Pictorial Logic." *YFS*, 52 (1975).

Lotringer, Sylvere. "The 'Subject' on Trial." *Semiotext(e)*, 1 (1975).

Lycan, William G. "Gombrich, Wittgenstein and the Duck-Rabbit." *JAAC*, 30 (1971).

Lycan, William G., and Peter Machamer. "A Theory of Critical Reasons." In *Language and Aesthetics*, edited by Benjamin Tilghman. Lawrence, Kans., 1973.

MacCormac, Earl R. "Metaphor Revisited." *JAAC*, 30 (1971).

MacDonald, Margaret. (1) "Art and Imagination." *PAS*, 53 (1952–53).

———. (2) "The Language of Fiction." *PAS*, Supp. 27 (1954).

———. (3) "Some Distinctive Features of Arguments Used in Criticism of the Arts." *PAS*, Supp. 23 (1950).

McFarland, Thomas. "The Originality Paradox." *NLH*, 5 (1973–74).

McGann, Jerome. "Formalism, Savagery, and Care; or, The Function of Criticism Once Again." *CI*, 2 (1976).

McGlynn, Paul D. "Point of View and the Craft of Cinema." *JAAC*, 34 (1976).

McGregor, Robert. "Art and the Aesthetic." *JAAC*, 32 (1974).

Mackie, A. "The Structure of Aesthetically Interesting Metaphors." *APQ*, 12 (1975).

Macksey, Richard. "The Artist in the Labyrinth: Design or *Dasein*." *MLN*, 77 (1962).

de Man, Paul. (1) "Action and Identity in Nietzsche." *YFS*, 52 (1975).

———. (2) *Blindness and Insight: Essays in the Rhetoric of Contemporary Criticism*. Oxford, 1971.

———. (3) "The Epistemology of Metaphor." *CI*, 5 (1978).

———. (4) "Genesis and Genealogy in Nietzsche's *Birth of Tragedy*." *Diacritics*, 2 (1972).

———. (5) "Nietzsche's Theory of Rhetoric." *Symposium*, 28 (1974).

———. (6) "Political Allegory in Rousseau." *CI*, 2 (1976).

———. (7) "The Purloined Ribbon." *Glyph 1* (1977).

———. (8) "Semiology and Rhetoric." *Diacritics*, 3 (1973).

———. (9) "The Timid God: A Reading of Rousseau's *Professions de Foi du Vicaire Savoyard*." *GR*, 29 (1975).

Mandelbaum, Maurice. "Family Resemblances and Generalizations Concerning the Arts." *APQ*, 2 (1965).

Manns, James. (1) "Metaphor and Paraphrase." *BJA*, 15 (1975).

———. (2) "Representation, Relativism and Resemblance." *BJA*, 11 (1971).

Manser, Anthony R. "Games and Family Resemblances." *PHIL*, 42 (1967).

Marcuse, Ludwig. "Freud's Aesthetic." *JAAC*, 17 (1958).

Margolis, Joseph. (1) "Aesthetic Perception." *JAAC*, 19 (1960).

———. (2) "Art as Language." *Monist*, 58 (1974).

———. (3) "Critics and Literature." *BJA*, 11 (1971).

———. (4) "The Identity of a Work of Art." *Mind*, 67 (1959).

———. (5) *The Languages of Art and Art Criticism*. Detroit, 1965.

———. (6) "The Mode of Existence of a Work of Art." *RM*, 12 (1958).

———. (7) "Mr. Weitz and the Definition of Art." *PS*, 9 (1958).

———. (8) "Numerical Identity and Reference in the Arts." *BJA*, 10 (1970).

———. (9) "Proposals on the Logic of Aesthetic Judgments." *PQ*, 9 (1959).

———. (10) "Recent Work in Aesthetics." *APQ*, 2 (1965).

Marotti, Arthur F. "Countertransference, the Communication Process, and the Dimensions of Psychoanalytic Criticism." *CI*, 4 (1978).

Martin, F. David. "The Persistent Presence of Abstract Painting." *JAAC*, 28 (1969).

Martland, T. R. "Art?" *APQ*, 15 (1978).

Mast, Gerald. *Film/Cinema/Movie: A Theory of Experience*. New York, 1977.

Mayberry, Thomas. "Aesthetic Pleasure and Enjoyment." In *Language and Aesthetics*, edited by Benjamin Tilghman. Lawrence, Kans., 1973.

Mayo, Bertram. "Poetry, Language, and Communication." *PHIL*, 29 (1954).

Mead, Hunter. *An Introduction to Aesthetics*. New York, 1952.

Meager, Ruby. (1) "Seeing Paintings." *PAS*, Supp. 40 (1966).

———. (2) "Tragedy." *PAS*, Supp. 34 (1960).

Mehlman, Jeffrey. (1) "The 'Floating Signifier': From Lévi-Strauss to Lacan." *YFS*, 48 (1972).

———. (2) "How to Read Freud on Jokes: The Critic as *Schadchen*." *NLH*, 6 (1975).

———. (3) "*Poe Pourri*: Lacan's Purloined Letter." *Semiotext(e)*, 1 (1975).

———. (4) *Revolution and Repetition: Marx/Hugo/Balzac*. Berkeley and Los Angeles, 1977.

———. (5) *A Structural Study of Autobiography: Proust, Leiris, Sartre, Lévi-Strauss*. Ithaca, N.Y., 1974.

Mew, Peter. "Metaphor and Truth." *BJA*, 11 (1971).

Meyer, Leonard B. (1) *Emotion and Meaning in Music*. Chicago, 1956.

———. (2) *Explaining Music: Essays and Explorations*. Berkeley and Los Angeles, 1973.

———. (3) *Music, the Arts and Ideas*. Chicago, 1967.

Michaels, Walter Benn. (1) "The Interpreter's Self: Peirce on the Cartesian 'Subject.' " *GR*, 31 (1977).

———. (2) "Walden's False Bottoms." *Glyph 1* (1977).

Michelis, P. A. "Aesthetic Distance and the Charm of Contemporary Art." *JAAC*, 18 (1959).

Miller, J. Hillis. (1) "Ariachne's Broken Woof." *GR*, 31 (1977).

———. (2) "Ariadne's Thread: Repetition and the Narrative Line." *CI*, 3 (1976).

———. (3) "The Critic as Host." *CI*, 3 (1977).

———. (4) "Deconstructing the Deconstructors." *Diacritics*, 5 (1975).

Miner, Earl. "That Literature is a Kind of Knowledge." *CI*, 2 (1976).

Mitchells, K. "Aesthetic Perception and Aesthetic Qualities." *PAS*, 67 (1967).

Mitias, M. H. "Art as a Social Institution." *PERS*, 56 (1975).

Moffett, Kenworth. *Kenneth Noland*. New York, 1977.

Morawski, Stefan. "Contemporary Approaches to Aesthetic Inquiry: Absolute Demands and Limited Possibilities." *CI*, 4 (1977).

Morgan, Douglas. (1) "Creativity Today." *JAAC*, 12 (1953).

———. (2) "Icon, Index and Symbol in the Visual Arts." *PS*, 6 (1955).

———. (3) "Psychology and Art Today." *JAAC*, 9 (1950).

Morgan, William. "Feminism and Literary Study." *CI*, 2 (1976).

Morris-Jones, H. "The Logic of Criticism." *Monist*, 50 (1966).

Morton, Bruce. "Beardsley's Conception of the Aesthetic Object." *JAAC*, 32 (1974).

Mothersill, Mary. (1) "Critical Reasons." *PR*, 69 (1960).

———. (2) " 'Unique' as an Aesthetic Predicate." *JP*, 58 (1961).

Moutafakis, N. "Of Family Resemblances and Aesthetic Discourse." *Philosophical Forum*, 7 (1975).

Munro, Thomas. (1) " 'The Afternoon of a Faun' and the Interrelation of the Arts." *JAAC*, 10 (1951).

———. (2) "Form and Value in the Arts." *JAAC*, 13 (1955).

———. (3) "Form in the Arts." *JAAC*, 2 (1943).

Nahm, Milton C. *Aesthetic Experience and Its Presuppositions*. New York, 1946.

Nathan, Daniel. "Categories and Intentions." *JAAC*, 32 (1974).

Naumburg, Margaret. "Art as Symbolic Speech." *JAAC*, 13 (1955).

Neill, B. C. "Critical Study of *Languages of Art* by Nelson Goodman." *PQ*, 21 (1971).

Nelson, Cary. "The Paradox of Critical Language: A Polemical Speculation." *MLN*, 89 (1974).

Newcomb, James W. "Eisenstein's Aesthetics," *JAAC*, 32 (1974).

Norton, Richard. "What is Virtuality?" *JAAC*, 30 (1972).

Ohmann, Richard. (1) "Literature as Act." In *Approaches to Poetics*, edited by Seymour Chapman. New York, 1973.

———. (2) "Speech, Action, and Style." In *Literary Style: A Symposium*, edited by Seymour Chapman. New York, 1971.

———. (3) "Speech Acts and the Definition of Literature." *Philosophy and Rhetoric*, 4 (1971).

———. (4) "Speech, Literature and the Space Between." *NLH*, 4 (1972).

Olen, Jeffrey. "Theories, Interpretation, and Aesthetic Qualities." *JAAC*, 35 (1977).

Olson, Elder. *On Value Judgments in the Arts and Other Essays*. Chicago, 1976.

Osborne, Harold. (1) *Aesthetics and Art Theory*. New York, 1970.

———. (2) *Aesthetics and Criticism*. London, 1952.

———. (3) "Reasons and Descriptions in Criticism." *Monist*, 50 (1966).

———. (4) "Taste and Judgment in the Arts." *Journal of Aesthetic Education*, 5 (1971).

Palmer, Anthony. "Creativity and Understanding." *PAS*, Supp. 45 (1971).

Palmer, Richard. *Hermeneutics*. Evanston, Ill., 1969.

Panofsky, Erwin. *Meaning in the Visual Arts*. Garden City, N.Y., 1955.

Parker, DeWitt H. (1) *The Analysis of Art*. New Haven, 1926.

———. (2) "The Nature of Art." *Review Internationale de Philosophie*, 1 (1939).

———. (3) *The Principles of Aesthetics*. New York, 1946.

Paskins, Barrie. "On Being Moved by Anna Karenina and 'Anna Karenina.' " *PHIL*, 52 (1977).

Passmore, J. A. "The Dreariness of Aesthetics." *Mind*, 60 (1951).

Peltz, Richard. "Classification and Evaluation in Aesthetics: Weitz and Aristotle." *JAAC*, 30 (1971).

Pepper, Stephen C. (1) *Aesthetic Quality*. New York, 1938.

————. (2) "Art and Experience." *RM*, 12 (1958).

————. (3) "Art and Utility." *JP*, 20 (1920).

————. (4) "Autobiography of an Aesthetic." *JAAC*, 28 (1970).

————. (5) *The Basis of Criticism in the Arts*. Cambridge, Mass., 1949.

————. (6) "Feibleman's Aesthetic Theory." *Studium Generale*, 24 (1971).

————. (7) "Further Considerations on the Aesthetic Work of Art." *JP*, 49 (1952).

————. (8) *The Work of Art*. Bloomington, Ind., 1955.

Philipson, Morris. (1) *"Mrs. Dalloway*, 'What's the Sense of Your Parties?' " *CI*, 1 (1974).

————. (2) *Outline of a Jungian Aesthetics*. Evanston, Ill., 1963.

Poggioli, Renato. *The Theory of the Avant-Garde*. Cambridge, Mass., 1968.

Polanyi, Michael. "What is a Painting?" *BJA*, 10 (1970).

Pole, David. (1) "Art and Generality." *Mind*, 85 (1976).

————. (2) "Morality and the Assessment of Literature," *PHIL*, 30 (1955).

————. (3) "Varieties of Aesthetic Experience." *PHIL*, 30 (1955).

Portnoy, Julius. *The Philosopher and Music*. New York, 1954.

Poulet, Georges. (1) *The Interior Distance*. Baltimore, 1959.

————. (2) "The Self and Other in Critical Consciousness." *Diacritics*, 2 (1972).

Prall, D. W. (1) *Aesthetic Analysis*. New York, 1936.

————. (2) *Aesthetic Judgment*. New York, 1929.

Pratt, Carroll C. (1) *Meaning in Music*. New York, 1931.

————. (2) "The Stability of Aesthetic Judgments." *JAAC*, 15 (1956).

Pratt, Mary L. *Toward a Speech Act Theory of Literary Discourse*. Bloomington, Ind., 1977.

Price, Kingsley B. (1) "Is There Artistic Truth?" *JP*, 46 (1949).

————. (2) "Is the Work of Art a Symbol?" *JP*, 50 (1953).

Pursur, J. W. R. *Art and Truth*. Glasgow, 1957.

Quinton, A. M. "Tragedy." *PAS*, Supp. 34 (1960).

Rader, Melvin. (1) "The Artist as Outsider." *JAAC*, 16 (1958).

————. (2) "Dickie and Socrates on Definition." *JAAC*, 32 (1974).

————. (3) "The Factualist Fallacy in Aesthetics." *JAAC*, 28 (1970).

————. (4) "The Imaginative Mode of Awareness." *JAAC*, 33 (1974).

————. (5) "Isolationist and Contextualist Aesthetics: Conflict and Resolution." *JP*, 44 (1947).

————. (6) "Marx's Interpretation of Art and Aesthetic Value." *BJA*, 10 (1967).

Rader, Ralph. (1) "Explaining Our Literary Understanding." *CI*, 1 (1975).

————. (2) "Fact, Theory and Literary Explanation." *CI*, 1 (1974).

Radford, Colin. (1) "A Causal Judgment in Criticism." *Mind*, 85 (1976).

————. (2) "Fakes." *Mind*, 87 (1978).

Raleigh, Henry P. (1) "Art as Communicable Knowledge." *Journal of Aesthetic Education*, 5 (1971).

————. (2) "Film: The Revival of Aesthetic Symbolism." *JAAC*, 32 (1973).

Reid, Louis A. (1) "Aesthetic Meaning" *PAS*, 55 (1954–55).

————. (2) *Meaning in the Arts*. New York, 1969.

Richter, Peyton. *Perspectives in Aesthetics*. New York, 1967.

Riddel, Joseph. (1) "From Heidegger to Derrida to Chance: Doubling and (Poetic) Language." *Boundary 2*, 4 (1976).

————. (2) *The Inverted Bell: Modernism and the Counterpoetics of William Carlos Williams.* Baton Rouge, La., 1974.

————. (3) "A Miller's Tale." *Diacritics*, 5 (1975).

Rieser, Max. (1) "Problems of Artistic Form: The Concept of Art." *JAAC*, 27 (1969).

————. (2) "The Semantic Theory of Art in America." *JAAC*, 15 (1956).

Righter, William. *Logic and Criticism.* London, 1963.

Romo, Emilio. "The Scope of the Intentional Fallacy." *Monist*, 50 (1966).

Rorty, Richard. "The Philosophy of Jacques Derrida." *JP*, 74 (1977).

Rosand, David. "Art History and Criticism: The Past as Present." *NLH*, 5 (1973–74).

Rose, Mary Carman. "Linguistic Analysis and Aesthetic Inquiry: A Critique." *Southern Journal of Philosophy*, 9 (1971).

Rosenberg, Harold. (1) *The Anxious Object.* New York, 1964.

————. (2) *Art On the Edge.* New York, 1975.

————. (3) *Artworks and Packages.* New York, 1969.

————. (4) *The De-Definition of Art.* New York, 1972.

————. (5) *Discovering the Present.* Chicago, 1973.

————. (6) "Metaphysical Feelings in Modern Art." *CI*, 2 (1975).

————. (7) *The Tradition of the New.* New York, 1959.

Rosenberg, Marvin. "Drama is Arousal." *JAAC*, 27 (1969).

Roskill, Mark. "On the Recognition and Identification of Objects in Paintings." *CI*, 3 (1977).

Ross, Stephanie. "Caricature." *Monist*, 58 (1974).

Rothman, William. "Alfred Hitchcock's *Notorious.*" *GR*, 29 (1975).

Rowe, John Carlos. "Writing and Truth in Poe's *The Narrative of Arthur Gordon Pym.*" *Glyph 2* (1977).

Rubin, William. "Jackson Pollock and the Modern Tradition." *Artforum*, 5 (1967).

Rudinow, J., and R. I. Sikora. "Are There Art-Critical Concepts?" *Analysis*, 35 (1975).

Rudner, Richard. (1) "On Semiotic Aesthetics." *JAAC*, 10 (1951).

————. (2) "The Ontological Status of the Esthetic Object." *PPR*, 10 (1950).

————. (3) "Some Problems of Non-Semiotic Aesthetics." *JAAC*, 15 (1957).

Ryan, Michael. (1) "The Act." *Glyph 2* (1977).

————. (2) "The Question of Autobiography in Cardinal Newman's *Apologia Pro Vita Sua.*" *GR*, 31 (1977).

————. (3) "Self-De(con)struction." *Diacritics*, 6 (1976).

Sagoff, Mark. "The Aesthetic Status of Forgeries." *JAAC*, 35 (1976).

Said, Edward W. (1) *Beginnings.* New York, 1975.

————. (2) "On Originality." In *Uses of Literature*, edited by Monroe Engel. Cambridge, Mass., 1973.

————. (3) "Roads Taken and Not Taken in Contemporary Criticism." *Contemporary Literature*, 17 (1976).

————. (4) "What is Beyond Formalism." *MLN*, 86 (1971).

Sartre, J.-P. (1) *Critique of Dialectical Reason.* London, 1976.

————. (2) *Essays in Aesthetics.* New York, 1963.

————. (3) *Situations.* New York, 1965.

————. (4) *What is Literature?* New York, 1949.

Savile, Anthony. (1) "Nelson Goodman's 'Languages of Art,' " *BJA*, 11 (1971).

————. (2) "The Place of Intention in the Concept of Art." *PAS*, 69 (1968–69).

Saw, Ruth. (1) *Aesthetics*. New York, 1971.

————. (2) "Sense and Nonsense in Aesthetics." *BJA*, 1 (1961).

————. (3) "What is a 'Work of Art?' " *PHIL*, 36 (1961).

Saw, Ruth, and Harold Osborne. "Aesthetics as a Branch of Philosophy." *BJA*, 1 (1960).

Schleusener, Jay. "Literary Criticism and the Philosophy of Science." *CI*, 1 (1975).

Schneidau, Herbert N. "Style and Sacrament in Modernist Writing." *GR*, 31 (1977).

Scholes, Robert. "Towards a Semiotics of Literature." *CI*, 4 (1977).

Schrade, Leo. *Tragedy in the Art of Music*. Cambridge, Mass., 1964.

Schwyzer, H. R. G. "Sibley's 'Aesthetic Concepts.' " *PR*, 72 (1963).

Sclafani, Richard. (1) "Art and Artifactuality." *Southern Journal of Philosophy*, 1 (1970).

————. (2) "Art as a Social Institution: Dickie's New Definitions." *JAAC*, 32 (1973).

————. (3) " 'Art,' Wittgenstein, and Open-Textured Concepts." *JAAC*, 29 (1970).

————. (4) "Art Works, Art Theory, and the Artworld." *Theoria*, 39 (1973).

————. (5) "The Logical Primitiveness of the Concept of a Work of Art." *BJA*, 15 (1975).

————. (6) "Sensations, Feelings and Expressions." *Rice University Studies*, 58 (1972).

————. (7) "What Kind of Nonsense is This." *JAAC*, 34 (1975).

————. (8) "Wollheim on Collingwood." *PHIL*, 51 (1976).

Scobie, W. D. L. "Margolis on 'The Identity of a Work of Art.' " *Mind*, 69 (1960).

Scott, Nathan. *Negative Capability*. New Haven, 1969.

Scriven, Michael. (1) "The Language of Fiction." *PAS*, Supp. 27 (1954).

————. (2) "The Objectivity of Aesthetic Evaluation." *Monist*, 50 (1966).

Scruton, Roger. *Art and Imagination*. London, 1974.

Searle, John. (1) "The Logical Status of Fictional Discourse." *NLH*, 6 (1975).

————. (2) "Reiterating the Differences: A Reply to Derrida." *Glyph 1* (1977).

Seem, Mark D. "Liberation of Difference: Toward a Theory of Antiliterature." *NLH*, 5 (1973–74).

Segre, Cesare. "Narrative Structures and Literary History." *CI*, 3 (1976).

Sesonske, Alexander. (1) "Truth in Art." *JP*, 53 (1956).

————. (2) "Vision via Film Form." *Journal of Aesthetic Education*, 5 (1974).

————. (3) "The World Viewed." *GR*, 28(1975).

Sessions, Roger. *The Musical Experience*. Princeton, 1950.

Sheldon, Mark. "Metaphor." *Philosophical Forum*, 7 (1975).

Shell, Marc. (1) *The Economy of Literature*. Baltimore, (1978).

————. (2) "The Golden Fleece and the Voice of the Shuttle: Economy in Literary Theory." *GR*, 30 (1976).

————. (3) " 'What is Truth?': Lessing's Numismatics and Heidegger's Alchemy." *MLN*, 92 (1977).

Shields, Allan. "The Aesthetic Object as 'Objet Manque.' " *JAAC*, 30 (1971).

Shiff, Richard. "Art and Life: A Metaphoric Relationship." *CI*, 5 (1978).

Sibley, Frank. (1) "Aesthetic and Non-Aesthetic." *PR*, 74 (1965).
———. (2) "Aesthetic Concepts." *PR*, 68 (1959).
———. (3) "Aesthetic Concepts: A Rejoinder." *PR*, 72 (1963).
———. (4) "Aesthetics and the Looks of Things." *JP*, 56 (1959).
———. (5) "Objectivity and Aesthetics." *PAS*, Supp. 42 (1968).
Sibony, Daniel. "*Hamlet*: A Writing Effect." *YFS*, 55/56 (1978).
Silvers, Anita. (1) "Aesthetic Akrasia: On Disliking Good Art." *JAAC*, 31 (1972).
———. (2) "The Artworld Discarded." *JAAC*, 34 (1976).
———. (3) "How Art Instructs: Another Look at Cognitivism." *Anais Do VIII Congresso Interamericano De Filosofía E V Da Sociedad Interamicana De Filosofía*, 3 (1974).
Simpson, E. "Aesthetic Appraisal." *PHIL*, 50 (1975).
Sipos, George. "On the Reproduction of Works of Art." *JAAC*, 32 (1973).
Sircello, Guy. (1) *Mind and Art*. Princeton, 1972.
———. (2) *A New Theory of Beauty*. Princeton, 1975.
———. (3) "Subjectivity and Justification in Aesthetic Judgments." *JAAC*, 27 (1968).
Sirridge, M. J. "Truth From Fiction?" *PPR*, 35 (1975).
Skinner, Quentin. "Motives, Intentions and the Interpretation of Texts." *NLH*, 3 (1972).
Smith, Barbara H. (1) "Literature, as Performance, Fiction, and Art." *JP*, 67 (1970).
———. (2) "On the Margins of Discourse." *CI*, 1 (1975).
Smith, Robin. "On Eliminating the Art Object." *Dialectica*, 24 (1970).
Sparshott, Francis E. (1) " 'As' or the Limits of Metaphor." NLH, 6 (1974).
———. (2) "Basic Film Aesthetics." *Journal of Aesthetic Education*, 5 (1971).
———. (3) "Mr. Goodman on Expression." *Monist*, 58 (1974).
———. (4) "Mr. Ziff and the 'Artistic Illusion.' " *Mind*, 61 (1952).
———. (5) *The Structure of Aesthetics*. Toronto, 1963.
Spector, Jack. *The Aesthetics of Freud: A Study of Psychoanalysis and Art*. New York, 1973.
Spivak, Gayatri. "The Letter as Cutting Edge." *YFS*, 55/56 (1978).
Stahl, Gary. (1) "An Inductive Model for Criticism." *Monist*, 50 (1966).
———. (2) "Sibley's 'Aesthetic Concepts': An Ontological Mistake." *JAAC*, 29 (1971).
Stalker, Douglas. "A Good Poem." *PPR*, 38 (1977).
Starobinski, Jean. (1) "Considerations of the Present State of Literary Criticism." *Diogenes*, 74 (1971).
———. (2) "The Meaning of Literary History." *NLH*, 7 (1975).
———. (3) "On the Fundamental Gestures of Criticism." *NLH*, 5 (1973–74).
Stein, George. *The Ways of Meaning in the Arts*. New York, 1970.
Steinberg, Leo. *Other Criteria*. Oxford, 1972.
Stevenson, Charles L. (1) "Meaning: Descriptive and Emotive." *PR*, 57 (1948).
———. (2) "On the 'Analysis' of a Work of Art." *PR*, 67 (1958).
———. (3) "On 'What Is a Poem?' " *PR*, 66 (1957).
Stolnitz, Jerome. (1) *Aesthetics and Philosophy of Art Criticism*. Boston, 1960.
———. (2) "The Artistic Values in Aesthetic Experience." *JAAC*, 35 (1976).
———. (3) "Notes on Comedy and Tragedy." *PPR*, 16 (1955).
———. (4) "On Objective Relativity in Aesthetics." *JP*, 57 (1960).

———. (5) "Some Questions Concerning Aesthetic Perception." *PPR*, 22 (1961).

Strier, Richard. "The Poetics of Surrender: An Exposition and Critique of New Critical Poetics." *CI*, 2 (1975).

Subotnik, Rose Rosengard. "The Cultural Message of Musical Semiotics: Some Thoughts on Music, Language and Criticism Since the Enlightenment." *CI*, 4 (1978).

Sussman, Henry. "The All-Embracing Metaphor: Reflections on Kafka's 'The Burrow.' " *Glyph 1* (1977).

Tanner, Michael. "Objectivity and Aesthetics." *PAS*, Supp. 42 (1968).

Tejera, V. (1) "Contemporary Trends in Aesthetics: Some Underlying Issues." *Journal of Value Inquiry*, 8 (1974).

———. (2) "The Nature of Aesthetics." *BJA*, 1 (1961).

Tilghman, Benjamin R. (1) "Aesthetics Perception and the Problem of the Aesthetic Object." *Mind*, 75 (1966).

———. (2) *The Expression of Emotion in the Visual Arts: A Philosophical Inquiry*. The Hague, 1970.

———. (3) "The Literary Work of Art." In *Language and Aesthetics*, edited by Benjamin R. Tilghman. Lawrence, Kans., 1973.

———. (4) "Wittgenstein, Games and Art." *JAAC*, 31 (1973).

Tollefsen, Olaf. "The Family Resemblance Argument and Definitions of Art." *Metaphilosophy*, 7 (1976).

Tomas, Vincent. (1) "Aesthetic Vision." *PR*, 68 (1959).

———. (2) "The Concept of Expression in Art." In *Science, Language, and Human Rights*. Philadelphia, 1952.

———. (3) "Creativity in Art." *PR*, 67 (1958).

Tormey, Alan. (1) "Aesthetic Rights." *JAAC*, 32 (1973).

———. (2) *The Concept of Expression: A Study in Philosophical Psychology and Aesthetics*. Princeton, 1971.

———. (3) "Critical Judgments." *Theoria*, 39 (1973).

———. (4) "Expression in the Performing Arts." *Anais Do VIII Congresso Interamericano De Filosofía E V Da Sociedad Interamericana De Filosofía*, 3 (1974).

———. (5) "Indeterminacy and Identity in Art." *Monist*, 54 (1970).

Traugott, Elizabeth. "Generative Semantics and the Concept of Literary Discourse." *Journal of Literary Semantics*, 2 (1973).

Trilling, Lionel. (1) "The Legacy of Freud: Literary and Aesthetic." *Kenyon Review*, 2 (1940).

———. (2) *Sincerity and Authenticity*. Cambridge, Mass., 1973.

Tsugawa, Albert. "The Objectivity of Aesthetic Judgments." *PR*, 70 (1961).

Urmson, J. O. (1) "Literature." In *Aesthetics: A Critical Anthology*, edited by George Dickie and Richard Sclafani. New York, 1977.

———. (2) "What Makes a Situation Aesthetic?" *PAS*, 31 (1957–58).

Ushenko, Andrew P. (1) "Metaphor." *Thought*, 30 (1955).

———. (2) "Pictorial Movement." *BJA*, 1 (1961).

Vivas, Eliseo. (1) "Animadversions on Imitation and Expression." *JAAC*, 19 (1961).

———. (2) *The Artistic Transaction*. Columbus, Ohio, 1963.

———. (3) "Contextualism Reconsidered." *JAAC*, 18 (1959).

———. (4) "A Definition of the Esthetic Experience." *JP*, 34 (1937).

———. (5) "What is a Poem?" *Sewanee Review*, 62 (1954).

Vygotsky, Lev S. *The Psychology of Art*. Cambridge, Mass., 1971.
Wacker, Jeanne. "Particular Works of Art." *Mind*, 69 (1960).
Wallach, Michael A. "Art, Science, and Representation." *JAAC*, 18 (1959).
Walsh, Dorothy. (1) "Aesthetic Descriptions." *BJA*, 10 (1970).
———. (2) "The Cognitive Content of Art." *PR*, 52 (1943).
———. (3) "Critical Reasons." *PR*, 69 (1960).
Walton, Kendall L. (1) "Are Representations Symbols?" *Monist*, 58 (1974).
———. (2) "Categories of Art." *PR*, 79 (1970).
———. (3) "Fearing Fictions." *JP*, 75 (1978).
———. (4) "Languages of Art: An Emendation." *PS*, 22 (1971).
———. (5) "Pictures and Make Believe." *PR*, 82 (1973).
Wartofsky, Marx. "Art, Action and Ambiguity." *Monist*, 58 (1974).
Watkins, Evan. *The Critical Act*. New Haven, 1978.
Weber, Samuel. (1) "The Devaricator: Remarks on Freud's *Witz*." *Glyph 1* (1977).
———. (2) "The Sideshow, or: Remarks on a Canny Moment." *MLN*, 88 (1973).
Webster, William E. "Music is Not a 'Notational System.'" *JAAC*, 29 (1971).
Weitz, Morris. (1) *Hamlet and the Philosophy of Literary Criticism*. Chicago, 1964.
———. (2) "Interpretation and the Visual Arts." *Theoria*, 39 (1973).
———. (3) *Philosophy of the Arts*. Cambridge, Mass., 1950.
———. (4) "Professor Goodman on the Aesthetic." *JAAC*, 29 (1971).
———. (5) "Reasons in Criticism." *JAAC*, 20 (1962).
———. (6) "The Role of Theory in Aesthetics." *JAAC*, 15 (1956).
———. (7) "Symbolism and Art." *RM*, 7 (1954).
———. (8) "Wittgenstein's Aesthetics." In *Language and Aesthetics*, edited by Benjamin R. Tilghman. Lawrence, Kans., 1973.
Welsh, Paul. (1) "Discursive and Presentational Symbols." *Mind*, 64 (1955).
———. (2) "On Explicating Metaphors." *JP*, 60 (1963).
White, Hayden. "The Absurdist Moment in Contemporary Literary Theory." *Contemporary Literature*, 17 (1976).
Williams, Donald C. "Form and Matter." *PR*, 67 (1958).
Wilson, Patrick. "The Need to Justify." *Monist*, 50 (1966).
Wimsatt, William K., Jr. *The Verbal Icon*. Lexington, Ky., 1954.
Wimsatt, William K., Jr., and Monroe C. Beardsley. (1) "The Affective Fallacy." *Sewanee Review*, 57 (1949).
———. (2) "The Intentional Fallacy." *Sewanee Review*, 54 (1946).
Wimsatt, William K., Jr., and Cleanth Brooks. *Literary Criticism: A Short History*. New York, 1957.
Wittgenstein, Ludwig. *Lectures and Conversations on Aesthetics, Psychology and Religious Belief*, edited by Cyril Barrett. Berkeley and Los Angeles, 1972.
Wohlfarth, Irving. "On the Messianic Structure of Walter Benjamin's Last Reflections." *Glyph 3* (1978).
Wollheim, Richard. (1) *Art and its Objects*. New York, 1968.
———. (2) *On Art and the Mind*. Cambridge, Mass., 1974.
———. (3) "Representation: The Philosophical Contribution to Psychology." *CI*, 3 (1977).
Wolterstorff, Nicholas. (1) "Toward an Ontology of Art Works." *Nous*, 9 (1975).

————. (2) "Worlds of Works of Art." *JAAC*, 35 (1976).

Zemach, Eddy M. (1) "Thirteen Ways of Looking at the Ethics-Aesthetics Parallelism." *JAAC*, 29 (1971).

————. (2) "Why Prescriptivism in Aesthetics is Wrong." *Metaphilosophy*, 7 (1976).

Zerby, Lewis K. "A Reconsideration of the Role of Theory in Aesthetics—A Reply to Morris Weitz." *JAAC*, 16 (1957).

Ziff, Paul. *Philosophical Turnings*. Ithaca, N.Y,, 1962.

Zuckerkandl, Victor. *Sound and Symbol*. New York, 1956.

Anthologies and Collections

Aschenbrenner, K., and A. Isenberg, eds. *Aesthetic Theories: Studies in the Philosophy of Art*. Englewood Cliffs, N.J., 1965.

Battcock, Gregory, ed. (1) *Idea Art*. New York, 1973.

————. (2) *Minimal Art*. New York, 1968.

————. (3) *The New Art*. New York, 1966.

————. (4) *Super Realism*. New York, 1978.

Barrett, Cyril, ed. *Collected Papers on Aesthetics*. Oxford, 1965.

Beardsley, M., and H. Schueller, eds. *Aesthetic Inquiry: Essays on Art Criticism and the Philosophy of Art*. Belmont, Calif., 1967.

Coleman, Francis, ed. *Contemporary Studies in Aesthetics*. New York, 1968.

Dickie, George, and Richard Sclafani, eds. *Aesthetics: A Critical Anthology*. New York, 1977.

Elton, William, ed. *Aesthetics and Language*. New York, 1954.

Harari, Josue V., ed. *Textual Strategies: Perspectives in Post-Structuralist Criticism*. Ithaca, N.Y., 1979.

Hofstader, A., and Richard Kuhns, eds. *Philosophies of Art and Beauty*. Chicago, 1975.

Hook, Sidney, ed. *Art and Philosophy: A Symposium*. New York, 1966.

Hospers, John, ed. *Introductory Readings in Aesthetics*. New York, 1969.

Kennick, W. E., ed. *Art and Philosophy*. New York, 1964.

Levich, Marvin, ed. *Aesthetics and the Philosophy of Criticism*. New York, 1963.

Lipman, Matthew, ed. *Contemporary Aesthetics*. Boston, 1973.

Macksey, Richard, ed. *Velocities of Change: Critical Essays from MLN*. Baltimore, 1974.

Macksey, Richard, and Eugenio Donato, eds. *The Structuralist Controversy: The Languages of Criticism and the Sciences of Man*. Baltimore, 1972 (1970).

Margolis, Joseph, ed. *Philosophy Looks at the Arts*. New York, 1962.

Mast, Gerald, and Marshall Cohen, eds. *Film Theory and Criticism: Introductory Readings*. Oxford, 1974.

Meyer, Ursula, ed. *Conceptual Art*. Toronto, 1972.

Osborne, Harold, ed. *Aesthetics*. Oxford, 1972.

Rader, Melvin, ed. *A Modern Book of Aesthetics*. 3rd ed. New York, 1960.

Talbot, Daniel, ed. *Film: An Anthology*. Berkeley and Los Angeles, 1967.

Tilghman, Benjamin R., ed. *Language and Aesthetics*. Lawrence, Kans., 1973.

Tillman, F., and S. Cahn, eds. *Philosophy of Art and Aesthetics*. New York, 1969.

Tomas, Vincent, ed. *Creativity in the Arts*. Englewood Cliffs, N.J., 1964.

Vesey, G., ed. *Philosophy and the Arts*. London, 1972.

Vivas, E., and Murray Krieger, eds. *The Problems of Aesthetics*. New York, 1953.

Weitz, Morris, ed. *Problems in Aesthetics*. New York, 1959.

About the Editors

Morris Philipson was born in New Haven, Connecticut, in 1926. After spending a year at the Université de Paris, he did his undergraduate and master's work at the University of Chicago, and received his doctorate from Columbia University. He has taught English literature, cultural history, and philosophy at Hofstra College, the Juilliard School of Music, Hunter College, and the University of Chicago. For 1956-1957 he was awarded a Fullbright fellowship to study at the University of Munich. Dr. Philipson edited the volume of Aldous Huxley's writings *On Art and Artists* (1960); he is the author of three novels and numerous articles and short stories. He was editor of Vintage Books, and a member of the editorial staff of Random House, Inc., before becoming Director of the University of Chicago Press in 1967.

Paul J. Gudel is the William Rainey Harper Postdoctoral Fellow in the Humanities at the University of Chicago.

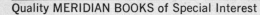

Quality MERIDIAN BOOKS of Special Interest

℗   Ⓜ

PLUME and MERIDIAN Books For Your Reference Shelf

Quality Books from PLUME and MERIDIAN

(0452)

□ **THE DANCE ANTHOLOGY edited by Cobbett Steinberg.** Introducing the principals, history, aesthetics, theory and milieu of the dance, this volume ranges from accounts by such seminal choreographers as Balanchine, Duncan, and Graham to vivid portraits of past and present dancers, from insightful criticisms on the dance to classic statements of aesthetic principles. "An impressive and illuminating introduction to the art of dance."—*Publishers Weekly.*

(252334—$8.95)

□ **GOTHIC ARCHITECTURE AND SCHOLASTICISM: An Inquiry Into the Analogy of the Arts, Philosophy, and Religion in the Middle Ages by Erwin Panofsky.** An important contribution to the history of art as well as to the history of ideas, Erwin Panofsky indicates with grace and humanistic breadth the profound correlation between the development of Gothic architecture and the growth of scholastic philosophy. Illustrated. (005817—$4.95)

□ **EXISTENTIALISM FROM DOSTOEVSKY TO SARTRE selected and introduced by Walter Kaufmann.** Revised and expanded. The basic writings of existentialism, many never before translated, including Kierkegaard, Nietzsche, Kafka and Camus. (006686—$6.95)

□ **EXISTENTIALISM, RELIGION, AND DEATH: THIRTEEN ESSAYS by Walter Kaufman.** With a special Introduction by the author. With essays spanning twenty years, this book blends critical scholarship with the voice of personal experience and is an invaluable companion to *Existentialism from Dostoevsky to Sartre.* (006481—$6.95)

All prices higher in Canada.

To order, use the convenient coupon on the next page.

Quality Books from MERIDIAN and PLUME

(0452)

☐ **THE FUTURE OF ARCHITECTURE by Frank Lloyd Wright.** In this volume the master architect looks back over his career and explains his aims, his ideas, his art. Also included is a definition of the Language of Organic Architecture as the architect has employed it throughout a lifetime of work. (005213—$4.95)

☐ **FRANK LLOYD WRIGHT: Writings and Buildings selected by Edgar Kaufmann and Ben Raeburn.** A survey of Wright's career, from his early years until his death in 1959. The architect's writings are accompanied by more than 150 drawings, photographs, plans and sketches, plus a list of locations of all Wright's buildings.
(005957—$7.50)

☐ **THE NATURAL HOUSE by Frank Lloyd Wright.** Here, shown in photographs, plans, and drawings, are houses for people of limited means, each individually designed to fit its surroundings and to satisfy the needs and desires of the owners. (004454—$3.95)

☐ **THE LIVING CITY by Frank Lloyd Wright.** Mr. Wright unfolds his revolutionary idea for a city of the future, a brilliant solution to the ills of urbanization, whereby man can attain dignity in his home, his work, his community. Includes Wright's amazing plans for his model community, Broadacre City. (006392—$6.95)

☐ **A FIELD GUIDE TO AMERICAN ARCHITECTURE by Carole Rifkind.** The first book of its kind to classify and illustrate every major form of American building style—from 17th-century wood houses to today's glass and steel skyscrapers. This invaluable handbook describes the historical background, construction materials, and basic structures and styles that will enable the reader to identify virtually any building in the United States. With over 450 black and white illustrations. (252245—$9.95)

All prices higher in Canada.

Buy them at your local bookstore or use this convenient coupon for ordering.

THE NEW AMERICAN LIBRARY, INC.
P.O. Box 999, Bergenfield, New Jersey 07621

Please send me the PLUME and MERIDIAN BOOKS I have checked above. I am enclosing $_____(please add $1.50 to this order to cover postage and handling). Send check or money order—no cash or C.O.D.'s. Prices and numbers are subject to change without notice.

Name_____

Address_____

City_____State_____Zip Code_____

Allow 4-6 weeks for delivery.

This offer is subject to withdrawal without notice.